SEXUAL LIFE
IN ENGLAND
PAST AND PRESENT

Drawing by Rowlandson [*Pl.* 1

HUG——MUG——GIN

SEXUAL LIFE IN ENGLAND

PAST AND PRESENT

———

IVAN BLOCH

ORACLE

Sexual Life in England Past and Present

First published in 1938 by Alfred Aldor., London

This edition published in 1996 by Oracle Publishing Ltd.,
2A Kingsway, Royston, Hertfordshire,
SE8 5EG, England.

ISBN 1 86196 003 4

Printed and bound in Guernsey by
The Guernsey Press Co. Ltd

PUBLISHERS' PREFACE

THE present work is a translation from the German, and readers might justifiably wonder why any publisher in this country should issue a history of English morals written by a foreign author.

The answer is as simple as it is surprising.

No comprehensive history of English morals written in the English language has ever been published ! As a result of a thorough search extending over a long period we have found that whereas all other branches of English history are adequately, and more than adequately, covered by authentic publications, the history of English morals has been almost completely neglected. There are numerous excellent books on England's political, economic and literary history, while the number of local histories—histories of particular localities, such as counties, cities, villages, and even individual buildings—is legion ; but books dealing with the morals and manners of the English people can be numbered on the fingers of one hand, and even then they relate to a particular period or a particular locality, and are of a documentary rather than of a historical character. And by issuing the present work we are making a first attempt towards filling this very serious gap in English historical literature.

The need for a comprehensive and authentic history of morals is obvious. Indeed, it is no exaggeration to say that a history of morals is an indispensable key to the understanding of the history of a people as a whole. For the acts and events that constitute history are inevitably influenced by the moral concepts prevailing in the periods in which they take place. The political acts of the states-man, the tendencies of the author, the style of the artist, even the relationship between master and servant—all these things are to a very considerable extent determined by the accepted moral standards of the age, particularly in so far as they relate to sex. And the same applies in almost every field of human activity.

Needless to say, a history of morals must deal, in the main, with immorality, particularly sexual immorality. The attitude of the average decent man and woman to love and marriage, their rigidly moral outlook, represent the taken-for-granted side of a nation's life, and do not influence —at all events not in any spectacular way—the shaping of the destinies of the people concerned. On the other hand, the gross immorality of a monarch like Charles II and the debauchery of the leading personalities of his court explain much that may be characteristic of a particular age, not only on the moral, but also on the social and political side. In the same way, prostitution in the lower social strata tells us more about the economic condition of the people than the puritanism of the masses.

The author of the present work has dealt with all the phenomena pertaining to his subject in a scholarly manner, conscientiously documenting all his facts, although, in the absence of English sources he has frequently had to rely on French and German publications of various periods. On the whole, however, he has given an authentic and com-prehensive survey of English sex life from the earliest Anglo-Saxon times up till the end of the nineteenth century, with detailed descriptions of the various types of sexual vice practised in England at various periods. In addition, he has traced the influence of sexual vice on literature and art in a manner calculated to give a complete picture of what might be described as the seamy side of English life throughout the centuries.

That the author was well qualified to write a history of English morals will be readily conceded. Ivan Bloch, the world-famous writer on the physiology and psychology of sex, is recognised throughout the world as an authority on all matters relating to sex, and this fact alone constitutes a guarantee of the scholarly quality of the present work.

In one respect, however, we emphatically repudiate the conclusions drawn by our author from his authentic and well-documented facts. In dealing with the prevalence of sadism and other forms of sexual vice in England at certain periods in the past, he states repeatedly that the examples quoted by him arose from a trait of harshness, even brutality, that was inherent in the English character. Apparently, it did not occur to him to ask himself what had become of that ' inherent trait ' when he wrote the present work, for even then England was far ahead of the rest of the world, and particularly Ivan Bloch's own native land, in all matters involving humaneness and true courtesy. One need only instance the question of animal protection, which was dealt with in England not only by legislation, but through the kindness inherent in the English character, many decades before it was even raised anywhere on the Continent.

The author's conclusion in this matter is really too absurd to require repudiation, and we only refer to it in order to point out that he was probably influenced by the view of England which was at the time in question deliberately propagated on the Continent for political reasons, and that his acceptance of that view does not detract from the factual contents of his present work. After all, Ivan Bloch made his world-wide reputation by dealing in facts, not in conclusions.

In collecting and collating facts he had few equals and no superiors, and we confidently offer SEXUAL LIFE IN ENGLAND PAST AND PRESENT as an authentic work, and we sincerely trust that it will serve the purpose for which we have intended it, namely, as the starting point of an adequate literature on the history of English morals.

THE PUBLISHERS

SUMMARIES OF CHAPTERS

PUBLISHERS' PREFACE

INTRODUCTION

General character of the English people. Historical stability. Causes of the individuality of the English race. English national pride. Realistic temperament. A people of action. Judge Jeffreys. Examples of coarseness from real life. Coarseness in Shakespeare, in 'Hudibras', in the novels of the eighteenth century, in Hogarth's pictures, in humorous drawings. Coarseness in specifically erotic literature. England the home of eccentricity. 'Spleen,' a psychological explanation. Examples of English 'spleen' (Gluttons' Club, louse races, etc.). English prudery. The psychology of this specific prudery. Its connection with immorality. The stamp of coarseness, the eccentrics and hyprocrisy in English sex life. Derivation of the essentially English peculiarities in sexual matters from this general character. 1. Marriage by purchase. 2. Defloration mania and child seduction. 3. Flagellomania. 4. Frequency and scandalous handling of trials for adultery.

BOOK ONE

CHAPTER I

THE ENGLISH WOMAN

English beauty. General remarks on the aesthetics of the female body. The beauty of the English woman. Why the English woman is the most beautiful in the world. Opinions of well-known observers (Archenholtz, Taine, Chesterfield, v. d. Decken, Rasch, Addison, Lavater, etc.). English women's large feet. The so-called ' Emancipation of Women ' originated in England. Why the English woman is especially predisposed to these activities. Her early maturity, great freedom and limited delicacy of feeling. England the ' Women's Paradise '. The Anglo-Saxon woman. Unfavourable influence of the Feudal System on the position of women. First appearance of self consciousness and of the sense of joint responsibility in the English woman. Women as members of the Merchants' Guilds. The breweries a monopoly of women in the Middle Ages. Women in the cloisters. The learned women of the sixteenth century. The ' Regnum vulvarum '. Retrogression in women's

CHAPTER II
MARRIAGE

CHAPTER III
PROSTITUTION

CHAPTER IX

CHAPTER X

BOOK TWO

CHAPTER XI

*table. Meat consumption in the nineteenth century. Gout specifically an
English disease. Drunkenness. Large proportion of women drunkards.
Aphrodisiac foods. George IV's predilection for truffles. Ginger as an
aphrodisiac. Love potions in medieval England. Cantharides at the brothels.
The Pinero balsam. Vendors of aphrodisiacs. The Dildoes. Historical
facts on the Godmiché. Dildoe business of Mrs. Phillips. Sale of Dildoes
in the nineteenth century. The turkey as Godmiché. Dildoe pamphlets.
Cosmetics. Cosmetics used by Anglo-Saxons. Heyday of cosmetics in the
eighteenth century. Make-up and powder. Powder tax. Bedford's powder
scene. Perfuming gloves. Perfumes. Contraceptives and preparations for
abortion. Dr. Conton and his invention. Frequency of artificial abortion in
London. Internal preparations for abortion. Pessaries and abortion. Secret
confinements. First scientific pamphlet on miscarriages. 'Lucina sine
Concubitu.' Venereal diseases. First appearance of syphilis in England.
John Hunter's famous experiments. Wide prevalence of venereal disease
around 1750. Precautionary measures by brothel owners. Prevalence in
nineteenth century. Hospitals for venereal diseases. Decrease in recent years.*

CHAPTER XII

FLAGELLOMANIA

*An evil peculiar to the English. Justification of this theory. Originated from
Anglo-Saxons. Prevalence of flagellomania among all classes and ages.
General causes. General observations on sexual flagellation. Literature of
flagellation. Existence of erotic flagellation in ancient times. Introduction of
religious element in the Middle Ages. Flagellantism and discipline are of
medieval origin. Development of the flagellation system by Teutonic Christian
nations. Incidence of sexual flagellation among animals. General observations on sexual flagellation among humans. Physiological explanation
(Bloch). Motives. Aesthetic attractions. Aesthetic significance of the
buttocks. Plastic attractions. Exhibitionism of the nates. The 'Posture
Girls'. Colour attractions. Biological significance of same. Movements of
flagellated part as excitant. 'Kallipygian games' of the ancients. Sadistic
elements in flagellation. Humans flagellating animals. Sight of blood.
Difference between antique and Christian flagellation. Masochistic element in
flagellation. Rôle of magic words. Magnetism. Purely religious causes of
flagellation. Flagellation as remedy. Therapeutic-medical employment.
Remedy against impotence. Descriptions by Doppet and de Renneville.
Roubaud's flagellating machine for impotence. Flagellation for sterility and
other complaints. As a beauty treatment. Significance of habit. Distribution
of blows according to a German scientist. Flagellating instruments. Various
kinds of rods. Rods at brothels. Urtication. 'Linaria cymbalaria.' Flagellation with flowers. With asbestos. With brushes. Flagellating machines in
early and modern times. Electrical flagellation. Flagellation part of professional prostitution in England. The governess. Flagellation as an art.
Subtlety and refinement in flagellation. Favourite points on the body.
'Higher' and 'lower' discipline. The 'cut-up' (flagellation of genital*

CHAPTER XIV

SADISM AND MASOCHISM   pages 432–455

CHAPTER XV

OTHER SEXUAL PERVERSITIES   pages 456–464

CHAPTER XVI

FASHION AS PROCURESS   pages 465–498

CHAPTER XVII

EROTIC LITERATURE

LIST OF ILLUSTRATIONS

INTRODUCTION

It was Henry Thomas Buckle who was the first to realise the value of a critical study of the influence of nature upon individuals and peoples. One glance at the map of Europe shows most clearly how the peculiar position of England must have influenced the character of the English. England is an island with precipitous cliffs, surrounded by an angry sea which makes navigation specially dangerous, by reason of storms and reefs. These circumstances have induced a more complete isolation of the country and its inhabitants than has been the case with other islands. Buckle remarked that England was seldom visited by foreigners up to the middle of the eighteenth century[1]. The nation's prolonged isolation is the actual explanation of its most outstanding characteristic, which is insularity: its wholly original independence of attitude both in business and government affairs. This marked independence, moreover, explains why the English awoke to the theory of 'political freedom' centuries before continental peoples and incorporated it in their lives. (Magna Charta, 15th June, 1215.) To this independence, this self-assurance, can be traced really most of the remaining qualities of the English race which have caused an unshakable stability throughout centuries as in no other European nation. English self-assurance does not

[1] Even under George III, when the Countess de Boufflers visited England her wish to become acquainted with England was regarded as a great service. 'Car on remarquait qu'elle était la seule dame Française de qualité qui fut venue en voyageuse depuis deux cent ans: on ne comprenait point, dans cette classe, les ambassadrices, ni la duchesse de Mazarin, qui y étaient venues par nécessité.'—L. Dutens, *Mémoires d'un voyageur qui se repose.* Paris, 1806. Vol. I, p. 217.

attract by its gay candour, but repels by a certain moroseness, a sullen earnestness, which has been attributed, not without justice, to the fog which is a feature of the country's climate. Jonathan Swift is an embodiment of this English gloom, both in his life and in his work.

The Englishman's self-assurance has resulted in a national pride of a vigour hardly to be found among any other people. According to von der Decken the knowledge of abiding by the law is one source of this national pride which is the possession of every Englishman and which is fed by the thought that no accident of birth or circumstance can veto his claim to wealth and honour[1]. All through their literature and public life the voice of this English national pride is continually in evidence. In Chauvinism John Bull leaves all other peoples far behind him.

A further characteristic, peculiar to the English people, is their realistic sense, the gift of keen observation, the ability to make practical use of the immediate present. Englishmen are born practical philosophers. This realistic sense gives something genuine, something solid to all creations of the English spirit, and finds expression too in the very cast of their features. It is no accident that England should be the home of Francis Bacon and John Stuart Mill, the discoverer and the exponent of the inductive method. The ideal of the English people at all times has been action, which in philosophy gives rise to induction.

Exaggerated self-assurance is apt to develop very easily into coarseness and brutality. As a matter of fact brutality was one of the most conspicuous traits of the English national character and was manifested in a vast variety of ways. The independence, the straightness and energy of the Englishman is apt to become insensitive coarseness.

[1] F. von der Decken, *Study of English National Character*. Hanover, 1802. Pp. 45-46.

[4]

The Englishman was downright, thorough and logical in his brutality as he was in everything else. Macaulay gives countless instances of this, especially in his brilliant description of the manners of the seventeenth century. The most notorious example of this English brutality was Judge Jeffreys. Macaulay gives the following picture of him:

' He was a man of quick and vigorous parts but constitutionally prone to insolence and to the angry passions. . . . Already might be remarked in him the most odious vice which is incident to human nature, a delight in misery merely as misery. There was a fiendish exultation in the way in which he pronounced sentence on offenders. Their weeping and imploring seemed to titillate him voluptuously; and he loved to scare them into fits by dilating with luxuriant amplification on all the details of what they were to suffer. Thus, when he had the opportunity of ordering an unlucky adventuress to be whipped at the cart's tail, " Hangman," he would exclaim, " I charge you to pay particular attention to this lady! Scourge her soundly, man. Scourge her till the blood runs down! It is Christmas, a cold time for Madam to strip in! See that you warm her shoulders thoroughly! " . . . To enter his court was to enter the den of a wild beast which none could tame and which was as likely to be roused to rage by caresses as by attacks. He frequently poured forth on plaintiffs and defendants, barristers and attorneys, witnesses and jurymen, torrents of frantic abuse, intermixed with oaths and curses. His looks and tones had inspired terror when he was merely a young advocate, struggling into practice. Now that he was the head of the most formidable tribunal in the world, there were few indeed who did not tremble before him[1].'

[1] Thomas Babington Macaulay, *History of England from the Accession of James II*, Vol. I.

It is a lifelike portrait in which the English brutality of that time is depicted in all its various aspects. A few examples make this clear. In 1790 the London crowd took delight in every kind of bizarre pastime. Donkeys were baited; little pigs were thoroughly greased all over and dogs set on them; old dogs were made to fight a mad donkey. One pastime was held weekly throughout the winter in the fields: a small pig was shaved close with a razor, and its tail thickly greased—the game was to catch it by the tail and swing it round your head. The prize was a lace hat which was paraded on a pole, and the points of the game consisted in the falling of the fellows as they struggled to seize the tail, in the squealing of the animal and the shrieking applause of the crowd. The following notice shows the favourite pastimes of the lowest class of the community on Whitmonday: ' A new hat will be the prize for men, a shift of dutch linen for girls—in a drinking competition: further there will be a ball-game for a fine ham, a sack-race for a pair of new trousers, wrestling for a big plum pudding, and for a guinea—to get a sound thrashing.' In Stepney a fighting bantam was matched against a 25-year-old raven, and the bantam lost. On the same occasion a donkey was baited by old dogs on a piece of waste land, and the barking of the dogs, the cries of the donkey and the shouts of the spectators combined to make a horrible concert. At the famous ' Bartholomew Fair ' held in London for the enter- tainment of the lowest class, the star turn was a so-called wild Irishman—a fake of the stupidest kind. As a matter of fact, an Irish coal-heaver had been hired, stripped naked, smeared with tar and rolled in cow-hair; then he was fastened to a post by two big iron chains and exhibited to the gaping, credulous populace as a freak[1]. The following

[1] J. W. von Archenholtz, *Annals of British History*. Hamburg, 1791 (in future quoted as *Annals*). Vol. V, pp. 390-391, 411.

example from Archenholtz probably touches the very peak of vulgar brutality. In a village near London there lived a half-wit by the name of James Trotter. He was among the poorest of the poor and was the father of three illegitimate children who had to be supported by the parish. What with the general worry, the upkeep of the idiot's bastards and his continous attempts on the chastity of every young woman and girl in the place, the Parish Council decided to take a most extraordinary step. They forced Trotter's mother, partly by promises, partly by threats, to consent to her son's castration, and in April 1790 it was actually performed—by the man who slaughtered pigs[1]. Taine recounts how in the year 1840, at a party in London, certain honourable gentlemen amused themselves by making beautiful women in their ball-dresses drunk and then dosing them with a concoction of pepper, mustard and vinegar[2]. Hector France, whose writings will often be cited, has collected other examples of former English coarseness and brutality; especially does he depict in lively colours the horrible brutality at boxing matches[3]; a favourite and also extremely characteristic pastime of Englishmen.

English brutality was manifested also in literature and art. According to Taine, Shakespeare possesses as complete a vocabulary of coarse expressions as Rabelais. His heroes take handfuls of muck and fling it at their foes without considering themselves sullied by it. And these barbarities are not confined to the rabble, but are to be found—and even more grossly—among people of position as well[4]. A type of such coarseness in Shakespeare is Caliban in *The Tempest*. Butler's *Hudibras*, and seventeenth-century

[1] Archenholtz, *Annals*, Vol. V, p. 365.
[2] H. Taine, *History of English Literature*, Vol. II, p. 8.
[3] Cf. the chapter ' Les Champions épiques de Maze Hill ' in *Les Va-Nu-Pieds de Londres*. Paris, 1887. Pp. 179-186.
[4] Taine, *loc. cit.*, Vol. I, p. 484.

novels (Swift, Smollett, Fielding and others) form really a
monument for ever to the brutality of the age. Hogarth
has pictured it in his work[1]. ' Punch ', too, their puppet-
hero, is a true type of their brutality[2].

Akin to brutality comes another degenerate growth of
the English feeling of independence: the tendency to
eccentricity, ' spleen ' as it was called; heightened self-
consciousness which ventures upon odd enterprises, peculiar
and eccentric things, in order to prove before the whole
world its originality and independence. Thus every
expression of English spleen was mixed with a good dash
of arrogance which makes these eccentricities appear even
more distasteful.

This is not the place to give many instances of spleen[3]. It
was exemplified in the seventeenth century by the Club of
Beef-eating Britons[4], whose members met weekly to indulge
their gluttony; or by the convalescents and invalids of
Chelsea and Greenwich, who organised races of—lice,
putting them on a table and laying wagers on their turn of
speed. The passion for betting was one of the most
characteristic expressions of English spleen. It occurred on
every possible occasion and often led to the most incredible
eccentricity and aberration[5].

[1] Cf. Taine's brilliant description, Vol. II, p. 448.
[2] It will be noted that in stating his case Ivan Bloch chooses fortuitous
and somewhat exceptional examples over a period of nearly two hundred
years, omitting to make any comparison with similar conditions in other
countries during these centuries, or to make any allowance for changing
humanitarian standards.—ED.
[3] Philarète Chasles treats the subject of English spleen exhaustively in
the second volume of his work *Le dixhuitième siècle en Angleterre*.
Paris, 1846.
[4] Archenholtz, *Annals*, Vol. V, p. 383.
[5] A large collection of examples, illustrating the English passion for
betting, is to be found in *Traits of English Originals* (Leipzig, 1796),
a book compiled chiefly from Archenholtz. There one finds, for instance,
on p. 64, one of the maddest wagers made in 1773. The bet was to

Finally, to these elements in the English national character which have been described so far, must be added one more, which at first sight appears almost contradictory—namely, that remarkable prudery and hypocrisy which permeated the whole of English life: that extreme puritanism which in this land of freedom and enlightenment made the people doubly difficult to understand. How can it be explained, this ' ultra-squeamishness ', this ' hyper-prudery ' which, according to one of their own countrymen, an authority on his people, the English of the last century possessed to such a pronounced degree?[1] On the one hand the Englishman carried his self-assurance and superiority with becoming gravity; but on the other hand, rightly aware of his own nature, he feared that the manifestations of his inborn brutality and eccentricity might sap and endanger his national superiority and independence. So he found himself forced to cling with the greatest care to the outward forms of propriety and to watch over them in order that no one might dare to break this shell of social formality.

This is the only psychological explanation of English prudery. It provided a counterbalance to those bad qualities: the hard schooling, to which the Englishman, naturally brutal and inclined to harmful eccentricity, had to submit in order to protect himself against their effects. For prudery and hypocrisy love only the surface veneer under which the darkest depravity may often lurk. I shall deal later with this connection between English hypocrisy and immorality after I have given one or two examples of prudery which appeared often in the strangest guise.

ride forty miles in three hours, drink three bottles of wine and untie the girdles of three girls. The stake was fifty guineas, and the challenger won triumphantly. One man crawls all over England on hands and knees; another wagers that he will chalk every tree in St. James's Park, and so on.

[1] Pisanus Fraxi, *Index Librorum prohibitorum*. London, 1877. P. xvii (cited in future as *Index*).

[9]

Gustav Rasch, in his book *London by Night*, wrote: ' I cannot help laughing whenever I think how carefully every man, young or old, sitting opposite each other on the narrow seats of an omnibus, endeavours to straighten the dress of any woman who passes between them so that on no account shall there be least glimpse of her foot or still worse of her garter. Each face wears such an earnest look—like a priest who in the morning preaches on the immaculate conception of the Virgin Mary and in the evening, over a glass of red wine, smiles at the simpleness of the faithful.'—' "I cannot walk down this street with you ", a friend said to me. I had been lunching with him at Bibra's Hotel in St. Martin's Lane and wanted to make a short cut down a side street to a small bookshop. "Why ever not ? " I asked him, astonished. The street was narrow but I saw nothing queer about it. "Well, in that public house over there rooms are let for rendez-vous." " But what does that matter? We have no intention of taking a room there." "No, but I might run into an acquaintance, you see; and my reputation would suffer." [1] '

Prudery was so deep-rooted in England that even Science, which should know neither shamelessness nor shame, was tainted by it. Dr. Bourneville, publisher of *Progrès Médical*, and one of the most distinguished French physicians, prints the following notice in No. 52 of his paper, dated 30th December, 1899 : ' We are informed that on December 19th the English police seized every copy of the English translation of Charles Féré's work *La Pathologie des Emotions*, on the ground that the book was " obscene " and likely to corrupt the morals of Her Majesty's subjects. The police had at the same time seized the second volume of Havelock Ellis's *Studies in the Psychology of Sex*[2].' Similarly, an article on

[1] G. Rasch, *London by Night*. Berlin, 1873. Pp. 83-84.
[2] It is an indication of the change in outlook since this book was written, that a condensed edition of Havelock Ellis's great work is now generally on sale.—ED.

'Medical Etiquette in England'[1] states that the review by a continental doctor of a strictly scientific book on sexual pathology, written by an accredited expert, was rejected by one of the foremost English medical journals with the comment: 'Not for English readers.' From the same source comes the following example of exaggerated prudery towards a doctor. 'A continental physician told me that an elderly lady, wife of a colleague, consulted him. The description of her symptoms pointed to some disease of an organ in the abdomen. The patient complained of pain and the doctor asked if the pain was in the abdomen, using the word "belly". The lady, though elderly, became embarrassed at this word; and later on, having become on friendly terms with the doctor and his wife, confided to the latter, that the blunt use of the word "belly" had affected her most unpleasantly; she went on, moreover, to add that the doctor, when treating English ladies, would be well advised never to use this dreadful word: it was absolutely taboo. "But in Heaven's name!" the doctor's wife exclaimed, "Whatever does an English lady do when she consults her doctor?" "She refers to her 'stomach'", answered the Englishwoman.'

In his excellent *Eclaircissement sur les Obscénités*, Pierre Bayle writes with much humour on a similar case of exaggerated prudery, and its intimate psychological connection with immorality has not escaped him. For it is obvious that a human being who is perpetually worrying about what is decent and what is indecent, must for ever be letting his thoughts dwell on indecency; whereas the naive and innocent person keeps easily without any bother within the bounds of decency; it never occurs to such a person to denounce anything as obscene when it is only the twisted thought of the prude that makes it so.

[1] *The Medical Weekly*. 1900. No. 7.

Few observers of the English scene have failed to note this close association of prudery and sexual hypocrisy with immorality. 'The more prudish and narrow the sexual outlook of a people or society is, the more criminal are natural aberrations considered; the more disgraceful and unregulated is the organisation of prostitution, that veritable spreader of poison, and of half-prostitution, the curse of big cities—then, I say, all the more rankly does " secret vice " flourish which lends its victims a spurious air of exquisite morality. And in England above all! Many pages would not suffice to recount my observations on that![1]' A diplomat has depicted this basis of prudery in England with point and vigour.[2]

Into the category of English prudery falls the case of Colonel Valentine Baker, which caused a great scandal in the 'seventies. The Colonel happened one day to be alone in a railway carriage with a pretty, coquettish girl. She flirted with him a bit: he flirted with her, and then she made as if to sleep. The Colonel instantly took his chance and began to caress her: she quietly accepted his caresses, like a nice respectable girl. But when he got above himself and went so far as to cry out ' My darling! My ducky ', the modest maiden, preferring acts of love to words of love, springs

---

[1] Gustav Jäger. *Discovery of the Soul.* Leipzig, 1884. Vol. I, p. 265.

[2] ' La pruderie londonienne a ses demangeaisons et ses curiosités impures. Elle aime à voler ou à se poser sur la frontière qui sépare les bienséances conventionelles de la franche débauche. Il n'y a rien qu'elle aime si cordialement qu'un soupçon de vice. Vous connaissez ce tableau célèbre intitulé le " Fruit Défendu " et representant deux jeunes filles regardant curieusement dans un volume qu'elles ont pris sur un rayon de la bibliothèque paternelle. Elles lisent des choses qui les font successivement sourire et rougir; eh bien! c'est la symbole vivant et gravé de la société de Londres. Qu'est en effet pour elle, le mystère de la pureté en comparaison avec le mystère du vice? Qui n'aimerait mieux connaître les vies des pécheurs que celles des saints? La société de Londres est infinément charitable parce que sa curiosité ne connaît pas des bonnes.'— *La Société de Londres par un Diplomate étranger.* Third edition. Paris, 1885. P. 301.

up and gives the alarm: people come rushing in, the poor
officer is arrested and thrown into prison and eventually
cashiered from his regiment in disgrace. Ten years elapsed.
British officers presented a petition for the reinstatement of
Baker Pascha, who had served with the Turkish forces in
the Russian campaign (1877) and had been promoted to the
rank of general for distinguished service in Egypt; whereupon
a counter-petition appeared, signed by thousands of English
ladies, who protested so indignantly that the Queen, in spite of
the intercession of the Prince of Wales (a personal friend of
Baker), simply did not dare to grant the original petition.
On this occasion the press opened its columns to sundry
screams of feminine indignation. One lady explained that
English womanhood had been insulted in the person of Miss
Dickenson. Another lady was overcome to think that a
British officer could bring himself to shake hands with such a
despicable creature as Baker, or to sit at the same table
with him. A third wrote: ' His presence is an insult to every
woman in the nation '; and a fourth held the opinion that even
the mention of such a profligate's name was a gross indecency.
To speak of him at all must therefore be forbidden[1].

It was necessary to dwell at some length on these salient
features of the English national character and to set them
in the right perspective because the knowledge of them and
their continual recognition is essential to any understanding of English sex-life and its peculiarities. For the
character of a people (or of an individual) is revealed
nowhere more clearly than in the realm of sex. Here those
noteworthy peculiarities in race and individual are seen in
sharpest, clearest outline, because a human being is most
completely himself in this sphere. Those prominent
elements in the national character to which I have already

---

[1] Presentation of the Baker Affair by Hector France, *La Pudique
Albion*. Paris, 1900. Pp. 180-183.

[13]

drawn attention—self-assurance, brutality, tendency to eccentricity, and hypocrisy gave English sex-life its particular stamp and cropped up everywhere in characteristic fashion, indeed, they generated four sexual phenomena which might have been considered typically English, namely, marriage by purchase; defloration-mania and abuse of children; flagellation-mania; frequency and scandalous treatment of divorce cases.

Up to the nineteenth century a very curious custom (I shall treat it at length in my first chapter) prevailed in England: a husband who was tired of his wife could sell her to the highest bidder in a crowd assembled in some public place. The Anglo-Saxons had practised this custom, which even then aroused astonishment among other nations.

But the English common people continued this revolting custom of the Middle Ages right on to the first decade of the nineteenth century. The fact that a man could lead his wife to market with a rope round her neck (such was the practice), offer her to the gaping crowd and sell her, frequently at a mock price, to the first comer—shows a mentality of indescribable coarseness and brutality: and also illustrates the tendency of the English to eccentricity, the spirit of spleen, the wish to astonish, to do something strange and unheard of. Both points will be seen clearly in the subsequent detailed account of marriage-sales.

In the realm of sex the self-assurance of the Englishman, coupled with his inborn brutality and eccentricity, often engendered defloration-mania and lust for virgins. In other lands, undoubtedly, individual men might be found who were especially attracted by a girl's innocence; but the really appalling revelations in the *Pall Mall Gazette* turned a searchlight on the matter. The Englishman, aware of the high value of virginity in the modern world (antiquity thought otherwise), gave rein to his appetite for the rare

[14]

and delicate in this field, and nowhere did brutal egoism and cold-heartedness appear in a more horrifying light.

A third manifestation of English brutality in the sphere of sex was the flagellation-mania—another heritage from the Anglo-Saxons. There is no more interesting chapter in the history of English sex-life than that which deals with the fascination the whip has exercised on the minds of men of every class and every age. From the standpoint of race-psychology the study of flagellation in England is undoubtedly most productive: such deep-rooted tendencies should receive closer attention than has hitherto been the case, for then many sexual perversions appear in quite a new light. Anyhow, brutality, eccentricity and hypocrisy found expression in the Englishman's flagellation-mania in nice proportion.

And now I come to the last sexual expression of those three qualities I have just named: that is, the frequency and scandalous treatment of divorce and so-called crim.-con. cases[1]. They illustrate English nature; their number since the time of Henry VIII is enormous, and they are reported in the columns of the newspapers at length and in intimate detail in the most shameless and brutal manner[2]. Whoever has studied even a small part of the vast English crim.-con. literature will be astonished how this people, with such an excessive feeling for propriety, could at the same

[1] Crim.-Con. is an abbreviation of the words ' Criminal Conversation '. Up to the Matrimonial Causes Act (1857), a husband could bring an action for damages against his wife's paramour (action for criminal conversation). It was a common law suit, and the damages were estimated according to the loss he was supposed to have suffered by the seduction and loss of his wife. This procedure was abolished by the 1857 Act and made part of the new divorce procedure, by way of a separate claim for damages against the co-respondent in a petition for dissolution of a marriage.—ED.

[2] Recent legislation on this point has, of course, forbidden the publication of any details in a divorce case apart from the names and the facts given in the judge's summing-up.—ED.

time permit this scandalous reporting of most immoral divorce cases to persist year after year; and also enjoy discussing them with the greatest imaginable relish. Just at this point the three fundamental traits of the English national character emerged in a glaring light, and combined to form an ensemble which a French writer described in the apt phrase the ' dessous de la pudibonderie anglaise '.

BOOK I

THE TWO MANIFESTATIONS OF THE SEXUAL LIFE

BOOK I

CHAPTER I

THE ENGLISH WOMAN

In the opinion of the most varied aesthetic experts, the English race as a whole, not only the English woman, carries off first prize for beauty among the nations of Europe. According to Finck the English, both physically and spiritually, are the most finely developed race in the world. ' The Englishman is far and away the most beautiful " animal in the world "[1].' The author of *London and Paris* remarked: ' Here beauty in both sexes is so general that only beauty of a high order attracts attention. It seems to me that from this viewpoint the British nobility at a court function must afford a glorious spectacle to any man, not poisoned by communist theories. Few courts can boast such natural grace, such health, such poise[2] '. Archenholtz went so far as to place the beauty of English men above that of the women. ' The beauty of English women has become proverbial in Europe, but the men are even better looking. There is a certain amount of justification in women being called the fair sex on the continent; but in England where the phrase is in use, many paradoxes are current to show that only male gallantry tolerates the distinction. For instance, if you were to walk

[1] H. T. Finck, *Romantic Love and Personal Beauty*. Breslau, 1890. Vol. II, pp. 532, 538.
[2] *London and Paris*. Weimar, 1799. Vol. IV, p. 104.

down a line of English soldiers on parade, you would be
amazed at their regular features, their beautiful eyes, their
fresh complexions, the predominating oval faces, and finally
at the slender disciplined build of their bodies. And what
manhood! Irish and Highland soldiers are even taller; they
have, too, a wild look in the eye which somehow suits their
height extraordinarily well. But better-looking men nobody
could hope to see than those of the London Volunteer Corps.
True, they are the fine flower of the capital: artists,
merchants, rich shop-keepers, townsfolk, all born and
bred in the lap of luxury for the arts of peace. This fine
appearance, this admirable build, can be seen too in other
companies of men in London. For example, firemen in green
uniforms with large silver breast-plates march through the
streets on certain days, with the band playing. What a lot
of fine manly-looking fellows! In truth, there is hardly a man
among them underdeveloped or misshaped. Take the
sailors on the Thames, the workmen in the large London
factories and workshops, the numerous porters and draymen;
have a look at the boys at Westminster, at Christ's Hospital,
at Charterhouse, at the schools of the London parishes, at
Eton, etc.; everywhere you will find that, with the possible
exception of Turkey, nowhere in Europe can so many
good looking men be seen as in England. Accordingly the
beauty of women, which reduces men to slaves on the
continent, does not produce anything like the same effect in
England. The witchery of women is rendered practically
ineffective by the same magic at work in the good looks of
men: and more than that—as the truth is that the effect of
male beauty on women is more powerful, swifter and more
lasting than that of women's beauty upon men. So no one
need be surprised that English girls, at least many of them,
pay rather open homage to men; that they not only
cast invisible nets for the hearts of men like our own lovely

countrywomen, but also themselves take all the steps which have been the privilege of men in love to take since the beginning of the world: such as declarations, letters, messages by go-betweens, and all the honourable arts of courtship. A young man of striking appearance—for where practically all men are well made, only a man of exceptional good looks can attract attention—is inundated with watch-chains, toothpick cases (with suitable devices and mottoes, and never made quite the same), scarves, handkerchiefs (worked with mysterious letters and arrows, and so on), tie-pins (containing a lock of the giver's hair), a regular collection of souvenirs, called keepsakes, and neat little editions of favourite authors, especially Shenstone, Gray, and Pope's *Rape of the Lock*, on the front page of which some telling verse is inscribed, and above all with letters. Such letters as the Widow Currie wrote to Tom Jones are certainly sent to hundreds of young men[1].'

This is the fullest tribute I have ever read to the good looks of Englishmen and to the effects of these good looks. Archenholtz especially appreciated the regular features, the fine complexion and the slenderness of the Englishman. As a matter of fact, the fresh and delicate colour of the Englishman, noticeable even in quite old men, is largely due to the mild damp climate, which preserves the tissues of the skin. Emerson is of opinion that it is the health of the whole bodily structure which speaks to us in the flash and power of the eye. The passion for long walks, for riding, for tennis, for rowing and other games and exercises, as well as great cleanliness, has a great deal to do, without any doubt, with increasing English beauty, but it cannot be denied that its main cause is to be found in climatic conditions, in precisely those natural influences which are responsible for the

[1] J. W. v. Archenholtz, *Annals*, Vol. VIII, pp. 247-250. Many letters of the kind referred to are quoted.

enchanting green of English lawns which have often been compared to the freshness of English complexions.

English women have long been considered the most beautiful women in Europe. It is extremely interesting to learn the effect which the overwhelming beauty of the English woman has produced upon different observers. Their descriptions are really more informative than any systematic analysis or any scientific study could be.

' Of all the beauties ', said Archenholtz, ' to be found in this island, none is so wonderful as the charm of the fair sex. This is so convincing that every foreigner, whatever his country, would not hesitate for an instant in awarding the prize for beauty to English women. In lovely build, in neat figure, in shape of breast, in the tender skin of the face, where the gentlest features glimmer—in all this does the English girl excel [1].'

Julius Rodenberg exclaimed in ecstasy: ' Oh! England's girls are beautiful! Let others go into raptures over the dark eye, the small foot, and the grace of the Parisienne. Give me a girl of England—with her aristocratic features, her two rows of white teeth, her two thick plaits of yellow hair, and her heart full of fire! [2] '

The art historian Wagen has described the beauty of women of the English nobility, together with its setting, in the following account of a ball given by the Duke of Devonshire which he attended in June 1835:

' A withdrawingroom, the walls of which were decorated with mirrors and rose-coloured hangings, in the centre of which was a wealth of flowers of every colour, filling the air with their sweetness, looked especially ornate and delightful. As though to complete the impression of a fairy world, and to add to its charm, the slender sylph-like forms of young

[1] Archenholtz, *England*, Vol. III, pp. 68-69.
[2] Julius Rodenberg, *Day and Night in London*. Berlin, 1862. P. 54.

English women of rank passed in and out, for this most fashionable ball had gathered them in rare numbers. Here I encountered women like living van Dyck portraits; with the fine regular features, the transparent, warm complexion and fair hair which he knew how to reproduce so incomparably. Still more striking were quite Southern types, with black hair and sharply defined foreheads, on which grew small velvety eyebrows, giving a piquant effect to the face. They might well have descended from the early Britons; at any rate the invading Saxons and Normans were blonde races.

'England possesses, for the highest class of society at any rate, a peculiarly favourable soil for such flowers. And this is easily understandable. The physical education of children is nowhere so sensibly and healthily organised as in England: nowhere have I seen such a number of children bursting with health as here. Great regularity of life, simple but nourishing food and much outdoor exercise form the main features of their upbringing, which is strictly adhered to until the children are grown up.

'One great advantage is that the children are not forced to live in terribly overheated rooms for half the year as children in other Northern countries are obliged to do; for the open fire in England does not cause the same complications. Thus the skin does not become blotchy and unhealthy; but one finds here as in Italy that the bone structure shows through in a marked manner, which gives at once greater definition to the face and finer distinctions. Finally, it is remarkable how a special type of beauty has persisted in some of the old families: many collections of family portraits bear witness to this fact. The English aristocracy, owing to their greater freedom in the choice of wives, have avoided the degeneration to caricature and the stunted growth which is noticeable here and there in other countries[1].'

[1] Wagen, *Art and Artists in England*. Berlin, 1837. Vol. I, pp. 241-244.

The famous Rotten Row in Hyde Park provides a fit setting for the beauty of the well-born Englishwoman. Gustav Rasch remarked with reference to this brilliant parade: ' I have never seen such lovely girls; not on the Passegiata of Monte Pincio where the red glow of sunset lights up the glittering dome of St. Peter's; not on the broad street of Posilipp, from which you may see the laurel-covered shore of the world's most beautiful bay and the fiery column of Vesuvius; not under the chestnut trees at Longchamps— Long live the girls of Old England[1].'

Not only in aristocratic circles is feminine beauty so remarkable: it is to be found quite as frequently in middle-class society: Rasch, the author just quoted, even asserted that he had seen the most beautiful girls among prostitutes, who are generally recruited from the lowest class. ' English women are the most beautiful in Europe; but the girls who walk nightly in Regent Street are the most beautiful in London. You cannot find such another promenade on earth as that from the colonnade of Her Majesty's Theatre to the Circus—not under the glittering arcades of St. Mark's Square, not on the Corso of the Eternal City, not in the Galerie d'Orleans, not in the gardens of the Palais Royal[2].'

The French are also great admirers of English beauty. Taine often referred to the delicate loveliness of English complexions: ' Many Society ladies put diamonds in their hair, and their bare shoulders have that incomparable whiteness which the candour of the lily hardly approaches.' And though he considered that ugliness can be uglier in England than in France, he yet acknowledged that 'English-women are generally more beautiful and healthier than Frenchwomen '. Out of every ten girls one is remarkable,

[1] Gustav Rasch, *Dark Houses and Streets in London*. Wittenberg, 1863. Vol. II, pp. 85-86.
[2] *Ibid.*, Vol. II, p. 81.

while a naturalistic painter would look at five or six with pleasure. ' When Lady Mary Wortley Montague visited the court of the Regent of France, she created a sensation among our painted and affected beauties, by proudly showing them the natural loveliness of lively colouring and an unspoilt English complexion! Faces remain young far longer than with us in France, especially in Paris, where they fade quickly: features remain fresh often to advanced old age.' Taine has, moreover, described the type of English beauty portrayed by the poets: Shakespeare's Virginia and Ophelia, Otway's Belvidera, and Richardson's Pamela. These girls and women are soft and fair; they have blue eyes and lilywhite skins; they blush easily; they are timorously tender and grave and gentle; they are intended to yield, and to be dependent and faithful.

Lord Byron, who preferred Italian women, is yet obliged to own that among a hundred English women thirty at least would be pretty[1].

Thackeray has created in Beatrix Esmond the ideal Englishwoman of the period, a brunette: ' She was a brown beauty; that is, her eyes, hair and eyebrows and eyelashes were dark; her hair curling with rich undulations and waving over her shoulders; but her complexion was as dazzling white as snow in sunshine: except her cheeks, which were a bright red and her lips which were of a still deeper crimson. Her mouth and chin, they said, were too large and full, and so they might be for a goddess in marble, but not for a woman whose eyes were fire, whose look was love, whose voice was the sweetest low song, whose shape was perfect symmetry, health, decision, activity, whose foot as it planted itself on the ground was firm but flexible, and whose motion, whether rapid or slow, was always perfect grace—agile as a nymph,

[1] Thomas Medwin, *Talks with Lord Byron*. Second edition. Published by H. Barsdorf. Leipzig, 1898. P. 18.

[25]

lofty as a queen—now melting, now imperious, now sarcastic—there was no single movement of hers but was beautiful. As he thinks of her, he who writes feels young again and remembers a paragon[1].'

But there is no quite perfect beauty on this earth; and many observers point out a striking defect in the beauty of Englishwomen—their large feet, which show to great disadvantage at the ballet. In operettas and ballets the dancers were ' mainly English; they have good fine figures, but their feet and ankle-bones are so large and coarse that no one who has an eye for beauty of line can look at them with pleasure[2] '. Of course, envious Parisiennes delight to jeer at this imperfection of the Englishwoman[3].

If you inquire into the reason of the English woman's supreme beauty, of course you will have to agree with Wagen and others that conditions of life (sport, food, outdoor exercise, climate, etc.) must have a great deal to do with it. For all that, the primal cause must be looked for in the crossing of race-stock, which has occurred in a very marked degree in England, and which is known to have a strong influence on the development of physical beauty. Finck draws attention especially to the fact that the English nose has in the course of time grown noticeably more beautiful as a result of this crossing. A second basic cause of their beauty is the mental ripeness of the English woman, due to the care expended on intellectual development in the education of a girl. The charming ' lines of intelligence ' which, according to Finck, can be traced in the countenance of an English lady, contribute much to the increase of her beauty.

The physical advantages of English women tally with the mental. In no country does the history of woman form so

---

[1] Finck, loc. cit., pp. 531-532.
[2] London and Paris. Weimar, 1803. Vol. XII, p. 235.
[3] Les Dessous de la Pudibonderie Anglaise, Vol. II, p. 28.

interesting a chapter in the history of general culture as in England: the country in which the modern woman's movement originated, those strivings which were designated under the name of the emancipation of women. This becomes clear if we look more closely at the character of the English woman who is predisposed to such striving. First to be noted is the early mental ripeness of English girls compared with French and German girls. This ripeness originates in no small degree from the greater freedom the English girl enjoys from her earliest youth onwards. However dry and proud and mannered an Englishman may be, nevertheless so far as intercourse between the sexes is concerned he has long retained the most admirable principles. This intercourse is of the freest imaginable. ' I am not a blind partisan of England and the English,' said Fanny Lewald, ' but I see here the germ of the future, in such belief in goodness as I have never met elsewhere. When one sees a young and pretty girl at the Whittington Club perfectly at ease among a number of men, with no other protection than mutual respect, one cannot deny that this people is far, very far, in advance of us on the way to the right goal[1].' Every girl is allowed, almost without exception, to walk for hours arm in arm with a young man, some friend of the family; or at a party to talk undisturbed to any man she chooses in any room she likes. She is her own mistress, does, and leaves undone, what she likes, without any fault being found with her behaviour, which is often not at all genteel. Primness is completely foreign to the English woman. Good round oaths are often heard from the lips of gentlewomen, who are quite familiar with the slang of the sportsman and the stable. One day the Duchess of Marlborough called on the Chancellor Lord Mansfield without giving her name; the man-servant went in to announce her

[1] Fanny Lewald, *England and Scotland*. Berlin, 1864. Vol. II, p. 126.

and said: ' I couldn't find out who she was, my Lord, but she swore so stiff that she must be a lady of quality[1] '. The subject of feminine conversation often gave occasion for criticism in the eighteenth century. Swift said:

Or how should I, alas, relate
The sum of all their senseless prate,
Their innuendoes, hints and slanders
Their meanings lewd and double entanders!
Now comes the general scandal charge,
What some invent, the rest enlarge.

William Alexander, in his *History of Woman*, said that in Scotland and other parts of Northern Europe a woman would be as embarrassed to be discovered on her way to the Temple of Cloaca, as to that of Venus. In England a visit to that Temple hardly sufficed to raise a blush on the tenderest cheek. In Paris, too, during the last century, a gallant would often accompany his mistress to the altar of this goddess, and stand watch at the door, entertaining her with jests and endearments, while she conducted the ceremony within. If a lady felt this natural need in her carriage, she ordered the coachman to stop, and whoever might be in her company proceeded to relieve herself and afterwards took her seat once more, quite unembarrassed in the carriage[2].

This early maturity, this lack of shyness and freedom of intercourse give the English woman a male quality which strangely enough finds expression in her handwriting. Most English girls and women have a distinctly manly hand-writing and do not employ the long thin strokes almost habitual to French and German girls.

These characteristics of the English woman make it clear why she has won greater respect for herself than have her

---

[1] Georgiana Hill, *Women in English Life*. London, 1896. Vol. I, p. 335.
[2] W. Alexander, *The History of Woman from the Earliest Antiquity to the Present Time*. London, 1779. Vol. II, p. 3.

Pl. 2]   *Designed by Wm. Hogarth*   *Engraved by T. Cook*

BEFORE

Pl. 3]   *Designed by Wm. Hogarth*   *Engraved by T. Cook*

AFTER

continental sisters. For that reason, even in the Middle
Ages, England was called the ' Paradise of Woman[1] '. A
glance at the history of English women will show how far this
claim is justified.

Thomas Wright proved that all the characteristics of
English women were to be found already in the Anglo-Saxon.
She was the careful housekeeper, the loving wife, the nurse
and consoler of her husband, the noble and virtuous matron.
The home was her domain. For we learn from a poem in the
Exeter Book that ' it becomes a woman to be at her table:
she who gads and chatters is full of faults. A man despises her
and often strikes her on the cheek[2] '. On the other hand,
Anglo-Saxon women varied the monotony of domestic
life by the study of Latin, which they not only read but also
wrote with considerable fluency. Especially in the seventh
and eighth centuries was interest in literature active: later,
war with the Norman invader interrupted such study[3]. The
Church, which branded ' the Eternal Womanly ' as sinful,
and the Feudal System also exercised a depressing influence
upon the position of women. She was regarded as a kind of
slave. Vassals and bondsmen were forced to pay a sum of
money to the overlord on the marriage of their daughters[4].

Nevertheless, the self-assurance and corporate sense, which
form the indispensable foundation of every struggle towards
emancipation, were evidenced in English women even in
the Middle Ages, and explain the reason why these struggles
should have originated in England. In the year 1429 (under
Henry VI) when the Duke of Gloucester had repudiated and
imprisoned his wife, the Duchess Jacqueline, and set Eleanor
Cobham in her place, a group of City dames came to the

[1] W. Alexander, *ibid.*, Vol. I, p. 289.
[2] Thomas Wright, *Domestic Manners in England during the Middle
Ages*. London, 1862. P. 52.
[3] G. Hill, *loc. cit.*, pp. 18, 22.
[4] *Ibid.*, p. 29.

House of Lords and presented a petition against this wanton and injurious treatment of a woman. A contemporary account relates: ' One Mistress Stokes with divers other stout women of London, of good account and well apparelled, came openly to the Upper House of Parliament and delivered letters to the Duke of Gloucester, to the Archbishop and other lords there present, containing matters of rebuke and sharp reprehension to the said Duke of Gloucester, because he would not deliver his wife Jacqueline out of her grievous imprisonment, being then detained prisoner by the Duke of Burgundy, and suffering her to remain unkindly whilst he kept another adultress contrary to the law of God and the honourable estate of matrimony. They felt as all good citizenesses should that they had part and lot in the affairs of the kingdom, and did not think it "going out of their sphere" to express their opinion on a matter of the gravest import[1].'

This independent attitude of women found expression also during the rise of the Merchant Guilds in the fourteenth and fifteenth centuries, for women were admitted to them and, as Miss Toulmin Smith points out in the introduction to her book on English Guilds, to the same extent as men. Out of 500 guilds at least 490 had as many women members as men. Even when a priest was at the head of affairs women were admitted as lay members and enjoyed much the same rights as men. These ' sisters ' of Guilds had the most varied vocations. The following ordinance of Edward III shows in how many branches of activity women were even then engaged, in the middle of the fourteenth century. ' But the intent of the King and his Council is that women, that is to say, brewers, bakers, carders, spinners and workers so well of wool as of linen cloth and of silk; brawdesters and breakers of wool and all other that do use and worke all handy works, may freely use and work as they have done before this time

[1] G. Hill, *loc. cit.*, pp. 35, 36.

without any impeachment or being restrained by this ordinance.' As a matter of fact breweries were almost entirely in the hands of women, also the sale of beer at inns. The ' alewife ' was a well-known character in ' merry old England '. At the present day, too, many public houses in country districts of England are kept by women[1].

Women deserve special mention in the English cloister of the Middle Ages. Up to the sixteenth century nuns enjoyed great freedom, and could choose whether they stayed for a long or a short time. For example, the nuns of Appleton in Yorkshire were very jovial little ladies, and their prioress in 1489 was recommended to see to it: ' that none of your sisters use the alehouse nor the· waterside, where scores of strangers daily resort[2].' Abbesses took part in great synods, as, for example, the famous Elfleda at the beginning of the eighth century. English girls in the Middle Ages were for the most part educated in the cloister, where they learned not only the humanities but also nursing, cooking, drawing, writing, music, singing, and so on. The so-called ' double monasteries ' worked disastrously—those cloisters where men and women lived together. Gabriel d'Emilianne related of the house founded by Gilbert in 1148, called the Gilbertine: ' He (Gilbert) in a short time got thirteen cloisters built in which 700 monks and 1,100 nuns lived together, separated only by the thickness of a wall. This hermaphroditic order, consisting of both sexes, soon produced worthy fruit. For these holy virgins, nearly all of them, became pregnant, which gave occasion to the following verses:

Harum sunt quaedam steriles, quaedam parientes,
　　Virgineoque tamen nomine cuncta tegunt.
Quae pastoralis baculi dotatur honore,
　　Illa quidem melius fertiliusque parit.

[1] G. Hill, *loc. cit.*, pp. 44-47.
[2] *Ibid.*, p. 75.

Vix etiam quaeris sterilis reperitur in illis,
    Donec ejus aetas talia posse negat.

Tho' some are barren Does, yet others,
By Fryars help, prove teeming mothers.
When all to such lewdness run
All's covered under name of nun.
The Abbess in honour as she excells,
Her belly too, more often swells.
If any She proves barren still,
Age is in fault, but not her will.

These nuns disposed of their children secretly to hide the scandal of their birth from the world; which accounts for the fact that at the time of the Reformation so many bones of little children were found, some in burial grounds, some in cesspools[1].'

The Reformation further confirmed and raised the status of English women. A contemporary traveller wrote: ' Women have much more freedom than in any other country. They are almost like masters.' A Dutchman observed: ' England is called the Paradise of married women.' Frederick, Duke of Wurtemburg, who visited England in 1592, also praised the extraordinary freedom which English women then enjoyed[2]. The desire for literary study became strong. No era, according to Dr. Wotton, was so rich in learned women as the sixteenth century. Study was so much the fashion that the fair sex seemed really to be convinced that Greek and Latin heightened their charms. Plato and Aristotle in the original lay on many a dressing-table. Georgiana Hill is of opinion that never in all history have there been so many great women as

[1] Gabriel d'Emilianne, *A Short History of Monastical Orders.* London, 1693. P. 133.
[2] G. Hill, *loc. cit.*, Vol. I, pp. 116, 118.

[32]

between the years 1500 and 1600. A contemporary poem, written by a man, gives the prize for learning to women:

> You men yt read the memoryes
> Of wonders done and paste,
> Remember will the historys
> Of women first and laste:
> And tell me if I saye not true,
> That women can do more than you.
>
> And more than any man can do
> So quicklie and so trym
> What counterpointes of polycie,
> Of arte and of artyfyce,
> But women with facylictie
> Can compass and forecaste.

Princess Mary (later Queen), the daughter of Henry VIII and Catherine of Aragon, was tutored by the famous Ludovicus Vives. Erasmus spoke with especial warmth in praise of her Latin. She wrote excellent Latin letters. Elizabeth, her step-sister, understood Latin, French and Italian, Greek too; studied theology, read with zest Plato, Aristotle, Xenophon, and translated a dialogue of Plato and two speeches of Socrates from Greek into Latin. Lady Jane Grey was also very learned, and was well grounded in Hebrew, Chaldee, Arabic, French and Italian. And not only princely ladies carried on these studies, but also noble women and burgesses like the daughters of Sir Anthony Coke, Henry VIII's tutor, one of whom became the mother of Francis Bacon; and the daughter of Thomas More and Mary Sidney, sister of the Sir Philip Sidney, the famous author of the *Arcadia*. In a word, the sixteenth century was very favourable to learning among women, perhaps because at that time so many women were in a position of authority. About 1561 the thrones of many kingdoms in Europe (including the English

and Scottish thrones) were occupied by women, and a
malicious satire appeared—'De regno vulvarum'. It was
written by D'Aubigné for François Hotmann. It begins as
follows:

Vulva regit Scotos[1], vulva ac tenet ipsa Britannos[2]
    Flandros et Batavos nunc notha vulva regit[3]
Vulva regit populos, quos regnat Gallia portu[4]
    Et fortes Gallos Itala vulva regit[5]
Hinc furiam furiis, vulvam conjungite vulvis,
    Et naturæ capax omnia regna capit.

The revolutions and Puritanism of the seventeenth century, combined with the licentiousness of the Restoration,
were unfavourable to culture among women, which indeed
received a marked setback in this century. Women found
themselves between two parties, both equally hostile to
their interests, libertines and ascetic Puritans. The former
won the day. The lighter pleasures came into vogue;
dancing and music were preferred to classical studies, and
fine and gross sensuality were developed side by side.
Priestesses of the latter like Lady Castlemaine, Francis
Stuart, Louise de Querouville, Nell Gwynn and others
carried all before them; and the few women like Lucy Aspley,
Anna Halkett and Margaret Lucas who strove for higher
culture attracted little attention. Mary Astell's attempt
to found a Protestant cloister, as well as her book *A Serious
Proposal to Ladies* (1700), in which she pleaded for the
mental and moral advance of women, can only be regarded
as an isolated curiosity. Moreover, the belief in witches
which flamed up for the last time in the seventeenth century

[1] Mary Stuart.
[2] Elizabeth of England.
[3] Margaret, Duchess of Parma, natural daughter of Emperor Charles V.
[4] Catherine of Austria, sister of Charles V, widow of John III, King of
Portugal, and regent during the minority of his son Sebastian.
[5] Catherine de Medici.

(especially fed by the Puritans) did not serve to increase the general respect for women[1].

At the beginning of the eighteenth century the position of English women in public life was far from satisfactory. Men held them in such scant respect at that time that a Mrs. Drake felt called upon to write an *Essay in Defence of the Female Sex* (London, 1696).

This state of affairs, however, soon underwent a change. The eighteenth century—the period of the Four Georges and of great writers and artists—is noteworthy also in the history of the English woman; indeed, of the whole female sex. The idea of all that is comprehended in the phrase ' the emancipation of women ' was first clearly formulated in England, developed and made into a lasting subject of public agitation. The study of the beginnings of this movement would make an interesting theme for a special book, as a good many matters in those beginnings still remain obscure. I intend to confine myself to presenting the chief moments in the history of English women's emancipation, and to passing a few critical remarks upon the subject of the emancipation of women in general.

The foundation, from which alone the modern woman's movement could arise, was enlightenment and awakened individualism, spread by the influence of Rousseau's writing (who curiously enough was an opponent of women's emancipation). The self-assurance of the woman became active, and in England, where it had always existed and was only at times suppressed, it advanced once more with renewed energy. Miss Bellamy said: ' The superiority of mind, of which men

---

[1] James I, that learned eccentric, asks in his *Demonologie*: ' What can be the cause that there are twentie women given to that craft where there is only one man? ' and gives his answer: ' that women are frailer than men '. And he cites Eve's fall as the beginning of Satan's lordship over woman. The last witch was executed in 1716, when a mother and daughter were put to death at Huntington.

boast, is in truth only a common prop for male arrogance. How many women I might cite whose profound acquirements refute this absurdity which is ever on the lips of men.' The initiative, thus taken by women, did not fail to have its effect on men, as the following poem shows:

> The rights of woman, says a female pen,
> Are to do everything as well as men.
> And since the sex at length have been inclin'd
> To cultivate that useful part, the mind;
> Since they have learnt to read, to write, to spell;
> Since some of them have wit and use it well;
> Let us not force them back with brow severe,
> Within the pole of ignorance and fear!
> Confin'd entirely to domestic arts,
> Producing only children, pies and tarts[1].

When a man writes an *Essai sur la Supériorité Intellectuelle de la Femme*[2], it is unlikely that the following poem, written at the same time and expressing the same opinions, contains any trace of irony:

> I wonder why, by foul-mouthed men
>   Women so slandered be,
> Since it doth easily appear
>   They're better far than we.
> Why are the graces, every one
>   Pictur'd as women be,
> If not to show that they, in grace,
>   Do more excel than we?
> Why are the liberal sciences
>   Pictur'd as women be,
> If not to show that they in them
>   Do more excel than we.

[1] *Memoirs of the Forty-five First Years of the Life of James Lackington.* London, 1793. Pp. 266-277.

[2] Dell' Acqua, *Essai sur la Supériorité Intellectuelle de la Femme.* Berlin, 1798.

> Why are the virtues, every one,
> Pictur'd as women be,
> If not to show that they in them
> Do more excel than we?
> Since women are so full of worth,
> Let them all praised be—
> For commendations they deserve,
> In ampler wise than we[1].

This self-assurance of women first found expression in the famous assemblies known as Blue Stocking Clubs. Where did the remarkable name Blue Stocking originate? It began by having no trace of the slighting significance with which it is now used. The real origin of the name is still unknown. I must confine myself to giving various theories upon it. John Timbs finds the oldest mention of a Blue Stocking or ' Bas Bleu ' in the Greek comedy which bears the title of *The Banquet of Plutarch*, where the name is applied to a woman with a strong liking for the business of literature. Mills, in his *History of Chivalry*, found the same designation in use in the ' Societa de la Calza ', founded in Venice in 1400, in which the members at their literary discussions differentiated themselves by the colour of their stockings, following the customary usage of Italian Academies in the Middle Ages to employ distinguishing marks. The colours were at first fantastically varied, but one colour, blue, eventually predominated; and this society lasted till 1590. Then the name Blue Stocking reached Paris, where it branded feminine pedantry. From France it was imported into England, where it was used to describe the pettiness of literary effort in feminine coteries. According to Timbs, however, the Blue Stocking of the eighteenth century is a home growth. Boswell noted in his *Life of Dr. Johnson*, under the date 1781: ' About

---

[1] *Doings in London*, p. 259.

this time it was much the fashion for several ladies to have evening assemblies where the fair sex might participate in conversation with literary and ingenious men, animated by a desire to please. These societies were denominated *Blue Stocking Clubs*; the origin of which title being little known it may be worth while to relate it. One of the most eminent members of these societies, when they first commenced, was Mr. Stillingfleet, whose dress was remarkably grave and in particular it was observed that he wore blue stockings. Such was the excellence of his conversation, that his absence was felt as so great a loss, that it used to be said, "We can do nothing without the blue stockings"; and thus by degrees the title was established [1].'

This assumption of Boswell is not quite correct. For, according to the Rev. Montagu Pennington, the biographer of Elizabeth Carter, Stillingfleet died in 1771[2] and had for fourteen years given up the habit of wearing blue stockings[3]. According to Doran, the term Blue Stocking was first used in 1757 in a letter written by Mrs. Elizabeth Montagu, and that too in connection with Stillingfleet. So it is possible that the name does actually originate from some definite personality.

The merit of first starting societies, reserved wholly for conversation to the exclusion of every game, is generally attributed to Mrs. Elizabeth Montagu, *née* Robinson (not to be confused with her celebrated kinswoman Lady Mary Wortley Montagu) to Mrs. Vesey, an Irish lady, and to Mrs. Ord (daughter of the celebrated surgeon Dillington). The name Blue Stocking Club was given not merely to their assemblies but to any over which a lady presided. Parties at

[1] John Timbs, *Clubs and Club Life in London.* London, 1872. Pp. 169-170.

[2] G. Hill, *loc. cit.*, Vol. II, p. 54.

[3] Doran, *A Lady of the Last Century.* London, 1873. P. 66.

Mesdames Montagu, Vesey and Ord were called ' bas bleu assemblies ', without distinction[1].

That was the heyday of the Blue Stocking parties, which lasted on into the nineteenth century but which gradually came to neglect more and more their original purpose. Lord Byron's diary, destroyed by Murray and Moore, contained a humorous account of a Blue Stocking tea party where young ladies on back seats ' tried hard to look wise and were only the prettier because they did not succeed[2] '.

The example of the Blue Stockings was soon followed. Girls and women plunged with zest into the most profound learned studies, so that towards the end of the eighteenth century the large number of learned women filled foreign visitors with astonishment. ' Without wishing to stir up that hornets' nest by asking : should womenfolk learn more than cooking, sewing and knitting, you only need a few years' experience of life in London to be convinced that the jest " She is a Blue Stocking " has quite lost its savour[3]. Above all, women eagerly studied English history. But numerous women read widely in physics, chemistry, surgery, medicine, botany, astronomy, mineralogy, the philosophy of Kant, dietetics, etc. They were especially attracted by the study of mineralogy and botany.

The ladies of good position who understood how to make themselves the centre of literary social life were imitated by middle-class women who founded so-called ' debating clubs ' to which only persons of the female sex were admitted[4].

[1] Doran, *ibid.*, pp. 264-271. According to Lady Crewe the ladies at Mrs. Montagu's parties are said to have actually worn blue stockings. Cf. the article ' Elizabeth Montagu ' in the *Dictionary of National Biography*. London, 1894. Vol. 38, p. 241.

[2] J. Russell, *Memories and Counsels*. Halle, 1876. P. 2.

[3] *London and Paris*. Weimar, 1799. Vol. IV, p. 296.

[4] Archenholtz, *England*, Vol. III, p. 142.

According to Archenholtz these clubs were not a success, partly because the fair sex has small talent for public speaking, and in consequence the speeches, on either side, had been learned by heart beforehand, and partly because many young men, dressed as women, found their way in![1]

More than by these distinguished Salons and the unfortunate Debating Clubs, the cause of women's emancipation was furthered by a book which, in spite of Mary Astell's and Daniel Defoe's pioneer work, must be described as the first book to treat the question in a comprehensive manner. The book, which was published in 1792, is *A Vindication of the Rights of Woman* by Mary Wollstonecraft (1759-1797).

She was an impulsive and enthusiastic woman of great charm, both in appearance and manner. Her portrait, painted by Opie, was owned by her son-in-law, who was no less a man than the poet Shelley. Mary Wollstonecraft's book has been almost forgotten in the flood of writing about the woman question with which we are inundated by modern literature. Most new books on the subject betray a complete ignorance of this admirable work. So I feel it is all the more important to draw attention to it, as I consider it is the best work that has been written upon the woman question. For the authoress recognises always the important and fundamental fact, which later J. S. Mill and after him many others have endeavoured either to dismiss or obscure, that man and woman are two different beings, and that in consequence there are limits to the emancipation of women. Mary Wollstonecraft's book still delights the reader of to-day by its sound understanding of human nature: it is the beautiful expression of a profound spirit. Moderate in tone, it is also moderate in its claims, and above all recognises those fundamental differences between man and woman which all the frenzied efforts of our modern viragoes can never alter. Mary

[1] Archenholtz, *Annals*, Vol. I, p. 469.

Wollstonecraft saw clearly that woman will never attain the same degree of emancipation as man, and men will always surpass them in many things. This thought permeates the whole work.

In sketching shortly the most important moments in the history of women's emancipation in England, I begin with literature. Among all the nations of Europe since the seventeenth century English women have possessed, relatively speaking, the largest number of writers. This is explained by the fact that English women take a much greater interest in literature, and read far more books than continental women. The girl, for example, who goes to town to shop, makes a practice of reading a book, just as an Englishman spends a great deal of his leisure in reading. An observer could collect many amusing incidents caused by this reading mania in the streets of London. There have been lending libraries from the earliest days—eagerly patronised by the feminine public—such as those of Hookham and Lackington in the eighteenth century. James Lackington writes in his *Memoirs*: ' Ladies do not now read only romances—though many of them are excellent productions which improve the heart as well as the mind, but they read also the best books in the English language, and many read the best authors in other languages as well. Many thousands of ladies who visit my shop know quite as well what books to choose and are quite as well acquainted with works of taste and genius as the gentlemen of fashion who are so ready to sneer at women novel readers [1].' Naturally, of course, the number of light readers was greater than those interested in serious reading[2]; and it is not otherwise to-day.

[1] James Lackington, *Memoirs*. London, 1793. P. 266.
[2] These novels were often of an extremely doubtful character. Jouy relates how he found a very erotic novel left behind by two ladies in Kensington Gardens (*The Hermit of London*, by M. de Jouy. Paris, 1820. Vol. I, p. 155). In a scene in *The Rivals* Sheridan pictures Lydia Languish

I shall only mention the most prominent among the vast number of English authoresses. Aphra Behn (1644-1689) (akin to Susanne Centlivre, her 'sister spirit in the Lord Priapus' as Johannes Scherr remarks[1]) was the only obscene woman writer that England produced, yet she possessed a talent by no means to be despised, and in her *Oronooko* pursued the same aim as, nearly two centuries later, Mrs. Harriet Beecher Stowe in *Uncle Tom's Cabin*. Miss Fanny Burney (1752-1840), who became Madame d'Arblay, achieved a high reputation in the eighteenth century, though she is known to-day mainly by Macaulay's famous essay, her novels *Evelina* and *Cecilia* being almost forgotten. Anna Radcliffe (1764-1823), on the other hand, lives yet; her thrillers are still asked for at lending libraries.

The two most prominent women-writers in the nineteenth century were without doubt Felicia Hemans and George Eliot. Mrs. Hemans (1794-1835) sings of God's mercy: her beautifully shaped 'songs, filled with devotion, are sweet-scented roses in the garland of English lyrics' (Scherr).

---

commissioning her maid Lucy to fetch frivolous books from different libraries and endeavouring to hide the forbidden fruit from her aunt:
'LYDIA: Wait. Somebody's coming. Quick. See who it is.
'LUCY: Oh! It's my Lord and your Aunt.
'LYDIA: Quick. Lucy, dear. Hide the books. Throw "Tanzai" under my toilet. Put "Adultère Innocent" behind "Human Duties". Push Ovid under the pillow, and "Bijoux Indiscrets" into your pocket.'
Crébillon, Scarron and Diderot were also popular. Hogarth, in his 'Marriage à la Mode,' portrayed Crébillon's 'Sopha' lying on the sofa of Lady Squanderfield; and Lichtenberg adds the comment that the book suits a lady's library as nicely as silver balls or sugar plums a Christmas tree. On the other hand, however, as Moritz points out, English classics were widely circulated in the eighteenth century and read by high and low. His landlady, a tailor's widow, read Milton by preference. English people, too, unlike Germans even to-day, bought the books they read. Cheap editions of the classics were owned by everybody. Cf. C. Ph. Moritz, *Travels in England in* 1782. Leipzig. Pp. 34-35.

[1] J. Scherr, *General History of Literature*, ninth edition. Stuttgart, 1895. Vol. II, p. 47.

George Eliot (1819-80) was perhaps the most important of all European women-novelists: in her novels (*Scenes of Clerical Life, The Mill on the Floss, Silas Marner, Middlemarch*) she endeavoured to solve contemporary problems, both philosophical and social, by bringing her genius to bear upon them; she was a poet whose name ' posterity will mention in the same breath with Dickens and Thackeray[1] '.

As regards art, English women have only excelled as painters during the last century. Fanny Reynolds, the portrait painter, ' merely imitates her famous brother's faults ', his pupil, James Northcote, remarked; Mrs. Conway distinguished herself as a miniature painter, Mrs. Carpenter as a painter of landscapes[2].

In 1859 Miss Herford, Mrs. Grote and Mrs. Lind-Goldschmidt founded the Society of Lady Artists, which held its fortieth exhibition in 1895[3].

There were opera-singers in England from the beginning of the eighteenth century, and composers from 1780, amongst others Mrs. Beardman, Kate Fanny Loder, Eliza Flower, Mrs. Barnard, etc.[4]

Ever since the beginning of the eighteenth century, when the Duchess of Marlborough played such an important part in political life, English women have taken a lively interest in politics and have been especially active at elections. Moreover, the ladies of the eighteenth century delighted to discourse on political topics in their letters[5]. In May 1738 there was an interesting debate, behind closed doors, in the House of Lords, to which only members of the Commons were to be admitted; a group of ladies determined to flout the order. At 9 a.m. they appeared at the door and Sir

[1] Ernst von Wolzogen, *George Eliot*. Leipzig, 1885. P. 228.
[2] G. Hill, *loc. cit.*, Vol. I, pp. 294, 296.
[3] *Ibid.*, Vol. II, p. 168.
[4] *Ibid.*, Vol. II, pp. 172-174.
[5] *Ibid.*, Vol. I, p. 336.

William Sanderson courteously informed them that the Chancellor had issued orders forbidding their admission. The Duchess of Queensberry, as 'leader of the squad', stormed at the ill-breeding of a mere lawyer, and begged Sir William to let them in on the quiet. He refused politely at first, and then swore he would never let them pass. Her Grace replied with noble warmth that enter she would in spite of the Chancellor and the whole House. When the Peers were told, it was decided to starve her out. Orders were given that the doors should be kept closed till the sitting was over. But the Amazons proved themselves stout besiegers.

They stood their ground till 5 p.m. without food, banging and kicking the door to such purpose that speakers in the House could hardly be heard above the din. When the Lords ignored this conduct, the two Duchesses, expert in the tactics of war, ordered half-an-hour's complete silence. The Chancellor took this for a sure proof that they had gone away, and gave orders for the doors to be thrown open, as members of the House of Commons were impatiently awaiting admission. On that, the ladies burst in and planted themselves in the front rows of the gallery. They stayed until 11 p.m., when the House rose; and throughout the debate applauded and booed, and made themselves generally conspicuous[1].

It can easily be imagined what an effect this political keenness of women produced at election times. Thus the Duchess of Devonshire worked hard for the return of Charles Fox in 1784. Fox won the election, in spite of the Tory poster: 'No murder! No club law, no butcher's law, no petticoat government!' John Stuart Mill's support of equal political rights for women is the most important event in the history of women's struggle for political power during the nineteenth century in England. In May 1866 he presented to Parliament a petition to this effect, signed by 1,499 women;

[1] G. Hill, *loc. cit.*, Vol. II, pp. 31-33.

MY WIFE!

Who in three Weeks after marriage
Did use me with uncivil carriage
And prov'd herself an arrant Baggage?
MY WIFE!

Pl. 4]

Artist unknown

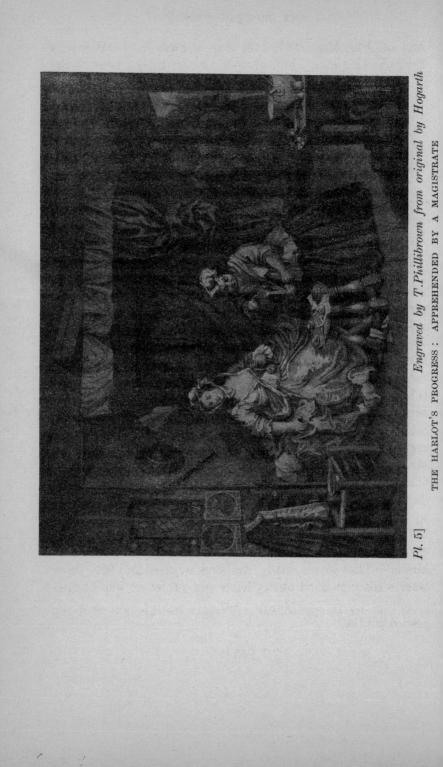

Pl. 5]

Engraved by T.Phillibrown from original by Hogarth

THE HARLOT'S PROGRESS : APPREHENDED BY A MAGISTRATE

and on 19th May 1867, ' the day of days in the Woman's Suffrage Calendar ', Mill proposed as an amendment to the ' Representation of the People Bill ', that the word *man* should be struck out and replaced by the word *person*. This was rejected by 202 votes to 83. Since then the Central Committee of the National Society for Woman's Suffrage, under the leadership of Mrs. Fawcett, worked actively to reach that goal towards which Mill strove[1].

Very interesting is the history of the part played by women in the medical profession in England. In the Middle Ages any woman who possessed knowledge of medicine was regarded as a witch. During the reign of Henry V a petition was presented: ' that no women use the practyse of fisyck under payne of long emprisonment.' Under Henry VIII women herbalists enjoyed special protection. Midwifery was practised by women in the Middle Ages. Not till 1518 were there accoucheurs, who however remained of inferior standing to the accoucheuses till 1750. But it was a man who by the discovery of the forceps made the greatest contribution to the *ars obstetrica* in thousands of years (Chamberlin about 1670). In 1671 a licensed midwife, Mrs. Jane Sharp, published the first book on midwifery: it went into four editions. As already mentioned, women's great dislike of male midwives persisted till the end of the eighteenth century. This is confirmed by recorded instances that are very quaint. Thus Miss Willughby, a midwife and daughter of Dr. Percy Willughby, wished on one occasion to bring her father into consultation on a very critical case. He did not venture to enter the room openly. ' At my daughter's request ', he says, ' I crawled in on hands and knees.' That was in 1618. And one hundred and fifty years later a distinguished obstetrician and professor was obliged

[1] G. Hill, *loc. cit.*, pp. 35, 331. [Women's franchise was, of course, granted in 1915.]

to crawl into a bedroom in the same surreptitious manner[1].
Amongst the many quacks who flourished during the
eighteenth century there were a few women who achieved
some renown. The first women doctors in the nineteenth
century were Dr. Elizabeth Blackwell and Miss Elizabeth
Garrett. In 1869 Sophia Jex-Blake started an agitation
for the admission of women to the study of medicine. At
length seven girls were permitted to attend medical lectures
at Edinburgh University. As they were about to enter the
lecture-room they were received by the medical students
and a specially hired mob with the vilest abuse—and pelted
with mud! Women were finally admitted to the study of
medicine in 1876 by the Russell Gurney Act[2].

In the nursing profession the name of the noble Miss Florence
Nightingale shines out for ever, since the days of the Crimean
War. To her England owes the magnificent organisation
known as the Nurses Training Institution at St. Thomas's
Hospital. Above all, have philanthropy and nursing been
benefited in England by women.

The most energetic champion of the complete emancipation of women was John Stuart Mill. His book *The Subjection of Women*, which was published in 1869 and roused
heated discussion, may be regarded as one of the most
extreme in the literature of this question. It contains
four chapters. In the first, the introduction, the author
begins by pointing out that the standing of the two sexes has
not been made different by nature. He instances as specially
important that the character of the modern woman has been
artificially produced and that no experience lies behind
woman in a state of emancipation. Thus the advantages
of men over women are one-sided. It is certain that the
emancipated woman would not act contrary to her nature.

[1] G. Hill, *loc. cit.*, Vol. II, pp. 271-275.
[2] *Ibid.*, Vol. II, pp. 284-285.

The second chapter describes modern marriage and pictures woman's subjection under it. For even if a woman may often rule her husband, yet to have power neither in the affairs of the family nor of the state is but a mock-freedom. The wife, according to Mill, has the greatest hardships to bear in marriage.

The third chapter of Mill's book deals with the admission of women to professions hitherto closed to them. He is of opinion that woman is equipped for every branch of human knowledge and activity, though he recognises the physical and mental differences between man and woman, which he believes can be explained by the long seclusion of woman.

In the fourth chapter, finally, he envisages the results of women's emancipation which will yield a marked increase of individual talent as well as the clearer effect on public life of the moral influence of woman which to-day is latent. The uplifting of the whole status of womanhood will prove no less full of blessing for marriage.

In my earlier works I have already stated my conviction that the complete removal of social, political and administrative distinctions between man and woman (that is, emancipation in Mill's meaning of the term) would not be advantageous, would be, in fact, frankly unworkable. I also drew attention to the veritable core of the modern woman's movement which consists in the fact women to-day can claim ' greater rights ' and ' more numerous opportunities of education '. I said that woman is man's companion with equal rights, but not with equal strength. Opponents and advocates of women's freedom both fall into the same error. They compare what is incomparable. Whoever wishes to pass a fair and unbiassed judgment upon the woman question must realise, in my opinion, that it is impossible merely to place man and woman upon an equality as extreme theorists like Mill suggest. It is customary to say they complete each other. Which is as much as to say that each has something that the other does not possess. But it is certain that these differences are more of a qualitative than of a quantitative kind. It cannot be said woman has less intelligence, is stupider than man, as those opponents of woman's emancipation assert who pride themselves so much upon their male 'superiority'. But one must say woman has a different intelligence from man. Woman is not 'less' or 'more' than man, she is merely 'different'. Buckle, in his fine essay on *The Influence of Woman on Science*, has offered one more convincing proof of his mind's penetrating acuteness. He here investigates these differences of quality in the purely mental sphere, and proceeds to make abundantly clear that it will be as impossible for women to adopt all man's capabilities as it is impossible for man to attain the merits of sheer womanliness. Buckle shows that Nature has made women more deductive and men more inductive. Women judge from the general, men from the particular. Women possess to a greater degree what is called intuition. They do not see so far as men; but what they see they grasp more quickly.

Will it be possible for women's emancipation to remove those differences between man and woman which are rooted in their innermost being? Even the most rabid advocates of women's rights must accept the undeniable fact that woman bears children, not man: that woman menstruates, not man[1]. It remains equally true that these primitive functions will always be a hindrance to complete emancipation, though they do not preclude advance and improvement in the intellectual and social position of women, which every fair-minded man willingly recognises as necessary.

[1] Though it has recently been asserted that man experiences ' something like menstruation '.

But if one looks at the final goal, one sees it must be for ever unattainable.

I hope and believe that John Ruskin will remain right in the future too. He held woman's work to be fivefold. (1) To please her fellow human beings. (2) To feed them appetisingly. (3) To clothe them. (4) To keep them clean and tidy. (5) To teach them. According to Mrs. Hawthorne, home is the woman's great arena, and will, she hopes, remain so. There she can exercise a sway that no king or emperor can rival. And it is compatible with culture, intellect and earnestness. I should like to cry aloud to the modern woman: Educate yourself; dedicate your time to science; take part in the thoughts and occupations of man, but do not seek to do as he does. For you will never be his equal, even as he will never be your equal.

CHAPTER 11

MARRIAGE

ACCORDING to Taine women in England are more womanly and men more manly than elsewhere. Each of the two natures reach their extreme development; the one, that of courage, resistance and initiative; the other, that of gentleness and self-sacrifice; the one is great in contentiousness, determination and dominance, the other inexhaustible in patience and self-effacement. Hence the happiness and permanence of married life in England. In France marriage is the union merely of two comrades on very much the same footing: hence the perpetual crossness and irritation. In contrast to the woman in Southern countries, the woman in England yields herself up entirely, without care for herself: she seeks her happiness in obedience, in generosity, in service. She preserves one wish only, to live day by day ever more fully in the life of the husband she has chosen freely and for ever. Witness a long procession of characters in German and English literature. This old Germanic instinct is portrayed by Beaumont and Fletcher (in the characters of Bianca, Ordella, Arethusa, Juliana, Euphrasia, Amoret), Webster (Duchess of Malfi, Isabella), Ford and Greene (Penthea, Dorothea), etc. All these and many other women display a wonderful power of sacrifice and generosity in the midst of the sorest trials and the strongest temptations. Their soul is at once primitive and grave. Here women remain loyal longer than elsewhere. Their love does not consist in tasting forbidden fruit; rather do they stake their whole life upon it[1].

Finck maintains that modern romantic love originated in England. ' Love in England and America is romantic love, pure and simple, as it was first presented by Shakespeare and after him, with more or less exactness, by a hundred other poets and novelists. This love does not lack colour, warm glowing colour, but it is no longer mere local colour, of a kind peculiar to nation or province: it is love in its very essence, in its universal form: love such as in the course of time will hold sway and must hold sway over the whole of this planet. England wears in the crown, which her many services to civilisation have won for her, many a jewel; but the brightest of them is the fact that she was the first country in the world—the world of antiquity, the world of the Middle Ages, and the world of to-day—to remove the bars from the windows of the great women-prison, to open all doors for the unhindered entry of Cupid and to make him everywhere at home and everywhere welcome[2].'

The sacredness of marriage, which Burke in his treatise on *The Sublime and Beautiful* praised in such glowing terms, is still to be met with in England, perhaps more frequently than in other countries. Travellers and writers have always praised this inwardness of English family life, as for example Goldsmith pictures it in the first chapter of *The Vicar of Wakefield*, or as Miss Burney shows us in her diary, where she describes a walk of the Royal family at Windsor[3].

The pessimistic conception of marital happiness which Byron expresses in the third canto of *Don Juan* (verses 5-10) is to be attributed rather to personal incidents than to any general experience.

[1] H. Taine, *History of English Literature*, Vol. I, pp. 407-409.
[2] Finck, *loc. it.*, Vol. II, pp. 40-46.
[3] Cf. W. M. Thackeray, *The Four Georges*.

In contradiction to these pictures of English love and marriage stands the remarkable fact that marriage by purchase and usages linked with it dishonouring to woman have persisted in England from ancient times right up to the last century. Nowhere has marriage by purchase assumed such repulsive forms as in England. The origin of this barbarous custom goes right back to the Anglo-Saxon era[1]. Jeaffreson gives a plausible explanation of the origin of English marriage by purchase. According to him, the English father brought up his daughters in the patriarchal period to very discreet ideas, so that on reaching marriageable age they were unused to expensive ways; enriched him rather by their work. They not only did his cooking, but made his clothes and helped on the farm. So it came about that the more daughters a man had, the richer he was held to be. They were a direct source of gain for him. For this reason marriage by purchase was introduced neither in the interests of women nor in the interests of intending bridegrooms, but solely in those of the father with marriageable daughters[2]. The custom was made possible by the lowly status of woman. According to Anglo-Saxon laws she was always obliged to live under the lordship of a man who was called her 'mundbora' or protector. The father was naturally the protector of the unmarried daughter. On his death the brother took the father's place. After him came the next of male kin, and in the absence of male kin, the King. The girl's value was decided by her rank, and the law fixed the price which had to be paid for her[3]. A widow was worth only half as much as a

[1] According to some, marriage by purchase is thought to have prevailed among the ancient Britons. Cf. *London As It is*. Leipzig, 1826. P. 85.

[2] J. C. Jeaffreson, *Brides and Bridals*. Second edition. London, 1873. Vol. I, pp. 33-35.

[3] F. Somner Merryweather, *Glimmerings in the Dark; or Shadows of the Olden Times*. London, 1850. P. 190.

virgin[1]. She was obliged, however, by a law of Canute to remain
unmarried for at least twelve months after the death of her
first husband. If she married within that period, she was
obliged to hand over the fortune of her first husband to his
next of kin. This was made law by Henry I. Every guest
at the wedding gave the bridal pair a present. The mundbora
conducted the daughter to the bridegroom with the words:
' I give thee my daughter, to be thy honour, and thy wife,
to keep thy keeps, and to share with thee thy bed and goods.'
Then the priest gave his blessing to this marriage by purchase.
On the morning after the wedding the bridegroom, before
he got out of bed, gave his wife a valuable gift, the
' morgaen-gife ', which remained her special property[2].

When Christianity reached England marriage by purchase
had already become general and the various marriage laws
applied directly to this institution. But a law of King
Ethelbert enacted that a young husband might return his
wife to her father and demand the repayment of the money
he had given for her[3], if he found her on closer inspection
in a different condition from that which the seller had
admitted. On the other hand, by a subsequent law, the
man who did not marry a woman he had bought was
obliged to forfeit the wedding price and to pay a fine as well[4].
Whoever had intercourse with a virgin was obliged to buy
and marry her; or in the event of the father not agreeing
to the marriage, at any rate pay her value in money. (Law of
King Alfred.) If a free man dishonoured the wife of a free
man, he was forced to pay the full ' weregeld ' and also to

---

[1] There were four grades of widow. First were worth 50s., second 20s.,
third 12s., fourth 6s. So a poor man was often in a position to purchase
a widow when he could not afford a virgin. Merryweather, *loc. cit.*, p. 192.

[2] Merryweather, *loc. cit.*, pp. 192-194.

[3] Jeaffreson, *loc. cit.*, Vol. I, p. 55.

[4] Thomas Wright, *Domestic Manners in England during the Middle
Ages*. London, 1862. P. 55.

purchase another wife for the wronged husband and bring her to the house[1]. Very speculative fathers sometimes even sold the same daughters to different men[2].

Marriage by purchase continued in England up to the nineteenth century. In its first decades the sale of women was still relatively frequent. But even so late as 1884 such cases are on accredited record. In an article in *All the Year Round* of the 20th December 1884, more than twenty cases were given from the preceding year, with names and all details in which prices were paid for women varying from five and twenty guineas and half a pint of beer, to a penny and a dinner[3]. Marriage by purchase was very frequent in the eighteenth century, especially towards its end, and at the beginning of the nineteenth century. ' Never was the sale of women so frequent ', says Archenholtz, ' as now. Scenes of this kind, once so rare, have become common. The sale of women among the common people is more frequent than ever[4].'

Jouy remarks that in his time (about 1815) all efforts of authority to remove this scandal proved vain[5]. Most often

---

[1] Merryweather, *loc. cit.*, p. 192.

[2] ' It was not uncommon for a greedy and unprincipled father, in this old period, to sell a handsome daughter to three or four different suitors, and, after receiving as many handsome payments for her without surrendering immediate possession of her person, to give her at last to another admirer for an adequate consideration.'—Jeaffreson, *loc. cit.*, Vol. I, pp. 39-40. The possibility of this repeated sale is explained by the fact the money could be paid long before marriage (even while the bride was still a child), and that, too, to cover the expenses of a good upbringing and good fare for the bride.

[3] Finck, *loc. cit.*, Vol. II, p. 47.

[4] Archenholtz, *Annals.* Vol. V, p. 329. Vol. XIX, p. 187 (of the years 1790 and 1796).

[5] ' Une coutume aussi infâme s'est conservée sans interruption, qu'elle est mise chaque jour à exécution; que si quelques magistrats des comtés, informés que de semblables marchés allaient se faire, ont cherché à les empêcher en envoyant sur les lieux des constables ou huissiers, la populace les a toujours dispensés, et qu'elle a maintenu ce qu'elle considère comme son droit.' Jouy, *L'Hermite de Londres*, Vol. II, p. 324.

husbands sold their wives; fathers sold their daughters more seldom than in earlier days.

The conduct of such sales was the roughest imaginable and most humiliating for the unfortunate woman. Commonly the husband led his wife with a rope round her neck, on a market day, to the place where cattle were sold, bound her to a post and sold her to the highest bidder in the presence of the necessary witnesses. Some quite lowly official, often the husband himself, fixed the price, seldom more than a few shillings; then he untied her and led her round the market place by the rope[1]. The people called this kind of sale 'the horn market'. The purchasers were usually widowers and bachelors. The woman became by such sale the authentic mate of the purchaser, and her children by him were looked upon as legitimate. Sometimes the new husband followed this purchase by a wedding in church. Thus a lord, for example, who had seduced the wife of a servant, bought her formally from the husband and afterwards married her. The law allowed such marriages, which were regarded as legal. Women were offered for sale, too, in the newspapers. The following advertisement appeared in a Dublin paper in May 1791: 'A bargain to be sold.' This was an expression which implied in Ireland the sale of a woman[2]. The ordinary place in London where these sales of women were held was Smithfield Market, where, too, as has been pointed out, the cattle market was held. In *The Times* of 22nd July 1797 the following notice occurs: 'By an oversight in the report on Smithfield Market we are not in a position to quote this week the price of women. The increasing value of the fairer sex is considered by various celebrated writers to be a

---

[1] Cf. Jouy, *loc. cit.*, Vol. II, pp. 317-319. Chapter 'Vente de Femmes à Londres'. Pp. 317-324. With a vignette showing such a sale-scene, in which the rope is to be seen.

[2] Archenholtz, *Annals*, Vol. VII, p. 177.

sure sign of increasing civilisation. On these grounds Smithfield may raise a claim to rank as a place of special advance
in refinement, for at its Market the price of women has lately
risen from half a guinea to three guineas and a half[1].' On
12th April 1817, at Smithfield Cattle Market, Jouy saw a
man, in the middle of a large crowd, struggling to put a rope
round the neck of a young and pretty woman, who offered
violent resistance. The noise attracted the attention of a
constable, who arrested them both and took them before
the magistrate. The man excused his conduct on the grounds
of his wife's infidelity, and she could not refute the
charge. There was nothing for the magistrate to do except
to deplore the barbarous scene and to caution the man to
keep the peace in future. The woman was acquitted and
both were released with the mildest warning[2].

I shall give a few examples of this shocking ceremony,
from which will be seen what slight value a woman had in
England. ' A farmer', so Archenholtz related, ' some time
ago, living in an English county, advertised the loss of his
horse in a London newspaper, and offered the finder a
reward of five guineas. Curiously enough it happened
that his wife too ran away the next day, and the farmer
in the same paper offered a reward for her recovery—of four
shillings![3]' A labourer in Oxford sold his wife to a bricklayer
for 100 shillings. He led her into the market-place, as usual
by a rope, which he held on to until he had pocketed the
money, whereupon he handed her over to her new husband
and wished him the best of luck. A similar incident occurred
in Essex where a man sold his wife and two children for
half-a-crown. The ceremony was performed to music and
the mother was obliged to walk three times round the

---

[1] Finck, loc. cit., Vol. II, pp. 47-48.
[2] Jouy, loc. cit., Vol. II, p. 319.
[3] Traits from the Character of English Criminals, p. 49.

market-place at Marchin Green with the rope round her neck.
A journeyman carpenter in London sold his wife to a mate,
who was overjoyed when a few weeks afterwards his new
wife inherited an unexpected legacy of £1,500. In Nottingham a man sold his wife three weeks after the wedding: a
blacksmith bought her for a shilling. A countryman living
near Thame in Oxfordshire had sold his wife a few years
back, but without any formalities. His neighbours told him
that the sale was not valid, and so he decided upon a
repetition of the ceremony, fetched his former wife and led
her seven miles round to Thame, where she was duly sold for
half-a-crown. The more remarkable thing about it was
that he had to pay fourpence tax on the woman, the same as
for the purchase of a beast. A donkey-driver in Westminster
sold his wife and his donkey together for 13 shillings and
two pots of beer to another donkey-driver, whereupon
they all three repaired to a public-house and drank up the
beer. In February 1790 the head of a parish by Swadlincote
had a woman sold in Burton. Her husband had absconded
from the woman, who in consequence had to be supported
by the parish. To be rid of this burden, the parish councillors
sent the woman to Burton market, where she was bought for
a florin. The purchase was carefully entered in the parish
accounts, and the cost of the rope was included[1]. In March
1796 a button-maker in Sheffield disposed of his wife to a
porter for the large sum of sixpence: the overseer of the
market acted as witness for a fee of fourpence[2]. On the
9th December 1819 a man sold his wife to a painter for
5s. 6d.; on 30th January 1817 a gentleman of private
means got rid of his wife for 1s. 6d., whereupon he stood the
buyer a glass of beer to drink his health in, he was so delighted.
In April of the same year a very brutal man dragged his

[1] Archenholtz, *Annals*, Vol. V, pp. 330-331.
[2] *Ibid.*, Vol. XIX, p. 187.

wife with a rope round her neck, with the utmost cruelty, into the market-place at Dartmouth and sold her for two guineas. The plight of the woman, who had been married a year and a half, roused general sympathy; she suffered, too, under his brutal treatment. But her luck was in; she was bought by her first lover. The lowest price paid for a wife was threepence—in Nottingham, the same year.

On occasions the custom of marriage by purchase was applied to men. Though very seldom, examples yet occurred up to the nineteenth century of the sale of husbands, which the courts severely reprimanded but could not forbid any more than in the case of women. A certain Margaret Collins complained before the Mayor of Drogheda that her husband was living with another woman. The husband submitted that his uncommonly strong and furious wife, who often bit him in her rage (and that, too, quite recently), had handed him over to another woman, his present wife, at a price, twopence being first offered and 1½d. taken[1]. At that the plaintiff, in the presence of the whole court, leaped at the newly married couple and went for them tooth and nail until she was dragged off[2].

There is no need of lengthy argument to estimate rightly the coarseness and brutality which underlay the institution of marriage by purchase. The fact that it could last so long in England speaks clearly enough of itself. According to Finck, even in the lowest classes, the sellers frequently came in for rough handling, so that they were pelted with stones and mud; while for the wives, the horror of the proceedings was mitigated by the fact that in all accredited cases of this kind they were only too glad to be sold and thereby be freed from their tyrants.

[1] Wives, it is to be noted, valued husbands at an even lower figure than husbands wives.
[2] Jouy, *loc. cit.*, Vol. II, pp. 321-322.

The frivolity with which marriage was treated in earlier days in England is strikingly illustrated by two curious phenomena in the sphere of matrimony, the so-called Fleet marriages and the notorious parsons of Gretna Green.

Fleet marriages take their name from Fleet Prison, in the City ward Fleet Ditch, in which the weddings were performed. Right up to the beginning of the eighteenth century a man walked about all day in front of the Fleet Prison, who asked the passers-by: 'Anyone want to be married?' as at fairs nowadays a showman will shout invitations to step up to see wax-works or a menagerie. On the doors hung a sign representing a man and woman with joined hands, and for a few pence the functioning parson married every couple who wanted to be united. In 1704 nearly 3,000 weddings were performed in this manner in four months[1].

In 1735 a woman correspondent wrote to the *Gentleman's Magazine* complaining about the number of ruinous marriages which were celebrated every year in the Fleet Prison ' by a crowd of drunken clergymen in black coats who purported to be " clerks " and " registrars to the Fleet," who walked up and down Ludgate Hill and persuaded those in ale houses and ginshops to marriage, thereby keeping them on the Sabbath from attendance at church[2] '. From October 1704 to February 1705, 2,954 weddings were performed; often twenty or thirty couples were mated in a single day. Pennant related that often, when he was a young man passing by the prison, he was accosted by a dirty fellow who urged him to come inside and get married. He saw the clergyman walking to and fro before the door—an unwholesome-looking, down-and-out creature clad in a dirty night-

[1] Fanny Lewald, *England and Scotland*. Second edition. Berlin, 1864. Vol. II, p. 79.
[2] *Doings in London*, p. 336.

gown, with a fiery red face, ready to couple anybody for a glass of gin or a twist of tobacco. The Governor of the prison and the Registrar got handsome incomes from these weddings.

Even in 1754 public advertisements read: ' With legal warrant. Marriages are celebrated in the ancient Royal Chapel of St. John the Baptist in the Savoy Palace with the greatest secrecy, despatch and regularity. There since the time of the Reformation to the present day (more than two hundred years) legal and authentic registers have been kept. Costs amount to one guinea only,—inclusive of the five-shilling stamp. There are seven secret approaches to this chapel, five by land and two by water[1].'

Even more famous than these Fleet marriages were the romantic weddings of Gretna Green at which that ' helper in romantic trouble ', as Fanny Lewald calls him, the blacksmith of Gretna Green, officiated. Gretna Green has been the Eldorado of unhappy lovers not only in novels (English and German) but also in real life. Archenholtz gave the following account of marriages made at Gretna Green: ' The marriage ceremony at Gretna Green on the Scottish border, whither people, anxious to be united, hasten with galloping post horses from all parts of the kingdom is so famous or rather notorious that a short description is necessary here. An Englishman, who played the part of bridegroom in a scene of this kind in 1790 writes as follows: After a tedious journey our coachman at length brought us to the cottage where the cement-master mixed his mortar to build the walls of Hymen's temple. He was not at home. He was sought for half an hour and at last found in a tavern from which this high-priest of Hymen and also of Bacchus came reeling

---

[1] Fanny Lewald, *loc. cit.*, pp. 79-80. Similar marriages were the so-called Mayfair marriages, which were celebrated at the London May Fair, and the Canongate marriages in Edinburgh. Cf. Jeaffreson, *loc. cit.*, Vol. II, pp. 203 *et seq*.

AFTER SWEET MEAT COMES SOUR SAUCE

OR GENERAL CASEY GOT INTO THE WRONG BOX.

Drawing by Rowlandson

[*Pl.* 6

in haste towards us. When I inquired about the price for which he coupled people, he made the modest demand of 30 guineas. But I gave him to understand that we would rather drive on another twenty miles to another clergyman than pay such an exorbitant fee. Whereupon he quickly changed his note, coming down to 10 guineas, to be paid, however, in advance. On this we agreed. But now he demanded a bottle of brandy from which during the ceremony, though it lasted hardly six minutes, he drank five glasses to strengthen his voice, as he put it. We asked for our marriage licence, which he immediately made out and signed with his name—Thomas Brown. It contained only a few lines to the effect that the persons Charles —— and Mary —— had been duly united by him according to the ritual of the English Church and the laws of the Scottish Church. When we desired the signature of witnesses, he said: This moment you shall have a couple of them; and gravely took a pen and with his hand wrote in two strange names. And we travelled back to England a properly married couple[1].' This incredible procedure was confirmed by Jeaffreson, who has given the most complete historical account of Gretna Green weddings. In the first place, according to him, the so-called smith is a fable which had its origin in the poetic idea of Vulcan, the smith forging the chains of matrimony. There is no proof that any Gretna Green marriage was performed in a smithy or that any of the famous ' couplers ' was a smith by trade. One of these so-called clergymen had been a common soldier, another was a tobacconist, and a third had carried a pedlar's pack. All were drunkards and knaves. There is no evidence of a blacksmith being found among them.

A certain Scott was the first to marry lovers. George Gordon, an old soldier, followed him. Gordon succeeded in convincing the simple bumpkins in the neighbourhood that

[1] Archenholtz, *Annals*, Vol. VII, pp. 250-252.

he had a special warrant to marry runaway lovers, for which
he had to pay the government ten pounds a year. As no
one wished to inspect this warrant, the knave was believed
to hold the monopoly of conducting weddings. But in the
year 1789 the fellow got a co-worker in Joe Paisley, once a
tobacconist, who made himself quickly popular in the
taverns of Gretna Green by his astonishing powers of
drinking. The innkeepers felt great gratitude towards this
' clergyman ', who did so much for them, and felt it also
their duty to do all in their power to support him.

At weddings Gordon appeared in the uniform of a soldier,
Paisley in complete clerical outfit. As he drank more and
more he became a monster of obesity and weighed in the
end over 21 stone. After his death many successors appeared.
A former pedlar, David Laing, got the lion's share. After the
scandal caused by the abduction of the rich Miss Ellen
Turner by Edward Jibbon Wakefield, he had to appear
on one occasion as witness before the court; his evidence
was most entertaining.

On the introduction of railways the number of marriages
at Gretna increased for a time; they were finally put a
stop to for ever, by law, in July 1856[1].

In the history of English marriage the phenomenon of
marriage advertisement deserves its place. England is the
home of the marriage advertisement. This is linked up
with the early and remarkable development of newspapers,
which in its turn was favoured by the reading mania of
English people. On 19th July 1695 Houghton, the father
of advertisement, printed in his *Collection for Improvement*

---

[1] Jeaffreson, *loc. cit.*, Vol. II, pp. 208-214. This law runs: 'After the 31st
December 1856 no irregular marriage contracted in Scotland by declaration, acknowledgement or ceremony, shall be valid, unless one of the
parties has at the date thereof his or her usual place of residence there or
has lived in Scotland for 21 days next preceding such marriage; any law,
custom or usage to the contrary notwithstanding.'

of Husbandry and Trade, the first advertisements of this kind: 'A gentleman, thirty years old, who says he has a very considerable fortune, would like to marry a young gentlewoman, who has a fortune of about £3,000 and he is willing to make a proper contract on the matter.'

'A young man 25 years old, with a good business, whose father is ready to settle £1,000 on him, would like to make a suitable marriage. He has been brought up by his parents as a dissenter, and is a useful man.'

It is clear that these first marriage advertisements do not forget the *punctum saliens* (on which I need not enlarge). Houghton attached to these advertisements the remark that if it were shown that he himself were disinterested and of great discretion and the inserters were of really good faith (which even to-day is very frequently open to question) these advertisements might prove themselves of great utility.

Houghton's idea caught on, and especially from the middle of the eighteenth century marriage advertisements rapidly increased in number. A close study of them is most amusing. For in them once more a great deal of English eccentricity is to be seen. Readers will be interested to know what a few of these marriage advertisements are like.

Archenholtz wrote: ' One of the strangest British customs is the method of seeking a companion in marriage by means of advertisement in the newspaper. In August 1788 an advertisement appeared in London papers which easily outdid hundreds of others of a similar nature: it ran as follows: " *Advertisement for a Wife.* Sir John Dimly, Bart., Lord of the Manor of Charleton near Worcester and of Henly Castle near Malvern Wells, wishes to make a contract of marriage with a young woman, and in the event of his death to settle on her £192,000 sterling, if she will take him for her husband. The young woman must possess a fortune of 300 guineas of her own. It is all one, be she virgin or widow, yes, even she be pregnant by her former husband. More intimate information may be obtained from Sir John Dimly either by seeing him personally or by letter, but in the latter event postage must be paid." You would consider the whole thing to be the invention of a practical joker if numerous circumstances had not substantiated its truth[1].'

In the *Hampshire Chronicle* of June 1791 the following remarkable marriage advertisement appeared: ' All those who read this or hear of it are requested to think carefully whether they know a young woman at all answering to this description: well developed and full of grace in her person; more a beautifully made woman than a pretty one; good teeth, soft lips, agreeable breath; the colour of her eyes, immaterial; further, a full firm and white bosom; affectionate and well educated but not witty; courteous and neat in speech, with looks that prove that she is able really to feel pleasure where she wishes to inspire it in others. If there be such a person, a gentleman 56 years old, but vigorous and strong, is determined to marry her, however small her fortune may be. He possesses an income of £800 a year and is ready to make a preliminary settlement on her of £100. But she must agree to live entirely in the country, to love the husband of her choice with all her heart, and withal she must not be more than seven years older or fourteen years younger than I am. Letters should be addressed, etc.[2] '

In a Bristol paper appeared, August 1795: ' A gentleman needs a companion to journey with him towards matrimony; his intention is to depart as swiftly as possible, to leave the main roads and highways and to stroll in the paths in the wood of love. His fellow-traveller must be healthy, not too

---

[1] Archenholtz, *Annals*, Vol. I, pp. 339-340.
[2] *Ibid.*, Vol. VII, pp. 203-204.

fat because that would make the journey troublesome, and to while away the hours of the marriage state, the chattier the better: etc.[1] '

On 22nd May 1797 a girl in London had the following advertisement printed in *The Observer*, a Sunday paper:

' TO WHOM IT MAY CONCERN:

'A young lady has been obliged for some years now to live secluded from the world for the pleasures of which she felt at least inclination, as her duty was to look after a sick relative. Now suddenly thrown among people, she finds that the possession of a large fortune in no way compensates her for the absence of the one person with whom she was accustomed to live. She is cut off from advantages enjoyed by others and is, in consequence, compelled to use the only means in her power, unusual as they may be, to find what she is seeking—a friend. Should a gentleman of breeding, who is not old, of good faith, pleasing, well-mannered and good family, or a lady who has such a brother or son, wish to know more of the undersigned, a few lines, should they prove agreeable, will receive careful attention: letters must be sent care of this newspaper which has the writer's address, as delicacy at first forbids any other course.

Eliza.'

Following this, for five consecutive Sundays many letters appeared in *The Observer*. The editor was obliged to issue an edition of his paper half as large again as usual, because everybody, especially the match-makers, were anxious to see how this public courtship would fare. All London talked of it, and in the papers as well as in society people liked to appear as though they knew well enough who this mysterious Eliza was.

[1] Archenholtz, *Annals*, Vol. XVI, pp. 138-139.

Eliza achieved her purpose, and had her choice among a large number of picked men. At first nothing was heard of the issue of the affair. But gradually in society people came along who pretended to know Eliza. Once at the opera the author of *London and Paris* was shown one of the most perfect beauties in a box, over whose chair a big handsome man was leaning. ' Have a good look at that couple; that is the famous Eliza, now Mrs. C., with her husband. She brought him a fortune of £70,000 and he is worth £30,000. They possess everything to make life delightful; but in themselves is their greatest wealth; they see little society and enjoy being with the boys she has borne him. I know from a fairly reliable source a few facts about the courtship. I'll tell you. She and her lady companion took a house and engaged new servants. Both were dressed in black and wore half-masks. Usually this surprised men, and they were unprepared for the serious, decided kind of talk. But as soon as ever Eliza saw that the man in her company deserved trust she opened her heart to him in the most delightful way, and said all she could to him—without betraying her identity. At the end she got each man's word of honour not to give her away, even if her choice did not fall on him. You can see few men can compare with Mr. C. in looks, and with the rest our Eliza, like other women, wasn't too much concerned[1] '.

Marriage advertisements of a doubtful nature appeared in early days as they still do to-day, for the cloak of anonymity was highly favourable to the secret ways of vice. It is known why prostitutes desire marriage. Archenholtz informs us: ' Nymphs of the street assumed the mask of virtue and desired in the papers to marry men of good repute. They advertised themselves usually as young, well-educated and of considerable means, and wanted only a small capital from

[1] *London and Paris*, Vol. IV. Weimar, 1799. Pp. 27-34.

the man or a decent business. People from the country and
other inexperienced folk often fell into the snare. They found
a charming creature with the tender look of innocence, who
knew how to draw a moving picture of the unkind treatment
she has received from friends and relations, whereby the
ease with which her fortune was to be had was not forgotten.
It worked, the man fell—and woke to find himself—but too
late, betrayed[1].'

Papers devoted entirely to marriage advertisements appeared first in England. The first of this kind was issued
in London about 1870. The oldest read the *Matrimonial
News* with the greatest delight, the ' journal le plus extraordinaire, le plus anglais, le plus excentrique, le plus original
et la plus amusant de la Grande-Bretagne ', as Hector France
said[2]. Of the 500 or 600 persons who sought their happiness
in its columns an average of 80 per cent. were women. The
men belonged for the most part to the category which
France, with bitter sarcasm, dubs the ' Alphonses du
mariage ', the bullies of marriage, and have become more
numerous—alas! even in Germany—since then. Here are
a few examples of these pitiful fellows:

' Albert, big, dark, 27 years old, without means except for
his income of £80 a year, would like to make the acquaintance
of a lady from 30-45 years old, who has the means to make
a comfortable home. Photograph wanted.'

' Hubert, age 26, height five feet eight, dark, is considered
a handsome man, has an affectionate and loving nature, is
agreeable in manner but possesses only a modest pittance. He
is anxious to correspond with an elderly lady, not older than
60 however [*sic!*] and intends to marry immediately. She
must possess the means to run a comfortable establishment.

' Robert, engineer, age 27, height 6 feet, a good-looking

[1] Archenholtz, *England*, Vol. I, pp. 100-101.
[2] Hector France, *Les Nuits de Londres*. Paris, 1900. P. 309.

fellow, dark, strongly built, well brought up, good references, is anxious to marry. His position is good but not very profitable. He wishes to correspond with a rich elderly lady or widow[1] '.

Marriage clubs and marriage agencies attached themselves to these matrimonial papers. There were marriage clubs as early as 1700; their members aided one another to make good marriages and took on the cost of weddings. Even then a lot of fraud and swindling became mixed up with it[2], which is the case still with more modern 'matrimonial clubs[3] ', so that the existence of their own 'Detectives for Matrimonial Cases' is explained. For example, I take from the *Daily Telegraph* of 23rd July 1900 the following advertisement:

' Slater's Detectives for Furnishing Matrimonial Details as to the social position, past character, future prospects, general habits and temper of the intended partner for life, in order to make marriage a success. Consultations free.—1 Basinghall Street, E.C.'

Matrimonial agencies were also the product of the eighteenth century; they were not confined to England but are to be found also in France. The most famous London ' Marriage Bazaar ' in the eighteenth century was the establishment at 2 Dover Street, St. James's. In its prospectus can be read what follows: ' Every visitor to Dover Street will be shown into a separate room. Whoever cannot state his wishes personally must do so in writing through a friend. Declarations must be drawn up with the greatest exactness, not only with regard to position but also to age, physical state and religion.' The matrimonial candidate had to pay a preliminary fee of £5 5s., and as much again after the wedding. According to Sampson, the establishment was a

[1] Hector France, *loc. cit.*, pp. 322-323.
[2] Jeaffreson, *loc. cit.*, Vol. II, p. 87.
[3] Sampson, *loc. cit.*, p. 500.

complete swindle. At one of Madame Cornelys' famous masked balls, on 16th July 1776, the following lampoon on it was distributed:

MARRIAGE TREATIES

Ye Nymphs forlorn who pine away in Shades!
Ye mournful Widows waiting for—Brocades!
Coxcombs who sigh for—Mode! and sighing Wits!
Bucks of St. James's and ye half-moon'd Cits!
Ye old and young—the ugly and the fair!
To Hymen's Shrine haste, sacrifice despair.
Let Law divorce, tyrannic Husbands rail,
Hence dare their ire!—for here's enough for sale.
Let Virtue's mask the Wife awhile pursue,
Here's fresh Supply—here Wives of ev'ry Hue!
Black, white, red, grey—the bright, the dull, the witty!
Here's Dames for Courtiers, misses for the City!

As a curiosity, the following quaint advertisement of this agency in the *Daily Advertiser* of 1777 may here find place: ' Wanted by a young gentleman who has just started a place of his own, a lady of 18-25 years old, well bred and with a fortune of not less than £5,000; sound in wind and limb, 5 ft. 4 in. high without shoes on ; not fat but not too thin; clean skin; sweet breath and good teeth; without conceit or affectation; not too chatty and not quarrelsome, but yet with character enough to pay back a score; generous; not over-fashionable but always decent and tidy; the sort of person who can entertain her husband's friends gaily and pleasantly, and make parties gay and attractive; who can keep his secrets so that he can open his heart to her on all occasions without restraint; who lets economy rule in the home, and can with a light heart reduce the budget if necessity requires[1].'

[1] Sampson, *loc. cit.*, pp. 481-486.

[69]

The frequency and nature of the so-called Divorce and Crim.-Con.[1] cases must now be examined as a second characteristic phenomenon of English sex life. They form one of the most interesting chapters in the history of English morals: a chapter which is of a specifically English quality, and throws a peculiar light upon the character of the nation, as I have already mentioned in the introduction. To understand the national character, Crim.-Con. cases must be studied mostly, if not wholly, because they have evoked, like another English speciality the flagellation-mania, an enormous mass of literature.

The frequency of divorce is remarkable even among the Anglo-Saxons, who seem to have derived it from their Celtic ancestors. ' Divorce plays a great rôle in all the Celtic sagas[2]', for example in the Arthur Saga, Mordred seduces Guinevere, the wife of his uncle Arthur. Anglo-Saxon marriage was so easily broken that husband and wife could separate in the event of mutual incompatibility without more ado. Accordingly, intercourse between man and woman outside marriage was extremely widespread[3]. Divorces were quite common[4].

There were two kinds of divorce. The first required re-marriage, the second did not[5]. Among the numerous Divorce Laws that of King Ethelred's is particularly remarkable: ' If a freeman have been familiar with a freeman's wife let him pay for it with his " Wergild " and provide another wife with his own money and bring her home to the other[6].'

There was a law of King Edgar, which ordered that an

[1] See footnote on p. 15.
[2] Carl Weiser, *History of English Literature*. Leipzig, 1898. P. 9.
[3] Thomas Wright, *loc. cit.*, p. 54.
[4] Jeaffreson, *loc. cit.*, Vol. II, pp. 294-295.
[5] W. Alexander, *loc. cit.*, Vol. II, p. 237.
[6] Thomas Wright, *loc. cit.*, p. 55.

adulterer or an adultress should live on bread and water three days a week for seven years[1]. In Canute's time the adulteress had her nose and ears cut off and was condemned to perpetual celibacy, which in any case the Romish Church enjoined at that time[2]. Gradually the latter developed the principle of the indissolubility of marriage as a sacrament. It is noteworthy that in spite of this, divorces persisted during the Middle Ages in England[3] though they became less frequent. On the introduction of Protestantism, divorces again became daily occurrences and the eighteenth century is especially notorious for the large number of Crim.-Con. cases.

In spite of the large number of these cases it was no easy matter to bring one to a successful conclusion. Above all, the man who brought an action against his wife must himself have been above suspicion. If he neglected her for a mistress, if he exceeded decency in speech or conduct, if he did not forbid the visits of a stranger and did not, as absolute master, drive his wife's gallants out of the house, if he shut his eyes to what was going on and had been too complacent a husband—the seducer escaped all punishment. There were interesting examples of this. My Lord ——, a complete fool, had a wife whose body, in his opinion, resembled that of the Venus de Medici. Proud of having such charms at his disposal, he showed one of his friends his wife in her bath, for the friend had told him that he himself was married to the Callipygian Venus. Unfortunately, the friend was so enflamed by what he saw that he determined to seduce the lady—which he succeeded in doing. On which the husband brought an action against

---

[1] W. Alexander, *loc. cit.*, Vol. II, p. 233.
[2] Wright, *loc. cit.*, p. 54.
[3] *Brockhaus Encyclopaedia.* Vol. V. ' Divorce.'

[71]

the friend, with the result that he was himself punished as the seducer of his wife[1] '.

An old colonel brought a young subaltern to his house. The subaltern fell in love with the wife of his superior officer. The husband informed the court that the subaltern after dinner had enjoyed his wife on the sofa in the next room. But it was also pointed out that the old colonel had sat on over his wine while this happened, not taking that care of his wife which is the first duty of an English husband. The jury accordingly awarded him damages of one shilling only[2].

In no country was the system of espionage on women so highly developed as in England, where detective-bureaus, especially in Crim.-Con. proceedings, flourished. The famous Henry Slater recommended his detectives, who watched suspicious persons in all their comings and goings. ' What they do, what company they keep, whether the club can really be responsible for his late nights, and whether shopping only takes up so much of her time[3].' A similar advertisement of the same bureau read:

' DIVORCE

'Before commencing divorce proceedings consult Slater, who will secretly obtain all reliable evidence. Successful in every case wherein engaged in the Divorce Court for 13 years.'

As soon as sufficient evidence had been collected for the opening of a case (partly with the help of these detectives), public proceedings took place. Crim.-Con. procedure in

---

[1] *Les Dessous de la Pudibonderie Anglaise*. Paris, 1898. Vol. I, pp. xviii-xix. In a brochure on this case appeared a caricature in which Mylord —— had lifted the other on his back in order to see his wife getting out of the bath, with one foot on the side, the other in the water. Cf. *Traits of Originals*, p. 57.

[2] *Ibid.*, p. xix.

[3] Advertisement in *Daily Telegraph*, 1900.

England was notorious for its scandalous nature. Prudish England became unrecognisable on hearing the depositions which were made and listened to with the greatest composure. I will give the gist of some of the depositions to show their general quality.

A witness deposes that he has watched his good lady through the keyhole being kissed and cuddled and thrown on the sofa and afterwards putting her hair in order in front of the looking-glass.

Milady is accused of misdemeanour with an actor. Two women friends state, after taking the oath on a Testament, that they bored a hole in the wall through which they saw how this clever actor raised the lady's dress and pressed a kiss on her knee *se altius non iturum esse promittens*.

Mrs. Harris told her housemaid to put fresh curtains up on her bed as her husband was coming. Not the husband, however, but the Reverend Mr. Craven came. Her young sister, her women friends, her maids stood watch all night in the passage. They heard the bed creak and the housemaid told the court that she recognised the same dreadful stains in the bed as Barbara Kreutz saw in that of the unfortunate Queen Caroline of England[1].

A footman observed his mistress in a field with her lover 'in a very extraordinary situation'. The judge said: 'Describe the position,' and the witness *se met à quatre pattes devant le tribunal*[2].

A bishop deposed that his wife had seduced a young man whom she introduced into the house under the pretence of marrying him to their daughter. He was informed by this same daughter that her mother spent the nights with the intended bridegroom, so he lay in hiding and heard kisses given and received. When silence fell, he broke open the

[1] *Les Dessous de la Pudibonderie Anglaise*, Vol. I, p. xiii.
[2] *Ibid.*, p. xiv.

door with the help of his daughter and footmen, with lights in their hands. They found ' the amorous couple naked in the same bed[1] '.

If the witness had not described a doubtful situation with sufficient accuracy, magistrates never wearied of digging out the most obscene details by plying the often very naive witness with questions. With some justice Hector France described Crim.-Con. magistrates as the worst pornographers[2].

The whole conduct of these divorce cases points to a remarkable insensitiveness among Englishmen to scandal, even if it touched with its taint members of their family who were dragged into the proceedings. An English husband did not hesitate to broadcast his own shame. Archenholtz gave the following illustration of this:

'A ship's captain came upon his wife and one of his sailors when they expected not to be disturbed in what they were doing. He had her stripped naked and, with her lover, set astride a mast which was decked with streamers and carried on the shoulders of a number of sailors. The procession went through the streets of East London while a band played and an amazing crowd of people followed.'

'A country nobleman, who had come with his wife to London on a pleasure trip, had strong suspicions of her infidelity. He gave out he was going a journey and surprised

---

[1] *Les Dessous de la Pudibonderie Anglaise*, p. xix.

[2] ' Mais de tous les pornographes il n'en est peut être pas de plus osés que les magistrats et les gens de la loi de la Grande-Bretagne. Dans les procès adultère et de divorce, les cas d'enlèvement et de séduction de mineures, les scènes les plus risquées de viol et d'assault sur les filles impubères, ils exigent des témoins et des victimes un luxe de détails et se complaisent à des questions à faire rougir les dragons de la Reine; et comme les débats sont publics, que le huis-clos n'existe pas, même dans les causes les plus grasses, les chercheurs de documents humains peuvent y puiser d'amples études pour l'histoire des mœurs du temps.'—H. France, *In the Police Court.* Paris, 1891. P. ix.

her in the night in the arms of an officer. He was provided
with cord and had them bound by men hand and foot
and tied by the neck to the bed-posts. He exhibited them
in this plight to all his friends and acquaintances. The
friends brought others along, for which permission was
gladly given and this strange spectacle lasted for four days,
during which time the loving couple got nothing but bread
and water[1].'

It was almost always the husband who gave the journalists
the first details about his cuckoldom in order ' to enlighten
the spirit of the nation '. His honour seemed to receive
satisfaction by just that which in other countries would
have been accounted public disgrace. In a divorce case the
husband never made himself ridiculous, but it was always
the wife's lover, well thrashed, who went pale. A duel,
which in other countries was the usual outcome of this
sort of scandal, was regarded in England as utterly superfluous, as, indeed, a *chose ridicule*.

The scandal of Crim.-Con. cases was to a certain extent
increased and made lasting by print. English Crim.-Con.
literature is vast. And the contents? A mass of moral ordure
is heaped in these countless works, brochures, journals,
songs, etc., concerning divorce cases. I should like to compare
their contents with that in the works on so-called ' Pastoral
Medicine,' in which theologians, under the cloak of morality,
complacently broadcast the most obscene and filthy things.
The whole immorality of old England is concentrated in the
twelve volumes of the *Crim.-Con. Biography, or celebrated
trials in the Ecclesiastical and Civil Courts for Adultery and
other Crimes connected with Incontinency, from the Period
of Henry VIII to the Present Time* (by Francis Plowden,
London, 1789). Not less obscene than the printed matter of
this vast pornographical work are the illustrations of the

[1] Archenholtz, *Annals*, Vol. I, pp. 398-399.

text which, for example, show Mrs. Draper on the knees of her clerk; Mrs. Harris offering the charms of her bosom to her loved clergyman; Mrs. Cibber *quae tactibus obscoenis amantem Slopper irritat*; Mrs. Abergavenny showing her huge bosom to Sir Lyddel, with the caption ' You are necessary to me as the air I breathe ', Milady Grosvenor surprised in bed with the Duke of Cumberland in an inn, and Milord avenging her infidelity with a servant girl on his knee[1].

To spread this sort of filth among the populace was the business of those innumerable Crim.-Con. brochures and Crim.-Con. lampoons. ' The most scandalous literature in London ', said the author of *London and Paris*, 'consists of the reports of Crim.-Con. and Divorce Cases which are printed without expurgation. No book is asked for so frequently in the lending library, and the editions, reprints and extracts from them prove their popularity[2].' These brochures and songs on ' Criminal conversations ' formed the main stock-in-trade of the so-called ' straw vendors '. Some time after it had been illegal to sell such writings publicly, the vendors offered straws for sale which they wrapped up neatly in the song in question. Often these efforts were read aloud[3]. The newspapers, too, gave very full accounts of divorce cases, in which the word crim.-con. stared in large type above the actual articles. For some time there was even a Crim.-Con. Gazette (or *Diurnal Register of the Treates* [sic] *and Follics of the Present Day*), which appeared in eighteen numbers from 20th November 1830 to 30th April 1831. It was illustrated, published by E. Elliot, and its contents were throughout obscene[4]. Byron has in the first canto of *Don Juan* (verses 188 and 189) lashed the

[1] *Les Dessous*, etc., Vol. I, pp. xvii, xviii.
[2] *London and Paris*, Vol. VIII, p. 243.
[3] Rosenberg, pp. 37-38.
[4] Pisanus Fraxi, *Catena Librorum Jacendorum*. London. Pp. 388-389.

Pl. 7]

Engraved by S. Davenport from original by Hogarth

THE HARLOT'S PROGRESS : SCENE IN BRIDEWELL

Pl. 8]

Engraved by G. Pressbury from original by Hogarth

fever of English newspaper writers for getting a crim.-con.
case published as speedily as possible:

> Here ends this canto.—Need I sing, or say,
>   How Juan, naked, favour'd by the night,
> Who favours what she should not, found his way,
>   And reach'd his home in an unseemly plight?
> The pleasant scandal which arose next day,
>   The nine days' wonder that was brought to light,
> And how Alfonso sued for a divorce,
> Were in the English newspapers, of course.
>
> If you would like to see the whole proceedings,
>   The depositions and the cause at full,
> The names of all the witnesses, the pleadings,
>   Of counsel to nonsuit or to annul,
> There's more than one edition, and the readings
>   Are various, but they none of them are dull;
> The best is that in short-hand ta'en by Gurney[1],
> Who to Madrid on purpose made a journey.

No class of English theatre has overlooked the drawing
value of divorce cases. The presentation of such crim.-con.
cases, which enjoyed a vogue right up to the 'seventies of the
nineteenth century, at the ' Coal Hole ' was the most
notorious. Faucher related of this: ' In a corner of London
there is a tavern, which gives a dramatic, musical evening
entertainment which has no precedent in any other place in
the world and could have none. The tavern is called the
Coal Hole. Every evening here for many, many years
magistrates and jurymen are caricatured; and propriety
outraged as nowhere else in the world. And this in seemingly
moral but really hypocritical England. The jurymen are the

---

[1] Gurney was a publisher of crim.-con. cases in Byron's time, notorious
for his shamelessness.

public, and the judge, who calls himself Baron Nicolson, is a
fat old ruffian who presides over the assembly in a huge wig
and black gown. Before him on the barristers' bench sit
three or four down-at-heel literary hacks who play their
parts in barristers' wigs and gowns. A mock divorce trial is
being performed. The opposing counsel call on witnesses
who appear in the box one after the other in suitable
costumes, amongst them many men dressed as women.
All the witnesses are obliged to kiss something which at a
distance resembles a Bible and to raise their hand for the
oath while the judge murmurs some gibberish. The witnesses
are mostly needy actors who have come down in the world.
The cross-examination to which they are subjected by the
barrister or rather mock-barrister is extremely spicy! Licence
has no limit here whatever. The judge finally sums up, puts a
question to the jury, one of whom answers and passes
sentence. Music follows and behind rises a curtain disclosing
a brilliantly lighted little stage on which girls are grouped
in flesh-coloured tights[1].' Especially in the eighteenth century,
which far exceeded the nineteenth in the enormous number
of divorce cases, the smaller theatres and touring companies
were sure to draw a numerous and appreciative audience by
producing plays and farces about adultery.

The list of famous Crim.-Con. cases[2] begins with that of
Mervin, Lord Audley, Earl of Castlehaven, in 1631 which
ended in the execution of the accused. Lord Audley,
evidently a sexual pervert, was accused of forcing his wife

---

[1] Julius Faucher, *Glimpses of Culture Compared in the Four Biggest
European Capitals*. Hanover, 1877. Pp. 428-429.

[2] Of course it is impossible, within the limits of this work, to give
complete accounts of these ' famous ' cases, so that I must confine myself
to giving a selection from the most characteristic. Those divorce cases
which have become historic may be found collected in the little work
*Crim.-Con. actions and trials and other legal proceedings relating to marriage
before the passing of the present Divorce Act*. London. Cited as *Crim.-con.*

to have frequent sexual intercourse with a footman in his presence, while using the same footman for pederasty. The case opened on 25th April 1631. The Countess, on being questioned, said that shortly after her marriage to the Earl, Amptil, a footman, came while she and her husband were in bed; and on this occasion Lord Audley spoke obscenely to her and told her that her body was his property, that she was to love Amptil in the same way as himself; that he would willingly take the responsibility if she slept with other men. She was forced to obey. He then attempted to force another footman on her. He called him into the room at night and revelled in looking at his private parts, forcing his wife to look also. On another occasion a servant, Broadway, was obliged to rape the Countess while the Earl himself held her arms and legs. Afterwards the Countess wanted to kill herself with a knife which Broadway wrenched from her hand. Skipwith had to do the same with her. And his master often told him he would be pleased if a son were the result of this intercourse. This evidence was confirmed by the footmen and other witnesses. The Countess also deposed that her husband *auxilio olei eam paedicavit*, and practised pederasty with the footmen. Lord Audley was found guilty of abetting a rape on his wife by the unanimous vote of the peers forming the court, and by 15 votes to 12 of committing pederasty in two cases. He was sentenced to death by strangling; but the sentence was modified to decapitation, which was carried out at the Tower on 14th May 1631[1].

I will mention next, amongst the Crim.-Con. cases of the

[1] Cf. 'The Tryal and Condemnation of Mervin, Lord Audley, Earl of Castlehaven, at Westminster April 5, 1631, for abetting a Rape upon his Countess, Committing Sodomy with his Servants and Commanding and Countenancing the Debauching of his Daughter.' London, 1699. *Crim.-Con.*, pp. 34-3⁻. Further, the erotic magazine *The Exquisite*, for the year 1843, contains a complete account of this case.

eighteenth century, that against Catherine Earle, who saw
Charles Holland, the actor, on the stage, fell violently in
love with him and invited him by letter to become her
lover, which the gallant actor immediately accepted. Mrs.
Earle had married in 1750 and brought her husband a dowry
of £10,850 besides ' very valuable plate and furniture'.   Mr.
Earle was also a very wealthy man with an annual income of
£2-3,000. It is remarkable that Mrs. Earle's dearest women-
friends bore witness against her in this trial. Thus Mrs.
Frances Nightingale deposed that she had frequently seen
Mrs. Earle with Mr. Holland at the house of a third friend,
Miss Gilbert, where Holland was invited to come by his
lover. The two were always left alone at these parties.
On 6th March 1765, when Mr. Holland was again at Miss
Gilbert's for supper, Mrs. Nightingale and Miss Gilbert
watched the guilty couple through a hole which had been
previously bored in the wall of an adjoining room. Mrs.
Nightingale saw Holland kneel in front of Mrs. Earle, raise
her skirts and kiss her knee. Miss Gilbert said she had seen
still more and described minutely the act of adultery. A
servant, Taylor, described how he acted as *postillon
d'amour* to them.   Edith Garlick, a maidservant, accompanied her mistress to a restaurant under the Piazza at
Covent Garden where Mrs. Earle drank tea with Mr. Holland
and then retired with him for ten minutes to an adjoining
bedroom. After this evidence a divorce was granted to
William Earle[1].

In 1771 the divorce of the nymphomaniac Mrs. Elizabeth
Draper created a great sensation. She was the eldest of the
ten children of a grocer named Hartnoll, and married
Richard Draper on 16th August 1764, being then no longer
a virgin. She was a perfect example of English beauty and

[1] *Crim.-Con.*, pp. 69-73. *Les Dessous*, etc., Vol. I, pp. 70-75.

bewitched everybody with her loveliness. The first who could boast of her favours was a small negro in the service of her father. She was ten years old when he seduced her. At fifteen she married Mr. Draper, a rich merchant who was unfortunately impotent, but even had he been otherwise he would hardly have been able to prevent his wife's daily increasing love-mania from finding extravagant expression. When she was first married and living on Mr. Draper's estate in the country, she took intense pleasure in watching the mating of mares and stallions, and is said once to have realised with a stallion Juvenal's verse—*Imposito clunem submittat asello*. Very soon after her marriage she began to lead a dissolute life. Her first liaison was in 1766 with a coachman, Charles Russell; then she made an apprentice, William Penfold, her victim, who at the age of fifteen entered Mr. Draper's service in London an innocent country lad. Three weeks after his arrival Mrs. Draper approached after dinner, kissed him, undressed him and then herself, *manu ejus genitalia tetigit*, and seduced him. In court the obedient apprentice declared that he had to perform this service for his mistress twice a week. The virility of coachmen also appealed to her, as the postilion John Haylock enjoyed her favours at the same time. A maid, Sarah Eliot, asserted that after Haylock had visited Mrs. Draper the condition of the bed proved that adultery had been committed.

Meanwhile, Mrs. Draper's nymphomania had reached its height. Miss Rutt relates that she once surprised three young fellows in her room. Mary Allen, a servant, watched through a hole in the wall[1] how her mistress sat with bare breasts in front of John Lancaster, a neighbouring land-owner. ' Lancaster was taking liberties with her. At this

---

[1] This plays an ominous part in Crim.-Con. cases.

time the boards on which she was standing, making a little
noise, she heard Mrs. Draper say, Somebody was coming;
on which she retired into the next room, but soon returned
and looked through again; they had then left the fireplace,
but the bed being near the door, she plainly heard them on it,
and heard it crack and make a noise as if persons were
pressing upon it; she also heard them whisper upon the bed.
She continued listening for some minutes, and believed that
they were commiting the crime of adultery together.'
One day a certain James Delegal was sitting in the theatre
at Islington when he suddenly felt the lady next him ' put
her hand on his private parts ', and try to attract him to her.
It was Mrs. Draper, who this time, however, was not
fortunate. As last witness the 17-year-old Edward Goode
gave evidence. He came to London about the middle of
1770 and saw Mrs. Draper for the first time at dinner in her
husband's house. At table she trod on his foot and secretly
pressed his hand. At first he thought it was a joke, but the
very next day she enticed him into a room, where there
was a bed, put her arms round his neck and confessed her
love. He tore himself away and fled, while she shouted
threats after him. On the following day she sent for him.
She lay in bed; and stopping by the door, he asked what she
wanted. She said come into bed with me; whereupon he
immediately went away. A little later she came down to
him dressed. ' Elle accourt, et s'assied sur mes genoux,
mêle des baisers au discours le plus tendre et coule une main
dans . . . mon sein, lève sa jupe et me dit " Voulez-vous? "
Et je commis le péché d'adultére. Le jour suivant, après
dîner, à peine le mari fut-il au bas de l'escalier, qu'elle
vint chevaucher sur moi.' The young man pictures in
lively colours how he and the apprentice Penfold shared the
ceaseless favours of this Messalina; and how at last, driven
by pangs of conscience, they revealed everything to the

master of the house. This remarkably scandalous case ended in complete divorce[1].

Dorothea Kinsman allowed herself to be seduced by a eunuch almost before she was of marriageable age. She lived with him for seven years without finding his impotence unpleasant. At last, in 1784, she wrote from Naples after a long silence the following letter which was read in court word for word:

' My honoured Father, I am deeply upset over what has happened between me and Tenduci. My misfortune is mostly due to youthful ignorance. For some years I was only bewitched by his beautiful voice. But it has pleased God to bring me to a better frame of mind so that what has happened between me and a eunuch by way of marriage is not a holy bond in the sight of heaven.'

The good father sent her 200 guineas at once to rescue her from the clutches of this impotent creature; on which the daughter brought an action against her poor husband. The wording of the petition was as strange as the letter to her father. 'Tenduci', so it ran, ' was born in Siena, he is now 40 years old and was deprived of his manhood at the age of nine; indeed, he suffered complete castration according to Italian practice. By this operation both testicles were removed, which makes it impossible for him to procreate and in consequence consummate a marriage. Tenduci came into the house of my father, who was a solicitor in Dublin, as my singing teacher eight years ago. It was not difficult for him to take advantage of my inexperience. We were secretly married by a Catholic priest and we fled as secretly. On our arrival in Italy, Tenduci gave out that I was a pupil, entrusted to him by my parents. He was very careful not to speak of a marriage as there is a law in Italy which condemns to the gallows eunuchs who marry.' The petition

[1] *Crim.-Con.*, pp. 100-105. *Les Dessous*, etc., pp. 79-90.

ended with the request that the marriage should be declared
null and void and that Tenduci should be ordered to pay
costs. But it was an untruth to declare Tenduci impotent.
For later with Parisian ladies who, like the Roman ladies
of Juvenal's time, had a weakness for eunuchs, the singer
proved to have manly qualities. This physiological truth[1]
seemed to be unknown to the English court which tried the
case. He used the evidence of many witnesses with regard
to his strange condition and they were astonishingly
outspoken in that evidence. Amongst others an old Irish
officer related how Tenduci had showed him a bad scar on
the left side of the groin, a little above the scrotum. As he
was present one day while Tenduci was dressing, he saw
him take a red velvet bag from a trouser pocket. He asked
him if it was a sacred relic from Rome. ' No, no,' answered
Tenduci, ' those are my testicles. I keep them with me in
this bag ever since they were cut off.' This drastic recital
impressed the court so much that the marriage was declared
null and void, especially as it had been solemnised by a
Catholic priest[2].

The most famous English divorce case of the eighteenth
century is that against Queen Caroline, wife of the Prince
Regent, later George IV, ' with its incredible scandal, which
flowed like a sewer from the floor of the House of Lords and
sank the lustre of the Crown and the fair name of the
reigning family in a sea of mud[3] '. Caroline Amalie Elizabeth
was the daughter of Karl Wilhelm Ferdinand, Duke of
Brunswick-Wolfenbüttel, and was born on 17th May 1768.
She married the Prince of Wales, later George IV, on 8th April
1795. The marriage was unhappy from the start. ' At their

[1] Cf. also A. Moll, *Libido Sexualis*, Vol. I, pp. 422-424.
[2] *Les Dessous*, etc., Vol. II, pp. 24-27.
[3] G. Brandes, *Main Currents of Literature in the* 18*th Century*. Eighth
edition. Charlottenburg, 1900. Published by H. Barsdorf. Vol. IV.
' Naturalism in England.' P. 34.

first meeting at St. James's Palace, when the Princess knelt before him, the Prince called out to the Ambassador, Lord Malmesbury: "Harris, bring me a glass of brandy, I don't feel well"; and when it was suggested that a glass of water would be more suitable under the circumstances, he rushed from the room, swearing, without saying a word to his bride. At the wedding he was drunk and hiccuped continuously during the ceremony. He not only treated the Princess with indifference, not only was outrageously neglectful and unfaithful; but with callous brutality he shut her up, surrounded her with spies, and by a false accusation deprived her of her daughter, which led to frequent scenes at Court. The conduct of the Princess does not seem to have remained blameless long. At first she was merely unwise, but in later years she attempted to console herself and not always in a becoming manner. So we find her, a lady of fifty, travelling through Europe with her courier and chamberlain, the former valet, Bergami—an Italian "Ruy Blas"—whom she loved tenderly, appointed to every possible position and covered with orders[1].' When the Prince came to the throne in 1820 as George IV, his consort came back to England, but was brought before the House of Lords and accused of infidelity by her husband, who had tried in vain to keep her out of the country. This tragic divorce trial lasted from 19th August 1820 till 10th November of the same year, and more has been written about it than about any similar affair. 'As witnesses in this case, the King brought over shiploads of foreign hotel-waiters and chambermaids to give evidence against the Queen, which roused the bitterest outcry from the English public'. The taking of their evidence became one of the greatest scandals in the world's history. Brandes says: 'I do not think I have ever read

[1] G. Brandes, *loc. cit.*, Vol. IV, pp. 259-260. It is very doubtful if the relations between the Queen and Bergami were really as intimate as Brandes assumes.

anything more shameless than the reports of this trial.
Cross-examinations about the positions of bedrooms and
beds, the state of the sheets in the morning; about a Queen
and her chamberlain in complete negligé, filled the columns
of English newspapers day after day[1]'.   In order to give
readers an idea of the repulsive nature of these cross-
examinations, a few examples will be quoted.

Examination of Alessandro Finetti: ' Were you ever present
when Bergami's bed was warmed?—I was not there when the
bed was warmed but I brought a hot-water bottle. Did you
see Bergami get out of bed to let it be warmed?—Yes.
Was the Princess in the room at the time?—Yes. Do you
remember your journey from Ancona to Rome?—I do. Do
you remember seeing the Princess and Bergami together
on any evening during that journey?—Not in the evening.
Then at some other time of the day or night?—Never at
night, but in the daytime. What time of day was it?—I do
not remember if it was before or after dinner. Did you observe
anything when you saw the two together?—Yes. What was
that?—As I went through the courtyard I saw the Princess
do this (made a movement). Who was with the Princess?—
Bergami. (Here the counsel for the defence, Lord Brougham,
objected to the witness merely making a sign. Only facts to
which a name and an exact description could be given had
up till now been permitted as evidence in English courts of
law. The Lord Chancellor allowed the objection, and told the
witness to answer in words not signs). Describe then how you
saw the Princess and Bergami as they walked through the
courtyard—The Princess was embracing Bergami. (A Peer
asks: What do you understand by the word "embracing"?—
She did this with her hands (makes a movement). Where did
she put her hands?—The Princess put her hands round his

[1] G. Brandes, loc. cit., Vol. IV, pp. 260-261.

arms. Do you mean by that round his waist?—Yes. (The Attorney-General asks) Were they looking at each other?—They were. Were their faces close together?—Their faces were some distance apart because she is little and he is tall.'

Evidence of Louisa de Mont: 'Do you remember Her Majesty taking a bath on board ship?—Yes. Did she do so more than once?—I only remember two occasions. Who went with her?—Mr. Bergami. Did they both come on deck afterwards, or did Bergami come first?—Bergami came first and told me to go to Her Majesty and help her to dress. When Bergami called you, how long had he been with her Royal Highness?—Nearly three-quarters of an hour.'

Evidence of Vincenzo Guargito: 'Did you ever have orders to close the deck-tent when the Princess and Bergami were inside?—Yes. While you were doing so did you ever see the Princess and Bergami lying on their beds? (Mr. Williams remarks here: " I think the question should run: Where did you see them? " The Solicitor-General replies: " I have no objection to putting two questions in place of one if Mr. Williams wishes.") As you closed the deck-tent did you see the Princess on the bed?—Sometimes in bed, sometimes standing. And Bergami?—He lay mostly on the little bed. Did you close the tent, leaving them thus?—Yes. How was Bergami lying? On his back or on his side or how?—He lay on his back. Did you see Bergami come out of the tent afterwards?—Yes. How long after?—That varied from a quarter or a half to an hour. Did Bergami accompany the Princess every time she went below to the bath?—Always, and not only when she went for a bath but whatever she went for. Did the Princess have to go below for any other reasons?—Generally she went to the closet below deck. And Bergami went with her there too?—Yes.'

The following testimony must also be given:

[87]

' At Karlsruhe Her Majesty was one day found in Bergami's room; she was sitting upon his bed, and he was in bed with his arms around the neck of Her Majesty. She was surprised in this extraordinary situation by one of the *femmes de chambre*, who was going into the room by chance . . . in that bed was found a cloak, which Her Majesty was afterwards seen wearing; and in that bed, also, certain marks were also observed by one of the servants. These marks, without his saying anything further at present, would leave their Lordships perhaps to infer that which he wished them to understand.'

' What was the state of Bergami's dress at the time you saw him in the passage going towards the bedroom of Her Royal Highness?—He was not dressed. When you say he was not dressed, what do you mean; what had he on?—He was not dressed at all.'

' On the 12th of that month she arrived at Salona. . . . A large bed was provided in the inner room for Her Majesty; the outer room assigned for Bergami had no bed. There was no access to the bed in the inner room except through Bergami's. It would be proved in evidence that, in the morning after Her Majesty had slept there, her bed had the appearance of having been slept in by two persons. There was only one passage to Her Majesty's bedroom; that passage led from Bergami's room, and in his room there was no bed.'

This scandalous trial ended with the complete acquittal of the unfortunate Queen, thanks chiefly to her brilliant defence by Lord Brougham, which culminated in his historic concluding speech, but she died in the following year in great measure owing to the mental and physical humiliations she had suffered in the course of her ordeal. The case astounded all Europe and inspired the poet Shelley to write his wonderful satire *Oedipus Tyrannus or Swellfoot the*

[88]

Tyrant, an ' Aristophanic comedy, as happily conceived as
Prütz' *Political Birth Chamber*. The action takes place
in Boeotia. English bulls appear here as swine. Mentality,
manners and government are described in terms of
hoggishness. The hypocrisy of the royal husband, the
shameless harrying of the Queen on the subject of her purity,
the perjury of Castlereagh and Sidmouth are all shown in
the satire with consummate skill[1] '.

A short time after this noteworthy Crim.-Con. affair, a
case in which the famous actor Edmund Kean was involved,
aroused almost as much interest. The trial took place on
17th January 1825. Robert Albion Cox claimed damages
from Kean on the charge of adultery with his wife. The
plaintiff, who had married in 1805, had lived happily with
his wife until she became acquainted with Kean in 1813.
Kean was at that time acting at Drury Lane Theatre.
Mrs. Cox was a cultured woman, fond of the theatre and
especially well read in Shakespeare; and she extravagantly
admired the genius of the accused. Kean, who visited Cox's
house with his own wife, soon started a love affair with
Mrs. Cox with such secrecy that the husband for a long
time had not the least suspicion. The reading of Kean's
many love-letters made the trial especially interesting, as
did also the evidence of witnesses to the clever manner in
which the guilty pair had deceived Mr. Cox. Kean was
sentenced to pay £800 damages[2].

Of worse character than Kean's letters were those which
the young Count de la Rochefoucauld wrote to Lady
Cavendish in 1859, when he was attaché to the French
Embassy in Rome; and they played an important part in
the divorce suit which her husband brought against her.
No pen can describe the dirt and obscenity of these letters,

[1] G. Brandes, *loc. cit.*, Vol. IV, p. 261.
[2] *Crim.-Con.*, pp. 38-47.

and from references which appear in them, the replies of the lady were even worse. At any rate twelve of the Count's letters have won the distinction of completing one of the most obscene English erotic books. They occupy the last twenty-six pages of the fourth volume of the notorious *Romance of Lust*, which was published in 1873-76. The author of this book comments thus on the letters: ' When the counsel for the injured husband handed in the letters with their translation, he remarked that in his opinion they were too scandalous to be read in open court. The Judge looked at one or two and said, turning to the court: "I entirely agree with my learned friend. I shall take them home and refer to them in my summing-up to the jury." Some of the letters revel in the most incredible fantasies. The Count continually mentions how far his descriptions fall short of those in her replies. As he retains possession of the lady's passionate assurances, one can only judge from his references to certain gross familiarities that she possessed as warm and licentious a temperament as my aunt and the divine Frankland (two heroines in the *Romance of Lust*). These interesting letters fell into my hands by chance, and I can assure the reader that they are the actual sworn literal translations which were found in Mrs. Chichester's bureau by her husband and handed into the court. The Count, apparently, feared such a contingency, because he begged her again and again to destroy his letters when read. But with the strange shortsightedness of her sex she kept them, and they formed the only proof by which she lost her position in society and was ruined. She was a woman of forty-five and the mother of several children, but it is just these undisciplined and licentious matrons who are most attractive to a young man who feels flattered and proud to have conquered a woman of society. It was certain that she was no novice in depravity and had probably passed through many hands before he won her. He appears to have been quite "woman-mad", one of the worst delusions a man can have[1].'

It is impossible to give the content of these excessively obscene letters; it need only be noted that La Rochefoucauld confesses to his lady that she picked 'the flower of his virginity'. 'I have never kissed another woman, and whatever misfortune may befall it will always be an indescribable happiness for me to remember that I lost my innocence through your enchanting caresses (*par tes délices*). This is perhaps the greatest happiness and the one consolation in my life—and will remain so. But before God, it is a great happiness and my delight such as cannot be found again on earth. I do not believe that he who took your innocence was as pure as I was, and if there is a greater joy than that which I know, I promise you never to seek or experience it, though I do not ask the same of you. I do not wish to hear other women spoken of: even to look at them disgusts me. You know it, and you know too that nothing in you disgusts me, but that everything that is you enchants me; and I love and worship it all. It is a kind of madness and you know it; for when you are kind you give me, at least in writing, the idea of that which you would not do, if you harboured the least doubt about it.' It is instructive to note to what lengths this passionate love leads the young man who had in fact been pure, for his assertion must be believed. He describes with fervour the joys of *Cunnilingus, urinam bibendi, faeces devorandi*, the *delicias omnium corporis partium* of the loved woman. 'As much as the odour of woman is repugnant to me in general, the more do I like it in you. I beg of you to preserve that intoxicating perfume; but you are too clean, you wash yourself too much. I have

---

[1] P. Fraxi, *Catena*, pp. 585-586.

often told you so in vain. When you will be quite my own I shall forbid you to do it too often, at most, once a day, my tongue and my saliva shall do the rest.' In all this can be plainly recognised that form of Masochism which I should like to describe as juvenile, because it is so often seen in a man's early love manifestations, even if it does not take such an extreme form as in this case. These aberrations are most often found when older women have seduced boys and youths. In this case at least the woman appears, as doctrix of the *ars amandi*, to have originated these perversions[1].

The most important divorce trial at the end of the nineteenth century was that of Colin Campbell—not only because it affected aristocratic circles. On Friday, 26th November 1886 began, at the Law Courts, the divorce suit of Lord Colin Campbell against his wife, and at the same time of Lady Colin Campbell against her husband. The Duke of Marlborough, Colonel Butler, Captain Shaw and Dr. Bird were cited as co-respondents in the one case, and Miss Mary Watson in the other. The Duke of Argyll, father of Lord Colin, and the Marquis of Lorne, his brother, and son-in-law of Queen Victoria, were present at the trial. Lady Colin had already brought a suit against her husband for brutal behaviour in March 1884. The court gave judgment for separation of bed and board, whereupon Lord Colin

---

[1] With reference to these private letters, perhaps H. France is right in saying: ' Que de singuliers et étonnants écrits enrichiraient la chronique des mœurs et les rayons des bibliophiles si des dérots et prudes ne les avaient fait disparaître, ou si à la veille du suprême voyage, le grand homme harcelé par le confesseur ou tourmenté par le scrupule n'avait anéanti les pages naturalistes en sans poser devant le public il diversait en riant le fonds de son sac.'—H. France, *En Police Court*, Preface, p. viii. This is confirmed by the incredible revelations regarding pornographic notebooks made by peasants and maids in the Stettin district. Cf. *The Sexual Social Conditions of the Evangelical Peasants in the German Empire.* Vol. I (by Pastor H. Wittenberg and Dr. E. Hückstedt). Leipzig, 1895. Pp. 104-105.

Drawing by Rowlandson   [*Pl.* 9

A TOUR TO THE LAKES

Whoe'er has travelled life's dull round
Through all its various paths hath been
Must oft have wondered to have found
This warmest welcome at an Inn.

Drawing by Rowlandson   [*Pl.* 10

CATCHING AN ELEPHANT

brought an action against his wife for adultery with the four accused, and Lady Colin against her husband for adultery with Mary Watson, her maid.

Of course, peeping through keyholes, suspicious position of beds, disordered bedclothes, and so on play a great part in this trial. In her evidence Lady Miles, a relation of Lady Colin, says: ' One day her Ladyship was ill. Dr. Bird was called in and remained for some time. The next time I saw Lord Colin he told me that Lady Colin had had a miscarriage. I did not believe it and said he was only slandering his wife. Lord Colin remained convinced of it, and believed that Dr. Bird only wanted to conceal the fact. I pointed out to Lord Colin that his wife had also been treated by Dr. Hicks, and that therefore it would be difficult for Dr. Bird to keep anything secret. But Lord Colin replied that the two doctors were friends and that made anything possible. On this I questioned Dr. Bird, who swore on his word of honour that there was no possibility of a miscarriage with her Ladyship; she was suffering from a disease and would never be blessed with children. It was wicked to make such accusations when her Ladyship had already suffered so much, and if Lord Colin did not withdraw he would not continue to attend her. I informed Lord Colin and he answered: "There must be some truth in the story"; but I was to beg Dr. Bird to continue to attend his wife. On June 7th, at a dinner at 79, Cadogan Place, Lord Colin suddenly complained of pains in his stomach. I told Mary Watson to make compresses for him, but got the rude answer: "Make the . . . yourself." When Lord Colin heard of it he laughed and said: "The little vixen is jealous of you." "What! jealous of me!" "Yes, of course! " Mary Watson laughed at me while I was making the compress. When I asked Lord Colin to reprimand her, he praised her and said she was a pretty poisonous little vixen! Which was an insult to me. Another time I saw Mary Watson

sitting on Lord Colin's bed with both arms round his neck[1].'
Drs. Godson and Gibbons declared on the contrary that they
examined Mary Watson in the morning and found her still
a virgin, which however does not mean that sexual intercourse
has not taken place[2]. Rosa Baer, formerly Lady Colin's
lady's maid, says that she saw her commit adultery with
Lord Blandford, which was confirmed by Lord Colin's servants
Delaroche and O'Neil. O'Neil once saw through the keyhole
Lady Colin lying on the floor with Captain Shaw[3]. Sir
Charles Russell's cross-examination of O'Neil about this
last occurrence is interesting and typically English. The
maid, Eliza Wright, gave evidence that Lady Colin suffered
from an infectious disease before she was married. ' Gonorrhea
or syphilis? ' asked the judge. ' Syphilis ' was the prompt
reply. It appeared from Lord Colin's own evidence that
he had been treated before marriage for venereal disease by
several specialists, amongst them the famous Sir Henry
Thompson, who admitted him to his clinic for operation.
Lady Colin declares that she was infected by her husband
after marriage. The doctors not only confirm this and
emphatically deny the alleged miscarriage, but stress
repeatedly that the character of Lady Colin's illness precluded the possibility of co-habitation, and that she could
not at that time have committed adultery. The verdict of
the jury acquitted the defendants. The costs of the trial,
amounting to £15,000, were borne by Lord Colin[4].

These few revelations about English divorce trials[5] are

[1] *Colin Campbell Divorce Case.* London, 1887. Pp. 3-4.
[2] *Ibid.*, p. 10.
[3] *Ibid.*, pp. 13-22, pp. 25-27.
[4] Cf. also the lively account of this trial by H. France, *En Police Court*,
pp. 129-196.
[5] I will mention among famous divorce cases which I shall not describe:
The Talbot case (1856, *Crim.-Con.*, pp. 11-33); the suit of Cranford *v.*
Dilke (1886, *En Police Court*, pp. 91-109); the divorce petition of Admiral
Parson (1890, *En Police Court*, pp. 119-128); and more recently the suit

sufficient to show clearly how immoral and scandalous they were, and how coarsely they were conducted. The devastating pronouncement which Lord Lyndhurst gave in May 1857 on English divorce cases was endorsed by all Europeans, but did not stop the rage for divorce scandals in England. He said amongst other things: ' Lord Campbell has more than once described this kind of case as a disgrace to our legal practice and has stated with perfect rightness that no European country would tolerate it; and that continental lawyers with whom he had spoken condemned English law for still maintaining it. I think I can confirm the opinion of my noble and learned friend. At least, I have talked with many expert foreigners on this subject and have never heard another point of view expressed. In a book which appeared lately, I find the following passage on divorce trials: " The husband shamelessly pockets the damages. The publicity in which these cases necessarily take place and all the details and evidence about the accusation are in the highest degree scandalous and improper. For instance, the evidence of servants, young ladies-maids, which they give in detail before the public in open court—what they saw, heard or guessed—is no less than a kind of prostitution, even lower than the common form " [1] '.

These are hard words but true, and their effect was soon felt. For it is noticeable that in the second half of the nineteenth century divorce cases became much rarer[2], which may well be regarded as a consequence of the proceedings in the House of Lords in 1857.

of Captain James Vivian Forbes-Smith against his wife (*Daily Telegraph*, 19th July 1900).

[1] *Crim.-Con.*, p. 9.

[2] *Ibid.*, Preface, p. 1. Another English speciality is the so-called ' Breach of Promise ' case. Cf. Katscher, *Land of Fog*, etc., pp. 275 *et seq.*, and Louis Blanc, *Lettres sur Angleterre*. Paris, 1866. Vol. III, pp. 121-125.

CHAPTER III

PROSTITUTION

THE general character of English, and especially of London, prostitution was, in keeping with the character of the people, extraordinarily coarse and cynical. An English observer, contrasting London prostitution with that of the Continent, said: ' In no continental capital is it possible to see society so shockingly in the grip of vice and debauchery as in our own metropolis; there recently in Waterloo Place, the Quadrant, Haymarket, Waterloo Road, not to mention the theatre foyers, scenes have been witnessed which one has never experienced in the most vicious of continental towns[1]'. Hector France also expresses himself strongly as regards the incredible shamelessness and coarseness of the English prostitutes; his countryman, however, Leon Faucher, finds that this coarseness has considerably diminished during the last thirty years. (His book *English Studies* appeared in 1856.) The Russian Tarnowsky also states that in no other European town does prostitution appear in so cynical a form as in London[2], and according to Hügel, in no other country was prostitution carried on so generally and in so disgraceful and so bestial a manner[3]. The following statement will prove the general correctness of these opinions,

[1] *The Lancet*, 1853. Vol. I, p. 347.
[2] H. France, *Les Va-Nu-Pied de Londres*. Paris, 1884. Pp. 8-9. Dr. B. Tarnowsky, *Prostitution and Abolitionism*. Hamburg and Leipzig, 1890. P. 35.
[3] Fr. S. Hügel, *On the History, Statistics and Regulation of Prostitution*. Vienna, 1865. P. 43.

but it must not be forgotten that the shocking character
of London prostitution had been called forth to no small
extent by foreign prostitutes, the lowest of whom, as we
shall see later, had flocked from abroad to London.   When
it is appreciated that with these prostitution necessarily
means degeneration and brutalising of the character, it
becomes obvious that no great distinction between English
and foreign prostitutes should properly be made.

As regards the number of prostitutes in London, the
estimates of different authors naturally differ considerably.
Everyone knows that it is difficult, probably impossible,
in any large town to obtain reliable statistical data on this
point, particularly in the largest town in the world.   To this
is added the fact that in England there has never existed a
system of control as on the Continent, so that for this
reason an accurate knowledge of the numbers of *public*
women is impossible to obtain, not to speak of private
prostitution.   All accounts therefore of the number of
London prostitutes can only be regarded purely as estimates.

Any estimated number can be divided naturally into
various categories.   As regards the different classes of
London prostitutes in the eighteenth century, Archenholtz
wrote as follows: ' Those of the lowest class live together in
open houses, under the supervision of matrons who provide
them with food and clothing.   Their clothes, in accordance
with English luxury, are, even in the case of common girls,
of silk, and many of them escape with them from their
prisons and start trade on their own account.

' By this step up, the unfortunate girl, in addition to
gaining her independence, obtains also the right to reject
lovers whom she dislikes, which was not allowed in the
open house.   On the other hand, she is exposed to the necessity of providing entirely for herself, which if her income is
poor or she is extravagant, may lead her to a debtors'

prison. The uncertainty of payment leads all landlords who let rooms to such girls to double their rent. The extortionate sums generally obtained, and which are usually paid regularly for safety's sake, induce people in reasonably good circumstances to open their houses to these unfortunate girls. They are given the best rooms and the best furniture for a weekly rent which far exceeds the yearly house rent with all taxes. Without these girls many thousand houses in the West End of London would stand empty. In the single parish of Marylebone, which is the largest and most thickly populated in England, there were a few years ago not less than 13,000 prostitutes, of which 1700 inhabited whole houses. These last live very respectably and are undisturbed in the exercise of their profession. They are so much lord in their own house, that should a distinguished magistrate even attempt to disturb them in it, they could throw him out of the door. So long as they pay their taxes as promptly as other householders, they enjoy the same rights. Their houses are always charming, often beautifully furnished. They have chamber and waiting maids, often liveried servants, and many even their own carriage. A large number have life annuities which they have received from their seducers or from rich and generous lovers when intoxicated. These annuities certainly secure them from need, but they are usually not sufficient to enable them to live sumptuously in the capital and to enjoy expensive pleasures; they therefore permit lovers' visits, but only those whom they like—the others are sent away[1].

It may also be noted, when the classes of London prostitutes are considered generally as Archenholtz here does, that they produced both main types, the brothel dweller and the independent prostitute.

[1] Archenholtz, *England*, Vol. II, pp. 246-248.

The author of *Doings in London* divides prostitution in 1830 into the following general categories: First came the completely ' hackneyed ' prostitutes, who haunted street corners, dark alleys, narrow streets and similar localities, prowling round in the dark of the night, prostituting themselves for the smallest sums, becoming infected with venereal disease and in alliance with the commonest criminals and bullies. The second class was composed of those girls who lived in ' houses of retreat ' for which they paid the proprietresses high fees, almost all their takings in fact, as they were usually provided with food and clothing. The only difference between these prostitutes and those of the first class was that those of the second are better dressed, for which advantage, however, they are kept under the strictest supervision by their extortionate mistresses. These houses of retreat were of the lowest kind, in which robbery, murder and drunkenness were the order of the day. Thirdly came the so-called bagnios and the brothels, the inmates of which were also under the care of matrons, but could not strictly be reckoned amongst the street prostitutes. Fourthly there were the so-called fashionable prostitutes with their own dwellings, dresses and servants, who were mostly kept by rich merchants, gentry and the like[1].

Ryan likewise divides prostitutes into those who have their own dwellings and those who live in houses of retreat. To this latter class belong sempstresses, servants, theatre prostitutes and such like, also the sailors' prostitutes of Thames-side—as everywhere, the dregs of prostitution—also canteen women and soldiers' prostitutes[2].

With which we come to the question of the recruiting of London prostitutes. Ryan gives the following useful list of the

[1] *Doings in London*, pp. 92-93.
[2] Michael Ryan, *Prostitution in London*. London, 1839. P. 179.

callings from which come the main contingent of prostitutes:
' Milliners, dress-makers, straw bonnet makers, furriers, hat-
binders, silk-winders, tambour-workers, shoebinders, slop-
women, or those who work for cheap tailors, those in pastrycook, fancy and cigar shops, bazaars, servants to a great
extent, frequenters of theatres, fairs, dancing-rooms which,
with almost all places of public amusement in large towns
and cities, are licentious. It is impossible to estimate the
number of those addicted to secret prostitution in the
different ranks of society[1] '.

In addition, there are young girls from the country with
no experience of a town, who fall an easy prey to the
procuresses and sink, with or without compulsion, into
prostitution. 'These vile procuresses like to keep their
eye on the country coaches which arrive daily in London in
great numbers from all the provinces, and usually bring in
country girls seeking service in the capital. Poor creatures
of this kind are overjoyed when, on arrival in such a
crowded place, of which they know nothing of the ins and
outs, they find someone making them the friendliest advances,
and out of what appears to be benevolence looking after
them (apparently) like a mother. Events now lead gradually
to their fall and thereafter to the receipt of instructions.
In the evening the girl is sent out on the hunt[2] '.

In former and also more recent times the daughters of poor
country parsons took to prostitution in London in large
numbers[3]. There are many examples of whole families
being kept on prostitution. Ryan tells of a certain Leah
Davis who brought up all her thirteen daughters to be

[1] Ryan, *loc. cit.*, p. 174.

[2] Archenholtz, *England*, Vol. II, p. 257. ' One of the causes of the
number of these " filles de joie " was probably the constant immigration
from the provinces of young friendless girls eager to taste the delights
of London.'—G. Hill, *Women*, Vol. I, p. 318.

[3] Archenholtz, *loc. cit.*, Vol. II, p. 252; and J. Rodenberg, *loc. cit.*, p. 255.

prostitutes, and kept brothels with them in different parts of London[1]. In the eighteenth century, particularly, many London families had their prostitutes, though in another sense. According to Georgina Hill, most married men kept mistresses in one form or another. Many took them into their houses and had them eat at the same table as their wives, from which arrangement discord hardly ever arose. They were even seen going out in the company of the wife, and the only difference between them was that the mistress was usually better looking, better dressed, and not so stiff.

Further, the factory system has to be considered, which began to develop in England in the second half of the eighteenth century, and very soon, with its resulting concentration of women and children, had the worst possible effect on public morality, so that as early as 22nd June 1802 the indiscriminate employment of children as factory workers had to be prevented by law. The factories, with their concentration of large numbers of people of different sexes, *mostly* young, were, first in England, later also on the continent, a ceaseless source of prostitution. Colquhoun estimated as early as the year 1793 that amongst the 50,000 London prostitutes, not less than 20,000 were factory workers, whilst only 3,000 came from the domestic servant class[2].

London and its suburbs[3] naturally take the lion's share of the English prostitutes, then comes Great Britain generally. All along, however, large numbers of foreign prostitutes have lent a special character to London prostitution. These, for the most part the dregs of the Continent which have drifted to London, form a ' hot-bed for the growth of

[1] Ryan, *loc. cit.*, pp. 137-138.
[2] *Tableau descriptif*, etc., Vol. I, p. 118.
[3] ' Some writers maintain that every one in three of the daughters of persons in the lower rank in life become prostitutes before they are twenty years of age.'—Ryan, *loc. cit.*, p. 169.

catinilaric existences[1] '. London, to a greater extent than all other capitals, harbours the lowest of this riff-raff, as it is further away and cut off by the sea. Besides which, both before and after the Revolution, all reprobates were expelled from France[2]. The hatred of the English for foreigners, which in this instance was quite justified, was aroused in particular at the beginning of the eighteenth and nineteenth centuries against the large number of French immigrants, who by many London families were not allowed over their doorstep, so afraid were they of their sexual excesses[3]. The Londoner still calls all foreign prostitutes ' French women '; like the Lesbians and Phœnicians of old time, they enjoy the reputation of special refinements in all the arts of love, which are not always despised by John Bull[4]. Hector France remarks that these popular *boulevardières* are often Germans and Belgians who come to London in almost as large numbers as the French, principally through the fast developing white-slave traffic, which must be considered later. In the fourth place are the Italians, then follow the other continental nations. Ryan has himself noticed some Greeks and East and West Indians amongst London prostitutes. The many negresses must not be forgotten, for whom the taste in London is almost as well developed as in Paris.

Yet one more category of girls must be mentioned, which has latterly unfortunately, to a great extent, become a prey to prostitution. This is that of waitresses. The waitress system is also of English origin. In the first chapter (p. 31) I mentioned that in the Middle Ages women played a great part in the life of English inns, that in those days the sale

[1] Henry Dorgeel, *The Germans in England*. London, 1885. P. 96.
[2] *London and Paris*, Vol. III, p. 14.
[3] *Ibid.*, Vol. VIII, p. 17.
[4] H. France, *Les Va-Nu-Pieds*, etc., pp. 11-12.

of beer was nearly always in the hands of women, and the
' ale wife ' was a well-known folk-type. In the seventeenth
and eighteenth centuries came the ' bar-maids ', women
and girls who sold drinks behind the bar of the inn. From
them the waitress evolved, at the beginning of the nineteenth
century, whose work it was to go round the rooms of
the inn, taking food and drink to the guests; out of this
situation familiar relations between guests and waitresses
developed spontaneously.

As regards the age of London prostitutes it was found,
according to Talbot's investigations, that in the year 1838,
amongst 3,103 prostitutes 3 were under 15 years of age,
414 from 14 to 20, 872 from 20 to 25, 525 from 25 to 30,
237 from 30 to 40, 88 from 40 to 50, and 19 from 50 to 60.
Talbot knew prostitutes of 10 and of 50 years of age. Those
over 50 years were usually procuresses and brothel keepers[1].
Nowhere was the youth of some of the prostitutes so astonishing as in London, and in no town was child prostitution
developed to such a shocking extent as in London. I shall
enquire later into the evidences and origin of this phenomenon[2].

What is the general impression given by London prostitution? What are and were the circumstances in which
prostitutes live, the public activities of prostitution
especially?

' So soon as it becomes dark ', wrote Archenholtz, ' these
girls (professional prostitutes), well turned-out, in all
seasons flood the principal streets and squares of the town.
Many go on the man-hunt in borrowed clothes which they
hire by the day from the matrons, who for safety's sake

---

[1] Ryan, *loc. cit.*, p. 21.

[2] ' Parmi les traits qui peuvent servir à caractériser la prostitution
à Londres, ce qui surtout révolte le cœur et excite l'indignation, c'est
l'âge auquel elle s'empare de ses victimes.'—G. Richelot, *De la Prostitution
en Angleterre et en Ecosse.* Paris, 1857. P. 15.

pay another woman to follow the huntress continously on foot in order to see that she does not run away with the clothes. If the girl makes no capture and comes home without money, she will be ill-treated and must go hungry. They therefore accost passers-by and take them either home or to taverns. They can be seen standing in groups. The best class of prostitutes, who live independently, are content to go on their way till they are spoken to. Many married women even, who live in distant parts of the town, come to the Westminster district where they are unknown, and carry on the profession, either from vice or need. I have been astounded to see children of eight and nine years offer their company, at least so far as it would serve. The corruption of men's hearts is so great, that even such children can find lovers to flirt with them. More than that: at midnight the girls leave the streets and old beggar women of 60 and more come out from their hiding places in order to serve drunken men returning heated from their revels, who must satisfy their animal needs blindly, as it were, " at the galop".[1]

Schütz similarly described this barbarous man-hunt: 'So soon as the streets are lamp-lighted, which lighting is not regulated by the changes of the moon, but by the fall of darkness, they begin to swarm with street girls who, well got-up and well dressed, display their attractions. Certain it is that no place in the world can be compared with London for wantonness, and even the strictest observer of chastity has many temptations to fight against; the number of evening and night prowlers is so unbelievable. Many of them stroll the streets alone, and it must be said to their credit that they are fairly discreet. Either they silently offer one their arm or they make use of all sorts of formulas, such as, for instance, " I should so much like to marry you ",

[1] Archenholtz, *England*, Vol. II, pp. 256-258.

"Your love would make me happy", and much more of the same kind of talk. A single repulsing word is enough to drive these street ladies away, or it suffices even to pass silently by; but one must be careful not to move the right arm, as this sign may be taken for consent. Many, however, are not content with soliciting, but try to force their affections on one. It is difficult to get rid of these, as sometimes four, five and more, in competition, attach themselves to one. The modesty which Herr von Archenholtz attributes to this class of women, I have never observed, and I think, on the contrary, that it would be easy to demonstrate conclusively that they exceed in shamelessness, at an earlier age, any other women of easy virtue. What struck me most was the shamelessness of the children who, with the grownups, roamed the streets and offered their services to passersby. Usually a crowd of female creatures stand in front of the theatres, amongst whom may be found children of nine and ten years—the best evidence of moral depravity in London. In general, the English nation oversteps all others in immorality, and the abuses which come to light through addiction to debauchery are unbelievable[1].' Sunday also, which was once kept so sacred in England, means no day of rest for the London prostitutes. On the contrary, it is a most important working day[2].

In this hunt for men there was no lack of ' trade rivalry ', and regular battles often took place amongst the prostitutes. Böttiger amusingly describes a scene of this kind: ' They cannot stand new " wares ", who have not purchased their

[1] F. W. v. Schütz, *Letters from London*, pp. 214-217.

[2] Voltaire described the English Sunday festival very correctly when he said: ' On Sunday in London there is no opera, no comedies and no concerts. Card playing is strictly forbidden. On these days people go to church, to the inns and to the prostitutes ' (*Œuvres*. Kehl, 1786. Vol. XIV, p. 61). According to v. Schütz, ' the prostitutes parade the streets on Sundays the same as on other days, and the tea-gardens are fuller of this class of women than on week-days ' (v. Schütz, *loc. cit.*, p. 119).

rights, invading the street where for some time they have been accustomed to offer their attractions. This fact came to light through a dispute between two such mercenary prostitutes which had to be settled by the Lord Mayor. One had insulted the other, and the reason for the attack was none other than that the complainant had ventured into a business district which was open to her: " You must pay your footing ", which meant you must first purchase your right to capture. The other thought she was on free ground, and thus she boldly defended herself in a practical manner as befitted a true Briton, till at last *esprit de corps* took a hand and other members of the numerous sister-hood did battle on the field with tongue, hand and foot[1].'

As von Schütz mentions, one of the favourite haunts of the street-walking prostitutes was the neighbourhood of the theatres. Other favourite buildings were the numerous churches, which was the case as early as the sixteenth century. Young people of the world gathered in St. Paul's Cathedral in London and walked about there to gossip, to laugh, to show off their new clothes. This procedure had become almost an institution, and the men paid compensation to the cathedral authorities for the noise their spurs made. Swindlers, prostitutes and other vagabonds came there, and everyone conducted his business in the church[2]. Ryan says that in 1840 there were numerous churches and sacred buildings which could be cited as places of prostitution. Young elegants and merchants congregated at the time of the services in the neighbourhood of the churches, accosted the women coming out and took them to one of the numerous brothels situated in the vicinity. Girls also waited for men outside the churches[3]. Prostitution was also active in the

---

[1] *London and Paris*, Vol. IX, p. 16.
[2] H. Taine, *loc. cit.*, Vol. I, pp. 360-361.
[3] Ryan, *loc. cit.*, p. 177.

neighbourhood of the Houses of Parliament and the Law Courts[1]. The ports have at all times been the haunt of prostitutes of the lowest class who, especially on the departure and arrival of ships, collect in crowds and take boats out to the ships. Numbers of prostitutes also travel from London to other ports as soon as the arrival of a ship is announced, and terrible scenes are there enacted. After such orgies a large number of sailors are always attacked with venereal disease[2].

Finally, one may note on the streets prostitutes belonging to a higher class, riding and driving about. In the eighteenth and up to the nineteenth century one could often see girls of this sort in fine phaetons drawn by beautiful ponies, driving round in the large parks[3].

Sitting at a window counted for a long time in England as a sign of prostitution. ' To show oneself at the window ', wrote Archenholtz, ' is considered very improper. Nothing less than some street incident which may arouse curiosity can excuse an honourable woman for opening the window. Public girls, on the other hand, interpret this morality the other way round[4] '. According to Ryan, the girls in the ill-famed Aubrey brothel often stood naked at the window and executed all manner of indecent movements and postures. The same thing happened in many other open houses in London. In contrast to this exhibition of attractions at the window there is the very popular use at one time,

[1] Ryan, *loc. cit.*, p. 189.
[2] *Ibid.*, p. 190. This repulsive form of prostitution at the ports must not be confused with the great marriage journeys to the East Indies which were formerly undertaken by girls who were anxious to marry, and who hoped there to find a man among the white people. ' The day after his arrival, the Captain would give a ball to which all the men came who wished to marry, in order to make their choice from amongst the newly-arrived beauties ' (Rosenberg, *loc. cit.*, pp. 196-198).
[3] Ryan, *loc. cit.*, p. 177.
[4] Archenholtz, *England*, Vol. III, p. 74.

namely in the Restoration period and in the first quarter of the eighteenth century, of the mask by professional prostitutes, mostly of the better classes, who thus sought to hide their calling, and also by married women who pursued amorous adventures.

In addition, many habitual prostitutes, in accordance with the custom of that time, used masks. This custom, according to Malcolm, gave a welcome opportunity to many immoral, curious and lascivious people to satisfy themselves by visiting places of ill-repute unrecognised, there to indulge in excesses of all kinds. An example of this happened in May 1724. The ' White Lion ' in Wych Street, one of the last of the hundred Drury taverns, and very renowned in the time of Charles II on account of the conviviality of the frequenters of the concert and dance rooms at the top of the house, had for a long time a bad reputation by reason of the immoral orgies which took place there under the cloak of a concert, and the neighbours awaited impatiently the time when the law would be openly transgressed by the frequenters of the tavern. The time came, and the police discovered, amongst the commonest prostitutes, ladies of rank, rich merchants' wives and their daughters; an assembly that surprised everyone, so that the prostitutes could hardly believe they were in such good company, and the distinguished newcomers were shocked when they saw the faces of the degenerate prostitutes. The latter went to Bridewell prison, the former were let off with a sharp warning[1].

One of the saddest manifestations of London prostitution was the existence of homeless girls, the number of whom was huge and who almost always fell victims to prostitution at an early age. As early as the eighteenth century these poor

[1] J. P. Malcolm, *Anecdotes of the Manners and Customs of London during the Eighteenth Century*. London, 1810. Vol. I, pp. 280-281.

children of misfortune filled the streets of London at night-time with their clamour. ' What a pitiful sight it is ', an old book says, ' to see a crowd of little creatures lying in heaps close to one another, how even in the severest weather they sleep in the streets, and how some of them, hardly big enough to reach a man's hip, are already pregnant and a burden on the parish whose dung-heap serves them as a refuge! I have often thought that the removal of these brats of prostitution from the gates of a great Protestant town might be a work not altogether unworthy of our reforming street cleansers[1].'

The growth of night life in London was encouraged to a great extent by the lighting of the town which, especially in the best districts, was really beautiful[2]. Numbers of oil lamps lighted the streets with a brilliance which was to be found in no other European town. The beginning of the nineteenth century brought gas lighting, which was first installed in Finsbury Square in the year 1808[3].

With general lighting of the town an important change took place in the external manifestations of prostitution. Whilst the public prostitutes had hitherto had their headquarters in the City, or more frequently on the borders of the City and the West End, they now spread over all parts of the town, principally in the West. The centre of prostitution in the eighteenth century was Covent Garden with Drury Lane, the centre in the nineteenth century lay further West, in the Haymarket and Regent Street. It was first observed in London not only how the night lighting of a big town encouraged the spread of prostitution to all its parts, but how greatly the nightly

[1] *Satan's Harvest Home: or the present state of Whorecraft, Adultery, Fornication, Procuring, Pimping, Sodomy,* etc. London, 1749. P. 2.
[2] Archenholtz, *England*, Vol. I, p. 197.
[3] Henry B. Wheatley, *London, Past and Present.* London, 1891. Vol. I, p. 45.

excesses in the higher grades of society also increased; but at the same time crimes which would be committed in darkness were thereby restrained. The appearence of the West End after midnight is thus described by an observer: ' Although it was already after 3 o'clock, the nymphs and shepherds still sacrificed on the altar of Bacchus, and the peak of lust was reached. Carriages drove one behind the other, bringing the ladies from their dwellings into the arms of their beloved admirers who awaited them with the utmost impatience at the different pleasure resorts[1].' The large parks also served as meeting places[2]. As already mentioned, Drury Lane and Covent Garden was the centre of prostitution in the eighteenth century. 'There is the good old market with its gabled church, immortalised by Hogarth, with its square which was formerly renowned as the gallant rendezvous of the town, and with its arcades in the middle, full of roots and oranges and bunches of mignonette.

' Covent Garden means Convent Garden; and this was originally the garden of the Abbey of Westminster, which under Edward VI was granted under patent to the Duke of Bedford, who still owns the whole of the land and property. From this time on, the quiet garden of the monks rapidly changed into one of the gayest and most fashionable quarters in London. The Duke built himself a palace here, and the Russells loved the neighbourhood. The square also was built. When we pass Covent Garden we think of Dryden, of Voltaire and the beautiful actresses of Drury Lane[3].'

The centre of modern London prostitution is the Haymarket and Regent Street in the West end, the most fashionable streets in London. In the introduction to an erotic novel,

[1] *The Midnight Spy*, p. 116.
[2] ' Here are also to be seen a number of tawdry misses, lying in wait for a fool of fortune, or an inexperienced countryman; in short, the walks exhibit a motley scene of vanity, folly and knavery ' (*ibid.*, p. 17).
[3] J. Rodenberg, *loc. cit.*, pp. 60-61.

Kate Handcock, which appeared in 1882, occurs the following: ' The subject of this short tale was a charming girl, whom I met late one night near the well-known Haymarket, the acknowledged centre of debauchery in London[1].' An idealised description of the activities in the Haymarket by that fine and sympathetic observer Julius Rodenberg, shows the character of the place only too plainly.

' Midnight is the hour of the Haymarket and the hour of the midnight tea-parties, to which beautiful sinners are invited for uplifting talks with bishops and nobles who wish to convert them to virtue. While sleep rules in London's huge circumference and even the dance halls are dark and still, the " Café de la Régence " is still lighted up, and on the wide pavement as far as the columns of His Majesty's Theatre begins the promenade which seldom ends before 2 or 3 in the morning.

' What a brightly-coloured intoxicating medley—what a hubbub of sound, what lights, stars, eyes, scarves, light footfalls and frivolous hearts! How the oyster houses fill up with elegant gentlemen from the theatre, their opera glasses still in their hands, and with ladies, hungry and thirsty from the dance, to keep them company. Past the slender tower of St. Martin's-in-the-Fields goes the crowd. The high columns of Charing Cross stand up in the night sky and the broad, majestic, ghostly façades of houses glimmer through the night; and in the high windows of the sleeping buildings the moon is reflected. But on Haymarket Hill the sounds of traffic are loud. At the corner by the Café de la Régence drone the bagpipes, and the old Highland melody "The Campbells are coming oho, oho! " shrills through the night, above the noise of laughing, greeting and jesting[2].'

[1] *Kate Handcock : or a Young Girl's Introduction to Fast Life.* London, 1882. P. 1.

[2] J. Rodenberg, *loc. cit.*, pp. 254-255.

Regent Street, perhaps the 'most effective street of the metropolis' as Wheatley calls it, was laid out at the command of the Prince Regent, later King George IV, by the famous architect Nash in the years 1813 to 1820, and soon developed into the favourite and most up-to-date street in London.

'In the daytime Regent Street belongs to the nobility and gentry of Great Britain, but as six o'clock strikes the scene changes. Thereafter no carriage bearing a crown or coronet may be seen, the liveries and the aristocratic countenances of the court ladies disappear. Another public comes on the scene; other ladies with eyes often no less beautiful and with silk dresses which rustle no less, and until long after midnight the wide pavement on the right-hand side resembles the floor of a dance hall, and the coloured arcade of the Quadrant an Attic night-scene, full of people and the sound of all the languages of Europe. But on that subject we will say no more[1].'

The author of the *Memoirs of a Singer* speaks of the 'so-called " stretch " in Regent Street' which she visited with her friends[2], indicating that Regent Street was the haunt of the best class of prostitutes.

We will close this sketch of the general impression given by London prostitution with a description of one of the nightly promenades in the Haymarket and Regent Street, which began about 1 o'clock and continued till 3.

'In no continental town does a similar promenade take place. The wide footpaths of the Haymarket, from the arcades of His Majesty's Theatre to the bend of Regent Street, shimmer in the reflection of the gas lamps and the mirrors of the cafés and restaurants which, like a sparkling belt, enclose the left-hand side of the street. All doors are open, all windows illuminated. From the small rooms

[1] J. Rodenberg, *loc. cit.*, p. 3.
[2] *The Memoirs of a Singer*, Vol. II, p. 205.

decorated in red and gold comes the sound of music, merry laughter and the clink of champagne glasses, and on their soft red velvet cushions the orgies of the London night are celebrated. Those small gaily decorated rooms, and the simplicity and quiet of the dining rooms in Cheapside, in which City merchants on the narrow seats behind the high brown settles consume their roast beef and drink their ale and porter from pewter mugs, silently, hat on head, the *Times* in their hand—what a contrast! And on the wide stone pavement the promenaders mingle, beautiful girls in shining dance frocks, pearls braided in their hair, promenaders of all nations, from all towns and countries, laughing, whispering, disappearing through the brown mahogany doors of the cafés, coming and going. The night air is impregnated with the scent of patchouli and " Eau de mille fleurs ". The trains of satin dresses rustle on the stone, scarves float, rose-coloured ribbons flutter; sparkling eyes, caressing words; there a greeting, here a whisper and a laugh !

'Ever more lively becomes the scene; often it is difficult to make one's way through the groups of girls and promenaders. All languages of the world are heard, French, German, English, Italian, as under the shimmering arcades of St. Mark's Piazza at 8 o'clock in the evening. Once again we see all the dancers from Cremorne. There is the beautiful tall girl in the white muslin dress with the rose-coloured scarf and the gold-embroidered Arab mantle. On the arm of a tall fair man in the forties, in light summer clothing, she comes from the mahogany door of one of the restaurants. A long line of cabs and hansoms stands in the middle of the street.

'Her companion beckons one of the drivers—the couple get in. The beautiful girl in the gold-embroidered Arab mantle has disappeared from the stage of the modern London night.

[113]

'And there through that window we can see the lovely girl with the dark eyes and the gold blonde curls. She lies on a divan against the wall of the small blue carpeted room; in front of her sits a man, his back turned to the window, handing her sherry. The small table is spread with oysters, lobster salad and wine bottles. Her arms are burning, her soft complexion is reddened by the champagne. How long since she forgot the printed paper which the serious silent man put into her small white hand in front of the fantastic door of the Magic Garden as she hurried here to her champagne, oysters and golden guineas! Or did she not read it at all? We go further. It is nearly 2 o'clock. The pavement of the Haymarket becomes ever more lively the nearer we get to Piccadilly Circus. In Regent Street it is dark. The glow reflected from the gleaming windows of the cafés and restaurants is diminishing, the street will soon be lighted only by the long row of gas lamps. But for all that it is no more deserted than the Haymarket. Here also silk dresses rustle on the wide pavements and here floats the scent of " Eau de mille fleurs " and here also dark eyes and frivolous hearts greet one another. In Oxford Street the night is lonely and quiet. For Oxford Street 2 o'clock is a late hour. We meet no one. But there a light still streams across the street, coming from one of the public houses which are open after midnight. From within we hear sounds of voices, brawling and cries. Let us go inside! Ragged creatures crowd round the bar, behind which a fat bald man in shirt sleeves serve sale, porter, gin and whisky. What figures and what faces! What torn coats and dirty dresses! What women, half drunk, sipping a glass of gin and water! And this public house after midnight there at the corner of Oxford Street is, after all, merely an offshoot of the glittering cafés in the Haymarket[1].'

[1] Gustav Rasch, *London by Night*, pp. 44-49.

CHAPTER IV

THE HAUNTS OF PROSTITUTION

THE places where prostitution was mostly carried on in the early and later Middle Ages in England, and especially in London, were the public baths, the so-called *bagnios*, which have retained the name up to modern times. According to Dufour, public baths came to the Europe of the Middle Ages principally through the Crusades, as a result of which a knowledge of the oriental warm baths was acquired[1]. The spread of the bath establishments was extraordinarily rapid in the Middle Ages. Dufour says that in Paris in the twelfth century nearly every street had its bath[2], and according to Rudeck, even very small villages possessed these establishments[3]. Nearly everywhere the sexes bathed together in these public establishments. Conditions in Germany are described by Rudeck as follows: 'In the early morning the bath-keeper announced in the street, by blasts on a horn, that all was ready. People of the lower classes then undressed almost completely at home and wended their way through the streets to the bath house. Guarinonius says that well educated burghers and their wives stripped in their homes and walked naked through the public streets to the bath house. " How often indeed does the father run naked from the house through the streets

---

[1] P. Dufour, *Histoire de la Prostitution*. Brussels, 1861. Vol. VII, p. 42.
[2] *Ibid.*, p. 42.
[3] W. Rudeck, *History of Public Morality in Germany*. Jena, 1897. P. 12.

to the bath with his naked wife and naked children? How often do I see (I do not name the town) young girls of 10, 12, 14, 16 and 18 years quite naked and with only a short linen bath robe, often torn, or as they say here in the country, with a ' Bath honour ' as sole covering in front and round the shoulders! With this and bare feet, and one hand held behind for propriety, out of the house they go, through the long streets in broad daylight, running to the bath! How often do the stark naked, 10, 12, 14 and 16 year old youths run by their side, accompanying these vagabonds." After this the last remnants of clothing are thrown off in the dressing room and the Turkish or water bath is entered stark naked. Hans von Schweinichen relates as follows: "When I was at the Court for a few days the old Duchess took a bath; I had to wait on her there as a youth. Before long a young girl came, called Katherina, stark naked, and called me to give her cold-water." Many bath houses had a single dressing-room, which was of course used by both sexes at the same time. From many descriptions it is evident that two-seater bath tubs were often used by persons of different sexes at the same time!" In France people did not go naked through the streets, but the conditions at the baths were, according to the evidence, even worse than in Germany, so that before long a respectable woman could no longer be seen there.

Whilst the public baths in Germany and France soon degenerated into places of free sexual intercourse and prostitution, London went a step further, and these baths were established as official places of prostitution. The organisation of the baths as brothels took place in the reign of Henry II (1154-1189). These bath-brothels were almost entirely confined to the Southwark district on the south

---

[1] W. Rudeck, *loc. cit.*, pp. 5-7.

bank of the Thames, outside the city walls, which district did not become a part of the capital until the year 1550. It was a sad quarter, full of old houses, their walls falling down, and only half of them inhabited. In addition there were gardens and places for dogs, bears and other fighting animals there.

In later times these bath establishments spread over the whole town, being then called ' Hothouses ' or ' Bagnios '. According to Wright, who also traces back to the Orient the introduction of the baths, they remained for a long time, up to the middle of the seventeenth century, the principal places of prostitution. They were usually called by the good English name ' hothouses '; sometimes, however, their oriental origin showed in the use of the Persian name *hummum*. This title is still preserved in the names of two modern hotels which are built on the site of similar establishments in Covent Garden[1]. Ben Jonson speaks of sweating in the hothouses, and a character in the old play *The Puritan* says, speaking of a difficult undertaking: ' Marry, I shall sweat as much over it as if I had been in sixteen hothouses.' These hothouses were principally the resort of women and, as in the East, were soon the favourite meeting-places for libertines with women and girls. Soon they were used to such an extent for these immoral purposes that the name ' Hothouse ' or ' Bagnio ' became identical with that of a brothel. This circumstance led to their gradual disuse. A very rare and remarkable woodcut of the time of James I, with the title ' Tittle-tattle, or the several branches of gossiping ', illustrates in different scenes the manner in which the young women of the day spent their time in idleness, and shows also the interior of a hothouse. In one of the rooms are women sitting in bath-robes and

[1] Compare K. Baedeker, *London and Environs*. Tenth edition. Leipzig, 1890. P. 8.

taking light refreshment, in another room they are enjoying themselves with men[1].

From the history of mediæval prostitution, which was principally confined to the bagnios, a few salient points may be mentioned.

Public morality in England took a serious turn for the worse during the Norman invasion. Just as in France the Norman influence was felt in this way—Dufour ascribes to them the first introduction on a large scale of pæderasty, which was later revived through the Crusades[2]—so England, directly after the invasion of the Normans, was inundated with vice of all sorts. The cordial relations between England and France later on during the Middle Ages resulted in the lax French morality regarding sex life finding its way into England, and especially in the upper circles, amongst the nobles and clergy. Alexander remarks: ' Neither the morals of the Englishwomen were much more restrained, nor was their character much more modest than that of the French-women. The same indecent familiarity was remarked in their public, and unbridled excess in their private behaviour. During the Christmas festivities nearly every nobleman entertained his vassals of both sexes, and a neighbouring clergyman was usually appointed by him to preside over these extravagantly lustful and indecent revels. He was, according to the character of his office, usually designated the " Abbot of Misrule ". In the houses of the great were usually to be found rooms for the sewing and embroidery maids. The name that was given to these rooms, in accordance with the use that was made of them, became in time synonymous with that of a brothel. Indeed, so shameless in those days were all men of position, that even the clergy did not hesitate to have inscriptions put over the doors of

[1] Th. Wright, *A History of English Culture*. London, 1874. P. 495.
[2] P. Dufour, *loc. cit.*, Vol. III, p. 269.

these rooms, plainly showing their purpose. The famous
Cardinal Wolsey had over the door of a room of this kind
in his palace the (Latin) words: "The house of the harlots of
his Excellency the Cardinal[1] ".' Nicolaus Poplau, a Schles-
wig nobleman, who in the year 1483 travelled much in
Europe, informs us that Englishwomen meeting strangers
were very free with their kisses, and remarks: ' Between
English people—devilish marriages.' All the songs of the
English troubadours likewise point to the debauched life led
by the nobles and clergy between the twelfth and the
fifteenth centuries[2]. The English priesthood, according to
an account in Fox's *Acts and Monuments*, before the
Reformation kept for itself more than 100,000 harlots (who
in the mediæval dialect were known as ' Lemmans ' from the
French ' L'amante '), besides the numerous women they
seduced in the confessionals[3]. When Henry II demanded that
a priest who had disgraced the daughter of a noble and murdered the father, should be handed over to the secular arm,
Archbishop Becket refused to do so as he had already
punished the criminal by suspension, and a guilty person
could not be punished twice for the same crime[4]. Of the
English kings it is said that Henry I, Henry II and Richard I[5]
lived in open polygamy and had more illegitimate than
legitimate sons and daughters. Edward IV lived in con-

[1] W. Alexander, *loc. cit.*, Vol. I, pp. 11-12.
[2] *Eros.* Stuttgart, 1849. Vol. I, p. 80.
[3] P. Fraxi, *Centuria Librorum absconditorum.* London, 1879. P. 208
(from now on referred to as *Centuria*). Here were described the many
children's skeletons which were found in the English convents, in the
streams and other places. There was an original proposal to castrate all
Catholic priests in England (!) which was made by the author of the
document, ' Reasons humbly offered for a law to enact the castration of
Popish ecclesiastics as the best way to prevent the growth of Popery in
England. London, 1700.'
[4] *Eros*, Vol. II, p. 553.
[5] The frontispiece of the fifth volume of Dufour's *History of Prostitution*
shows Richard I in a house of ill fame.

tinual lasciviousness and in the most intimate relations with London women and young girls[1]. According to Sabatier, many English kings and nobles of the Middle Ages had their own gynæceums. Under Henry VIII there was a room in the royal palace with the inscription ' Room of the King's prostitutes[2] '.

As regards the external history of mediæval bagnio-prostitution in England, the most important statute affecting it was the Act of Parliament of the year 1161, which was agreed by both the Upper and Lower Houses and sanctioned by King Henry II. This memorable document runs as follows:

' In a parliament holden at Westminster, the eighth of Henry II, it was ordained by the commons, and confirmed by the King and Lords, that divers constitutions for ever should be kept within that lordship, or franchise, according to the old customs, that had there used time of minde: amongst the which these following were some: videlicet.

' That no stew-holder or his wife should let or stay any single woman to goe and come freely at all times, when they listed.

' No stew-holder to keep any woman to boord, but she to boord abroad at her pleasure.

' To take no more for the woman's chamber in the weeke, than fourteene pence.

' Not to keep open his doores upon the holy-dayes.

' Not to keep any single woman in his house on the holy-dayes, but the bayliffe to see they voyded out of the lordship.

' No single woman to be kept against her will, that would leave her sinne.

[1] *Eros*, Vol. II, p. 553.
[2] Rabutaux, *De la Prostitution en Europe depuis l'Antiquité jusqu'à la fin du 16me siècle*. Paris 1851, fol. 24. ' Nor did gentlemen of considerable property blush to hold lands by, and bear commissions for, being marshal of the king's whores ' (Alexander, *loc. cit.*, Vol. I, p. 12).

'No stew-keeper receive any woman of religion, or any man's wife.

'No single woman to take money to lye with any man, except she lye with him all night, till the morrow.

'No man to be drawn or enticed into any stew-house. The constables, bayliffe, and others, every weeke to search every stew-house.

'No stew-holder to keep any woman, that has the perrilous infirmity of burning; nor to sell bread, ale, flesh, fish, wood, coal or any victuals[1]'.

This statute brings the conditions in a bagnio of this kind very clearly before us. In Southwark, in the twelfth century, there were eighteen bagnios, under the supervision and charge of the Bishop of Winchester. They had before the doors large signs with such names as: 'The Crane', 'The Boar's Head', 'The Castle', 'The Cardinal's Hat', 'The Bell.' In the year 1380 all the houses belonged to a certain William Walworth, a fish merchant and Mayor of London. He let them to procuresses who managed them. At one time they were broken into by rioters in Kent. In the meantime the Act of Parliament of 1161 was again confirmed by King Edward III and Henry IV, and, in addition, the municipal authorities of the City in the year 1351 issued an order against the ' communes soles femmes qui ont pris la gise d'estre vestu et attirée a l'appareille des bonnes et nobles dames et damoiselles '. This order enumerated the articles of clothing which public girls were forbidden to wear and appointed for them a costume of their own.

Henry VI, in the year 1506, had the bath-houses closed, but soon after was obliged to open them again. Only twelve, however, were allowed to remain, which Henry VIII in the

---

[1] John Stow, *The Survey of London contayning the originall, increase, moderne estate, and government of that city.* London, 1633. P. 448.

[121]

year 1546 finally closed[1]. This moral monarch, by means of a herald blowing a trumpet in the streets, invited disorderly women to ' keepe good and honest rule '. Stow, who recounts it, unfortunately does not say whether this categorical order was carried out[2].

Towards the beginning of the seventeenth century, as an enquiry organised by one of the Aldermen of London showed, disorderly women had already spread to all districts. The Aldermen received an order to bring to punishment all prostitutes arrested in inns. They were also to see that the bath establishments in different parts of the town were not visited by prostitutes, and that the baths specially reserved for women were not frequented by young men, vagabonds and people of ill-fame. Owners of such establishments disobeying these orders were liable to a £20 fine.

Thus in the seventeenth century, especially under the influence of the Puritans, the bath establishments remained relatively free from the taint of their earlier connection with prostitution. When in the year 1649 a doctor, Peter Chamberlen, petitioned parliament for permission to open bath establishments all over England and published a brochure on the subject, his request was rejected on the grounds of morality[3].

At the time of the Restoration at the end of the seventeenth century the bagnios awoke to new life. In the eighteenth century there were numbers of establishments of this kind in all parts of the town. Archenholtz gives the following picture of the bagnios of the eighteenth century: ' In London there is a certain kind of house, called bagnios, which

[1] As C. J. Lecour (*Prostitution in Paris and London.* Paris, 1882. P. 269) rightly conjectures, on account of syphilis which had newly appeared at that time and had been spread very rapidly by the bagnios.

[2] Rabutaux, *loc. cit.*, fol. 18.

[3] *Biographisches Lexicon der hervorragenden Arzte aller Zeiten und Völker.* Vienna and Leipzig, 1884. Vol. I, p. 695.

are supposed to be baths; their real purpose, however,
is to provide persons of both sexes with pleasure. These
houses are well, and often richly, furnished, and every device
for exciting the senses is either at hand or can be provided.
Girls do not live there but they are fetched in chairs when
required. None but those who are specially attractive in all
ways are so honoured, and for this reason they often send
their address to a hundred of these bagnios in order to make
themselves known. A girl who is sent for and does not
please receives no gratuity, the chair alone being paid for.
The English retain their solemnity even as regards their
pleasures, and consequently the business of such a house
is conducted with a seriousness and propriety which is
hard to credit. All noise and uproar is banned here; no loud
footsteps are heard, every corner is carpeted and the
numerous attendants speak quietly amongst themselves.
Old people and degenerates can here receive flagellation,
for which all establishments are prepared. In every bagnio
is found a formula regarding baths, but they are seldom
needed. These pleasures are very expensive, but in spite of
this the many houses of the kind are full every night. Most
of them are quite close to the theatres, and many taverns
are in the same neighbourhood[1].'

The centre of this bagnio prostitution in the eighteenth
century was the Covent Garden neighbourhood. The most
fashionable bagnio was that of Molly King, in the middle
of Covent Garden. ' Ce rendez-vous était le réceptacle général

---

[1] Archenholtz, *England*, Vol. II, pp. 261-262. It can be seen from this
description that the bagnios of the eighteenth century fully resembled
those of the Middle Ages in this feature, that they did not provide the
inmates with board, and thus differed from actual brothels. The bagnios
of the eighteenth century were more a type of ' temporary lodging '.
and were therefore suitable for use as amorous rendezvous. For this
purpose they were very largely employed by men and women of all
classes. Compare also *Les dessous*, etc., Vol. I, pp. 91-92.

des prostituées et libertines de tous les rangs.' When the proprietress gave up her business she had 'through the foolishness, the lasciviousness and the debauchery of the time' acquired a large fortune. The second principal bagnio was that of Mother Douglas, also called 'Mother Cole', who only received debauchees of the highest standing in her establishments. Princes and peers visited it, also many distinguished women came there incognito. Mrs. Gould, the proprietress of a bagnio also in the neighbourhood of Covent Garden, catered for aristocratic and well-bred ladies. Women who swore or carried on indecent conversation were thrown out without further ado. Her principal clients were rich merchants who, under the pretence of going to the country, usually came to the house on Saturday evening and stayed till early on Monday. She treated these with extreme courtesy, providing the 'most excellent liquors, very refined courtesans, the most elegant beds and furniture'. Her best friend was a public notary whom she loved tenderly, and who with his qualifications was very useful to her. The fourth high-class Covent Garden bagnio belonged to Mrs. Stanhope, known as 'Hellfire Stanhope', because an intimate friend of hers was President of the Hellfire Club. She was a gifted woman and laid the greatest stress on the fact that she always provided her guests with the most beautiful girls.

The introduction of brothels proper, or, as they were called at that time, 'Seraglios', occurred in the year 1750 through a certain Mrs. Goadby. She had made several journeys to France, and had been initiated into the secrets of the famous Parisian *sérails*, especially those of Justine Paris[1] and

---

[1] With reference to the Paris, compare my book *Der Marquis de Sade und seiner Zeit* (Vol. I of the 'Studies in the history of the sex life of man,' pp. 127-132).

Montigny. The principles on which the last two were conducted, and which Mrs. Goadby to a great extent made her own, were the following:

The brothel proprietors accepted as far as possible only the most beautiful girls, and preferably those from different countries and of different faiths. All, however, were equally subject to the rules of the brothels and had to submit unconditionally to the orders of the brothel keeper, whose authority was supreme. It was also the duty of the girls to show ' le zèle le plus sincère pour les rites et les cérémonies de la déesse de cypros ' and to satisfy all fantasies, caprices and extravagances of the male visitors, carrying out their wishes in every particular. Finally, they must avoid all gastronomic and alcoholic excess in order that their behaviour should be modest and decent even in the pursuit of pleasure. It was an unpardonable crime to conceal from the brothel mistress gifts and monetary remunerations which were received over and above the very moderate fixed price. A night with a girl, together with a good supper, etc., cost a gold louis, a sum which, in comparison with the price paid in England up to that time for the same privileges, was very small. Usually these handmaids of Venus spent their time from the midday meal till the evening in a large salon, where some of them played the guitar, others accompanying them with songs, while some embroidered or plaited wreaths. During this time intoxicating drinks were forbidden; at the most, almond milk or similar harmless sweet liquors were allowed in order to avoid any chance of excess. Guests appeared in this salon usually after the theatres were over, when their custom was to offer a handkerchief to the lady of their choice. If this was accepted, she belonged to the man for the night.

Mrs. Goadby carried on this system after her return from France. She rented a very elegant house in Berwick Street, in the Soho district[1], engaged the most famous London prostitutes and a surgeon to look after their health; no one was accepted about whom there was any suspicion in this connection. She had brought with her much fine French silk material and lace, so that her girls should be distinctively dressed. She did not, however, charge the low prices of the French brothels or prohibit alcoholic drinks.

Goadby's establishment, which in every respect fulfilled its claim to ' refine our amorous amusements ', soon achieved a great reputation and received large numbers of visitors of good standing, who could here indulge in any extravagance or perversity they wished. In a very short time Mrs. Goadby became a rich woman and later retired to a country property which she had acquired[2].

She had numerous imitators who all tried to run their brothels on the same luxurious lines[3]. Malcolm says these

[1] The peculiar name ' Soho ' comes from an old cry, ' So-ho ' or ' So-how ' which hunters gave when they found the hare. See Wheatley, *loc. cit.*, Vol. III, p. 262.

[2] *Les Sérails de Londres ou les Amusements Nocturnes.* Brussels, no year, pp. 10-12. This book is an exact French translation (original edition, Paris, 1801) of an important English work *Nocturnal Revels : or, The History of King's Place, and other Modern Nunneries, etc.* By a Monk of the Order of St. Francis. London, 1779 ; two vols. Pisanus Fraxi (*Index*, pp. 319-21) considers this work one of the few authentic sources for prostitution in London in the eighteenth century. It will be cited henceforth as *Sérails.*

[3] Doppet remarks with regard to the requirements of a well-managed brothel: ' As the Temple of Love depends for its existence on the appetites which are therein aroused, those who serve the goddess must employ in their persons every possible means of attracting men's eyes to themselves. All their thought and effort must be concentrated on a suitable wardrobe, and their dresses must be so cut that the attractions of the body may be fully displayed. Their smile is inviting, their movements are voluptuous, their dwelling elegant, the pictures which decorate it stimulate desire, their books are chosen with the same end in view, etc. In short, nothing is forgotten which may arouse sexual impulses. In addition, the prostitutes know thousands of ways in which to further their desires, and to invest the sexual act with ever-fresh attractions.'— Doppet, *Flagellation and its effects on sexual impulse* in *The Treasure-*

were really remarkable[1].

Charlotte Hayes, a *demi-mondaine* well known on account of her many amorous adventures, first followed the example of Mrs. Goadby and rented in King's Place, Pall Mall, a house which she furnished beautifully and opened soon after Mrs. Goadby's *sérail*. Under the name of the Charlotte Hayes 'Cloister[2]', it soon achieved a great reputation on account of its *marchandises choisies* (as Charlotte Hayes called her girls). The 'nuns' were very beautiful girls whom she zealously initiated into the mysteries of the goddess of Cyprus, so familiar to her, and the sensual value of which she well understood. She gave them dresses, watches, gold ear-rings, and other expensive adornments, accounted to them also for their food, lodging and washing, so that they were soon loaded with debt and bound to their 'Abbess', nor could they obtain their freedom without the greatest difficulty.

The visitors to Charlotte Hayes' *sérail* were nearly all impotent debauchees who required every possible stimulation for the satisfaction of their lusts. The brothel mistress had

Digger, etc., by I. Scheible. Stuttgart, 1847. Vol. IV, pp. 375-376. The most luxurious brothel in the world was that known in Amsterdam as 'The Fountain'. It consisted of a large building with restaurant, dance-hall and private rooms, café, and a billiard-room on the roof of the house, where the most beautiful girls played billiards stark naked. At small tables round sat serious, blinking old gentlemen, comfortably smoking their long pipes, drinking their glass of grog and enjoying the remarkable spectacle. See *Untrodden Fields of Anthropology*. Paris, 1898. Vol. I, pp. 129-130.

[1] 'These seraglios or whatever else the reader pleases to term them, are in many instances large and handsome houses.'

[2] It is characteristic that in earlier times the brothels were known as 'cloisters', 'abbeys', and their inmates as 'nuns'. Avignon and Montpellier had similar immoral abbeys. Toulouse had in the Rue de Comenge a brothel, the 'Grant-Abbey', etc. (see P. Dufour, *loc. cit.*, Vol. IV, p. 181). William IX, Duke of Aquitaine, the 'Goliath of Prostitution', was interested in a plan to found a huge brothel on the lines of a convent, conducted by the most famous harlots of Poitou (Dufour, *loc. cit.*, Vol. IV, p. 131).

also to provide a supply of virgins which, as we shall see later, was an essential requirement for a good brothel.

This kind of pleasure must, of course, be paid for, and Hayes understood perfectly how to extract money from her visitors, as the following price-list shows:

Sunday the 9th January.

A young girl for Alderman Drybones. Nelly Blossom, about 19 years old, who has had no one for four days and who is a virgin ...	20 guineas.
A girl of 19 years, not older, for Baron Harry Flagellum. Nell Hardy from Bow Street, Bat Flourish from Berners Street, or Miss Birch from Chapel Street	10 guineas.
A beautiful lively girl for Lord Spaan. Black Moll from Hedge Lane, who is very strong ...	5 guineas.
For Colonel Tearall a gentle woman. Mrs. Mitchell's servant, who has just come from the country and has not yet been out in the world	10 guineas.
For Dr. Frettext, after consultation hours, a young agreeable person, sociable, with a white skin and a soft hand. Polly Nimble-wrist from Oxford, or Jenny Speedyhand from Mayfair	2 guineas.
Lady Loveit, who has come from the baths at Bath, and who is disappointed in her love affair with Lord Alto, wants to have something better, and to be well served this evening. Capt. O'Thunder or Sawney Rawbone	50 guineas.
For His Excellency Count Alto, a fashionable woman for an hour only. Mrs. O'Smirk who came from Dunkirk, or Miss Graeful from Paddington	10 guineas.

[128]

For Lord Pyebald, to play a game of
piquet, for *titillatione mammarum* and so on,
with no other object.   Mrs. Tredrille from
Chelsea[1]...   ...   .   5 guineas.
A husband and wife often met by chance at rendezvous in
the same infamous brothel.

One day Mrs. Hayes sent the following circular to her
clients: ' Mrs. Hayes commends herself respectfully to Lord
. . . and takes the liberty of advising him that this evening at
7 o'clock precisely, 12 beautiful nymphs, spotless virgins,
will carry out the famous Feast of Venus, as it is celebrated
in Tahiti, under the instruction and leadership of Queen
Oberea (which rôle will be taken by Mrs. Hayes herself).'

Cook's travelling companion, Hawksworth, tells that in
Tahiti young men and girls often copulate publicly before
the people, receiving good advice from the bystanders,
usually women, amongst whom the most important
inhabitants are to be found.   Thus the girls (of 11 years)
receive their information at an early age[2].

Mrs. Hayes had evidently read this report, and now
decided to carry out the same ceremonies before her guests
with the help of the 'Inventions, Imaginations and Caprices
of Aretino ', with which those taking part in the ceremony
had to make themselves perfectly familiar.   Twenty-three
visitors of the highest standing came, amongst them five
members of the House of Commons.   Punctually at 7 o'clock
the feast began, for which, for the men's parts, Mrs. Hayes
had engaged twelve athletic youths.   These youths, with the
nymphs, now celebrated the Tahiti Venus Feast before the
eyes of the entranced audience[3], after which a sumptuous

---

[1] *Sérails*, pp. 18-19.
[2] See Ploss-Bartels, *Das Weib in der Natur und Völkerbunde.*   Sixth
edition.   Leipzig, 1899.   Vol. I, p. 433.
[3] ' On avait étendu sur le carreau un beau et large tapis, et on avait
orni la scène des meubles nécessaires pour les différentes attitudes dans

meal was taken. Charlotte Hayes retired from business with a fortune of £20,000[1].

King's Place, Pall Mall, was the site of most of the new seraglios[2]. Mrs. Mitchell's brothel was there, with the famous inscription *in medio tutissimus*[3], also that of Mrs. Prendergast.

Amongst the brothel keepers of King's Place was a negress, Miss Harriot, who had been brought to England by a rich planter from Kingston in Jamaica. After the death of her master, who died suddenly of smallpox, she very soon started her career.

Mrs. Nelson, formerly a famous ' beauty ', began her work when the last traces of her own loveliness had disappeared as the result of her excesses. She therefore had to make up for lack of personal attraction by special refinements in the service of her clients. She first had a brothel in Wardour Street, Soho, at the corner of Holland Street, into which she managed by various means to entice young girls. She was bound in honour continually to provide fresh ' wares ',

lesquelles les acteurs et actrices dévoués à Venus devaient paraitre, conformément au système de l'Arétin. Après que les hommes eurent présenté a chacune de leur maîtresse un clou au moins de douze pouces de longueur, en imitation des présents reçus, en pareilles occasions par les dames d'Otaïti qui donnaient à un long clou la préférence à toute autre chose, ils commencèrent leurs dévotions et passèrent avec la plus grande dextérité par toutes les différentes évolutions des rites, relativement au mot d'ordre de santa Carlotta, en conservant le temps le plus régulier au contentement universel des spectateurs lascifs, dont l'imagination de quelques-un d'eux fut tellement transportée, qu'ils ne purent attendre la fin de la scène pour exécuter à leur tour leur partie dans cette fête Cyprienne, qui dura près de deux heures, et obtint les plus vifs applaudissements de l'assemblée. Madame Hayes avait si bien dirigé sa troupe, qu'il n'y eut pas un manœuvre qui ne fut exécutée avec la plus grande exactitude et la plus grande habilité ' (*Sérails*, p. 116).

[1] *Sérails*, p. 118.

[2] ' Nous revenons maintenant au grand endroit d'amour, de plaisir et de bonheur, au célèbre sanctum sanctorum, ou King's Place ' (*Sérails*, p. 150).

[3] *Ibid.*, pp. 24, 50.

and did not hesitate even to take a position as pseudo-governess in a school in order to entice young girls away. So soon as a newcomer arrived, her alleged husband, Mr. Nelson, wrote round to all important clients—and did not have to wait long for them to make their appearance.

Other brothels were those of Lucy Cooper in Bond Street[1], Susannah Adams in Westminster[2], and a certain Hannah, who had a large number of licentious houses in Johnson's Court[3]. In Holborn there was a brothel in which meals could be obtained at midday[4].

A special kind of brothel, consisting of three houses, was established by Miss Fawkland, the former mistress of a Major in the ' Black Guards '. She called these *sérails* in St. James's Street the Temples of Aurora, Flora and Mystery. The principal entrance was in the ' Temple of Flora ', the middle one of the three. On the left was the ' Temple of Aurora ' and on the right the ' Temple of Mystery '.

The Temple of Aurora contained twelve young girls in ages from 11 to 16. As soon as they were 16 they went over to the Temple of Flora, but never before this age. They were at once replaced by other girls of not more than 11, so that the Temple of Aurora, which Miss Fawkland called the ' first noviciate of pleasure ', always held the same number of ' nuns '. These were elegantly dressed and excellently fed and had two governesses who were always with them. The small girls were taught to read and write, embroider and sew. They had a dancing master, and a library of entertaining books, amongst which were such works as *Memoirs of a Woman of Pleasure*, which they were allowed to read primarily in order to inflame their senses at an early age.

[1] *Sérails*, p. 15.
[2] Archenholtz, *Annalen*, Vol. XVII, p. 197.
[3] *Ibid.*, p. 198.
[4] *Ibid.*, Vol. VII, p. 263.

[131]

The governesses also gave them theoretical instruction as to the relations between the sexes. Masturbation was, however, forbidden, and they were strictly watched in this connection. Walking out was not allowed. In this way Miss Fawkland brought up a stock of virgins, creatures early initiated into the mysteries of Venus, from whom, later on, considerable profit might be expected. In the meantime, even these young inmates of the Temple of Aurora had to receive visitors. Miss Fawkland, to be sure, satisfied herself beforehand as to their impotence, and they had to be over 60 years old, so that there should be nothing to fear as regards the virginity of the little girls. Lord Cornwallis, Lord Buckingham and Mr. Simpson were amongst the most zealous visitors to this temple of platonic love where so many ways of giving them satisfaction were known.

The Temple of Flora contained the same number of young ' nuns ' who, as the result of their previous education, were extremely lively, merry, agreeable and ' indescribably sensual '. In short, the visitor was so bewitched that he often had great difficulty in making a choice amongst so many attractions. In order to prevent jealousy and favouritism, Miss Fawkland arranged that all presents and sums of money received should be pooled and later divided equally amongst all. In contrast to other ' Abbesses ', Miss Fawkland was very generous to her ' nuns,' who could easily leave the brothel without stealing her clothes or her money. Once they had left, however, no return was allowed. Her generosity brought to Miss Fawkland a large throng of beautiful girls, from which, however, she only took enough to make up her always strictly adhered to number of twelve for each temple. Of the twelve 'nuns' of the Temple of Flora, six came from that of Aurora. The author of the *Sérails de Londres* describes in detail the origin and attractions of the remaining six inmates of the flower temple, amongst the ' subscribing ' visitors to which were Sheridan, Lord Hamilton, Lord Bolingbroke and Smollett.

The Temple of Mysteries justified its name on account of the scenes of secret and unheard of debaucheries which were enacted there. Neither the inmates of the other two temples nor those of other brothels were allowed to enter it[1].

Near these brothels were many lodging places for ladies of good position. The most renowned was the *buen retiro* of Mrs. Redson in Bolton Street, Piccadilly, who never admitted regular prostitutes, but lived on better-class ladies, mostly married, who came to her to amuse themselves with a *beau garçon*[2].

Mrs. Banks in Curzon Street, Mayfair, also provided ' vigorous men '; at the same time, though, she arranged for the presence of large numbers of the *belles voluptueuses* of the town, so that the men in this case also became her clients.

A speciality of the eighteenth century was the harems which some well-known rich men established for themselves. Archenholtz cites two examples of these harems.

' An Englishman who had recently returned from India rented a large house in London, not far from Soho Square, where he established a regular harem. He had a legal wife, but six odalisks besides, who all slept near her in separate beds. These beds stood in a circle, in order to facilitate the nightly round(!) which he made with his wife's consent. The most extraordinary thing was that in this little society the greatest harmony reigned. They ate their meals at the same table, and only in one particular was it unlike an Oriental harem, the women were allowed to go out alone

[1] *Sérails*, pp. 229-242.
[2] *Ibid.*, p. 223.

when circumstances required; otherwise they were always in the company of the wife, who thereby acted as duenna[1].'

In the eighth year of the eighteenth century Lord Baltimore's *sérail* became well known on account of a famous lawsuit which one of the inmates brought against her master. Lord Baltimore was a very rich and benevolent man. ' He had adopted the principle of living according to his whim, and he accordingly renounced all high offices and honours in his country, and never went to Court. His worst fault was his predilection for the fair sex, which was increased by his journeys to the East. After his return to England he had a very beautiful house built in the extreme West of London, towards the open fields, in a charming situation, on the model of a famous harem in Constantinople. Here he established a *sérail* and peopled it with beautiful girls, all of whose wishes were gratified, except that they were not allowed to go out. They had their prescribed rules which had to be punctually observed, and old women were their warders. Thus Baltimore lived the life of a Turkish Pacha. When he tired of one of his odalisks, he either gave her a handsome present or provided richly for her.'

Amongst the ' famous ' brothel keepers of the nineteenth century, two especially stand out (if we here omit the true ' flagellation ' brothels), Mary Wilson and Marie Aubrey.

Mary Wilson, the ' second Aloysia ', the ' reviver of erotic literature ', was at the height of her powers from 1815 to 1830. She was the Gourdan of the nineteenth century, one of the ' queens ' of prostitution, as Octave Uzanne calls this woman who, in the practice and improvement of her profession, made use of every modern device and refinement[2].

Mary Wilson kept brothels successively in different parts of London—in Old Bond Street, Tonbridge Place, New

[1] Archenholtz, *Annalen*, Vol. I, p. 389.
[2] O. Uzanne, *Correspondance de Madame Gourdan*. Brussels, 1883. P. 13.

Road, St. Pancras, and finally lived in Hall Place, St. John's Wood. She was indefatigable in her efforts to furnish this last Temple of Venus with every comfort and refinement, and achieved a considerable reputation in certain circles on account of her collection of flagellation instruments. This was further increased in that she was always endeavouring to augment her ' armaments of love ' and also gave much attention and zeal, which might have been better employed, to the increase and spread of erotic literature in England.

The second part of the first volume of the *Voluptarian Cabinet* (London, 1824), published by Mary Wilson with the significant motto ' Dum fatuimus vivimus,' contains on pages 61-76 a very interesting project for an entirely new ladies' brothel[1], a so-called ' Eleusinian Institute '. ' Any lady of rank and means may subscribe to this Institute, to which she shall always have the entry incognito; the married to commit what the world calls adultery, the unmarried to obey the commands of all-powerful nature, and to offer a sacrifice to the oldest of the gods, Priapus. I have bought a very convenient piece of land, lying between two main streets, from both of which it can be reached through shops in which only women's goods are sold. In this space, between two rows of houses, I have erected a very elegant temple, in the centre of which are large salons, surrounded by charming and comfortable boudoirs. In these salons, arranged according to their class, can be seen the most attractive men of all types that I can obtain, expert in all forms of pleasure to suit all tastes, and all in a state of great exaltation produced by good living and inertia. The ladies never enter the salons, but are shown

---

[1] These designs and reform projects for brothels are very numerous in the history of erotic literature. I need only mention the Marquis de Sade's plan for a brothel, which has been preserved, and Rétif de la Bretonne's *Pornography*.

the occupants through darkened windows in the boudoirs. In one room can be seen beautiful, elegantly dressed young men playing cards or music, in others, athletically built males, completely naked, wrestling or bathing. In short, there are so many kinds of these animals (*sic*) for them to look at that they cannot tell which to choose. As soon as their minds are made up, they ring for the chambermaid, call her to the window and show her the object of their desire, and he is forthwith brought to the boudoir.'

Of the erotic books which Mary Wilson published and had translated I might mention a translation of the *Puttana errante* of Aretino (' The Accomplished Whore ', London, 1827); the *Education de Laura* by Mirabeau (' The Curtain Drawn Up, or the Education of Laura,' as Vol. III of the *Voluptarian Cabinet*, London, 1824); also *The Spirit of Flagellation*, London, 1827. One erotic book, *The Mysteries of Venus*, which bears the name of Mary Wilson, was not written by her, but first appeared in Naples at a much later date, 1882.

Wilson found a worthy successor in Marie Aubrey, a Frenchwoman, who with her bully, John Williams, kept an infamous and celebrated brothel in Seymour Place, Bryanston Square, in the years 1825-37. This establishment was very largely frequented both by foreigners and natives, and according to Ryan was as fashionable a resort as ' the dwellings of the richest and noblest families '. The house consisted of twelve or fourteen rooms (apart from the staff quarters), every room being most elegantly appointed. The salon especially, a very large room, was a most imposing sight, with its many valuable and beautiful pictures and costly furniture. Marie Aubrey allowed her guests the use of her beautiful solid silver table-ware. When the brothel was closed about twelve to fourteen young girls were found there, mostly French and Italian.

[136]

Besides Williams, who lived in the house and was supposed to carry on business as a coal merchant, there was a doctor living in the neighbourhood who acted as agent, and who used to visit the brothel frequently. He was often sent to the London suburbs and to France and Italy to procure girls, and frequently also visited the shops in Oxford Street and the vicinity, procuring girls who were seduced immediately upon their arrival in the brothel.

Ryan estimates the number of brothels in London in the year 1840 as 1,500! And this must have been only half the real number, as many of these houses concealed their true character under other designations, such as ' Institution for the Care of Children ', in the rooms of which, every night, an incredible number of young women prostituted themselves[1]. Talbot counted at that time 5,000 brothels, whilst the number of schools, churches and charitable institutions was only 2,150[2], outstanding evidence of the colossal and widespread influence of the sexual factor in the social life of mankind. This is demonstrated further by the fact (as the same author tells us) that the brothels were preferably erected in the neighbourhood of the churches, and did good business there, ' so that often the preacher from the chancel could see the happenings in a neighbouring brothel[3],' a picture which would have rejoiced the soul of a Marquis de Sade. ' One of the most notorious and infamous houses in London', says Ryan, ' is opposite to a very much-frequented place of divine worship, and can be seen from its windows[4].'

It is not necessary to call attention to the fact that the dock district possessed a particularly large number of brothels[5].

[1] Ryan, *loc. cit.*, pp. 150-152, 154.
[2] *Ibid.*, pp. 132-133.
[3] *Ibid.*, p. 188.
[4] *Ibid.*, p. 189.
[5] *Ibid.*, p. 189.

In Leicester Square and the vicinity, which for this reason were very favourite resorts of the French, were many semi-fashionable brothels.

I now come to the places of assignation of London prostitution[1], which are as numerous as they are various. In the first rank are the inns, restaurants and lodging-houses of all kinds, but first and foremost the taverns, that is the beer and wine houses of high and low standing.

Rétif de la Bretonne, in his *Pornography*, says that London could quite well dispense with her brothels, as there are the taverns where ' both sexes meet without supervision, and those who have a lively inclination to pleasure can command agreeable satisfaction in a manner which cannot be found so easily anywhere else[2] '. The taverns are scattered all over the town. In the seventeenth and eighteenth centuries the neighbourhood particularly of Drury Lane and Fleet Street were full of these inns.

Since the Restoration the London taverns have been a favourite resort of light women and prostitutes. Casanova writes: ' I went for distraction to the Star Tavern. Lord Pembroke had told me that I should find the most beautiful women and the most agreeable virtue in the capital there[3].' George Alexander Stevens, who had an accurate knowledge of amorous London, describes a certain type of tavern prostitute, the so-called ' Tavern plyers '. When a company of young men had feasted well in a tavern, the waiter came in to ' inform your honours that four or five beautiful women

[1] Places of assignation may be anywhere, and a complete enumeration of them is therefore impossible. I am here concerned with dealing, as in my *Studies*, only with the important ones, and those characteristic of the time, people and town.

[2] Rétif de la Bretonne, *Le Pornographe*. Edit. H. Mireur.   Brussels, 1879.   P. 173.

[3] J. Casanova's *Memoirs*. Edit. Alvensleben u. Schmidt.   Vol. XV, p. 109.

had come to the door to enquire for your honours, and had
left a message that they would call again. Upon which the
bar was instructed to let the young men know when such
and such ladies came again, and to bring them in. Now
these women have a definite standing in the tavern, and all
wait in a small room in which they are cooped like sheep at
Smithfield, waiting to be let out. This is the nightly occupation of these unfortunate women, and if they are counted
amongst the best, what must be the life of the worst![1]'

The 'Weatherby' tavern was famous in the eighteenth
century (1750), the resort of all ' good-for-nothings, men of
the world, thieves and scoundrels'; a rendezvous for a
' great number of daughters of Venus of all classes, from the
kept mistress to the common prostitute '.

Other well-known taverns in the eighteenth century were
the ' Shakespeare ' tavern[2], the ' School of Venus ', as
Bob Derry's tavern was called, and the ' Golden Lion ' in
the Strand, known as the ' Cat '[3].

In the nineteenth century prostitutes were accustomed to
assemble in the ' long rooms ' and ' saloons ' of the taverns.
Ryan says in this connection: ' There were also many glittering saloons in different parts of the town, in each of which
often as many as 200 prostitutes assembled at the same time.
Rich and fashionable young men visited these places and
chose their "friend" from amongst the girls gathered there.
The taverns also possessed "saloons" and they brought much
profit to their proprietors. They were not altogether confined
to the West End of London, nor to that side of Temple
Bar, but were known in other parts of the town as " long
rooms", especially in the neighbourhood of the river, where

[1] G. A. Stevens, *The Adventures of a Speculist; or a journey through
London*. London, 1788. Vol. II, p. 213.
[2] *Sérails*, p. 81.
[3] P. Fraxi, *Catena*, p. 121.

many sailors are to be found. One of these long rooms was capable of holding 500 people. The prostitutes were stationed in rows in them, like the cattle at Smithfield Market[1], till the sailors and other guests had chosen their " women ". The couples then went to another large room in the tavern, and after revellings, drinking and dancing, the poor Jack Tars were taken to the brothels where they were stupefied with strong drink, robbed and turned into the street with or without their clothes, or murdered by bullies and secretly put out of the way. The proprietors of these taverns did a good business in the sale of refreshments and other " goods" and enticed prostitutes by promising them food and drink or money[2].'

Besides the taverns there were the ' gin palaces ', those ' breeding grounds of vice and evil[3] ' which Talbot puts on the same level as the brothels, and of which he counted in 1838, in London, no less than 5,000[4] ; further, the ' night-houses ', an offshoot of the taverns[5]. The oyster houses, where in the eighteenth century female ' pals ' robbed young men[6], and the ' dining rooms ', especially numerous in the neighbourhood of Drury Lane and Covent Garden Theatre, served as rendezvous, and to this end displayed a transparent white placard in their windows, on which was written in large green letters the word ' Beds '[7]. In addition the restaurants in the vicinity of Leicester Square served this immoral purpose. In the course of disclosures made by

[1] See above the same comparison by G. A. Stevens.
[2] Ryan, loc. cit., p. 189. Archenholtz also notes the spaciousness of the taverns. England, Vol. III, p. 146.
[3] Doings in London, p. 155.
[4] Ryan, loc. cit., p. 188.
[5] The Midnight Spy, pp. 98-110. He tells of one near Whitehall, and one in Newgate Street, where men of the world used to carry on philosophical discussions.
[6] Doings in London, p. 77.
[7] Rosenberg, loc. cit., p. 121.

Artist unknown

[*Pl.* 11

the *Pall Mall Gazette*, a scene in a similar restaurant was described[1].

Further assignation places of prostitution were the lodging-houses, which let private rooms such as those described by Cleland in *Memoirs of a Woman of Pleasure*[2]. Malcolm[3] and Ryan also state that in the lower houses of this description fifty beds were often in use in which males and females from ten to forty years were found sleeping together. In St. Giles and Whitechapel, especially, the worst type of prostitution was practised in these lodging-houses[4].

The term ' Boarding House ', too, often concealed a clandestine brothel, and strangers observed with astonishment young ladies in these ' Girls' Schools ' standing at the windows attracting passers-by with unambiguous gestures[5].

Tobacconists, provision merchants and bakers' shops, principally in the vicinity of the theatres and public places of amusement, also accommodated prostitutes during the day and evening, charging the most exorbitant prices[6].

London, like most other large European towns, possessed up-to-date assignation places for prostitution in the so-called Massage Institutes, which did not provide for ordinary prostitution only, but first and foremost offered opportunities for the gratification of the various perversities of sexual activity. The abuse of masseuses in the large towns comes under the head of sexual chicanery (see my exposition in Chapter IV); certain popular tendencies in this therapy have been carried to the point of actual

---

[1] *Der Jungfrauentribut des modernen Babylon* (' The virgins' tribute to the modern Babylon '). Budapest, 1885. P. 36.
[2] J. Cleland, *Memoirs of Fanny Hill*. Paris, 1888. P. 67.
[3] Malcolm, *loc. cit.*, Vol. I, p. 333.
[4] Ryan, *loc. cit.*, p. 201.
[5] H. France, *Les Nuits de Londres*, p. 60.
[6] Ryan, *loc. cit.*, p. 189.

immorality, and vice is practised under the cloak of
' Hypnotism ' (also ' Spiritualism '), ' Magneto-therapy '
and ' Magnetism ', ' Sexual friction baths ', ' Massage ',
' Mechano and Electro-therapy '. In England, and especially in London, illicit activities were pursued under the
pseudonym ' governesses ', ' manicure ', and the like. In
the columns of the journal *Society*, which ceased publication
in July 1900, were to be found many suspicious advertisements of the following type:

Manicure and Treatment for Rheumatism.
Miss Desmond,
39, George Street, Baker Street, W. (side door).
Hours 2-8.   Late of 11a, Air Street, Regent Street, W.

Rheumatism and Neuralgia, Nerve and Insomnia
Treatment.
School of Modern Discipline.
By
Augusta Montgomery, 27, Edgware Road, Oxford
Street, W.
Hours 11 till 9.

The conduct of these London massage establishments
was shown up some years ago by the so-called ' Massage
Scandal '. A certain George Frederick Robertson, a
musician, had been sent to a Massage Institute by the
' National Vigilance Society ' (for the suppression of
prostitution), but there committed the grossest immorality,
extorting money from the girls, and was later sentenced
to four years' imprisonment. The descriptions he gives
in his letters to the Society, of the various massage establishments, appear to be founded on fact. About one of
these institutes he writes: ' Madame M. is very inventive,
and anyone who is willing to pay a pound or more can get
there any sort of beastliness and immorality. The girls

[142]

practise all known sexual perversities and Madame M. is a harlot of no small ability.' In a second letter the following appears: ' Your letter confirmed my fears as regards the practices carried on in establishments for the treatment of rheumatism and for manicure, etc. I strongly suspect that shameless women are engaged in these practices.' The letter closed with a description of a massage institute in which he saw twelve naked girls prostituting their charms for all imaginable purposes[1].

Shortly after this a case came before the courts with regard to a massage establishment kept by a negro, James Davis, at 120 Marylebone Road. Davis was summoned for bodily injury to a girl and also on the ground of article 1 of the new law with regard to bullies. The trial is interesting in so far as it shows that institutes of this sort in London mainly served the English mania for flagellation. Hansen says, with regard to the case: 'Mr. Freke Palmer (the prosecutor) remarked during the hearing that it would perhaps be a good thing if the court were informed of the details of the case. The plaintiff had known the defendant for several years. She had lived formerly near Portland Road, but for two years now with the defendant at 120 Marylebone Road, and during the whole of that time he had lived on the money she earned as a dressmaker. In Marylebone Road the defendant kept a so-called massage establishment called the Balneopathic establishment for the treatment of rheumatism, gout and neuralgia by dry hot-air baths, massage and discipline, etc. The plaintiff could tell the judge that the women engaged in the institute as attendants had been domestic servants of the defendant against whom he had behaved immorally, and had thereafter taken them on as attendants, providing them with

[1] *Raped in the Railway.* London, 1894 (1900). Pp. 178-184.

the usual uniform. On the arrest of the defendant, amongst other letters, was found one which read as follows: "Dear Mr. Davis. I cannot come to you to-day as I have made another appointment. I am sorry I was not at home when you called upon me. I should like to see you and will come to-morrow at this time. Have ' Kantschus ' ready, one for me and one each for the two Spanish women. One shilling for each stroke." The plaintiff said that she was often unmercifully whipped by the defendant. Men had also come to be massaged and were always alone with the attendants, and she herself had had to put up with various demands which were made of her. Further evidence showed that the defendant had made a considerable income from the foregoing, and that he had allowed gentlemen, on payment of a large entrance fee, to be present at the chastisement of his massage attendants.'

Resorts of gallantry and ' Bon Ton', particularly character-istic of the eighteenth century, were the coffee-houses. These, however, at the height of their popularity, i.e., at the end of the seventeenth and the beginning of the eighteenth centuries, existed essentially for the entertainment of men, and may be regarded more as the forerunner of the later clubs. A short reference may, however, be made here to the most famous of the English coffee-houses, in view especially of conditions in later years[1].

An Englishman, a merchant in the Levant named Edwards, brought coffee to London in the year 1652 and opened the first coffee-house[2]. The new custom spread rapidly; the coffee-houses were the meeting-places of the upper and

---

[1] For anyone who is interested in the extremely engrossing history of the English coffee-houses from an intellectual point of view, an excellent book by Edward Forbes Robertson, *The Early History of Coffee Houses in England* (London, 1893), with a good bibliography, is recommended.

[2] Lecky, *History of European Morals*, p. 167.

middle classes, and all news was first disseminated there. ' Strangers remarked ', says Macaulay, ' that the coffee-houses are an institution which distinguishes London from all other towns ; that the coffee-house is the home of the Londoner, and that anyone looking for a gentleman usually does not ask whether he lives in Fleet Street or Chancery Lane, but whether he frequents the Grecian coffee-house or the Rainbow.' Every gentleman had at that time his special coffee-house where he was to be found at certain times and where he could get his letters. There were Tory and Whig coffee-houses and those for the different faiths[1]. Strangers were not admitted[2]. The most famous coffee-houses at the beginning of the eighteenth century were those of White, Will, the Grecian and the St. James's coffee-house. In the first issue of the *Tatler*, 12th April 1709, they were sketched as follows:

' Everything pertaining to gallantry, entertainment and conversation can be found at White's chocolate house; poetry in Will's coffee-house; learning in the Grecian coffee-house[3]; English and foreign novelties in St. James' coffee-house '.

---

[1] ' There were Puritan coffee-houses where no oath was heard, and where straight-haired men in their nasal voices discussed predestination and damnation; Jews' coffee-houses, where black-eyed money-changers from Venice and Amsterdam met; papist coffee-houses where, according to the notions of good Protestants, Jesuits made plans for another great fire and cast silver bullets to shoot the king with.'—Macaulay, *History of England*, Vol. II, p. 100.

[2] Paul Hensel, *Englische soziale Zustände zu Anfang des 18 Jahrhunderts* (' English social conditions at the beginning of the eighteenth century '), in *Neue Heidelberg Jahrb.*, 1899, Vol. IX, p. 6. The author rightly regards the exclusion of strangers as a sign that the coffee-house was taking on the character of the club.

[3] ' Grecian Coffee House ' in Devereux Court, Strand. ' I visited the Royal Society, at which the President, Sir Isaac Newton, the two secretaries, the two Oxford Professors, Drs. Halley and Keil, as well as others were present, whose company we afterwards enjoyed at the Grecian Coffee House.' Thoresby's *Tagebuch*, Vol. II, p. 117, of the 12th June 1712 (after Wheatley, *loc. cit.*, Vol. II, p. 148).

White's Chocolate and Coffee-House (called 'White's' for short) was opened in 1698 in St. James's Street, No. 37-38, and was very soon famous as the resort of the gallant *Jeunesse dorée* of London, and also as a playhouse.

At the beginning of the eighteenth century, in particular, all love affairs were arranged at White's. Pending the publication of the *Tatler*, Richard Steele thought to obtain all news of love intrigues from White's. Jenyns says about White's in the *Modern Time Gentleman* (1746):

> From hence to White's our virtuous Cato flies,
> There sits with countenance erect and wise,
> And talks of games of whist and pig-tail pies[1].

Perhaps the most famous of the coffee-houses was Will's at 1 Bow Street, Covent Garden (called after the proprietor, William Urwin), which was the meeting-place of poets, wits and fashionable men of the world at the time of the Restoration, and became particularly celebrated through the poet John Dryden. 'Nowhere do they smoke with more perseverance than in Will's coffee-house; this well-known house, lying between Covent Garden and Bow Street, was dedicated to high intellectuality. The talk there was of freedom, of poets and of the unities of time and place; there was one faction for Perrault and the moderns and another for Boileau and the ancients.

'Under no other roof could greater variety in the appearance of the visitors be seen. Earls with stars and orders, clergy in priests' robes and bands, malicious lawyers, bashful young people from the universities, translators and compilers of indexes in torn frieze coats. Everyone crowded round the

---

[1] H. B. Wheatley, *loc. cit.*, Vol. III, pp. 491-496. Rush recounts a characteristic anecdote about White's (*Residence at the Court of London*) under the 2nd March 1818: 'Let me relate what I heard of one of the Clubs—White's—the great Tory Club in St. James. Somebody spoke of the lights kept burning there all night: "Yes," said a member, "they have not been put out I should think since the reign of Charles II." '

chair where John Dryden sat, in the winter in the warmest corner near the fire, in the summer on the balcony. It was counted a privilege to stand and listen to him and to hear his opinion on Racine's latest tragedy or Bossu's discussion on epic poetry; a pinch from his snuff-box was an honour which would turn a young enthusiast's head[1].

John Wilkes liked to go with his immoral companions to Wildman's coffee-house in Bedford Street, Strand[2], and a rendezvous used by the *demi-monde* in 1702 was the ' Cloisters ' coffee-house[3]. To-day the coffee-houses seem to have a more universal character compared with their earlier individuality[4]. Casanova mentioned the ' Orange ' coffee-house as the most ' infamous place in the capital '[5]. In later times the type of the modern ' café ' came into fashion near the old coffee-houses, in which were to be found many prostitutes, *demi-mondaines* and similar dubious elements. In 1870 the ' Turkish Divan ' was particularly

---

[1] Macaulay, *loc. cit.*, pp. 99-100. In a poem called ' A day's ramble in Covent Garden, 1691 ' (in *Poems in Burlesque*, 1693), the *galanteries* at Will's are described as follows:

> To Will's I went, where Beau and Wit
> In mutual contemplation sit;
> But which were Wits and which were Beaus,
> The Devil sure's in him who knows.
> For either may be which you please,
> These look like those who talk like these;
> To make amends, there I saw Dryden.

Similarly E. Smith (in ' On John Phillip's Death '):

> Rail on, ye triflers, who to Will's repair,
> For new lampoons, fresh cant or modish air.

See Wheatley, *loc. cit.*, Vol. III, pp. 519-521.

[2] Wheatley, *loc cit.*, Vol. III, p. 515.
[3] Malcolm, *loc. cit.*, Vol. II, p. 121.
[4] ' Thus you see that the coffee-houses in this metropolis comprehend a great variety of characters, are frequented by all kinds of people, and also that they afford a stranger a very good notion of the inhabitants in general ' (*The Midnight Spy*, p. 26).
[5] Casanova, *loc. cit.*, Vol. XV, pp. 92-93.

well known, also the ' Café de la Régence. ', both of them in the Haymarket[1].

In all large towns the big gardens and places of amusement are a focus of prostitution, affording an opportunity for the assembly of crowds of people.

In London and the rest of England the most widespread types of these pleasure resorts were the tea-gardens. As early as the eighteenth century there were an ' astonishing number ' of these in and around London, and the small towns also had them. The most celebrated London tea-garden was ' Bagnigge Wells ', where over a thousand people drank tea at the same time on Sundays[2]. Others were Shakespeare's tea-garden, where were numerous summer-houses containing paintings of scenes from the poet's works[3], and ' White Conduit House ' in Pentonville, a sort of small Vauxhall[4].

In the year 1700[5] there existed many of these dubious tea-gardens in St. George's Fields, on the Surrey side of the Thames, between Southwark and Lambeth. This place had been since olden days the favourite goal of Sunday strollers in London, and Puttenham, as early as 1598, says:

I crost the Thames to take the cheerful aire,
In open fields, the weather was so faire[6].

The neighbourhood, towards the end of the eighteenth century, lost its rural character and was built over. Archenholtz remarks with regard to this: ' St. George's Fields in the South of London, which a few years ago was a charming place and much frequented on account of

[1] E. G. Ravenstein, *London*, etc. Hildburgh, 1871. P. 67.
[2] ' 'Tis drinking tea, on Sunday afternoons—At Bagnigge Wells, in china, and gilt spoons' (*Doings in London*, p. 235).
[3] Archenholtz, *England*, Vol. III, pp. 216-217.
[4] Wheatley, *loc. cit.*, Vol. III, pp. 496-497.
[5] Malcolm, *loc. cit.*, Vol. II, p. 129.
[6] Wheatley, *loc. cit.*, Vol. II, p. 99.

its walks and tea-gardens, had now become the prey of speculative builders. The whole of the fields are covered with small houses with six windows, three in front and three at the back, the tenants of which pay only £12 a year rent. These miserable huts serve as dwelling places for professional beggars, thieves, prostitutes and many poor families[1].'

Pennant mentions, in this connection, that in the year 1790 fine new footpaths had been laid out in this area[2].

The most celebrated of the tea-gardens in St. George's Fields was the ' Dog and Duck ', a place which had been known and frequented since 1643, but which suffered from an increasingly bad reputation as a centre of immorality and in 1812 was closed[3].

St. George's Fields, with taste and fashion struck,
Display Arcadia at the Dog and Duck;
And Drury Misses here in tawdry pride,
Are there ' Pastoras ' by the fountain side;
To frowsy bowers they reel through midnight damps,
With Fauns half drunk, and Dryads breaking lamps.

(Garrick, *Prologue to the Maid of the Oaks*, 1774.)

V. Schütz mentions a pleasure boat at the 'Dog and Duck' which was specially adapted for music, and which sailed around on a canal in the middle of the garden. He also found in one part of the gardens a building with nine suitably adapted rooms, ' in each of which there was a row of contiguous receptacles, on which eight persons could at the same time relieve their natural needs[4]'. According to Malcolm, the company which frequented the ' Dog and Duck ' evening after evening consisted of ' some of the

---

[1] Archenholtz, *Annalen*, Vol. I, p. 417.
[2] Wheatley, *loc. cit.*, Vol. II, p. 99.
[3] *Ibid.*, p. 100.
[4] V. Schütz, *loc. cit.*, pp. 53-54.

most beautiful middle-class women of the town, their bullies and such-like young men, who could there, with no thought for the consequences, refresh the thirsty throats of their girls with fiery drinks. What, reader, do you think was the result of all this?[1] '

The second of these ' incorrigible places of lascivious amusement ' (Malcolm) in St. George's Fields was the Apollo Garden. It was founded in the year 1788 by Mr. Clagget, the proprietor of the Pantheon in Oxford Street, as an imitation of Vauxhall, but it only existed for a few seasons[2]. In the middle of the gardens was a fine large orchestra. Malcolm and the author of *Doings in London* say that prostitution increased in these gardens to such a shocking extent that finally people of good standing were hardly to be seen there at all[3].

A place which was particularly frequented by the *demi-monde* from 1700 to 1730 was Belsize House, near Hampstead, in the north of London, celebrated on account of its springs, its beautiful gardens, its playhouse, its race-course and dance halls, and last but not least, the activities of the prostitutes. In 1730 Belsize House was closed, as ' more gallantry than anything else went on there ' and there was altogether too much ' licence[4] '.

Another tea-garden was ' Jenny's Whim ', the Vauxhall of the lower classes, but also frequented by people like Horace Walpole and others. This was situated near the wooden bridge between Chelsea and Pimlico, which is now part of Victoria Station[5].

[1] Malcolm, *loc. cit.*, Vol. I, p. 332. It is worth mentioning that there were mineral springs at the ' Dog and Duck ' which had long been in use for skin disease and scrofula and also to arrest the growth of cancer. See Campbell, *Political Survey of Britain*. London, 1774. Vol. I, p. 81.

[2] Wheatley, *loc. cit.*, Vol. I, p. 55.

[3] *Doings in London*, p. 236 ; Malcolm, *loc. cit.*, Vol. I, p. 332.

[4] *The Foreigner's Guide*. London, 1730. Pp. 128, 148.

[5] Wheatley, *loc. cit.*, Vol. II, pp. 305-306.

Between Piccadilly and South Audley Street lay May Fair, a celebrated place of amusement in the eighteenth century, and the source of many bad scandals[1]; in Islington was 'Sadler's Wells', so called after a mineral spring in the possession of a certain Sadler who opened an establishment there in the year 1683. In the 'long room opposite to Sadler's Wells', G. A. Stevens in July 1765 delivered his celebrated 'Lecture on Heads'. 'Sadler's Wells' still exists on the same site in Islington between New River Head and St. John Street Road[2]. 'Sadler's Wells', together with another place, 'Islington Spa', where was much dancing, and 'White Conduit House', also in Islington, were favourite resorts of Londoners who, particularly on Sundays, went there in crowds, as the following old poem shows:

Human beings here
In couples multitudinous assembled,
Forming the drollest group that ever trod
Fair Islingtonian plains—male after male,
Dog after dog, succeeding—husbands—wives—
Fathers and mothers—brothers—sisters—friends—
Around, across, along the shrubby maze
They walk, they sit, they stand[3].

Very remarkable, on account of the women who frequented it, was the 'Temple of Flora' in the 'Garden of Venus', which Archenholtz mentions. It was almost entirely the resort of fashionable prostitutes who had invented a new way of making their charms known. They 'paraded sitting in high phaetons through the streets, in wonderful Amazon costume, and accompanied by other girls, similarly dressed, riding alongside the phaetons[4]'. Men were allowed in the

[1] Wheatley, *loc. cit.*, pp. 515-517.
[2] Wheatley, *loc. cit.*, Vol. III, pp. 199-201.
[3] *Doings in London*, pp. 236-237.
[4] Archenholtz, *Annalen*, Vol. V, p. 282.

[151]

gardens only on payment of an entrance fee. It seems likely that these riding-crop swinging Amazons belonged to the ranks of the active flagellants.

Amongst the larger pleasure gardens of the eighteenth century were Marylebone (or, for short, Marybone) Gardens in the neighbourhood of the present Beaumont and Devonshire Streets. It was laid out in the second half of the seventeenth century. Pepys remarks in his *Diary*, under date 7th May 1668: ' Then we went out to Marrowbone and walked in the Garden. I was there for the first time, it is a beautiful place.' In the middle of the garden was a level green for bowling, a great attraction which the philosopher John Locke enjoyed. The garden was enlarged in 1730, and a spacious orchestra erected where, in the evenings, concerts and plays took place. In the middle of the eighteenth century John Trusler, the father of Dr. Trusler, was for many years proprietor of the gardens. He was a cook, and his dinners and breakfasts soon brought him a great reputation. Magnificent fireworks were often displayed here, creations of the famous pyrotechnician, Torré[1], who worked here for many years. Marybone Gardens were much frequented by the gallant world, and were often mentioned in *Sérails de Londres*. From 1746 on the proprietors were obliged to engage a guard of soldiers in order that visitors could get safely back to London. In the year 1778 the garden was closed[2], and at the beginning of the nineteenth century fine streets and squares had already been built on the site[3].

All these and many other pleasure resorts of the eighteenth century served the purposes of both secret and open prostitution. So-called ' Charity Concerts ' were often held

[1] See also Vol. I of these *Studies* for Torré, p. 167.
[2] Wheatley, *loc. cit.*, Vol. VI, pp. 511-513.
[3] *Doings in London*, p. 235.

in them, which many young men attended in all innocence, only to find themselves surrounded suddenly, as Malcolm tells us, by crowds of notorious procuresses and daughters of Cyprus. In 1757 the following Bill, presented by Sir John Fielding, was passed by Parliament: 'Any house, room, garden or other place which in London and Westminster or within 20 miles of the environs, not being licensed as a public dancing place, allows music or other entertainment of the same kind, shall be regarded as a disorderly house or place, and any authorised servant of the law may enter and arrest all persons found therein. Every person who owns such an unlicensed house, shall pay £100 sterling, and in addition suffer the punishment that the law has ordained in the case of bawdy houses[1].'

We saw that many of the ' tea-gardens ' and places of amusement fell victims to this law, especially towards the end of the eighteenth century. Those that remained disappeared with the outward spread of the town.

Of this charming series of pleasure gardens which beautified the whole of the nearer environs of London, and which in the eighteenth century gave the town such a distinctive character as compared with other European capitals[2], two not merely achieved world fame but were actually in existence up to the nineteenth century. These were the celebrated Gardens of Vauxhall and of Ranelagh, described by countless visitors to London, and astonishing and delighting all. These places are very interesting historically,

[1] Malcolm, *loc. cit.*, Vol. I, pp. 331-332.
[2] ' There was nothing that more distinguished the environs of the metropolis a few years since (before the building rage commenced), than the number of gardens open for public entertainment. I do not mean simple tea-gardens, but places of the plan of Vauxhall Gardens, where concerts of vocal and instrumental music were to be heard, and where the eye was regaled with displays of fireworks, illuminated walks and other embellishments ' (*Doings in London*, p. 234).

and also deserve special consideration as regards the subject of this book.

Just as there is only one London, so there was only one Vauxhall, says O. von Rosenberg[1]. Vauxhall lay on the south or Surrey side of the Thames, in the Borough of Lambeth. The derivation of the name has been attributed to various sources—some believed that the site belonged formerly to the celebrated Papist conspirator, Guy Fawkes, and that Vaux Hall is a corruption of ' Fawkes Hall '; others have proved convincingly that the ground was the property in the year 1615 of a widow called Jane Vaux[2]. The latter is a more reasonable explanation of the unusual name ' Vauxhall ' which, as is well known, was adopted later on in other towns to designate the same kind of place[3].

This celebrated, or one may safely say the world's most celebrated, pleasure garden was laid out in the year 1661, and known both as the ' New Spring Gardens ' and ' Vauxhall '. It soon developed into one of the principal haunts of London prostitution. As early as 30th May 1668 Pepys, in his *Diary* of that date, clearly indicates the nature of the company at Vauxhall: ' But oh lord! what a loose company it was there to-night, one need only to go there once to perceive the kind of doings there are.' Two days after he went there again, and writes about it on 1st June 1668: ' Alone to Fox Hall, went walking there and saw young Newport and two other good-for-nothings from the town and saw them overtake two girls, who walked round with them for an hour, their masks before their faces.' On 27th July 1668: ' Over the water with my wife and Deb and Mercer to Spring Garden, and eat there and walked;

[1] O. v. Rosenberg, *loc. cit.*, p. 148.
[2] *Doings in London*, p. 234.
[3] See Vol. I of these *Studies*, p. 167, for the Parisian pleasure resort of the eighteenth century called by the same name.

and observed how coarse some young gallants from the town were. They go into the arbours where there is no man and ravish the women there, and the audacity of vice in our time much enraged me. And so we to the water and with much pleasure home again.' In Congreve's comedy *Love for Love* (1695), Mrs. Frail says very revealingly: ' That's a thing to do, to drive to Covent Garden Square in a hired coach and walk there with a friend! If I were to go to Knightsbridge or Chelsea or to Spring Garden or Barn Elms and walk alone there with a man, people would certainly make something of it.' Wycherley also speaks of the bad reputation of Vauxhall, and Vanbrugh lays a very lively scene there. Etherege speaks in *She Would If She Could* and other dramas with sufficient clarity of ' Foxhall '. The *Spectator* describes in No. 383 how a masked prostitute accosted the walkers in Vauxhall and tried to attract their attention.

From 1712 to 1732 Vauxhall was little frequented. On 7th June 1732 it was again opened by Jonathan Tyers with a *ridotto al fresco* at which the Prince of Wales was present. The garden was strikingly embellished and lighted with thousands of lamps. Hogarth painted several pictures of Vauxhall, and Roubiliac created his celebrated statue of Handel, the most interesting thing to see there. Up to 1792 the entrance fee was 1 shilling, from then on 2 shillings and finally as high as 4 shillings. From 1850 on it was again 1 shilling. The last night of Vauxhall was 25th July 1859. The advertisement announced: ' Farewell to Vauxhall! The last night for ever! The last dance! The last supper! The last punch! and no extra charge![1]'

The arbours and dark bushes in Vauxhall particularly served the purpose of prostitution and were always mentioned

[1] Wheatley, *loc. cit.*, Vol. III, pp. 426-430.

as a great attraction. Tom Brown says: ' The ladies, who are only too glad to be alone, are delighted with the secluded paths in Spring Garden, where both sexes meet, and each acting as guide, manage in time to lose the way. The winding and side paths in these wildernesses are so confusing that the most experienced mother has often lost her way herself when looking for her daughters[1].' The *French Observer* (1769) says: ' A great many small isolated bushes have been put there, which are convenient for lovers. These perhaps attract the English women most.' In the year 1759 many complaints were made about the behaviour of the prostitutes and their male companions, who made an uproar in the dark bushes like 'Cavalcanti's bloodhounds', and men were accused of taking women by force to these lonely spots and there raping them[2]. Casanova, that resourceful gallant, when at Vauxhall, offered a girl 20 guineas if she would 'give me a quarter-of-an-hour's conversation in an arbour', and another time proposed to her ' a walk amongst the bushes[3]'. Canning, in *Loves of the Triangles* (1768), describes a scene in these secluded arbours of Vauxhall:

There oft returning from the green retreats
Where fair Vauxhallia decks her sylvan seats;
Where each spruce nymph from city counters free,
Sips the frothed syllabub or fragrant tea;
While with sliced ham, scraped beef and burnt champagne,
Her prentice lover soothes his amorous pain.[4]

Von Rosenberg describes Vauxhall in the nineteenth century, towards the end of its supremacy: at that time the gardens were only open three times a week, on Monday,

---

[1] Tom Brown, *Amusements*. London, 1700. P. 54.
[2] Malcolm, *loc. cit.*, Vol. II, p. 178.
[3] Casanova, *loc. cit.*, Vol. XV, pp. 156, 165.
[4] Wheatley, *loc. cit.*, Vol. III, p. 429.

Wednesday and Friday evenings, from the middle of May till the middle of August. People generally came from Westminster Bridge or Whitehall Stairs upstream to the gardens. 'Before one can get into the garden one has to buy a ticket at a ticket office which can hardly be seen for the darkness, which ticket is changed twice and more whilst one gropes about in half-dark, narrow boarded ways leading to the gardens. These long winding entries are evidently badly lighted and painted in such dark colours on purpose to astonish strangers to the greatest possible extent by the contrast when they enter the gardens through them. The darkness having already caused the curious to utter a half-dozen God-dams or other edifying expressions in his mother-tongue, he at last enters, as if by magic, the garden wherein all the senses are stunned. When I came to this place for the first time I could not persuade myself that I was not in a dream, but on earth. . . . Thousands of people, for the most part expensively dressed, are strolling in Vauxhall in a fiery sea of radiance from the brilliantly tinted gas lamps, the lights of which almost overshine the sun. Everywhere is music heard; here in a magic temple, the light of the countless lamps shining in through its pillars and arches, the most famous Italian voices sing their triumph; there musicians dressed as Turkish soldiers perform a noisy symphony in another similar temple, led by two genuine Moors skilfully beating their tambourines. In a Rotunda with three exits to the gardens, lighted by a huge bronze chandelier (20 ells square), Miss Peton, Madame Vestris, Herr Braham, delight the wandering crowd with their songs. And hardly is the last sound uttered, than all turn towards a near-by corner of the garden to see a pantomime or a national or tight-rope dance in a specially constructed theatre. So soon as the dancers have finished, everyone turns to the great curtain behind which the French rider

[157]

Du Croix, who performs daily in the circus of the Astley Theatre, stands ready with his wonderful horses to enact for them on an enormous terrace, the Battle of Waterloo, in which rider and horses show almost incredible skill. Fireworks usually mark the end of the evening's enjoyment, which lasts about 4 hours, so that by this time it is almost midnight. The vocal and instrumental music in the afore-mentioned temples continues uninterruptedly, and latterly till towards morning. After the end of the show pieces everyone, even the light-shy night birds from abroad with their admirers, strolls for a time about the lighted winding paths. Here and there families are sitting at supper in separate decorated wooden arbours which, for I don't know what purpose, seem to be intentionally in half darkness, and of which there are 30 to 40 in a row, completely hidden from each other by dividing walls. These arbours appear to me to be primarily intended for amorous adventures, rendezvous, etc., yet one sees respectable people in them. Silver plate is used in them, and one is waited on by men in scarlet livery, each with the number of the arbour he has to serve on his arm. The charge is one pound sterling per head, or rather per stomach. Besides these refreshment arbours, there are large, most brilliantly lighted rooms with galleries opening on to the gardens, raised 4 to 5 feet above the ground and built in Italian style. Here the tables are decked with silver, and flowers which scent the air and delight the eye, and beautifully prepared dishes are served. The respectable elements in the company seldom stay after 2 o'clock in the morning at the latest, and the evening must be very fine to keep them till then. The low females with their equally low admirers who have drunk, some to the limit of their thirst, some to the limit of their purses, sleep in the gardens or the guard-room quietly till the morning, and should they be asked how things went last night, they would say:

" after all they felt themselves pretty comfortable." It would not be surprising to hear that they had experienced again in their dreams the wonders of Vauxhall; it would be as difficult to give anyone the smallest conception of what they are like, as to try to make a blind man grasp the idea of colour[1].'

During the last years of its existence Vauxhall seems to have revived its power of attraction by holding great masked balls there, as we are told by the authoress of *Memoirs of a Singer*, who stayed in London at the end of the year 1850.

Casanova carried out his ' erotic projects ', as he called them, during his stay in London not only at Vauxhall but often at Ranelagh with its popular Rotunda[2].

Ranelagh was laid out in Chelsea in the year 1742 to the design of the architect William Jones, on land which formerly belonged to Lord Ranelagh. The great Rotunda of Ranelagh measured 150 feet across, had an orchestra in the middle and boxes for spectators round the sides. The principal amusement was the so-called ' promenading round and round ' the orchestra, whilst music was played and people took refreshments in the boxes. It was a sort of ' covered ' Vauxhall. Samuel Johnson described Ranelagh as the most beautiful spot he had ever seen. It lasted for 60 years and was first closed in 1803 and pulled down in 1805[3].

Walpole writes to Mann on the 26th May 1742 about the opening of Ranelagh: ' Two evenings ago Ranelagh Gardens in Chelsea were opened; the Prince, the Princess, the Duke, many of the nobility and a crowd of common people were there. There is a colossal amphitheatre, charmingly gilded,

[1] O. v. Rosenberg, *loc. cit.*, pp. 140-148.
[2] Casanova, *loc. cit.*, Vol. XV, p. 110.
[3] Chelsea Hospital now stands on the site.

painted and lighted, where anyone who cares for eating, drinking, looking on and crowds, can enter for 12 pence. The building and the laying out of the gardens cost £15,000. There are to be two masked balls there, admission a guinea for which you get supper and music. I was there yesterday evening, but did not think much of it. Vauxhall is better, for the garden is pleasanter and one gets there by water.' Soon, however, Ranelagh was so popular and the discontented Walpole so reconciled to it, that he writes to Conway on the 29th June 1744: ' I go every evening to Ranelagh, which has quite beaten Vauxhall on the field. No one goes anywhere else. Lord Chesterfield likes it so much that he has all his letters sent there.' According to Archenholtz, Ranelagh had no equal as a pleasure resort. ' The majestic shape and amazing size of the round salon, the marvellous lighting, the astonishing crowd of well dressed people moving about, the beautiful music, taken altogether makes a great show. The floor is covered with carpet so that no footfall is heard. Round the whole circle of the side walls are alcoves with tables laid ready for any of the spectators who wish for coffee or tea; similar tables stand also in the middle of the salon near a huge fireplace ornamented with lamps[1].' Archenholtz found the prices charged for food and drink at Ranelagh very high, but according to Moriz this was not the case.

A few of London's amusement centres which were primarily resorts of the *demi-monde* in the second half of the nineteenth century are mentioned by the authoress of *Memories of a Singer*; i.e., Canterbury Hall, the Argyll Rooms, the Piccadilly Saloon, the Holborn Casino, Black Eagle, Caldwell and Cremorne Gardens[2].

[1] Archenholtz, *England*, Vol. III, p. 201.
[2] *Aus den Memoiren einer Sangerin*, Vol. II, pp. 196-198.

As regards the entertainment in the ' Portland Rooms '
she says: ' In the Portland Rooms balls were held in the
winter season only. They began after midnight and went
on till four or five in the morning. The ladies and gentlemen
came in ball costume. English Bohemianism at its most
elegant could there be seen, all the ladies in low dresses,
no longer wearing mantillas and hats, the gentlemen also
in ball costume with white waistcoats and collars. The
Cancan was danced there, in a very unrestrained form, the
women behaving in a more bacchantic fashion than in other
places, but the police did not interfere.'

Of the places mentioned here[1] the most celebrated in the
sixth and seventh years of the nineteenth century were the
' Argyll Rooms ', ' Cremorne Gardens ' and the ' National
Assembly Rooms', which have not yet been referred to.

The ' Argyll Rooms ' (now the Trocadero) in Great
Windmill Street[2] were at the height of their popularity in
1850—' the Argyll Rooms provided glittering entertainments.
Behind the golden trellis work of the orchestra lively dance
music was played until midnight, and in the charmingly
decorated halls hundreds of beautiful girls, such as can
only be seen in England, were dancing. But those days are

[1] Smaller places of amusement of the *demi-monde* and the masculine
world of London which I may mention are the Hippodrome in Notting
Hill (1837-1841) (Ryan, *loc. cit.*, p. 115); the Nova Scotia Gardens in Bethnal
Green, one of the ' Black Spots of London ', which was done away with
in 1860 (Wheatley, *loc. cit.*, Vol. II, p. 606); Dibdin's 'Sans Souci' in Leicester
Square (*ibid.*, Vol. III, p. 209); Highbury Barn in Islington; Royal
Pavilion Gardens in North Woolwich; Rosherville Gardens above
Gravesend; People's Garden near Willesden Junction (Ravenstein,
London, p. 81; Baedeker's *London* (1890), p. 45). All these gardens
and places were carefully avoided by ladies of good standing.

[2] Not to be confused with the ' Argyll Rooms ' on the east side of Regent
Street at the corner of Little Argyll Street, a well-known concert house
in which Spohr in 1820, C. M. von Weber in 1826, and Felix Mendelssohn
in 1829 gave concerts (Wheatley, *loc. cit.*, Vol. I, p. 60).

[161]

gone—the Argyll Rooms are forsaken and the "National Assembly Rooms" in Holborn have taken their place[1].'

These were, from about 1860 to 1870, a dancing centre for prostitution. The walls were brilliantly decorated, the orchestras enclosed in gilded trellis work, and Italian music was played. The most beautiful ball *toilettes* were to be seen there. They were situated at No. 218, High Holborn[2]. Julius Rodenberg describes an evening at the 'National Assembly Rooms', with all its splendour, which in reality was so illusory.

'"The National Assembly Rooms"—a twinkling gas globe like a star before the door—tells us that we are at the right spot. I am not taking the reader to the "Argyll Rooms"— they are once more deserted and their long forgotten rival (Holborn Casino was its former unpretentious name) has decked itself anew in beauty and splendour. A medley of bright lights, warmth and sweet scents stream out to meet us. The eye is dazzled by the green and gold colouring and the wall-high mirrors, in which the dream-like reflection of this bright world of dance and beauty is doubled and trebled. Sounds of Italian music come from the gilt trellis-enclosed orchestra. This is the home of Verdi, and the women, lovely and sensual, who recline in the green damask armchairs, are his Bacchantes. Everywhere is light, perfume and enjoyment, but it is all an illusion—if the light of day could but shine suddenly through the curtains, how grey, how dull, how pale and faded it would all appear—the velvet, the gold, the mirrors and the women themselves. But it is night, and the gas-light sheds its deceptive lustre over them[3].'

If a London pleasure garden at the end of the nineteenth century could be compared with the Vauxhall of the

[1] G. Rasch, *London bei Nacht*, pp. 25-26.
[2] Ravenstein, *loc. cit.*, p. 78.
[3] J. Rodenberg, *loc. cit.*, pp. 252, 254.

eighteenth century, Cremorne Gardens on the banks of the
Thames at Chelsea had at least an outward similarity.
'Cremorne Gardens! Can it be a garden from some fairy
tale to which those dark arboured ways lead? Still, silent
foliage, wide lawns, colourful flower-beds shimmering, blue
mirrors of water, dark alleys, kiosks in Moorish style, Turkish
minarets, Arabian columned ways, modern dance halls with
open galleries into which the moon shines, theatres with
scenery in which genuine waterfalls splash, and where green
wooded valleys, dark ravines and white snow-capped
mountains are piled in perspective one behind the other,
Gangways with artificial caves, rushing water, crumbling
ruins and shell grottos, views of wide distances with a
background of blue hills, wonderfully decorated rooms
so large that in them a hundred knights and squires in
glittering, shining steel armour on caparisoned horses can
do battle with swords and lances; over all, the star-bespangled
canopy of the dark blue night sky, and the whole fantastic
scenery of a magic garden lighted by a thousand sparkling
gas lamps and flares held by garlanded statues—that is
Cremorne Gardens.

'We walk slowly towards the other end of the magic garden.
There also music is heard, not battle music, nor solemn
marches, but lively dance music. The magnificent dance
halls of the Argyll Rooms and the "National Assembly
Rooms" are here to-night under the blue star-spangled
night sky, amidst the rustling of the trees and the whispering
of the wind, in the soft air of the warm summer night,
amongst shrubs and foliage and shimmering flower beds over
which the white statues cast the coloured reflection of their
torches, and quiet lakes whose dark mirror the night wind
stirs. A great glittering room is before us, as light as day,
and the eye must first get used to it, before it can distinguish
the details of the fairy-like scenery. The dance hall is

[163]

round and surrounded on all sides by open arches, through which the dancers can see the gleaming flower beds, the minarets, the kiosks and the arboured alleys. All the arches and pillars are hung with coloured lamps, every pillar is entwined with illuminated garlands of flowers, and festoons of these connect the bright ceiling of this fairy-like dance hall with the arches. All the light is concentrated in the middle of the gay building and the corners are hidden by flower-decked grottos in which the dancers rest on fantastically decorated seats. The orchestra is not visible, and the music appears to come from the foliage-covered kiosks How lovely the dancers are, their light beautiful feet moving on the shining parquet floor to the rhythm of a Strauss waltz. England's women and girls are the loveliest in Europe; and those dancing there are the loveliest in London. What dark fiery eyes, what golden hair, what red lips, what classic features, what sensual lovely figures! They are all in magnificent ball toilettes, hair adorned with pearls and flowers, beautifully formed necks and shoulders bare, bare arms clasping their partners, leaning upon them and following the ever-quickening music. And who are they, these beautiful women in lovely ball toilettes, their hair threaded with pearls? Do they live in the tall stone palaces of Belgravia, with the solid balconies before the windows, past which we drove? Or do they come from the quiet distinguished streets looking on the flowers and lawns of Hyde Park and Regent's Park? May not that lovely girl in the embroidered Arab mantle, over a white pink-veiled muslin dress, be a Duchess? With what aristocratic negligence she lies on that ottoman on the right, her sandalwood fan in her white soft hand, cooling her hot face. Her small feet, in soft grey elastic boots rest on the velvet cushions. The white frock is caught up and shows an embroidered petticoat and delicate stockings; dark locks shade a high, aristocratic forehead; large, sad blue eyes gaze out from under the shadow of a black silk wimple. Her lovely full bosom is heaving from the exertion of the dance, and how the white shoulders rise from the rich lace of the dress! And, on the arm of her partner, a young midshipman, that blonde who is fanning herself with her perfumed handkerchief to cool herself! Her pale gold hair waves unadorned in rich natural curls over neck and shoulders—curls which are only to be seen in England—her black eyes sparkle like diamonds: pale gold hair, dark sparkling eyes, a blossom-white complexion, rosy with the exertion of the dance! A few more bars! It is midnight—the dance is ended. One after another the gas lamps are extinguished. The magic gardens of Cremorne become darker every moment. Everyone makes for the exits. Who were those dancers? We shall see them all again to-night. The girl with the pale gold curls with the fiery dark eyes, wrapped in a black silk mantilla, hurries past us alone through the dark arboured alleys to the exit. She calls a cab to drive to the town—if we like we can accompany her. As she sets her lovely foot on the step of the carriage, a silent dark-clothed man thrusts a folded leaflet into her hand. On the leaflet are the words: " I know whom I have believed, and am persuaded that he is able to keep that which I have committed unto him against that day. 2 Timothy 1, 2." Who is the silent, serious-looking man who thrusts the leaflet into the hand of the girl with the long pale gold curls? He also is an example of one of the contrasts in which London is richer than any other town in Europe. He is a member of an organisation which for some years has been trying to save the beautiful sinners who dance in Cremorne and after midnight crowd the pavements of the Haymarket and Regent Street from the bottomless pit of destruction into which, in a few years' time, pleasure and indulgence will cast them, who preach repentance to them after the midnight dances, at the midnight tea-parties, who seek them out under the arches of His Majesty's Theatre offering them home, fireside and employment. Will the beautiful sinner read the folded leaflet? Or shall we see her again in a dark room in the oyster house in the Haymarket, drinking sherry and champagne and laughingly throwing the folded leaflet of the black-clothed man on to the table?[1]

[1] G. Rasch, *London bei Nacht*, pp. 36, 39-43. See also the description of Cremorne Gardens in J. Rodenberg's *Alltagsleben in London* (' Round the Clock in London '). Berlin, 1860. Pp. 59-63.

CHAPTER V

PANDERING, BULLIES, AND TRAFFIC IN YOUNG GIRLS (DEFLORATION MANIA)

PROCURATION was developed to a greater extent and in more varied ways in London than in any other town; nowhere else were the agents of this deplorable, debased business so much in evidence. As regards also the cunning displayed in the practice of procuration, London, the central market for international traffic in young girls, took the first place and stood out in this connection in a way which can only be regarded as repulsive.

Colqhoun[1] reckons the number of panders in London in 1790 at 2,000. Richelot believes that in 1850 there were 5,000 procurers and procuresses in London. According to Ryan there were no less than 400,000 people directly or indirectly connected with prostitution[2].

This large number is divided into different categories and types for which the English have distinctive names.

The most widespread class of panders (mostly women) is the ' Bawds ' and ' Procurers ' or ' Procuresses '. The ' Bawd ' is almost always a former prostitute, and usually the proprietress of a brothel. Richard King describes in his *Frauds of London* the activities of the ' Bawds ' as follows: ' These old bawds frequent our religious gatherings and other public places with a young nun (as they themselves

[1] P. Colqhoun, *loc. cit.*, p. xxxi.
[2] Ryan, *loc. cit.*, p. 192.

call her) on their arm who, whilst the old creature, with eyes cast upwards, simulates piety and utters hypocritical prayers, tries to lead astray some man suitable for her purpose. When the service is over, the old woman on going out stumbles suddenly, falls down or faints as suits her purpose; the gentleman offers his help or his arm, or a coach to take her home; this she accepts, apologises for the trouble caused him, and begs her ' daughter ' to thank the gentleman for his great kindness. This she does, and surreptitiously takes the stranger's hand or shows her regard for him in some other way so as to establish intimacy with him. At the house the new acquaintance is invited to share a meal (long standing ready for this very purpose), during which the old woman on some pretext or other goes out of the room and leaves the couple alone, which opportunity the young man does not fail to make use of [1].' ' Procurers ' or ' Procuresses ' are people who, while not actually owning a brothel, undertake to provide ' wares ' for those who do or for independent people. They frequent churches, taverns, theatres, shops, balls, masks, public gatherings and the like in order to ensnare their prey. In particular they keep their eyes on young men and girls come to London for the first time from the provinces; and in former times on the arrival of each mail coach from the country, quite a crowd of these panders would assemble at the terminus or even at the previous stopping-place, in order to entice the girls during their stay at the inn [2]. Panders of this type obtained and still obtain a large part of their supplies through newspaper advertisements.

The ' Pimps ' were mostly of French origin and attached themselves to noblemen or other distinguished people, whilst

[1] Richard King, *The Frauds of London detected, or a new Warning-Piece against the iniquitous Practices of that Metropolis.* London, 1770. Pp. 13-14.
[2] *Ibid.,* pp. 56-57.

they masqueraded as fine gentlemen and set themselves to provide their patrons with every sort of sensual pleasure, and also to make known to them the loveliest girls in Paris with whom they pretended to be on the most intimate footing. Many noblemen employed these ' Pimps ' who acted as ' Commissaries of Vice ', and often at the same time carried on liaisons with the lady of the house, insinuated themselves into other houses to pick up what they could and usually ended as brothel agents. According to King, no Englishman could play this rôle with the success of a Frenchman[1].

Richelot includes amongst the modern London panders those who travel on the Continent procuring young girls as dressmakers, governesses and so on, paying them their first quarter's salary and then selling them at a high price in London to brothels. Shopkeepers (women) often belonged to the pander class, hung notices in their windows announcing vacancies for workgirls and then introduced them to prostitution. They themselves often kept a clandestine brothel. Many London procuresses went into the country, took jobs as farm workers, etc., and led astray the young girls who worked with them. Drivers and mail coachmen very largely assisted the panders. Finally the fortune-tellers[2] and dealers in obscene books[3] belonged to this class[4].

The Restoration was a golden time for the panders, who enjoyed an esteem such as did not fall to their share even in the licentious century of the Renaissance. For the frivolous King Charles II himself in person honoured procuresses, such as the famous Creswell, with his visits. According to Philarete Chasles it was a flourishing time for these ladies, and scholars of that epoch have written of

---

[1] R. King, *loc. cit.*, pp. 53-56.
[2] See Chapter V.
[3] See Chapter XVII.
[4] G. Richelot, *loc. cit.*, pp. 31-36.

the life and activities of nine representatives of the, in
those days, highly honoured profession, amongst whom were
Mother Ross, Mother Bennett, Mother Moreley and first
and foremost Mother Beaulieu, which last sued the Archbishop of Rheims because he had placed ' orders ' with her
and had not paid her for them[1]. Creswell carried on
procuration by means of a wonderful administrative
system, and sent her emissaries and spies throughout
England and France. She died a prisoner in Bridewell,
and bequeathed £10 to the minister on condition that he
only spoke ' well ' of her. After a sermon on morals in
general, the preacher closed as follows: ' In accordance
with the will of the departed, it is expected of me that I
should mention her and should only speak well of her.
All that I shall say of her is the following: she was born well,
lived well and died well, in that she was born with the
name of Creswell, lived in Clerkenwell and died in Bridewell[2].'

A very notorious procuress of the eighteenth century was
Mother Needham, who, in spite of her great piety, was
placed in the pillory on the 5th May 1731, and was so ill used
by the populace that she died a few days after.

Every prostitute or woman who prostituted herself in
London had her ' bully ', who lived on her earnings, and
seldom restricted himself to one woman. The ' bullies '
were thieves, pickpockets and often murderers. Girls of
not more than 13 years already had their bullies. The
business of these vagabonds was partly to protect the
prostitutes and partly to rob or murder visitors to the
brothels. They were the most desperate characters,
every one capable of the most horrible crimes. Usually
they came from the lowest classes, but there were also

[1] Ph. Chasles, Vol. II, p. 88.
[2] Ph. Chasles, *loc. cit.*, p. 89. J. Timbs, *The Romance of London*. London.
P. 275.

bullies in the middle and higher classes. They all spent the
day in beerhouses and inns, the nights in brothels where
they committed the worst atrocities. Ryan reports the
terrible fact that a great number of skeletons were found in
London brothels, the victims of the 'bullies'[1]. These were
particularly numerous in the fourth decade of the nineteenth
century in the 'bullies' ' quarter of the town, ' Fleet Ditch ',
where ' every house is the lowest and most infamous
brothel '. There was a very large aqueduct, in which the
bodies of those murdered by the bullies were thrown and
thus washed into the Thames, so that discovery was
impossible[2].

London was for a long time the central market for the
traffic in young girls, which was carried on there on a huge
scale and under the most shameful conditions. 'London,
representing free prostitution, was also the chief central
market for the export (and import) of young and older
prostitutes to all European and American countries[3].'

As regards the methods of this deplorable trade, the
' Disclosures of the *Pall Mall Gazette*' in the year 1885 and
Alexis Splingard's book *Clarissa: Out of the dark houses of
Belgium*, with its introduction by Otto Henne am Rhyn, in
which this subject is dealt with in a particularly detailed
manner, have shed much light. Many facts are also found in
the ' Report from the Select Committee of the House of
Lords on the Law relating to the protection of young girls,
Session 1881 '.

The *Pall Mall Gazette* stated with reference to the export
and import of human wares as follows: 'London, or rather
those who carry on the White Slave Traffic, provides the
largest market in the world for the sale of human flesh. As

[1] Ryan, *loc. cit.*, pp. 176-178.
[2] *Ibid.*, p. 1 7.
[3] Tarnowsky, *loc. cit.*, p. 201.

with any business, the traffic is export and import. There is a great difference between England and other countries in that, whereas in England vice is entirely free, that on the Continent is carried on under strict regulations. The ruin, however, of young innocent girls, their poverty and complete helplessness, their destitution and absolute ignorance of the language, are as compelling a force as the savage horrors of the state brothels and the unfeeling barbarity of the doctors. The girls are usually brought from France, Belgium, Germany and Switzerland to London for the purpose of seduction[1].'

Belgium, the ' land of model prostitution ', as O. Henne am Rhyn calls it, is the principal importing country for English ' wares ' of this kind—' English parcels' as they are cynically called by the traffickers in young girls[2].

In the year 1880, after repeated representations, the attention of the British Government was called to the fact that this traffic was in full swing, and that young Englishwomen were being taken by false pretences to Belgium, there to be used for the purposes of prostitution, and kept by force in houses of ill fame. Through the efforts of Sir William Harcourt, the lawyer T. W. Snagge was sent to Belgium to enquire into these circumstances, which fully bore out the communicated facts. A Dutchman named Klyberg, with his wife, was the principal importer, during the whole of the ' seventies ', of girls from London to the owners of houses of ill fame in Holland, Belgium and France. Henne am Rhyn quotes several ' business letters ' of this Dutchman, amongst which the following is noteworthy. It was written by Klyberg when in hospital, as ' he had sprained a foot

---

[1] *Der Jungfrauentribut des modernen Babylon* (The Virgin Tribute of Modern Babylon). Extracts from the *Pall Mall Gazette*. Budapest, 1885. Pp. 78-79 ; p. 85.

[2] H. France, *Les Nuits de Londres*, p. 52 ; *Jungfrauentribut*, p. 86.

Pl. 12]

Artist unknown

INTRUSION ON STUDY, OR THE PAINTER DISTURBED

CRIM·CON:

Get out of My House you Hussey, Thave't you to do your own buisnefs, not Mine.

Published with its direction by T.Bradford 48 Cock Fair Tho: Smithfield 20 Nov.

Pl. 13]

Artist unknown

when travelling' (a pity he had not broken his neck):
'My dear Quoilin,

'You will find me in London early on Tuesday, when you come to fetch your wares. You can take these away the same evening. Everything will be in readiness, and I can guarantee that if you fetch them from London it will only cost you the half of what it would in your own house. I have a lovely tall brunette girl, with glorious teeth, faultless bust; in a word, a beautiful woman and a good girl. My wife has had her for three weeks, and therefore wrote you. I have also a tall blonde girl when you have room. I am sorry I cannot go over, but I have business in Holland. I have been offered a house in Leyden, and should like to talk to you about it. Sarah, the woman who has the house in Amsterdam, has asked me about two lots, and the people in two other houses are also requiring goods, so that as soon as I can travel I shall make some money, and when I take over the house in Leyden I shall be my own agent and travel continuously. I shall have a lodging in London, where I can come to fetch girls[1]'.

Courtney, a Frenchman, was nearly as active as Klyberg in the export of English girls. Letters were found from many others living in the ill-famed 'French quarter' of London, with the same contents as that of Klyberg. Other traffickers in young girls were Carrotty Jack and a very dangerous gang consisting of John Sellecarts (also 'Sells' or 'Selly'), Mrs. Sellecarts (also 'Mrs. Vero'), Friedrich Schultz (also 'Marks'), Emile Regnier and the infamous wife of the last. Sellecarts took girls from London and brought them to Brussels, where he was in league with all the brothel keepers. The woman with whom he lived, an Irishwoman called

---

[1] *Clarissa, aus dunkeln Häusern Belgiens.* After the French original of Alexis Splingard. With introduction by Dr. Otto Henne am Rhyn. Leipzig. Pp. viii-x.

Raphael, whose real name he had no idea of, collected the girls and carried out the correspondence with the brothel keepers, as Sellecarts could not write. Amongst others she wrote the following significant letter:

> ' Greek Street,
>
> ' Soho Square, London, W.C.,
>
> ' 3rd April 1878.

' Madame,

' I hasten to inform you that I have two lovely English girls who wish to go into a " House ". Their true age and all papers are quite in order. I have not the honour to be personally known to you, but I beg you to believe that I do not do business like Kleber. I insist upon everything being properly (!) done, as since the Kleber affair it has become altogether too dangerous to send English girls abroad under false declarations and without carrying out the necessary formalities. My price is 300 francs for one girl, or 600 for the two. I shall bring them to Ostende, where you can fetch them yourself.

> ' I have the honour to greet you,
>
> ' Raphael[1].'

H. France gives a list of similar brothels in Brussels which took girls mainly from England, and the ages of whom were not more than 12 to 14 years[2].

The investigations of the Commission appointed by the *Pall Mall Gazette* in 1885 showed that this appalling traffic in young girls still continued after the enquiry instituted by Sir William Harcourt in 1880. The Commission reports: ' A few weeks ago a consignment of three " parcels " was sent from the neighbourhood of Leicester Square to Belgium. Two of them are now in Antwerp, the third in Brussels. A much larger consignment is expected shortly.'

---

[1] *Clarissa, aus dunkeln Häusern Belgiens*, pp. x-xi.

[2] H. France, *Les Nuits de Londres*, pp. 52-53.

A trader in these goods explained that usually a dozen young English girls are sent every month to the above-mentioned town, that is 250 a year, of which a third had already become prostitutes.

The celebrated Register of Girls, or so-called ' Lists of Ladies', was used by the traffickers in girls and by prostitution generally, in the eighteenth and part of the nineteenth centuries. Von Schütz remarks in this connection: ' I might refer again on closing this letter to the remarkable leniency of the English police, demonstrated by the fact that from time to time lists of names of the most celebrated " ladies of the town " are printed and openly sold in London. How eagerly these " lists of ladies " are bought can be judged from the fact that 8,000 to 10,000 copies are issued, and sometimes sold out in a few days[1].'

Archenholtz's statement that in his time the famous Register of Girls, which could formerly be obtained openly in the taverns of Covent Garden, had completely disappeared as the police were watching it, and would allow no more to be printed, is an error[2]. For every number of the erotic periodical appearing in the year 1795, *The Rangers' Magazine*, contained a ' Monthly List of the Covent Garden Cyprians; or the Vade Mecum of the Man of Pleasure ', in which the physical attractions and the charms of individual girls were described in detail[3]. C. de Méry also speaks of similar catalogues of prostitutes in the year 1828, and in the erotic periodical *The Exquisite* (London, 1842-1844), under the designation ' Stars of the Salons ', ' Sketches of Courtesans ' and 'Seduction unveiled', was a list of names, addresses and descriptions of popular harlots. In the year 1860 the Register of Girls still existed in the form of advertisements

[1] v. Schütz, *loc. cit.*, p. 217.
[2] Archenholtz, *Annalen*, Vol. VIII, p. 243.
[3] P. Fraxi, *Catena*, pp. 337-338.

which the brothel keepers published in the newspapers, still under the heading 'lists of ladies', in which they informed the public that fresh young girls were to be found in their brothels in all parts of the kingdom[1].

The most celebrated of these lists was the one which Harris, a tavern keeper in Drury Lane, published every year from 1760 to 1793. Archenholtz states: 'A tavern keeper in Drury Lane publishes every year a printed list of prostitutes who frequent his house and are otherwise known to him. This book bears the title "Harris's list of Covent Garden Ladies[2]"'. It contained their names, descriptions of their features, figures, manners, talents, etc., often showing much partiality. 8,000 copies were printed every year and were rapidly disposed of[3].' A complete series of this remarkable almanack is one of the greatest bibliographical rarities. The Brussels Library possesses a copy, No. 29883, published in 1765.

The London traffic in girls had a unique character and a decided bent in a certain direction on account of the widespread demand in England for virgins, i.e. the specifically English defloration mania, which was met with nowhere else in the world to such a great extent and accompanied by such brutal practices. The study of this morbid demand for virgins throws a surprising light on the influence of suggestion and on the fact that sexual customs and perversities are spread through imitation, and that it is not always necessary to look for a pathological reason for these abnormalities. ' Forty years ago', says Tarnowsky, 'not less than £50 was paid for a *virgo intacta*, now one can be had for £5. Forty years ago one did not dare demand a medical proof of virginity, now one can get this for £1. Formerly the training

[1] Fr. S. Hügel, *loc. cit.*, p. 146.
[2] *Harris's List of Covent Garden Ladies or A New Atlantis for the year*. London, 1760-1793.
[3] Archenholtz, *England*, Vol. II, pp. 266-267.

of young girls for prostitution was not understood, now a speciality is made of it. One deduces from these facts that with time further progress will be made in this direction[1].'

One man requires 70 virgins a year, but would willingly take 100, and a doctor deflowered three virgins in a fortnight[2].

If an explanation is sought of the reason why, amongst the English, defloration mania should have reached such epidemic dimensions, account must not only be taken of the horrible results of this passion, in which the worst side of the British national character came into play, but the deeper psychological basis must be sought for. For the Englishman, only the best is good enough. He must have something which can only once, and by only one person, be possessed, and of which he can boast before others. This is the case as regards the virginity of a girl, which attracts the Englishman primarily as something select and unique. According to an English author of the eighteenth century, who discourses in detail on the pleasures of defloration, the desire to seduce a virgin is an acquired taste, but none the less the acme of sensual pleasure. ' I hold truly that the enjoyment of a virgin, from the point of view of the physical as well as the psychic experiences of the seducer, is the highest peak of sensual pleasure. In the first place a man's fancy will be inflamed by the prospect of the enjoyment of a woman whom he has long desired and tried to win, and who has never before (as he believes) been in bed with a man, in whose arms no man has yet lain, and whose virgin charms he will be the first to see and triumphantly enjoy. This exquisite work of the fancy prepares the body in the highest degree for sensual pleasure.' The author then describes in great detail the delights of defloration, and with special

---

[1] Tarnowsky, *loc. cit.*, p. 44.
[2] *Der Jungfrauentribut*, pp. 48, 58.

[177]

enjoyment dwells on the cries of pain and the resistance to seduction made by a virgin[1].

In conjunction with the above-mentioned motives, the sadistic element in defloration mania may be cited as especially noteworthy. An English author points out that debauchees who pay large sums to procuresses for virgins for the purpose of seduction, are nearly always flagello-maniacs and, in fact, active flagellants, who obtain unique enjoyment from whipping young girls so brutally that the blood flows[2].

This mania for virgins was, as we saw, an old English vice, and had as its natural corollary child prostitution which, according to the unanimous evidence of all observers, had grown to frightful proportions in England. Von Schütz and Archenholtz have mentioned the astonishing number of very young prostitutes in London in the eighteenth century. Ryan mentions a brothel in Crispin Street, Spitalfields, that in the year 1810 was conducted and solely intended for the purpose of procuring and prostituting little girls of under 14[3]. In 1830 there were many children's brothels in London, amongst others that of a certain Maxwell in Betty Street, Commercial Road, Catherine Keeley in Dock Street, Commercial Road, and other brothels in the neighbourhood of Bedford Square and Mile End Road[4]. A certain John Jacobs and his wife kept a very well-known children's brothel for 25 years[5]. The children's brothel of David Romaine in Mile End was famous; when it was closed by the police, three girls of 15 years were found, on whose prostitution the worthy pair lived. Every possible

---

[1] *The Battles of Venus.* Haag (London), 1760. Pp. 24-26.
[2] *Venus' School Mistress or Birchen Sports.* Paris, 1898 (privately printed). Appendix.
[3] Ryan, *loc. cit.*, p. 109.
[4] *Ibid.*, p. 124.
[5] *Ibid.*, p. 138.

method of seducing children of both sexes was employed in
this establishment. There were often assembled there on
Saturday evening ten to fourteen boys, in ages from 10 to
15 years, for the purpose of the most horrible immorality
with the girls. Usually one of the three little girls was sent
out on the streets on Saturday evening in order to entice
the boys into the house, when, the number and the total
sum represented being large enough, they were let into
the den of immorality, where the other two girls naturally
visited them. This custom was frequently observed by the
police, who often saw twelve boys go into the brothel
together. Ryan rightly surmises that the results of these
excesses would mean ruin for the boys[1]. The most depraved
activities were carried on by William Sheen, who had
numerous brothels in the worst districts of the town
(Wentworth Street, Spitalfields and others). He organised
regular pornological clubs where men and women practised
the most horrible immorality with the children! There were
always from thirty to forty children in his brothels[2].

Hector France makes the most shocking disclosures with
regard to child prostitution in London in later years.
The chapter ' Marché aux enfants ' in *Va-nu-Pieds de
Londres* should be read[3] ! A correspondent of the *Figaro*
says: ' Every evening towards midnight more than 500 girls
in ages between 12 and 15 years parade between Piccadilly
Circus and Waterloo Place, that is on a stretch of ground no
more than 300 yards long[4].'

[1] Ryan, *loc. cit.*, pp. 138-139.
[2] *Ibid.*, pp. 149-150.
[3] *Ibid.*, pp. 30-40. See also ' Le Gagne-Pain de Lily,' *ibid.*, pp. 192-198.
[4] Faucher remarked forty years earlier : ' Entre Spitalfields et Bethnal
Green, sur une route dont l'accroissement de la population a fait une rue,
se tient, les lundis et les mardis, entre six et sept heures du matin, un
marché aux enfants ' (*Les Va-nu-Pieds*, p. 33). Children could be bought
here for any purpose. Thus Hadji Ali ben Mohamed, owner of an acrobatic

The famous revelations of the *Pall Mall Gazette* in the year 1885, however, have thrown the most light on the prostitution of very young girls and the sale of children for the purposes of immorality. As Tarnowsky rightly says, the accurate circumstantial evidence given leaves no ground for suspicion as to their truth. They made such a deep impression that the price of single copies of the paper rose to 5s., and 20,000 copies were distributed[1]. W. H. Stead[2] was the leader of the investigations of the secret commission set up by the *Pall Mall Gazette*, which began its work on Whit Monday 1885 and continued uninterruptedly thereafter day and night. The first official suggestion for such an investigation was received by the office of the paper from the City Treasurer, Mr. Benjamin Scott, President of the London ' Committee for the Prevention of Traffic with English Girls '. The secret commission was formed under the auspices of the *Pall Mall Gazette*, and it was instructed to investigate the facts independently of the police, although it worked in conjunction with the Home Office and the Local Government Board. Stead presided over the details of preparing the work of the Commission and over the enlistment of the support of distinguished people. The Archbishop of Canterbury, the Bishops of London and Westminster, and also the prison chaplains, took their share. ' Besides the churches, I obtained the help of those societies

troop which performed in Westminster Aquarium in 1879, bought twenty young English children in ages from four to twelve years, at 25 francs per head (*ibid.*, p. 36).

[1] Tarnowsky, *loc. cit.*, p. 41.

[2] William Thomas Stead, born on 5th July 1849 at Howden-on-Tyne, took over in 1880 the post of Assistant Editor to the *Pall Mall Gazette* under John Morley, and in 1883 became Editor of the paper. At the beginning of the year 1890 he retired from this post and founded the *Review of Reviews*. In latter years he became well known both as a pacifist and through his intercession on behalf of the Boers in connection with the South African War.

which exist for the suppression of this traffic, of ladies working for hospitals and asylums, and of all those whose philanthropic and religious zeal brings them in direct contact with actual conditions.' The result of the enquiry, according to Stead, spoke for itself, though he says that the disclosures made are never so terrible as the facts themselves. Then also the Commission could only ' skim the surface of the proposition '. The whole thing was carried through in less than six weeks, with a total outlay of £300 sterling, ' less than a rich man would spend on the corruption of a single shop girl of the better class, say the daughter of a coachman or a doctor[1] '.

The revelations of the Pall Mall Gazette principally referred to those crimes which Stead rightly classed as ' sexual outrages ' in contradistinction to ' sexual immorality '. To these outrages belong: (1) Buying, selling and seduction of children. (2) Procuring of virgins. (3) Enticing and ruin of women. (4) International girl-slave trade. With regard to the first point in particular, the enquiry has collected definite information which it is impossible to go into here in detail. I must confine myself to a short analysis of the important contents of the report of the Pall Mall Gazette.

According to Stead it was a fact that in London a system was in full operation under which the rape of virgins was one of the most ordinary events, that these virgins were mostly of tender years, actually too young to understand the nature of the crime whose victims they were against their will; that these atrocities were continually being perpetrated and practically never punished, and that the arrangements for procuring these victims of London's lust, certifying their virginity, seducing them, and destroying the traces of the seduction, were carried out with a facility and an efficiency which to those

[1] Der Jungfrauentribut, p. viii.

[181]

who have not had actual experience of the ease with which crime can be perpetrated, is almost unbelievable. A brothel keeper made the following confession to Stead: 'There is always a demand for virgins as you call them, " fresh girls " as we call them in the trade, and a pander who understands his business has his eyes open in every direction.

'His stock of girls is always being exhausted, so that he has to be continually filling it up and looking out for suitable "numbers" in order to keep up the reputation of his house. The hunt for "fresh girls" takes a good deal of time, but it is simple and fairly easy once one knows the ropes. I myself have been into the country and have disguised myself in all manners of ways in order to get girls; occasionally I have worn the dress of a minister, let the girl believe that I intended to marry her and so obtained possession of her in order to oblige a good client. How was this done? When I had paid court for some time to my girl, I proposed to her that I should take her to London to show her the sights of the town. I brought her up with me, took her about and gave her a great deal to eat and drink—particularly to drink. I took her to the theatre and so arranged that she should miss the last train. She was now very tired, a little muddled with drink and excitement and very frightened at finding herself alone in the town without friends. I offered her a suitable lodging for the night, she went to bed in my house, and thus the business was done. My client had a virgin, I received my commission of 10 or 20 pounds sterling and the next morning the girl, who had lost her character and did not dare go home, would in all probability do what the others do, she would become one of my "numbers", which means that she would earn her living on the streets for the benefit of my house. That is a very simple example of the way in which we recruit girls. Another very easy way of obtaining virgins is to breed them.

[182]

Many women who live on the streets have female children, and they have to earn their living. When they are 12 or 13 years old they are saleable. For a very attractive "number" of this sort they receive 20 to 40 pounds sterling. I send my own daughter from my own brothel on to the streets. I know now a couple of very pretty little girls who will soon be sold. They have only to take the first step, and it would be bad business not to make as much out of it as possible. Parents who are given to drink often sell their children to brothel keepers. In the East End of London you can buy as many "fresh girls" as you want. In one street in Dalston you can buy a dozen of them. Sometimes the supply is greater than the demand and you have to seduce your girls yourself or get someone in to do it, which is very bad business. There is a man named S. who has an appointment at a well-known house to seduce the young girls and fit them for the needs of the house when there is no demand for virgins but for girls who have already been seduced[1].'

In the year 1885 there was a systematically organised traffic in virgins in London. Particularly infamous was the ' firm ' of the procuresses X. and Z., whose speciality was the provision of virgins. The house was founded in 1881 (almost immediately after her own defloration) by Miss X., a young, energetic and very cunning person. She was then 16 years old! She was introduced to a man by a young girl who had already been seduced, and who pocketed half the price of her innocence as commission. The ease with which her go-between had made a couple of pounds was a revelation to her, and immediately after her own fall she began to look for young girls. In two years' time the business had reached such proportions that she was obliged to take Miss Z., a somewhat older girl, as working partner. ' We deal in virginity,' said this worthy maiden to Stead, ' but not in

[1] *Der Jungfrauentribut*, pp. 10-12.

[183]

virgins. My partner procures the girls, who are seduced and taken back to their relatives. The business is then at an end so far as we are concerned. We deal only in " first seduction "; a girl only goes through our hands once. Our customers desire virgins, not damaged goods, and usually they only see these once[1].' Most of the virgins in this institution were recruited from amongst children and shop girls, governesses, cooks and servants. ' Young girls from the country, fresh and rosy, are easily found in the shops or out walking. But the principal source of supply is the nursemaids. My old client always says to me: ' Why don't you supply nursemaids? In Hyde Park there are as many as you want, and they are all virgins[2].' The large parks were systematically searched by these procuresses for ' fresh girls '; Hyde Park and the Green Park gave the best results in the mornings in this respect, Regent's Park in the after-noons. ' As we go on our way, we look out for a pretty girl; once found, we talk to her; during the next few weeks we try to meet her as often as possible, till we have won her confi-dence to such an extent that we can persuade her into considering how easy it is to make a pound sterling by receiv-ing a visit from a man[3].' Certain it is that a great percentage of the girls submitted of their own free will to the enticements of the procuresses, knowing very well the fate that awaited them. Stead describes a scene at a procuress's, when she made a young girl go through ' all sorts of movements ' in order to show off her good qualities to the best advantage. He asked the poor victim why she had let herself be seduced, whereon the girl told him candidly that it was on account of the money[4]. The prices paid by men of the world for the

[1] *Der Jungfrauentribut*, p. 50.
[2] *Ibid.*, p. 53.
[3] *Ibid.*, p. 54.
[4] *Ibid.*, p. 41.

provision of virgins was much higher in the West End of London than in the East End. In the wholesale house of the firm X. and Z. the price for a virgin was £5, in a brothel in the East End £10, and in the West End £20 sterling[1].

In the case of a girl who was given to a man by force for defloration against her will, various methods were employed. Some brothel keepers made use of narcotics. ' She slept when he did it—she was fast asleep. To tell the truth she had been put to sleep, as often happens. I gave her a sleeping draught—it is a mixture of laudanum and something else, chloroform is often mixed with it, but I use either snuff or laudanum. We call it " black draught "; they lie there almost as dead, and the girl first knows in the morning what has happened. And then? Oh, then she cries a great deal with the pain, but she is surprised and hardly knows what has happened, except that she can hardly move for pain. We naturally tell her that everything is all right; all girls have to go through it once; she is over it now without knowing anything about it and no amount of crying will help[2].' Others tried to avoid any scandal by carefully choosing the situation of the house or the room. Many houses had an underground room from which no sound could be heard, and which would never be discovered. Or the room was thickly padded and thus the cries of the children were inaudible. ' In my house ', said a highly respectable woman who had a villa in the West End of London, ' you can gloat over the cries of the girls with the certainty that no one will hear them besides yourself.' In order to taste the full complete voluptuousness caused by the cries of the immature child, there was no necessity for a padded or underground room. ' Here is a room where you

---

[1] *Der Jungfrauentribut*, pp. 38-39.
[2] *Ibid.*, p. 16.

will be quite safe. The house itself stands in its own grounds, the walls are thick, a double carpet covers the floor. The only window, which looks on the garden at the back, is doubly protected, first with shutters then with heavy curtains. You can lock the door and do what you like. The girl can shriek murder till all is blue but no sound will be heard. The servants will be far away at the other end of the house, I only will be about to see that all is quiet. If some means of stopping the cries is at hand, a cushion, a bed-cover or even a handkerchief, there is no danger at all. To many men the cries of pain of the tortured girl are the essence of their enjoyment[1].'

In order to facilitate this abominable act for an impotent debauchee who no longer had strength to overcome the resistance of a powerful girl, the binding of the unfortunate child was often carried out. 'In order to oblige a rich client, who had so dissipated his vitality in debauchery and excesses, that none but very young girls could satisfy his exhausted senses, an exceedingly worthy lady undertook to bind a girl, of 14 or 15 years old, hand and foot to the four corners of the bed, so that any resistance, with the exception of her useless cries, would be impossible. Before it was finally decided to bind the girl, the lady of the house, a strong woman, placed her services gladly at the disposal of her client, holding the girl down forcibly while her rich patron carried out his desire. Even that was too much for him, and he requested that the lower part of the girl's body should be strapped down. Tying down for the purpose of rape is not at all unusual in Half Moon Street and in Anna Rosenberg's brothel in Liverpool[2].'

How well organised down to the last detail this seduction

---

[1] *Der Jungfrauentribut*, pp. 21-22.
[2] *Ibid.*, pp. 23-24.

traffic was in London, is shown by the fact that the brothels and procuresses had their own doctors (*sit venia verbo!*), who had to supply so-called ' certificates of virginity ' after a thorough examination of the girls in this respect. Stead bespoke one day at the house of the procuresses X. and Z. no less than five virgins, and relates in a lively manner the course the negotiations took, particularly in regard to the examination for virginity:

' The business was concluded, the advance payment handed over and the procuresses undertook to deliver the goods the following Saturday. At a certain place in the Marylebone Road I awaited the company at half-past four. A minute later I saw the women X. and Z. coming, but with only three girls. One was big, pretty and seemed to be about 16 years old; the others were younger with somewhat clumsy figures. Two of them were shop girls, the third was learning the trade of a dressmaker. The procuresses were full of profuse apologies. They had been to Highgate to make up the number of five virgins, but two of those in prospect could not go out that day. They would bring these on Monday without fail, and, indeed, to make up for loss of time, they undertook to bring three girls on Monday instead of two, altogether six virgins. We went in to the doctor's. The girls, who did not know one another, and did not dare to speak to one another, were examined separately, making no objection. After the examination they signed a paper agreeing to their seduction. To the great surprise of the girls two of them failed to obtain the certificate of virginity. The doctor could not be sure that they were not virgins, yet they were not "virgo intacta" in the technical sense. I gave the two girls five shillings for their trouble in coming, paid X. and Z. their commission for the one genuine virgin, and went away with the following document in my pocket:

[187]

' "—— St., London, W.

' " 17th June 1885.

' " I hereby state that I have to-day examined D., sixteen years old, and confirmed her virginity.

' " Dr.. "

'Nothing could have been simpler or more business-like than this deal, which differed from the usual method of procedure of the firm X. and Z. only in that the doctor's examination took the place of seduction. Equipped with my scrap of paper, I could take my virgins to whom I liked. Last Friday morning they brought four young girls to the doctor; three were fourteen and one eighteen years old. The last was an assistant cook in one of the best-known hotels in the West End. The three younger girls were rejected by the doctor, only the eighteen-year-old received the certificate. " Can the little rascals have been seen already! " Mrs. Z. exclaimed in annoyance. " It is always the young ones who cannot pass the examination." In ten days I have had nine girls delivered to me, of which four received a certificate of virginity, whilst five were rejected[1].'

The investigations of the *Pall Mall Gazette* revealed the astonishing fact that in London at the end of the nineteenth century a method was in use which was customary in the Middle Ages and up to the seventeenth century, neglected and rare in the eighteenth century and then revived. I mean the artificial restoration of lost virginity. Stead's investigations showed that the sale of patched-up girls in London was quite a usual thing. Reading this part of the disclosures, one might imagine oneself taken back to the time of the Middle Ages.

Although in olden times in the Orient, and in classical days, such practices were carried on, the scholarly monks

[1] *Der Jungfrauentribut*, pp. 55, 57.

Designed by Wm. Hogarth

STROLLING PLAYERS

Engraved by T. Cook

Pl. 14]

BITTER FARE
OR
SWEEPS REGALING

Pl. 15]

Artist unknown

and Arabian doctors of the Middle Ages first raised to a fine art the restoration of virginity. All later writers on this subject rely on Avicenna or Albertus Magnus and other representatives of scholastic medicine for their information. These medical scholars had drawn up a list of so many ' Signa vel probae virginitatis ' that in the case of failure they were obliged to relinquish some of the methods by which they re-established the appearance of virginity, that is the concealment of the 'Signa corruptionis virginitatis'. I once extracted from the writings of the French doctor, Heinrich von Mondeville, published by J. Pagel, a typical collection of these methods, amongst which astringent plants, pieces of broken glass and leeches, or sponges or fish bladders soaked in blood and inserted in the vulva, etc., may be mentioned. This type of treatment was much resorted to during the whole of the Middle Ages. The writings of Albertus Magnus have been widely disseminated since the sixteenth century in volumes of extracts from the so-called *Albertus Parvus* ('Alberti Parvi Lucii Libellus de mirabilibus Naturae arcanis '), so that according to Dufour all the great ladies and gentlemen of the seventeenth century knew recipes for the restoration of virginity. In particular, the barbers and bath-keepers were skilled in this art, and no less the old prostitutes and procuresses. Venette mentions the steam from a little vinegar, in which has been thrown a red-hot iron or brick, an astringent decoction of acorns or of sloes, myrrh, Provençal roses, cypress nuts, *unguentum adstringens fernelii*, water distilled from myrrh, etc., as means by which ' the normal female parts, now too wide open, may be drawn together and closed '. Artificial uniting of the parts seems also to have been much used as a means of restoring virginity.

In the eighteenth century these practices were still general in all fashionable brothels. In London, Charlotte Hayes enjoyed a great reputation in this connection. In the *Sérails de Londres* it is told how the celebrated Don Juan, George Selwyn (see the third chapter), once at the brothel asked Hayes about the virginity of her nuns. Alderman Portsoken had told him that he had been surprised to find at the Hayes' one night previously a genuine virgin. Charlotte Hayes, Selwyn relates, gave it as her opinion that a woman could lose her virginity 500 times and yet continue to pass as a virgin. Dr. O'Patrick had restored most satisfactorily her own thousand times lost virginity[1].

England seemed to be the only country in Europe which could boast of the existence of these mediæval malpractices within its borders. One finds it hard to believe that such things as are reported by Stead should have been possible at the end of the nineteenth century: ' When I was carrying out investigations in Ostend I became very uneasy on account of discoveries which were made by a trustworthy agent at the other end of the town. These related to a house which was kept by a seemingly highly respectable midwife, where children of panders were brought before being seduced in order that their virginity might be established, where after the seduction they were brought back to be "patched up", and where abortions could be carried out. The existence of this house was no secret. It was well known in the trade, and my agent was directed to it without any trouble by a "gay woman" whose acquaintance

[1] ' Que quant à l'Hymen, elle avait toujours entendu dire que c'était un dieu, et que par conséquent il ne faisait point partie de la formation de la femme; qu'elle hasardait donc de dire, qu'elle avait maintenant dans son séminaire autant de virginités qu'il en fallait pour contenter toute la cour des Aldermans, et la Chambre des Communes par-dessus la marché; qu'elle avait une personne, Mlle Su . . y, arrivant justment de la Comédie avec le conseiller Pliant, qui, dans une semaine, avait fait trent-trois éditions de virginalité: que Mlle Su . . y, étant la fille d'un libraire, et ayant travaillé sous l'inspection de son père, connaissait la valeur des editions nouvelles ' (*Les Sérails de Londres*, p. 47).

he had opportunely made. The respectable old woman had doubtless another business of a less doubtful character, but in the trade her calling was unquestionably, in the first place, the certification of virginity, and in the second place the reparation of injuries caused by brutality, in which she possessed great skill and dexterity. She knew how these were done, but was powerless to prevent them; all she could do was to alleviate the pain and, so far as possible, repair the damages of debauchery for which she was not responsible nor was she able to control it. She would provide a virgin in order to oblige a client, or rather she delivered as a virgin a girl who had long taken leave of her virginity. The number of patched-up virgins which Madame Jeffries delivered to her aristocratic clientele in the neighbourhood of the Quadrant was regarded as one of the most remarkable sidelines in the business of the great dealer in human beings of Chelsea.'

The disclosures made by the *Pall Mall Gazette*, the most important of which have been reproduced in the foregoing, aroused tremendous excitement. The indignation in England was so great that the prosecution of the editorial staff of the paper was threatened, principally in order to prevent the publication of the names of those accused. Many meetings were held with this object, but the Government gave up the idea of prosecution and answered that they themselves would take steps to investigate the matter in conjunction with the police. In the meantime the *Pall Mall Gazette* demanded that a Commission should be set up, composed of persons of high standing, by which the truth of the facts revealed might be proved. This Commission sat from 11 in the morning till 5 in the evening of 29th July 1885, and its President announced afterwards that the following resolution had been passed:

' In the course of our enquiry we decided to set aside the charges that have been brought against private persons, certain associations and the methods of the police. We confined ourselves to proving the existence of organisations illegally carrying on an immoral trade. Having carefully examined the witnesses and the evidence submitted to us, we have come to the conclusion that, apart from the accuracy of the details—for which we cannot vouch—the facts revealed by the *Pall Mall Gazette* are on the whole correct in their essentials.'—Signed: Edward Benson, Archbishop of Canterbury, A. Temple, Bishop of London, Cardinal Manning, Samuel Morley, M.P., and R. Reid, Q.C.[1]

After the enquiry there was a change over of popular feeling in favour of the *Pall Mall Gazette*, and a general crusade against this criminal traffic was demanded with the object of putting a permanent stop to it.

Hector France described very vividly the celebrated meeting which was held in Hyde Park at the end of August 1885, on the strength of the *Pall Mall Gazette* disclosures. It was one of the largest gatherings within memory. More than 250,000 people of both sexes and all ages and classes took part in it. From 5 o'clock on, on a Saturday afternoon, an enormous crowd of people streamed along Piccadilly to Hyde Park, in the midst of which was borne a large white banner with the inscription ' Honour the *Pall Mall Gazette* ', whilst William Stead rode on a waggon in triumph, through the crowd, who everywhere greeted him with the enthusiastic cry 'Long life to Stead!' Each person carried a bouquet of white roses, the symbol of purity. To be sure, shoulder to shoulder with members of all the religious organisations were prostitutes in large numbers, making up to the men in a free and easy manner and with

[1] Tarnowsky, *loc. cit.*, pp. 41-42.

licentious coarseness. The effect of the religious and moral tracts which were distributed on this occasion was nullified by a pornographic journal *The Devil*, which was also distributed, and on the first page of which three girls in tights displayed their voluptuous charms. Speech after speech from men, and still more from women, continued into the night, and finally the following resolution was unanimously passed:

'The citizens of London declare their shame and indignation with regard to the evils which have been exposed.

'They declare through this meeting that they will support the authorities and will help them in the strict carrying out of the penal laws.

'It is the duty of every good citizen to look social and moral evils resolutely in the face, evils which are the cause of those appalling vices, the victims of which are their own daughters, in order that these evils may be stamped out[1].'

A short time after this meeting there appeared in *Lloyd's News* an article entitled 'A mother who is looking for her daughter'. Stead and his companions were accused of having stolen, seduced and kidnapped the 13-year-old Eliza Armstrong. Stead published in the *Pall Mall Gazette* the particulars of his purchase of the little Eliza, for which he made use of the services of an experienced procuress, took on himself the whole responsibility for the matter, and travelled at once to England from Switzerland, where he then was.

Eliza Armstrong was, as Stead accurately described in the 'Disclosures of the *Pall Mall Gazette*', bought by him through a former prostitute named Jarett, examined by a midwife, Maury, as to her virginity, and drugged with chloroform. Stead was in the room with her, but did not

[1] H. France, *En Police Court*, pp. 18-27.

interfere with her in any way. She was then taken to Paris to be received into the Salvation Army there. Later, when much excitement over the case had been aroused, she was taken back to her parents, who were paid double the amount of the previously agreed sum. Notwithstanding, the case against Stead and his associates, amongst whom was the ' General ' of the Salvation Army, Mr. Booth, was proceeded with zealously, just as if the disclosers of these atrocities were themselves the greatest criminals, whilst the infamous procuress was allowed to proceed peacefully with her horrible work. Stead and his fellow accused, with the exception of Booth, after a long trial full of incidents grave and gay, were sentenced to several months' imprisonment[1].

On 12th January 1886 Stead, at the expiry of his sentence, was released from prison. A great meeting was held in his honour in Exeter Hall the same evening.

The disclosures of the *Pall Mall Gazette* and the perhaps too zealous investigations of Stead, did no damage at all to the London traffic in girls. At first, probably as the result of the uproar which was caused, the price of living wares was somewhat increased. This crisis, however, soon passed over, the business went quietly on its way, and it was possible to say that ' the market has been lively and the demand and number of orders have increased: the supply of " patched up " girls exceeds the demand[2] '.

---

[1] See H. France, *loc. cit.*, pp. 28-90 (' Le Cas d'Elisa Armstrong').

[2] Tarnowsky, *loc. cit.*, p. 43. H. France tells of the case of a certain Louisa Hart, an infamous young procuress, who enticed young girls from the street into her house and gave them over to old men for defloration. (*En Police Court*, pp. 212-220.)

CHAPTER VI

PROSTITUTION AND CRIME

THE relation of prostitution to crime was closer in England than in other countries because English prostitution enjoyed a greater measure of freedom than was possible elsewhere. In England the good of the community was sacrificed to the freedom of the individual. Whilst the spiritual and physical health of the individual was more carefully regulated than his sexual activities, the irregular sex life of society, as one might appropriately term prostitution, could never be kept within bounds nor reduced without causing a great deal of harm, but it could not be allowed to develop free and unhindered. It was in point of fact regarded favourably by the police.

In order to understand the circumstances we must bring to mind the legal inviolability of domestic authority granted by the Habeas Corpus Act, under which the English police dare only enter a dwelling when a crime had been committed or they were authorised by a magistrate's warrant. If it was desired to proceed against a brothel keeper, the law required that two tax-paying plaintiffs living in the same parish should make their complaints to a constable or a tax collector, on which they would be taken before a Justice of the Peace, where they would be obliged to pay £20 security for the costs of prosecution and £50 for the collection of evidence for the trial. Only then would the authorities issue an order for the arrest of the defendant. The plaintiffs

[195]

A HISTORY OF ENGLISH SEXUAL MORALS

appeared before the court, which set the defendant free
against his promise to appear at his trial to defend himself.

At the trial the plaintiffs must furnish circumstantial
evidence. If the defendant was condemned, each of the
plaintiffs had the right to an indemnity of £10; if he were
acquitted, they lost their deposits. As evidence, it was
necessary that one person should declare before the
court that he had committed an act of immorality in the
brothel in question. It can be imagined how difficult it
was to obtain such evidence. If the defendant feared
condemnation, he left the parish where he was accused,
whereupon the trial had to be discontinued and the
defendant who had removed to another parish had to be
proceeded against once more by residents therein in the
same way. If the condemnation of a brothel keeper finally
resulted, he was given only ten days' imprisonment[1].

This legal protection and the great measure of individual
freedom gave a unique character to the social position of
prostitution in England. It might be said that English
prudery tried to regard the situation as non-existent and
to veil its nature, insomuch as the prostitute is no prostitute
before the world. ' Before the law, the evidence of a
prostitute, whatever her class, is as good as any other.'
These anomalies show that there is difficulty in reconciling
ideals and principles with actual facts, which is a common
situation[2].

[1] Hügel, *loc. cit.*, pp. 145-146.
[2] Archenholtz, *England*, Vol. II, p. 249. The authoress of the *Memoirs
of a Singer* says with regard to the relatively good social position of the
London prostitute: ' The street girls, although they are called prostitutes
in the police reports, are at the same time not such social pariahs as on
the continent, and they are better protected by the law than elsewhere;
if they are insulted by anyone, or called dishonourable names, the offender
is punished; they are also not so shunned as a class as elsewhere, and for
this reason they do not call themselves prostitutes, but independent
ladies.' From the *Memoirs of a Singer*, Vol. II, pp. 196-197.

[196]

Another reason for the unrestricted character of English prostitution was the open leniency of the police who, in some ways, played the rôle actually of official bullies to the prostitutes. In the eighteenth century complaints were made about these corrupt conditions. The police then consisted for the most part of the unreliable, sleepy 'parochial watchmen', the 'night constables', whom the people jokingly called 'Charlies'. The modern London police, however, founded by Sir Robert Peel in 1828, had on the whole preserved the old patriarchal attitude towards prostitution. There still existed, as Stead termed it, an 'unnatural alliance' between prostitutes and police[1].

In theory the policeman certainly possesses no power over the house of ill fame. Though if he likes he can make it almost impossible for an open house to do business.

'"The police are the brothel keeper's best friend ", said a former proprietor to me', wrote Stead.

'" In what way? "

'" Because they shut their eyes. And the brothel keepers are the best friends of the police, because they pay them."

'" How much have you paid the police? " I asked him.

'"Three pounds a week whether the times were good or bad," he answered, "and my establishment was only a small one."

'In Edinburgh I received the report of a missionary, who told me that he knew of a case in that town of a gentleman rescuing a girl from the hands of a policeman who had continually threatened her with arrest until she finally acceded to his wishes. He very rightly concluded that for this one known case there were probably hundreds of unknown ones. Many policemen are bachelors and live in barracks

---

[1] It must be pointed out that the days of Stead only are here referred to, i.e. the 1880's, and that Scotland Yard of to-day has nothing to do with the 'unnatural alliance' here referred to.

like soldiers, and to them are entrusted the unconditional control of the streets, which after all are the drawing-rooms of the poor[1].'

Hector France mentions more than once the bribery of the police by prostitutes[2].

In view of all this it is not surprising that prostitution and crime were nowhere so intimately related as in London, where robbery, theft and murder were practised under the eye of the police and went unpunished. The danger of London prostitution is an ever-recurring theme in all accounts of the morals of the English capital.

No less dangerous in London were the conditions in the brothels. The author of *London and Paris* reports: ' The disorderly conduct of the paid prostitutes is so gross that one can hardly speak of it with propriety; it is therefore no wonder that such a fertile source of evil of every kind is so seldom referred to in public. For instance, in Castle Street, Oxford Street, there is hardly a house where from early morning till night-time, it is not possible to see the most revolting spectacles. In particular, there is a house there kept by an old sinner which is remarkable on account of its monstrous licentiousness; to go by appearances, however, this should soon cause its downfall. As many stories are told privately about this house as about an enchanted castle. My gossip had the following at first hand. Yesterday at midnight, he said, a man was thrown out of the window by three women. He fell in the gutter and was half dead before the night watchman discovered him and raised the alarm. The man was drunk, had let himself be enticed into the murderous den and apparently would not pay what he was asked. A quarrel followed and finally the rough

[1] *Der Jungfrauentribut*, pp. 63-66.
[2] *Les Va-nu-Pieds de Londres*, p. 10.

handling[1].' R. Cruikshank has drawn a similar typical brothel scene. A man sits between two prostitutes, one of whom drinks with him while the other takes his money and watch, handing them to a bully hidden in the background. The accompanying text says that the victim will later, completely drunk, be put outside, where he will wake up the next morning[2].

In earlier times the inexperienced provincial immediately on his arrival in London became the victim of rogues and prostitutes. Macaulay gives an exquisite description of the arrival of one of these pitiable ' greenhorns ' in the British metropolis.

' When a landowner from Lincolnshire or Shropshire appeared in Fleet Street, it was as easy for the populace to tell where he came from as if he were a Turk or a Lascar. His dress, his gait, his speech, the way in which he gazed at the shops, stumbled in the gutters, ran up against sack carriers, and stood under the gutters of the roofs, showed him to be a prime subject for the operations of the practical jokers and rogues. Bullies pushed him into the gutter, hackney coachmen bespattered him from head to foot, thieves investigated at their ease the great pockets of his riding coat, while he stood entranced at the glitter of the Lord Mayor's Show.· Swindlers, still sore from a flogging, introduced themselves to him and appeared to him the most respectable and worthy gentlemen he had ever seen. Painted women, the off-scourings of Lewkner Lane and Whetstone Park, represented themselves to him as countesses and noble ladies[3].'

[1] *London and Paris.* Weimar, 1801. Vol. VIII, pp. 171-172.
[2] *Doings in London,* p. 81.
[3] Macaulay, *loc. cit.,* Vol. II, p. 101. It is characteristic that most English descriptions of the morals of London are in the form of the enlightenment of a provincial by one born with a knowledge of all the secrets of the capital. Such is the *Midnight Spy,* Ned Ward's *The London Spy, Doings*

Amongst the criminals and vagabonds connected with prostitution the beggars and receivers should next be mentioned. The London beggars were perhaps the greatest swindlers and cheats in the world. Since the time of the Middle Ages they had their headquarters in the (now rebuilt) neighbourhood of St. Giles and were a well-organised band, which was again divided into different classes, and had its own languages, the so-called ' cant ' or ' slang '. Every day these beggars divided up into single small groups scattered throughout the town. The beggars of St. Giles were once famed as ' men of the world ' amongst the London populace, and carried on regular orgies with the prostitutes, giving themselves up to the most debauched immorality. As Urbanus and Fidelio in the *Midnight Spy* draw near to the vicinity of St. Giles, they hear from afar singing and dancing and learn that here the ' Beggars' Club ' of St. Giles holds its nightly revels; the members during the day received from charitable rich folk the means by which they could spend the night in revellings and excesses[1]. Archenholtz, too, mentions this jovial ' Beggars' Club ' of St. Giles[2].

There was also a ' Beggars' School ' in which an old woman instructed children in the art and the secrets of begging. This ' Academy ' was primarily intended for girls[3].

The receivers, of which Colqhoun in his time counted 3,000, were also in league with the prostitutes, indeed thieves often brought stolen goods into the brothels[4].

in London, etc. Richard King also, in his *Frauds of London*, is specially concerned for the welfare of the poor ' greenhorns ', whom he cannot warn sufficiently against the great number of dangers and rascals of the capital.

[1] *The Midnight Spy*, p. 33.

[2] Archenholtz, *England*, Vol. I, p. 170.

[3] *Doings in London*, p. 119. King William IV was supposed, as Prince of Wales, to have once been present at a ' Beggars' Carnival ' in St. Giles.

[4] *Ibid.*, p. 250.

The ' trappers ' worked with a ' big-bellied ' harlot for the purposes of their swindling and blackmailing operations. One of these girls, noticeably big in the body, would with the help of the 'trapper' and his accomplices, who act as witnesses, get hold of a young man, by whom she would pretend to be pregnant. A policeman was called and the prostitute swore that the man in question was the father of her child, on which there was nothing for him to do but to pay up if he wished to avoid the most unpleasant consequences. Richard King says that the ' trappers ' were in particularly close alliance with the brothels of Covent Garden, Drury Lane and Hedge Lane, and were set by the harlots, bullies, ' setters ' and pickpockets to watch any particularly promising prey. Should the person in question be found sitting one day in a public place, the two ' trappers ' would join him and start the following conversation: ' Jack, that is the gentleman who at such and such a time did so and so to me.' ' Yes, I recognise him quite well. I will give him a good thrashing.' A third scoundrel now comes on the scene and proposes to the gentleman that he should pay these youths money to hush up the matter, as they are capable of committing any crime. He whispers this quietly in his ear. If he refuses the third man begins to argue and there is a quarrel. A crowd collects and often the gentleman gets the worst of it. If he lets himself be persuaded to pay hush money, the trappers have him safe and continue to extort money from him by means of letters and messages which they send him. Nearly always, however, it is the regular frequenters of brothels who fall into the hands of these rogues, as they do not dare to tackle persons they know nothing about[1].

Child substitutors were nearly always recruited from the procuresses' and prostitutes' class. The author of *Doings in*

[1] R. King, *loc. cit.*, pp. 89-91.

London relates the following as a characteristic story of the methods of these infamous individuals: ' A young " green-horn ", fresh from the country, met a street girl in the Haymarket, who in a friendly manner offered him a lodging for the night. He willingly agreed and accompanied her, after much feasting, to her dwelling, No. 2, Union Court, Orchard Street, Westminster, where they spent the night together.

When he awoke in the morning the youth was very much surprised to find that the girl had disappeared and in her place a young baby was fast asleep in the bed. He discovered further that she had taken with her his stockings, with their contents of thirteen sovereigns and some silver. In his dilemma he called the owner of the house, but no one could give him any enlightenment. He protested and swore that the child did not belong to him and that he would not have anything to do with it, and after a stormy scene ran out of the house without stockings to inform the police, who pretended to take steps to find the girl. He was obliged to return home the greater part of the way on foot, in a sad frame of mind, thinking of his foolishness and repenting of it at his leisure[1].'

London was particularly ill-famed for the huge number of pickpockets, both men and women, to be found there. King's belief that there were more pickpockets in London than in the whole of the rest of Europe held good for many years[2]. These criminals were mostly connected in some way with prostitution. Prostitutes were nearly all most skilful pickpockets and generally had male assistance in their thefts. Robbery in the brothels, and also in the dwellings of the independent prostitutes, was an everyday occurrence in

[1] *Doings in London*, p. 91.
[2] R. King, *loc. cit.*, p. 61.

London[1]. As many as thirty or forty prostitutes, dressed as fine ladies, often managed to get into large gatherings in the eighteenth century, especially masked balls, and robbed the guests to their hearts' content. In the year 1795, indeed, on the King's birthday, a common prostitute smuggled herself into a Court ball and took away valuable property to the amount of 1,700 pounds sterling[2]. Moriz tells of his visit to Vauxhall Gardens: ' As all the people came out in a crowd, there was a great cry: "Take care of your pockets!" which meant that a pickpocket in the throng had had a lucky haul[3].'

The last class of London criminals to be considered is that of the professional burglars, robbers and murderers, the ' outbreakers ', ' footpads ' and ' highwaymen '. Whilst the first belonged to the lowest bullies' class, the ' highway-man ' was regarded as the aristocrat of criminals. ' To ensure his success and safety it was necessary for the highway robber to be a bold and skilful rider, and for his manners and his external appearance generally to be those of the owner of a fine steed. For this reason he generally led an aristocratic life, appeared in fashionable coffee and gambling houses, and laid wagers with prominent men at horse races. Sometimes he was in any case a man of good family and breeding; there was, and perhaps still is, a romantic admiration for some of the freelances of this profession. The common man eagerly swallowed the tales of his wildness and dexterity, of the occasional proofs of his generosity and good-heartedness, of his love relationships, of the wonders of his riding, of his desperate fights and of his manly bearing before the court of justice and on the way to the gallows. The highwayman was found on every main country road;

[1] See similar cases in *Doings in London*, p. 91, etc.
[2] *Tableau descriptif de Londres*, Vol. I, pp. 121-122; *Doings in London*, p. 153.
[3] Moriz, *loc. cit.*, p. 36.

the waste land in particular, through which ran the main roads in the vicinity of London, was infested by robbers of this kind. Hounslow Heath on the Great West Road and Finchley Common on the Great North Road were perhaps the most famous of these districts[1].'

One of the most celebrated of the highwaymen was Claude Duval[2], a one-time French page to the Duke of Richmond in the seventeenth century, notable for his gallantry to pretty ladies; on account of his attacks on travellers, Holloway between Islington and Highgate was for a long time unsafe. After his death a street there was named ' Duval's Lane '.

' It was told how Claude Duval took to the woods, was the leader of a terrible gang and had the honour of being cited in a King's Proclamation as the foremost amongst known criminals; how he, at the head of his band, held up the carriage of a lady from which a booty of 400 pounds was taken, how he only kept 100 pounds for himself and promised to give the rest back to the fair owner if she would dance a Coranto with him on the heath; how his bewitching gallantry won the hearts of the women, how his skill in the use of the sword and pistol made him the terror of all men; how at the end of 1670 he was overpowered when full of sweet wine, and how ladies of the highest rank visited him in prison and pleaded for his life[3]. Equally loved by the ladies was M'Lean, the " fashionable highwayman " in the first half of the eighteenth century. Horace Walpole was overtaken and robbed in Hyde Park by this man on a November night in 1749[4].'

---

[1] Macaulay, *loc. cit.*, Vol. II, pp. 112, 113.
[2] A full account of him is given in the chapter ' Notorious Highwaymen ' in the *Romance of London* by John Timbs, pp. 241-269.   See also J. Rodenberg, *Studienreisen in England* ('Instructive Excursions in England '). Leipzig, 1872. Pp. 285-293.
[3] Macaulay, *loc. cit.*, Vol. II, p. 114.
[4] *The Romance of London*, p. 249.

The close relationship between the criminals of London and prostitution is shown particularly clearly by the fact that in the ‘ Thieves’ Clubs ’ and the thieves’ quarters, prostitutes play a prominent part. Archenholtz says that girls (‘ whose beautiful form is intended by nature to be honoured ’) belong to most of the robber gangs. During the daytime these girls acted as spies, at night as assistants. The Parish of St. Giles had many thieves’ clubs, i.e., houses where the thieves congregated in large numbers and held licentious orgies with their prostitutes. There was a particularly ill-famed public-house in St. Giles which bore the inscription ‘ Here you may get drunk for a penny, dead drunk for twopence, and get straw for nothing ’. In the cellars of these houses men and women held debauches day and night[1]. The ‘ Blood Bowl House ’ in Smithfield was another of the same kind, which Hogarth represents in the ninth number of *Industry and Idleness*. There was a beer-house in the cellar which was a meeting-place for the most abandoned male and female rogues.

In those days the two main headquarters of London criminals were the ‘ Golden Lane ’ district and that of Whitefriars. Of Golden Lane, Stype writes as early as 1567: ‘ Of no great account either for buildings or inhabitants[2].’ Whitefriars, on the borders of the City and the Temple, sheltered in every house, from the cellar to the roof, rogues and infamous creatures whom ‘ women even worse than they had followed into their retreats[3] ’.

The gambling houses were also centres of crime and prostitution in London in the eighteenth century, and were at that time at the height of their prosperity. Sexual activity is often combined with gambling, as is anything

[1] Archenholtz, *England*, Vol. I, p. 173.
[2] Wheatley, *loc. cit.*, Vol. II, p. 121.
[3] Macaulay, *loc. cit.*, Vol. II, p. 93.

which will induce a state of high nervous excitement. C. J. Weber remarks: ' Play leads to other excesses—little good comes from easily got money; one. is in the mood for pleasure, and he who loses seeks to drown his care—and so takes refuge in both wine and women![1] '

Card sharpers and big gamblers were very glad to make use of the services of pretty women in order to heighten the attractions of the game, and to console unlucky players for their losses and encourage them to lay fresh wagers. The French emigrants in London not only increased the number of gambling dens to a considerable extent, but also introduced to them a large and dubious female element[2]. ' Here at the gaming tables many ladies ape the sirens of old times. They use the influence of their beauty to lead men to ruin[3].'

According to Colqhoun there were at the end of the eighteenth century about 2,000 professional gamblers, sharpers and ' black-feet ' in London, and in Westminster alone 40 gambling houses, where Faro-banks were held the whole day long and ' Rouge et Noir ' and other games of chance were played. From this place five ladies of fashion received for each ' rout ' 50 pounds and also one-eighth of the winnings. Seven gambling houses were supported by subscription, six admitted only their own clients, and three were open to any stranger or debauchee. Wine and food were to be had in any quantity in all[4]. In addition, in nearly all public places of amusement and at balls there was gambling. Archenholtz says: ' Never was gambling so general in England. In very many prominent houses

[1] Carl Julius Weber, *Deutschland, oder Briefe eines in Deutschland reisenden Deutscher* ('Germany, or Letters from a German travelling in Germany '). Third edition. Stuttgart. Vol. IV, p. 145.

[2] Colqhoun, *loc. cit.*, p. xliii.

[3] Archenholtz, *Annalen*, Vol. XI, p. 422.

[4] Colqhoun, *loc. cit.*, p. xxix.

assemblies and balls were held simply for the purpose of gambling[1].'

Some of the ill-famed gambling dens which existed up to the middle of the nineteenth century were those in St. James's Street, Waterloo Place and Park Place. Amongst the worst in the eighteenth century was ' Mordington's ', a gambling house in the vicinity of Covent Garden, whose owner was a certain woman named Mordington, and which was referred to by the Middlesex jury in the year 1744 as ' a place of debauchery, idleness and evil[2] '. This gambling house was closely connected with the brothel kept by Molly King, which was usually visited by players from the house[3].

Mention should also be made here of the remarkable ' Blasphemous clubs ', clubs [4] for special pornographic purposes which combined sexual excesses with atrocities of all kinds. These were gatherings, mostly of men, but also of women and men, who aimed at suitably combining immorality and outrage[5]. Smollett lays the responsibility for the demoralisation and depravity of his time to a large extent on these clubs[6]. Macaulay says that thieves and robbers were hardly so dangerous to peaceful citizens as the members of these clubs, who, like the sadists, combined crime with excess.

These ' blasphemous societies ' originated in the time of the Restoration. It was then a favourite pastime ' for licentious young gentlemen to go about the streets creating an uproar, breaking windows, overturning sedan chairs,

[1] Archenholtz, *Annalen*, Vol. V, p. 337.
[2] Wheatley, *loc. cit.*, Vol. II, p. 563.
[3] *Sérails de Londres*, pp. 3-4.
[4] With regard to these, so far as sexual perversities are concerned, see Chapters VI and VII.
[5] ' They added blasphemy to riot.'—J. Timbs, *Clubs and Club Life in London* (1872), p. 38.
[6] *Ibid.*

thrashing peaceful men, and importuning pretty women with their coarse pleasantries'. Since the Restoration various different bands of these tyrants had ruled over the streets. Pepys mentions in his *Diary* the 'Ballers' of this time: 'Harry Killigrew explained to me what the latterly much-discussed society, the " Baller ", really is. It consists of some young fools amongst whom he himself is included and of Lady Bennet with her women; they indulge in all imaginable immoralities and excesses and dance there completely naked[1].'

Somewhat later, in the time of Queen Anne, the Mohocks or Mohawks led their crazy existence. They dragged people into the streets at night time, beat them up and stabbed them, cut pieces off them and ' roasted ' others. The most barbaric members of the Mohocks Club were called ' Tumblers '. They stood girls and women on their heads. Yet other unique outrages were practised by the ' Sweaters '. Six of them surrounded the victim and placed the points of their swords against him. Those ' Sweaters ' to whom the back of the attacked man was turned, pricked him with their swords on ' that part where the schoolboy is punished ', and when he turned round for pain, the other 'Sweaters' repeated this ' pricking operation '. In No. 332 of the *Spectator* an adventure of this kind was described. Another wild pastime of the Mohocks was to put women in casks and let them roll down Ludgate or Snow Hill.

The principle of the ' Bold Bucks ' was to act in ' flaming lust ' in the same manner as their animal namesakes. They dragged all females indiscriminately into the streets— mothers and grandmothers as well as daughters. Even their own sisters feared their lust and avoided their vicinity.

---

[1] Macaulay, *loc. cit.*, Vol. II, pp. 90-91. J. Timbs, *loc. cit.*, p. 33, mentions ' Mums ', ' Nickers ', ' Hawkabites '.

' Blind bold love ' was their motto, and they behaved like the beasts after which they were named[1].

The ' Hell-fire Club ', the head of which was the Duke of Wharton, was very celebrated in the first half of the eighteenth century. It specialised in more ' transcendental wickedness ' in that its members used the ritual of religious cults at their gatherings; these were held in small taverns, and the ceremonies were carried out with ' the greatest regularity ' and with ' Obscenities, curses, blasphemies ' [2]. According to Archenholtz' description it must have been a sort of ' Satan's Club ', and probably celebrated ' black masses '. He said: ' A few years ago a society was formed, the object of which was to make fun of all religions. They called it the Hell-fire Club. Their assembly hall was turned into a sort of temple in which stood an altar where they prayed in secret to the devil. Every gathering of members of this hellish Order began with an invocation, entreating the invisible help of Satan's godhead. The well-known Lord Sandwich and many other prominent Britons were members of this peculiar club, which is however done away with[3] '. Arthur Dinaux says that the Hell-fire Club was a company of roués who, unconcerned with politics, employed their time in eating and drinking and enjoying life *per fas et nefas*[4].

The Hell-fire Club became so mischievous that a Bill for its suppression was brought in in the Upper House, during the discussion of which the Earl of Peterborough declared that he stood for a parliamentary king but not for a parliamentary religion, and the Duke of Wharton, with an old family bible in his hand, tried to belittle the charges made against the club[5].

[1] Malcolm, *loc. cit.*, Vol. I, p. 264.
[2] *Ibid.*, p. 265.
[3] Archenholtz, *England*, Vol. I, p. 279.
[4] Arthur Dinaux, *Les Sociétés Badines*. Paris, 1867. Vol. I, p. 319.
[5] J. Timbs, *loc. cit.*, p. 38.

In March 1788 a club was discovered with the significant name of the ' Cock and Hen Club '. ' Under this title ', says Archenholtz, ' licentious creatures gathered together in the parish of Clerkenwell in the northern district of the capital. The club had a male and a female president. Here unbridled excesses were carried on, disturbing the neighbours, and after much difficulty fifteen constables succeeded in raiding the club. There they found 157 persons of both sexes, mostly hopelessly drunk, who defended themselves with sticks, tongs and shovels, but were overpowered. Most of them then threw themselves out of the window or off the roof, but sixty were captured and taken to prison.'

The most fashionable of all the clubs of this kind which were carried on in distinguished circles was the ' Order of St. Francis of Medmenham Abbey ', so called after the founder.

He had studied exhaustively in Italy the communities of monks and nuns which seemed to him to go so much against nature and reason, and after he returned to England he decided to found a burlesque institution in the name of Saint Francis which would clearly demonstrate the absurdity of the cloister and would be the home not of asceticism but of happy jollity and unrestrained sociability. He therefore associated himself with several other prominent men of the world with this end in view. They rented a small island in the Thames near Hampton, built a fine house containing many comfortable rooms, a library, a music room, a gaming room, etc., and called it Medmenham Abbey. The company spent several months here in the summer, and so that Adam should not be alone, it was incumbent on every member to bring with him a lady of ' lively, easy and agreeable charac- ter'. Opulent dinners were given there, at which the wine conduced much to the enlivenment of the company, and after which the ladies usually withdrew with their chosen.

[210]

The talk during the meal was transparently licentious and full of double meanings, increasing the excitement of the company. A special dress was worn with great piety by both male and female 'Franciscans'. Reception into the Order took place in a special chapel, with peals of bells and music, before twelve ' knights ', to whom the candidates made their confession of faith and swore fealty[1]. So long as the ladies stayed in Medmenham Abbey they regarded themselves as the legitimate wives of the monks, and each monk took care not to disturb the honeymoon of the others. In order that a woman should not be discovered there by her husband, father or other acquaintance, these unique priestesses of Venus arrived masked, passed all the monks in review, and only unmasked when they were sure that there was no danger. Otherwise they could at once withdraw unhindered. At these gatherings of the monks and nuns of Medmenham Abbey, all ' forms of physical and platonic love ' were tried out, and the conversation was often so obscene and licentious that the ladies used their fans to hide their blushes, and very often made the pretence of shyness an excuse to ' retire for a time with their lovers '. Particularly noteworthy was the fact that this pious cloister availed itself of the services of midwives and doctors to a great extent. In certain cases the ladies, when they thought it necessary, could retire for a time from the world, and in Medmenham Abbey contribute to the increase of the population. The children resulting from these unions were ' sons and daughters of the Holy Francis ' and were brought up at Medmenham Abbey[2].

---

[1] John Wilkes indulged in a rough joke at the admission of Jemmy Twitcher (Lord Sandwich). See W. F. Rae. *Wilkes, Sheridan, Fox, the Opposition under George the Third.* London, 1874. P. 58.

[2] *Les Sérails de Londres,* pp. ix-xv.

CHAPTER VII

THE MAGDALEN HOUSES, SOCIETIES FOR THE SUPPRESSION OF PROSTITUTION, AND ABOLITIONISM

THE oldest ' Rescue Houses ' for prostitutes were in France, where Archbishop William as early as the year 1226 founded the ' Maison des Filles-Dieu ', towards which King Louis the Holy gave a considerable sum on condition that 200 girls should be taken in. In 1490 a monk, Jean Tisserand, founded the ' Maison des Filles-pénitentes '. The first ' Magdalen Establishment ' was erected in 1618 by a merchant, Robert de Montry[1].

In England the ' Magdalen Institutions ' or ' Asylums ' have only been in existence since the eighteenth century.

The oldest is the celebrated Magdalen Hospital, which is still in existence, and which in the year 1758 was founded by the unfortunate Court chaplain (who ended on the gallows), Dr. William Dodd, its first home being in Prescot Street, Goodman's Fields. Horace Walpole visited it from Northumberland House with a large party shortly after it was opened on 27th January 1760, and thus writes about it: ' Prince Edward, Colonel Brudenel, his groom, Lady Northumberland, Lady Mary Coke, Lady Carlisle, Miss Pelham, Lady Hertford, Lord Beauchamp, Lord Huntingdon, Mr. Bowman and I. . . . The Magdalens sang a hymn, you cannot think how

[1] Dufour, *loc. cit.* Hügel, *loc. cit.*, p. 219.

beautifully. . . . Dr. Dodd, the unfortunate minister, preached in the French manner, very eloquent and stirring. When closing, he turned to His Royal Highness, whom he addressed as " Most Illustrious Prince ", and begged his protection, and I suggested to the " illustrious one" that he should ask for the sermon to be printed[1].

In the year 1772 the Magdalen Hospital was removed to St. George's Fields. At that time a very interesting description of it appeared in the periodical *London and Paris* as follows: ' If you go out over Blackfriars Bridge, after about half-an-hour, you come on the right-hand side to the Hospital of this name for repentant sinners. . . . London has amongst other virtues, the merit of trying to reduce the number of these hindrances (to betterment), although only a few amongst the many "women of the town" make use of the philanthropic establishment at Magdalen House. Admission is obtained on a written petition only. As there are many amongst these unfortunate women who are of good family and upbringing, a distinction has been made between them, so that the better sort will not be frightened away, and these are put together, as also those of the lower class. Each one does a certain amount of work, and what she earns from it, in accordance with the decision of the committee for the time being, is added to the small capital which is given to her on leaving, so that she may be able to support herself. It is left entirely to her own choice as to what she does in this direction, and the sale of the articles is arranged by certain people outside the establishment. The women are treated with the greatest consideration and kindness, so that no unpleasant thoughts of prison may be connected with the house. After three years they often go into service or return to their parents.

[1] *Walpole's Letters to George Montagu*, Vol. III, p. 282. Quoted according to Wheatley, *loc. cit.*, Vol. II, p. 454.

[213]

'On admission, the woman is required to sign the rules which are to be observed, and she engages either to pay a yearly sum of £10 for board, lodging and necessaries, or to stay in the hostel for three years; the Board has power to discharge anyone should it think fit. In any case, no female who has once been admitted may leave the house without a permit from the Superintendent. Each one has her own bed and locker, of which she keeps the key herself. In many rooms there are small cabinets or alcoves, which as a reward for good behaviour are allotted to the best of the inmates, so that in their leisure hours they may be alone. Their real names are written in the register, but they prefer to be known by fictitious names. No reference is made to their former way of life, and the slightest hint of it even is forbidden. In the institution they are all dressed alike in light grey uniform; their other clothing is equally simple and extraordinarily clean; on the whole their appearance must be very attractive. A young man who had the opportunity of seeing all the Magdalens assembled together could hardly describe the effect made on him by the sight of so many attractive women, whose simple clothes, modesty proper to the place, serious cloister-like demeanour, and consciousness of guilt, lent them an irresistible, winning charm. He felt, on thinking it over afterwards, that the forms, faces and spiritual characteristics he had seen there must melt the cold heart of any conscientious judge and move him to acquit the beautiful sinners unconditionally.

'The life is strenuous and regular. Excess and licentious conversation is punished with arrest and forfeiture of wages.

'And what use is made of this kindly philanthropic institution? Published reports state that from 1758, when it was founded, to Christmas 1786, no less than 2,471 women had been admitted. Of this number 300, accustomed to an independent life, could not tolerate the restrictions of the

[214]

community and were obliged to leave; 45 came either because they were out of their minds or had incurable diseases; 60 died; 52 never came back to the establishment from the hospitals where they had been sent for treatment; 338 were dismissed for various faults and disorderly behaviour, but 1,608 were either sent back to their parents improved(?), or they married, or took up some useful calling[1].'

The other principal institutions for repentant prostitutes in London were the Lock Asylum, founded in 1787 for girls who had left the hospital of the same name, and admitting 18 to 20 persons; the 'London Female Penitentiary' in Pentonville, founded in 1807, which took in 93 girls; the Guardian Society, which was founded in 1812 for the admission of 31 prostitutes; the 'Maritime Penitent Refuge' for sailors' prostitutes, which was founded in 1829; and further the 'British Penitent Female Refuge', the 'Female Mission South London Penitentiary', etc.[2]

According to Ryan, from the foundation of the first five Magdalen Hospitals till 1838, about 11,000 persons altogether were admitted, whilst during the same time four million were submerged in prostitution! During the same period 462 million pounds was spent in the pursuit of excesses, and not the tenth part in the reduction of them[3].

Alongside the Magdalen Houses were the Foundling Hospitals, of which there was only one in London. At the end of the eighteenth century it could take in 550 foundlings. But from each mother, who was obliged to legitimatise it, only one child was taken, in order not to encourage immorality[4].

---

[1] *London and Paris.* Weimar, 1799. Vol. III, pp. 110-116. Most of the girls when they were discharged were not yet twenty years old. See *The Picture of London*, 1818, p. 209, where there is also a description of this old Magdalen house.

[2] Ryan, *loc. cit.*, p. 127. Hügel, *loc. cit.*, p. 220.

[3] Ryan, *loc. cit.*, p. 187.

[4] *London and Paris*, Vol. XII, p. 237.

In connection with these institutions there have always been in England, and especially in London, many so-called ' Morality Societies '[1], which exist for the suppression of the evil of prostitution and its accompanying vice.

As early as the beginning of the eighteenth century there was a ' Society for the Reformation of Manners '. The Bishop of London preached for it in the year 1726 against the excesses and immorality of the masked balls[2]. ' The Society for the Suppression of Vice,' founded in 1802, became of considerable importance. The philanthropist, Wilberforce, states the aim of this society in his preface to the ' Report of the Society for the Suppression of Vice '.

The minimum annual subscription was one guinea. The aims of the institution were:

1. Prevention of the secularising of Sunday.
2. Obeying the precepts of the Scriptures.
3. Suppression of obscene books and pictures.
4. Supervision and extermination of open houses.
5. Taking of measures against fortune tellers, male and female.

So far as the fourth point is concerned, the Society does not appear to have been very successful. From 1802 to 1817 eleven brothels in all were suppressed through the ' Society for the Suppression of Vice '; in the year 1837 it was only able, in spite of all its efforts, to obtain the legal suppression

---

[1] A modern author criticises these societies very sharply: ' He belonged to a self-constituted Society of National Purity, which rather helped to spread unclean practices and create impure thoughts; as, for the rest, is the natural tendency of all such Associations. These men sometimes took upon themselves to apply the necessary correction or antidote, and the world at large would be indeed startled did it know of the impure punishments inflicted in its name and for its social purification' (*Raped in the Railway*, p. 177). It is indeed possible that doubtful elements were sometimes smuggled into these societies and, under the cover of the fight against vice, carried out their unsavoury projects.

[2] H. D. Traill, *Social England*. London, 1896. Vol. V, p. 141.

of 18 out of the 2–3,000 brothels in London[1]. A clearer example could not be found of the folly of attempts to suppress prostitution by force.

In May 1835 the ' London Society for the Protection of Young Females and Prevention of Juvenile Prostitution ' started its activities. It received much support, especially from the higher ranks of the clergy[2].

In the year 1847 Naval Lieutenant Blackmore associated with a City Missionary, Mr. John Vanderkiste, in a ' courageous effort to save or improve a handful of these victims of battle '. He founded, with his own money and with the support of many friends, two houses for the admission and care of unfortunate girls, the so-called ' Female Temporary Homes '. ' The hardest part of the work, which required the complete surrender of the soul, was the seeking out of the victim of social evil in her haunts, so glamorous by night and so melancholy by day, talking to her quietly and—once she had recovered sobriety—knowing how to persuade her through unremitting kindness of the underlying virtues of purity and modesty. These Franklins and MacClintocks of morality went on their moonlight expeditions from Gray's Inn Lane, through Holborn Hill and Fleet Street to Regent Street, Oxford Street and Tottenham Court Road, the great centres of vice, frivolity and misery, and they repeated these journeys evening after evening for some years, parting company at certain places and meeting again at others.

' They distributed amongst the people whom they were trying to get hold of, leaflets with the address of a guest house in which they could find shelter, a fire and a little food. Like ships at sea, these brave travellers kept their "Log-books" in which they recorded the details and the results of their expeditions. The "Log-books" were printed

[1] Ryan, *loc. cit.*, pp. 90, 108, 148.
[2] *Ibid.*, p. 118.

from time to time, and distributed to friends and supporters of the Moonlight Mission. No novel reads so interestingly as these pages, in which the deepest misery, the lowest depravity and the deepest remorse are depicted; none however could arouse so powerfully in the breast of the reader such a growing sense of pity, of abhorrence, of hate and of love. It often happened—the reports in the "Log-book" mention this—that readers became lovers; in one case a conversion led to three offers of marriage, one of which, that of a minister of the Evangelical High Church, was accepted. Here we have reality and the tragic grandeur of fate. Here we have as scenery the beautiful streets of London in the gaslight and moonlight; here we have as heroines the loveliest and unhappiest girls in England, and for heroes two men, saving souls in this medley of dance, glitter, music, wine and patchouli[1].'

The first approach to the girls to be saved was generally through the giving of a religious book, tract or leaflet, as G. Rasch (see above) tells us. North Peat says in this connection in his *Stars of the Night, or Humorous Curiosities in England*: ' It was ten o'clock in the evening. We were furnished with small religious and moral tracts which had, besides the good advice contained in them, the address of our house on the wrapper, and on another page an invitation to the lost girl to visit us. It is curious to note that these brochures, in order to make it more likely that they would be accepted, were usually so done up as to give them the appearance of a letter or note[2].'

Later, girls who were amenable to this religious influence were invited to the so-called ' Morality teas ', where, to the accompaniment of tea, food and pious songs, repentance

---

[1] J. Rodenberg, *Day and Night in London*, pp. 256-262.
[2] Extract from C. J. Lecour, *La Prostitution à Paris et à Londres*. Paris, 1882. P. 274.

was preached[1]. Hector France describes one of these *Thé moralisateur* very vividly if satirically. It was given by the ' Blue Ribbon Army ' to a number of ballet dancers, and ten sermons were preached one after another at short intervals in one and the same evening. A great tumult arose, which finally developed into a regular fight[2]. Also an indication of how far one can get by these methods. Do people really believe that prostitution can be prevented by sermons?

The conclusions that Tarnowsky drew from the efforts of the English Magdalen Houses and morality societies are in this regard very instructive. In his opinion, none of these societies is of the slightest use in the matter of prostitution, nor can ever be. This is clearly to be seen from the financial reports of the most genuine of these societies. The 'Guardian Society', for example, from 1812 to 1850 provided 1,932 prostitutes with shelter, of which 843 left the institution or had to be sent away for improper behaviour, 533 were returned to their families, that is to the same relatives who had sold them or given them to prostitution, 53 were sent to their own parishes by the society, whereby their later fate was unknown, 17 died in the institution, 31 remained in the institution and 455 took posts, or in any case, after they left the asylum, supported themselves more or less respectably. Their fate is also unknown. Tarnowsky concludes from this report that three-fourths of the prostitutes who are admitted to asylums go back to prostitution and that the last fourth is not finally rescued from prostitution. ' What proportion of those who are "Turned to Truth" fall into prostitution again after a month or two, the philanthropic society is unable to say. It has fulfilled its task, it has helped the unfortunates in need of help, has made the

[1] Lecour, *loc. cit.*, p. 273.
[2] H. France, *En Police Court*, pp. 228-237.

immorality of their position clear to them, showed them the possibility of honest service, and provided them with the means of continuing on this path, also promised them future support. The society is in the right; but the prostitute is also in the right, who, after a month or a year in the path of virtue exclaims: ' Kill me rather once and for all, but I cannot live this life any longer, my soul yearns for the old ways[1].'

In face of these facts, the efforts made by the so-called ' Abolitionists[2] ' are highly irrational if not dangerous. The idea of Abolitionism is the removal from prostitution of all supervision and the abolition of the former as a lawful and tolerated institution.

Mrs. Josephine Butler founded in the year 1875 the ' Ladies' National Association for the Repeal of the Contagious Diseases Act ' as well as an International League, the ' Fédération britannique, continentale et générale ', with the object of suppressing the regulation of prostitution in some English towns which had resulted from the passing in 1864 of the ' Contagious Diseases Act '. This Association has since then organised assemblies every year in different European countries. In the year 1889 its principles were laid before the Congress in Geneva in the form of eighteen theses, which have since been established as the programme of abolitionism at congresses in Genoa, The Hague and in London. These run:

1. Moral principles for both sexes are inseparable and alike.
2. The natural rights of the man are the same as those of the woman.

[1] Tarnowsky, *loc. cit.*, pp. 111-112.
[2] Not to be confused with American Abolitionism, which means the abolition of slavery, and which ceased to exist on the 1st January 1863, when its object was accomplished.

Artist unknown

DAYS OF PROSPERITY IN GLOUCESTER PLACE OR A KEPT MISTRESS IN HIGH FEATHER.

CARTOON OF 1809 REFERRING TO THE DUKE OF YORK AND HIS MISTRESS

[*Pl.* 16

3. Offences against purity are as culpable on the man's side as on that of the woman.

4. Self-control in matters of sex is one of the most important principles of health for individuals and for the community.

5. The State, as the representative of justice, should in no case countenance evil, and least of all ally itself with vice.

6. Prostitution is a basic infringement of the laws of nature and hygiene; its organisation is directly opposed to the laws which penalise instigation to immorality.

7. The legal guarantees of personal liberty must be the same for both sexes.

8. The law should allow no infringement of the right which every woman possesses to control her own affairs.

9. Any regulation of prostitution is not only powerless against the spread of syphilis, but is favourable to this; in addition it encourages immorality, leads to an increase in the percentage of illegitimate births, to the growth of secret prostitution and the decrease of social and individual morality. The regulation of prostitution as a prophylactic against disease which is produced through prostitution, must be unconditionally rejected.

10. The State, whose duty it is to protect both sexes in the same measure, demoralises the prostitutes themselves by regulation and therefore lowers the status of women. The compulsory medical examination of harlots—the foundation of any regulation—is an insult to the woman, and calls for so much the greater opposition, because it leads to the complete submerging of the unfortunate creature who is forced to submit to it, in extinguishing the last rays of modesty, which even the most outcast do not altogether lack.

11. Compulsory medical examination is a false guarantee of the health of the woman examined. It is a betrayal of society under the cloak of medical sanction and at the same time an attack upon personal liberty which, if at all, should be made upon both sexes alike.

12. Compulsory medical examination of men or women applied under regulation does violence in a revolting manner to the rights of man, is an insult to the best achievements of civilisation and an unfortunate hygienic error. The licensing of open houses sanctions an immoral convention which regards immorality as necessary for the man.

13. The open house leads to degradation of morality, is dangerously stimulating, and a school of dishonour.

14. The women of the open house are kept there by force and become regular slaves; they are subject to the caprices of the owner, who has complete control over their minds and bodies.

15. The State should use no hygienic methods for cleansing prostitution, inasmuch as there is no question here of danger which is external as in an epidemic, but of one which men risk of their own free will, knowing of its existence.

16. The State must prohibit all collective organisation of prostitution in all forms and prosecute all those connected with it; it must stamp out vice instead of allying itself with it and regulating it.

17. The concepts which arise from the regulation of vice are not consistent with the salvation of the victims of prostitution.

18. The regulation of prostitution is, as experience teaches, a very great hindrance to the conversion of prostitutes, inasmuch as registration and medical examination

injure the modesty to which no harlot is a stranger, and make more difficult the possible and desirable conversion of the fallen to the path of honour[1].

In order to pronounce a correct judgment on these points, it must be borne in mind, as Blaschko very rightly shows, that there are two kinds of abolitionism, which may be designated pious and radical abolitionism.

Pious abolitionism, which regards prostitution as an immoral arrangement and extra-marital sexual intercourse as a sin, thinks to exterminate prostitution through *abolition* of regulation. According to its tenets, regulation cannot be consistent with the moral or Christian idea of the State; they describe it as an immoral pact between the State and vice, which latter should not be regarded as an unavoidable social phenomenon, but should be destroyed and penalised.

Radical abolitionism certainly recognises the necessity for, and the impossibility of exterminating, prostitution, and it does not become indignant over the immorality of ' State as pander ', but it holds that regulation is injurious to the liberty of the citizen and an encroachment on the rights of the individual, also that it entails oppression of the possessionless for the benefit of the possessor, and of the female sex for the benefit of the male. It therefore demands the freedom of prostitution[2].

Professor Benjamin Tarnowsky, in his important book on *Prostitution and Abolitionism* (Hamburg, 1890), has clearly shown the complete futility of the principles of the latter. I can only advise the reader who wishes for further information on this important subject to go to his book. The

[1] Tarnowsky, *loc. cit.*, pp. 16-18.
[2] A. Blaschko, *Syphilis and Prostitution from the point of view of public health regulation.* Berlin, 1893. P. 144. The same writer in the 'International Conference on the prophylaxy of syphilis and venereal diseases'. *German Medical Weekly.* 1899. No. 39.

author indicates therein that to desire the extermination of prostitution is a Utopian idea, also that it is a grave error to suppose that State supervision has in itself a demoralising effect on society, and that the brothels in no way favour the spread of prostitution. Also that supervision neither constitutes any guarantee nor is a suppression of the right of the individual to prostitute herself. According to Tarnowsky it is also indisputable that rational regulation prevents the spread of syphilis.

Blaschko has also severely criticised the ideas of the abolitionists, in that he declares the opinion of the ' pious ' abolitionists that the State should have nothing to do with prostitution in any way but should suppress and penalise it in all its branches, is not open to discussion, as the State must make allowances for the actual needs of society, and must mitigate or lessen as far as possible the consequences of the satisfaction of these needs. With ' radical ' abolitionism Blaschko agrees to this extent that he would do away with the whole institution of ' moral police ' as it exists to-day, and in its place provide sound sanitary supervision. That ' the danger of prostitution, in consequence of professional operations—in conformity with the law that the danger is increased fourfold in ratio to the number of sexual relationships—is so excessively great that, in face of the impossibility of the individual protecting himself adequately, it is necessary and right for society to do this[1].'

I must say that I have great sympathy with Blaschko's opinion that that melancholy institution, the ' moral police ', should be done away with. But I cannot understand how it is possible to carry out a regular sanitary supervision without police help. A certain amount of coercion must be used with prostitutes in this connection, and as the doctors

[1] Blaschko, *loc. cit.*, pp. 144-146.

[224]

themselves cannot use it, the help of the police organisation in the regulation of prostitution, the necessity for which the humane and philanthropic Blaschko himself recognises, cannot be dispensed with.

There is no doubt in any case that the present methods of regulating prostitution can be considerably improved. The ' brothel slaves ' who are spoken of in the 14th thesis of the Abolitionists should not exist. Procuresses and bullies must be punished unmercifully. I am, in spite of all attacks upon brothels, of the opinion that a State-housed prostitution offers the greatest safeguard against all these evil conditions.

If society is to be forcibly cured of the unfortunate errors which at the same time are certainly not answerable for its sickness, and submitted to regular supervision in order to protect it from ill health, the State is justified in preventing as far as possible prostitution and sexual excesses and irregularities of every kind (even the morbid) which are liable to injure society. It is not necessary to be a criminal in order to endanger the well-being of the community. And therefore it is the duty of the State to protect society from evil, whatever its origin. In this the idea of abolitionism is justified.

I close with a few antitheses which Tarnowsky has opposed to the Abolitionists:

The good of the community is the principal aim of all legislation.

In the name of this good the interests of the individual must be sacrificed to those of society.

Prostitution cannot be suppressed either by penalisation nor by regulation, nor by complete freedom in the traffic of the body.

Unconditional penalising of prostitution leads to the

growth of its more hidden forms, to the development of family prostitution.

Free prostitution leads to unhindered competition in the strengthening and multiplication of the arts of provocation to immorality and at the same time to the combining of prostitution with other licentious activities.

Failure in regularising prostitution, that is failure in compulsory supervision and hospital treatment of the infected prostitutes, leads undeniably to an increase in the spread of syphilis through these last.

Syphilis is not only a bodily disease which is acquired in the course of guilty sexual relationships as, so to speak, a merited punishment for vice. On the contrary, the worst consequence of syphilis is that it causes the innocent to suffer.

A well-governed society is bound, through the taking of appropriate measures for the protection of its members, to look to the future as well as the present as regards the consequences of syphilis.

Regulation of prostitution, by means of which the demoralising influence of the latter on society is lessened and the mischief caused by the spread of syphilis reduced—such regulation does not aim at depriving those women who practise immorality as a profession of the right to prostitute themselves, but on the contrary to limit this personal right through a series of practical regulations.

Just as limitation of the sale of wine and regulation of licences does not take from the drinkers the right to get drunk, so the legal supervision of prostitution and the brothels is not an encouragement but a limitation of the freedom of immoral and licentious persons.

Legal impartiality and not the caprice of the administrators must govern the registration of prostitutes.

For the purpose of limiting the spread of syphilis and venereal infections through prostitution, strenuous measures must be taken to: 1. Reduce the mortality of prostitutes themselves; 2. Protect the community from the spread of the disease through already infected prostitutes; and 3. Bring into operation the most suitable methods of treating diseased prostitutes.

In the present condition of society I hold that the doctrine which teaches that freedom of prostitution is a criminal weakness is unworthy of true philanthropy[1].

[1] Tarnowsky, *loc. cit.*, pp. 215-218.

CHAPTER VIII

THE RESTORATION

THE immorality of English sexual life reached its culminating point during the Restoration period. Never before—nor since—have such orgies been indulged in. Crude and vulgar sensuality and brutish lust prevailed to a greater extent in the reign of Charles II than ever before.

Despite their efforts to imitate French manners, Charles's court and the whole society of those times were far from showing the elegant refinement and wit which caused French corruption to appear in so attractive a light. One should not be misled by reading the *Memoirs of Grammont* by Hamilton, in which the state of affairs is considerably idealised. When Hamilton says 'At court all was happiness and pleasure, refinement and splendour such as may be called forth only by a prince of gentle and noble character. Beauties sought only to be enchanting, men tried to please and everyone made the most of their natural gifts. Some of them distinguished themselves by the grace of their dancing, some in the magnificence of their appearance and some by their wit, but most of them by their love affairs and very few of them by their faithfulness[1]', he gives with concise brevity a brilliant picture of the frivolity and cynicism of that society. One important feature, however, was passed over, one which impressed its specific English

---

[1] *The Memoirs of Count Grammont*, by Anthony Hamilton. Jena, 1853. P. 143.

character on each of 'the merry, thoughtless days of Charles II': this was the boundless coarseness and brutality in their debauchery. Grammont is not the book to read in order to learn of this, but the *Diary* of the good Pepys, the poems of Rochester, the comedies of Etherege, Wycherley, Vanbrugh, Farquhar and others. From all these, Taine's thoroughly correct judgment on the immorality of the Restoration period was certainly drawn. He makes a very interesting comparison between French and English corruption of this period: 'The polish of the French deceives and blinds us. In a Frenchman debauchery is not entirely shocking; when the animal in him is released it is not accompanied by boundless excesses; fundamentally he is not really so coarse and brutal as the Englishman. The glittering layer of ice by which he is covered may be broken through without releasing the boisterous, turbid, muddy stream that rages and foams within his neighbour. In England the contrary is the fact. As soon as the external varnish of morality is scratched off, there appears the animal in man in all its passionate coarseness and hatefulness. An English statesman declared that in France the rage of the captive mob could be calmed by appealing to their humanity and honour, whereas in England raw flesh must be thrown to them in order to calm them. Violation, blood, orgy: this is the element in which this society mob feels at home: they lack everything that might make an excuse for carnival, above all wit (*esprit*)[1].'

I believe that a reading of the *Memoirs of Grammont* would convince anyone of the fact that love was never coarser and more vulgar than in the English society of the Restoration. Women had never before been treated so roughly and unscrupulously by men. The purely sensual cult of woman-worship was never before performed in

[1] H. Taine, *loc. cit.*, Vol. II, pp. 8, 11.

such a disgusting manner. Macaulay rightly remarks: 'Unbridled debauchery, the natural consequence of unnatural severity, was the prevailing fashion in those days, involving, of course, the moral degradation of women. It was good taste to idolise feminine beauty in a coarse and shameless manner. Admiration and desire aroused by women was very rarely combined with respect and real attachment or with any kind of chivalrous feeling for them, and the qualities which fitted them to play the part of companion, adviser and trustworthy friend, repelled the libertines of Whitehall instead of attracting them. Any lady of the court exhibiting her white throat and bosom at balls and parties, distinguishing herself by quick and appropriate repartee, flirting with chamberlains and captains of the Guard, singing ambiguous songs with an ambiguous expression in her eyes, slipping occasionally into a page's dress to perform some mischievous prank—had more chance of being worshipped by a devoted circle of admirers, of being honoured by the Royal attention, of marrying some rich and distinguished nobleman, than Johanna Grey or Lucy Hutchinson would ever have had[1].'

Anyone wanting a contemporary account of those times in order to obtain a true, clear and memorable picture of them in their real colours, should read the famous *Mémoires du Comte de Grammont* by Anthony Hamilton[2]. This book, written in French by an Englishman, is one of those which should be read regularly every year[3]. I do not hesitate to compare Hamilton with Tacitus. He, like the famous

[1] Macaulay, *loc. cit.*, Vol. II, pp. 196-197.
[2] First edition: *Mémoires de la vie du Comte du Grammont, contenant particulièrement l'histoire amoureuse de la cour d'Angleterre, sous le règne de Charles II.* (Cologne, 1713.) Good edition (with notes and index) by G. Brunet (Paris, 1859) and H. Motheau (Paris, 1876). I have used the French edition, *Mémoires du Comte de Grammont par A. Hamilton*: new edition, with essay by Sainte-Beuve (Paris, Garnier Frères, no date).
[3] C. A. Sainte-Beuve, *Causeries du lundi*. Paris (Garnier Frères, no date). Vol. I, p. 102.

Roman historian, stands above events; and, like the latter, can express himself vividly but concisely, thus deepening the impression he makes on his readers and giving them food for much thought on his subject.

According to Sainte-Beuve it is impossible to analyse the *Mémoires de Grammont*. They have to be read consecutively in order to get a clear idea of the Restoration period. In describing this period I shall refer also to various other sources, so that a more vivid picture may be obtained of the characteristics of the time and people.

Restoration society was the creation of Charles II, and its existence depended on him. There was never a king, not even Louis XV, who impressed the stamp of his personality upon his surroundings so deeply as did Charles II. The theory that only energetic characters are able to exercise much influence on their contemporaries seems here to be at fault. Even lack of energy may sometimes prove infectious, especially in the case of such an artist in pleasure and lust as Charles. It must also be remembered that on his return from exile the people welcomed in him the liberator who would release them from the fetters of the Puritanism which had weighed so heavily upon them, and the beginning of a new, happier and easier epoch dates therefrom.

The proverb ' Idleness is the mother of sin ' proved to be very true in the case of Charles II. In an old edition of Rochester's and Dorset's works, a noteworthy characteristic of the King is mentioned which seems to have been little appreciated, but which, in my opinion, helps very much to give a clear picture of his personality. According to this book the King was more negligent and idle than lascivious, and like many female libertines of those days let himself be led into debauchery rather in order to please others than for the satisfaction of his own desires. Especially towards the end of his life indolence played a much more important part than love in the hours he spent with his mistresses. These latter served chiefly to fill his *sérail*—what he really wanted was amusement and flirtation[1]. As regards the psychology of debauchees it must be remembered that it is not always lust which produces idleness. Often enough the contrary may be the case: idleness is the cause of sin. Charles II was thus a lover of idleness and frivolous pleasures. He was quite unable to control or restrain himself. He did not believe in human virtue, or in human sympathy; he had no desire for success and no sense of guilt. His frivolous weakness was of a type possessed by no other man of his intelligence. He was a slave, although not a deceived one, and, in addition, devoted beyond measure to sensual gratification[2].'

Hamilton gives a very true picture of Charles: ' The King was inferior to no one as regards figure, carriage and apparel. He was versatile and of gentle and kindly disposition. His mind was open to all impressions, he was sympathetic to sufferers, inexorable to evil-doers and, if anything, too soft-hearted. Capable of any exertion when need arose, so long as events pursued their ordinary course, he would take nothing seriously and could not become deeply absorbed in anything. Often he was a victim, but even more often the slave of his inclinations[3].'

Although this unprincipled king, lacking character and energy, was of a sensual nature and possessed a regular harem of mistresses, love with him was more of a pleasant pastime than a passion. Love to society in those days was a coin which could be made use of. Mrs. Manley writes in her *Atalantis*: 'People nowadays do not love for the sake of

[1] Macaulay, *loc. cit.*, pp. 181-182, 183.
[2] " A Short Character of King Charles II " in *The Works of the Earls of Rochester, Roscommon, Dorset, etc.* London, 1714. Vol. I, pp. lii to lx.
[3] *Mémoires du Comte de Grammont*, p. 75.

love, but chiefly on account of its use and profit to them[1]. It was to the interest of the women to make everyone fall in love with them, and the mere indifference of a young man was looked upon as an insult[2]. The King, by his own example, encouraged this view. The "vapours", the hysteria of to-day, were made use of even at that time to usher in changes in the affections and to dupe and console deceived husbands. Any disease, the cause of which was not known, was, according to the fashion of those days, called the "vapours". If a lady ran short of money to play bassette with and her husband refused to give her any, she immediately summoned the "vapours" to her aid, and the same thing happened whenever occasion arose. For instance, if she were not allowed to attend a party with her friends, she would drive incognito in a hired cab to her seamstress on the pretext of having a dress made. But her lover would join her there and thus the husband was deceived. What was he then to do? Did he oppose the will of the lady he must expect the "vapours" to set in in force. In short, the "vapours" were so fashionable that they served as excuse and often enough as remedy for all kinds of diseases[3].'

After these preliminary remarks on the external character of Charles's court, let us try to depict some of its outstanding personalities, and first of all the ladies.

Of all the numerous mistresses of Charles II, three were undoubtedly the most famous: Lady Castlemaine, the Duchess of Portsmouth and Nell Gwynn.

Barbara Villiers, Countess of Castlemaine and later Duchess of Cleveland, daughter of William Villiers, second Viscount Grandison, was born in 1641 in Westminster. As

---

[1] *The Atalantis of Mrs. Manley, or a secret Report on the most distinguished Persons in England.* Haag, 1714. P. 631.

[2] *Ibid.*, p. 488.

[3] *Ibid.*, p. 484.

early as 1656 she was surrounded by a great number of admirers. On the 14th April 1659 she married Roger Palmer, later Earl of Castlemaine, but he does not seem to have been the father of any of her many·children. Intimate relations between Charles II and Mrs. Palmer began on the 28th May 1660, the day of the King's return to Whitehall.

On the 25th February 1661 her first child, Anna, was born, whom the King acknowledged as his daughter, although her existence had been attributed to the Earl of Chesterfield, to whom she bore a striking resemblance. On the 13th May 1662, the day of the arrival of Katherine of Braganza, whom the King had chosen for his wife, he was staying, according to Pepys' *Diary*, at the house of Lady Castlemaine. But there appears to have been no light before her house, and this caused a great sensation. The King and his lover had sent for scales to have themselves weighed, and the lady, being pregnant, was the heavier of the two. She drew attention to herself by speaking very arrogantly to the new Queen. Pepys writes: ' The Queen, in the presence of her ladies, remarked to Lady Castlemaine, that she was afraid the King would catch cold by staying until so late at night at her house. Whereupon the Countess answered in a loud voice that he never stayed long, he always left early enough (although he very seldom went away from her before two or three in the morning), so he probably spent his nights somewhere else. The King just then entered the room, and hearing her insolent answer, whispered in her ear that she was a vulgar, impertinent woman and commanded her to leave the court. This she did immediately and moved into a hired apartment in Pall Mall, where she remained for two or three days. Then she sent a message to the King asking whether she might have her things fetched. He answered that she must come and see to them herself. She did so, the King joined her, and they were again good friends.'

Such temporary partings were frequent, but the strong-minded woman on these occasions always knew how to handle the King so as to bring him to his knees. Another passage from Pepys' *Diary*: ' Although the King and Lady Castlemaine are reconciled, she no longer lives in Whitehall, but at the house of Sir D. Harris, where the King visits her. He says she expects him to ask forgiveness on his knees and to promise that he will never again so insult her. She threatened to send his natural children to him, which almost drove him out of his senses. In her fury she shouted that she had had enough of him and would have all his letters to her printed.' Despite the objections of the Queen, the Countess was appointed a member of her own Royal household. In June 1662 she bore the King a second child, a son, Charles. She then began to have many other love affairs, but the King still visited her four evenings a week, 'when he stole back to her alone and secretly through the private garden, so that even the sentinels knew and talked about it, which is certainly a bad thing for a king ' (Pepys).

On the 20th September 1663 a third child was born to Lady Castlemaine (Henry), but the King refused to own him. He nevertheless loaded her on this occasion with valuable gifts. Two more children followed: on the 5th September 1664 and on the 28th December 1665. In 1666 Lady Castlemaine moved into her sumptuous apartment at Hampton Court. At that time her love affair with the worthless Sir Harry Jermyn led to very frequent quarrels with the King.

In 1668, when several brothels in the City were done away with, a very ingenious pamphlet was published, bearing the title: *Petition of the poor Whore to the most serene, illustrious, august and excellent Lady of pleasure, Countess of Castlemaine. Signed: Madame Creswell*[1]. This was followed somewhat later

---

[1] A notorious procuress in the time of Charles II.

by a burlesque answer: ' given at our closet in King Street *die Veneris*, 24th April, 1668.' After 1674 Lady Castlemaine was supplanted in the King's affections by the Duchess of Portsmouth, but she soon consoled herself with a number of new admirers, among whom was John Ellis. A great stir was roused by her liaison with the rope-dancer, Jacob Hall, and with John Churchill, who later became the famous Duke of Marlborough. Hamilton writes of the former in his concise but most expressive way: ' Jacob Hall, a famous rope-dancer, was very fashionable in London in those days, and delighted the spectators with his skill and strength. The Countess wished to convince herself privately of his physical attributes, for his figure in his professional dress appeared to be that of an athlete, and his legs were very different from those of the ever-victorious Jermyn. Judging from the rumours spread all over the City, and from the numerous derisive poems, more flattering to the dancer than to the Countess, she was not at all disappointed in him. But she did not mind gossip, and her beauty became ever more radiant[1].' In her *Atalantis* Mary Manley gives a very detailed description of the relations between Lady Castlemaine and Marlborough. She calls the Countess here very pertinently ' Duchesse de l'Inconstant '. ' Fortunatus ' is John Churchill, later Duke of Marlborough. One of his aunts was ' Controller of the household of the Duchesse de l'Inconstant, favourite of the Emperor Sigismund the second[2] and she was the most distinguished member of the family. Young Fortunatus visited her frequently. One day the Duchesse met him there, and being very impulsive fell in love with him and commanded him to come and see her after the King had gone to bed. The clever aunt, who knew her mistress only too well, was quite aware of what

[1] *Memoirs of Grammont*, p. 89.
[2] This is supposed to be Charles II.

she wanted from her nephew; she was very glad of his good fortune, and spent the whole day adorning and perfuming him in order to ensure his success. After reminding him of various important points, she led the young Adonis to the bed of her beloved Venus. The Duchess was delighted, and later she seems to have discovered that this was the first time his young heart had been kindled by the flame of love. The youth's obvious confusion, which so overcame him that he hardly knew what he was doing, and his evident lack of experience, were a fresh attraction for her, and she was very well satisfied with her first trial of him. He too, however, was well aware of how to turn this unexpected luck to his own advantage[1].' Bishop Burnet writes: ' As soon as the Duchess of Cleveland believed herself to have been jilted by the King, she consoled herself with numerous love-affairs. On one occasion she was surprised, by Buckingham's arrangement, by the King himself; her lover sprang out of the window.'

William Wycherley, the writer of comic poetry, a very handsome man, was also caught in the net of this Messalina, and Mrs. Manley relates in a very vivid manner her liaison with Lord Dover. Churchill, who was in love with Sarah Jennings, later his famous wife, had long tired of his affair with Lady Castlemaine, and was waiting for a favourable opportunity to part from her. He therefore asked his friend Lord Dover to keep an appointment he had made with her instead of himself. 'The next day the Duchess was to go to Churchill immediately after dinner. She was so anxious to be with him that she had not the patience to dine properly, and arrived just at the appointed time. As she was expected the servants had been, as usual, sent out of the way, except one who was in the secret. This man told her that his master was awaiting her in a small room where he had gone

[1] *Atalantis*, pp. 580-582.

to rest after his bath. She hurried in. The windows were closed, the curtains drawn and the small room was dark. She, however, made out the shape of a male figure lying on a couch stretched out in a very indecent position on account of the summer heat, and having nothing on but a thin wrap covering his body. He had been cautious enough to cover his face with the laces of the pillow, lest he should be recognised. His joy at the arrival of the Duchess caused him to make some movement which pleased the Duchess so that she could not delay taking advantage of the situation.' It is easy to guess what happened next. On the 16th June 1672 she again—*patre incerto*—bore a child: her third daughter, Barbara. In 1677 she went to Paris, whence she corresponded regularly with the King.

She returned in 1685 to England to start an affair with the actor Goodman, by whom this most prolific of all mistresses bore a son in March 1686. After that she had a number of liaisons. Her husband, who in the reign of James II had acted, not too successfully, as ambassador to the Pope, died on the 21st July 1705. Four months later the nympho-maniac widow of 64 married young Robert Fielding, one of the most handsome men of his time, who was also known as ' Beau Fielding '. He was, however, a coarse fellow who treated his old wife very roughly. It turned out fortunately that he was already married to another woman, so she sued him for divorce. In the course of the proceedings some of her letters were read, and their appalling indecency was not at all surprising to those who had heard the stories of her incredible depravity. She survived this last event by only a few years, and died on the 8th October 1709 of dropsy. This woman, who was referred to by Macaulay as the ' most extravagant, despotic, and most shameless of all depraved women[1] ' was of an extraordinary beauty of figure and face.

[1] Macaulay, *loc. cit.*, Vol. III, p. 278.

According to Oldmixon 'she was the most beautiful and most voluptuous of all the Royal concubines '. She had a lovely round face with a childlike expression, red-brown hair and marvellous dark blue eyes. Many pictures have handed down to posterity a record of her famous beauty. By or after Lely alone there are five portraits of Lady Castlemaine, one of them in the well-known Hampton Court Gallery[1].

Louise Renée de Kérouaille (Kéroualle), Duchess of Portsmouth and Aubigny, daughter of a Breton nobleman, was born in 1649. She became Maid of Honour at the Court of Duchess Henriette of Orleans, a sister of Charles II, with whom she came to England in 1670. By that time the King had become tired of Lady Castlemaine. In 1670 Evelyn for the first time saw ' this new famous beauty, who however, in my opinion, has a stupid babyish face '. In October 1671 she became the official mistress of Charles II, on which fact Louis XIV congratulated her. On 29th July 1672 she bore the King a son, Charles Lennox, first Duke of Richmond.

As a Frenchwoman and a Catholic she was very unpopular in England. The people called her ' Carewell ' or ' Madame Carwell '. On 19th August 1673 she received the title of Duchess of Portsmouth, to which Louis XIV added that of Duchesse d'Aubigny. She influenced Charles in his friendly approaches to France[2]. She kept her position, a very brilliant one externally, until the death of the King. She had received from the King £136,668 in all. Her house was

---

[1] The whole description chiefly after *Dictionary of National Biography*. Ed. by Sidney Lee, London, 1899. Vol. 58, pp. 312-318. Compare further G. S. Steinmann, *Memoirs of Barbara, Duchess of Cleveland* (London, 1871); Mrs. Manley's *Atalantis*; *Grammont's Memoirs*; Macaulay's *History of England*; Pepys' *Diary*.

[2] Macaulay ascribes to the sister of Charles II, the above-mentioned Duchess Henriette of Orleans, the greater part in this *rapprochement* (*loc. cit.*, p. 221). 'The sister's persuasion and the witchery of her friend succeeded in influencing the weak Charles in the short space of ten days to do just as Louis wished.' Grammont (comment), p. 311.

furnished with the greatest luxury. According to Evelyn,
' Her apartment in Whitehall was ten times as beautiful as
that of the Queen'. He tells of a visit which he paid her in
company with the King. ' I followed His Majesty through the
galleries and went with a few members of his suite to the
dressing-room of the Duchess, next to her bedroom. She
had just got out of bed, was dressed in a light morning
gown, and His Majesty with the gallants stood around
whilst she was combed by her maids. What I found most
surprising was the rich and magnificent furnishings of her
room[1].' After the death of Charles II the Duchess returned
to France and spent the rest of her life on her estate in
Aubigny. She lived until 17th November 1734. Voltaire
saw her as an old woman, and found her very beautiful.
George Selwyn also saw her then. Lely, Kneller, H. Gascar
and Mignard painted portraits of this unusual beauty,
whose ' gentle, soft and childlike features were increased in
charm by her French liveliness ' (Macaulay). Her motto,
' En la rose je fleuris ', was adopted by her descendants,
the Dukes of Richmond and Gordon[2].

Undoubtedly the most attractive figure of all Charles's
mistresses, and also the most popular, was Nell Gwynn.
She was in her lifetime the most generally beloved of the
Royal mistresses on account of her kindly, child-like, naïve,
and withal true English character. On the whole, according
to Thomas Campbell, amongst Charles's mistresses his
' Loves of the theatre ' were the least costly and unpopular[3].
Nell Gwynn was one of these ' theatre loves '.

Eleanor Gwyn (or Gwynn), generally called ' Nell Gwynn ',

[1] Compare also Macaulay's description of the room, Vol. II, p. 169.
[2] Description after *Dictionary of National Biography*. London, 1892.
Vol. 31, pp. 59-62. J. H. Jesse, *Literary and Historical Memorials of
London*. London, 1847. Vol. II, pp. 210-211. Evelyn's *Diary*. H.
Forneron, *Louise de Kéroualle, Duchesse de Portsmouth*. Paris, 1886.
[3] Thomas Campbell, *Life of Mrs. Siddons*. London, 1834. Vol. I, p. 99.

the daughter of a fishwife, was born in London on 2nd
February 1650. Until her thirteenth year she sold oranges
in the Theatre Royal, and also, according to a satire of
Rochester's, herrings. Later a travelling actor took her
into his company and she sang in public-houses. Her
beautiful face induced the notorious procuress, ' Mother
Ross ', to take her into her brothel, where she was given
lessons in spelling, arithmetic and singing. The actor
Charles Hart and John Lacy were her lovers. Hart undertook to train the talented Nelly for the stage. She first
appeared in 1665 as Cydaria in *Indian Emperor*, by Dryden.

She was not a first-rate artist, but her natural liveliness and
grace were combined with a talent for singing and dancing.
Pepys frequently expresses his admiration for her. He calls
her the 'pretty, witty Nell ' (3rd April 1665). ' The ladies
act very well, especially little Nelly.' After having seen her
in *Celia*, he kissed her. So did his wife, and he added:
'. . . she is an exceptionally pretty creature' (23rd January
1666). She drew the attention of the King to herself in 1671.

Dryden had written for her an epilogue to his play
Tyrannic Love. Such epilogues, containing the most frivolous verses, were preferably recited by women. ' The tone
of the Epilogues was always very free, and they were almost
always recited by the most popular actresses. Nothing
delighted the audience more than to hear the most indelicate
verses recited by a pretty young girl, who was supposed
as yet to be innocent[1].' In this particular case there were
some unusual circumstances. William Preston, a mediocre
actor of a small company, had appeared in a new play in an
extremely large hat which brought the play a wholly
unexpected success. Dryden therefore made Nell Gwynn
appear in ' a hat of the size of a very large cart-wheel ',
which made her little figure look so funny, and her so lovely,

[1] Macaulay, *loc. cit.*, Vol. II, p. 134.

that everyone was enchanted, and the King took her home
and then and there made her his mistress. She still, however,
continued her profession; Dryden gave her his best parts,
and she remained the favourite of the public. Pepys writes
of her appearance in Dryden's *Virgin Queen*. ' In this play
there is a comic character, Florinel, which I never hope to
see again played so well as it was played by Nell Gwynn,
equally when she appeared as a savage girl and as a young
fop. She took off the bearing and manners of a conceited
young coxcomb in a way no actor can.' Many anecdotes,
especially in Tom Brown's *State Poems* and in poems by
Etherege, show how popular she became within a very short
time. She was called ' The poor man's friend ', and her
position as mistress was less resented than in the case of
the aristocratic loves of the King. It was considered by
the people to be more the result of fate than of vice, and
they took her part passionately in the incessant quarrels
between herself and the Duchess of Portsmouth.

Many illuminating stories were related about these quarrels.
The mob one day gathered before the shop of a jeweller in
Cheapside to see the Duchess of Portsmouth fetch a splendid
silver service, the gift of the King, and broke out in abuse of
her. They cried out that they would like to see the silver
melted and poured down her throat. The presents really
belonged to the beloved Nell. ' What a pity it should not
be bestowed on Madame Ellen! ' On another occasion Nell
drove in her carriage through the streets of Oxford. The
mob took her for her rival, and abused and threatened her.
She then laughed and put her head out of the window,
crying to them: ' Pray, good people, be civil; I am the
Protestant whore.' She was well able to make her rival look
ridiculous. The Duchess of Portsmouth asserted that she
was closely related to the most aristocratic French families,
and each time one of these relatives died she went into

mourning. On one occasion a French prince had died and she, of course, appeared in black. On the very same day the news of the death of a Tartar Chan happened to reach England. Nelly appeared at the court in mourning. She was standing close to her rival when a friend of hers asked her the reason for this. ' Oh,' she said, ' didn't you know of the loss I have suffered through the death of the Chan?' ' What the devil was the Chan of Tartary to you? ' answered the friend. ' Oh, exactly the same as the Prince de . . . was to Mademoiselle de Quérouaille.' Madame de Sévigné mentions in her letters the relationship between these two famous mistresses. ' The Duchess had not foreseen that she would one day find an actress in her way. And this actress is just as haughty as Mlle. herself. She often insults her, makes faces at her, deprives her of the King and boasts each time he gives her the preference. She is young, indiscreet, wild, good-humoured. She sings, dances and plays her parts with an extraordinary charm. She has a son by the King and hopes that he will own the child. Of the Duchess she says: " This person wants people to believe that she is a lady of rank and is related to the first families in France. If this be true, why does she degrade herself by being a courtesan? She ought to die of shame. As for me, it is my profession, and I don't want any better. I have a son by the King whom his father ought to own, and he will, for he loves me as much as her." ' Nell had two sons by the King, one of whom later was given the title of Duke of St. Albans. The King loved her fondly till the end of his life, and, according to Burnet, his last words (to the Duke of York) were: 'Let not poor Nellie starve[1].' She survived the King by a short

[1] This is not quite correct, as these were neither the last words of Charles nor did they refer to Nell Gwynn. Macaulay says: ' During the night Charles earnestly commended the Duchess of Portsmouth to the care of James; "and do not let poor Nellie starve ", he added kindly. The Queen sent her excuses for her absence through Halifax; she was

time only. She died on 13th November 1687, when only thirty-seven, of apoplexy. Nell Gwynn was a typical English girl: frank, not sentimental, kindhearted and grateful to her old friends, amongst whom were the poets Otway and Dryden. She never interfered in politics and was, unlike Lady Castlemaine, faithful to the King, although he was not her first lover. He was her ' third Charles '. Whether it was Dorset or Captain Hart who had the honour of being her ' first Charles ' is, according to Macaulay, uncertain. But Dorset seems the more likely. According to Bishop Burnet, Nell Gwynn was ' the most high spirited and absurd creature that ever lived at a Royal court '. She had a pretty, graceful little figure, red-brown hair and very small feet; when she laughed her eyes nearly disappeared. There are very many pictures of Nell Gwynn. One of them, by Lely, is in the Garrick Club; a second is in the Lely Room in the Hampton Court Gallery; a third in the National Portrait Gallery. No. 306 of King James's Gallery was ' Madame Gwynn, naked, with a Cupid ', by Lely. Many others besides have painted her portrait. Algernon Charles Swinburne wrote a beautiful memorial to Eleanor Gwynn in the following poem in his *Poems and Ballads*:

> Sweet heart, that no taint of the throne or the stage
> Could touch with unclean transformation, or alter
> To the likeness of courtiers whose consciences falter
> At the smile or the frown, at the mirth or the rage,
> Of a master whom chance could inflame or assuage,
> Our Lady of Laughter, invoked in no psalter,
> Adored of no faithful that cringe and that palter,
> Praise be with thee yet from a hag-ridden age.

too overcome by sorrow to take her place at the bedside of the King, and begged his forgiveness for all the offences she had committed contrary to his wishes. " She begs my forgiveness, poor woman," cried Charles. " I beg hers with all my heart ".' Macaulay, *loc. cit.*, Vol. II, pp.176-177.

Our Lady of Pity thou wast: and to thee
All England, whose sons are the sons of the sea,
Gives thanks, and will hear not if history snarls.
When the name of the friend of her sailors is spoken:
And thy lover she cannot but love—by the token
That thy name was the last on the lips of King Charles[1].

Around these three famous mistresses of King Charles II
were grouped the many other inmates of the harem of this
woman-mad king, whose names for the most part have not
come down to posterity; those beauties who, competing
with the above-mentioned in lust, love and pleasure, gave
to this court such a characteristic stamp.

Miss Stewart, who later became the wife of the Duke of
Richmond, early tried to oust Lady Castlemaine from the
King's favour[2]. She was remarkably beautiful, but not
equally interesting. ' It is strange that such unusual
physical charms should be combined with such dullness of
mind. All her features were regular, but her figure was not

---

[1] Compiled from *Dictionary of National Biography* (London, 1890,
Vol. 23, pp. 401-403); *Memoirs of the life of Eleanor Gwinn* (London, 1752);
Cunningham, *Story of Nell Gwynn*; Thomas Campbell, *Life of Mrs.
Siddons* (London, 1834, Vol. II, pp. 99-101); Grammont's Memoirs;
Macaulay; Pepys; A. C. Swinburne, *Poems and Ballads* (third series,
London, 1897, p. 132).

[2] ' Lady Castlemaine noticed that the King followed Miss Stewart with
his eyes, but instead of being jealous, she encouraged him as much as
she could, perhaps out of the carelessness of a woman who is very conscious of her charms, perhaps in order to remove suspicion from her new
love-affair with Jermyn. She regarded this budding passion, which must
surprise the whole court, not only without anxiety, but she went so far
as to make a favourite of her rival, and invited her to all the suppers she
gave to the King; trusting to the power of her own beauty, she often
invited the young lady to spend the night with her, and as the King came
every morning to see Lady Castlemaine before she got up, he found Miss
Stewart with her in bed. Early passion finds irresistible charm in the
smallest things, but the unwary Castlemaine had no anxiety about letting
her rival be seen in such a position at her side; trusting no doubt that
whenever she chose, she would be able victoriously to divert the King's
attention from Miss Stewart' (*Mémoires du Comte de Grammont*, pp. 57-88).

perfect; she was slender, rather upright and exceeded the average height of women. She was charming, danced very well and spoke French better than her mother-tongue.

With courteous manners she combined a fine taste in dress which is impossible to acquire unless one has been brought up in France. She was of such a childish disposition that she laughed at everything. She enjoyed the simplest jokes with a vivacity which was more suitable to a child of 12 or 13. Except for playing with dolls, she was like a child —blindman's buff was her favourite game, she would build card houses whilst others were playing for high stakes, and the courtiers were often to be seen helping her[1].' Pepys describes her as one of the most beautiful creatures he ever saw. ' If any woman can surpass Lady Castlemaine in beauty and charm, this is the one, and I shall not be at all surprised if the King changes. She is the cause of his coldness to the Countess[2].' Miss Stewart distinguished herself by her lasciviousness[3] and cynical shamelessness. Hamilton remarks that the bathing negligees of the court ladies served only to exhibit their charms without being actually indecent.

[1] *Mémoires du Comte de Grammont*, pp. 88, 112.
[2] *Ibid.*, p. 328.
[3] ' Old Carlingford and the mad Crofts, those lively wits, used to tell her the most wonderful yarns at every opportunity. I know no stories, and if I did I have no talent for telling them. For this reason I was embarrassed when she asked me for them. One day when she was teasing me I said: " I don't know any, Madam." " Then invent one ", she said. " I am still less capable of doing that, but if you like I will tell you a dream, a more extraordinary one than usual." Her curiosity was aroused and it had to be satisfied at once. I told her, therefore, that in my dream the most charming creature in the world, whom I dearly loved, came to see me in the night. I then drew her own picture under the cover of this wonderful beauty, but I told her also that the spirit had come to me with the most favourable intentions, and had not behaved badly. But this did not satisfy Miss Stewart's thirst for knowledge, and I had to describe all the proofs of her favour which the lovely phantom had shown me; she did not seem either surprised nor embarrassed, and attentively listening to the story, she made me repeat many times a particularly nice bit.' *Ibid.*, p. 270.

Miss Stewart was so thoroughly convinced of her own superiority that if any of the other court ladies were praised for their nice legs or arms, she immediately gave a practical demonstration of her own. ' Indeed, with a little skill I don't think it would be difficult to get her, all unsuspecting, completely unclothed.' Hamilton gave Miss Stewart a very nice horse in order to enjoy her charming figure mounted. The King preferred hawking to all hunting sports, because the ladies also could easily take part in it, and on such occasions he was surrounded very often by all the beauties of the court. On these occasions hard riding often gave the ladies opportunities to exhibit—intentionally or unintentionally—their secret charms. Hamilton describes a scene like this with Miss Stewart. She left the court in 1667 in order to marry the Duke of Richmond. Evelyn writes of this marriage in his *Diary* on 26th April 1667[1].

The gentlemen of the court were no better than the ladies—on the contrary, they surpassed them in frivolity. It is difficult to say whether the men or women were better depicted in Hamilton's classic description. Seldom has so small a frame contained so many varied and unique figures.

The relations between men and women of the type we have been discussing must have been incredibly coarse. Gossip of the lowest kind and the filthiest slander were the weapons employed by men and women against each other in their usually very unequal disputes. The women despised

[1] The marriage was made necessary by the fact that the King—in consequence of Lady Castlemaine's disclosures—had surprised Miss Stewart with the Duke of Richmond. Hamilton writes: ' It was near midnight. The King came on his mistress's maids, who curtseyed profoundly on his entrance and told him in a whisper that Miss Stewart felt suddenly ill after he had left her, but had gone to bed and was now, thank God, sleeping peacefully. " I must make certain of this ", exclaimed the King, pushing back those who stood in his way. Miss Stewart was actually in bed, but by no means asleep. The Duke of Richmond was sitting at the head of the bed, and he was also far from asleep.'

the men no less than they were themselves despised, and the honour of women was trodden underfoot. The systematic libel actions, for instance, brought against Miss Hyde solely in order to prevent James II from marrying her, were outrageous. One Talbot says she granted him an interview in her father's private room which turned out to be so lively that they both forgot the things on the table in their interest in what they were doing, and unfortunately spilt a whole bottle of ink on a five-page despatch, 'whereupon the King's monkey, having been accused of this mischief, was for a long time in disgrace'. Jermyn mentioned in several places longer and more fortunate appointments with Miss Hyde. Both stated, however, that they had enjoyed ' but the small pleasures of love '. On the other hand, Killigrew declared that he enjoyed Miss Hyde's favours to the utmost limits. ' He was a merry, sly fellow, and had a talent for telling anecdotes in a most amusing fashion. His rendezvous, he said, took place in a different small room, built right above the water and intended for quite other purposes than lovemaking. They had two or three swans for witnesses, who had probably had the same luck on several other occasions, for the lady frequented this room and enjoyed much pleasure therein[1].'

Conversations about the charms of the opposite sex were always vulgar and shameless either with men or women. Women liked to discuss the physical abilities of famous wooers; men, on the other hand, analysed exhaustively the constitution of the female body. Men sometimes handed over their wives to their friends to make what use they liked of them, as Mr. Cooke did to Sir William Baron[2].

Deceived husbands sometimes revenged themselves in a very queer fashion ' without poison or iron ', but thor-

[1] *Mémoires du Comte de Grammont*, pp. 134-135.
[2] Mrs. Manley's *Atalantis*, p. 483.

oughly satisfactory to them. Southesk went to the most notorious places in order to pick up ' the most disgusting of all diseases. But he only half succeeded in revenging himself because, after he had undergone the most drastic treatment to get rid of the disease, he was the only one to have his gift returned to him by his wife, for she carried on no more intercourse with the man for whom the present was intended[1].' It was lucky for the Marquis de Flamarens that the only ' present ' he was given by Lady Southesk was her fond heart[2].

There were frequent scenes of jealousy between the ladies, especially the numerous mistresses of the King[3].

Pregnancy and child-birth were everyday events. The haughty Miss Warmestré, ' apparently mistaking the date, took the liberty of being confined at court '. Miss Bellenden, warned by this example, was prudent enough to leave court shortly after, in order to avoid being turned out[4]. Lady Castlemaine's ' figure was distorted by a third or fourth

[1] *Mémoires du Comte de Grammont*, p. 139.

[2] *Ibid.*, p. 175.

[3] Grammont presented the King with a splendid coach with glass windows. ' The Queen had a feeling that this wonderful carriage would bring her luck, and wished to be the first to use it with the Duchess of York. Lady Castlemaine saw her in it and, being convinced that she would look much prettier in it than in any other, she asked the King to lend her the magic carriage to be driven in it in Hyde Park, on the first fine day. Miss Stewart expressed the same desire and asked for the carriage for the very same day. The King was at a loss, for there was no means of arbitrating between the two Goddesses, whose former friendship had changed to mortal hatred, for each wanted to be the first to have the carriage. Lady Castlemaine was pregnant and threatened to bear her child prematurely should her rival be granted the favour. Miss Stewart, on the other hand, assured the King that she would never let herself be put in that condition if he did not fulfil her wishes. This latter threat won the fight, and Lady Castlemaine was so upset and furious that she almost kept her word. It was also said that the triumph cost her rival a little of her innocence ' (*Mémoires du Comte de Grammont*, p. 119).

[4] *Ibid.*, pp. 183, 184.

A HISTORY OF ENGLISH SEXUAL MORALS

pregnancy, and the King was good enough to put it to his own debit[1]'.

Pepys was told by Captain Ferrers that ' at a ball at court about a month previously, a maid of honour had dropped a baby whilst dancing '. It is said to have been carried off in a handkerchief, and the King kept it in his private room for about a week and dissected it, making coarse jokes[2]. The Queen knew only too well that the King was not specially anxious to have legitimate children as long as his lovely mistresses would provide him with illegitimate heirs[3].

Amusements never lacked at this court of lascivious debauchery. But of all these, riding was especially popular, when the ladies could display all their charms. ' There were outings on horseback when mounted ladies did their best— with or without success—to display their charms[4] ', as, for instance, when Miss Arabella Churchill was given the opportunity to show the Duke of York the contrast between her face and her body[5]. Pepys one day saw a troop of ladies returning from their riding and followed them to the Court of Whitehall, saw them trying on each others' plumed hats and heard their peals of laughter. ' It was the loveliest sight, with their beauty and their gorgeous costumes, that I have ever seen in my life. But the loveliest of all was Miss Stewart in her riding dress with her red-feathered hat on the side of her head, her sweet eyes, her little Roman nose and splendid figure, the loveliest I have ever seen[6].' Indeed, the King loved her best when he saw her on horseback.

[1] *Mémoires du Comte de Grammont*, p. 259.
[2] Taine, *loc. cit.*, Vol. II, p. 23.
[3] *Mémoires du Comte de Grammont*, p. 262.
[4] *Ibid.*, p. 116.
[5] *Ibid.*, p. 247.
[6] J. H. Jesse, *Literary and Historical Memorials of London*. London, 1847. Vol. II, p. 247.

The most pernicious fact about this distinguished society was that the people followed its vicious example. No other epoch in the history of public morals shows so clearly the unhealthy influence of a corrupt upper class on the morals of the people as this, when special pleasure was taken in maintaining constant touch with the common burghers and people of the lower classes. Rochester, for instance, settled down in the City for a short time, originally with the intention of becoming acquainted with the secrets of the citizens; that is, he intended ' to take part under an assumed name and in disguise, in their amusements and parties and occasionally in the enjoyment of their wives. He was invited to all the parties, and while he discussed with the men the faults and the weakness of the Government, he joined with the women in criticising the court ladies and mistresses of the King. He upheld their opinion that these shocking abuses rankled in the marrow of the poor people.

The pretty ladies of the City were in no way inferior to those of the West End, yet in their part of the town one husband was generally content with one wife. Finally, outdoing their complaints, he declared his astonishment that fire from heaven had not fallen on Whitehall and consumed it, whilst good-for-nothings like Rochester, Killigrew and Sidney were tolerated, who asserted that all London husbands were cuckolds and their wives painted their faces. This kind of thing made him so popular with the men, and sought after, that he soon grew tired of the banquets and the importunacy of the merchant-folk[1].' Miss Frances Jennings and Miss Price, disguised as ' orange girls ', offered and sold their fruit in the City, and, of course, had all sorts of adventures, according to Hamilton. The ladies of the court often disguised themselves, and even the Queen mixed amongst the people at fairs, disguised as a peasant woman.

[1] J. H. Jesse, *loc. cit.*, p. 221.

Bishop Burnet writes: ' The court in those days took part in the most licentious masquerades. King and Queen, ladies and courtiers, went about in disguise, entered the houses of unknown people and danced there, making bad jokes. It was not easy for them to be recognised by such as did not know the secret. They were carried about in common hired chairs, and the Queen was once lost by her chairmen, not knowing her identity. She was left all alone and did not know what to do. In the end she had to drive to Whitehall in a hired coach[1].'

But this hobnobbing with the lower classes went even farther than that. John Evelyn writes about the ladies of rank, that they frequented taverns in which a courtesan would never have set her foot. ' But you will be even more astonished to hear that they passed their large glasses round, drank each other's healths, danced to the music of the violin, freely distributed kisses, and called this a decent form of amusement[2].' De Cominges, French Ambassador at Charles's court, reports that indulgence in excesses in taverns and brothels was common amongst people of rank, and even ladies of very distinguished families would accompany their gallants to such places to drink Spanish wine[3].

J. H. Jesse, in his *Literary and Historical Memorials of London*, interspersed with verses, gives a poetic description of life during the Restoration period, which may be included here as a fitting close to this section[4]:

' Live while we live ', the frolic monarch cries;
Away with thought in joy's delicious hours,
Of love and mirth, of melody and flowers!
Lo! on the ear voluptuous music falls,

[1] *Mémoires du Comte de Grammont* (Comment), p. 330.
[2] G. Hill, *Women in English Life*. London, 1896. Vol. I, 184.
[3] *Ibid.*, p. 187.
[4] J. H. Jesse, *loc. cit.*, Vol. II, pp. 204-205.

The lamps are flashing on the mirrored walls;
How rich the odours and how gay the rooms
With sparkling jewels and with waving plumes!
Bright names that live in history's page we trace,
Hyde's mournful look, and Monmouth's angel face;
Portsmouth's dark eye, and Cleveland's haughty charms
That chained a monarch to her snowy arms;
There royal Catherine cheeks the jealous tear,
While pleads her lord in beauty's flattered ear;
There gleams the star on graceful Villiers' breast,
Here the grouped courtiers laugh at Wilmot's jest:
There glittering heaps of tempting gold entice
The wealthy fool to chance the dangerous dice;
Here floats young beauty through the graceful dance,
Feigns the fond sigh, or throws the wanton glance;
There the soft love song to yon group apart,
Steals with delicious sweetness o'er the heart;
The easy monarch glides from fair to fair,
Hints the warm wish, or breathes the amorous prayer.

CHAPTER IX

DEBAUCHERY IN ENGLISH SOCIETY IN THE EIGHTEENTH AND NINETEENTH CENTURIES

THE influence of the spirit of the Restoration period upon English social life was tremendous. The general constitution of the upper classes, as they were established in the reign of Charles II, has, on the whole, remained unchanged up to the present day. The expulsion of the Stuarts did not alter the character of English society life. The beginning of the eighteenth century exhibits the same tendencies in this society, but in an ennobled form, becoming gradually, in the course of the eighteenth century, through intellectual interests, more refined and established. Paul Hensel remarks in his interesting essay on English social conditions at the beginning of the eighteenth century: ' A return of Puritan austerity was not to be feared. It was, and remained, a worldly generation, thinking more of getting on in the world than of seeking the way to salvation. But religion was no longer scorned and the idleness of the upper classes was condemned.' Nevertheless, Hensel considers the main characteristic of that period to be ' the absence of the most important element in our lives to-day': work, although it was not so bad as in the days so faithfully described for us by Pepys in his *Diary*[1]. The disinclination to regular

---

[1] P. Hensel, *English Social Conditions at the Beginning of the Eighteenth Century*. Neue Heidelb. Jahrb., 1899. Pp. 2-3.

occupation still prevailed in England during the eighteenth century.

Due to their long sojourn in France, the Stuarts had brought with them to England a predilection for French habits and manners, and the intimate relations between French and English society were personified by individuals like Grammont and St. Evremond. Francophilia is the most noteworthy bequest of the Restoration period, giving undeniably a peculiar flavour to the eighteenth century.

Next to Francophilia, sentimentality is a prominent characteristic of English society. The idea of sentimentality is a peculiarly English one. The first literary manifestation of this idea which, to a certain extent, popularised it, was Laurence Sterne's *Sentimental Journey*. The second representative of this school is Samuel Richardson (1680-1761). He was the founder of the sentimental family novel, describing the everyday conflicts of private life. Richardson sought to depict this life with its noble sentiments, its good deeds, its fine humanity, but also with its need, its vices, its meanness.

The sentimentality of the eighteenth century often manifested itself in a strange manner, which we can scarcely understand nowadays. The floods of tears which, for example, flow unceasingly in the heartrending books of the German Miller, flowed in reality. When Casanova recited a touching passage of Ariosto's *Orlando Furioso* to an audience including, amongst others, Voltaire and Madame Denis, he modulated his intonations according to the emotions he wished to call forth. ' My violent efforts to hold back my tears were visible to everyone, and the eyes of the listeners were full, but in the end I cried so unrestrainedly that my audience sobbed in sympathy. M. Voltaire and Madame Denis fell on my neck, but their embraces could not stop my tears. Voltaire remarked: " I have always said that the secret of calling forth tears is to weep oneself, but the tears must be real ones and they must come from a deeply moved soul "[1].'

A yet more remarkable example of sentimentality can be found in *Sérails de Londres* (a work playing more or less the same rôle in English society of the eighteenth century as did *Grammont's Memoirs* in that of the seventeenth century). It is a story of a young count who frequented the brothel of Mrs. Dubery solely in order to carry on sentimental conversation with one of the prostitutes, giving her each time a note for twenty pounds. The reason for this peculiar caprice was his sexual impotence, and this was his way of seeking some substitute for physical pleasure[2]. Sentimentality in this case is obviously a means of sexual satisfaction, a substitute and equivalent for natural sexual activity, and is a positive proof of the morbid character of these artificial emotions.

The general character of society of the eighteenth century was, in comparison with that of the Restoration period, decidedly more refined and ennobled. Men like Rochester or Dorset seem, in spite of their brilliant talents, common and vulgar fellows in comparison with Selwyn and March, with their polished manners and elegant, well-bred behaviour. This later society, too, was ruled by the spirit of Rococo. The prevailing mode of entertainment was light, pleasant conversation, accompanied, of course, by ' gossip '. The so-called ' demi-reps[3] ' of the eighteenth century in England must not be confused with the French *demi-mondaines* of the nineteenth century. The demi-reps were ladies of not perfectly irreproachable reputation, and they were exposed to the permanent danger of being ' dissected alive at the tea-tables[4] '. The gossiping women of London

[1] Casanova, *Memoirs* (Leipzig), Vol. XI, p. 33.
[2] *Les Sérails de Londres* (Brussels, no date), new edition, pp. 160-162.
[3] From ' demi-reputation '.
[4] G. Hill, *loc. cit.*, Vol. I, p. 343.

were a favourite topic for the moralising authors of the eighteenth century, Addison, Steele, Sterne, for example, and the good Richard King, who emphasised particularly in his *Frauds of London* the destructive effect of their gossip[1].

The aristocracy and the common people in the eighteenth century were more widely separated from each other than in the seventeenth century, when a kind of patriarchal relationship still existed between them. In addition, the court, according to Archenholtz, no longer frequented common brothels, but the courtiers maintained brothels of their own.

' There are other houses as well, in the vicinity of St. James's Palace, where a number of nymphs are kept for the pleasure of the courtiers. There is a street called King's Place, containing charming houses, inhabited solely by priestesses of Venus living under the supervision of well-to-do matrons. They go to public places of amusement, even the most expensive ones, and are always very well dressed. Each of these " nunneries[2] " has its own carriages and liveried servants, for the girls never go on foot except for their walks in the Park. They pay for their apartment and food and are treated as boarders although, however, obliged to submit to the rules of the house. The high price paid even for entry to these temples kept the mob from frequenting them, and for this reason rich and distinguished people came the more. The famous Fox, before he became a Minister, was one of the many visitors to these houses, and often hurried straight from there to Parliament, where he affected all by his eloquence. It is remarkable that so long

---

[1] R. King, *The Frauds of London*, p. 30.
[2] ' Nunnery ' was a mediaeval name for brothel, first used in France. See the chapter, ' Women's Houses ', in Iwan Bloch's *Prostitution*, Vol. I. Berlin, 1912.

as this man lived the life of a libertine he was respected for his justice and uprightness and for his true patriotism. But when he devoted himself entirely to politics he renounced his debaucheries and his virtues at the same time[1].' This is a very interesting psychological manifestation. For the virtues and faults of the individual have a very close connection with his or her sexual life. If the former are to be understood, the latter must be taken into account, and what applies to the individual applies likewise to society. The sexual life of a society, with its various symptoms, is always a true reflection of the culture of the age.

The grand fancy-dress balls, at this time at the height of their popularity, were the rallying point of the best society.

The precursors of these balls were the ' masques ' of the seventeenth century, and three of the most famous authors of these were Daniel, Campion and Ben Jonson. This last had, according to Taine, really invented these plays, at which sumptuous luxury was displayed.

' His hands shuffle all things together: the Greek gods, the whole Olympus of olden time, allegorical figures as depicted by the painters of those days, the divine, the human, the abstract, and the real, the antique and the modern. He brings them all on to the stage, creating a mixed brew of harmonious grouping, songs, allegories, to excite or intoxicate the artistic senses of the onlookers. The élite of the kingdom appears on the stage—no buffoons in borrowed, ill-fitting costumes, moving uncouthly about, but ladies of the court, queens in the full splendour of their rank and pride, decked with real diamonds. They make a show of the luxuries they possess, so that the whole splendour of national life may be concentrated, like jewels in a jewel-case at the opera. What dresses! What pomp!

[1] Archenholtz, *England*, Vol. II, pp. 260-261.

What a gathering of queer individuals ! What a crowd of gipsies, magicians, gods, heroes, priests, gnomes! What transformations, dances, wedding-songs and fights! What a shifting of scenery, landscapes, buildings, floating islands, triumphal arches, symbolic spheres! Gold glitters, jewels sparkle, the purple catches the light of the big chandelier in its rich folds, the ruffled silk reflects the light, flashing diamonds adorn the ladies' bosoms. The brocaded costumes are covered with silver embroidery and decorated with strings of pearls, appliquéd with golden flowers and fruits and all kinds of bizarre arabesques, giving the impression of a picture within a picture. The steps of the throne are adorned with statues of the God of Love holding torches. Musicians in scarlet and purple wraps, with laurel-wreaths on their heads, play in the arbours, crowds of masked players pass up and down in ever-changing groups. Some of them wear silver and red-brown costumes, others sea-green and orange. The short white jackets are embroidered with gold, and all costumes and jewels are surpassingly rich. The throne floats in a sea of light[1].'

But these masques of the seventeenth century were mere show pieces, and thus differed from the masquerades of the eighteenth century, in which the whole of the distinguished company took part, The fancy-dress balls were essential components of the richly coloured picture of English High Society in the eighteenth century; and Fitzgerald rightly picks them out as ' the note ' of the general taste, mentioning at the same time the large buildings erected for this special purpose, such as Ranelagh[2], the Pantheon[3], Almack's, and the famous building of Madame Cornelys in Soho Square[4].

[1] Taine, *loc. cit.*, Vol. I, pp. 460-461.
[2] Seé Chapter IV.
[3] *Ibid.*
[4] P. Fitzgerald, *Life of George IV*, Vol. I, p. 52.

The fancy-dress balls helped to a very great extent to spread immorality. Complaints were made at the very beginning of the excesses indulged in at such festivals. The Bishop of London in 1726 preached from the pulpit against fancy-dress balls. Three years later the ' Grand Jury of Middlesex ' declared that the fancy-dress balls were the chief promotors of vice and immorality[1]. Great scandals were often caused by the behaviour of the mob, on which Archenholtz reports as follows: ' The English mob takes part in fancy-dress balls in a curious and such an unpleasant way, that it is surprising how refined ladies can, under such circumstances, seek such dearly-bought pleasures. Owing to their great number, many of the carriages were compelled to wait for a time in the street, and the masked passengers were at the mercy of the crowd. All the waiting carriages were illuminated with torches by these outcasts of the nation, deriding those inside with the wit of the fish market, obscenities and bawls of laughter. They climbed on the wheels of the carriages, holding their torches under the noses of those inside. But the amusement usually went no further than curiosity and derision[2].'

The costumes at such fancy-dress balls were mostly rich and very expensive; some of the ladies, however, distinguished themselves by their lack of costume. Lady Elizabeth Montague gives a description of the costume of a certain Miss Chudleigh at a fancy-dress ball in 1750: ' Miss Chudleigh's dress, or rather undress, was very interesting. She represented "Iphigenia before her sacrifice ", but she was so unclothed that the High Priest had no difficulty at all in closely examining the victim. The ladies, who themselves were not too strait-laced, were so revolted at this that they

[1] H. D. Traill, *Social England*. London, 1896. Vol. V, pp. 141-142.
[2] Archenholtz, *England*, Vol. III, pp. 215-216.

refused to speak to her[1].' 'Spleen', too, was often expressed in curious ways. King George III, who was not especially fond of the fancy-dress balls, once in 1771 induced Colonel Luttrel to terrify the company at a ball by appearing in a coffin clad in a shroud; he accordingly did this, frightening the guests and especially the ladies, until he was finally turned out by a man disguised as a sailor[2].

The most famous fancy-dress balls of the eighteenth century were those at Almack's, and those arranged by Madame Cornelys (or Cornelis).

Almack's was so called after the name of a Scotchman who had the ballroom built in 1764, on the southern side of King Street, St. James's, and inaugurated it by giving a sumptuous festival ball attended, amongst others, by the Duke of Cumberland, the victor of Culloden. The great ballroom held 1,700 persons. The fancy-dress balls at Almack's were organised by a committee of distinguished ladies, and only members of the ' upper ten ' were admitted. Gilly Williams describes in his letter to George Selwyn on the 23rd February 1765: ' A new subscription of 10 guineas has been inaugurated at Almack's for which, in three very elegant, newly-built rooms, one can attend a ball and supper a week for twelve weeks. Considering the rather high entrance fee, it is to be presumed that the company will be a select one.'

Almack's existed until after the middle of the nineteenth century, and was later called Willis's, this being the name of its new proprietor. Until 1850 the entertainments held there were distinguished by their exclusiveness. After that time the reputation of this old and famous establishment

---

[1] Doran, *A Lady of the Last Century*, p. 57.
[2] Archenholtz, *England*, Vol. III, pp. 213-214.

gradually declined owing to the ' plebeian invasion ', and finally it was closed in 1863[1].

The fancy-dress balls arranged by Madame Cornelys (Cornely or Cornelis), the ' Empress of Taste and Voluptuousness[2] ', one of the most interesting adventuresses of the eighteenth century, were even more sumptuous than those at Almacks.

Madame Cornelys, as she was called in London, was originally Teresa Imer. She came from the German Tyrol, and was the daughter of the actor Imer, whose troupe performed in Italian theatres in the first three decades of the eighteenth century. Teresa was a striking beauty, and in her early years had had love affairs with distinguished Italian gallants, such as Senator Malipieri, at whose house she became acquainted with Casanova in 1740. We learn from the *Memoirs* of the latter that she was his lover for a short time, and that he adopted her son, born in 1746, whom he took to see her after her emigration to London in 1763[3].

The clearest picture of her personality and life may be obtained from descriptions of her by some of her contemporaries.

Archenholtz writes: ' This German-Tyrolean woman of low origin attained to a good position in London by the recitals she gave, although she was but a very mediocre singer. Having made the acquaintance of several distinguished ladies, she rented a large fine house and had it

[1] Since the beginning of the nineteenth century Almacks had served as a concert hall. Concerts were given here from 1808 to 1810 by Mrs. Billington, Mrs. Braham and Signor Naldi, the rivals of Catalini who sang in the ' Hanover Square Rooms '. Charles Kemble's famous Shakespeare recitals were given here in 1844. See J. Timbs, *Curiosities* of *London*, p. 3.

[2] *Sérails de Londres*, p. 215.

[3] See Victor Ottmann, *Jacob Casanova von Seingalt, his Life and his Works.* Stuttgart, 1900. Pp. 19-20, 22-23, 62, 76.

furnished in princely fashion[1]. The entertainments here consisted of recitals, balls and masquerades. No one but subscribers were admitted, and even these had to produce a written permit from one of the presiding ladies. Less than twelve tickets could not be bought, and these at first cost only six guineas, but later the price was raised to nine guineas. For the first year the number of subscribers was 2,700. The anniversary of the foundation of the establishment was celebrated every year by a fancy-dress ball, on which occasion anyone was admitted without distinction. The entrance fee was two guineas, but for this sum a fine supper was served at two o'clock in the morning. She told me herself that more than 8,000 tickets were sold on such occasions.'

All these festivals differed considerably from one another, thanks to the inventive genius of this woman of extraordinary talents. Illuminated arcades, triumphal arches, rooms transformed into gardens with orange-trees, fountains and lovely flowers were seen here; transparent paintings and inscriptions, flights of stairs and avenues with coloured lamps arranged in pyramidal and other designs, festooned with garlands; specially arranged tables for the repast, a series of splendid rooms, each furnished luxuriously in some oriental style—Persian, Indian, Chinese, etc. The greatest ceremony prevailed, augmenting considerably the splendour of the entertainment. Nine thousand artistically arranged wax candles burnt in the rooms on these anniversaries.

Madame Cornelys was not avaricious; she was always in debt and was, as a rule, imprisoned after each party, until at last these entertainments had to be discontinued, and

[1] This house was called ' Carlisle House ', and was in Soho Square by the present Greek Street. See Henry Sampson, *A History of Advertising*. London, 1874. Pp. 483-484; and Jouy, *L'hermite de Londres*, Vol. I, p. 6.

henceforth she, the former ' Empress of Taste ', depended entirely on the kindheartedness and charity of her friends[1].

The Soho masquerades were in vogue for about twenty years, during which time Madame Cornelys was repeatedly in the debtor's prison, and, after a final bankruptcy, she disappeared from the scene for ever. The famous house at 20-21 Soho Square existed for many years and preserved some of its former splendour in its interior decoration. Its last owners were a firm—equally celebrated in its way—Crosse and Blackwell of ' Pickles ' fame[2]!

The game ' Faro ' mentioned in *Humphrey Clinker* as a special attraction at Cornelys' house, was one of the indispensable fashionable amusements of distinguished English society in the eighteenth century, and had passionate devotees, particularly in the higher-class *demi-monde*. Some idea of how widely this vice was spread amongst women is given by the correspondence of George Selwyn, which contains several descriptions on the subject, and these are confirmed in the memoirs of Casanova[3].

The distinguished courtesans of the eighteenth century can be compared in every respect to French ' Maîtresses ', these having indubitably been their models. The same wit, the same elegance, the same splendour, and not infrequently the same cunning. The search for pleasure held men and women equally in its grip. Lady Mary Wortley Montague writes in one of her letters: ' I deplore the unpopularity of the married state, which is scorned by our young girls nowadays, as once by the young men. Both sexes have

[1] Casanova's *Memoirs*, Vol. XV, pp. 91, 108-109.

[2] Adrian, in his *English Sketches*, gives a very vivid description of a masquerade under George IV (Frankfurt a.M., 1830), Vol. I, pp. 82-124; also Pierce Egan in his *Life in London*, ed. Hotten, London, 1900, pp. 230-250, with the ' Masquerade song ', pp. 240-242.

[3] See E. J. Roscoe and Helen Clergue, *George Selwyn, his letters and his life*. London, 1899. P. 18.

discovered its inconveniences, and many feminine libertines may be found amongst young women of rank. No one is shocked to hear that " Miss So and So, Maid of Honour, has got nicely over her confinement "[1].'

The actress Anna Bellamy was the most talented of all these English courtesans. She was beautiful and clever, and her house was a regular ' Bureau d'Esprit ', a gathering place of all distinguished and learned men, and even ladies of high rank[2], and she is worthy of mention in the history of the emancipation of women. At the same time, she was one of the most amorous and lascivious women of her age. She was born in 1731, the illegitimate daughter of Lord Tyrawley, an old _roué_. She became an actress at Covent Garden Theatre, and died in 1788, after writing her rightly famous memoirs[3].

Archenholtz describes Miss Bellamy as follows:

' Whilst we are on the subject of distinguished courtesans, we must mention the brilliant actress who played for 30 years in London theatres, Miss Anna Bellamy, who is still alive and has just finished her " Memoirs ", containing the very interesting and instructive history of her life. She was perhaps not quite an Aspasia, but more a Maintenon. Her beauty, her wit, her intelligence, her talents, her generosity and refined manners irresistibly attracted everyone to her. Her house was a gathering place of great and celebrated men. She was an intimate friend of Young, Thomson, Littleton, Garrick and Chesterfield. Ministers of State, generals, ambassadors, visited her daily and sat at her table,

[1] Quoted from Johannes Scherr, _History of English Literature._ Second edition. Leipzig, 1874. P. 125.

[2] _Sexual Debaucheries in the Countries of the Old and New World_, etc. New edition, without place or date, p. 137.

[3] See P. Fitzgerald, _The Romance of the English Stage_ (London, 1874), Vol. I, p. 106; Archenholtz, _Annals_, Vol. I, p. 402; Walter Thornbury, _Haunted London_ (ed. Walford, London, 1880), pp. 317-318.

at which the choicest food for mind and body was abundantly offered them, adding to the refined pleasures of social life. She took an active part in court affairs, and in the elections. She could scarcely be quoted as a model of feminine virtue, for she always had a favourite lover with whom she lived. But so great was the power of her extraordinary merits and her well-proved nobleness of spirit, that even irreproachably virtuous ladies of the highest rank maintained social intercourse with her and permitted their daughters to do the same, for the good of their minds and hearts[1].'

It is of psychological interest that this woman, who had loved and was loved by so many—even by the famous Fox[2] —came in the end to the knowledge which is spared to no man or woman of pleasure: ' Les jouissances que la vie offre à nos sens, à de grandes intervalles, sont souvent perfides, presque toujours équivoques et jamais durables; mais les peines sont sûres, elles semblent plus s'identifier avec notre existence[3].' It is a pity that this observation, of particular interest considering the mouth from which it came, should have escaped the attention of Schopenhauer, the great philosopher of pessimism, whose habit it was to collect and quote such-like sayings.

Besides Miss Bellamy, Kitty Fisher and Fanny Murray were regarded as the most accomplished courtesans of that period; they are mentioned in many writings of their day[4],

[1] Archenholtz, *England*, Vol. II, pp. 255-256.
[2] Miss Bellamy, *Memoirs*, Vol. I, pp. 260 ff. [3] *Ibid.*, Vol. II, pp. 27-28.
[4] For example, in a book which appeared at Geneva in 1785, *Les Amours et les Aventures du Lord Fox*, at the close of which the following remarkable reflection appears: ' Les femmes qui, dans les siècles plus reculés, ont fait commerce de leur vertu, peuvent-elles se comparer à celles de nos jours? Les Flora, les Laïs, etc., ont vécu dans l'éclat de la magnificence: encore laissèrent-elles après leur mort d'immenses richesses. Flora, en mourant, a légué au Sénat de Rome une somme considérable pour l'institution d'une fête annuelle sous le nom de Jeux Floraux. En Angleterre, une contemporaine de Fanny Murray et de Kitty Fisher devint assez riche pour se donner 30,000 livres st. de rente.'

admired by their most celebrated contemporaries for their extraordinary beauty, and vied with each other in gallantry and unparalleled luxury.

Archenholtz writes of Kitty Fisher: ' One of these girls, Kitty Fisher, distinguished herself—about 25 years ago—by the unique manner in which she served the goddess Venus. By nature endowed in the highest degree with beauty and intelligence, wit and liveliness, she was greatly admired and desired by all such as preferred the joys of sexual contacts to all the other pleasures of life. This priestess was well aware of her value, and fixed therefore the sum of 100 guineas as the price of her favours for one night; she had, nevertheless, plenty of admirers, who did not appear to be discouraged by this large amount. The late Duke of York, brother of the present king, was amongst them. After having spent a night with her, he gave her a bank-note for £50 sterling, for he happened to have no more on him. Miss Fisher was very much offended, and gave him to understand that she did not wish any further visits from him, and to show her contempt for his present she sent the bank-note (which, as everyone knows, is made of a specially thin paper) to a pastrycook, who put it into a tartlet which she afterwards ate for breakfast[1].' This anecdote, reminiscent of the history of Cleopatra's pearl[2], is consistent with other reports of the unlimited pride of this ' Flora of London '. She chose her lovers only from amongst men of good position, as was seen when she was once taken ill. Amongst other celebrities, six members of the House of Lords had their names entered in the list of visitors. She was very extravagant, and in luxury did her best to surpass the highest classes of society. She did not, for instance, deny herself the pleasure of once eating fresh strawberries

[1] Archenholtz, *England*, Vol. II, pp. 251-252.
[2] This is perhaps why Reynolds painted her as Cleopatra.

in winter, for which she had to pay the enormous price of twenty guineas! One night she surprised the audience of a theatre by having tea served in her box during the performance. In short, she resembled an English Dubarry[1].

Fanny Murray (died in 1770) was the daughter of a musician in Bath, and had been married to a Mr. Ross. She was renowned between 1735 and 1745. Horace Walpole mentions her in a letter to Conway in 1746 as a ' famous beauty '. She was the mistress, amongst others, of John Spencer and Beau Nash. Her name was immortalised in a very doubtful fashion by the rôle she was given in the obscene satire of the well-known political agitator and author, John Wilkes, *An Essay on Woman*, dedicated to her, in which she is represented in sexual activity[2].

There were many other beautiful and intelligent courtesans in the eighteenth century, such as Miss Lucy Cooper, frequently mentioned in *Sérails de Londres* and in other similar books on courtesans; further, Mrs. Harriet Errington, who used to honour her numerous (mostly military) lovers by presenting them with locks of her hair[3]; and Miss Parsons, the lover of the Duke of Grafton[4].

---

[1] *Tableau descriptif, moral, philosophique et critique de Londres en* 1816. Paris, 1817. Vol. I, p. 118.

[2] See ' Wilkes and the Essay on Woman ' in *Notes and Queries*, second series, No. 79, 4th July 1857, p. 1; No. 80, 11th July, p. 21; and No. 81, 18th July 1857, p. 41. A German book, *History of the famous Miss Fanny Murray*, translated from the English (Nuremburg, 1780), was not accessible, nor the English original.

[3] See the *Memoirs of Mrs. Harriet Er-g-n, containing her amours, intrigues and tête-à-têtes with the Colonel M-n, Colonel T-l-n, Captain Sm-th, etc.* London, 1780-90. On the title-page the heroine is depicted holding a pair of scissors, with which she has just cut off a lock of her hair for her gallant. This lies on a piece of paper.

[4] *Memoirs of the amours, intrigues and adventures of Charles August du Fitz-Roy, Duke of Grafton, with Miss Parsons.* London, 1769; also under the title: *Intrigues à la mode. Biographical memoirs of the Duke of Grafton, including some particulars in the life of the celebrated Miss Anna Bella Parsons.* London, no date. With coloured portrait of Parsons.

These priestesses of Venus generally had, besides the lovers who supported them, a great number of admirers, some of whom fell desperately in love with them, and were driven by jealousy to commit terrible deeds, as in the tragic career of Miss Ray, who was murdered by the preacher Hackman.

James Hackman, son of an officer and at first himself an officer, later a preacher, became acquainted at Lord Sandwich's house in Minchinbroke with Miss Martha Ray, daughter of an artisan in Holywell Street, London. When eighteen years old she had become the mistress of John Montagu, fourth Earl of Sandwich, by whom she afterwards had several children. She was unusually pretty, and everybody was charmed with her exceptional beauty and by her marvellous voice, which had been trained by Giardini for the stage. Hackman immediately fell passionately in love with this attractive young woman and pursued her for years with proposals of marriage which, however, always met with refusal. He ended by putting a bullet through her head on the 7th April 1779 in a fit of jealousy, as she left the theatre after a performance of *Love in a Village*. She was killed on the spot. He then turned the pistol against himself, but was not severely wounded. This affair made a great stir, and reports on it were published next day in all the London newspapers. But he very soon atoned for his crime, for he died at the age of twenty-seven on the gallows at Tyburn. Miss Ray was thirty-four[1].

The English theatre also contributed to the number of

---

[1] See *Dictionary of National Biography*, ed. Stephen and Lee (London, 1890), Vol. 23, pp. 422-423; J. H. Jesse, *George Selwyn and his contemporaries* (London, 1882), Vol. IV, pp. 59-65 (with picture of Ray by Dance on p. 59). Boswell describes, in the Life of Johnson, the execution of Hackman, whom he accompanied to Tyburn. Sir Herbert Croft in 1780 published a fictitious correspondence between Hackman and Miss Ray, under the title *Love and Madness—a story too true, in a series of letters between parties whose names would perhaps be mentioned were they less known or less lamented.* London, 1780, 8vo.

the courtesans of the eighteenth century. The ladies of the theatre allowed themselves almost unlimited sexual freedom, which in smaller towns and in itinerant troupes of players, differed little from genuine shameless prostitution[1].

The author of *London and Paris* writes of the famous singer (of Drury Lane and Covent Garden), Mrs. Billington: ' I have seldom seen the gifts of the gods and goddesses so lavishly bestowed on one woman as on this musical Pandora. Apollo gave her the magic gift of music and mime; Bacchus dissected ten of his fresh, round-limbed, plump maenads and nymphs and created of them a picturesque, lovely, rosy form to be his faithful servant; the goddess of Cyprus rewarded her devout priestess for the abundant clouds of incense which she burnt at secret altars in her honour, by yoking royal princes, dukes and nobles to her chariot.'

' When she first cast her magic net in Dublin the Duke of Rutland, Viceroy of Ireland, was caught in it. She had long arrived at a mutual tolerance with the man whose name she took on giving up her maiden name of Weichsel. " Her obliging temper cannot resist the importunities of afflicted swains ", writes the author of the secret theatre chronicles, *Secret History of the Green Room* (London, 1795, Vol. II, p. 73), in which the curious will also find a list of the parts she took at Covent Garden.

' Cyprus also sent her youngest maidens and graces to adorn her firm, rosy, plump limbs with glittering jewels, her throat and wrists with strings of oriental pearls and topaz pendants, her fingers with diamond rings, her figure with gems and golden girdles; Minerva, the goddess of plastic and graphic arts, had her portrayed by a hundred painters and copper-plate engravers (last winter her portraits in small and large copper-plate, in water colour,

---

[1] See *A Secret History of the Green Room*, by Hazzlewood (London, 1795), Vol. I, p. 318.

in charcoal, were the favourites in London print shops).
Mercury, finally, led the god of wealth and opulence, Pluto,
to her house, and the little blind god likewise found his
way in[1].'

A somewhat tempestuous career was that of another
heroine of the stage, Mrs. Abington (Fanny Barton).
Daughter of a soldier, she was at first a flower-girl. She
had many love-affairs, which resulted in her inevitable
infection with venereal disease; she was later on introduced
by the *demi-mondaine* and procuress, Sall Parker, proprietress
of a fashionable brothel, into distinguished society. Here
she became a friend of the notorious brothel-keeper and
courtesan, Charlotte Hayes, and became well known as
such ' at the genteel houses about Covent Garden '. In 1752
she appeared for the first time as ' Miranda ' in *The Busy-
body* on the stage of the Haymarket Theatre, where she
was very successful. She married the conductor, Abington,
with whom she had previously been surprised in intimate
tête-à-têtes. Her wedding-day—or rather, her nuptial night—
was marked by a tragi-comic event.

Not long before her marriage she had a liaison with
a very rich and extravagant Creole. He happened to
return from a voyage on the night of her wedding to
Abington, and hoped to spend some happy hours with her.
He rapped at her door at about midnight, and inquired if
Miss Barton were in. The maid informed him that Miss
Barton, in the meantime, had become Mrs. Abington, and
had just retired to rest with her newly married husband.
The unhappy Creole made an infernal noise, and insisted
on speaking to his unfaithful mistress. She finally appeared,

[1] Böttiger, *London and Paris* (Weimar, 1805), Vol. IX, pp. 73-75. See
also the *Secret History of the Green Room*, Vol. II, pp. 67-76, where her
love-affair with the impresario Daly is described, and it is told how her
husband caught her *in flagranti* with him. Her liaisons with the Duke of
Rutland, old Mr. Morgan and others are also related.

dressed rather scantily, and assured him that the maid had told him the truth, but that she would nevertheless henceforth visit him every evening and would spend the whole night with him! But he called her foul names and left her for ever. Her husband, too, was soon obliged to part from her because of her scandalous behaviour in Ireland, where she earned a great many laurels for her art, but became famous also on account of her love affairs, and by her shameless attire, in which her almost entirely naked bosom was exposed to lascivious, leering glances[1].

The actress Mrs. Edwards had also been, like Mrs. Abington, a prostitute in a Covent Garden brothel before she went on the stage[2].

The actress Mrs. Williams of Drury Lane was a permanent visitor to the fashionable brothels in Duke and Berkeley Streets, and her private income resulting therefrom amounted to a considerable sum[3]. Mrs. Curtis, a very ' vicious ' woman, sister of the famous actress Mrs. Siddons, delivered lectures in Dr. Graham's ' Temple of Health ' on certain topics that ' would make decent people blush[4] '.

Mrs. Harlowe, of Covent Garden Theatre, was notorious for her numerous love-affairs with very old men. She evidently suffered from the abnormal condition which Krafft-Ebing lately designated as ' gerontophilia[5] '.

The actress and courtesan Harriet Wilson, the ' English Ninon ', who became the mistress of Lord Craven when only fifteen, and afterwards had many love-affairs with men of high rank, such as the Duke of Wellington, the Duke of Argyle, and others, lived in the first quarter of the nineteenth century, in the reign of George IV. In her *Memoirs*,

---

[1] *Secret History of the Green Room*, Vol. I, pp. 41-58.
[2] *Ibid.*, Vol. I, p. 248.
[3] *Ibid.*, Vol. I, p. 353.
[4] *Ibid.*, Vol. II, p. 18.
[5] *Ibid.*, Vol. II, pp. 262-264.

describing her extremely eventful career as a courtesan, she gives a very clear picture of the frivolous lives of society people of this period.

The unlimited sexual freedom of actresses ceased in the reign of Victoria. This freedom, by the way, had been severely condemned by the most famous of all actresses of the eighteenth century, Mrs. Siddons, the most perfect interpreter of Lady Macbeth, who moved George III to tears by her wonderful performance; her hand had been respectfully kissed by Samuel Johnson; according to the lawyer Erskine she was a model of eloquence; and she was immortalised by Sir Joshua Reynolds as the famous 'Tragic Muse'[1]. The absolute unapproachableness of some of the actresses often called for desperate measures on the part of passionate, rejected lovers. The beautiful tragic actress, Miss Kelly, was twice shot at from the audience by rejected lovers[2]. In Victorian English society, actresses led a most respectable domestic life. Badly-paid chorus girls and ballet dancers only were for sale, and even the most beautiful of the more renowned actresses were ' de simples et bonnes bourgeoises[3] '.

There were ample opportunities, apart from the theatres, of becoming acquainted with prominent courtesans: at Ranelagh, Vauxhall, at fancy-dress balls and promenades, and especially in the elegant confectioners' shops, such as Hickson's (in Piccadilly), renowned for its wonderful cakes, consumed standing, while the eye roamed over the gallery of assembled beauties, and the internal heat was cooled with soda-water, fashionable since about 1810[4]. The so-called 'Alpha Cottages' between Regent's Park and

---

[1] Thornbury, *Haunted London*, pp. 319-320.

[2] *Ibid.*, p. 336.

[3] Rémo, *La vie galante en Angleterre*, p. 179. See also *Aus der Londoner Gesellschaft* (Leipzig, 1885), p. 309.

[4] Jouy, *L'hermite de Londres*, Vol. I, p. 336.

Paddington, the *petites maisons* of distinguished English society, were likewise rendezvous for amorous adventures[1].

But the best and easiest opportunities for gallant ladies to exhibit their charms were presented by evening parties or ' routs ', called ' arenas of fashion in the upper classes ' by the author of *Doings in London*.

Gambling was the chief amusement here according to Hüttner, but as is known all over the world, gambling and love are almost inseparable.

Jouy and von Rosenberg in the nineteenth century give a detailed account of these routs. Von Rosenberg describes in a particularly sarcastic and emphatic manner the fashionable behaviour of young people here, the flirtations of the fair sex and the bored cynicism of juvenile greybeards.

' Some booksellers and print-sellers, such as Ackermann and others, had a great collection of caricatures, drawings, sketches, copper-plates and the like, which they hired out for routs: three, four and up to five guineas were paid for them on each occasion.

' A number of elegant ladies and gentlemen sit around a table laden with pictures, caricatures, copper-plates, discussing the problems of light and shade, form and colour, of Rubens, Van Dyck, Raphael and so on. Form and colour had probably been thoroughly studied by these ladies before their mirrors. They keep themselves upright in their tight corsets, and the finest Chinese paints give them colour enough in the candlelight to prevent the rest of the ladies from casting a shadow upon their beauty. See, there is a novice, just come from school, perusing some nicely bound volumes and, seeing that mamma is absent, she quietly turns over the leaves in search of forbidden passages of Byron's *Don Juan*. A well-made but poorly dressed demi-god in high collar and stiff cravat lies stretched comfortably on a sofa, gazing

[1] Jouy, *loc. cit.*, Vol. II, p. 162.

nonchalantly through his lorgnette at the fairies standing about who, nearly fainting with fatigue, would give half the world for the quarter of a chair. All the means which beauty and an eloquent eye can invent they employ to make this recumbent Adonis abandon his composure and still more his comfortable position, but all in vain. He remains cool and prostrate.'

This is a quite good representation of the British Don Juan who, in the society of the eighteenth century and of the reign of George IV, played a very prominent but not at all creditable rôle. The study of English Don Juans gives a very interesting psychological insight into the character and peculiarities of the English men of pleasure who were the models for French and German novels of the nineteenth century.

One of the main features of the British Don Juans, who are completely distinct from the libertines of the Latin and of the other Teutonic countries, is the cool, brazen calmness with which they indulge in the sensual pleasures of life; love to them is much less an affair of passion than one of pride and of the gratification of their consciousness of power. The French, the Italian Don Juan is driven from conquest to conquest by his passionate sensuality. This is the principal motive for his actions and for his mode of life. The English Don Juan seduces on principle for the sake of experiment; he pursues love as a kind of sport[1]. Sensuality plays but a secondary rôle and in the midst of his sensual enjoyment the coldness of his heart is still painfully apparent.

This is the ' rake ' described by Richardson in his *Clarissa Harlowe*. Taine writes of this type of English Don Juan:

---

[1] Queensberry writes in 1766 to Selwyn: 'Bully (that is, Lord Boling-broke) is appearing again in society, and swears that he will seduce any innocent girl whatever. I do not doubt that he will.' See Jesse, *George Selwyn*, Vol. II, p. 66.

' What a character! How very English! How different
from Mozart's or Molière's Don Juan! Unyielding pride, the
desire to subjugate others, the provocative love of battle, the
need for ascendency, these are his predominant features.
Sensuality is but of secondary importance compared to
these. He will spare a young innocent girl because he knows
the conquest would be too easy and because her grandmother begs him not to seduce her. His slogan is: humiliate
the proud! " I like opposition ", he writes in one of his
letters. Pride, nothing but limitless, insatiable, absurd pride
is the main, the only, the central motive of his whole being.
He confesses that he considers himself the equal of Cæsar
and he condescends to private conquests out of mere caprice.
" I'll be damned if I'd marry the world's highest-born and
most beautiful princess if I knew or only suspected that she
had hesitated but for a second between me and an emperor! "
He is generally a jolly and witty talker but his humour is
only an outward symptom; he is coarse and immoral, he
jests like a hangman, harshly and cruelly, over the evil deeds
he has committed, or is about to commit. It can truly be said
of the libertines of this country and of those times, that they
threw human flesh into the carrion-pit. One of Lovelace's
distinguished friends decoys a young innocent girl, makes
her drunk, spends the night with her in a brothel[1], and
departs, leaving her there in payment of the bill, and rubs his
hands serenely in learning that she had been imprisoned
and had gone out of her mind and died. In France libertines
were but frivolous fellows, whereas here they were mean
brutes. Knavery had poisoned their love[2].'
  In view of the fact that an unmarried young man of the

---

[1] It was not much better in the *Midnight Spy* (p. 62), when Don Juan
Bamwell, son of an apothecary in Red Lion Square, systematically seduced
young girls and passed them on to his friends. Thus he alone furnished
a whole crowd of prostitutes.
[2] H. Taine, *loc. cit.*, Vol. II, pp. 406-7.

eighteenth century, with an annual income of £2,000, spent £1,800 on his private amusements, in which 'girls' took the first and last place[1], no one will be surprised at Lichtenberg's description of such a ' rake '.

' The real rake gambles, drinks, f . . . s, speaks of amorous pills and bougies, as one of us would speak of candied fruits or sweets; turns night into day and day into night, hence the eternal assaults against street lanterns and active and passive fights with the guard; he ruins innocent creatures who love him, fights duels with persons whose honour he has injured, spends money extravagantly, his own and that of other people, and all this is for the purpose of acquiring a reputation for himself[2].'

A distinguished man of the world of this type generally got up at noon or very frequently not until 3 p.m.; he took his breakfast and then went out on foot or on horseback. He dined with a few of his friends at 8, chatting with them until 11, and afterwards went to Vauxhall to spend another £20 on bad wine. He finally visited one or more brothels and went home at 4 in the morning[3].

These evening visits to brothels were signs of *bon ton.* All famous libertines of the eighteenth century, such as Foote, Selwyn, George Alexander Stevens, Lord Pembroke, Gilly Williams, and others, were to be found there.

The frequency of suicide is a conspicuous symptom of English Society. Montesquieu, even, was struck by it[4]. Archenholtz was greatly amazed by the appalling frequency of suicide cases amongst London libertines. ' In other countries young people of wealth and rank very seldom

[1] Archenholtz, *England,* Vol. II, p. 266.

[2] Lichtenberg's descriptions of Hogarth's engravings, published by Kottenkamp (Stuttgart, 1882), p. 224 (to the first page of the *Rake's Progress*).

[3] Jouy, *loc. cit.,* Vol. I, pp. 330-331.

[4] Taine, *loc. cit.,* Vol. II, p. 203.

seem to tire of their lives. It is not at all unusual in England, where great freedom prevails and people are able to satisfy their desires without fear of police interference, as in Paris; thus the nerves of these libertines soon get worn out and satiety steps in, leading at last to tragedy[1].

According to Schütz, climate and food were less responsible for these phenomena than the satiety, the profound melancholy, which comes from disappointment at the futility of all sensual pleasures. ' Luxury in London is extraordinary, and a youth who has thus rioted his passions in a perpetual frenzy, on reaching the age of manhood is seldom able to endure the adversities of life, these being in most cases the results of his early follies and debaucheries. We cannot, then, be surprised at his desire to make an end of it all[2].'

But a hypochondriacal disposition, as well as the heavy, gloomy elements of the English character, are equally important causes of these suicides, committed mostly, according to Rosenberg, in November, the notoriously foggy month. Suicides were often enough committed in brothels! A son of Lord Milton thus went one night to one of the fashionable brothels, had twelve of the most attractive girls sent in and gave them a sumptuous meal. He then closed the doors, ordered the girls to undress and entertain him with voluptuous poses and dances for a few hours. He then rewarded them in princely fashion, and shot himself[3].

The famous and notorious Duke of Queensberry, better known under the nicknames of ' Old Q.' or ' Lord Piccadilly ', was one of those whose lives really consisted of nothing but an endless series of love-affairs and amorous rendezvous[4].

---

[1] Archenholtz, *England*, Vol. III, p. 128.
[2] v. Scühtz, *loc. cit.*, pp. 171–172.
[3] Archenholtz, *loc. cit.*, Vol. III, pp. 131-132.
[4] The following description is chiefly from Jesse, *loc. cit.*, Vol. I, pp. 194-210, and the *Dictionary of National Biography*, ed. Stephen (London, 1888), Vol. XV, pp. 373-374.

He resembled the Don Juans of Latin countries in his insatiable lust.

William Douglas, third Earl of March and fourth Duke of Queensberry, was born in 1724. As a schoolboy he betrayed unusual and eccentric sexual inclinations, and later on he was to surpass all libertines of his age in this respect, being much assisted by his high rank and his princely fortune. He was a very elegant and perfect libertine, passionately devoted to gambling and horse-racing, a connoisseur and patron of arts and artists, a model of taste and elegance as regards his attire, and, in addition, kind-hearted, charitable and jovial. But these good points were negligible in comparison with his unparalleled debaucheries. The older he got, the crazier he became in this respect.

His house in Piccadilly (afterwards No. 138, near Park Lane) and his villa in Richmond were the Capri of this modern Tiberius. Sitting in the porch or at the window of his house in Piccadilly, this old man of eighty-six could be seen every day looking down at the passing beauties with amorous glances[1]. If he saw an acquaintance amongst the passing girls, or if one of them aroused his special interest, he ordered his groom—standing always at the door—to go and call her in. Incredible debaucheries, insane eccentricities in the realm of sexual pleasure, went on under the roof of this house, to which only sly allusions were made by his contemporaries, who spoke of it as the home of ' Oriental voluptuousness ' and ' refined sensuality ' ! Woman was everything to him, the only aim, the only reason for existence; although at the last he became deaf in one ear and blind in one eye, he paid his French physician Elisée

[1] ' This wrinkled, paralysed, toothless old Don Juan died the same corrupt unrepentant fellow he had been in the most fiery days of his youth. In a house in Piccadilly there is a low window where old Queensberry is said to have sat in order to leer at passing women with voluptuous eyes.' Thackeray, *The Four Georges*.

(former physician of Louis XV) large sums for each day his life could be prolonged. Elisée had to assist him at his love-affairs and help him in making preparations for his happy hours. Old Q. did not die of love, but of eating too much fruit, over 86 years old, on the 23rd December 1810. He faced death calmly and coolly, unlike the pious Samuel Johnson. He was, like Selwyn, never married, and bequeathed his immense fortune to his relatives, though one million was left by him to his servants and to some of his former lovers[1].

Sir Nathanial Wraxall, who was personally acquainted with old Q. during the last period of his life, writes of him: ' He sought for pleasure in all its forms, and was as eager for it at 80 as he had been when only 20. Having exhausted all the imaginable pleasures of human life, he settled down in his house near Hyde Park Corner, looking out of his windows at what Johnson had called " the full stream of human life ". I saw him nearly every day during the last seven years of his life. His body became a ruin, but his mind remained young. The fact is that in December 1810, when at the point of death, his bed was literally covered with at least 70 *billets doux* and letters written by women of the most varied social positions, from duchesses to semi-prostitutes. Being unable to open and read the letters, he ordered them to be left on his bed unopened, and they lay there until his death. Several fabulous stories about him were related—and believed—in the City, as, for instance, that he had a glass eye, that he used to take milk baths (in consequence of which belief Londoners had, according

[1] Catalogue of the legatees in Jesse, *loc. cit.*, Vol. I, pp. 206-210. The apothecary Fuller, in Piccadilly, claimed in addition £10,000 for 9,340 visits which he said he had paid to the Duke in the last seven and a half years of his life, and for 1,215 nights during which he had watched by him! The judge awarded him £7,000. *Gentleman's Magazine*, Vol. 81, Book II, p. 81.

to Jesse, an insurmountable distaste for milk), and other absurd things. It is, however, a fact that he performed the scene of Paris and the three goddesses in his dressing-room: three of the most wonderfully beautiful girls in London were brought there, dressed like the Homeric goddesses on the Mount of Ida, whilst he, in a shepherd's costume, rewarded the one he considered the most beautiful with a golden apple. This classic scene took place in his house opposite the Green Park. Neither the Duke of Buckingham—mentioned by Pope—whose whole life passed in an ecstasy of voluptuousness, nor any other contemporary libertine, ever indulged in such eccentric performances as took place in this rakish period[1].'

Old Q.'s passion for music accounts for his predilection for opera-singers and ballet-dancers. Owing to this passion for prima donnas and ballerinas, he supported the Italian opera in London financially to a considerable extent. The dancer Zamperini (born in Venice 1745) was one of his best-known mistresses, whose charming features were immortalised by the painter Hone (reproduction of portrait, Jesse, Vol. II, p. 69). In 1766 the Duke of Queensberry wrote to his friend Selwyn in France: ' I love this little girl, but how long the love will last I cannot tell. It may increase or be over before you are back[2].' This declaration is very characteristic of the Don Juans of those days. Indeed, ' Lord Piccadilly ' was notorious for the number of love-affairs he ' wound up ' every year, and for his extraordinary experience in erotic matters, in consequence of which he plays an important part in English decadent and pornographic literature[3].

[1] Jesse, *loc. cit.*, Vol. I, pp. 200-203.
[2] *Ibid.*, Vol. II, p. 106.
[3] The first place must be given here to the interesting work of J. P. Henstone, *The Piccadilly Ambulator, or Old Q., containing memoirs of the Private Life of the evergreen Votary of Venus* (London, 1808), with a picture

A curious mixture of depravity, eccentricity and scholarly inclinations, combined with a love of travel inherited from his mother, are found in the character of Edward Wortley Montague, son of the famous Lady Mary Wortley Montague, referred to in a work of Coates[1] as ' the British Don Juan '.

His life (1713-1776) was a series of curious adventures in all the countries of Europe and Asia. As a boy he escaped several times from his parents' house. Once he went to a chimney-sweep to serve as his apprentice; another time he went on board a ship as a cabin-boy; yet again he fled to Spain as a mule-driver[2]. His parents forgave him several times, but finally they had enough of his escapades, and when his mother died she bequeathed him one guinea[3]. After the death of his parents he left England for ever, travelled, especially in the East, changed his religion more than once, and died a Mohammedan. He had many love affairs in each country and many children by different women. But at last he longed for a legitimate heir. His plan was to marry a poor woman already pregnant, and to

of the Duke on the verandah of his house in Piccadilly. Further, old Q. was mentioned in the *Memoirs* of Bellamy, Vol. I, p. 59 (of the French edition); in Thackeray's *Virginians* as the Earl of March; in *Sérails de Londres and* another erotic book, *The Wedding Night or Battles of Venus, a Voluptuous Disclosure, etc.* (London, about 1830), which contains a long description of the Duke; in Wraxall's *Memoirs*; Horace Walpole's letters; Wheatley's *Round about Piccadilly.* The *Memoirs of the Life of the Duke of Queensberry* are worthless. Jesse included in the fourth volume of his great work on the period of George Selwyn, a picture on the title-page which brings before us the features of the famous old Q., after a plate by J. Cook. It is a jovial, smiling face with a great eagle's nose, which latter seems to confirm the old saying that men with great noses are great in love.

[1] Henry Coates, *The British Don Juan; being a narrative of the singular amours, entertaining adventures, remarkable travels, etc., of the Hon. Edward W. Montague, son of the celebrated Lady Mary Wortley Montague* (London, 1823).

[2] Archenholtz, *England*, Vol. III, pp. 81-82.

[3] Doran, *A Lady of the Last Century*, p. 130.

adopt the child born after the marriage. For, owing to his age and weak physical condition, he was convinced that he could not venture to hope for a child of his own[1]. He therefore declared, a few months before his death, his intention to marry a ' widow or a lonely lady of good family, and of refined manners, who must be in the fifth, sixth, seventh or eight month of her pregnancy[2] '. His cousin, Elizabeth Montague, writes of this queer fellow: ' When I first became acquainted with him, he was a dandy and a libertine; I little knew then that one day he would be engaged in rabbinical studies, wandering through the Orient as one of the travelling scholars of the world[3].'

A counterpart to Edward Montague was the notorious Baltimore, who had a regular Turkish harem in London. An action was brought against him for rape, but he was acquitted. Thereafter, he left England and never again returned. Casanova met him in Naples. Barthold describes this libertine as follows: ' This eccentric British libertine had been wandering through Europe for years, and was determined to travel as long as he could, for he did not wish to know where he was to be buried. Like a sultan he travelled in 1769 with eight women, a physician and two negroes, whom he called his Corregidores, because they policed his wandering *sérail*. With the assistance of his Aesculapius he acquired interesting experiences regarding his houris. He fed the fat ones only with acids, the thin ones on a milk diet and beef-tea. When he arrived in Vienna with his suite, Count von Schrottenbach asked him which out of the eight ladies was his wife. He answered that

[1] Coates, *loc. cit.*, p. 209.
[2] *The Encyclopaedia Britannica*, eighth edition (Edinburgh, 1860), Vol. XV, p. 506.
[3] Doran, *loc. cit.*, p. 130. He wrote also several treatises for the Royal Society and greater works, amongst others a book on *The Rise and Fall of the Ancient Republics*.

he was an Englishman, and as he did not care to stay in
a country where he was called to account for his being or
not being legally married, and where he could not settle
the affair by a fight, he chose to leave immediately for some
other country[1].'

It is obvious from these descriptions of the most prominent types of aristocratic English libertines of the eighteenth
century that they belonged to a very curious species of
Don Juan, and their adventures and their doings generally
were stamped with the eccentricity of the English. The fact
that these *roués* were, in most cases, immensely rich,
enabled them to satisfy all their desires without restraint.

Beside these aristocratic libertines, those of the middle
classes were of comparatively less importance, although, like
the former, they were seen everywhere: in the brothels, in
the parks, in music-halls, at the races and the theatres.

One of these middle-class libertines was Charles James
Fox, the famous statesman, one of the ' best dressed men of
his day ', a leader of the ' Maccaronis ', and at the same
time one of the most notorious rakes. ' The worst libertines
were outdone by him in his passion for every kind of vice,
insane luxury, wild pranks, pursuit of women and excessive
drinking[2] '. Samuel Foote (1720-1777) must also be mentioned here, the ' modern Aristophanes ', an actor at the
Haymarket Theatre, a dramatic poet, a very extravagant,
jovial libertine, who took an active part in all the mad
pranks of his good-for-nothing friends. In *Sérails de Londres*[3],
a visit he, George Selwyn, and Price paid to the brothel of
Charlotte Hayes is described, the curiosity of the two former
having been for some time excited by Price's enthusiastic
description of the pleasures to be found there. They became

[1] F. W. Barthold, *loc. cit.*, Vol. II, pp. 305-306.
[2] Jesse, *loc. cit.*, Vol. II, p. 220.
[3] *Sérails de Londres*, pp. 34-46.

[Pl. 17

Drawing by Roberts   A BARGAIN

acquainted there with a well-known Spanish courtesan, ' Countess of Medina ', who told them the eventful story of her life. Samuel Foote made a short speech to Mrs. Hayes, in which he enlarged upon the excellent qualities of the brothel, whilst George Selwyn was engaged in exploring the virginity of the inmates.

We postpone until later the description of George IV and his friend George Brummell as being typically representative of English High Society at the close of the eighteenth and beginning of the nineteenth century, and we will close this long list of English Don Juans with a few words on Lord Byron, whose love-life has been so much discussed.

In spite of his fiery, passionate soul and of his early desire for love, which set him aflame for Mary Duff when only eight, and for her beautiful cousin, Margaret Parker, when twelve, Lord Byron cannot be said to have been a typical Don Juan. He was not ' a lover of many ', but rather ' loved by many ', a man to whom women were always more devoted than he to them. His genius, his passion, his beauty, attracted women and took their hearts by storm. But in most cases his own was untouched, as with Lady Caroline Lamb, and with the charming Jane Clara Clairmont, mother of his daughter Allegra.

Walter Scott writes of Lord Byron: ' His was a face one might dream of.' One of England's most beautiful women exclaimed on seeing him for the first time: ' This pale face will be my destiny! ' Ackermann, one of the many Byron biographers, writes of him that in many cases ' he cast a downright spell over his lady worshippers ', but he himself was not the slave of woman[1]. The memoirs of Frances Ann Kemble give an idea of the irresistible impression he made on women. Under these circumstances, it can be imagined how

---

[1] Richard Ackermann, *Lord Byron. His life, his works, his influence on German literature.* Heidelberg, 1901. P. 59.

difficult it must have been for him to be guided by the ordinary principles of respectable convention in his relations with women. They followed him wherever he went, and, in their jealousy, those he rejected tried to damage his moral reputation by malicious gossip and lies. Thus, in public opinion Lord Byron was regarded as a lascivious Don Juan, and English society turned from him when the mysterious tragedy of his marriage with Annabella Milbanke became known: she left him quite unexpectedly after a year, and sued for divorce on the strength of ' secret information ' of a spy. This ' secret information ' is unknown to this day[1]. It is a fact, however, that Lady Byron later accused her husband of having carried on an incestuous liaison with his stepsister, Mrs. Augusta Leigh. She related this story, regarded even by Jeaffreson as ' monstrous and absolutely false[2] ', to Mrs. Harriet Beecher Stowe, who published it in her libellous book[3]. The complete falsity of this charge is satisfactorily proved in the Byron biographies written by Elze, Jeaffreson, Ackermann and others.

A peculiar contribution to the question of Lady Byron's divorce proceedings is given in two obscene poems published in 1865-1866, which must naturally be taken with some reserve as regards the cardinal point, but they must not be omitted from the history of this marriage, and should be discussed in detail[4]. The title of the volume containing these poems is: *Don Leon; a poem by the late Lord Byron, author of Don Juan, Childe Harold, etc., etc. And forming part of the private journal of his lordship, supposed to have been entirely destroyed by Thos. Moore.*

[1] See Ackermann, *loc. cit.*, pp. 74-75.

[2] J. C. Jeaffreson, *The Real Lord Byron.* London, 1883. Vol. II, p. 355.

[3] H. Beecher Stowe, *Lady Byron vindicated, etc.* London, 1870.

[4] After Pisanus Fraxi, *Index librorum prohibitorum.* London, 1877. Pp. 189-193.

Pardon, dear Tom, these thoughts on days gone by;
Me men revile, and thou must justify.
Yet in my bosom apprehensions rise,
(For brother poets have their jealousies)
Lest under false pretences thou shouldst turn
A faithless friend and these confessions burn.

To which is added : *Leon to Annabella; an epistle from Lord Byron to Lady Byron.* London: Printed for the Booksellers. 1866. 8vo, 52 + 57 + 17 pages.

The first poem, *Don Leon*, consists of 1,455 verses and it is an enthusiastic apology for paederasty. Lord Byron describes therein his various paederastic love affairs, excusing and defending himself for his tendency to paedication, this latter being—according to him—the reason for his conflict with his wife, in that he attempted and practised paedication with her during her pregnancy.

Ah, fatal hour! for thence my sorrows date:
Thence sprung the source of her undying hate
Fiends from her breast the sacred secret wrung,
Then called me monster; and, with evil tongue,
Mysterious tales of false Satanic art
Devised, and forced us evermore to part.

Lord Byron pleaded in excuse that he had committed the act because coitus could not be performed in the usual way owing to his wife's advanced pregnancy.

The second poem: *Leon to Annabell; an epistle from Lord Byron to Lady Byron, explaining the real cause of eternal separation, and forming the most curious passage in the Secret History of the Noble Poet.* Here the verdict of Lady Byron's lawyer, Lushington, is quoted: ' Lady Byron cannot live any longer with her husband. He has given her cause for divorce, which must remain for ever unrevealed.

Her honour as a woman forbids any further intercourse with him.' In the poem allusion is made to the reasons for separation:

> Oh, lovely woman! by your Maker's hand
> For man's delight and solace wisely planned.
> Thankless is she who nature's bounty mocks,
> Nor gives Love entrance whereso'er he knocks.
>
> Matrons of Rome, held ye yourselves disgraced
> In yielding to your husband's wayward taste?
> Ah, no!—by tender complaisance ye reigned:
> No wife of wounded modesty complained[1].

Neither of the two poems, of course, were really written by Lord Byron. Pisanus Fraxi learned from an acquaintance of the publisher, William Dugdale, that on the purchase of the manuscript in 1860 Dugdale really believed the poems were written by Lord Byron himself and was about to demand from Lady Byron a considerable sum as the price of his promise not to publish them. He, however, gave up the idea on the warning of a gentleman who, on examining the poems more closely, found passages in them containing allusions to events which happened after Lord Byron's death.

Another accusation had been brought against Lord Byron, previously to that of Mrs. Beecher Stowe. He was, in both cases, accused of sexual crimes. Whether incest or paedication was the graver of the two, remains an open question. No evidence whatsoever was produced to sustain either of them, or his alleged homosexuality, which was enlarged

[1] A new edition of ' Leon to Annabell ' was published bearing the title: *The Great Secret Revealed! Suppressed poem by Lord Byron, never before published, Leon to Annabella. Lord Byron to Lady Byron, an epistle explaining the real cause of eternal separation, and justifying the practice which led to it. Forming the most curious passage in the secret history of the noble poet, influencing the whole of his future career, etc*. A yet later edition appeared in Brussels in 1875.

upon by Moll[1]. Jeaffreson's report on Byron's ' Harem ' in
Venice[2] is, owing to this author's prejudices against Byron,
to be accepted with caution, although there is no denying
that the poet led a very debauched life in Venice and this
period of his life was the main reason for the great output
of literature on his ' love adventures ' [3].

With George IV (died 1830), who indulged in debauchery
until the last few years of his life, this gallant period, which
included the second half of the eighteenth and the first third
of the nineteenth century, came to an end, and was followed,
with the exception of the short interval of the reign of
William IV, by the Victorian era, lasting sixty-five years, in
which the whole character of society completely changed for
the better as regards morals. That is, it became more *moral*,
although this description, as will be seen, must be subjected
to certain limitations.

The influence and conduct of the court has always been of
the greatest importance in the character and morality of the
aristocracy, which is always imitated by the middle-class for
its social life generally. Thus the pure and happy domestic
life of the Queen naturally could not fail to exercise a great
influence, and an abrupt end was put to the previous period
of dissipation. The gambling houses, the gallant promenades
of Vauxhall and Ranelagh, the taverns and brothels, gave
place to a number of strictly moral fashionable clubs; while
the routs, which gave so many opportunities for flirtations,
love adventures and seduction, were replaced by blameless
receptions and garden parties. Duels were done away with,

---

[1] A. Moll, *Die Konträre Sexualempfindung*. Third edition. Berlin, 1899.
Pp. 136-137.

[2] J. C. Jeaffreson, *loc. cit.*, Vol. II, p. 68.

[3] For example, *The Loves of Byron, his intrigues with Celebrated Women;
Amours of Lord Byron* (London, 1848); *Private Intrigues of Lord Byron;
Private Life of Lord Byron;* C. Reiter, *Lord Byron's Liebesabenteuer,*
ca. 1858, two parts.

theatres were thoroughly reformed, and thus distinguished society was and is, to all outward appearance, a model of morality and purity. But unfortunately an occasional flash of lightning sometimes reveals a very dark side to things!

Such flashes are seen in the shape of repeated scandalous trials for adultery, or of the *Pall Mall Gazette's* revelations on the epidemic of defloration-mania in the 'eighties, this being in its way a unique and specifically English feature; or in the shape of the so-called annual ' elopement season ', when some distinguished lady would run off with her groom or coachman.

Neither is the 'gallant life' completely done away with. Only, the Don Juan of to-day prefers Paris to London for the scene of his love affairs and especially at the time of the second Empire, rich and distinguished Englishmen were much sought after by famous Paris hostesses. And there are even now certain pretty and elegant ladies, possessing fine houses and considerable incomes, who are neither respectable middle-class wives nor real courtesans. ' C'est une femme qui garde sa liberté et sa dignité, qu'on n'approche que difficile-ment, qui choisit ses compagnons de tendresse non sur la livrée mais d'après son goût. Elle garde son indépendance, ne dédaigne ni les cadeaux ni l'argent offert, mais ne lie pas son existence. Elle aime le plaisir en femme du monde, exquise et raffinée, et flanquerait à la porte le goujat qui se per-mettrait des plaisanteries grossières. Elle ne ruine pas les hommes comme nos sauteuses parisiennes, et se livre à l'amour pour l'amour, y apportant tout autant de feu que le partenaire[1] '. Here we have a realisation of the ideals of ' free love '.

Besides these women there are still always distinguished *cocottes* to be seen at fashionable hours in Bond Street and

---

[1] Rémo, *La vie galante en Angleterre*, pp. 44-45.

in Hyde Park, often enough carrying on social intercourse with respectable women.

The picture drawn in the well-known book *London Society by an Acclimatised Foreigner* (Leipzig, 1885), by a foreign diplomat, was, on the whole, true enough. He does not fail to stigmatise the frivolity hidden behind the prudishness which was especially conspicuous in discussing delicate topics. Much light is thrown upon this dark background of English social life by the authoress of a book published in 1861, by the well-known Berlin publisher Otto Janke, and entitled *Memoirs of a German Governess*. These memoirs, to all appearances authentic, give a true account of real events and impressions. They contain also examples of the appalling corruption of morals in certain English aristocratic circles. These ' black sides ' of the social life of the English upper classes must not be hushed up, neither because they are usually hidden by the oft-mentioned prudishness, nor because, on the other hand, they are in contrast to the highest and noblest forms of pleasure which in England can be enjoyed as in no other country. And therefore I gladly complete these descriptions by giving a pleasant picture of this fine art of living drawn by the art connoisseur Wagen[1].

' On the whole the assertion is justified that none know as thoroughly the art of enjoying life so finely and nobly as the English of the upper classes, who are not only rich but generally accomplished. They possess beautiful surroundings, ample opportunities for enjoying music, excellent private libraries, lovely country houses, are able to travel in the most interesting and beautiful parts of Europe and of the whole world. Finally, they can enjoy the most varied and interesting social intercourse, and it must be admitted that they have not much left to wish for.'

[1] Wagen, *Kunstwerke und Kunstler in England*, Vol. II, p. 78.

CHAPTER X

LADY EMMA HAMILTON

THE loveliest and most extraordinary amongst the many beautiful gallant women of the eighteenth century was 'that incarnation of healthy animal beauty[1]' Emma Hamilton, whose wonderful life and fate is a remarkable contribution to the history of English Society morals and must therefore be dealt with in special detail.

Emma Lyon was born in 1761 in Cheshire, the daughter of poor parents. At the age of twelve she became a nursery-maid in the house of a physician, Thomas, at Hawarden. She liked the family and never forgot them. At sixteen she entered the service of a greengrocer in London. Later on she was with a rich lady in whose library she had an opportunity of satisfying her desire for reading; she read all the bad novels she could get hold of, which prematurely excited and heated her fancy. Her ever-increasing charm was the means of her getting a situation in a family where she was treated as one of themselves; she took part in all their entertainments, and her talent for the stage was awakened.

Her future career was determined by her incomparable beauty. A contemporary's description of her is as follows:

'She had a perfect figure, fine regular features, and an indescribable charm and attractiveness about her face and in her expression. Her movements were light and graceful. She was joyous and gay, but far from giving an impression

[1] Traill, *Social England*, Vol. V, p. 299.

of frivolous flirtatiousness. Her lovely, clear voice, her expressive singing, soon charmed everyone around her and she began to take part in dramatic performances arranged at the house, winning general admiration and universal praise. She also soon began to show signs of the courage and self-reliance which were to dominate her character ever afterwards[1].'

Her first love affair had begun in a very curious way. A relative of hers was taken by the press-gang for a sailor, and when she applied to the Captain, John Willet Payne, for his freedom, he granted it but at the price of her own body. Thus she became the Captain's mistress. Later on a very rich and respected nobleman, Sir Henry Featherston, fell in love with her, and she was taken by him from her first lover. He took her to his country residence in Sussex, where she lived for a few months in splendour and enjoyment. In the autumn he took her to London, but soon left her alone, and she was threatened with poverty. She then became acquainted with the notorious charlatan Dr. Graham, proprietor of the famous ' Temple of Health ', of which we shall learn later. Graham was fascinated with her beauty and decided, in order to give new life to the exposition of his theories and to widen the already shrinking circle of his pupils, to employ at his lectures, as a means of illustrating his points, a young woman who was the perfect example of beauty and health. He sought, and found Emma, who suddenly found herself the representative of the blessed deities, enchanting the rapidly increasing circle of pupils. She sat as model to several painters and sculptors. Many valuable *objets d'art* of those times were copies of her beautiful face and figure. The number of her admirers was steadily growing and by this time she was free from all financial troubles.

[1] *History of Lady Hamilton* (Leipzig, 1816), pp. 25-26.

A great friend of the arts, Sir Charles Greville, also made Emma his mistress, further improved her talents, and took her to Ranelagh, then the 'most fashionable place of amusement and gallantry, where she immediately became the centre of attraction, everyone being charmed by her beauty, her dramatic talents and her lovely voice[1]'. She had her mother to live with her, took the name of Emma Harte, and by Sir Charles had two daughters and a son whose aunt she was supposed to be.

Sir Charles Greville was a nephew of the celebrated diplomat and connoisseur, Sir William Hamilton, British Ambassador at the Court of Naples.

He was one of those learned English epicureans who had, since the middle of the eighteenth century, settled down in sunny Italy to enjoy his life in a milder climate, surrounded with works of art, in contact with learned men, scholars and artists. He was ' engaged in philosophy, poetry, studied (like the elder Pliny) the phenomena of Vesuvius and, as a modern Pausanias, the ruins of Pompeii and Herculaneum. At the same time he was a passionate huntsman, and would roam the woods for whole days with the King, or go fishing with a line in an open boat under the scorching sun, although he was seventy years of age. Even later, in 1801, on cele-brating Lord Nelson's victory at Copenhagen, he danced the tarantella with his wife, forty years his junior, and quite wore her out. He also took pleasure in the sight of young people of both sexes, as we learn from Goethe's *Voyage*; the author saw, after dinner, a dozen youths swimming in the sea; a pleasure which was paid for by Sir William every afternoon[2]'.

This lover of art and life came to London in 1789, and at the house of his nephew Greville became acquainted with

[1] *History of Lady Hamilton*, p. 33.
[2] *Ibid.*, p. 309.

his beautiful mistress. He was immediately taken by her beauty and artistic mind, and most lively desires were aroused in him. The fulfilment of his wishes was made possible by the unsatisfactory financial situation of Greville, and so Hamilton found, as Goethe in his *Voyage in Italy* writes, 'after his long study of art and nature, the summit of all joy in nature and art in a beautiful young girl'.

Emma accompanied him to Italy, where she so perfected herself in her art under his guidance that her enchanted teacher married her the following year, and thus she was admitted at court. Here she soon became of influence, due mainly to her intimate friendship with Caroline, Queen of Naples, whose debaucheries made the court of Naples a modern Capri, as described in a rather exaggerated fashion in the Marquis de Sade's *Justine et Juliette.* According to the result of the critical revision of Gorani and Coletta's statements by Moritz Brosch, Caroline undoubtedly deserved to be named the ' Messalina of Naples ', for besides many love-affairs with different men, she was passionately in love with her friend Emma Hamilton. They were inseparable, and vied with each other in organising luxurious feasts and in devising and planning new and artistic amusements. There, also, Emma found many admirers, and was in no wise insensible to them: Lord Bristol, the Bishop of Derry (an ingenious, lively, coarse-witted man, whose rich assortment of anecdotes and *bon mots* seemed to be inexhaustible), had the honour of being one of her lovers.

The most celebrated and most portentous of all her love affairs was the one with Nelson, the great British admiral and victor of Aboukir. He first came to Naples in 1798, where a great festival in his honour was given by Sir William and Lady Hamilton, and attended by 1,800 guests. The relations between Nelson and Lady Hamilton soon became very intimate; they made excursions in disguise, wandering through the streets of Naples, visiting public places where they enjoyed themselves with the girls.

A revolution broke out, the court fled to Palermo, and Nelson accompanied his mistress there. Sir William and Lady Hamilton returned in 1800 to London with Nelson. They rented a house together in Piccadilly, where Emma bore her lover a son, Horatio Nelson. During the periods of separation due to Nelson's expeditions to Copenhagen and Boulogne, he wrote most passionate letters to his beloved. ' You need not be afraid of any woman in the world; besides yourself, not one is anything to me: I know but one, for who could be compared with my Emma? May Heaven soon give me the blessing of seeing your dear angel face again. You are unparalleled—there is no one worthy of cleaning your shoes. I am, always was and shall always be, your most devoted and constant friend.' On the 6th September 1802 Sir William Hamilton died, and Emma was compelled to leave the house in Piccadilly and moved into Clarges Street. Nelson settled on her an annual allowance of £1,200 after the birth of a girl. The hero's death at Trafalgar (21st October 1805) put an abrupt end to their union. Before his death he exclaimed: ' I am dying, it will soon be all over with me. Give my hair and all I possess to my beloved Lady Hamilton! ' And once more, already dying, he said to his physician: ' Hardy, take care of my beloved Lady Hamilton! Take care of my poor Lady Hamilton! '

After the death of her beloved hero, Emma very soon started on the downward path. She led a dissipated life, plunged into debt, was imprisoned in 1813 in the debtors' jail, and died in Calais in 1815 of a disease of the liver[1].

[1] *History of Lady Hamilton* (Leipzig, 1816); *The Letters of Lord Nelson to Lady Hamilton* (London, 1814, two volumes); J. C. Jeaffreson, *Lady Hamilton and Lord Nelson* (London, 1887, two volumes).

This extraordinary woman attained an important position
in the history of morals and art in another field, rather than
through her amorous and adventurous career; she was the
inventor and the first perfect presenter of the so-called
plastic poses or *tableaux vivants*, still in favour and
frequently seen in variety and music-halls even in our own
times, and which, performed by this plastic sorceress,
reached the level of the most noble and highest art.

' But the genius of Mrs. Hamilton ', writes Archenholtz[1],
' was manifested especially in a new invention. It consisted
of the imitation of the attire and poses of antique female
beauties as portrayed by well-known statues and pictures.
She herself personified them with great art. She appeared
in the graceful pose of a pensive Madonna of Guido; a few
minutes—a slight change of raiment—and the Madonna
vanished and changed into a Bacchante reeling with happiness, a Diana of the chase or a Medicean Venus. She thus
represented all the greatest statues and pictures, so long as
the subject was a woman.'

Goethe, in his *Voyage in Italy*, left an incomparably
beautiful memorial of Lady Hamilton's poses with their
conciseness and light grace.

' She is an Englishwoman of about 20 and is very beautiful and well built. She has a Greek dress made for her which
suits her wonderfully. She lets her hair down, takes a
couple of shawls, and presents such a variety of poses,
gestures, expressions, etc., that one finally wonders whether
one is dreaming. Accomplishments vainly attempted by
many artists were here seen finished, spontaneous and in
surprising variety: standing, kneeling, sitting, lying, serious,
sad, teasing, voluptuous, repentant, enticing, menacing,
anxious and so on, one follows after another. She changes

[1] Archenholtz, *British Annals* (1791), Vol. VII, pp. 167-168.

the drapery of her scarves and makes a hundred different head-dresses with one and the same piece of material. The old Knight holds the lights for her, and is wholly absorbed in the business. He sees in her all the antiques, the beautiful profiles of Sicilian coins, and even the Apollo of Belvedere. Anyway, it is a delightful entertainment, and we enjoyed it two evenings. This morning she is being painted by Tischbein.'

The most beautiful poses of Lady Hamilton were drawn and published in a volume of twenty-four engravings by the Prussian historical painter Friedrich Rehberg[1].

According to Henry Angelo's statement in his *Memoirs*, Emma once posed as a model at the Royal Academy of Art[2]. It is possible that this is the subject of a very spiteful etching by the caricaturist Thomas Rowlandson, formerly in possession of the bibliophile Pisanus Fraxi, now in that of the South Kensington Museum, London. Its title is ' Lady H . . . Poses ', and represents the interior of a painter's studio. An old man lifts a curtain and points to a young, naked girl standing as a model before a youth sitting at an easel, drawing with one hand and with the other holding a glass to his eye. In the background on the right two figures are embracing, and in the foreground, to the left, on the floor, two heads kissing each other are seen. The composition is very clever and the naked girl is especially well drawn[3].

---

[1] *Drawings faithfully copied from Nature, etc.* By Frederick Rehberg, Historical Painter in His Prussian Majesty's service at Rome (1794).

[2] *Reminiscences of Henry Angelo, with Memoirs of his late Father and Friends* (London, 1830), Vol. II, p. 242.

[3] See Pisanus Fraxi, *Centuria librorum absconditorum* (London, 1879), pp. 357-359.

BOOK II

BOOK II

CHAPTER XI

APHRODISIACS AND PREPARATIONS FOR ABORTION

A FULL study of the history of human sexual life necessitates the examination of internal and external sexuality in the widest sense of the word: by which is meant, natural and artificial, alimentary and medicinal means of stimulating one's own or attracting another's sexual instinct, and also for the removal of and protection against certain consequences of legitimate and illegitimate sexual intercourse.

Stimulation and attraction of the *libido sexualis* has been brought about in the alimentary sphere by alcoholic and gastronomic excesses; in the medicinal sphere by aphrodisiacs and cosmetics.

Among undesirable consequences of intercourse, against which special measures are taken, pregnancy, venereal diseases and impotence are the most important. From the earliest times a whole mass of quack remedies for abortion and prevention have been in evidence; and this has brought into being a special class of criminal, often most injurious to the general health and life of the community, namely, the quack.

This natural connection is to be seen in the study of the history of sexuality in England.

There is no doubt that the manner in which a people eats and drinks exercises a very strong influence upon its sexual life. The sort and choice of food and drink must not be ignored. In general it may be stated that an excessive consumption of meat and alcohol in the diet acts as a sexual stimulant, whereas a predominatingly vegetable diet—from which certain vegetables, acting as aphrodisiacs, have been excluded—produces a soothing effect upon the *vita sexualis*.

With this in mind it is clear that the Englishman's diet must exercise considerable influence upon his sexual life. For English diet has from ancient times been characterised by an unusually large consumption of meat and alcohol, accompanied by widespread intemperance at table. There can be no doubt that this has influenced the form and expression of the *vita sexualis* of the English, and helps to explain the frequency of such phenomena as, for example, flagellation-mania[1].

The well-known English folk-song, ' Oh, the roast beef of Old England', points to the age of this preference for meat. Johann Joachim Becher, a doctor of the seventeenth century, refers to this in his *Psychosophia* as a generally accepted fact: ' It is well known how unhealthy and smelly Englishmen are with their perpetual devouring of meat[2].' Boisguillebert, a French writer of the seventeenth century, describes the English in the same way as powerful beer-drinkers and meat eaters right down to the lowest classes, while the French of his time consumed almost nothing but bread[3]. Another Frenchman of that time, H. Misson de Valbourg, who published (The Hague, 1698[4]) an extremely interesting

[1] Hüttner, *loc. cit.*, p. 170, speaks of the ' deleterious effect of the frequent enjoyment of animal food on the blood and the consequent degeneration in morals '.

[2] J. J. Becher, *Psychosophia*. Second edition. Frankfurt, 1673. P. 200.

[3] Wilhelm Roscher, *System der Volkswirtschaft* (National Economy). Twentieth edition. Stuttgart, 1892. Vol. I, p. 628.

[4] H. Misson de Valbourg, *Mémoires et observations faites par un voyageur en Angleterre*. The Hague, 1698. Pp. 392-393.

description of the country, people and customs of England after staying there for some years, relates: ' Les Anglais mangent beaucoup à dîner. Ils mangent à reprises et remplissent le sac. Leur souper est leger. Gloutons à midi, fort sobres au soir. J'avais toujours ouï dire qu'ils étaient carnassiers; et j'ai trouvé que cela est vrai. En m'a parlé de plusieurs personne en Angleterre qui n'ont jamais mangé de pain; et pour l'ordinaire, ils en mangent très peu. Ils grignotent de temps en temps quelque miette, pendant qu'ils machent la chair à grandes bouchées.'

English authors corroborate foreign observers. Traill remarks that intemperance was so great in the reign of James I that ladies and gentlemen of the court frequently became dead drunk and rolled on the floor[1]; Macaulay refers to the enormous consumption of beer among the middle and lower classes from the fifteenth century, with a corresponding consumption of wine among the upper. After the end of a meal it was usual for the men to be lying drunk under the table[2].

Paul Hensel, in his valuable studies of English life at the beginning of the eighteenth century[3] describes the state of affairs at that time: ' Everybody drank then, and by preference, heavy wines. Burgundy was preferred to light red wine. Port wine and Sherry ran Burgundy close . . . Ladies did not refuse heavy wines at dinner, and the rest of the day did not pass without liqueurs of various kinds.'

Gastronomical themes were treated by celebrated writers. William King wrote for the Beefsteak Club an Art of Cookery[4].

---

[1] Traill, *loc. cit.*, Vol. IV, p. 161.
[2] Macaulay, *History of England*. German by W. Besseler. Brunswick, 1859. Vol. II, pp. 47-48.
[3] P. Hensel, *Englische sociale Zustände zu Anfang des achtzehnten Jahrhunderts* (English Social Life at the Beginning of the 18th Century). New Heidelberg Annual, 1899, Vol. IV, pp. 4-5.
[4] Gräss, *loc. cit.*, Vol. III, p. 374.

As the eighteenth century progressed there was an increase rather than a decline to be noticed in attention to the pleasures of the table. The lower classes especially shared the interest in food and drink in a marked manner.

From 1775 the taking of brandy increased to a formidable degree[1]. Moriz found the commonest sign in London to be 'Dealer in Foreign Spirituous Liquors'. He maintains that at the last uprising more men were to be found dead by empty casks of brandy than were shot by the soldiers[2]. There were, too, special drinking parties who met regularly for the enjoyment of a particular spirituous drink. Such, for example, at the end of the eighteenth century was that of The Eccentrics who foregathered with a man called Fulham in Chandos Street, St. Martin's Lane, to partake of a certain kind of ale known as ' Brilliant '[3].

Very favourite places for gastronomical and alcoholic indulgence were brothels, and bagnios and taverns frequented by prostitutes, which calls attention to the close connection between excesses in either sphere. These various temples of Venus generally possessed food and drink licences; and orgies were celebrated in honour of Venus and of Bacchus.

In the eighteenth century a strange rôle was played by the chamber-pot at table. Forster[4] recounts: ' The difference of food between the east end and west end of the town is remarkable. The total stranger however would find little difference; for everywhere people are stiff and unhelpful. Before dinner they sit motionless in their chairs, say little, fold their arms and are bored, until it is time for the meal. Then the women flock into the dining-room, no one gives them an arm. They start immediately to drink as at an inn, or drink one to

[1] *London and Paris*, Vol. III, pp. 16 ff.
[2] C. Ph. Moriz, *Reisen eines Deutschen in England im* 1782. Berlin, 1783. P. 21.
[3] John Bee, *loc. cit.*, pp. 15-17 and 73.
[4] Forster, *loc. cit.*, pp. 227-8.

another, separately; and afterwards healths are drunk.
Also, as soon as the ladies go, the chamber-pot is brought
in everywhere.'

There was little change in the nineteenth century: indeed,
things got much worse in the matter of indulgence in alcohol.
The consumption of meat, too, increased. Economic reports
are really astonishing. Porter reckoned the consumption of
a decent family, including children and servants, at 370
pounds each a year! While the yearly consumption of
meat per head from 1868 to 1871 amounted to 102·1 lb.,
it increased to 110·7 lb. in the years 1872 to 1883. In various
orphanages in London the daily allowance of meat for each
child was on the average between 0·23 and 0·438 lb. In
France a soldier gets a daily meat ration of 350 grams on
active service: in England he gets twice as much, namely
670 grams.

This excessive consumption of meat is not only responsible for the prevalence of gout, a specifically English
complaint, but without doubt exercises a stimulating effect
upon the *vita sexualis*.

The general endeavour of men to increase their natural
abilities in regard to the function of the sexual instinct is
probably one of the causes of the use of aphrodisiacs in the
narrower meaning of the word: particularly in cases where this
need exists because of the loss or diminution of the ' potentia
coeundi et generandi '.

Of the food which in England is considered specially
stimulating, Ryan mentions in particular: Fish, turtle,
oysters, crab, lobster, eggs, artichokes, truffles, mushrooms,
celery, cocoa, onions, ginger, pepper, apricots, strawberries
and peaches[1].

King George IV prized the aphrodisiacal property of
truffles so highly, that his ambassadors at Turin, Naples,

[1] M. Ryan, *Prostitution in London* (1839), p. 384.

Florence, etc., had instructions to keep the royal kitchens well supplied by special courier with large delicate and tasty truffles[1].

In England ginger was not only taken inwardly as an aphrodisiac, but it was thought that its outward application had a stimulating effect upon the *libido sexualis*. Thus, in an erotic pamphlet *The Amatory Experiences of a Surgeon* (London, 1881), the hero seduces two women, whilst he touches them with his hands rubbed in ginger.

Medicinal love-means, especially in the Middle Ages, were administered in the form of potions and powder. In the fifteenth century, for example, on the accusation of Richard III, Lady Elizabeth Grey was arraigned before Parliament for having enticed King Edward IV into marriage by means of a love-potion[2]. In later times cantharides were used almost entirely as medicinal stimulants, and especially in the eighteenth century they were the chief aphrodisiac. On this two-edged and dangerous expedient Venette writes: ' Spanish flies (cantharides) have so violent an effect upon the natural organs of both sexes. For if only two or three grains are taken, such burning and inflammation ensue that actual illness intervenes. This happened to a friend of mine some time ago who is still alive: his best man, in despair at seeing his own beloved married, resolved to put such cantharides in a cake which was to be eaten on the evening of the wedding. As the night passed, the bride-groom was so strong on his wife that at length she was almost worn out. But this pleasure was changed to distress: the groom at midnight was so inflamed that he could only make water with the greatest pain, and passed blood. Fear added to his suffering and he actually fainted. The

[1] John Davenport, *Aphrodisiacs and Anti-aphrodisiacs*. London, 1869. P. 88.
[2] *Ibid.*, pp. 72-73.

greatest care had to be taken of him until he was restored to health[1].'

This well-described case illustrates the almost typical consequences of the use of cantharides—the extreme inflammation of the urinary passage. Moreover, in many instances the expedient fails, as for example in the *Sérails de Londres* a nobleman had to have recourse to scourging with a birch when cantharides had failed to awaken his potency[2].

In another erotic pamphlet, *Randiana or Excitable Tales* (New York, 1884), marvellous powers are ascribed to Pinero-Balsam. At present such medicinal aphrodisiacs are sold generally by ' rubber-goods ' shops in the neighbourhood between Oxford Street and Leicester Square, but in England they have as little repute as in other northern countries, and mainly because the Englishman in need of a stimulant prefers flagellation to all other means.

As last group of aphrodisiacs certain appliances must be mentioned which women use to excite their *libido sexualis*, and which may be described as surrogates of the man. They are artificial reproductions of the male organ in the form of phalli, ' *godemichés* ', ' *consolateurs* ', ' *bijoux indiscrets* ', ' *bijoux de réligieuse* ', ' *Cazzi* ', ' *parapilla* ', etc. In England they were sometimes used under the name of dildoe or indiscreet toy.

According to an English author they are of great antiquity. Pictures of them in the hands of women are to be found in ancient Babylonian sculptures. For ' far away in those mystic times, among those primeval civilizations, one thing was then as it is to-day, one thing was destined to continue unaltered, the same, the passions, the loves and

---

[1] Nicolai Venette, *Abhandlung von Erzeugung der Menschen*. (A Treatise on the Generation of Men). Königsberg and Leipzig, 1738. Pp. 187-200.
[2] *Sérails de Londres*, p. 175.

the lusts of women '. In ancient India women made use of them also; and we know the ancient Greeks knew of godemichés from the plays of Aristophanes and other writers of comedy.

The countries of Western Europe learned of godemichés from the ancients. The physicians of the Middle Ages mention these appliances. In a catalogue of ecclesiastical punishments compiled by Bishop Burchard of Worms in the twelfth century occurs the following: ' Fecisti quod quaedam mulieres facere solent, ut faceres quoddam molimen aut machinamentum in modum virilis membri, ad mensuram tuae voluntatis, et illud loca verendorum tuorum, aut alterius, cum aliquibus ligaturis colligare, et fornicationem faceres, cum aliis mulierculis, vel aliae eodem instrumento sive alio tecum?[1]' From this description it is clear to what refinements of use for various purposes (masturbation, coitus, etc.) the godemiché was put.

During the Renaissance these appliances were made mostly in Italy and introduced into France. ' C'était l'Italie des Borgia et des Médici,' says Dufour, 'qui avait enseigné à la France, toutes ces pratiques, tous ces instruments, tous ces stimulants de prostitution; c'était la cour qui avait toujours la main dans ces jeux obscènes; c'était elle qui, ardente à s'emparer de ses innovations impures, les accréditait et les popularisait dans la nation, où il ne resta bientôt plus rien de la vieille candeur gauloise[2].' Catherine de Medici once found no fewer than four such *bienfaiteurs* in the box of one of her court-ladies[3]. In the seventeenth century godemichés were made in France of velvet or glass[4]. A refinement was introduced by way of

---

[1] Ploss and Bartels, *loc. cit.*, p. 453.
[2] P. Dufour, *loc. cit.*, Vol. V, p. 251.
[3] *Ibid.*
[4] *d'Ecole des Filles* (Cologne), p. 126.

novelty in the eighteenth century and was much appreciated. That was the addition of an artificial bag filled with hot milk, the compression of which simulated the act of ejaculation. Pictures of such *consolateurs* are often to be seen in erotic books of the eighteenth century. In Germany, too, these appliances were known. In 1701 Maria Cillie Jürgens was accused in Hamburg of having unnatural intercourse with Anna Elizabeth Buncken with the help of such an instrument[1].

In England dildoes, as they were called, were in great request, at any rate from the eighteenth century. John Bee remarks that they were originally called ' dil-dols ', and that these instruments had formerly been used far more frequently than in his time[2] (1835). Archenholtz gives further details over the commerce in dildoes in the eighteenth century: ' A woman, Mrs. Phillips, used this means to get her stock in trade known, for her shop is unique in the world. It consists of wares which are never sold publicly, which indeed can hardly be found at all in ordinary towns, and are only made and used in London and Paris. In Paris they are sold secretly in fancy shops; in London this woman has a shop near Leicester Square with them as her only wares[3].'

Ryan[4] refers to the use of godemichés in London brothels about 1840. According to a later authority they are sold at present by purveyors of erotic literature. They usually cost £2 10s.[5] and are made of india-rubber. There are different kinds; one that can be used by two women at the

[1] C. Trummer, *Studies of Torture and Witch Trials*, etc. Hamburg, 1844. Vol. I, pp. 81-82.
[2] Bee, *loc. cit.*, p. 205.
[3] Archenholtz, *England*, Vol. III, p. 125.
[4] Ryan, *loc. cit.*, pp. 198-199.
[5] *Love and Safety*, p. 60.

same time, another with appliances for several *orificia corporis*, a third with an attachment for the chin, etc.[1]

Superstition appears at times to play a part in the practice of these and similar appliances. Thus in a pornographic book, *Nunnery Tales; or Cruising under false Colours. A Tale of Love and Lust* (London, 1866-1867, 3 vols.) there is an exact portrayal (Vol. I, p. 70) of the way in which girls suffering from green sickness obtain relief by the use of the neck of a turkey.

An account of present use of the dildoe in England is to be found in the *Story of a Dildoe, a Tale in Five Tableaux* (London, 1880), in which three girls purchase such an instrument from their milliner. All details of its purchase and preparation and use are here fully described.

The ' Wonderful and Edifying History of the Origin of the Godemiché or Dildo ' which is printed at the end of an erotic work *The Schoolfellows; or Young Ladies Guide to Love* (London, 1830) is not an original, but is translated from *L'Histoire merveilleuse et édifiante du Godemiché* in the second part of *L'Aretin ou la Débauche de l'Esprit* of Abbé Dulaurens (Rome, 1763 and 1768)[2].

The use of cosmetics is less widespread in England than in other, especially romance, countries. Archenholtz remarks: ' English women rely on their natural beauty so much that they despise artificial aid. Only a few *filles de joie* put rouge on. Many, even on the most festive occasions, never put powder on their hair. Cleanliness, which is very carefully attended to, increases not a little the natural charms of the fair sex.'

The Celtic inhabitants of Britain knew, however, certain

---

[1] *Love and Safety*, p. 65.
[2] On the present use of the godemiché see I. Bloch, *The Sexual Life of our Time*. London, 1908. P. 412.

cosmetics, such as hair-lotion, rouge and hair dye[1]. According to Wright, small tweezers are to be found in the graves of Anglo-Saxon women: these were clearly used for the removal of superfluous hair. They knew, too, about colouring the hair. After the Danish invasion it was men who principally used cosmetics[2].

The century of gallantry and refinement led to the renaissance of cosmetics in England. Numerous perfumed waters and soaps were imported from Spain, Portugal, Italy, France and Turkey. But Windsor and Bristol soap was also much in use, and the famous ' Washballs[3] ' which contained injurious substances like white lead, quicksilver, etc. Especially celebrated was a Danish cosmetic which contained a mixture of numerous beauty-waters compounded with borax, vinegar, bread, eggs and—the heads and wings of doves. By its agency, women of fifty were said to be able to recover the fresh complexion of a girl of twenty[4]. In the eighteenth century face-powder and rouge came into prominence as cosmetics; and according to Hüttner, English women brought the application of rouge to a fine art.

Powdering, which has been known in England since the sixteenth century, was used almost to excess during the eighteenth century. In 1795 a tax was put upon powder, which caused much bitterness. Up to the middle of June in this year 300,000 persons had paid a guinea each for the right to use powder for one year. Others gave up powder for themselves, but had their horses or dogs powdered who were not taxed[5]. The tax, however, had this good effect: it roused energetic opposition to the excessive use of powder,

[1] Trill, *loc. cit.*, Vol. I, p. 114.
[2] Wright, *loc. cit.*, p. 80.
[3] G. Hill, *loc. cit.*, Vol. II, pp. 82-84.
[4] *Ibid.*, Vol. II, p. 83.
[5] Archenholtz, *Annals*, Vol. XVI, pp. 183-184.

which was led by the Duke of Bedford. Archenholtz relates[1]: ' The Duke of Bedford was responsible for a remarkable scene; in September 1795 he organised a pleasure party near Woburn Abbey among many of his friends, including Lords Russell, Villers and Paget, and Mr. Lambton, Mr. Day, Mr. Vernon, members of Parliament, and other prominent men. Here in the open a solemn ceremony took place of combing out of powder and cutting off of hair. All heads were cropped close and all the company agreed to pay a forfeit if any of them within a stated time used powder or ribbon for his hair. This example was very soon followed by the gentry of Bedfordshire and Hampshire, and the ladies vied with the men in no longer using powder, if not in cutting their hair.'

In the history of means of prevention and abortion in England, the very prototype of the first named is the condom, that sheath for the covering of the male organ before coitus, made out of the appendix of lambs, of fish-bladder, or rubber and so on, which is supposed to have been invented by a doctor named Conton in the reign of Charles II and which serves as a preventive against venereal disease and conception[2]. In spite of careful research I can trace no such person as Dr. Conton in the seventeenth century. In the sixteenth century, moreover, Dr. Fallopia had recommended sheaths of linen, and that such sheaths were in use in the seventeenth century is seen from the pornographical brochure, already mentioned, *L'Ecole des Filles* (published in the reign of Charles II), where Suzanne informs Fanchon that men put ' *un petit linge* ' over their member to prevent pregnancy. For all that the improvement of these sheaths by the use of animal skin may be attributable to the

---

[1] Archenholtz, *Annals*, Vol. XVI, pp. 184-185.
[2] For further details of the condom see I. Bloch, *Sexual Life of our Time*, pp. 378-79.

Dr. Conton who gave his name to the condom. Casanova also speaks ' of the little shields which the English have invented to keep the fair sex from worrying[1]'. In the eighteenth century, at all events, the condom was everywhere in use. As English specialities of more recent times, Hector France mentions condoms decorated with the portraits of Gladstone and even more eminent persons[2].

Bee mentions the word ' relieved ' as in popular use for the practice of abortion. Even then such criminal advertisements appeared in the papers. A certain White living in St. Paul's Churchyard practised abortion as his calling[3]. At a later date Pisanus Fraxi[4] refers to the widespread increase of this criminal practice in England, which was far greater than would be supposed from legal cases. A gentleman who had studied the question wrote to him: ' I know a case where a girl went to a doctor in the West End and found six or seven girls in the waiting-room, awaiting their turn to be operated on. The same occurred on two other occasions when she consulted that doctor. They were for the most part ballet girls or women in some way connected with the theatre. The fee was £5.'

Means for abortion, taken internally, are also in use. According to Taylor, English women use mainly Juniperus Sabina, the needles of the yew, iron-sulphate and iron-chloride, and in some cases even cantharides[5]. Maiden-pills made by a French doctor are much used; as is the apparatus for the prevention of conception, invented by an American doctor[6].

[1] Casanova, *Memoirs*, Vol. XIII, p. 208.
[2] Hector France, *Les Va-Nu-Pieds de Londres* (Paris), p. 65.
[3] John Bee, *loc. cit.*, p. 212.
[4] P. Fraxi, *Index Librorum Prohibitorum*. London, 1877. P. xxxvi.
[5] Ploss and Bartels, *Woman*, Vol. I, p. 764.
[6] Rémo, *loc. cit.*, p. 253.

Both in England and America pessaries are a favourite means of prevention; they often work, too, quite mechanically as means of abortion. The transactions of the National Medical Association for 1864 described no less than 123 kinds of pessary, ' from a simple stopper to a patent thrashing machine ' which could only be worn under the largest crinoline and looked like a water wheel. Dr. Buck, who gives the information, remarks acidly[1]: ' Pessaries, I suppose, are sometimes useful, but there are more than there is any necessity for. I do think that this filling the vagina with such traps, making a Chinese toy-shop of it, is outrageous. Hippocrates said that he would never recommend a pessary to procure abortion—nay, he swore he never would. Were he alive now he would never recommend one at all. If there were fewer abortions there would be fewer pessaries, and if there were fewer pessaries there would be fewer abortions. Our grandmothers never knew they had wombs only as they were reminded of it by the struggles of a healthy foetus; which by the by they always held on to. Nowadays, even our young women must have their wombs shored up, and if a baby accidentally gets in by the side of the machinery and finds a lodgment in the uterus, it may, per-chance, have a knitting-needle stuck in its eyes before it has any.'

For women and girls who are afraid of such criminal methods or by whom they have failed, there were even in the eighteenth century places and arrangements for secret deliveries. ' We have here ', says Hüttner[2], ' a large number of nursing homes in which young ladies can, unknown by the world, produce their illegitimate children. Nearly every newspaper receives announcements of one or more of such houses and their owners are in quite good odour with this

[1] *New York Medical Journal*, Vol. V, p. 464.
[2] Hüttner, *loc. cit.*, pp. 180-181.

honourable profession.' Archenholtz[1] gives further details about this: ' There are houses in London where women can be secretly confined, where they are provided with every comfort and well looked after. Their name and station remain unknown not only to their attendants but even to the owners of the house, so that the patient is as secure as if the confinement had taken place in another country, especially should she have chosen a house at some distance from her own home. The position of such houses is made known partly through the papers and partly by printed slips distributed in the streets.'

In the chapter on Pregnancy belong two interesting brochures of that time.

The first, by John Henry Mauclerc, who wrote under the pseudonym of James Blondel, is epoch-making in the history of the teaching in the so-called ' overlooking ' of women, which Mauclerc subjected to a brilliant criticism in his treatise on the power of imagination in pregnant women[2], which appeared in 1727, so that very little was actually left of this ancient superstition.

The second work is obviously an amusing satire by Sir John Hill (or, according to the bibliographer Lowndes, by F. Coventry) on the dispute taking place at that time between Albrecht v. Haller and Caspur Friedrich Wolff with regard to different theories of fertilisation. The title speaks for itself. In the German edition it runs: '*Lucina sine concubitu*, that is, a letter to the Royal Society of Science, wherein it is proved in an incontrovertible manner both by reason and experience that a woman can become pregnant without the aid of a man and bring forth a child ' (Frankfort and Leipzig, 1751, 8vo). Hereupon Richard Roe

---

[1] Archenholtz, *England*, Vol. III, p. 124.
[2] J. Blondel, *Three Remarkable Reports on the Power of the Imagination in Pregnant Women and its Effect upon the Foetus.* Strassburg, 1756.

wrote a second satire called after the French edition of
Combes: *Concubitus sine Lucina, ou le Plaisir sans peine.
Réponse à la lettre: Lucina sine concubitu* ' (Londres, 1752,
8vo. Later translated by Mercier de Compiègne under the
title *Lucine affranchie des lois de concours.* Paris, 1799[1]).

Diseases of the sexual organs are mentioned in middle
English medical works. But from the end of the fifteenth
century only purely local complaints are named, swellings
and running sores which are mostly designated under the
universal name ' Burning '. Syphilis was first brought into
England in 1496, probably by English mercenaries who
fought under Charles VIII in Italy in 1495. The new
disease was called 'Spanish pox', later ' French pox ', and
in Bristol ' *Morbus Burdigalensis* ', because it was introduced
there from Bordeaux in 1498[2]. The error of classing
all venereal diseases as identical was thoroughly established
in the eighteenth century in England by the famous
experiments of John Hunter: the Hunter Museum, called
after him, has made his name familiar to visitors to
London. Ricords' clever experiments were the first to
prove that syphilis is *toto caelo* a different disease from
the local venereal infections[3].

Owing to the vast expanse of English trading activities
venereal diseases became very widespread, especially as
from the beginning of the seventeenth century London was
sought out by foreigners more than any other town in the
world. In an old work which appeared in 1749, *Satan's*

[1] Bibliographical material is given by H. Hayn, *Bibliotheca Germanorum
gynaecologica et cosmetica.* Leipzig, 1886. P. 73. Also J. Gay, *Bibliographie
des ouvrages relatifs à l'amour.* Fourth edition. Lille, 1897. Vol. II, par. 917.

[2] Cf. I. Bloch, *The Origin of Syphilis. A medical and historical enquiry.*
Jena, 1901. Vol. I, p. 276.

[3] Cf. on Hunter's experiments E. Lang, *Lectures on Syphilis.* Second
edition. Wiesbaden, 1896. Pp. 34-39.

Harvest Home, or the Present State of Whorecraft, Adultery, Fornication, etc., we read: ' The greatest evil which accompanies prostitution and which can befall mankind is the spread of that infectious disease called French pox, which has caused such ghastly ravages in Europe for two hundred years. In this country it is so seldom absent from whorecraft, which is nowadays termed gallantry and genteel behaviour, that a healthy robust constitution is regarded as a mark of bad breeding and lack of gentility; and a healthy young fellow is considered as a boor who has spent his days in a peasant's hut. . . . In general our aristocracy seems to be distinguished by bad health, probably caused by the effects of this ruinous disease. Husbands infect their wives, wives their husbands or even their children: these infect their nurses who pass it on to other children so that no age, no sex, and no rank is completely free from this scourge[1].' The author of *Sérails de Londres* confirms the prevalence of syphilis among English upper classes during the eighteenth century[2]. London was feared by foreigners for this reason. Schütz[3] relates: ' The illnesses to which foreigners are sometimes subject after a few months' stay in London are no proof of this; for if these gentlemen were to give us an honest account of their conduct, we should soon find that the sensual pleasures for which London caters so richly are more to blame for their illnesses than the much abused climate.'

In Gay's *Beggar's Opera* Mrs. Trapes, the brothel keeper, complains of ' having eleven genteel clients in the surgeon's hands[4]'; but other brothel keepers took better care of the health of their clients. For example, the famous Mrs. Goadby kept a doctor to examine the girls before admission and to

---

[1] *Satan's Harvest Home,* etc. London, 1749. P. 31.
[2] *Sérails de Londres,* p. 213.
[3] Schütz, *loc. cit.,* p. 69.
[4] Taine, *loc. cit.,* Vol. II, p. 209.

reject all of those whose health was open to question[1]. According to Girtanner it was the fashion in London ' for young sparks always to carry with them a piece of grease in a little box so that if necessary they could smear the glands with it before intercourse[2] '.

Even the old motive of revenge by infection crops up sometimes. A nobleman told the procuress Charlotte Hayes that he had wagered a rival for his wife's affection that he would catch syphilis within a month, and asked Hayes to procure a syphilitic girl so that through her his rival might be punished. Hayes hired him such a girl for £30, who actually infected the man in question[3].

Until the middle of the nineteenth century the spread of syphilis among children was appalling. When Ryan states that brothels were visited yearly by 100,000 boys[4], we need not be surprised that during the years 1827-1835 no fewer than 2,700 cases of venereal disease occurred amongst children between the ages of 11 and 16. Logan confirms this and remarks: ' In one of our hospitals I found five little girls aged 13, 12, 11, 9, and 8 suffering from a shameful illness. The mother of the last was also suffering from the same disease. Three of these girls lived at home with their mother and had not been seduced by other children[5].' In London there are even special nursing homes for infected children between the ages of 10 and 14. The Lock Hospital in Harrow Road (founded as early as 1746) is the best known for venereal disease. Lecour in his book on prostitution in Paris and London[6] reveals facts about the number of persons

---

[1] *Sérails de Londres*, p. 12.
[2] Christopher Girtanner, *Treatise on Venereal Disease*. Göttingen, 1788. Vol. I, p. 275.
[3] *Sérails de Londres*, pp. 20-21.
[4] Ryan, *Prostitution in London*, p. 186.
[5] Ryan, *loc. cit.*, p. 120. H. France, *Va-Nu-Pieds*, p. 40.
[6] C. J. Lecour, *La Prostitution à Paris et à Londres*. Paris, 1882. Pp. 270 ff.

treated in this and similar hospitals. According to Ryan, 44,973 sufferers from venereal disease were admitted to the Lock Hospital from January 1747 to March 1836[1].

In the last decades of the nineteenth century the spread of venereal disease in London and English ports became so great that so-called ' health-bureaus ' were established to supply healthy prostitutes, who were given a certificate by the examining doctors[2].

Jeannel (confirmed by Tarnowski) pointed out that England was, in the nineteenth century, the main source of infection, and spread sexual disease because of her enormous overseas trade and her Colonial empire in all parts of the world.

However, these conditions appear to have undergone considerable improvement as much in consequence of a saner outlook on social questions and the instruction of the people on the dangers and effect of venereal disease whereby the number of the infected has greatly decreased, as of the present repugnance of unmarried English people to unregulated satisfaction outside marriage, which leads to earlier marriages.

[1] Ryan, loc. cit., p. 186.
[2] Lecour, loc. cit., p. 273. A. Blaschko, Syphilis and Prostitution. Berlin, 1893. P. 147.

CHAPTER XII

FLAGELLOMANIA

FLAGELLATION-MANIA (the desire to beat and flog) and preference for the use of the rod may be described as a specifically English abuse; it was so widespread among all ranks and ages that it formed one of the most interesting features of their sexual life. True, beating as a punishment and the rod as a sexual stimulant have played a part (and still do) amongst other races; any study of the subject reveals the fact that the desire to mishandle another by flogging is latent in human nature, being connected with the sexual instinct. Undoubtedly flogging, beating and whipping have been practised as punishment everywhere in the world since the dawn of history, both among the civilised and the savage; and this form of correction frequently acted as an aphrodisiac, and was employed by the person who administered it from sexual motives. The connection between active or passive flagellation and the sexual impulse has always been a matter of universal knowledge. Nevertheless it is possible to maintain that England was at one time the classic land of flagellation. For this assumption rests on factual evidence. In no other country had the passion for the rod been so systematically practised and developed; nowhere else had the whole of literature since the seventeenth century—poetry and prose, decent and indecent—been so occupied with this theme. At the same time no stage or daily newspaper elswhere had handled the theme with such openness—which is specially remarkable in view of English prudery concerning sexual matters. Finally, no other people possess so many artists who have devoted their talent to this strange subject. The greater prevalence of flagellation in England is largely due to the fact that in other European countries this passion is nearly always concealed under the cloak of religion and remains in that sphere, whereas in England its purely worldly character was calculated to give it considerable prominence—and, in fact, did so.

' Countless English books are devoted to this subject alone: no English erotic writing is free from accounts of flagellation, and many single pictures present scenes of whipping. The rod has separated man and wife; its devotees have been found in the most high-class girl schools, and in earlier times it was spoken of on the stage without concealment[1].'

The strongest evidence for the prevalence of flagellation-mania in English education is the fact that far the greatest part of earlier literature on flagellation in Germany and France was compiled from translations and reproductions from English sources. Neither France nor Germany has produced such a spate of erotic and non-erotic literature on the subject as England. In other peoples it is always a question of isolated sensualists and the impotent, who employ the rod as an aphrodisiac. ' All tender considerations of modern humanity ', says Taine, ' have failed to abolish boxing-matches and the use of the rod among this people[2].'

That it is the specifically English element (i.e. Anglo-Saxon, not Celtic or Norman) which is prone to this tendency is

[1] P. Fraxi, *Index librorum prohibitorum*, being notes bio-biblio-icono-graphical and critical on curious and uncommon books. London, 1877. Pp. xl-xli.

[2] H. Taine, *History of English Literature*. Leipzig, 1878. Vol. I, p. 43. Also Eulenburg calls England ' the promised land, the temple of flagellation'. (Eulenburg, *Sadism and Masochism*. Wiesbaden, 1902. P. 60.)

proved by the fact that the old Anglo-Saxons introduced the use of the rod into England, and that both Anglo-Saxon men and women used it with passion[1]. This fact has always been noted by historians. Hector France also calls the use of the rod an 'institution ancienne et vraiement nationale' and an 'usage tout saxon' which has been handed down from one generation to another as a sacred tradition, but has survived chiefly by the force of example and imitation[2].

The spread of flagellation-mania among people of every rank and age in English society affords further evidence that it was a specific national quality and not a passion limited to a small circle of sensualists and the like. The author of the introduction to one of the best-known English books on flagellation remarks: ' Many people, insufficiently acquainted with human nature, believe that the passion for flagellation must be confined to the aged or to men exhausted by sexual perversion. But this is not the case. For there are just as many youths and men in the prime of life who are victims of this passion as there are old men and weaklings.' The author then instances generals, admirals, colonels, captains, bishops, judges, barristers, lords, members of the House of Commons and doctors as devotees of the rod[3]. The same can be said of the female sex, amongst whom the use of the rod was not confined to the lower classes but was prevalent in the highest circles, as will be seen in later pages[4].

Taine appears inclined to attribute their excessive use of the rod to their way of life, above all to their over-indulgence

---

[1] J. Wright, *Domestic Manners in England during the Middle Ages.* London, 1862. P. 56.

[2] H. France, *Les Nuits de Londres.* Paris, 1900. P. 229.

[3] *Venus' Schoolmistress or Birchen Sports.* Reprinted from the edition of 1788, with a Preface by Mary Wilson, containing some account of the late Mrs. Berkley. Paris, Société des Bibliophiles, etc., 1898. P. viii.

[4] Cf. also H. France, *loc. cit.*, p. 229.

in meat and alcohol, which I also have referred to, and which certainly serves to encourage the use of a strong stimulant like flagellation. After drinking, and eating an incredible amount of meat, ' the coarse human animal finally satisfies itself with noise and sensuality[1] '.

Besides the manner of life, another factor comes prominently into the history of English flagellation—namely, the sexual. And in order to understand this, it is necessary to examine the universal connection between flagellation and sexuality.

There is, of course, something abnormal in sexual flagellation, though it has a natural connection with the accomplishment of the sexual act among human beings.

Flagellation has become the main method of activity of sadistic tendencies, just ' because all physiological sadistic accompaniments of sexual intercourse are united in it, and come to light with renewed force. Only by means of flagellation can the sadist enjoy the full ensemble of etiological impulses which his sadistic feelings demand. Flagellation therefore is generally best explained as the imitation and conscious synthesis of all physiological sadistic accompaniments of coitus[2] '.

Certain expressions, movements, colour-changes of the person flagellated resemble phenomena in the sexual act and awaken the same association of ideas as sexual sensations arouse.

When we examine separate motives for sexual flagellation, we discover that in its most usually practised form, the whipping of the posterior, the purely aesthetic charm of that portion of the body is a direct cause of flagellation. Delolme[3]

---

[1] Taine, *loc. cit.*, pp. 43-44.   [2] I. Bloch, *loc. cit.*, p. 76.
[3] Delolme, *The History of the Flagellants, or the Advantages of Discipline : being a Paraphrase and Commentary on the ' Historia Flagellantium '* of the Abbé Boileau, Doctor of the Sorbonne, etc. By One who is not Doctor of the Sorbonne (J. L. Delolme), London, 1777, pp. 328-329.

recalls how an elderly lady, shocked at the wrinkles of her face, surveyed the rest of her body in a large mirror and discovered to her delight that the shape of that part remained flawlessly beautiful. He points out further that many people find great attraction in the sight of the posterior, and so, thinking of it creates a predisposition to flagellation-mania. He thinks ' sight in love ' plays a great part in the matter.

The ancient Greeks knew well the aesthetic significance of the posterior, as is proved by the creation of Aphrodite Kallipygos. Anthropologists and aestheticians of a later date refer clearly to the beauty of this part. Moreau remarks: ' Les reliefs qui les (les cuisses) surmontent posterieurement, ces formes, dont la Vénus Callipyge offre le plus parfait modèle, ont un genre de beauté qu'il serait difficile de décrire, et qui paraît consister principalement dans le passage agréable que ces renflements établissent entre le torse et le membre[1].'

An authority on aesthetics, Schasler[2] calls the posterior a quite unjustly despised part of the body, and when not despised, derided, and proceeds as follows: ' Its high aesthetic significance, even in comparison with the bosom, does not rest only in the fact that like the tail in animals, it serves to hide the opening used for emptying, but that it seems made by its plastic beautiful roundness to distract the attention from that natural but none the less unaesthetic function, and to make us forget it, a contingency which does not arise among shameless animals.' According to Frusta, this explains the fact that the ' artistic sense ' is aroused in both sexes by ' the sight the callipygean charms uncovered

[1] J. L. Moreau, *Histoire Naturelle de la Femme*. Paris, 1803. Pp. 306-307.

[2] Max Schasler, *Aesthetics*. Leipzig and Prague. Vol. I, pp. 175-176.

and this leads to the enchantment of the sensibility of the organs of sight and touch[1] '.

Later poets, too, have celebrated the aesthetic charm of this part of the body. Delolme and Bertram (Cooper) name Rabelais, Lafontaine, Rousseau, Scarron, Lord Bolingbroke as its admirers. Pavillon, a *bel-esprit* in the reign of Louis XIV sings its splendour in a poem *La Métamorphose du Cul d'Iris en Astre*[2] '.

Apart from the general aesthetic significance of the posterior as explained by Moreau and Schasler, the more actual plastic charms of this part exercise a distinct influence by its shape. G. Jaeger thinks that this accounts wholly for its fascination. Vischer is of the opinion that the peach-like shape of the posterior awakens aesthetic satisfaction[3]. De Sade, too, explains that the 'rondeur, conformation forme enchanteresse' form the attraction which surrounds this place (*Justine*, Vol. I, p. 42). Then, too, excessive size of posterior, such as is frequently to be found among Hottentots and Negro races[4], exerts a certain charm on some persons. In consequence, flagellants effect the artificial enlargement of this part. Such a ' philopodex ' in the ' Exhibition of Female Flagellants ' requested the painter to portray the women's

[1] Frusta, *Flagellation and the Jesuit Confessional.* Stuttgart, 1834. P. 311.

[2] Delolme, *loc. cit.*, pp. 234-238. Rev. Wm. Cooper, B.A., *Flagellation and the Flagellants. A History of the Rod in all countries from the earliest period to the present time.* Illustrated. London, 1896. P. 4. There is an analysis of Pavillon's poem in J. Gay, *Bibliographie des ouvrages relatifs à l'amour, aux femmes et au mariage.* Lemonnyer, Lille, 1899. Vol. III, p. 215.

[3] G. Jaeger in the *Yearbook of Sexual Studies.* Leipzig, 1900. Vol. II, p. 65.

[4] Cf. W. Reinhard, *Under the Stick.* Dresden, 1903. Pp. 176-180. In this respect woman is put before man. ' Natibus gaudent majoribus feminae, id quod jam Cercidas poeta de Venere et Atheniensibus feminis. Inde Καλλιπυγους a se dictis praedicavit". J. Rosenbaum, *De sexuali organismorum fabrica*, etc. Halle, 1832. P. 51.

[325]

posteriors as over rather than under the size which the artist
or sculptor is accustomed to allow their proportion. Others
watch scenes of flagellation through magnifying glasses in
order to have the flagellated part as gigantic as possible
before their eyes[1].

In the *Venus Schoolmistress* occurs a very remarkable
comment on the human posterior. The author maintains
that boys up to 16 have very similar posteriors but that
afterwards they assume an ' individual ' character. Some
retain their childish shape, others become large and
take on a hard and rough quality. The author also maintains
that men with well developed posteriors marry earlier than
others, as these callipygean Adonises exercise a great
fascination upon women and surpass other men in their
potentia coeundi et generandi[2].

The influence of this plastic attraction explains the fact
that many persons find great satisfaction in seeing the
posteriors merely uncovered without resorting to flagellation,
and obtain sexual pleasure from the sight. ' Flagellation
and uncovering ', says Ryan, ' are inseparable, and often
cause erection even in children[3].' Uncovering with no
consequent whipping is frequently sufficient to attain this
end.

Thus in a German brochure on flagellation several persons
are shown watching the callipygean charms through opera
glasses[4]; and in *Justine*, by the Marquis de Sade (Vol. III, p. 34),
a great callipygean revue occurs for the libertine Verneuil,
comprising girls, boys and women, young and old. In
certain country districts of Brittany this exhibition of nates

[1] Such a scene is described in *Memoirs of a Russian Dancer*. Milwaukee,
1898. Vol. II, pp. 81 ff.

[2] *Venus Schoolmistress*, pp. 97-99.

[3] Ryan, *loc. cit.*, p. 382.

[4] *In Venusberg, or Experiences in a Pension*. Budapest, no date. P. 49.

is arranged in most extraordinary manner, namely, in the middle of a so-called *Toull ër c'has* (French *chatière*), that is, a large apparatus in the form of wooden spectacles, through which the spectator pushes his head, while a woman uncovers her posterior before him[1].

In England this liking for the mere pleasures of sight has produced a special sort of prostitute, the so-called ' posture girls '. This type appears to have sprung up about 1750. They crop up first in various erotic writings of the time. Thus, in the *History of the Human Heart, or The Adventures of a Young Gentleman* (London, 1769, p. 116), there is talk of ' posture girls who stripped stark naked and mounted themselves upon the middle of the table ' to show their beauties. In the fifth tale (' The Royal Rake ') of the *New Attalantis for the Year* 1762, ' Posture Nan ' is celebrated as ' the greatest mistress in her sex at this art '. The behaviour of these girls in a brothel in Great Russell Street has been very openly described in the *Midnight Spy*. ' Behold an object ', says Urbanus, ' which rouses at once our disgust and our pity. A beautiful woman lies stretched on the floor and offers to the view just those parts of her body that, were she not without all shame, she would most zealously seek to conceal. As she is given to drink, she arrives usually half drunk, and after two or three glasses of Madeira exposes herself to men in this unseemly manner. Look, she is on all fours now, like an animal. She is ridiculed, and men gloat over such prostitution of incomparable beauty[2].'

When we pass on to the subject of the actual act of flagellation, we must chiefly draw attention to the charms exercised by pigmentation, which before and during the performance

---

[1] *Glossaire cryptologique du breton.* Paris, 1899. Vol. VI, pp. 65-66.

[2] *The Midnight Spy.* London, 1766. P. 67. ' Posture Masters ' must not be confused with ' Posture Girls '. They were jugglers and contortionists, who bore this name from the time of Charles II. Cf. I. Strutt, *The Sports and Pastimes of the People of England.* London, 1830. Pp. 235-236.

affect the eye of the active flagellant. Colouring plays a great part in the *vita sexualis* of both sexes.

When the flagellant brings about a reddening of the nates he is only seeking to produce a natural accompaniment of the *libido sexualis*. Confirmation of this is found in the fact that savage races paint their posteriors red to make them conspicuous, as is the case with apes[1]. Perhaps the contrast of colour between the beaten and unbeaten parts has a sexual effect[2].

The special and very strong sexual attraction aroused by the flow of blood to the flagellated parts, and their consequent reddening, is given great prominence in all works on flagellation[3]. Frusta relates: ' A famous and highly respected German count of the eighteenth century, who was madly in love with his young and beautiful wife, never found her so attractive as when he had properly punished her with the rod. She received—for she herself got no pleasure from the affair— anything she liked to ask, if she submitted. What is supposed to have roused him most was the change in colour of the skin. For hours he gazed and could not have enough of the sight.' Brantôme relates similar occurrences in his *Dames Galantes*[4].

Bloch points out that pictures of flagellation scenes, in which the flagellated parts are mostly painted a brilliant red, also provide proof of the attraction of this discoloration by beating[5].

The author of the *Romance of Chastisement* (London, 1870, p. 72) thinks that the *posteriora* of human beings possess the inherent power of reddening, even without flagellation, and

---

[1] Delolme, *loc. cit.*, p. 234.
[2] Bloch, *loc. cit.*, p. 80.
[3] E.g., *Raped on the Railway.* London, 1899. P. 140.
[4] Frusta, *loc. cit.*, p. 312.
[5] Bloch, *loc. cit.*, p. 81.

claims himself to have seen the alternate paling and reddening
of these parts.

A further attraction is provided by the violent movements
and twitchings which affect the parts during chastisement,
and which may be regarded as the simulation of certain
movements during coitus[1]. The ' quivering ', the ' oscilla-
tion ', the ' voluptuous twitching ' of the flagellated part are
invariably mentioned in accounts of flagellation scenes. A
letter from Alkiphron, speaking of the movement of the
posterior at the ' callipygean games ' (after the French translation by Abbé Richard), says: ' Dans leur jeu rapide, dans
leurs convulsions aimables, ces sphères n'ont pas le tremble-
ment de celles de Myrrhine. Leur mouvement ressemble au
doux gémissement de l'onde. Aussitôt elle redouble les las-
cives crispations avec tant d'agilité, qu'un applaudissement
universel lui décerne les honneurs du triomphe[2].' In the
' Kallipyge ' the movements of the *posteriora* were even to
a certain extent reproduced in a spectator, who said it was
as though that part of him wished to describe the sensations
aroused by the flogging[3].

A very important, perhaps the chief, cause of active
flagellation is the sadistic tendency of the flagellant.
Cooper[4] says: ' Amongst the elements which compose the
passion of the flagellant, the chief one appears to be—
according to an old writer—a sensation of satisfaction at
the sufferings of others, arising from the evil tendencies

---

[1] 'The ancient Indians,' says Bloch (*loc. cit.*, p. 79), 'who accomplished
wonders in the observation and co-ordination of the outward manifestations of libido sexualis, define as a symptom of the sexual ardour of women
the " twitching of the posterior ". The same twitching of this region is
magnified at the moment of orgasm. They resemble closely the reflex
movements caused by pain or death-throes, and just for that reason
arouse the sadist because they appear completely involuntary.'

[2] P. Dufour, *loc. cit.*, Vol. I, pp. 190-191.

[3] *The Callipygian*, Milwaukee, 1898. P. 142.

[4] Cooper, *loc. cit.*, p. 164.

which linked with the good are to be found in the heart of every man; and the close connection between cruelty and lust, which finds pleasure in the sight of the frequently ridiculous movements and convulsions of some one who is being flogged.'

Those cases in which persons delight in watching the greatest number of floggings possible can also be traced to predominating sadistic tendencies. An officer who had often watched the chastisement of his younger brothers and sisters, developed a quite insane passion for flogging. He used to bribe the warders in a Dutch reformatory to let him act as flogging-master; and when that was not possible he would watch while the female prisoners were whipped[1].

These sadistic flagellants were chiefly roused by seeing the whipping fetch blood; for which reason the punishment had always to be continued up to that point in order to give the flagellant the desired satisfaction. This was portrayed, for example, in the *Justine* of the Marquis de Sade (Vol. I, p. 265). Dufour perceives in this thirst for blood the main difference between the flagellation of antiquity and that of the Christian era.

The masochistic element is prominent in passive flagellation. The person flagellated is filled with ' a mystical sensation (a mixture of sensuality and fantasy) of subjection to the strength of another, of reversion to childhood of his personality, as well as simultaneous deep shame and delight at the ill-treatment administered[2] '. According to Krafft-Ebing[3], passive flagellation serves the man inclined to the perversion of masochism mainly as an expression of his desire to be dominated by the woman. Such a situation is sharply portrayed in the famous picture of Hans Baldung

[1] Cooper, *loc. cit.*, p. 165.
[2] Frusta, *loc. cit.*, p. 312.
[3] Krafft-Ebing, *Psychopathia sexualis*. Tenth edition. Stuttgart, 1899. P. 90.

in which Aristotle serves Phyllis as a horse and is urged on with the whip. The following case, noted by Cooper, also illustrates the masochism of the person flagellated: A nobleman in the reign of George II hired a house in London and a pretty housekeeper. Once a week she had to prepare everything necessary for scrubbing a room, and also engage two women, of whom one was obliged to represent the housekeeper and the other the housemaid and help him with the work. While the nobleman scrubbed the room he behaved as though he were a girl from the poor house, and did the work so badly that one or both of the women had to whip him as the poor-house children were whipped by their mistresses![1]

Further, in Otway's comedy *Venice Preserved* (Act III, Sc. 1) a similar masochistic whipping scene takes place. The senile senator Antonio visits his mistress Aquilina in order to romp with her. He asks her to spit in his face; then behaves like a dog, crawls under the table and begs her to treat him like a dog, to kick him and so on, till finally the courtesan fetches a rod and whips him from the room[2].

The 'magnetic theory' of flagellation is exhaustively treated in the English book *The Romance of Chastisement*. When the flogging is carried out by a practised female hand, the author says that a kind of magnetism runs from her to the victim (N.B. often male) and back again. A woman, flagellated, described the magnetic condition as follows: ' Fear and shame went. It was as if I gave myself to the embraces of a man whom I loved so much that I anticipated his wildest desires. But no man was in my thoughts, rather Martinet (the governess) was the object of my worship, and I felt that I shared her passion through the rod. The rapport, as exponents of magnetism call it, was so

[1] Cooper, *loc. cit.*, pp. 167-168.
[2] Cf. P. Fraxi, *Centuria librorum absconditorum*, p. 450.

[331]

strong that I could guess her thoughts. Had she desired me to offer the front of my body to her blows, I should have tried to obey, in spite of being bound. A magnetic shudder ran through us both which increased with every blow. It was, however, quite impossible for me to say whether pain or pleasure predominated.'

The main characteristic of religious flagellation, asceticism, self-abasement, shows very distinct sexual elements. Bloch remarks on this: ' Asceticism originates in the opposition between spirit and matter, rooted in primitive man, which causes the latter—in man his physical being, especially its most intense expression, sexual desire—to be regarded as something impure, to be fought, overcome and if possible destroyed, in order to save his purely spiritual being. With the vow of poverty, sexual abstinence, the fight against the " flesh " (the church fathers always referred to the genital organs as " caro ") is the chief psychological feature of asceticism. But in order to overcome the " flesh ", to fight the often intensively increasing sexual urge and if possible stamp it out, the ascetic was obliged to be always on his guard against it, always to be thinking of it. Consequently he occupied himself far more with sexual desire than the normal man. Sex mortification and sex perversion . . . these are the two poles between which the ascetic's life swings—which in any case points to a strong admixture of sexuality. Asceticism is often only the means of obtaining sexual satisfaction in another form and in a higher degree[1].'

James II of England may be mentioned as another example of the connection between religion and lust; he was one of the greatest sensualists of his time (*vide* above) and, at the same time, a bigoted Catholic. Macaulay relates that his consort, Mary of Modena, whom he shamefully neglected and betrayed, kept till the end of her life the rod with which he atoned for

[1] I. Bloch, *loc. cit.*, pp. 95-96.

his ill-treatment of her on his back, and bequeathed it on her death as a relic to the convent of Chaillot[1]. Religious discipline brought sexual abuses most quickly in its train when it was practised together by persons of different sex, and the man beat the woman or *vice versa*. A Puritan writer says with justice: ' It is not seemly for a man to let himself be beaten by a woman, and a girl is ruined when she receives blows from a man[2].'

Passive flagellation plays a great part as a simple preliminary to intercourse. Pisanus Fraxi is of opinion that flagellation, if it has any value at all, should be only a preparatory act, 'an incentive to higher pleasure ', a means to an end, not the end itself[3].

The purely physical effects of whipping on the sexual system are explained by the reflex excitement in the sexual sphere, especially the sympathetic nervous centres in the spine, caused by sharp and painful blows on the skin, particularly in the neighbourhood of the sexual organs. Dr. Meibom even asserts that the effect of flagellation on the coming of erection can be accurately observed, and that the *oscillationes membri* are regulated according to the number of strokes applied[4]. John Davenport says: ' As an erotic stimulant, more particularly, it may be observed that, considering the many intimate and sympathetic relations existing between the nervous branches of the extremity of the spinal marrow, it is impossible to doubt that flagellation exercised upon the buttocks and the adjacent parts has a powerful effect upon the organs of generation[5].'

[1] T. B. Macaulay, *History of England.*

[2] Cooper, *loc. cit.*, p. 174.

[3] P. Fraxi, *loc. cit.*, p. 242.

[4] Henry Meibomius, *A Treatise of the use of Flogging at venereal affairs*. . . London, 1718, pp. 310-311.

[5] Davenport, *loc. cit.*, p. 113.

[333]

The Duchess Leonora Gonzaga of Mantua may be mentioned as an example of the preparatory effect of passive flagellation; she made her mother whip her in order to feel more warmth in intercourse and so conceive[1].

At the same time, active flagellation is often used as a quick preparatory means of putting a person into a favourable condition for the practice of coitus. This applies to women as well as men. The activity of female flagellants often ends by the summoning of a man to satisfy the desires roused in them by the whipping. In the same way male flagellants often have recourse to their wives or a brothel after active flagellation. Thomas Bartholinus relates: ' Persians and Russians chastise their wives with blows from a stick on the posterior before they perform their marital duty. Barclay assures us that with the Russians the love of the husband is measured by the number of blows he gives. The bride in Russia would rather be without any other piece of household goods than rods. These rods are never used for punishment, but only for the purpose mentioned[2].'

The stimulating effect of active, and even more of passive, flagellation has been utilised for therapeutic purposes. Physicians of olden times incorporated flagellation in all seriousness into their therapy, as a proved means against hindrances to normal sexual intercourse, and to assist pregnancy; but, above all, in cases of impotence, both *generandi* and also *coeundi*. Arabian physicians are said to have prescribed it to patients suffering in this way.

' During my stay in Paris I was called to one of the many brothels in the Rue St. Honoré to attend to a prostitute who had been taken ill at her profession. As I entered her room I heard the angry voice of a woman in the next room; the

[1] A. Eulenburg, *Sadism and Masochism*. Wiesbaden, 1902. P. 58.
[2] Th. Bartholinus by J. H. Meibom. ' On the Utility of Whipping', etc., in *The Treasure-seeker*, Vol. IV, pp. 257-258.

woman who needed my assistance did not give me time to ask the cause of the noise. In a low voice she begged me to keep quiet, carefully moved the curtain and let me look through a small opening, where I saw a comedy of the most absurd description—which, by the way, was repeated twice a week. The chief character, a charming brunette, had her neck and legs and posterior quite uncovered. Four old men stood round her in official wigs. Their costume, their condition, their expression forced me to bite my lips to keep from bursting into laughter. These white-haired old libertines were playing at " school ", as little boys sometimes do among themselves. The whore, holding a bundle of rods, chastised each in turn: and the one who received the most strokes was the weakest among them. They kissed their mistress while she worked away with the beating; and the comedy only came to an end when tired nature mocked further efforts. My patient was much amused at my astonishment, and told me several anecdotes of an even more comic description, as happened daily in their " cloister". " We have got ", she declared, " the most important office in Paris, for we enjoy the privilege of venturing to apply the rod to the most distinguished members of the clergy, of the official world and of business"[1].'

In the pornographic work *On the Venusberg*, flagellation is put to an extremely strange therapeutic usage. Here an old, nearly blind, man was brought in whenever girls were being whipped, because ' the sound of the swish of the rod and the crying of the beaten girl strengthened his sight for a little while by lust; so he longed to attain this happiness as often as possible! '

Not less fantastic are the applications of the rod in lunacy

[1] *Traité du Fouet, et de ses effets sur le physique de l'amour, ou Aphrodisiaque externe. Ouvrage médico-philosophique, suivi d'une dissertation sur les Moyens d'exciter aux Plaisirs de L'amour par D. . . .* (F. A. Doppet), *Médicin.* Paris, 1788, and Stuttgart, 1847. Pp. 381-383.

(*Caelius Aurelianus*), hypochondria, epilepsy, gout; it may be useful certainly as a preventive measure or as a means of suggestion, though it is better replaced by other less harmful methods. Cooper tells of a doctor who regarded the rod pretty well as Dr. Sangrada did cold water and the letting of blood. It was a panacea in his eyes, as it ' brought sluggish veins into activity, loosened acid deposits, cleansed the body of the vapours, made the head clear, the bowels active, the blood flow and the nerves strong[1]'.

Not less interesting is the fact that a certain cosmetic effect is ascribed to flagellation. It is said to develop a certain *embonpoint* in the parts flagellated by bringing the blood circulation from inside out to the skin. Galen relates that horse-dealers administered regular beatings to their horses in order to make them fat[2]. Flagellation is said to be especially favourable to the development of callipygean charms. This belief comes out in the work of an ancient writer of comedy where a procuress is shown beating her girls to get them larger posteriors.

But it is the habitual practice of flagellation, combining with all these various motives, which raises it to the point of a veritable passion. Pico della Mirandula pointed this out[3]. Both active and passive flagellation can by frequent repetition assume an overwhelming attraction both for the flagellant and the flagellated.

Bloch remarks: ' Concerning the teacher and the warder, either may at the start of his activity be entirely free from any sadistic tendency, which is rather introduced during the course of his habitual use of corporal punishment so that gradually it becomes a pleasure[4].'

[1] Cf. the interesting chapter ' The famous therapeutic and medicinal properties of the rod ' in Cooper, *loc. cit.*, pp. 67-70.
[2] *Ibid.*, p. 68.
[3] Meibom, *loc. cit.*, p. 265.
[4] Bloch, *loc. cit.*, Vol. II, p. 86.

Carlier, the former Chief of Police of Paris, writes of the
'material' for whipping and flogging: 'Among certain
prostitutes a veritable arsenal of instruments of torture
can be found: Whips, rod, knotted sticks, leather thongs
in which nails have been driven, etc., etc. The dried blood
which covers these instruments offers proof that they
are not kept merely as playthings and for show, but are
actually used for the satisfaction of monstrous lusts[1].'
A patient of Krafft-Ebing stated as a fact that ' every
experienced prostitute was accustomed to possess some
instrument for flagellation, usually a rod[2]'.

Flagellating with flowers is a tender love-service, as
described in the *Kallipyge*, and a picture of such a scene
has been made by a celebrated French artist as the title-
page of de Villiot's *En Virginie*.

Even more extraordinary materials have been used for
flagellation. In the erotic brochure *On the Venusburg*, it is
mentioned that fine asbestos, rubbed to powder and applied
to the human skin, induces a prickling and burning sensation
which increases in strength the more the part in question is
rubbed and scratched. By this means the same effect is
produced as by whipping without so much damage to the
skin.

The brush is an instrument quite often employed for
flagellation. This is mentioned in an erotic brochure,
Lascivious Gems (London, 1866, pp. 48-56), where the impotent Edward Tracy is bound to the bed-post by his lady and
belaboured first with a rod and then with a brush. ' Still I was
not satiated. Seizing a hand-brush, I struck the raw flesh
with the bristles and scrubbed it with them. I then took the
eau-de-Cologne bottle from the dressing-table and poured
the contents over the parts and resumed the use of the hair-

[1] Ullo, *The Flagellation Mania*. Dresden, 1901. P. 48.
[2] v. Krafft-Ebing, *Psychopathia Sexualis*, p. 95.

brush.' The unfortunate lover, naturally enough, fainted under this barbarous treatment.

Refinements of flagellation have been thought of; for example, whipping by machines, so that where possible several persons can be whipped at the same time. These fantasies are mainly of Anglo-American origin. In the eighteenth century an English *bon vivant*, Chace Price, tried to construct a machine which could flagellate forty persons simultaneously. The famous actor Samuel Foote had a long discussion about it with the inventor in the brothel of Charlotte Hayes, as Price was anxious to get his invention patented[1]. In 1830 Talbot saw such a machine for flagellation at work in a London brothel[2]. Lately, Americans have taken up the idea again. In the English paper *Society* the following letter from Henry Rowlands was published on 14th October 1899[3]: ' If the American press can be believed, our cousins in the United States have invented nothing less than a machine for the infliction of corporal punishment. This invention, however, can make no claim to originality, as I have long possessed a book, at least eighty years old, which I picked up second-hand in the Rue Montmartre, and in which a wooden contrivance is described: to this two rods are fixed and a boy and a girl can be beaten at the same time. Mr. Croquemitaine undertakes the necessary handling of the boys, while Mrs. Croquemitaine attends carefully to the girls. To judge by a picture it is possible to deal with a large number of delinquents in a comparatively short space of time without fatigue or becoming unduly overheated.'

Americans, at the summit of civilisation, attempted to break all records in this sphere by applying electricity to the

---

[1] *Les Sérails de Londres*, p. 46.
[2] Ryan, *loc. cit.*, p. 381.
[3] *Education of John Bull*. Dresden, 1901. Vol. II, p. 125. Cf. concerning ' Whipping-machines ' Hansen, *Stick and Whip*, pp. 121-122 (and two satirical prints, pp. 122 and 124).

operation of these machines for flagellation. Chicago papers
reported that an industrial school at Denver had introduced
an electrically driven whipping contrivance. De Villiot[1] described it as follows: ' The contrivance in question has the form
of a chair which lacks the seat or cane bottom. The patient
seats himself on this after having uncovered what is dis-
respectfully termed his posterior. This up-to-date chair is
sufficiently raised to allow four beaters fixed beneath it to
operate freely in a rotatory movement more or less rapid
according to the wish of the operator, who has only to switch
on an electric battery fixed to the chair with metal wires.
The beaters, set in motion, do their job most conscientiously,
and possess the advantage of working in a regulated, orderly
manner and without the least fatigue to the operator. As to
the feelings of the principal party—that is to say, the pupil—
who is held in the chair by a vice gripping ankles and wrists,
American papers say nothing. The operator has only to
press a button and the whipping chair does the rest.'

From flagellation instruments we must turn to the *personnel*
of flagellation, as it is not a matter of indifference who wields
the rod or how the rod is wielded.

With regard to the last point, flagellation had been raised
in England to a veritable art and had produced a special
branch of prostitution, the so-called ' governesses ' who got
their name from governors with authority to inflict frequent
corporal punishment. In the introduction to *Venus Schoolmistress* occurs the following: ' Women who give most
satisfaction to lovers of the discipline are called governesses
because they have acquired by experience a tact and a *modus
operandi* which the common run do not possess. For a woman
will not get the custom of lovers of the rod by mere wielding
of the rod or readiness to flagellate. She must rather be

[1] De Villiot, *Etudes sur la Flagellation*. Paris, 1899. Pp. 364-365.

well educated by an experienced woman and made perfect in the art. She must possess a quick and intense method, to recognise the various aberrations of men's fancy, and show instant readiness to meet and satisfy them[1].'

In consequence, sexual flagellation requires great delicacy and a certain *savoir faire* on the part of both men and women flagellants. The author[2] of a brochure on flagellation which appeared in London in 1868 (*The Merry Order of St. Bridget*) remarks: ' There is a huge difference in the manner of whipping. The application or toleration of the rod brings no enjoyment if it is done in the ordinary way, as when a woman strikes out in a temper. But if an elegant and well-dressed lady handles the rod proudly and gracefully, then whipping or being whipped becomes a real pleasure[3].'

The English practice of flagellation developed refinements in the application of the rod; above all, the notorious ' cut up ', which is flagellation of the genital and perineal sphere. It is described at length in most English brochures on flagellation: for example, *The Romance of Chastisement, or Revelations of the School and Bedroom* (London, 1870, p. 62), and in *The Romance of Chastisement, or the Revelations of Miss Darcy* (London, 1866). In a later brochure it is suggested that the ' cut up ' was then still in use in schools[4]. The Marquis de Sade, that refined martyr, certainly knew about it (*Justine*, Vol. II, p. 197).

The practice of flagellation receives quite special peculiarities and an individual character owing to the fact that it is

[1] *Venus Schoolmistress*, p. ix.
[2] Probably Bertram, who wrote *The History of the Rod* under the name of Cooper.
[3] *The Merry Order of St. Bridget. Personal Recollections of the Use of the Rod. By Margaret Anson. York. Printed for the Author's Friends.* 1857. London, 1868. P. 181.
[4] *With Rod and Bum; or Sport in the West End of London. By Ophelia Cox. A true tale by a young governess.* London and New York, 1898. P. 16.

accompanied by certain other eccentricities and adornments. Apart from the sadistic and masochistic propensity of most flagellants, other perversities function in the practice of flagellation. The author of *Venus Schoolmistress* remarks: ' I could fill a whole book with an account of the many and various strange whims to which men are prone in flagellation[1]'.

Clothing, for example, plays a great part—both in the case of the woman flagellating and of the man flagellated. Numerous active flagellants, both men and women, want the full uncovering of their victims only in part, as this affords them greater pleasure. The author of *The Romance of Chastisement* (London, 1870, p. 80) rightly terms ' bath-nakedness ' decent compared with the extremely improper partial uncovering of girls or boys to be flagellated.

Similarly, in the *Exhibition of Female Flagellants* it is written: ' Nakedness must be partial during flagellation in order to obtain the highest degree of satisfaction ', and the suggestion is made so to arrange the clothing of different people that each one presents a different part of the body to the eye of the flagellant.

Costume as such, the general arrangement of clothing, has a great effect frequently upon flagellants, as well as the contrast which clothing affords to the part unclothed. This is the case with both active and passive flagellants. Thus a passive flagellant requires the woman who is to beat him to be dressed in the habit of a nun[2]. In the *Romance of Chastisement* the flagellated girls wear Empire costume; in a book of anecdotes, *The Sublime of Flagellation*, a young devotee of the rod is driven to beg his mistress to beat him when she is wearing her gala robes. Shoes covered with gold spangles, gold-threaded silk stockings, skirt, necklace, bracelets, have proved his undoing. Often women's underclothing

---

[1] *Venus Schoolmistress*, p. 55.
[2] *The Merry Order of St. Bridget* (London, 1868), p. 25.

and dresses were specially decorated where they end in the neighbourhood of the thighs and posterior in order to draw attention to this part.

In another brochure the ' Lady in White ' is mentioned as a special attraction. ' Frau Hautville made a very pretty toilet for the occasion (flagellation); she was entirely in white, in the dress of a novice taking the veil. The frock was considerably changed as it was too flowing for the occasion, but all was white silk and lace; and she looked like a little angel when her toilet was finished. From top to toe she wore nothing that was not pure white. White shoes with diamonds sparkling on the bows; white silk stockings, tied above her round knees with white silk garters with white bows; white underclothes of the finest linen embroidered with lilies. Her frock was of silk—the soft, spun kind which does not crumple, richly embroidered with Mechlin lace, and over her head she wore a four-cornered veil[1].'

The nosegay belonged to the outer adornment of women flagellants in England. It was worn usually in the bosom, and its perfume roused the feeling of the striker and of the person, man or woman, struck.

Nosegays, worn in a special manner, appear at an earlier date to have served as signs among prostitutes, so that men with such tendencies might know that the woman wearing such a nosegay would satisfy their desire for flagellation. These ' nosegays of lechery ' were much worn in the eighteenth century at the great pleasure gardens of Vauxhall and Ranelagh.

The so-called *voyeurs*, that is persons who find sexual satisfaction in merely looking on at the flagellation of others, form a special group of devotees of the rod.

Thus Frusta relates that an officer, in his later years,

[1] *Flagellation Experiences.* German by E. Weber. Dresden, 1901. Pp. 130-131.

well known to him and of high rank, quartered in W. and
in M., paid one or other of the police-agents a ducat to be
allowed to watch every time when prostitutes, arrested by the
police, were flogged[1]. The same author knew a respected
police official who ordered females by the dozen to be beaten
with rods on the bare or partly bare lower part of the body.
'He watched the spectacle with society ladies, and took snuff.
In his earlier years he gave the police agents of M. and V.
a ducat each time for permission to watch the flogging of
girls and women who had been seen after eight o'clock in the
streets and had therefore been brought to the police-station.
In 1819, at one of the " Hepp! Hepp! "—also in brilliant
company—he ordered over twenty servant-girls, including
some very respectable ones, who had been brought in, to
be unmercifully whipped.   He fell into disgrace later because
a lady took a pinch of snuff from a box inside which was a
picture of a young woman being flogged[2].'

The existence of feminine *voyeurs* is proved by a very
remarkable passage from the *Memoirs of John Bell, a Domestic
Servant* (London, 1797), which Pisanus Fraxi[3] quotes: ' The
next place which I took was with a rich widow whose family
consisted of two schoolgirl nieces and a twelve-year-old
nephew.   She had been a beautiful woman and was still
pretty.   When she engaged me, she remarked that she relied
on my doing all she might require of me.   To this I agreed.
It soon became apparent what " all " meant: for when I
brought in breakfast the next morning she asked me if I had
ever been a servant in a school, and helped to whip the
children?   I said No; but remarked that I had often whipped
my brother whom I had taught to read.   About half an hour
later her nephew ran into me while I was carrying a plate,

---

[1] Frusta, *loc. cit.*, p. 266.
[2] *Ibid.*, pp. 305-306.
[3] P. Fraxi, *Centuria*, pp. 460-461.

which fell and broke. " Now, John," she said, " hold the boy tight while I fetch a good rod." She quickly fetched one from the cupboard and gave it to me with the words: " Sit down and give him the rod as you did to your brother." I gave the little lad a thorough beating, which my mistress watched with evident pleasure. " Very good ", she said. " You see what the boy needs, and you can always give it to him when he deserves it, but, mind you, only in my presence." Then I understood that she had a great passion for watching children being whipped, but in spite of that I must admit I was much astonished when on the same evening after tea she ordered me to perform the same ceremony on her two nieces. It was, as a fact, something new for the young ladies of the house to be whipped by a servant. When my mistress noticed my hesitation she looked at me sternly and called: " At once. On this sofa, or you quit my service." ' On which the servant whipped the two girls and the boy again, as much as his mistress wished. ' It is needless to recount the different ways in which I carried out my new and unusual duties. In the morning she liked the whipping to be performed while she sat sewing, and counted the stitches and the strokes. In the evening she enjoyed the pleasure at tea-time, sipping from her saucer, at the same time saying quietly: " Please, John, a little more to the right. That will do." ' Finally, a fifteen-year-old page was engaged, who was often whipped in the presence of the mistress.

In an old English collection of anecdotes, mostly drawn from life, *The Cherub, or Guardian of Female Innocence* (London, 1792), the activity of a *voyeur* is recounted in detail. It deals with a rich old banker of Broad Street who made an arrangement with the heads of two girl-schools (one at Hackney, the other at Stratford), whereby on the weekly payment of a large sum of money he indulged in a strange pleasure. In each school the customary punishment of the children took place on the day of his weekly visit. While the old gentleman looked through an opening from a neighbouring room, the children were brought in one after the other, uncovered and whipped[1].

Of course the sexual nature of flagellation is most frequent and most apparent when it occurs between persons of different sex.

Even a beating given to a woman by a man without lust will always, just because of the difference of sex, take on a certain sexual nuance, while it is much more rarely the case with beating between persons of the same sex, and only enters in after frequent repetition.

On the other hand, when sexual relations exist between persons of the same sex, as with homosexuals, flagellation will, of course, have exactly the same erotic character as with persons of a different sex.

Moll mentions cases of flagellation between urnings[2]. But the parallel is specially interesting which he draws between passive flagellation and passive pederasty, both of which he attributes to the desire for special excitement in the posterior region affected by them[3]. This connection has not escaped the Marquis de Sade also. He asserts that passive flagellation provokes the tendency to passive pederasty and *vice versa* (*Juliette*, Vol. VI, p. 228, note). Doppet, too, proves that chastisement on the posterior with rods very often brings out the tendency to pederasty in boys[4].

In the same sexual flagellation often occurs between female homosexuals, known as tribads. Moll assumes that

---

[1] *The Cherub, or Guardian of Female Innocence. Exposing the Arts of Boarding Schools, Hired Fortune Tellers, Corrupt Milliners, Apparent Ladies of Fashion.* London, 1792. P. 17.

[2] Moll, *Sexual Sensibility in Opposites*. Berlin, 1899. Pp. 280-287.

[3] *Ibid.*, pp. 240-241.

[4] Doppet, *loc. cit.*, p. 403.

homosexuality in women heightens the tendency to it[1]. The Hungarian women who came to Germany in the fourteenth century, undressed themselves in public, and, while singing all kinds of strange songs, beat themselves with rods and sharp goads, were possibly among these homosexually inclined women. In the eighteenth century in France and England several flagellant clubs of tribads were known to exist. About Paris, Frusta[2] remarks: ' Finally there were young females who beat themselves in gardens with rose-twigs, and struck Milesian attitudes. In Paris during the revolution several similar associations were discovered, to which respectable women had been enticed. In them Sappho was honoured as protective goddess: her picture adorned the altar in the hall where everything was calculated to make sense and fantasy reel. The orgies opened with flagellation; the most shameful sex perversions ended them. Deep hatred against man was the first principle to be impressed upon them. *La Galerie des Femmes* (Jouy, Hamburg, 1799) contains an artistic representation of the facts, true in the main[3].'

After this account of the universal causes and manifestations of erotic flagellation, which contains many glimpses of English conditions, we will turn to the consideration of its history in England in particular.

One fact stands out in the history of English flagellation-mania—the extraordinarily strong tendency to active flagellation in English women.

It is very difficult to decide the question whether cruelty is more frequent in men or in women: one can, however, state with certainty that cruelty in women is far subtler

[1] Moll, *loc. cit.*, p. 565.
[2] Frusta, *loc. cit.*, p. 40.
[3] In Tableau VII, entitled ' Sappho, ou les Lesbiennes '.

than in men. 'Woman,' says Virey, 'blood-thirsty and insatiable in revenge, carries cruelty to the point of insanity just as she attains to the very peaks of virtue[1].' According to Bloch[2] man is more inclined to follow passionate impulse in cruel actions, while calculated 'cold' cruelty is peculiar to woman; and linked as it is with fiendish malice, awakes more horror than the less considered cruelty of man. Nobody has more clearly recognised and portrayed the nature of female cruelty than Leopold von Sacher-Masoch in his romances and novels, of which I will only mention the cycle, first published recently, called *Cruel Women* (Dresden, 1901, 2 vols.). Sacher-Masoch, this remarkable apologist of female cruelty, describes in all his literary creations 'the woman with Sphinx eyes who is cruel because lustful and becomes lustful through cruelty[3]'.

It appears that female cruelty makes preferential use of flagellation to satisfy her desires[4]. Pisanus Fraxi states that there is sufficient evidence to prove that woman finds pleasure in chastising others, that she has a greater tendency to flagellation than man, and is more insatiable and unfeeling during its performance[5]. Zimmerman says the same thing in

---

[1] J. J. Virey, *Woman*. Leipzig, 1827. Pp. 188-189.

[2] I. Bloch, *Sexual Life of our Time*. Pp. 565 ff.

[3] L. von Sacher-Masoch, *Cruel Women*. Dresden, 1901. Vol. I, p. 5.

[4] But female cruelty shows itself very clearly in other forms. Virey quotes authentic instances. Thus in many savage tribes it is mostly women who find pleasure in murdering and torturing prisoners of war. (*Vide* Hearne, *Voyage*, Vol. II, p. 32.) Cf. also Eulenburg, *Sadism and Masochism*, p. 72. In the beginning of the nineteenth century, as Abbé Richard relates in his *Description of Italy*, Vol. V, p. 242, Roman women took nightly walks in summer to all the butchers to see the oxen killed and watch their still twitching bodies. It may also be recalled that women of ancient Rome gave the sign by a movement of the thumb to kill gladiators; and that in Spain women patronise bloodthirsty bull-fights more eagerly than men. Cf. also the interesting and instructive chapter 'Female Cruelty' by Eulenburg (*Sadism and Masochism*, pp. 68-77).

[5] P. Fraxi, *Centuria*, p. 461.

his *Travel Notebook*. ' In the study of mankind, especially in the psychological sense, it is most remarkable that the fair sex is distinguished for its cruelty of this kind. Many of its members make a practice of being present at the flogging of slaves, and even go so far as to use the ox-whip themselves or take it from the overseer if he is not striking hard enough. Negro servants are veritable martyrs to white women[1].'

From all accounts we possess, English women are constituted by nature so as to possess slightly greater coldness of heart and inclination to cruelty than her continental sisters.

It was these proud and imposing figures[2], who have always by means of the rod subdued English male arrogance, who ' delighted in administering the birch '. For it must be emphatically stated that the English female flagellant was nearly always active, whether she belonged to the highest rank or the lowest. An acquaintance of Pisanus Fraxi, a devotee of the rod and well known in flagellistic circles, told him: ' I have personally known several ladies of high rank who had a remarkable passion for flagellation, and carry it out with pitiless cruelty. I also know the young and pretty wife of a preacher who has the passion to excess. I only knew one woman who liked passive flagellation; she, however, came from the lower classes. When she was intoxicated, she had her posterior whipped till the rod dripped with blood, calling out all the time, " Harder, harder! " and scolding if the punishment were too gentle[3].' Only in England are there rich gentlewomen who without being prostitutes practise active flagellation for pleasure. Cases like that of ' the flogging widow', which is recounted in *Experiences of Flagellation*, are

---

[1] Frusta, *loc. cit.*, p. 291.

[2] Such a woman is admirably portrayed in the picture of an English artist as ' Lady Termagant Flaybum '. She is about to whip her stepson. Reproduction in P. Fraxi, *Centuria*, pp. 456-457. Also in D. Hansen, *Stick and Whip*, Second edition, p. 177.

[3] P. Fraxi, *Index*, p. 46.

by no means exceptional in English society. The following is the story of the ' flogging widow ' in the book mentioned:

' Not long ago a rich, or apparently rich, widow appeared suddenly in society. Mrs. W. lived very well, kept her carriage and had a beautifully furnished house with a number of well-trained servants. No one knew the source of her wealth or whence she came; but she was soon received in the best society and won a prominent place by her downright manner and her appearance. Like many fine ladies she had a secret passion for the rod; and strange stories became current amongst her maids of the way in which she satisfied it on herself and on the girls; it was also rumoured that she had been accustomed to use the rod very freely upon her late husband. After his death she became acquainted with a young student who visited her under pretext of giving her lessons, but really to receive a sound beating at her hands[1].'

As has already been mentioned in the introduction, the history of flagellation-mania amongst English women can be traced to the Anglo-Saxon epoch. Here this tendency in women is the more noticeable because Anglo-Saxon penal laws were very mild as regards corporal punishment. One of the best authorities on this period, Thomas Wright[2], draws attention to the cruelty of Anglo-Saxon women towards their dependants as a strange fact. It even happened, on occasions, that menservants and maids were whipped to death by their mistresses. Many accounts speak of the accomplished manner in which these women wielded the rod. Pictorial representations of such flagellation scenes have also survived.

In the eighteenth century it is possible to point to regular clubs for female flagellants from which the conclusion may be

---

[1] *Experiences of Flagellation*. Dresden, 1901. P. 80.

[2] Thomas Wright, *Domestic Manners*, pp. 56-57 (picture of flagellation scene, Plate 37, p. 57). Cf. also Wright, *History of English Culture*, pp. 69-70.

drawn that the number of women with this tendency had noticeably increased.

A detailed description of such a club which met every Thursday evening in Jermyn Street can be read in the *Bon Ton Magazine* of December 1792: 'These female members are mainly married women who, tired of marriage in its usual form and the cold indifference which is wont to accompany it, determined by a novel method to re-awaken the ecstasy which they knew at the beginning of their married life. . . . The honourable society or club to which we refer never has fewer than twelve members. At each meeting six are chastised by the other six. They draw lots for the order of procedure: then either a written speech is read or an extempore one delivered on the effects of flagellation, as it has been practised from the earliest ages up to the present day, in monasteries and convents, brothels and private houses; after which the six patients take their places and the six flagellants begin the practical demonstration, first uncovering those parts which though less visible and less within reach of mishandling, are yet more sensitive and lively than others. The president of the club hands to each a stout rod, and begins the chastisement herself, with any variation she likes while the others watch. Sometimes, by order of the president, the whipping starts on the calves and goes up to the posterior, until the whole region, as Shakespeare says, from milk-white " becomes one red ". After the president the other flagellants take their turn.'

The most notorious female flagellant of the eighteenth century was Elizabeth Brownrigg, an obvious sadist, who was executed at Tyburn on 14th September 1767. She was the wife of James Brownrigg, a plumber, of Fleur-de-Luce Court, Fleet Street, London. She was a midwife in the parish of St. Dunstan's, and took girls as apprentices. On the outside she appeared a thoroughly respectable, God-fearing woman, but

at home she figured as fiercely cruel mistress to the apprentices; she had in 1765 three of these, Mary Mitchell, Mary
Jones and Mary Clifford, and ' trained ' them by means of
daily brutal floggings. ' She beat the children as a drunken
coster beats his donkey.' Mary Jones succeeded in escaping,
but Mary Mitchell was brought back, after an attempted
flight, by Mrs. Brownrigg's son. Mary Clifford was treated
worst: every day she was beaten with a stick, a broom-
handle or a horse-whip; and with Mitchell she was often
undressed and bound for several hours and kept in the cellar
on bread and water. One day Mary Clifford was undressed,
bound and beaten five times, and after being in hospital a
few days, died from the effects of her dreadful maltreatment.

The Brownriggs were arrested. The husband and son
were sentenced to six months each, and Mrs. Brownrigg to
the gallows[1].

Nowhere has flagellantist prostitution started so soon or
been developed to such a degree as in England. Speculation
on men's masochistic tendencies to passive flagellation, combined with their own preference for active flagellation, led
many women to develop a subtle skill in the art of whipping
and in the application of the rod; and eventually to the
establishment of special brothels for flagellation. From the
end of the eighteenth century (formerly, about 1760, a Mrs.
Jenkins had won great renown as a flagellant) and throughout the nineteenth century, they form a characteristic feature
of prostitution in London[2].

These brothels, which increased in London from 1800
onwards[3], were devoted solely to flagellation, and their

[1] Cf. for this *cause célèbre* Cooper, *loc. cit.*, pp. 174-175. *Experiences of
Flagellation*, pp. 125-128.
[2] *Etude sur la Flagellation*, p. 178.
[3] Yet there were institutions devoted solely to flagellation in the
eighteenth century, such as the ' White House ', that of ' Mother Cum-
mins ', the ' Elysium in Brydges Street ', etc. Cf. Fraxi, *Index*, p. 312.

description as ' flagellation-brothels ' is accurate. They were generally luxuriously appointed, and served not only as places where men could submit to their heart's content to passive flagellation, but also as educational institutions (*sit venia verbo*) where girls and women could acquire the gentle art of whipping and the graceful application of the rod.

Pisanus Fraxi has collected absolutely authentic details about these flagellation-brothels. He maintains that many of the female assistants themselves took a great interest, even a passion, in their calling[1]. There were not only women who merely, *lucri causa*, satisfied men's flagellation-mania, but many who wielded the rod with the greatest pleasure, quite unlike prostitutes in general. They took pupils too, as has been mentioned[1] in the *Ars flagellandi*.

According to Fraxi it would be easy to compile a long list of these keepers of flagellation-brothels. He confines himself, however, to naming the most notorious. At the beginning of the nineteenth century Mrs. Collet enjoyed such renown as a subtle flagellant that even George IV visited her, which is an established fact. She had a brothel at first in Tavistock Court, Covent Garden; from which she moved to the neighbourhood of Portland Place; from there she migrated to Bedford Street, Russell Square, where she died. She brought up her niece to the same calling: she later, as Mrs. Mitchell, carried on a flourishing business at 22 Waterloo Road (later 44), and at last in St. Mary's Square, Kennington. She was followed by Mrs. James, who started life as a maid in the family of Lord Clanricarde. She established a brothel in Soho (7 Carlisle Street) for flagellation, and made a large fortune, so that later she retired from ' business ' and took a luxuriously furnished house in Notting Hill, full of pictures, while she herself appeared in public loaded with jewels.

But without doubt the queen of flagellation was Mrs.

[1] P. Fraxi, *Index*, p. xlvi.

Theresa Berkley, who kept a famous establishment at 28 Charlotte Street, Portland Place. She was past-mistress of her art, an expert in knowing the various whims of men clients, which she satisfied in the most refined manner; at the same time, she was an excellent business woman and put by a considerable fortune.

' She possessed the first great requirement of a courtesan. namely lubricity. For without herself being licentious, a woman cannot long keep an inclination to such activity, and it is soon obvious that she is only anxious to fill her pockets with pounds, shillings and pence. She could be jovial and amusing; and used to find out every inclination, every whim, every mood, every wish of her clients, and satisfy them, as soon as ever she was suitably paid. Her arsenal of instruments was vastly more complete than that of any other governess. Her care of the rods was extraordinarily thorough.

' They were always kept in water so that they should be green and supple. She had a dozen tapering whip thongs, a dozen cat-o'-nine-tails studded with needle points, various kinds of thin supple switches, leather straps as thick as traces, curry-combs and ox-hide straps studded with nails, which had become tough and hard from constant use, also holly and gorse and a prickly evergreen called " butcher's bush ". During the summer, glass and Chinese vases were kept filled with green nettles with which the "dead were often brought to life again". Thus in her establishment anyone provided with reasonable means could have himself beaten with canes, scourges, whips and straps, pricked with needles, half-strangled, scrubbed with many kinds of harsh brushes, scourged with nettles, curry-combed, bled and tortured until he had had enough of it.'

Theresa Berkley became particularly famous in her profession through her invention of the ' Berkley Horse ' or

[353]

' Chevalet '. She invented this apparatus for the flogging of men early in 1828. It was really an adjustable ladder which could be extended to a considerable length, and on which the victim was securely strapped, openings being left for the head and genitals[1]. In Mrs. Berkley's *Memoirs* there was a copperplate showing the ' horse ' in use. Mrs. Berkley herself is seen flogging the posterior of a man strapped to the Chevalet, while a very *decolleté* girl sitting on a chair underneath acts as ' Frictrix ' to him.

This new and unique invention brought the Berkley a large clientele and enormous profits. When she died in September 1836 she left a fortune of £10,000 which she had amassed in eight years. In her *Memoirs* there was also a picture of another speciality of her establishment, a compound pulley on the first floor, to which a man could be attached by his hands and flogged in this position.

A very interesting insight into the eccentricities of her male clientele is given by the following letter from a flagellomaniac to the Berkley which was first published in *Venus Schoolmistress*:

January 1836.

To Madame T. Berkley,
    28 Charlotte Street, Portland Place.

Honoured lady,
    I am an ill-behaved young man and quite incorrigible! The most celebrated tutors in London have chastised me but have been unable to correct my wilfulness. A gentleman of

---

[1] An illustration of the 'horse' appeared in the 1836 edition of *Venus Schoolmistress*, which P. Fraxi reproduced in his *Index Librorum prohibitorum* on p. xliv. After this reproduction the picture was repeated in Hansen's *Stick and Whip*, p. 167, and Eulenburg's *Sadism and Masochism*, p. 61. The Chevalet is also found in modern flagellation pictures. In Paris during the Exhibition of 1900 it was made much practical use of and greatly appreciated by men of the world. Compare Hansen, *loc. cit.*, p. 171.

the name of Brunswick recommended me to a Madame Brown, who was supposed to have remarkably strong arms. Another sent me to Madame Wilson in Marylebone, who was even less slenderly built. The old hotelier Jaunay, of Leicester Square, took me to Mrs. Calmers, who is supposed to be very experienced in the use of the stick, and I was invited to dinner with this lady. She received me in her elegantly appointed house, but to no purpose! In spite of her imposing form and the strength of her arm, she could make no impression on me! Another advised me to go to Mrs. Jones. But she, like all the others, tried in vain to belabour my back with sticks. Captain Johnson recommended me to Betsy Burgess, who is supposed to be a skilful governess. The bookseller Brooks, of Bond Street, gave me one of Mrs. Collett's cards and also Mrs. Beverley's. I am aware that all these ladies understand their profession, but their united efforts failed to make any impression on me.

Finally, honoured lady, I received an introduction from your close friend, Count G., which is causing me to jump for joy, because I have been told of your famous apparatus, the Chevalet, which should succeed in punishing sufficiently undisciplined young men like myself.

I will come to see you at the beginning of February, when I am in London with my friend the Count, where Parliamentary duties await us; but in order that there shall be no misunderstanding between us, I herewith give you a list of my requirements.

1. It is necessary that I should be securely fastened to the Chevalet with chains which I will bring myself.

2. A pound sterling for the first blood drawn.

3. Two pounds sterling if the blood runs down to my heels.

4. Three pounds sterling if my heels are bathed in blood.

5. Four pounds sterling if the blood reaches the floor.

[355]

6. Five pounds sterling if you succeed in making me lose consciousness.

I am, honoured lady,

Your quite incorrigible,

O.

In the second half of the nineteenth century, also, flagellation establishments flourished in London. Amongst others, Mrs. Sarah Potter, alias Stewart, was very well known in the 'sixties. There is a remarkable little book about her which was incidentally published with the object of making public the facts of her arrest in the year 1863, on the charge of a girl whom she had beaten against her will[1].

' Her method of carrying on her business was that the girls received board, lodging and clothing, and in return were expected to minister to the lusts of the clientele of her " Boarding House ". The girls were flogged in many different ways. Often they were bound to the ladder, at other times whipped round the room or laid on the bed. Any idea or innovation which the perverted fancy could imagine was made use of to vary the orgies, for which the lady of the house received 5 to 15 pounds sterling. The income from the " School " enabled Stewart to rent a country house and to keep a lover, to the great scandal of the neighbours.'

More recent flagellation brothels are described by Pisanus Fraxi; among them one to which twenty young women came

---

[1] *Mysteries of Flagellation, or a History of the Secret Ceremonies of the Society of Flagellants. The saintly practice of the birch! St. Francis whipped by the Devil! How to subdue the passions by the art of flogging! With many curious anecdotes of the prevalence of this curious pastime in all nations and epochs, whether savage or civilised. Printed by C. Brown, 44, Wych Street, Strand. Price 2d.* On the title-page was a woodcut of a girl undressing herself, while on either side stand an old man and an old woman, both holding a rod in their right hand, the man, in addition, holding a rope in his left; in the background is a ladder. Compare P. Fraxi, *Index*, p. 311.

to go through all the different stages of a ' schoolmistress ',
and powerfully to wield the rod. The written requests of
their ' pupils ' were often quite remarkable. Some men
wished to be laid over the knee like children, others whipped
on the back of a servant maid, still others wanted to be tied
up[1].

An article by Otto Brandes entitled *Die Auspeitscherin*
(The Female Flogger) in the *Zeitgeist* (a supplement to
the *Berliner Tageblatt*) of 23rd October 1893, together
with the letters which appeared in the English paper
Society during the year 1900, point to the widespread
tendency at that time to active flagellation among English
women. 'During my stay in London in 1901 a shoe shop
in W——— Street was said to be a secret flagellation brothel.'
But in general the old ' flogging establishments ' have
changed to modern ' manicure institutes ' and the like, of
which one could see elegant examples in the West End,
especially in the neighbourhood of one particular street.

The following invitation card, an original device, is for
' Gentlemen Flagellants ' and was printed at the end of the
book *The Sublime of Flagellation*:

' A short time after the appearance of the " fashionable
lectures " in Paris, the following card was passed on by
booksellers to each purchaser of the work.

' " All purchasers of the 'lecture' who are curious to judge
of its effects, will, if they go the proper way about it, be
directed to a lady of outstanding bodily and spiritual culture.
If the proper compliments are made to her, she will deliver
each of the ' lectures ' with a rare eloquence and a happy
union of a powerfully sympathetic voice and movement.

' " This lady has her own house. Her 'lecture room' is
furnished with rods, with cat-o'-nine-tails, and with some

[1] Fraxi, *Index*, pp. xliv ff.

[357]

of the finest flagellation pictures. She also has a strong woman who is quite capable of taking a man on her back, in case he wishes to be treated like a schoolboy. She and her servant will also lend themselves to passive flagellation, if it be so desired. The price of the first lecture is one guinea, each succeeding one half-a-guinea, and to the servant, if acting as ' mount ', half-a-crown.

' " N.B.—Single gentlemen, who like to represent themselves as schoolboys, can also be visited by the lady and servant at any hour, but especially in the early morning before they get up. They can then have the enchanting entertainment of being taken out of bed, set upon the ' mount ', and whipped: all of which will be carried out with astonishing art." '

From the foregoing, it is clear that the male flagello-maniac usually requires to be whipped himself, but also practises active flagellation frequently, extending this both to girls and boys.

In the introduction to *Venus Schoolmistress* (p. viii), male flagellants are divided into three classes:

1. Those who like to receive a more or less severe chastise-ment from the hand of a woman who takes pleasure in wielding the rod with power and skill.

2. Those who like to apply the rod themselves to a female.

3. Those who are neither active nor passive flagellants, but who get sufficient sexual excitement from just looking on at a flagellation.

The old-time poet Christopher Marlowe (1564-1593) describes even in his own time a disciple of passive flagella-tion in the following characteristic epigram:

When Francis comes to solace with his whore,
He sends for rods and strips himself stark naked;

For his lust sleeps, and will not rise before
By whipping of the wench it be awaked.
I envy him not, but wish I had the power,
To make his wench but one half hour[1].

There was also the notorious individual who made the streets of London unsafe at the end of the seventeenth century, and who would lift up the clothes of any women he met and give them a slap or a blow. He went about his work so skilfully that popular belief invested him with supernatural powers. He was called ' Whipping Tom '. Pisanus Fraxi[2] mentions a literary curiosity dealing with this peculiar flagellant, entitled: *Whipping Tom Brought to Light, and exposed to View: In an account of several late Adventures of pretended Whipping Spirit. London, printed for Edward Brooks* 1681.' In this book Whipping Tom's pranks are described as follows:

' Whipping Tom for some weeks past has lurked about in alleys and courts in Fleet Street, Chancery Lane, Shoe Lane, Fetter Lane, the Strand, Holborn and other places, and at unawares seazes upon such as he can conveniently light on, and turning them up as nimble as an Eel (*sic*), makes their Butt ends cry Spanko; and then (according to the report of those who have felt the weight of his Paws) vanished; for you must know, that having left the Country, he has not the advantage of getting Rods, and therefore is obliged to use his hands instead thereof. His first adventure, as near as we can learn, was on a Servant Maid in New Street, who being sent out look her Master (*sic*), as she was turning a Corner, perceived a Tall black Man standing up against the wall, as if he had been making water, but she had not passed for, but with great speed and violence seized her and in a trice

---

[1] *The Works of Christopher Marlowe.* London, 1826. Vol. III, p. 454.
[2] P. Fraxi, *Centuria*, p. 469.

laying her across his knee, took up her Linnen, and lay'd so hard upon her Backside as made her cry out most piteously for help, the which he no sooner perceiving to approach (as she declares) but he vanished; and although diligent search was made no person could be found.'

As mentioned, the ' flogging cullies[1] ', that is the devotees of passive flagellation, undoubtedly formed the greater proportion of male flagellants, but there were active flagellants as well amongst these, and very frequently the tendency to passive is combined with that of active flagellation.

The doings of such male flagellants are apparently, according to actual facts, very clearly described in a completely sadistic work: *The Experimental Lecture of Colonel Spanker* (London, 1879)[2].

It deals with a company of aristocratic flagellants, under the leadership of ' Colonel Spanker ', who rent a house in Mayfair near Hyde Park which they entrust to the care of a former brothel keeper, who assists in flagellation orgies held in it and procures the young women to be whipped. At first they engage poor women from the streets (flower girls and the like), who are ready if well paid to allow themselves to be whipped. But ' the lack of all sensitiveness and modesty in such poorly educated young women became quite disagreeable. . . .'

So two young women of gentle birth are enticed into the house and cruelly beaten and tortured.

' This book,' remarks an English bibliophile, ' which we can fairly assert is the most coldly cruel and unblushingly

---

[1] ' Cull ' or ' cully ' meant either bully or frequently the customers of a brothel who paid money for ' secret, sweet and costly pleasures '. Poll Ellis (a prostitute) laid a large net in order, as she ironically said, the better to catch the ' culls '. Compare John Bee, *Sportsman's Slang*, etc., p. 61.

[2] Cf. P. Fraxi, *Catena*, pp. 246-251; Hansen, *Rod and Whip*, pp. 196-206.

indecent of any we have ever read, stands entirely alone in the English language. It seems to be the wild dream, or rather nightmare, of some vicious, used-up old rake, who, positively worn out, and his hide tanned and whipped to insensibility by diurnal flogging, has gone mad on the subject of beastly flagellation.'

Male flagellants who practise active flagellation are described, in the same terms as in the *Lecture of Colonel Spanker*, in another book, *The Convent School, or Early Experiences of a Young Flagellant*, by Rosa Belinda Coote (London, 1876), in which a woman is whipped and tortured in the most cruel way by two men.

Sexual flagellation and an ardent passion for the rod in England are not only manifested in brothels, but appear in almost all social activities, where they play a more important part than is the case in other countries.

In this respect, the English schools demand first consideration. Many men have left us their memories of ' school miseries ', and have so clearly described the chastisements given by the teachers, that we may almost assume that they have found pleasure therein, in the same way as their masters. Mention of these beatings in schools are to be found in *Specimens of Table-Talk* by S. T. Coleridge (27th May 1830), in *Essays of Elia* and *Recollections of Christ's Hospital* by Charles Lamb, in the *Autobiography of a Working Man* (London, 1848) by Alexander Somerville, in *Self Formation, or the History of an Individual Mind* (London, 1837) by Capel Loft, in *Memoirs of a Cape Rifleman* by Colonel Whitehorn, in the works of Leigh Hunt, and of many others.

Further rich material for a history of flagellation in English schools exists in many novels and romances and other works of belletristic literature, written from both experience and observation, such as Richard Head's *English Rogue*, Fielding's *Tom Jones*, Smollett's *Roderick Random*,

Captain Marryat's *Rattlin' Reefer*, Charles Dickens' *Nicholas Nickleby*, Kingsley's *Westward Ho!*

Very outspoken descriptions of corporal punishment in schools is given in the two books *Settlers and Convicts* (London, 1847) and *Twelve Years a Slave* (London, 1853). Frusta states: ' Whipping, scourging and beating have been very common from olden times in England, the classical land of freedom, and still are to this very day, though there are no Jesuits there. Home education is carried on with extreme severity and is accompanied by the whipping of both sexes, which lasts longest in the case of males. In the large colleges, until recent times, eighteen to twenty-one-year old young people were thrashed. The memoirs of Trelawney, the well-known friend of Byron, give a surprising picture from the inside of English school punishments in many establishments, and remove the need for further evidence[1]'.

Schoolmasters such as Dr. Gill[2] (beginning of the seventeenth century) and Dr. Colet of St. Paul's School, Dr. Drury and Dr. Vaughan of Harrow, Dr. Busby, Dr. Keate and Major Edgeworth of Eton, and Dr. James Bowyer[3] of Christ's Hospital, have become proverbial. They all appear to have agreed with Edgar Allen Poe in regard to the handling

[1] Frusta, *Catena*, p. 254. Cf. also Delolme, *loc. cit.*, pp. 69-70, with quotations from the works of the writers Fielding and Gay, and the lines :
The Schoolboy's desire is a play-day,
The Schoolmaster's joy is to flog.

[2] Cf. *Gill upon Gill, or Gill's Ass uncased, unstript, unbound* (London, 1608); or Davenant, *On Doctor Gill, Master of Paul's School*.

[3] When the poet Coleridge heard of the death of his old schoolmaster, Bowyer, he remarked that it was lucky that the cherubim who would conduct him to Heaven had but head and wings. Otherwise he would have undoubtedly have beaten them on the way Cf. W. H. Blanch, *The Blue Coat Boys* (London, 1877), p. 90, with an illustration showing various famous and influential people who had experienced the rod at Eton and at Christ's Hospital; and also anecdotes of Lamb and of Leigh Hunt. The above story has been also told of Dr. Busby.

of the cane, when he said: ' Children are never too tender to
be beaten. They are like tough beefsteaks that become the
more tender the more they are beaten.'   Or perhaps with
Lord Byron, who in *Don Juan* (Canto II, Stanza I) admonishes
the schoolmaster:

> Oh ye, who teach the ingenuous youth of nations,
>   Holland, France, England, Germany or Spain,
> I pray ye flog them upon all occasions.
>   It mends their morals, never mind the pain.

Westminster School had a bad reputation from olden days.
According to Cooper[1] they did not use a birch rod there, but
one made of apple twigs in a wooden holder. Two juniors
held the office of ' rod maker ' and had to provide the school
with rods. The inventor of the Westminster rod was supposed to be Dr. Bacher, who was in charge of the school from
1454 to 1487. For his punishment the delinquent had to kneel
on a block, his posterior was exposed and the teacher gave
him either four strokes, the so-called ' scrubber ', or six
strokes, the ' biblical '.

The two best-known flagellants of Westminster were Dr.
Busby and Dr. Vincent. Busby's rod was the 'sieve which
separates the chaff of learning from the wheat[2] '. Vincent's
rule was nearly as bad as Busby's ' reign of terror '. Cooper
says: ' He was not content with the prescribed punishments,
but also cuffed the boys and boxed their ears. Coleman took
up the cudgels against this, and said that a pedagogue had
the right to colour his scholars red in the proper places, but
that he had no right to make them black and blue with his
fingers. Under Vincent's rule the school founded a periodical
which was called the *Flagellant*, and which so aroused his
wrath that he threatened to take legal proceedings against

[1] Cooper, *loc. cit.*, p. 137.
  Ibid., p. 136.

the publisher. Then Southey, who had also held him up to ridicule in an article, came forward and announced himself as the author, and Vincent was unable to take any further steps against the school[1].'

An eccentric flagellant of Westminster School was Dr. Parr. His rod supplier was a man who had been taken down from the gallows and brought back to life, and from this man Parr always received the rods with a ' well-pleased smile[2] '.

There is no doubt that the practice of flogging at Westminster School produced many flagellomaniacs. As early as the seventeenth century a poet, Thomas Shadwell, introduced the subject into a comedy of his, *The Virtuoso* (Act 4). The old *roué*, Snarl, comes into a brothel to be flogged, and is asked by the girl: ' I wonder that a thing which I like so little should give you so much pleasure? ' To which he answered: ' I got so used to it at Westminster School that I have not been able to do without it since.'

This custom was undoubtedly bound up with the unbridled immorality and sexual freedom which, according to Hüttner[3], was rife at Westminster School and at Eton in the eighteenth century.

At the latter school it appears that in each boy's account there was a charge of half-a-guinea for birches. Dr. Keate held office here with merciless severity from 1809 for a quarter of a century. His insatiable passion for the stick was the subject of many stories in contemporary and later literature. As one anecdote relates, he knew the posteriors of his pupils better than their faces[4].

At the Universities, too, up to the eighteenth century, the students were given corporal punishment. Milton and

---

[1] Cooper, *loc. cit.*, p. 137.
[2] *Ibid.*
[3] Hüttner, *London Customs*, pp. 188-189, 192.
[4] Compare Cooper, *loc. cit.*, p. 138.

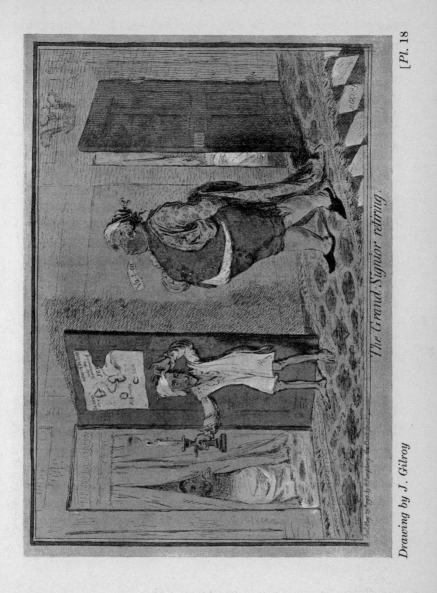

Drawing by J. Gilroy

The Grand Signior retiring.

[*Pl.* 19]

INDUSTRY & IDLENESS.

Designed by Wm. Hogarth

Johnson both appear to have been punished in this way
coram publico[1].

The ' whipping stocks ' and the ' whipping horse ' played
a large part in these punishments. Thackeray[2] tells of the
floggings that the poet Steele had to undergo at the old
Charterhouse School at Smithfield: ' He was very idle. He
was whipped deservedly a great number of times. Though
he had very good parts of his own, he got other boys to do
his lessons for him, and only took just as much trouble as
should enable him to scuffle through his exercises, and by
good fortune escape the flogging block. One hundred and
fifty years after I have myself inspected, but only as an
amateur, that instrument of righteous torture still existing,
and in occasional use, in a secluded private apartment of the
old Charterhouse School; and have no doubt it is the very
counterpart, if not the ancient and interesting machine itself,
at which poor Dick Steele submitted himself to the tormentors.

The rod was used no less in girls' boarding schools and
pensions than in the boys' schools.

These ' Ladies' Boarding Schools ' existed in England from
the end of the seventeenth century, but even in those days
seem to have had a bad reputation on account of the way in
which they were managed. Writers of that period condemn
most bitterly the excessive whipping of young girls in these
schools on the naked posterior, and the lascivious habits
necessarily resulting therefrom[3]. William Alexander complains of the frivolous education received by the girls in these
expensive schools[4]. The principals of the numerous ' Academies for Young Ladies ' had in most cases unlimited power
over the minds and bodies of the girls entrusted to them by

[1] Cooper, *loc. cit.*, pp. 139-140.
[2] W. M. Thackeray, *English Humorists of the Eighteenth Century*.
London, 1853.
[3] Malcolm, *Anecdotes of the manners and customs of London*, Vol. I, p. 328.
[4] W. Alexander, *History of Women*, Vol. I, p. 48.

the nobility and the rich burghers, and used these powers zealously and unscrupulously.

As regards the English girls' schools in the eighteenth century, we learn many interesting particulars from Cooper. Lady Frances Pennoyer of Bullingham Court in Hertfordshire writes in her diary under date 2nd January 1766: ' Went to the school as I intended, and met Dr. Aubrey on the way. Found the school girls all assembled and the teacher anxiously looking out. She is a charming young girl, but I should think too pretty for such a position. Dr. Aubrey went in with me and assured me that he had had much experience of whipping in girls' high schools, and was glad when the girls blushed. " It showed very seemly modesty ", he said. The two girls who were to receive punishment were prepared by the teacher. They knelt down and begged forgiveness. I was glad to see how nicely they took their punishment, which I gave them myself, in order to show the teacher how best to use the rods[1].'

Cooper also quotes the experience of an English lady in a girls' pension, which she described in a letter at the end of the eighteenth century. The writer relates, amongst other things: 'Punishment in girls' schools was already being reduced, but Miss Pomeroy still believed in it and made great use of it. If one of us had to be accused of a fault (and you can imagine the trifles that were called faults!), and it was considered that we ought to be punished, we had to go to the teacher's desk, and after a deep curtsey, ask to be allowed to fetch the cane. Permission was given with much ceremony, and we went out and came back without gloves and with the cane on a cushion. Then we kneeled down and presented the cane, which the teacher took and gave us a few strokes on the naked arms and neck. There were two kinds of cane; one made of birchrods and one of fine whalebone wound round

[1] Cooper, loc. cit., pp. 125-126.

with waxed thread.   Both gave much pain, but the one made of whalebone, which we called "soko", was the most feared.

'The strokes were like those made by the cat-o'-nine-tails and went deep into our flesh. " Soko " was used for serious faults, that is for any lack of respect for either of the two principals. This was a particularly fine school, in which 30 young girls were taken from the best families. It was not unusual for them to stay at school till they were 18 or 19 and a good marriage had been arranged for them, or until an older sister married and made room for them, so that they could be introduced to society. But young or old, none could escape the cane when Miss Pomeroy had made up her mind. There were so many punishments in Regent House that even the most zealous adherent of the proverb " Spare the rod and spoil the child " would have been satisfied.

'There were two or three grades of severe punishment. The first took place in Miss Pomeroy's room in the presence of herself and the servant. The second was the public preparation for punishment before the whole school, which was, however, followed by forgiveness, and the third was the public carrying out of the punishment. The only occasion when I received punishment in Miss Pomeroy's room, I remember as if it were yesterday, old woman as I am to-day! I was told to bring the cane to a room which the principal called her study. There I found the two ladies, knelt down before them and offered them the cane.

'This was taken by the elder of them who, as it seemed to me, fondled it gently with her fingers. Then she rang and ordered the maid to prepare me. This consisted simply in lifting up my frock and fastening my hands. I was terribly frightened as I had never in my life been whipped, and the shame of it so overcame me that a bad attack of hysteria was the result of my first punishment at school. Alas! I got used later on to seeing the cane used and to feeling it! I have seen

[367]

half-clothed girls of marriageable age whipped before all their schoolfellows for any small misdemeanour. There was a special dress, like a nightdress, which was put on for public punishment, and the culprit was brought out in this when her schoolfellows were assembled. She then had to bend over a desk, her hands were fastened and her feet stuck in the stocks.

'One young girl was punished in this way shortly before she left school to be married. I will call her Miss Darwin. She had naturally very little ability, and she was always stealing. Nothing was safe from her. It was what is now called kleptomania, but we had no grand names for crimes when I was young, and stealing was stealing, and there was an end of it! One afternoon Miss Pomeroy said: "Ladies, you will dress half-an-hour earlier this afternoon and be in class at half-past 4 o'clock instead of five." We looked at each other and Miss Darwin blushed but said nothing, and we went to our rooms. Then we found out what had happened, as the girl who curled my hair had to provide the canes, and had that day bound a perfectly new one specially for the occasion. At the appointed time we were all assembled and Miss Pomeroy took her place. Miss Darwin was made to stand in the middle of the room and then the principal related what she had done and what she must undergo.

'She was a very pretty girl and in size and appearance quite grown-up, but she stood there as if a caning were quite a natural occurrence. She was beautifully dressed in green brocade with a white silk underdress, and many pretty ornaments. Miss Pomeroy rang and said to the servant: "Prepare her!" The girl curtseyed and asked permission to take off her gloves. Miss Darwin bowed and the undressing proceeded. Then the robe of punishment was put on and the young lady offered Miss Pomeroy the cane on her

[368]

knees, after which she was led by two teachers to a desk and
fastened as has been related. Miss Pomeroy then beat her so
severely that red weals were to be seen all over the white
skin. After the punishment all her limbs trembled, her face
glowed and her eyes sparkled. She gave the cane back to the
teacher on her knees and went out to change her clothes[1].'

These two stories need no further comment in order to
make perfectly clear the sexual element contained in them,
and are sufficient, although one could add to them a large
number of similar authentic reports, to justify Hüttner's
remarks[2] on the great and universal immorality in the
English boarding schools of the eighteenth century.

The application of these punishments was naturally most
dangerous in those schools which were frequented by both
boys and girls and where the boys were punished *sans gêne*
before the girls and vice versa. This was the custom, for
instance, in the eighteenth century in the English charity
schools, where the noble patronesses themselves often
were present when punishments were given, and had so-
called ' punishment days '. The ladies themselves gave the
cane to boys and girls indiscriminately. This seemed, as a
' true, unadulterated report ' of that time says, to give them
quite exceptional pleasure[3]. Pisanus Fraxi[4] quotes the
following authentic letter from a gentleman who was
known to him, dated 13th May, 1859, which throws
considerable light on these conditions:

' In my childhood it was the custom in the preparatory
schools for boys and girls together to be under the authority
of a woman, and for the cane to be used on all occasions
with the utmost severity. We were whipped in the presence

---

[1] Cooper, *loc. cit.*, pp. 144-146.
[2] Hüttner, *loc. cit.*, p. 170.
[3] Cooper, *loc. cit.*, pp. 130-133.
[4] P. Fraxi, *Centuria*, pp. 458-459.

of both sexes, the girls laid on the knee or held under the arm, the boys on the back of a servant maid. This last often came to our (the boys') room and played " schoolmistress," and the girls did the same. I have a lively recollection of an extraordinary scene in this connection, which convinced me that many women are slaves to this particular passion.

'In the school I have mentioned, the woman who helped the teacher evidently much enjoyed seeing punishment given, although she was very fond of all of us and was herself a great favourite with the boys. But every morning she would tell some of the boys, never without an accompaniment of jokes and giggling, that they must not leave until " Missus " had paid them a visit, or in the evening that they must wait so long until "Missus" had had a " little conversation with you," and that the latter was to be expected any minute with a couple of terrifying canes. This girl took a lot of trouble with us, and I am afraid brought our puberty much too soon to its full development. She had a large bust and arranged her dress always so that when we were punished by being whipped, and had to put our hands round her, we could feel her bosom, the movements of which gave us a very pleasant sensation. Many boys got themselves punished purposely in order to experience this sensation. Although forty years have passed since then, my recollection of it is as clear as if it had been yesterday.'

In the *Memoirs of a Schoolmaster* (Bath, 1790) there is a remarkable chapter, 'My Marriage', in which the teacher relates how he fell in love with a widow, whom he surprised punishing her daughter, and to whom, after their marriage, he gave absolute authority to punish his pupils, which she did in her boudoir with all her might.

Even more remarkable are the flagellantic fantasies of an English schoolmaster in an account published by

Pisanus Fraxi[1] of an anonymous author, entitled: *Schoolmaster's little Dinner*. In this is described the visit of a teacher in north Yorkshire to a neighbouring colleague, a widower, who was passionately fond of the use of the cane, and who satisfied this passion in the most peculiar ways. His housekeeper was called 'Mother Birch' on account of her exceptional skill in making rods with good prickles. The teller of the story found with his colleagues two other pedagogues, a Dr. S., well known as a fanatical flagellant, and a Mr. T., who looked somewhat boyish. On going into the dining-room these met with a remarkable sight. In the four corners of the room were four candelabras, apparently held by four boys with naked posteriors. They were tied up and the hands so fastened that it looked as if they held the candelabra. After the first course the four worthy pedagogues set themselves to flogging the bare posteriors of the boys, in which work Dr. S. and the host were the most zealous. They then sat down with great appetite, and ' Dr. S. crunched the bones with his teeth as if they were those of the boys whom he had punished! ' The dessert was brought in by four other boys in blue jackets trimmed with silver, and white breeches. The host then took out 'four beautiful little canes bound with blue ribbon' and the peculiar quartette again began their questionable activities.

Thereafter Mr. T. was bound on the ' horse ' and his gestures and grimaces during the punishment highly amused his three lovable colleagues. The host himself carried out the whipping of his guest, in which he employed the method of the famous Dr. Keate, which was very uncomfortable for the victim. Mr. T. roared with pain and begged to be let loose, which, however, did not disturb the second Dr. Keate in his favourite occupation. Dr. S. continued the flagel-

[1] P. Fraxi, *Centuria*, pp. 453-456. The author calls himself ' Thackeray Pedagogus '

lation of his colleague till the poor T., half fainting with pain, was set free, on which a hand of whist finished off this edifying ' little dinner '.

Under such conditions it is no wonder that sometimes, as we saw by the example of the ladies in the charity school, flagellomaniacs who did not belong to the teaching profession gained entrance to schools in order to be present when punishments were given or to carry them out themselves. The best known case was that of Lieutenant Sir E. C——, who often went to Christ's Hospital to punish the children and to be caned by them[1].

The impropriety and the serious consequences of the methods of punishment used in the schools could not long remain hidden. For this reason all corporal punishment in English schools has many times been forbidden—it was prohibited for example in all the best schools and colleges in the year 1838[2]. But so deeply rooted in the English was the passion for the cane, that corporal punishment in the schools and pensions was retained until recently and nearly to the same extent as in former times. If the English magazine *Society* could fill columns during two years of publication with reports, communications and letters on the use of the cane, it seems clear that the so-called pedagogic flagellomania, which is of course nothing more than disguised sensuality must have been general in England.

The same may be said of the detailed reports on flogging in the London schools which are to be found in the *Etude sur la Flagellation*[3]. Hector France also, and he can be relied upon in this connection, says: 'Il ne faudrait pas croire qu'il s'agit ici d'un épisode isolé, cas particulier à une école dirigée par une vieille fille hystérique qui passe ses rages de

[1] Cooper, *loc. cit.*, pp. 166-167.
[2] Ryan, *Prostitution in London*, p. 382.
[3] *Etude sur la Flagellation*, pp. 303-324, 365-383.

chair sechée et les colères de ses attentes deçues en meutris-
sant des chairs fraîches; il est, sinon général, au moins très
commun, ainsi que le prouveront surabondamment les pages
qui vont suivre,' and he then quotes a large number of very
bad examples[1].

In one of the letters reported to *Society* is the following: ' Your correspondents often ask whether corporal
punishment is still in force in the better class girls' schools.
I can assure you that it does still exist and that for various
reasons it grows daily in popularity. Many schools in which
corporal punishment had hitherto not been known are
gradually taking to it, at first only in the form of what is
called " slapping ", that is hitting the hands with a stick. I
do not believe in these methods, as they may easily cause
injury to the bones and sinews. It would be much better
to use a pliant reed cane than an unyielding stick, which only
injures without causing the sharp pain desired. Others of
our better class girls' schools use the old-fashioned canes,
sticks and scourges, sometimes on the upper and sometimes
on the lower parts of the body[2].'

Conditions in the secular schools were repeated in the
convent schools, convents and churches. The Reverend
Zachary Crofton, a minister who was also a flagellant, was
mentioned by Delolme; in the year 1660 he was Vicar of the
Parish of St. Botolph, Aldgate, London, and a very truculent
gentleman both in religion and politics. Bishop Kennet
relates in his Chronicle, according to Dr. Calamy's account
of it, that Crofton must have been a great devotee of flagellation; he once gave his servant maid a very severe punishment, and later published a work in praise of flagellation[3].

---

[1] See the chapter ' Filles fessées ' in *Nuits de Londres*, pp. 203-215; also
the following ' Dompteuse de filles ', pp. 217-225.

[2] *The Education of John Bull*. Dresden, 1902. New edition. Vol. IV, p. 44.

[3] Delolme, *loc. cit.*, pp. 200-201.

In *Experiences of Flagellation* a scene in a convent school is described, when the Mother Superior acted as flagellant, and much enjoyed the shrieks of the little girls she ill-treated[1].

Andrew Steinmetz in his work on the English Jesuits[2] reports on the use of the rod under them. He writes as follows: ' During the fasts we used scourging twice a week. The doorkeeper announced: " Mortification " and we understood what he meant. When he had made the round with the " deo gratias " we prepared ourselves by baring our shoulders—every novice sat on his bed—and grasped the scourge. The time which the porter required for these preliminaries was supposed to suffice for the other novices. We were always ready when he rang a small bell and then, oh! if it edifies you, friendly reader, then be edified, if it makes you laugh, then laugh to your heart's content at the sound of the twenty scourges falling like a shower of hail on twenty innocent shoulders. I think we were limited to twelve blows, which were given as quickly as possible, and all finished at the same time. In the excitement produced, which was very like that of a shower bath, we could not refrain from throwing the scourge down on to the desk and then creeping with very pleasant sensations under the bedclothes! After the flagellation chorus, a young novice might be heard to giggle: "It was quite natural." He could not help it! Why have I described these scenes of folly so vividly? Because it is folly, and the " holy fathers " must regard it as such. But further, I regard it as very dangerous folly, which has results quite other than those intended. The reader must understand what I mean.

> *Manat*
> *In venas animumque!*

---

[1] *Flagellationserfahrungen*, pp. 111-113.
[2] Andrew Steinmetz, *The Novitiate, or a year among the English Jesuits.* London, 1846. Pp. 248 *et seq.*

If my own experience is worth anything, then I declare to the Jesuits that their " Discipline and chains " defeats its own object, and I reinforce my opinion with the help of the laws of physiology. In this matter we can say with truth: *nocet empta dolore voluptas!* '

As regards the domestic use of the rod, this should be considered next in connection with marriage. A correspondent of the periodical *Society* says: ' With my whole heart I endorse the opinion of your correspondent with regard to the reciprocal punishment of man and wife; family discords of many sorts can be easily avoided thereby, and I think it is a wonderful excuse for the renewal of old healing remedies—the kissing habit, etc. There is a unique attraction in whipping one's own wife or in being whipped by her hand. I hope that a time will come when all quarrels will be settled by the rod[1].' The ideal of this devotee of the rod would apparently be those people of whom it is reported that they regard the rod in marriage as a token of great tenderness[2].

According to Cooper, during the whole of the Anglo-Saxon period the husband had the right to beat his wife. By the civil law he could for any fault ' Flagellis et fustibus

---

[1] *The Education of John Bull.* New edition. Vol. IV, p. 44.

[2] According to Frusta, *loc. cit.*, p. 276, blows are regarded as caresses by the Indians of Guyana, which taste they share with the Russian women. The latter ' used to take it, and still do so, as a mark of contempt and a sign of diminishing affection if they are not punished from time to time. And these customs belong not only to the lower but to the higher classes of society also. In the *Toilette der Grazien* an interesting Frenchman, who married a beautiful Russian lady, tells how after fourteen days of the tenderest marital relations, she suddenly became pensive, sad and melancholy and uttered the deepest sighs. After much urging and insistence on the part of the husband, she at last explained in the fourth week, blushing with shame: "How can I believe that you love me? Have we not been married four weeks, and you have not beaten me once?" The husband, glad enough that that was the only obstacle to his happiness, did not delay in satisfying her. He provided himself with a fairly humane and elegant cane, and the lady complained no more.'

acriter verberare uxorem ', in other cases only ' modicam castigationem adhibere '. In the time of Charles II this right was only taken advantage of by the lower classes of the people. On a stall in the church at Stratford-on-Avon is a wood carving showing a man who is giving his wife something more than a ' modicam castigationem ', her position being as original as uncomfortable[1].

More frequently than between married couples, punishment was used between parents and children, that is the former carried this out on the latter. The correspondence in *Society* gives very detailed reports on the frequency of punishment by parents, and sees in this an obvious method of causing a tendency to flagellation. The latter is strikingly demonstrated in the already mentioned and very authentic *Memoirs of a German Governess*. The authoress tells of her experience in the house of Lady Georgiana N. at No. 7 Park Crescent, London, mother of several children, the most striking of which were a girl of 12 years, as pretty as a picture, and a boy of 11, whom she treated with quite exceptional cruelty. The governess shall tell her story herself:

' In my relations with her I found this lady on the whole quite agreeable, except in certain moods, to which I also attributed the inconsistency with which she treated her daughter. I could not understand how on some mornings when she had been to see her mother she came back crying and so badly beaten that she could neither sit nor walk. I should have had a heart of stone if I had not been most terribly pained, as I could not see the smallest reason for such barbaric punishment of the charming child. For a long time I could find no solution to my problem, and usually an hour after her mother would be smothering her with kisses and presents.

[1] Cooper, *loc. cit.*, pp. 172-173.

'One day Mrs. M., Lady Georgiana's maid, came to me and said that her mistress had asked her speak to me about a matter which as a mother was painful to her, and at the same time to ask me to watch Georgiana and, later, all the children, with the utmost care, as they were addicted to a sin which would ruin their bodies and finally also their souls.

'"But what is this sin?" I asked with the utmost astonishment. "She is always under my eyes and I have never seen the slightest sign of evil in her."

'"Oh, you would not believe how depraved all these children are! There is not a single day when they do not practise their vices. Milady and I see it with our own eyes, and then they have to confess it, and not being willing to do so, we beat them till they tell us everything. You cannot think how hard it often is, sometimes we are both so worn out with the beating that we cannot move our arms."

'At this revolting recital I saw red. "Is it possible", I cried, "that a mother should so beat her children? You say yourself that the children are beaten till they confess; that is a torture that is not employed over the whole civilised world for the worst crime, and how is it possible for anyone to make use of it with children? What sort of a sin are the poor little creatures guilty of?"

'The woman then told me, with the fury of an inquisitor, that the children were all addicted to the vice of self-abuse, and when I doubted this she threatened me with the wrath of Lady Georgiana. However sharply after this I watched Georgiana and kept her under my eye, I could never see anything unseemly in her behaviour. One day Lady Georgiana called me; Sir Charles was also there, and they addressed me rudely: "I engaged you to supervise my children and in order that you might do this satisfactorily, have told you of their bad habits. But you do not seem to do your duty, as Georgiana indulges her vice as wickedly as ever. You must either prevent this or we must part, as if you cannot watch one child, what will happen when the others are under your care? "

' " My Lady," I answered quietly, " I have watched Georgiana as the apple of my eye, and can guarantee that she has never done anything wrong."

' " There is, however, evidence to the contrary, is there not, Sir Charles? " she said, turning to him.

' " Certainly," said he, and the lady gave me such a detailed description of the facts that I nearly fainted; she also gave me, for my instruction, a book by the Frenchman Dr. Riofray, and asked me to read it carefully.

' Every morning after breakfast Mrs. M. fetched Georgiana and Charlotte to their mother, and there were few days that they were not beaten till the blood flowed. Miss J. and I heard their cries of pain, which tore our hearts, without our being able to do anything to help. The second boy, George, was also accused of this fault, and treated with the same cruelty. Only Lavinia, the eldest, a girl of thirteen years, was never called to her mother and therefore never beaten. When I once remarked how glad I was that Lavinia was free from this habit, she said: " Ah, she is as bad as the others, but she is too ugly for me to take any trouble with her."

' On the orders of Lady Georgiana, Mrs. M. then had to have some incredible machines made for the children by a well-known mechanic in Oxford Street. In the autumn we were again brought back to London, and here the children's sufferings, together with our own, continued as ever. Each one was cruelly ill-treated every day, and, incredible as it may seem, it is yet true, that when they had been beaten till the blood flowed, Mrs. M., on the orders of the mother, was obliged to rub in pepper and salt. And all this devilish cruelty was practised by Lady N. on the pretext of curing her children of an unnatural sin!

' I did not cease my care, but to my deepest sorrow I noted an increase in her cruelty to her children. They were tied at night by the hands and feet to the bedposts, and the mother invented all sorts of other cruelties; she also tried all she could to make me take my share in these atrocities and threatened me with her anger when she saw her plans fail. Thus she had me called one day as Charlotte lay bound hand and foot on her bed, quite naked and beaten and bleeding all over her body. When I came in the poor child gave me a look which I shall never forget; the mother handed me a birch rod which had been broken and was covered with blood, and invited me to " do my duty for once " [1].'

No further quotation is necessary to reveal from this very vivid description the true nature of the cruelty shown by a mother to her children. That it was purely sexual is most clearly obvious from the clever goading of the children, by which the mother suggested sexual misdeeds to them, and from the circumstance that only the pretty children were ill-treated, whilst she left the ugly ones in peace. Further examples of the flagellation of grown daughters by their mothers are to be found in the *Etude sur la flagellation*[2].

More frequent and more understandable, although none the less inexcusable, is flagellation of children by their stepmothers. Frusta remarks generally with regard to this: ' A remarkable psychological trait appears in the tendency of many step-parents to chastise the children entrusted to them; the words " stepfather " and " stepmother " are in many countries synonymous with " much beating ". Selfishness and lack of affection, cruelty and sensuality are

---

[1] *Memoirs of a German Governess in Belgium, England, Spain, Portugal, Poland and Germany.* Berlin, 1861. Pp. 30-31, 33, 34, 36, 40-41.

[2] *Etude sur la flagellation*, pp. 446-452.

mingled in this phenomenon, and the female sex is certainly the worst. The author knows many stories which emphasise this point and throw light enough on the peculiarities and compulsions of the human heart. Such instances were more frequent in past days, when corporal punishment was often continued over the age of majority, and these traits are found more often, as we have pointed out, in the more refined personalities than in the commoner, and in peculiar temperaments and humours. There is evidence from female mouths showing how seldom satisfactory relations are established between stepchildren and parents as regards their domestic discipline. There were women who had a passion for beating their stepsons and daughters as often as possible under the pretext of motherly correction, whilst with men this tendency showed itself more clearly towards the females. Seduction and adultery, onanism and suicide often resulted therefrom. The author once knew a celebrated officer who, not only at the age of twelve and fourteen, but even when he was twenty years old and had his epaulettes, received the rod from his stepmother, who carried out his punishment with the greatest zeal. Another who received incredible punishment, and frequently besides saw his grown-up sisters and cousins punished for episodes which had occurred at dances or for love affairs, became in the highest degree addicted to excessive sexual love combined with the most unbridled flagellation-mania; he began with page boys and kitchen maids and ended with anything he could get hold of. A few years ago a young man of sixteen who in his father's absence had been obliged by his step-mother to strip and undergo horse-whipping, hung himself from shame and despair. The author also knew twelve years ago a pretty dressmaker who up to a short time previously had been beaten by her stepfather, who was in love with her, daily or as often as she gave him cause for

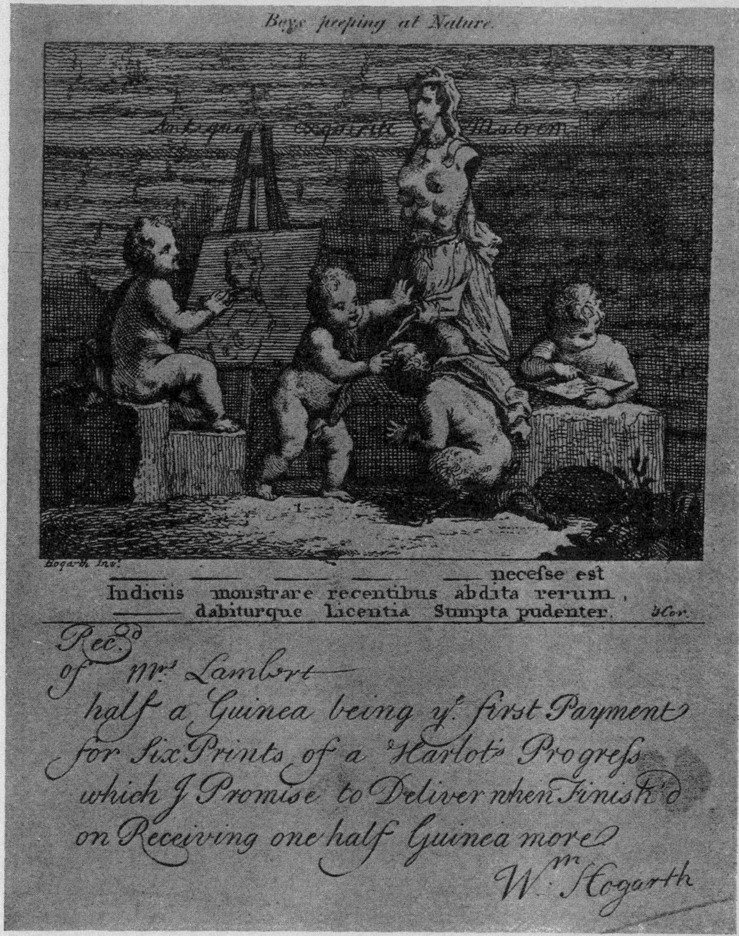
Boys peeping at Nature.
Antiquam Exquirite Matrem
Hogarth Inv.
——— ——— ——— ——— ——— necesse est
Indiciis monstrare recentibus abdita rerum,
——— dabiturque Licentia Sumpta pudenter. Hor.
Rec.d
of Mr. Lambert
half a Guinea being ye first Payment
for Six Prints of a Harlot's Progress
which I Promise to Deliver when Finish'd
on Receiving one half Guinea more
Wm. Hogarth

Pl. 20] *Artist unknown*

BOYS PEEPING AT NATURE

Drawing by Rowlandson [*Pl.* 21

LAND STORES

jealousy[1].' A typical pictured representation of these
relationships is the above-mentioned drawing of Lady
' Termagant Flaybum ' who beat her stepson after meals, a
' Scene which is enacted every day in Grosvenor Square to
the disgust of the neighbours[2] '.

There was a similarity between the relationships of step-
mother and stepchildren and those of lady and servant or
page, who, especially when she was beautiful, often enjoyed
the rod for sexual motives when given by the lady.
' In the days when it was the custom to chastise pages and
other servants with the rod, the passion for this was often
developed to an alarming extent, and many ladies excelled
in this branch of domestic authority. When a lady was of a
serious turn of mind, she felt convinced of the usefulness
of punishment, although an anatomical curiosity and an
indefinite inner feeling about it were never quite absent. If,
however, she was not of an honest nature, she usually tried
in this way to satisfy her sensual tendencies[3].' Hector
France says that many English ladies even invited their
friends to their boudoirs when they were going to punish
their servant maids or pages[4]. In *The Merry Order of
St. Bridget*, a lady at her toilet, in which he had to help her,
gave her servant the rod. Also in *The Quintessence of
Birch Discipline* (London, 1883) a page was beaten by both
his mistresses.

Tutors also, and factory owners, often flogged their
pupils, workpeople, factory girls, etc., out of sensuality.
Cooper reports on the following cases: ' The owner of a
straw-plaiting factory in a village in Bedfordshire, who was
always accustomed to beat the young girls in his factory,
was one day to his great astonishment sentenced to six

[1] Frusta, *loc. cit.*, pp. 265-266.
[2] P. Fraxi, *Centuria*, p. 456.
[3] Cooper, *loc. cit.*, p. 164.
[4] H. France, *Les Nuits de Londres*, pp. 229-230.

months' imprisonment because he had indecently beaten
one of the young girls with rods. All girls who worked in
dressmaking establishments, mantel, corset and similar
shops, were liable to flogging, and during their apprentice-
ship these punishments were often very severe. A dressmaker in Pall Mall, who a hundred years ago supplied the
highest class goods, had a bad reputation for severity.
She learnt the use of the rod in Paris, where she served as
chambermaid in the house of a prominent family[1].'

Flagellomania can most easily be satisfied in those
institutions where the victims are obliged to submit unconditionally and where public interference is impossible or at
least very difficult. To these belong primarily the houses of
correction, prisons, workhouses and the army and navy.

In England in the olden days the most frightful punishments were given in the prisons, with regard to which
Macaulay, Ryan and Cooper supply exact details. The
master of a workhouse in England was dismissed because he
had beaten several of the women under his charge in the
most improper manner. In the year 1841 James Miles, the
master of a workhouse in Rochester, was prosecuted because
he beat the children, especially girls of 12 and 14, with
heavy birch rods.

The Courts of Justice came to recognise that it must be
regarded as grossly indecent for a man to whip a girl[2].

The sexual element was very clearly to be seen in the
celebrated flogging of the prostitutes in the London prison
of Bridewell. Edward Ward, at the beginning of the
eighteenth century gives a very lively description of this
flagellation of the prostitutes[3].

' From thence my friend conducted me to Bridewell, being

---

[1] Cooper, *loc. cit.*, p. 176.
[2] *Ibid.*, pp. 170-171.
[3] *The London Spy*, pp. 129, 136, 139, 140.

Court-day, to give me the diversion of seeing the lechery of some Town Ladies cooled by a Cat of nine Tails. We followed our noses and walked up to take a view of their ladies, who we found were shut up as close as nuns; but like so many slaves, were under the care and direction of an over-seer, who walked about a very flexible weapon of office, to correct such hempen journey-women, who were unhappily troubled with the spirit of idleness. These smelt as frowzily as so many goats in a Welsh gentleman's stable, or rather a litter of piss-tail children under the care of a parish nurse; and looked with as much modesty as so many Newgate saints canonised at the Old Bailey. Some seemed so very young that I thought it very strange they should know sin enough at those years to bring them so early into a state of misery. My friend reconducted me back into the first quadrangle, and led me up a pair of stairs into a spacious chamber, where the court was sitting in great grandeur and order.

'A grave gentleman, whose awful looks bespoke him some honourable citizen, was mounted in the Judgment Seat, armed with a hammer, like a change-broker at Lloyd's Coffee House, when selling goods by inch of candle; and a woman under the lash in the next room; where folding doors were opened, that the whole court might see the punishment inflicted; at last down went the hammer and the scourging ceased; that I protest, till I was undeceived, I thought the offenders had been Popish penitents, who by the delusion of their priests, were drawn thither to buy lashes by auction.

'The honourable Court, I observed, were chiefly attended by fellows in blew-coats, and women in blew-aprons. Another accusation being then delivered by a flat-cap against a poor wench, who having no friend to speak in her behalf, proclamation was made, viz., all you are willing E-th T-ll, should have present punishment, pray hold up your hands:

[383]

Which was done accordingly: and then she was ordered the civility of the house, and was forced to show her tender back and tempting bubbies, to the grave sages of the august assembly, who were moved by her modest mien, together with the whiteness of her skin, to give her but a gentle correction.'

In the English army and navy the cat-o'-nine-tails played a regrettable part up to modern times, together with punishment with the rod[1]. When such horrible things could occur as the beating to death of a negress by Captain Kimber, for his own pleasure and with no fault on her part[2], it must be realised that the sexual element prevailed in these punishments to a very serious extent[3].

In earlier times flagellation scenes were even staged at the best English theatres, and the theme was discussed with the greatest candour on the stage, for example in the opera *The Boarding School, or the Sham Captain*, which was presented at Drury Lane Theatre in 1733, and in which the verse occurred:

> While she is stripping to get a good whipping,
> I'll away, dance and play,
> Yes I will, that I will;
> While she is stripping to get a good whipping,
> I'll go and romp with the girls and the boys, etc.

I myself in the year 1901 saw on the stage of a London suburban theatre with a bad reputation, the Standard Theatre, a similar whipping of the naked torso of a man by a woman in the play, *A Wold's Revenge*. Red stripes even appeared after each blow of the whip to the delight of the very questionable public!

Representations of punishments were very popular at

---

[1] H. France, *loc. cit.*, p. 235.
[2] Archenholtz, *British Annals*. Hamburg, 1795. Vol. XI, pp. 158-160.
[3] Compare Cooper, *loc. cit.*, pp. 112-121; *Flagellationserfahrungen*, p. 76.

annual fairs[1]. The tendency to flagellation was also satisfied frequently in the form of party games. To this class belong primarily the so-called ' school games ', which in England were eagerly played by the children, and in which the child taking the part of the teacher gave punishment with hand or cane[2]. According to Frusta, juvenile flagellation clubs have sometimes resulted from these, first with homo- then with hetero-sexual tendencies[3]. Amongst such may be mentioned ' la main chaude ', ' das Schäften ', ' beating the ham '[4] and a bad forfeit game in which the clothing was taken off garment by garment and the rod used[5].

Flagellation formed further a popular theme for discussion in English periodicals to an extent which is known in no other country and would not be possible. In the old *Spectator*, in the *Rambler*, *The Original Rambler*, in *Notes and Queries*,the subject was dealt with. Detailed discussions were found in the *Gentleman's Magazine* of January and February 1735 and October 1780, in *The Bon Ton Magazine* of November 1791, March, April, July 1792, August 1793, February, March 1794, November, December 1795, January, February 1796, in· the *World* 1856, No. 22; *The Coventry Herald*, 17th October 1856; *The Times* 1856, November 16-21, 1861, 18th March; in *The Leader* 11th February 1860; in *The Star* 6th May 1860. *The English Woman's Domestic Magazine*, April to December 1870, contained most of the contributions, also *Society* 1899 and 1900. *Town Talk* also gave a good deal of space to this subject in the 'eighties. It naturally appeared in the advertisements, usually disguised as ' Manicure ' but also often quite openly as ' Discipline '.

[1] P. Fraxi, *Centuria*, pp. 469-470.
[2] Compare *Stock und Peitsche*, pp. 144-145.
[3] Frusta, *loc. cit.*, p. 265.
[4] Hansen, *loc. cit.*, pp. 146-147.
[5] Frusta, *loc. cit.*, p. 267.

We have already spoken in the introduction to this chapter of the extraordinary exploitation of the subject in literature. Even that king of English literature, Samuel Johnson, ' lost no opportunity of praising the rod and was regarded as an authority in this domain[1] '. George Coleman's *The Rodiad* (London, about 1820) is generally held to be one of the most remarkable specimens in the anthology of the rod. This was not published by Coleman, but by a client of Sarah Potter[2]; the quintessence of English flagellatism is proclaimed in the much-quoted verses:

> Delightful sport! whose never failing charm
> Makes young blood tingle and keeps old blood warm.

---

[1] Cooper, *loc. cit.*, p. 172.
[2] Compare P. Fraxi, *Centuria*, pp. 471-474; Cooper, *loc. cit.*, pp. 150-153.

CHAPTER XIII

HOMOSEXUALITY

ALTHOUGH, as we shall see, the history of English morals
provides interesting details and examples of the occurrence
of sexual love between persons of the same sex, or homosexuality (uranism, paederasty, and tribady)[1], yet, according
to the experience of Pisanus Fraxi[2], the number of homosexuals in England must be very small compared with those
of other, especially Latin, countries. Havelock Ellis does
not venture to make any precise statement on the number
of English homosexuals and declares excessive an estimate
that they amount to five per cent. of the well-educated
middle-class people[3]. He thus leaves us, and rightly, in
complete uncertainty regarding the proportion of homosexuals in England.

Neither does J. L. Pavia's work on *Masculine Homosexuality in England* (published in Magnus Hirschfeld's
Quarterly Review, Leipzig, 1909) give any exact information
regarding their number. But judging from his statements,
it is quite considerable not only in London, but also in the

---

[1] A more technical term for homosexuality is sexual inversion. Paederasty is commonly called sodomy. The paederast is also termed a ' bugger '
(similar to the French ' bougre ', which is derived from the paederastic
sect of the Bulgars in the eleventh century) or ' catamite ': the effeminate
passive paederast is known by the name of ' Miss Nancy ' or ' Nancy boy '.

[2] Pisanus Fraxi, *Index librorum prohibitorum*. London, 1877. P. xxxiv.

[3] Havelock Ellis, *Studies in the Psychology of Sex: Sexual Inversion*.
Philadelphia, 1901. P. 30.

provincial towns, giving rise to exactly similar manifestations as in other European capitals (specifically homosexual haunts and theatres, public baths frequented only by homosexuals, and so on). Thus the statement of Pisanus Fraxi that homosexuality in England has not increased to the extent it has in Latin countries appears doubtful, at least demanding a close investigation, taking into account the fact that in all countries the big towns form the meeting-place of the greater number of homosexuals, some of whom come in from the provinces.

In England, as in other Teutonic countries, an occasional apparent increase in homosexuality in certain circles can be observed. It is then a question each time of the effect of external influences such as corruption at court (as in the time of Charles II), or certain degenerate fashions such as those met with in the eighteenth century. Times, for instance, like those represented very clearly in Rochester's notorious paederast drama *Sodom*, are very favourable to a real epidemic increase in homosexual tendencies, which are sometimes manifested in a slight and uncertain fashion but, at other times, are strongly roused and can lead to an apparent perversion of natural feeling. In such instances it is a question of a ' pseudo-homosexuality ', to the apparent large increase of which in England Pavia also refers, particularly among such bodies as sailors, schoolboys and university students, mine and street workers, footballers, athletes, members of certain men's and boys' associations and the like. Lack of intercourse with woman, and especially indulgence in alcohol, here play an important part.

The development of pseudo-homosexuality has probably been helped by the unique nature of the English club, frequented exclusively by men. The intensive cultivation of games in England may also have something to do with it, in the same way as this was regarded by the Greeks as

[388]

having given the original impetus to the cult of homosexuality. On the other hand, there is a serious obstacle
to the spread of homosexuality on a large scale amongst
the English in that no other people is so opposed to the
practice of this vice. Archenholtz wrote: ' Since English
women are so beautiful and the enjoyment of them is so
general, the revulsion of these Islanders against paederasty
passes all bounds. Attempted homosexuality is punished
by the pillory and several years of imprisonment, the act
itself by the gallows. The pillory, however, is almost as
good as death[1].'

This revulsion finds expression sometimes in erotic
writings. It is significant that the publisher of the *Voluptarian Cabinet*, Mary Wilson, announced in the Preface to the
third volume of this work, which contains a translation of
Mirabeau's ' le Rideau levé ', that she had taken the
liberty of replacing a paederastic scene in the original by
a flagellation scene. ' It is regrettable, indeed, that one of
the best French works should be disfigured by descriptions
of socratistical love. But it is even more regrettable that
such ideas should be translated into our language. I do not
speak thus only because I am a woman—if I were a man
I should consider it equally criminal to encourage the spread
of doctrines the adoption of which has such terrible
consequences[2].'

This was, however, written by the proprietress of a
brothel, by whom love between men must *a priori* be
condemned as damaging to her business.

The extraordinarily severe punishments meted out show
that paederasty is regarded in England as one of the most

---

[1] J. W. v. Archenholtz, *England and Italy*. Leipzig, 1787. Vol. II,
p. 267. Compare also his *Annalen der britischen Geschichte*. Hamburg,
1791. Vol. V, p. 352.

[2] Compare P. Fraxi, *Catena librorum tacendorum*. London, 1885.
Pp. 296-297.

hideous of crimes. Numa Praetorius has collected in the
first volume of the *Annual of Sexual* (*Zwischenstufen*) the
respective definitions of the English Penal Code of the
forms of this vice[1]. According to the Code they are distinguished as follows: 1. Buggery (unnatural immorality)
including (*a*) Sodomy (referring only to immissio penis in
anum, irrespective of whether it takes place between members of the same or of different sexes). (*b*) Bestiality. The
act itself is punished by imprisonment for life, an attempted
act by imprisonment up to ten years. 2. Immoral practices
between men (mutual onany, practices resembling co-
habitation). These are punished by imprisonment with hard
labour up to two years. Assistance in, instigation to and
attempts at these practices are punished in the same
manner. (In Scotland up to 1889 culprits were sentenced
to death for these crimes.) We need hardly mention that we
consider these measures barbarous and unworthy of a
civilised country, and as a preventative of the spread of
homosexual practices they are quite useless. In a general
sense the State is empowered through the immorality clauses
of the Penal Code to deal with homosexual seduction of
children in the same way as hetero-sexual immorality with
children.

Blackmail directed against homosexuals is punished in
England as severely as paederasty, that is with penal
servitude of from three years to a life sentence, or imprisonment with or without hard labour up to two years. If the
defendant is under sixteen, with or without flogging. It is
stressed by the law that the blackmail or attempt at blackmail must be accompanied by a direct accusation of

[1] Numa Praetorius, ' Punishments prescribed for homosexual inter-
course ' in *Jahrbuch für sexuelle Zwischenstufen*, published by Dr. M.
Hirschfeld, Leipzig, 1899, Vol. I, p. 142. Compare also Pavia, *loc. cit.*,
Vol. II, pp. 397-408.

paederasty, particularly a written accusation. Despite these severe measures, blackmail against homosexuals flourishes in all its forms, as shown by Pavia.

The first historical traces of homosexuality in England date back to the Norman period. According to Havelock Ellis the second Norman King of England, William Rufus (1087-1100), was undoubtedly a homosexual[1]. He does not say what evidence he has to support this assertion, and it must therefore be taken with some reserve. Another English king suspected of having been a homosexual was Edward II (1307-1327), who was accused of very intimate relationships with his favourites, especially with the Frenchman Gaveston[2]. Christopher Marlowe, in his famous drama *The troublesome Reign and lamentable Death of Edward II* (London, 1593), alluded to these relationships. Indeed, it is easy to perceive in reading the drama that the homosexual character of the relations between the King and Gaveston was intentionally stressed by the poet. In addition, both men are described as bisexuals. Before the passion for handsome men and boys had taken hold on the King he had dearly loved his wife, and Gaveston also had hetero-sexual tendencies. His love-affair with the King's niece is described in detail by Marlowe (Act II, Scene 1), and the King himself wanted his favourite to marry her. It cannot therefore be concluded from Marlowe's representation that Edward II was purely a homosexual.

That Marlowe (1564-1593) himself, as Havelock Ellis supposes, was a homosexual, is not proved. The fact is that he liked to frequent brothels and had numerous passionate

[1] Havelock Ellis, *loc. cit.*, p. 22.

[2] Compare Ellis, *loc. cit.*, p. 22; W. P. Dodge, *Piers Gaveston* (London, 1898).

A HISTORY OF ENGLISH SEXUAL MORALS

love relationships with women[1], and was said to have been stabbed finally on account of a soldier's whore whom he was waylaying[2]. This of course, does not mean that he did not occasionally indulge in homosexual love.

Another English poet of the sixteenth century had a much greater right than Marlowe to be considered a homosexual. This was Nicholas Udall (died 1557), the author of the first English comedy: *Ralph Royster-Doyster*. An article on him in the *Dictionary of National Biography* states that he was, as a teacher at Eton, very ill-famed amongst the pupils for his predilection for the administration of corporal punishment. Tusser reports that on one occasion he received fifty-three blows from Udall for a slight or non-existent fault. This was probably a case of homosexuality combined with sadism. In 1541 he was accused of unnatural sexual immorality, which he admitted before a Court of Justice.

He was dismissed from Eton and imprisoned for a short time, but the affair does not seem to have affected his reputation unfavourably, because later on he was appointed Vicar of Braintree and was highly esteemed by King Edward VI and Queen Mary. The former gave him a Prebendaryship at Windsor and the latter appointed him Director of Westminster School[3].

According to Havelock Ellis, Richard Barnfield, lyric poet of Elizabeth's time, also betrayed homosexual tendencies in some of his poems addressed to his friends, by which even the most tolerant of his contemporaries were greatly outraged. He was a landowner in Shropshire and apparently died a bachelor[4].

[1] Prölsz regards the other evil deeds of which Marlowe is accused as inventions (*loc. cit.*, pp. 144 ff.)
[2] Compare H. Taine, *History of English Literature* (Leipzig, 1878), Vol. I, p. 378.
[3] Compare H. Ellis, *loc. cit.*, p. 23.
[4] *Ibid.*

oryC

Another prominent personality amongst homosexuals in the seventeenth century was King James I (1603-1625), of whom it was said: ' Rex fuit Elisabeth, nunc est Regina Jacobus[1].' Havelock Ellis says he was undoubtedly an urning[2]. Becker and Weber declared in their works on *The History of the World* that James always had a great predilection for handsome young men and that his favourites were chosen accordingly[3]. The King's homosexual tendency was the subject of H. von Schaeffer's comedy *Check to the King*, in which he describes how James was taken in by the beauty of a young girl disguised as a boy.

Mervin, Lord Audlegh, Earl of Castlehaven, was a typical homosexual *voyeur* who carried on sexual intercourse with his footman and compelled his wife and daughter to cohabit with this and other men servants in his presence[4]. He was executed on the 14th May 1631.

In a very strange and rare English document of 1643, which was published with the permission of Parliament for the purpose of branding sundry priests for their vices, an account (No. 94) is given of the charges against a certain John Wilson, Vicar of Arlington, in accordance with which he ' repeatedly attempted, in the most beastly manner, to practise paederasty with National Browne, Samuel Andrews and Robert Williams, belonging to his parish, and induced them by persuasion and violence to commit this abominable sin, thereby, as he was not ashamed to boast, bringing the number of his victims up to eighteen. He declared, moreover, that he preferred men to women as regards sexual intercourse, because of the shame and dishonour that might arise from begetting bastards. He had further attempted to abuse

[1] *Jahrbuch für sexuelle Zwischenstufen* (Leipzig, 1900), Vol. II, p. 68.
[2] H. Ellis, *loc. cit.*, p. 22.
[3] Compare Moll, *Konträre Sexualempfindung* (Sexual Sensibility in Opposites), third edition, pp. 112-113.
[4] Pavia, *loc. cit.*, Vol. III, pp. 32-34.

a mare, and finally declared in public that paederasty was not a crime[1].'

The Restoration period was also very favourable to the spread of paederasty. We learn from numerous allusions in contemporary literature how frequent homosexual relations were in the reign of Charles II. In the first place, Rochester, in his notorious homosexual drama *Sodom* (detailed mention of which will be found later on in this book), gave us a terrible satire on the true activities of the homosexuals in his time, regarding the sexual act of the paederasts as a new and exciting ' raffinement ' compared to the boredom engendered by hetero-sexual intercourse.

In the second half of the seventeenth century the number of homosexuals increased to such an extent that they were able to form their own clubs. In any case, the existence of the first of these clubs has been proved at the end of the seventeenth century. It was called ' The Mollies' Club '. Edward Ward writes in his *History of London Clubs*, published in 1709: ' There is a curious band of fellows in the town who call themselves " Mollies " (effeminates, weaklings), who are so totally destitute of all masculine attributes that they prefer to behave as women. They adopt all the small vanities natural to the feminine sex to such an extent that they try to speak, walk, chatter, shriek and scold as women do, aping them as well in other respects. In a certain tavern in the City, the name of which I will not mention, not wishing to bring the house into disrepute, they hold parties and regular gatherings. As soon as they arrive there they begin to behave exactly as women do, carrying on light

[1] *The first Century of Scandalous, Malignant Priests, etc.* London, 1643. Compare P. Fraxi, *Centuria librorum absconditorum* (London, 1879), pp. 40-41. On the 5th December 1640 Atherton, Bishop of Waterford, was executed in Dublin for paederasty. Compare *The Crimes of the Clergy, etc.*, with an appendix entitled ' The Scourge of Ireland ' (London, 1823), p. 25. The paederast J. Childe met the same fate in 1640 (*ibid.*).

gossip as is the custom of a merry company of real women.
Later on, one of their brothers—or rather " sisters "—
(in their feminine jargon) would be dressed in a woman's
nightgown with a silken night-cap, and thus representing a
woman, bears a " child " (a dummy being to hand for this
purpose), which is afterwards baptised, while another man
in a large hat plays the part of a country midwife, a third
that of a nurse, the rest of them acting as unseemly guests
at a christening. Each had to discourse at length and with
great impropriety of the pleasures of a " husband " and
children, and praise the virtues of the former and the wonderful talents of the latter. Some others, in the rôle of
" widows ", lamented the deplorable loss of their
" husbands ". Thus each imitated the petty feminine faults
of women gossiping over coffee, in order to disguise their
natural feelings (as men) towards the fair sex, and to
encourage unnatural lusts. They continued these practices
until they were discovered and driven away from their
hiding-place by some agents of the Reform Society. Several
of them were publicly punished, and this fortunately ended
their scandalous orgies[1].'

The spread of paederasty which began during the Restoration period, still persisted in the eighteenth century, and
was specially favoured by degeneration in certain customs of
the time. The historian must not overlook the impetus
given to depravity by fashion and custom, and must clearly
define the relevant connections between these and sex life.
As fashion has a sexual origin, it reacts on the sexual life of
its time, giving it in its turn special characteristics.

It is very significant that in one of the works written at
that time against paederasty the prevailing luxury in

[1] *The History of the London Clubs, etc. By the author of the London Spy.*
Printed by J. Detton, Near Fleet Street, 1709. New edition, London,
pp. 28-29.

articles of clothing is severely criticised as one of the causes of unnatural lust. The author says: ' I must admit that no age ever produced anything so perverse as the clothing of the men of the present time who call themselves " pretty fellows " Their coiffures require nothing more than a row of hairpins to make them look completely feminine. It is easily realised why they always take great care to be as " pretty " as possible when they meet their companions, and all manliness is diametrically opposed to this unnatural behaviour. Consequently they try their best to imitate the mannerisms and dress of the opposite sex. By reason of all this our young gentlemen's dress at the present time is most vulgar and in very bad taste. It is very difficult nowadays to tell a gentleman from a servant. Their shoes, with low heels, are the emblems of their low minds, and the large buckles on them equal the extent of their affectation. The waistcoat, made of silver cloth, abundantly trimmed with lace, worn with a common blue jacket resembling a livery, has something so miserably perverse about it that it revolts me. I feel ashamed when I see them aping the servants about, carrying a big oaken stick, more suitable for an usher than for a gentleman. But the most intolerable thing is their hair, brushed high above the forehead and drawn together behind with a large comb as if it were a regular coiffure. I am told that some of our tip-top " beaus " wear frilled bonnets to give them a more womanly appearance, so that Master Molly has nothing to do but put on his frilly little bonnet and he will pass for a lady, except for his deplorable face. But even this can be remedied by means of powder and paint, which last is as much used by our men as by the French women. There is nothing more amusing than their new " joke " hats of the latest fashion, which are ridiculously dandyish. But to see them at balls or in evening dress—in silk jackets of many colours, revolts me beyond all measure. They had much better put on real women's dresses and petticoats instead of doing things by halves.'

The author scourges further the then very general bad habit of men kissing one another, which fact he rightly regards as one of the possible causes of an inclination to homosexuality:

' Of all the customs accompanying this wave of effeminacy, there is none more hateful, prevalent and injurious than that of men kissing one another. This habit was imported from Italy, the mother and nurse of paederasty, where a love affair between master and page is more often seen than between the master and a pretty girl. But this scourge has spread not only in Italy, but in France, where it was first imitated, and women in convents burn with a passionate and unnatural love for each other in a manner too indecent for description. I must take the part of my countrywomen to this extent that I assert, or at least hope, that this charge cannot be brought against them. However, I must admit that I feel revolted and scandalised whenever I see two ladies falling in each other's arms and kissing each other in a lascivious manner. Still, the sight of two repulsive lads, holding and caressing each other's hands and exchanging tender kisses, is even more disgusting. Although many quite distinguished gentlemen may be seen acting in this way, only because it is fashionable, the country will not be rid of infamous practices until these customs are done away with. For this is the first step in the direction of the abominable sin of paederasty. Under the cloak of fashion, catamite prostitutes offer their perverse services in the open street. I cannot imagine anything more repulsive than the sight of a couple of men caressing and kissing each other, as is to be seen daily in our most frequented public places, and not a single word of reproach may be said against them, for they have the excuse " It is the fashion now". Oh, cursed fashion!

[397]

Imported from Italy with a lot of other unnatural vices!
Are our own original sins not sufficient? Are we to add to
them those brought from abroad to fill up the measure of our
iniquities and prepare us still further for the judgment of
God?[1] '.

Very rightly, in these remarkable descriptions, the effeminacy of men and their mutual kisses in the fashion of the
time are regarded only as a sort of general symptom of
homosexuality, and could not be taken as a positive proof
of any one's immorality. It was emphasised only that these
bad habits were favourable to the spread of homosexuality,
and this is the only point of view from which the question
may be regarded. The simple fact that men choose to wear
women's dresses or kiss each other cannot be regarded as a
sign of their homosexuality, but this fashion surely supports
and facilitates such tendencies in the form of pseudo-
homosexuality. And above all, it will be taken advantage of
by genuine paederasts who may now, under the cloak of
fashion, show their feelings openly and unhindered.

This intimate and tender method of greeting between men
must evidently have had unpleasant results, for it seems to
have gone out of fashion towards the end of the eighteenth
century. A. v. Schütz remarks: ' No embrace is admitted
between men, and laughter would be aroused by so doing,
as a bow and hand-shaking are the only forms of civility
recognised[2].'

According to Bornemann, the connection between kisses
and homosexuality was clearly recognised at the beginning
of the nineteenth century. ' The kiss of friendship between

[1] *Satan's Harvest Home or the present state of Whorecraft, Adultery,
Fornication, Procuring, Pimping, Sodomy, and the Game at Flatts, and
other Satanic works, daily propagated in this good Protestant Kingdom.
Collected from the memoirs of an intimate comrade of the Hon. Jack S . n . r*
etc. London, 1749. Pp. 50 et seq.

[2] v. Schütz, *Briefe über London* (Letters from London), p. 122.

men is strictly avoided as inclining towards the sin regarded in England as more abominable than any other[1].' When Amireau in *London As It Is* wishes to greet the Doctor by embracing and kissing him, the latter gently wards him off, and contents himself with giving him a hearty handshake with the words: ' My friend, you must give up the habit of kissing one of your own sex; it is not the custom in England, and is only done by women[2].'

The spread of paederasty in the eighteenth century is evidenced by the existence of regular boys' brothels and several secret paederastic clubs.

According to the reports of the Old Bailey from 1720 to 1730, the paederasts had brothels of their own, with boy prostitutes at the disposal of their masculine lovers. Interesting particulars on this subject are found in a rare booklet, printed probably in Paris: *A Free Examination into the Penal Statutes: XXV. Henry VIII, Cap. 6 and V. Eliz., c. 17, addresst to both Houses of Parliament by A. Pilgrim, London,* 1833[3].

Several authors of the eighteenth century have written of the secret paederastic clubs. Archenholtz[4], for instance, tells us the history of one of these clubs, whose members gathered in a public-house near Clare Market, London.

---

[1] W. Bornemann, *Einblicke in England und London im Jahre* 1818 (Glimpses of England and London in the Year 1818). Berlin, 1819. P. 179.

[2] Santo Domingo, *London wie es ist, usw* (London as it is, etc.), Leipzig, 1826, p. 15. Thackeray remarks: ' In the poems of Shadwell, Higgons, Congreve and the comic poets of their time, the gentlemen, on meeting, fall into each other's arms: " Listen, Jack, I must embrace you ", it goes: " By God, George, Harry, I must kiss you, my lad! " And in the same way the poets greeted their brothers. The gentlemen of literature no longer kiss each other. I doubt if they love each other any more.'—*England's Humorists* (Hamburg, 1854), p. 79.

[3] P. Fraxi, *Index librorum prohibitorum.* London, 1877. P. xxxiv.

[4] *Originalzüge aus dem Charakter englischer Sonderlinge* (Original Traits of English Eccentrics), Leipzig, 1796. Pp. 158-160 (after Archenholtz).

' In October 1794 Bow Street Police Station received an anonymous letter to the effect that a group of men were accustomed to gather every Monday night in an inn called the " Bunch of Grapes ", near Clare Market, for the most unnatural and hideous purposes. The report stated further that the members of this club were nearly all thieves and forgers.

' The police naturally considered it their duty to verify the truth of these statements, and two policemen were sent the following Monday to the inn, with instructions to mix with the members of the club.

' This they did, stayed for a while and had ample opportunity of witnessing the disgusting proceedings.

' Next Monday the magistrate, Bond, sent the police-watch to the public-house. They burst open the door, guarded the windows and doors to prevent the monsters escaping and overpowered them.

' On entering the room the guard found two fellows in women's attire, with muffs and wide shawls and most fashionable turban-like bonnets, silken pinafores, etc. Their faces were painted and powdered, and they were dancing a minuet in the middle of the room, whilst the others were standing round watching them in the most improper attitudes.

' They were all arrested, a total of 18, and the following morning, clad in their women's dresses, they were taken before the magistrate to be questioned. It turned out that each member of the club had a woman's name, such as " Lady Golding ", " Countess Papillon ", " Miss Fanny ", etc., by which he was known to the other members of this shameful company.

' An enormous number of people gathered outside the Police Station and threatened to lynch the prisoners. These latter were handcuffed in pairs and chained together, and thus led away to prison accompanied by a strong escort of soldiers to protect them from the wrath of the mob. It was, however, impossible to prevent the people throwing stones and mud at the culprits the whole way there.'

Another paederasts' club held their meetings about 1785 in Clement's Lane, near the Strand. The worst sexual debaucheries went on here also, but the scene in the midst of which they were discovered was so ridiculous that it aroused laughter and merriment rather than revolt and wrath: they were caught in the act of nursing and feeding some of their suffering ' sisters ' lying in ' childbed'! the new-born babies being represented by big dolls. The new ' mothers ' played their part so well that one of them succeeded in misleading a policeman, and was released by him on the supposition that it was a woman[1].

At the same period there was a paederastic society in Exeter, whose members were nearly all men of rank and wealth. These also were caught in the midst of their orgies, and legal proceedings were started against fifteen of them, which, naturally, ended in their acquittal. But the incensed people were so convinced of their guilt that they burnt them in effigy without respect for their rank[2].

A third proof of the appalling spread of paederasty in the eighteenth century is afforded by the numerous actions against paederasts. According to *Satan's Harvest Home*, ' paederasty in former times was a vice almost unknown to our people. And, indeed, one would suppose that in a country possessed of such angelically beautiful women no such hateful aberrations could exist. Now, however, our papers are often full of the crimes committed by these brutes, and despite their having been severely punished on many occasions, we have every reason to fear that many of

[1] *The Phœnix of Sodom, etc.* (London, 1813), p. 27.
[2] *Ibid.*

them are undiscovered as yet, and this terrible vice may thus take root more firmly day by day'. The majority of actions were taken against individuals of the lower classes, probably because these had gone to work less cautiously, but men of high rank were also called to account by the law for their paederastic practices. The trials ended comparatively often in acquittal for lack of evidence.

The course of one of these paederast trials is described by Archenholtz: ' Two Englishmen, Leith and Drew, were accused of paederasty or, according to the English formula, of the " horrid, brutish crime, the name of which must not be pronounced amongst Christians". As the details of these delicate affairs must be discussed and explained fully and circumstantially, the judges were careful to clear the Court of women and youths. The evidence given by the plaintiffs was, as was generally the case in these trials, very imperfect. On the other hand, the defendants denied the accusation, and produced witnesses to prove their predilection for women. They were in consequence acquitted[1].'

Some of the well-known trials of this nature were those of Briggs and Bacon in 1790[2], of the actor Samuel Foote[3], of the innkeeper Thomas Andrews in 1761 for active paederasty with the sleeping John Finimore[4], of teachers in colleges for paederastic assaults on their pupils (as, for instance, the Reverend Dr. Thistlethwayte and Mr. Swinton of Wadham College, Oxford[5]), and finally of men of high position in society such as Mr. Beckford, Richard Heber,

[1] Archenholtz, *British Annals* (1789), Vol. III, p. 13.
[2] *Ibid.*, Vol. V, p. 150.
[3] Archenholtz, *England und Italien*, Vol. II, p. 268.
[4] Pavia, *loc. cit.*, Vol. III, p. 34.
[5] This is reported in *A Faithful Narrative of the Proceedings in a late Affair between the Rev. Mr. John Swinton and Mr. George Baker, etc. To which is prefixed, A Particular Account of the Proceedings against Robert Thistlethwayte, late Doctor of Divinity, etc., for a sodomitical attempt upon Mr. W. French, Commoner of the same college.* London, 1739. 8vo, 32 pp.

Gray Bennet, Jocelyne, Bishop of Clogher, Bankes and Baring Wall[1].

In Mrs. Manley's *Atalantis* (p. 723) Sir William Cowper was stated to be a paederast. In the *Crimes of the Clergy* (London, 1823), Lord Courtney (p. 730), who fled to France; John Fenwick, Vicar of Bryall in Northumberland (p. 8), who in 1797 fled to Naples; the Methodist preacher John Holland, alias Dr. Saunders; the Earl of Leicester (p. 730); Saudelands, Rector of Five Fields Chapel, Chelsea (p. 723); Captain Sawyer, who was imprisoned for ' indecent behaviour with men ', and many others are accused of paederasty.

The history of homosexuality in England in the nineteenth century begins with the discovery of the ill-famed ' Vere Street Coterie ' which, in the first decade of the century, carried on its immoral activities in a public-house in Vere Street, near Clare Market, London. This district seems to have been favoured in homosexual circles[2].

A detailed report on this paederast club may be read in the following rare book, a copy of which is to be found in the British Museum:

The Phœnix of Sodom, being an Exhibition of the Gambols Practised by the Ancient Lechers of Sodom and Gomorrah, embellished and improved with the Modern Refinements in Sodomitical Practices by the members of the Vere Street Coterie of detestable memory. Sold by J. Cook at . . .[3] *and to be had at all the Booksellers, 1813. Holloway, printer, Artillery Lane, Tooley Street.* (8vo, *pp.* 71.)

[1] P. Fraxi, *Index*, p. 340.

[2] Baker, *Stories of the Streets of London* (London, 1889), p. 154, calls Clare Market ' the once notorious haunt of vice '.

[3] A space appears to have been left here for Cook's more exact address, which he was perhaps supposed to fill in himself.

This book was written by a lawyer, Holloway (6 Richmond Buildings, Soho), probably a relative of the printer. It was written in defence of James Cook, innkeeper of the ' White Swan ', in Vere Street, Clare Market, the gathering-place of the paederasts. Cook, when he was imprisoned in Newgate, was badly fleeced by a lawyer named Wooley, under the pretext of ' getting him through ' the Court, and who used him at the same time as a scapegoat. He was not found guilty as regards the main part of the charge, and his accusation was limited to the fact that he had let his house be used for immoral purposes. In the hope of obtaining a milder sentence, he offered to give the names of the rich and distinguished visitors to his house, but this further incensed the judge, and he was sentenced to the pillory. Had the judge availed himself of Cook's offer, many well-known distinguished men would have been compromised, for ' even men in priest's attire went straight from the chancel to that sink of iniquity in Vere Street and other similar places[1] '.

The arrangements and management of the Vere Street house were described by the author of the above-mentioned book as follows:

' The ill-famed house in question was arranged most appropriately for its purpose. One of the rooms was equipped with four beds, another was furnished in the style of a lady's boudoir with dressing-table and all conveniences, paint, powder, etc. A third room was called the " Chapel ", where marriages were celebrated, sometimes between a " feminine " grenadier, six foot tall, and a " petit maître " who was half the height of his " beloved wife "! These weddings were celebrated in proper style with " brides-maids ", best men, etc., and the nuptial night was often spent in the same room with two or three other couples

[1] *The Phœnix of Sodom*, etc., p. 27.

[404]

and under the eyes of the rest of the company. However incredible this may sound, the reader may be assured that such was the perfect truth. In the upper part of the house lived the fellows who were always at the disposal of occasional visitors. They employed all those enticing methods which are used by feminine prostitutes in a brothel, the only difference between the former and the latter being a greater lack of decency in the men. Prominent men of honourable professions could be seen with lads of the lowest type "in" or "supra lectum". But the performance of such abhorrent acts was more bearable by far than the disgusting conversation which accompanied it, and which, according to Cook, was some of it so obscene that it could not possibly be reproduced either in words or in writing. It seems that some of these fellows were married and took pleasure, when together, in making fun of their wives, whom they called "Tommies", boasting of having compelled them to do things too loathsome for mention. I must quote one example, a case which brought a peer of the realm and his infamous associate to the gallows. I refer to the case of Lord Audley, who was accused of violence and paederastic abuse of his own wife. The husband himself used to relate this at Vere Street to many of the visitors, in the presence of his wife and accomplice, who took part in the narration as if it had been a praiseworthy act. This unfortunate woman was so deeply abased that she frequently submitted herself to this act. The miserable fellow was one of three depraved creatures who lived in the same house in the City. One of them was known by the name of " Venus ".

' The majority of these reptiles seem to have taken fictitious names which, as a rule, did not harmonise with their profession. For instance, " Kitty Cambric " was a coal merchant, " Miss Selina " an errand boy in a police-station, " Black-eyed Leonora " a drummer, " Pretty

[405]

Harriet " a butcher, " Lady Godiva " a waiter, the " Duchess of Gloucester " a gentleman's servant, the " Duchess of Devonshire " a blacksmith, and " Miss Sweet-lips " a country shopkeeper.

' It is widely and very naturally supposed that those possessed by such passions were usually very effeminate persons. But Cook's report teaches us that this was a false supposition and the contrary is often the case; that, for instance, Fanny Murray[1], Lucy Cooper[2] and Kitty Fisher[3] are now represented by an athletic sailor, a herculean porter and a deaf smith respectively. The last of these had two sons, very good-looking young men, both of whom were, as he himself boasted, as corrupt as their father.

' These were some of the ordinary members of the club. The occasional members were, however, more numerous and, if possible, even worse, because they occupied higher positions in society. These " ladies ", like the real ones, had their favourite men. One of them, White, a drummer of the guard, was executed some time ago for a repulsive crime committed against a certain Lieut. Hebden[4]. White, as a general favourite, was very well versed in the secrets of the fashionable members of the club, with regard to which, immediately before his execution, he made a detailed written report, the truth of which he maintained to the last. It is impossible to reproduce this because the person who copied it in the presence of a police-officer declared that the narrative made him so ill that he could write no further[5].' Cook recounts further that a gentleman from a respectable

[1] See p. 268 for this famous courtesan.
[2] See p. 268.
[3] See p. 267.
[4] Lieut. John Newball Hepburn, not ' Hebden ', and Thomas White were in December 1810 in the Old Bailey accused of an unnatural crime which had been committed on the 27th May of that year, found guilty, and both sentenced to death.
[5] The Phœnix of Sodom, pp. 10-14.

house in the City often visited one of these inn-brothels, staying there for several days and nights, during which time he usually enjoyed himself with eight, ten or even a dozen different men and boys[1].

'Sunday was the usual great day for appointments, to which some came from a long distance, sometimes 30 miles from London, in order to take part in festivities and elegant amusements with grenadiers, servants, waiters, drummers and the whole band of catamites in human form, from the sweepings of Sodom to the refuse of Gomorrah[2].'

Pisanus Fraxi quotes from a daily paper of that period details of the discovery of this paederasts' club and the capture of its members[3]. The existence of such an association could not long be concealed. The suspicions of the authorities at Bow Street were aroused long before the actual break-up, which took place in July 1810. Contemporary newspapers write of it as follows: 'Last Sunday night at 11 o'clock, three divisions of the Guard, accompanied by policemen, were sent out with this end in view. The secret was so well kept that the object of the raid was unknown to all, except Mr. Reed's confidant who led the divisions. The result was most successful.' Twenty-three individuals were arrested and brought to the police station of St. Clement Dane, whence they were taken to Bow Street in cabs on Monday morning between ten and eleven o'clock, for their hearing. A 'raging crowd collected, consisting chiefly of women', who were so incensed and aggressive that ' it was with the greatest difficulty that they were prevented from lynching the prisoners '.

The trial of seven of these took place at the Middlesex Court of Justice in Clerkenwell on Saturday the 22nd

---

[1] *The Phœnix of Sodom*, p. 17.
[2] *Ibid.*, p. 22.
[3] P. Fraxi, *Index librorum prohibitorum*, pp. 333-338.

September, namely William Amos, alias Sally Fox, the innkeeper James Cook, Philip Kett, William Thomson, Richard Francis, James Done and Robert Aspinal. All were found guilty. Amos, who had been twice convicted previously for similar misdemeanour, was this time sentenced to three years' imprisonment and to the pillory in the Haymarket opposite Panton Street. Aspinal, who seemed to have been less active than the others, was sentenced to one year's imprisonment, and the rest to two years' imprisonment and to the pillory in the same place.

The sojourn in the pillory proved to be an excruciating torment for the unfortunate prisoners. A newspaper describes it as follows:

' All classes of society were filled with disgust at the detestable doings of these creatures to such an extent that many thousands of people came to see them punished. Quite early in the morning the Old Bailey was literally besieged, and the thronging crowds put an end to the business of the Court at 12 o'clock. The shops from Ludgate Hill to the Haymarket were closed, the streets crowded with people who wished to see the villains pass by. Four of them had been taken from the House of Correction to Newgate on the Wednesday night, where Cook and Amos joined them, so that they might go together to the scene of their punishment.

' Shortly after 12 noon the " ammunition carts " started from the neighbouring market places. These were a number of carts drawn by butcher boys, who had previously filled them with offal and dung from the slaughter houses. Street vendors were also in readiness, carrying on their heads baskets filled with rotten apples, pears, cabbages and other vegetables and corpses of dogs and cats. All these articles were sold at high prices to the onlookers, who spared no expense in order to provide themselves with missiles.

' A group of fishwives were there, armed with stinking flaunders and decaying guts. But these were not sold, as their zealous owners wished to keep them for their own use.

' The Sheriffs and officials of the City arrived at 12.30 with more than a hundred mounted men, armed constables, and a hundred policemen on foot. These men were sent to Old Bailey Yard, where a wagon, generally used for transporting prisoners from the London prisons to the galleys, was waiting ready for the culprits. The wagon was drawn by two horses, led by two men armed with a pair of pistols. The gates of the Old Bailey were closed and all strangers shut out. The prisoners were brought out and seated in the wagon. Amos laughed, and was thereupon reproached by his companions. They all sat erect and apparently calm, but as they glanced up and saw the mass of spectators, covering even the roofs of the houses, they appeared to become alarmed. As the church clock struck half-past twelve the gates were opened. At the same time the crowd endeavoured to rush in, but they were driven back. A large posse of policemen, about sixty officers, armed and mounted as aforementioned, headed the procession, with the City officers. Next came the wagon, escorted by about forty officers and the Sheriffs. The first greeting the prisoners received was a volley of mud and a serenade of hissing, shouts and curses, so that they were obliged to bend down towards the floor of the wagon in order to try and avoid the missiles. The mob, and especially the women, had collected and piled up a great quantity of mud from the streets with which to give the villains a warm welcome. These heaps looked like ammunition dumps in a shooting ground. They were soon exhausted, and by the time the wagon came to the old house which once belonged to the ill-famed Jonathan Wild, the prisoners looked like

[409]

bears just emerged from a pool of mud. The rain of mud
continued all the way to the Haymarket, and before half
the way was done they resembled human beings no longer.
Had the journey been a more lengthy one, the wagon would
have been filled to the brim with dung and dirt. The innkeeper, who sat a little apart from the others, was a big
strong fellow and could not hide himself as easily as the other
smaller men. Therefore, and because he was very well known,
he was bombarded twice as furiously as the rest of them.
Dead dogs and cats, offal, rotten potatoes, etc., showered
upon him from every direction. His apparently manly
attitude called forth increased wrath, and only the passing on
of the wagon prevented his being lynched. At one o'clock
four of them were put into a new pillory specially made for
this occasion—the two others, Amos and Cook, enjoyed
the privilege of a pillory to themselves, and they were
accordingly driven to St. Martin's Police Station. Long
before any of them reached the places where the pillories
awaited them, their faces were totally disfigured by blows,
missiles and mud, and looked like living dung-hills. About
fifty women obtained permission to form a circle round them,
and these incessantly bombarded them with dirt, rotten
potatoes and eggs, with dead cats, offal, mud and dung from
slop-pails and buckets brought by some of the butchers of
St. James's Market. The villains were treated very cruelly,
but as the first party consisted of four, they had less to
endure than was the case with the other two. In an hour's
time these four were re-seated in the wagon and taken by
way of St. Martin's Lane, Compton Street and Holborn to
Cold Bath Fields Prison—welcomed in the same way as on
their journey from Newgate. After their release from the
pillory, the fishwives and butcher boys who had shown such
zeal were treated handsomely to brandy and wine, the price
of which was collected on the spot. A few minutes later the

last two, Cook and Amos, alias Fox, were put into the pillory. Cook covered his face with his hands and lamented deplorably because of the terrible blows he received. Amos likewise moaned piteously and showed a large brick-bat which had been thrown at his face. The Under-Sheriff declared that the sentence must be carried out, and they started slowly for the pillory. Cook did not say a word, but at the sight of the preparations which were being made, Amos solemnly declared his innocence. The mob, however, furiously hissed and shouted at him, so he, also, was put into the pillory, and in a few minutes they were both covered with filth and mud and their faces were more badly injured even than those of the other four men. Cook received several blows on his face and a big bruise on his brow, and both of Amos' eyes were terribly swollen and stuck together. When they were finally released Cook nearly fainted, and they had to be helped to their wagon, which took them back to Newgate by the same route, the same welcome accompanying them. Cook lay down again on the seat, but Amos was recumbent in dirt and dung until their arrival at Newgate, where they finally took refuge from the wrath of the most furious mob ever seen. As they passed the end of Catherine Street, Strand, a coach-man stood up in his vehicle and gave Cook five or six blows with his whip.

' It is impossible to reproduce here the abusive language of the mob and the insults that were poured on these monsters during their journey. Fortunately, the weather was dry or they would have been suffocated. From the moment the wagon had started, the wrath of the mob began to pour on them in the shape of regular showers of filth and dirt. Before they reached Temple Bar the wretches were covered with such a thick layer of mud that they appeared inhuman. They were fettered and seated in such a manner that they could not lie down and at the most could only protect their heads to a limited extent from the missiles by bending them. Some of them were badly injured by brick-bats and their faces bled horribly. The streets through which they passed reverberated with the shouts and curses hurled at them by the mob.'

Even those who approved of the State taking severe measures against the ever-increasing spread of paederasty would condemn scenes such as those described above, provoked by the State and legal authorities themselves. The only, and very doubtful, extenuating circumstance was that the pillory, with all its cruel and repulsive accompaniments, was a general method of punishing other misdeeds also, until about the beginning of the nineteenth century, the culprits being completely abandoned to the wrath of the mob. In any case, as early as 1830 the punishment for paederasty had become much milder. Adrian remarks: ' Paederasty is progressing to an appalling extent, and I have heard many public trials of these cases before the Courts; that, for instance, of a man who one day enticed a boy to go with him behind St. Giles's Church, and who was arrested and sentenced to seven months' imprisonment. An upholsterer, a husband and father, who had attempted to interfere with one of his fellow-workmen, was sentenced to a year's imprisonment, although all his acquaintances gave most favourable evidence as to his character. Three boys accused of the same crime were sentenced to eight months' imprisonment[1].'

A few more scandalous cases of this period are worth mentioning.

Mr. Greenfield, one of the most respected ministers in Edinburgh, and like many Scottish priests in receipt of a small income, decided to increase it by establishing a boarding

[1] Adrian, *Skizzen aus England* (Sketches from England), Frankfurt a.M., 1833. Vol. II, p. 11.

Artist unknown [*Pl.* 22

MISERIES OF BATHING

After bathing in the river—on returning to thê bank
for your clothes, finding that a passing thief has taken
a sudden fancy to the cut of every article of your dress.

house for university students. He was taken in the act of unnatural sexual intercourse with one of these young men. For the sake of the reputation of both parties, the affair was hushed up and it was treated as a case of mental disease. Greenfield renounced his position and spent the rest of his life in retirement under nominal supervision.

The last Earl of Findlater and Seafield died in 1820. He was a gifted and intellectual man, but when some of his other characteristics became known he was obliged to leave England and thereafter spent most of his time on the Continent, where he could more easily satisfy his desires. After his death the title of Findlater expired, but that of Seafield was inherited by Colonel Grant. Nearly the whole of his fortune was bequeathed to a Saxon family of the name of Fischer, especially to a young member of the same who, during his lifetime had been his page, and later on became his private secretary. The relatives of Lord Findlater refused to pay this legacy, and Fischer sued them for the money in the Scottish Courts. The family refused payment because the legacy was bequeathed ' ob turpem causam '. The trial went on for a long time, and two commissioners were sent to Saxony to ascertain the truth of the matter. But the scandal caused by the members of such a prominent family bringing disgrace upon their good name for pecuniary reasons was so great, that friends interfered and an arrangement was made whereby Fischer received £60,000, that is, nearly the whole of his claim[1].

A few years later Mr. Muirhead, a rich landowner in Lanarkshire, near Glasgow, had to leave the country on account of paederasty[2].

Mr. J. Wood, a lawyer in Edinburgh who moved in the best circles and was much esteemed as a philanthropist, devoting

[1] P. Fraxi, *Index*, p. 341.
[2] *Ibid.*

a great part of his time to the promotion of education and spending for some years a few hours daily teaching in the schools, was caught in the act of paederastic practices with his pupils. He availed himself of a hint which was given to him and fled to America, whence he never returned[1].

Thereafter paederasty appears to have had many devotees, particularly in Scotland and in Lancashire, where, according to the English police-surgeon Taylor, socratic love is extremely often to be met with. In Manchester and Liverpool there is hardly a session of the courts when one or more of these cases does not come up for trial. It is, likewise, also very common amongst English sailors[2]. According to Pavia, the Duke of Cumberland (son of George III) and Lord Castlereagh, later Marquis of Londonderry, Minister of War, were homosexuals[3].

The doings of the London paederasts at the beginning of the second part of the nineteenth century are described very vividly in a book published about 1850 or 1860, *Yokel's Preceptor*, in the section: ' A few words on Margeries in order to become acquainted with the ways and hiding-places of these brutish beings. . . . In the last few years the number of these brutes in human shape generally called " Margeries ", " Pooffs ", etc., has increased in the capital to such an extent that for the sake of public safety an exact knowledge of them is necessary. The punishment for their abominable crimes is not nearly severe enough, and so long as the law will not treat them more drastically, there can be no hope of their suppression. The fellows are too well paid (mainly because they are—as is generally known—supported by their rich associates) to care a jot if they have to spend a few months in prison. Why was punishment in

<hr/>

[1] P. Fraxi, *loc. cit.*, pp. 341-342.
[2] *Untrodden Fields of Anthropology*, Vol. II, p. 356.
[3] Pavia, *loc. cit.*, Vol. III, p. 36.

the pillory abolished? Would it not be very wholesome for such brutes? They cannot be sufficiently disgraced and humiliated. The reader must believe that it is a fact that these monsters walk the streets just like feminine prostitutes on the look out for opportunities.

' Indeed, the Quadrant, Holborn, Fleet Street and the Strand are full of them. Not so very long ago signs and bills were hung in the windows of respectable hotels in the vicinity of Charing Cross with the notice: " Beware of paederasts! "

' They usually gather near the picture shops, and are recognisable by their effeminate appearance, fashionable clothing, etc. When they see anyone whom they think might be a good catch, they put their fingers in a curious way under their coat-flap and move them about there: this is their way of offering their services.

' Many of them hang about in saloons, theatres, cafés, etc. We could report many disgusting cases of the brutish activities of these wretches, but we do not wish to trespass on the reader's time with such a repulsive topic. There are, however, one or two anecdotes which we must relate.

' The Quadrant is visited by a great number of the most notorious paederasts, who parade there in search of their " prey ", just like so many feminine prostitutes. One of them was called " the Fair Eliza ". This fellow lived in Westminster and had a mistress who was not ashamed to live on the income derived from his disgusting practices. Another fellow named " Betsy H.", who frequented the Strand, Fleet Street and St. Martin's Court, is one of the most notorious and shameless paederasts. He is often seen in music-halls reciting obscene poems. His father was a notorious pander for men, and he himself has been imprisoned several times. Nevertheless, he still carries on his disgraceful occupation.

[415]

' There have been many homosexuals amongst actors, some of them enjoying a very good reputation. We could give the names of many of them, but from a sense of pity we will not do so. A very rich director of one of the big theatres is said to have carried on paederastic intercourse with one of his actors, and it is also generally known that another actor, playing French parts in a circus on the other side of the river, belongs likewise to that miserable and repulsive brotherhood[1].'

Whether the above-mentioned paederast, known under the name of ' Fair Eliza ', be identical with the homosexual actor Eliza Edwards referred to by Tarnowsky and the English physician Taylor, is not known[2].

A description of paederasty in London was published in 1881: *The Sins of the Cities of the Plain; or The Recollections of a Mary-Ann. With short essays on Sodomism and Tribadism.* The author remarks in the appendix that as he was crossing Leicester Square on a sunny November afternoon in 1880, his attention was drawn to an extraordinarily handsome and effeminate-looking lad who was walking up and down, casting occasional glances at shop windows, and turning back again in order to attract and interest passers-by. This youth was a ' Mary Ann ', as paederasts were then called by the people. His doings and adventures are related in this work, and the book reveals very interesting particulars of the sexual life and intercourse of paederasts, which is by no means confined to members of their own sex. Particular attention is given by the author—obviously from personal experience—to the prominent paederasts Bolton and Park, arrested in 1887, who, disguised as women, had numerous

---

[1] *Yokel's Preceptor: or more sprees in London, etc. London. Printed and published by H. Smith*, 37 *Holywell Street, Strand.* Pp. 5 et seq.

[2] B. Tarnowsky, *Die krankhaften Erscheinungen des Geschlechtsinnes.* Berlin, 1886. Pp. 15-16.

love-affairs with men. They got off lightly and, later on, pursued their former profession in Lisbon[1].

To complete the presentation of nineteenth-century homosexuality in London contained in this book, we might mention F. Rémo's *Delineations*, also of the beginning of the 'eighties[2], and the already cited reports by Pavia (one of the greatest experts on homosexuality) on the life and doings of urnings in London.

The former mentions amongst other things the 'Dublin Scandal' of 1884 and the 'Cleveland Street Affair' of 1889, which was the result of an article in the *North London Press* declaring that No. 19, Cleveland Street, Tottenham Court Road, was frequented by certain aristocrats for homosexual purposes. Although legal evidence was produced in court which completely justified the article, *i.e.*, that a brothel for men was run in that house by a certain Hammond, and a male prostitute gave the names of earls and other nobles who frequented the house, nevertheless the Editor was sentenced to a year's imprisonment for slander. Pavia cites several other meeting-places, the resorts, past and present, of homosexuals, such as Holborn Casino, Argyll Rooms, the auditory of the Empire Theatre, St. James's Buffet, Piccadilly Buffet, Marble Arch, near Hyde Park, 'The Enterprise' in the East End, a homosexual resort near the Elephant and Castle, etc., etc.

The following passage from Johannes Schlaf's *Third Realm* (1900, page 73) is probably also based on personal observation. Describing London night life, he says: 'There were old gentlemen who would enter into love-affairs with young soldiers, good-looking, strong, healthy fellows, willing for a

[1] See also Hirschfeld, *Jahrbuch für Sexuelle Zwischenstufen* (1900), Vol. II, p. 63.

[2] F. Rémo, *La vie galante en Angleterre*. Paris, 1887. Pp. 14-15, 260-261.

pound sterling to comply with any request, and the devil knows what other freaks.'

As in other countries, monasteries, colleges and boarding-schools in England are favourable to the development of homosexual tendencies. In an article in the *New Review*, July 1893 (' Our Public Schools, their Methods and Morals '), the anonymous author compares the morals of English public schools with those of Sodom and Gomorrah[1], and W. F. Stead writes in the *Review of Reviews* on the 15th June 1895: ' Should everyone found guilty of Oscar Wilde's crime be imprisoned, there would be a very surprising emigration from Eton, Harrow, Rugby and Winchester to the jails of Pentonville and Holloway. Until then, boys are free to pick up tendencies and habits in public schools for which they may be sentenced to hard labour later on[2].'

In contrast to the comparatively mild punishments given for paederasty about the middle of the century, more severe measures have been taken against it during the last decade, as may be seen from some of the trials of later days.

The trial of the poet Oscar Wilde in 1895 was undoubtedly the most sensational of all[3]. Oscar Wilde, a remarkably gifted poet, gave expression to a purely aesthetic tendency in modern English poetry. This was evident in all his works, espe-

[1] See *Jahrbuch für sexuelle Zwischenstufen*, Vol. III, p. 404.
[2] *Ibid.*, p. 506.
[3] See the detailed necrology by Numa Praetorious in *Jahrbuch für sexuelle Zwischenstufen*, Vol. III, pp. 265-274; also O. Sero, *The Wilde Case and the Problem of Homosexuality* (Leipzig, 1896); Handl, ' The Wilde Trial' in *Die Zeit*, Vienna, 15th June 1895, No. 37; H. Rebell, 'Défense d'Oscar Wilde ' in *Mercure de France*, 1895; Tybald in *Echo de Paris* of the 29th May 1895; Paul Adam, ' L'Assaut malicieux ' in *Revue Blanche* of the 15th May 1895; Henry de Régnier, ' Souvenirs sur Oscar Wilde ' in *Revue Blanche* of the 15th December 1895; W. F. Stead in the *Review of Reviews* of the 15th June 1895, pp. 491-492; notice in *Jahrbuch für sexuelle Zwischenstufen*, Vol. III, pp. 550 and 608; Bernstein in *Die Neue Zeit*, 1895, Nos. 32 and 34; Havelock Ellis, *loc. cit.*, p. 212; Robert H. Sherard, *Oscar Wilde, the Story of an unhappy Friendship*, Popular edition, London, 1908.

cially in the novel *The Picture of Dorian Gray*[1]. Wilde, a married man, appears to have developed—for the same reasons as the ancient Greeks—a preference for homosexual activity. In *Dorian Gray* he describes the love of the painter Hallward for the youth Dorian Gray; this attachment was ' perfectly idealistic and spiritual, purely artistic and aesthetic, but nevertheless homosexual '. The poet himself describes it to the judges in the following idealistic form: ' The love, which in our day must not be called by its real name, the love of a man of riper years for a younger one—as for instance that of Jonathan for David—the foundation of Plato's philosophy, sung by Shakespeare and Michelangelo in their sonnets, this pure and profound attachment, spiritual and perfect, by which the greatest artists were inspired to create their most magnificent works—this love is, in our century, so misunderstood that it has brought me before a Court of Justice. Nevertheless, it *is* beautiful, august and sublime, the noblest of all forms of attachment. It is purely spiritual and can exist only between an older and a younger man, provided that the older is spiritual and highly intelligent whilst the younger still possesses intact freshness of soul, a capacity for hope and the ability to find pleasure and joy in life. It must be so, but the world will not understand it. It brings scorn on those who practise it and sometimes even puts them in the pillory.'

Unfortunately this theory suffered shipwreck when transposed into reality, just as in the time of ancient Hellas. For these attachments cannot possibly be looked upon as purely psychical. And a really pure and noble friendship between men will not stand the slightest admixture of sexuality without assuming a homosexual character. With Wilde the sexual side predominated. Numa Praetoria writes of him

---

[1] See J. Gaulke, ' Oscar Wilde's " Dorian Gray " ' in *Jahrbuch für sexuelle Zwischenstufen*, Vol. III, pp. 275-291.

that he ' led the life of a true sensualist and always let his sensuality take its course without any repression whatsoever.' He frequented aristocratic circles, where he entered into what may doubtless be considered sexual relationships with young men. His relations with the twenty-year-old Lord Alfred Douglas resulted in his imprisonment, on the accusation of the young man's father. Wilde was, in 1895, sentenced to two years' penal servitude for lascivious practices with men. After having served his time, the unhappy man went to live in Paris, where he died on the 7th December 1900, abandoned by all his friends.

Although Wilde cannot be acquitted of all guilt, it must be admitted that his punishment was much too severe.

The physician and author John Addington Symonds, the well-known authority on the Renaissance and collaborator with Havelock Ellis in his works on homosexuality, is said to have himself displayed homosexual tendencies, although he was a married man[1]. The excellent chapter in Ellis' book on homosexuality in Greece was written by him. Further particulars regarding the individuality of Symonds are given in his biography by Horatio Brown[2].

According to the following report in *Jahrbuch für sexuelle Zwischenstufen*[3], the late Marquis of Anglesey, who died in 1905, seems to have had homosexual tendencies, or at least to have been exceedingly effeminate.

' The divorce suit recently brought by the beautiful young Marchioness of Anglesey against her husband caused no astonishment. The young bride, who parted from her husband during their honeymoon, was long ago expected to try to regain her freedom. The Marchioness, *née* Chetwynd,

[1] Moll, *Konträre Sexualempfindung*, third edition, p. 143.

[2] H. Brown, *The Life and Letters of J. A. Symonds*, London, 1894.

[3] Vol. III, pp. 543-544. See also Pavia, *loc. cit.*, Vol. III, p. 48.

daughter of Sir George Chetwynd and the Marchioness of
Hastings, was only eighteen years old when she, two years
previously, consented to be the wife of the then Earl of
Urbridge. With her lovely finely-chiselled features, framed
by a mass of reddish-golden hair, her beautiful violet eyes,
she was one of the most admired beauties in England. She
was always surrounded by groups of enthusiastic admirers,
but she was impressed by the soft and gentle individuality
of the Marquis, and preferred him to anyone else. Little
did she know how much her future husband resembled a
pampered, spoilt, eccentric woman, possessed of all the
foibles and caprices of the fair sex. Indeed, the then twenty-
five-year-old nobleman, who on his father's death became
the fifth Marquis of Anglesey, looked like a beautiful young
woman, in man's dress, more than anything else. He was not
at all ashamed to powder his face in order to look paler and
more interesting. He was always perfumed, and his fine
slender fingers were always covered with rings. He was seen
promenading in Piccadilly or on the Boulevards in Paris
with a snow-white, pink-ribboned poodle in his arms, who
was just as abundantly perfumed with patchouli and Eau
d'Espagne as his master. In this aristocratic young Croesus
a fine serpentine-dancer was lost. To appear on the stage of
theatres or music halls as an imitator of the famous and
graceful danseuse Loie Fuller was one of the Marquis's
greatest pleasures.'

According to Spitzka[1], Lord Cornbury, who was British
Governor of New York in the reign of Queen Anne and a
notorious waster, was in the habit, in spite of his exalted
position, of walking in the street dressed as a woman and
behaving like a courtesan.

[1] Spitzka in the *Chicago Medical Review*, 20th August 1881, quotes
Krafft-Ebing's *Psychopathia sexualis*, tenth edition, Stuttgart, 1899.

One of the earliest references to homosexual relations between women (tribady) is contained in Sir Philip Sidney's pastoral romance *Arcadia*, dating from the sixteenth century. One passage relating to two princesses who go to bed together reads as follows: ' They adorned the bed with their prettiest clothes, so that on this night it surpassed the couch of Venus. Then they caressed each other, exchanging tender, though chaste, embraces and sweet, though cold, kisses. It seemed as though the God of Love were playing with them without his arrow, or that, tired of his own fervours, he had come to refresh himself between their sweet lips.'

At the voluptuous court of Charles II conditions were extremely favourable for the spread of Lesbian love. It appears that, in particular, a certain lady of the court had made advances to other women. The lady was Miss Hobart Hamilton, who is mentioned in the *Memoirs of Count Grammont*.

' Miss Hobart was a type of woman up till then unknown in England, just as her appearance must have been striking in a country where it was an exception for a young person not to be good-looking. She had a good figure, a resolute manner, and also intelligence, but she was not prudent enough. Her imagination was too vivid and somewhat unbridled. Her burning glance was the reverse of attractive. She was tender hearted, but, so it was said, only towards the fair sex.

' The first to attract her attention and tender solicitude was Miss Baggot, who reciprocated innocently and un-suspectingly. But on realising that all her friendship was not sufficient to satisfy the passion of a Hobart, she renounced her conquest in favour of the small niece of the governess, who felt greatly honoured by this.

' Rumours concerning this irregularity—whether true or not—soon began to circulate at court, but the people of the court were too uncultured to know about this refinement of

the tender affections which was so familiar in ancient Greece,
and they formed the opinion that the august Miss Hobart,
with her preference for the fair sex, was something different
from what she appeared to be.

' Owing to her new gift they began to sing satirical songs
about her, and as a result of the innuendoes her friends finally
deserted her.

' One day the ladies went for a ride, and upon their return
a certain Miss Temple dismounted at Miss Hobart's house for
rest and refreshment after the fatigue of the ride. However,
first of all she asked permission to change her underwear,
that is to say, to undress in the presence of her hostess. Her
wish was, of course, readily granted.

' " That's exactly what I was going to suggest to you ",
said Miss Hobart. " Although you look as lovely as an angel
in your riding habit, there is nothing like fresh linen and
comfort. I can't tell you ", she added, placing her arm round
Miss Temple's shoulders, " how glad I should be if you would
feel at home here. What I specially appreciate in you is
your sense of cleanliness. In this respect, as well as in many
others, you're very different from some of the other ladies.
Take, for instance, that little fool Miss Jennings. You must
have observed that she was admired by most of the dandies
at court on account of her marvellous complexion, which is
probably not entirely natural, and on account of her follies
which, on the contrary, are very natural, and for which she
is regarded as very witty. I have spent a great deal of time in
her society and was on good enough terms with her to know
something about her intellectual gifts; but the fact that they
are no better than her feet does not mean much. I have
been told some edifying little stories about her unclean
habits. She is said to abhor water like a cat. Just imagine,
she never washes her whole body, but only those parts that
are visible—her face, neck and hands ".

[423]

' Miss Temple was even more pleased with this than with the sweets she was offered, and in order to waste no time Miss Hobart undressed her before the maid had come in. At first Miss Temple made a few remonstrances, for she did not wish to accept such a service from a lady of Miss Hobart's standing at Court, but Miss Hobart insisted that she was only too pleased to help. When they had finished eating sweets and Miss Temple was undressed, her hostess said: " Let us go to the bathroom, where we can have a nice chat without being disturbed by a possible visitor." Miss Temple consented and the two of them sat down on a couch. " You are too young, my dear," began Miss Hobart, " to know anything about the terrible and dangerous character of men ", etc.'

Follows a vivid description of the manner in which Miss Hobart endeavoured to present the male sex in the worst possible light, in order to convert her guest to the idea of love between women, and, in particular, to the idea of love for herself (Miss Hobart). She spoke of the gentlemen of the Court and depicted Rochester, in particular, in the darkest colours imaginable. An eavesdropping maid overheard the conversation and repeated it to Rochester, who had Miss Hobart ' dressed down ' by Killegrew in the presence of Miss Temple.

' Your inclinations and your passion for young Miss Temple are known to everyone except herself, but if she had an inkling of what you want of her, she would surely treat you in the same way as Lady Falmouth had done. I advise you not to continue setting traps for a young girl who is too chaste to fall in with your wishes. I further advise you to reinstate your maid, in order to stop her objectionable gossip. She tells everyone that she is pregnant, and ascribes it to you (*sic*) and charges you with the basest ingratitude. You may rest assured that I have not invented these things.

However, should you disbelieve that I have heard this from her own mouth, let me inform you that she overheard your entire conversation in the bathroom and gave me a detailed account of it, not omitting your witty descriptions of all our friends at Court, and the improper couplet you recited to this lovely girl, also how you finally lured poor Miss Temple into the trap which you only set her in order to see her charms.

The author of *Satan's Harvest Home* (London, 1794) dealt with London's Lesbians of the eighteenth century. At that time Lesbian love was called ' game of flats ', which probably meant a special mode of sexual intercourse between women. This ' new kind of sin ', so widespread among ladies of high social position, was said to be just as common in Twickenham as it is in Turkey.

Hüttner writes about the occurrence of homosexual practices at girls' boarding schools[1], while Archenholtz even records the existence of Lesbian clubs[2].

' There is no limit to libidiousness in London. There are females who avoid all intimate intercourse with the opposite sex, confining themselves to their own sex. These females are called Lesbians. They have small societies, known as Anandrinic Societies, of which Mrs. Y. . . . [3], formerly a famous London actress, was one of the presidents. These Lesbians offer up their unclean sacrifices at these places, but their altars are not worthy of the secret groves where Dionne's doves were united in love; all they deserve is a thick veil to obscure them from the sight of men.'

[1] ' . . . And these inexperienced young creatures, full of sensuality, are left together without any supervision whatever, especially when they are in bed, and they spend their time reading obscene novels or in even more shameful amusements that are unmentionable.' Hüttner, *Sittengemälde von London* (London Morals), pp. 183-4.

[2] Archenholtz, *England*, Vol. I, pp. 269-270.

[3] This was most probably Mrs. Yates of the Drury Lane Theatre (d. 1787).

On the 5th July 1777 a woman was sent to prison for six months for wearing male attire and for ' marrying ' three different women[1].

According to H. Ellis, Lesbianism was in his day mostly indulged in by the ladies of the London stage and by prostitutes. A friend of his gave him the following account of the goings-on at the big London theatres and music-halls:

' Passionate friendships between girls—ranging from the most innocent associations to Lesbian love—are very common among the actresses, chorus and ballet girls. The latter seem to have a special bent for it. The confusion in the crowded dressing rooms, where the girls frequently have to wait for hours between calls in an over-stimulated state, presents ample opportunities for the development of such emotional aberrations. In nearly every theatre there is a group of girls who are avoided by the rest, or isolate themselves from the rest, though they are inordinately devoted to each other within the group. The majority of them are prepared to flirt with the opposite sex as well. But I know a few who would never speak to a man, and who are never seen without a permanent girl friend. If the latter belongs to another company, her " lover " waits for her at the stage door each night. However, these relations in most cases do not go very far. The English girl of the lower and middle classes, whether chaste or not, is always completely governed by tradition and conventional ideas. Ignorance and convention prevent her from accomplishing the logical consummation of this perverse association. Among the upper classes, as well as among better class prostitutes, these perverse practices have developed to their full extent, owing to the greater liberty of movement and action and to the prevailing freedom from prejudice.'

[1] P. Mantegazza, *Historico-Anthropological Studies of Sexual Life*. Jena. P. 98.

Thus it is clear from the above that these homosexual tendencies may sometimes be traced to accidental origins, and are often due to circumstances similar to those described here. The same may be said of prostitutes. The homosexual tendency is not necessarily congenital with them and is frequently only a form of compensation for the absence of normal love. Ellis's informant said the following about the practice of homosexuality among London prostitutes: ' In London such things are far less obvious and this phenomenon is less frequent, but by no means very rare. A considerable number of well-known prostitutes are reputed to have a homosexual tendency, but this does not affect their attitude towards their profession. I do not know of any prostitute who confines herself exclusively to Lesbianism, but I have heard hints to the effect that there have been one or two such abnormal creatures. One night I visited the Corinthian Club (a *locale* frequented by better-class prostitutes) and heard a fashionably dressed prostitute announcing that she would go home with a girl, and no one present doubted her word. Another prostitute had quite a number of female clients who bought photographs of her. But among lower-class prostitutes such practices are extremely rare. Many of them have never heard of any such practices, except, perhaps, of paederasty. They are usually shocked and even outraged when they hear about it, and consider it as part of " French bestiality ". Naturally, every prostitute has a girl friend with whom she sleeps occasionally, but as a rule this signifies no more than in the case of all other girls.'

In addition to homosexual persons of both sexes there are also numerous cases of physical and psychical hybrides, such as the viragines, hermaphrodites, and persons of dual sex, whose tendencies are neither expressly heterosexual, nor expressly homosexual, and in whom the two tendencies prevail sometimes alternately and sometimes simultaneously.

[427]

Butler, in his *Hudibras*, mentions such a 'man-woman'. In his age he had many models for a virago, such as the woman bandit Moll Cutpurse, who lived in the time of Charles I. She never indulged in the pleasures of feminine adornments, never dressed stylishly, and generally displayed no feminine characteristics. She wore male dress and committed her thefts and hold-ups in the neighbourhood of London[1]. One day the notorious highwayman Thomas Rumbold (executed in 1689) met a colleague who robbed him of his purse. In the ensuing fight Rumbold proved the victor. He bound his enemy hand and foot and searched him for his lost purse. Unbuttoning his adversary's coat he was amazed to find that 'he' was a woman. The virago then told him that she was the daughter of an armourer. 'In my youth', she said, 'my mother wanted me to be a seamstress; but all her pleadings, warnings and reprimands failed to diminish my martial spirit. I was no use in the kitchen, either. I was always hanging about in my father's workshop, enjoying the sight of the instruments of war which he was producing. It was my greatest pleasure to be allowed to brandish a nice sharp sword'.

When she was twelve years old she took fencing lessons in secret. In her fifteenth year she married an innkeeper, but her married life was very unhappy. Every now and then she donned a man's suit, made excursions to the highways and held up travellers[2].

It is interesting to note that there was another virago, the woman pirate Mary Reed (eighteenth century), whose sexual tendencies—as in the case of the above-mentioned Amazon—were determined by external circumstances. Her mother deliberately and systematically brought her up as a

[1] E. Whitehead, *Life, Deeds and Fates of the Most Remarkable English Highwaymen and Pirates*, Part I, pp. 93-96.

[2] *Ibid.*, Part I, pp. 186-189.

boy and she was made to enter the service of a French lady as a groom. This naturally contributed very considerably in the course of the years to the development of her masculine characteristics. Finally she enlisted in the Navy and served on board a warship. However, in spite of all this, she was hetero-sexual, for she fell passionately in love with a soldier, whom she later married[1].

The well-known Chevalier d'Eon played a notorious part as a man-woman, or rather woman-man, in the 'seventies of the eighteenth century. He lived in England for a long time. Everybody thought he was a woman, except Archenholtz, who happened to be in England when the d'Eon affair was causing a stir in that country. He suggested that d'Eon might in fact be a man, since he had been admitted as a member to a Masonic Lodge. Archenholtz further records: ' He (d'Eon) declared in 1777 that he would on a certain date produce proofs as to his sex.

' He fixed the place and the hour. The scene was to be a large coffee-house in the City during Exchange hours, probably in order to make sure of a large audience. There was an almost incredible rush. He appeared in the full dress uniform of a French captain, with the Louis Cross on his tunic. He made a speech, declaring that he had come to prove his manhood to all who doubted and would do so by the use of either his sword or stick. But as the challenge was not taken up by anyone, the Chevalier went home triumphantly[2].'

Subsequently d'Eon gave a display of swordsmanship. 'It was in January 1793 that he exhibited his skill as a fencer at Ranelagh. This strange creature, now sixty-seven years old, appeared on this occasion in the costume of Minerva, in full armour, with a helmet adorned with plumes. He fought with

---

[1] Whitehead, *loc. cit.*, Part II, pp. 75-81.
[2] Archenholtz, *England*, Vol. II, pp. 108-113, 117-123.

another Frenchman, a certain Sainville, who was a great artist and an expert swordsman, and displayed extraordinary skill. This new kind of entertainment attracted a large crowd of distinguished spectators. The scene of the contest was a stage erected for the purpose. Present was an English girl named Miss Bateman, a beautiful young woman who was devoted to the art of fencing, and who later became d'Eon's pupil and intimate friend[1].' Hannah Moore, who had long wanted to make the Chevalier's acquaintance, finally met him at a dinner party and was quite charmed with his, or rather her, gift for conversation, her wit, culture and gaiety.

He was of a gay disposition, especially after he had drunk one or two bottles of Burgundy. Hannah Moore found it most ridiculous that this female creature should be discussing with General Johnson with the utmost thoroughness, sometimes observing ' . . . quand j'étais colonel d'un tel régiment. . . .' One Chevalier d'Eon, the pious lady finally concluded, was enough[2].

Chevalier d'Eon also played a part in English eroticism. Thus, for instance, it is recorded in the *Adventures of an Irish Smock* (London, ca. 1875, pp. 51-53) that Chevalier Madame d'Eon confessed the truth concerning her sex to a courtesan. According to Adrian, an author who wrote in the first decade of the nineteenth century, Englishwomen have a greater natural propensity for viraginity than women of other nations. He was struck with the long, soldierly stride of the Englishwoman, as being characteristic of her. 'When you see two Englishwomen taking a walk together, you are reminded of a drummer and a corporal on the march. Their

[1] Archenholtz, *British Annals*, Vol. XI, pp. 426-427. Cf. also v. Schütz, *Letters from London*, pp. 50-52.

[2] Jesse, *George Selwyn and his Contemporaries*, Vol. I, p. 283. Cf. also on d'Eon *History of Pope Joan* by M. J. A. L., Leipzig, 1788 ; and J. Larwood, *The Story of the London Parks*. London, 1881. Pp. 436-438.

steps are so even, so regular and measured, lacking all feminine gracefulness and possessing a resolute, masculine character[1].

Bornemann, on the other hand, holds that viraginity is but rarely to be encountered in England as compared with other countries, and mentions among its principal manifestations wild riding, an enthusiasm for hunting, and the like. ' The ladies are far too much in favour of the slogan " the wilder the better ", and take a keen pleasure in thunder and lightning, scorching heat and pouring rain, whereas a fashionable gentleman does not like to go riding without a large parasol or umbrella to protect him from the sun or rain. The Master endeavours to play the part of a delicate creature, while the Mistress likes to appear strong and bold. Both strive to attract attention and admiration in the wrong direction[2].'

A certain London cattle-drover named Bob Bussicks (died 1792) achieved a certain notoriety among real hermaphrodites in the middle of the eighteenth century. He was one of the ' sights ' of London. A whole book was devoted to this pitiable creature, an obscene work entitled *Letters from Laura and Evelyne, giving an Account of their Mock Marriage, Wedding Trip*, etc. (London, 1883).

Both Laura and Evelyne were hermaphrodites, each being capable of playing both the active and the passive parts in sexual intercourse. They relate the incidents preceding and following their ' wedding ' with their ' super sexual consorts '. An orgy held in their honour at a London pornological club is also described in the most obscene manner at the end of this hermaphroditic novel.

[1] Adrian, *loc. cit.*, Vol. II. p. 16.
[2] W. Bornemann, *Glimpses of England and London in* 1818. Berlin, 1819. Pp. 194-5.

CHAPTER XIV

SADISM AND MASOCHISM

HARSHNESS is said to be one of the most prominent of all the English national characteristics. This assertion is based on the views of perfectly unbiassed observers who are, like the author of the present work, firm friends of the English. Archenholtz, Macaulay, and Taine are among those who hold this view. Taine writes that this brutal trait of the ancient Anglo-Saxons still persists in their descendants, as evidenced by the prevalence of blood sports, the excessive use of the 'cat', etc. Macaulay also admits that the principal traits of the English character have remained unchanged for many generations, though it must nevertheless be agreed that a considerable part of the brutalities of earlier times have been eliminated as a result of education.

However, cruel punitive measures like the pillory mentioned in the previous chapter, public whippings, and bloody boxing contests[1] lasted until the middle of the nineteenth century. All the foreign observers, from Lichtenberg to Steffen, remark on the disagreeable impression they gained of the peculiarly English sport of 'pugilism'. Lichtenberg,

---

[1] Fights, compared with which boxing may be regarded as a gentle, refined and harmless pastime, were the favourite amusement of many people. Great masses of spectators assembled to see the gladiators massacring each other with lethal weapons, and they screamed with pleasure if one of the fighters lost a finger or an eye (Macaulay, *History of England*).

[432]

in a letter addressed to J. C. Dieterich on this subject, in 1725 wrote: ' The morning before yesterday two men were fighting in the street where I live. One of them was knocked down by his opponent right at the beginning of the fight, and died on the spot. I removed the body, but had not seen the whole brutal contest[1].' Another boxing match is described by Lichtenberg in a letter dated the 28th September 1775. Hüttner, in the summer of 1802, saw a boxing encounter in Wimbledon, near London, between the Jew Elias and the notorious pugilist Tom Jones. The former, after a terrible combat lasting twenty minutes, landed a blow to Jones's ear, knocking him down.

Prize-fights were staged by pugilists around 1830 at the smaller theatres, especially in that at Catherine Street, Strand. Adrian describes one of these pugilistic performances at the above-mentioned theatre in his *English Sketches*, in a chapter entitled ' Boxers ', in which he writes of the almost incredible coarseness of the spectators.

In the 'forties of the nineteenth century boxing was prohibited by the police.

' But news of a proposed prize fight between two brutish fellows always leaks out to the public, who go along in large numbers to see them, encouraging them by applause, and honouring them by betting on the result. It is a repulsive sight. When the exhibition is over the result is published in the newspapers. The Press helps to glorify this worst of nuisances. Foreigners are requested to note that summary arrests follow if the police learn about these spectacles and arrive in time[2]. Yet in spite of the fact that public boxing

[1] *Letters of Lichtenberg*, edit. Albert Leitzmann and Carl Schüddekopf. Leipzig, 1901. Vol. I, p. 219.

[2] J. Gambihler, *Handbook for Visitors to London*. Munich, 1844. Pp. 142-3.

contests were prohibited and pursued by law, they continued to attract a large section of the English public[1].'

These facts alone are sufficient to show to what extent sadistic tendencies were developed in the English people. But a still more striking contribution to the history of Sadism, *i.e.*, the lustful joy experienced by perverts at the sight of pain and suffering in human beings or animals is provided by the public executions, which have exercised a powerful attraction and ghoulish fascination on the English from earliest times.

'This secret lust, which attracts so many people to the horrible spectacle of public executions, is a type of excitement in which the sexual element predominates and actually takes possession of the spectators during the act of execution. This is the subject of the Marquis de Sade's notorious novels, which are by no means pure fiction, but are, on the contrary, a reflection of the truth[2].'

This unholy pleasure in killing and torturing is too conspicuous a feature of 'Merry Old England' to require a more detailed description. We need only think of the plays of Marlowe and Shakespeare, or of those of Ford, Massinger and others, in which the horrible blood lust of the age is so clearly depicted. We will only quote here a few examples from more recent times of this fanatical lust for executions.

During the Restoration period the noble knights took considerable pleasure in attending the most horrible executions. Even 'gently nurtured' ladies came to feast their eyes on the horrible spectacle. 'The good Evelyn applauded them, the courtiers praised them in song. They had sunk so

---

[1] G. Steffen, *City of Five Million Inhabitants*, p. 201. Compare re history of pugilism in England Pierce Egan's *Boxiana, or Sketches of ancient and Modern Pugilism*. London, 1824. Four Vols.

[2] Ivan Bloch, *Contributions to the Aetiology of the Psychopathia Sexualis* (Dresden, 1903), Vol. II, p. 48, and *The Sexual Life of Our Times* (Berlin, 1909), p. 621.

low, and their senses were blunted to such an extent that
they were not in the least nauseated by the awful proceedings, which would have filled with horror anyone
possessing normal feelings of humanity. Some even went
further than that. When John Coke, the learned lawyer, was
being quartered, Captain Turner, who was in charge, ordered
the executioners to bring another prisoner named Hugh
Peters on the scaffold to be quartered, and to ask him whether
he was satisfied with their work, which the executioners,
rubbing their bloody hands, duly did. Characteristically
enough, immediately after experiencing the pleasures of
the spectacle of torture and execution, these bloodthirsty
noblemen hurried away to indulge in the most incredible
debaucheries and orgies[1]. This is one of the most patent
proofs of the sexual origin of their cruel lust[2].'

Tyburn, where the executions in London took place, was a
recognised venue of entertainment in the eighteenth century.
Seats were booked in advance, as at cock fights and boxing
matches. No Monday passed without an execution. Very
often several prisoners, up to fifteen at a time, were tortured
to death, and on such occasions the crowd of spectators was
always more numerous[3]. Tom Browne records that an old
lawyer who had offices in Holborn always used to grant his
clerks leave of absence on execution days, so that they might
have some ' fun '[4]. Lady Hamilton considered it a delightful
experience to have attended in Naples the executions of
Prince Caraccioli, the physician Cirillo, and others[5]. Thackeray writes: ' A hundred years ago crowds assembled in large
numbers to witness the last appearance of a highwayman

[1] H. Taine, *loc. cit.*, Vol. II, p. 18, 19.
[2] Mrs. Manley, *Atalantis*, p. 672.
[3] J. Rodenberg, *Studienreisen in England*. Leipzig, 1872. P. 289.
[4] W. Thornbury, *Haunted London*. London, 1880. P. 374.
[5] *The Story of Lady Emma Hamilton*. Leipzig, 1816. P. 118.

and to make fun of him. Swift, with grim humour, advised him to obtain a white shirt and to tie a black or red ribbon round his white cap, so as to enter the cart cheerfully. The same hero inspired Gay to some of his loveliest ballads and other poetical works[1].'

But he was mistaken when, further on, he wrote: ' Conditions are different now (1850). If a victim were brought out to be executed in a public place, all the windows would be hastily closed and the people, sick with horror, would withdraw into their houses and bar the doors.'

Executions in England, up to the last decades of the nineteenth century, were a favourite entertainment for the masses.

Schlesinger writes on this subject as follows:

' So you want to hear something about our national festivals? ' said a highly educated English lady who was a frequent visitor to the Continent, and was only too keenly aware of the shortcomings of her beloved country, which she saw clearly and without bias. ' So you want to know where our festivals are held? The grape harvests, Shrovetide frolics, and other events which are celebrated by country folk in your sunny land with wine, dancing and general merrymaking? Well, I will tell you. They are held at Newgate, sir, if there happens to be an execution, or in Horsemonger Lane, or at some other nice place outside the jails. Crowds of people assemble there from daybreak until the moment when the hangman performs his horrible duty. Your fairs and festivals are sparsely attended as compared with the multitudes who assemble at these places. The windows of the surrounding houses are let at high prices; stands for spectators are erected; stalls for the sale of food and drink spring up in the vicinity like mushrooms. The people pay good prices for beer and brandy. People come along from great

[1] Thackeray, *English Humorists*, pp. 108-109.

distances on foot and on horseback, or in carriages, to witness
the barbarous performance. And the first rows are occupied
by women, by my countrywomen. But they are by no means
women of the lower classes only. They also include smartly
dressed ladies, pretty girls with golden locks. Oh, it is a
terrible shame, but it is true. And, of course, it is the
deplorable duty of our newspapers to give a complete account
of the horrible event, not omitting even the most minute
detail of the victim's last agonised convulsions—their
readers would never forgive them if they did[1].'

This description is by no means exaggerated. That was
the true position until comparatively recently not only in the
big cities but also in the provinces. A passage in Holzen-
dorff's excellent work on the uselessness of capital punishment refers to this subject in the following terms:

' The otherwise peaceful and good-natured population of
a small town displays unusual malice on the occasion of an
execution, and it may therefore be asserted that attendance
at the performance of capital punishment brings to the
surface the basest instincts not only in the case of wicked
and corrupted people, but also in those who are otherwise
of a gentle disposition. Dymond reports that an execution
carried out at Chelmsford was made the occasion of a
" veritable carnival of debauchery " by the populace. The
executioner was entertained to dinner at a public house the
night before the execution in order to make him relate
incidents from his professional experience. People were
streaming to the scene from a radius of twenty miles. Young
men and women formed merry groups and enjoyed themselves thoroughly[2].'

[1] M. Schlesinger, *Wanderings through London* (Berlin, 1852), Vol. I,
p. 164.
[2] Quoted in Bloch, *Beiträge zur Aetiologie der Psychopathia Sexualis*
(Dresden, 1903), Vol. II, pp. 49-50.

It would be difficult to demonstrate more clearly than does the latter fact that this gruesome delight in execution had a sexual basis, which in turn proves that the tendency was a sadistic one.

Under the influence of such ' shows ', which were repeated again and again, some individuals developed into regular ' execution fans '. The latter included a large proportion of persons of high rank.

In *Aspects of the Character of English Eccentrics*[1] the following passage occurs: ' The sight of executed criminals affords a different, but just as extraordinary kind of pleasure to S. . . ., a gentleman who is otherwise universally respected for his sterling character. Executions have an indescribable fascination for him and exercise an inexplicable effect upon him. One of his friends reproached him with this; S. . . . made excuses and wagered that he would not attend the next execution, a thing he had never done before. The day of the next execution arrived, and brought with it an irresistible urge for S. . . . to indulge in his favourite recreation. He rode to Tyburn (the place of execution) and paid the wager. When the regicide Damiens was torn in pieces by horses in Paris[2], S. . . . travelled to the French capital for the sole purpose of witnessing the event, and paid the executioner to allow him to be present on the execution platform, in order to obtain a close view of the gruesome proceedings. After witnessing the execution he immediately returned to England.'

' S.' was most probably George Selwyn, one of the most notorious execution fans of the eighteenth century.

---

[1] Leipzig, 1796-1798, p. 48.

[2] See detailed description of this fearful execution, ' Assassinat de Louis XV et supplice de Damiens '. Extrait par Lemonty des *Mémoires manuscrits du Duc de Croy*. *Revue Retrospective*. Paris, 1883. Tome 1, pp. 357-370.

The most gruesome details of a suicide or murder, a view of the distorted corpse, the appearance of dying people, were objects of keen interest to him and filled him with a strange, painful glee. Horace Walpole tells numerous anecdotes about the peculiar pleasures of his friend. When the first Lord Holland lay dying, Selwyn, as one of his intimate friends, insisted on seeing him. ' If Mr. Selwyn calls again,' said Lord Holland to his butler, ' show him in. If I am still alive I shall be pleased to see him, and if I am dead he will be pleased to see me.'

Some of Selwyn's friends were themselves addicted to this peculiar sport and encouraged Selwyn to indulge in it. Thus Gilly Williams wrote to Selwyn: ' Harrington's doorkeeper was condemned yesterday. Cadogan and I have already booked seats at Brazier's, and I hope the Rev. Digby will arrive in time to witness the show with us. I assume that we shall also have the company of your honour, unless your palate is too spoilt for such simple fare[1]:'

Another friend, Henry St. John, begins a letter to Selwyn by recounting what he and his brother saw at an execution: ' We enjoyed a full view of Mr. Waistcott as he mounted the scaffold with a white cockade in his hat.'

It appears that there have also been execution fans in England in more recent times. Hector France writes of an English baronet who, for several years, collected knives and daggers used by murderers and hangman's ropes, and who subsequently sought for even more intense emotional experiences and acted the part of executioner himself. This man was known in Essex by the nickname ' Amateur Hangman '. One day the official executioner was prevented from carrying out an execution, and the baronet immediately volunteered to officiate in his stead. After that

---

[1] E. S. Roscoe and Helen Clergue, *George Selwyn, his Letters, and his Life*. London, 1899. Pp. 17-18. Also Timbs, *Curiosities of London*, p. 744.

he found pleasure in the work, and at every execution he requested the Sheriff of the county to entrust him with the task of the executioner, which he performed with aristocratic elegance and with obvious pleasure, and also gratis. Thus within a short space of time he executed with rare skill three ordinary murderers, two patricides, two conjugal murderers, four child murderers, as well as two women poisoners. He appeared to experience particular pleasure in executing women, and at such times he wore a peculiar, cruel smile on his face. This gentleman was a member of the exclusive ' Army and Navy Club ', before which he once had to justify himself on account of his gruesome activities, which he did to such good purpose that he was allowed to retain his membership of the Club.

Hector France once witnessed a sale of hangman's ropes at an auction room in the Euston Road. Each rope bore a label marked by the executioner Marwood with the name of the condemned person, the date of the execution, and the nature of the crime. Thus it was possible, according to the purchaser's taste, to buy a souvenir of a poisoner, a strangler or a patricide. The ropes with which wife murderers had been hanged were in great demand. Many gentlemen and young ladies of poetic aspect fought for the possession of these doubtful mementoes. One old maid bought an entire collection of the ropes. The part of the rope which had been in actual contact with the criminal's neck were most eagerly bid for[1].

Among the really sadistic criminals of the late seventeenth and early eighteenth centuries the highwayman Tom Dorbel deserves to be mentioned. Having committed a series of robberies, and having with great difficulty escaped the gallows, he took service as butler to a lady in Great Ormond Street, London. One day this lady sent him to Bristol to

[1] H. France, *loc. cit.*, pp. 248-249.

[440]

escort her young niece back to London. On the last stage of the journey he remained alone with her in the coach, raped and assaulted her in the most brutal manner, and satisfied his bestial lust on the gravely injured girl. Then collecting all her valuables, he ran away, but was captured and executed on 23rd March[1].

The notorious prostitute Miss Annabella Parsons was once assaulted by a sadist and wounded on the genital organs with a penknife (*Letters of the Duke of C.*, etc., Frankfurt and Leipzig, 1770, p. 272).

One of the earliest examples of a so-called 'Ripper' was the 'Monster', a man named Williams, who in April and May of the year 1790 rendered the streets of London unsafe for girls.

'The most remarkable court case of the year 1790', relates Archenholtz[2], 'was the case of the so-called "Monster", who had wantonly injured an incredible number of women. As plaintiffs there appeared at the court Lady Walpole, Mrs. Bourney, Mrs. Smyth, Mrs. Blany, Mrs. Newman, Miss Porter with her two sisters, Miss Toussaint, Miss Godfrey, the two Misses Boughano, and many other less prominent persons of the female sex, all of whom had either been wounded or had had their clothes cut by the "Monster's" knife. The criminal's name was Remrick Williams. The case was heard on the 8th of July at the Old Bailey, which was practically full of women. The elder Miss Porter appeared as one of the plaintiffs. Her counsel, a man named Pigot, invited the court to listen to the most remarkable story upon which a prosecution had ever been based. He said: "I must call your attention to a scene that is so new in the annals of humanity, a scene so inexplicable, so unnatural, that one might have regarded it, out of respect for human nature, as impossible, and might still be so regarded, but for

[1] C. Whitehead, *loc. cit.*, Vol. I, pp. 361-365.
[2] Archenholtz, *British Annals*, Vol. V, pp. 175-183.

the fact that the proofs are of a kind that cannot fail to convince the senses." This creature, charged with a nameless crime, the possibility of whose existence no legislator had ever dreamt of, a creature who stood alone among all human-kind, deserves to be described as to his physical appearance. He was five and a half feet tall and slightly built. He had a dark brown complexion, a long face, a long nose, and a wild look in his eyes. His features were not irregular, and his hair was naturally curly. However, he was not charged with bestial lust for the blood of women, but for " damaging clothes ". He was charged on three counts and was sentenced to two years' imprisonment on each, or a total of six years, to be served at Newgate. On the expiration of his sentence he was bound over in £400 sterling to be of good behaviour." '

Further details of this case are reported—in a very sceptical sense—by Georg Forster, who was staying in London at the time. He mentions the ' Monster ' in his diary under the date of 12th May 1790:

' For the past four weeks the whole of London has been talking about the " Monster ". The newspapers are full of him; the playwrights entertain audiences with his exploits from the stage; the ladies are afraid of him; the mob give every pedestrian a keen look in case he is the " Monster "; all the walls are covered with posters advertising a reward for the apprehension of the " Monster "; a fund has been opened to finance the hunt; Mrs. Smith, a society lady, has shot him with a pistol behind the ear; he disguises himself, goes about in various different guises, wounding beautiful women with a specially invented instrument, with hooks hidden in bouquets of flowers, with knitting pins, etc. And this " Monster " is nothing more nor less than a phantom invented to amuse the bored inhabitants of London town. A pickpocket who may have learnt to turn pockets inside out and empty them with the aid of an instrument might perhaps have injured a woman while picking her pocket in this manner; and this insignificant incident was sufficient as a basis for the story of a " Monster " who is supposed to be enraged with feminine beauty, sufficient to render probable a conspiracy between a number of similar creatures, who out of sheer cussedness or out of revenge, or perhaps out of perversity, are intent on destroying the whole feminine sex, or at any rate the beautiful portion of it[1].'

In view of Archenholtz's detailed report of the trial, and, above all, in view of the numerous similar cases in our own times, there is no reason to doubt the truth of Archenholtz's statement. Archenholtz describes in a delightful manner the temporary beneficial effect of the appearance of the ' Ripper ' on public morals.

' The nocturnal scenes in the streets between pleasure-seeking men and prostitutes, which went a great deal further here than in Paris, received a severe setback, for no man could, after dark, approach even a respectable girl in order to speak to her. The fair creatures fled in terror; and even the priestesses of Venus, who were waiting in the street for sacrifices, solicited less readily, for fear that they might be confronted by the " Monster ". The " peripatetic " passions disappeared. The order of things was reversed, and only those men were safe from suspicion who appeared in the street " after dark under the protection of a female ". Lady Wallace always carried a gold-mounted pistol for fear of the " Monster "[2].'

A true ' English Girard ', whose case bore a striking resemblance to that of the notorious French Jesuit Girard[3],

---

[1] *Letters and Diaries of Georg Forster of his journey on the Lower Rhine, in England and France in the spring of* 1790. Halle, 1893. Pp. 224-225.

[2] Archenholtz, *British Annals*, Vol. V, pp. 332-333.

[3] *Historie von Pater Girard und Madem. Cadière* (Cologne, 1732).

was the clergyman Scoolt, who read obscene books with the daughter of Inspector Reddic, took her to the theatre, and finally to a brothel, where he introduced her to every kind of vice, after which he left her in the lurch in the most shameful manner, having first administered to her, as Girard had done to Catherine Cadière, an abortive medicine[1].

The act perpetrated on the 9th July 1824 by the Catholic priest John Carroll, in Ballymore, does not belong to the same category, because he was subsequently found to be insane. He had already ' exorcised the devil ' from several people by jumping about on their bodies! On Friday the 9th July 1824 he called at the house of the nail-maker, Thomas Sinnot. The latter's daughter, a pretty little creature of three or four years, who was lying in bed in the same room where Carroll was, happened to start screaming. Carroll immediately declared that the child was possessed by the devil, and jumped on the bed and on to the unfortunate child. Hearing the child's screams, her father tried to restrain the priest, but several fanatics who happened to be present, including the girl's own mother, prevented him from doing so, and the mother even assisted the priest in the performance of his shameful ceremonial. She had to bring a barrel of salt water, the contents of which he poured over the unconscious child, and when the water became mixed with the blood streaming from the child's body, he cried in insane ecstasy: ' Witness the miracle! I have changed water into blood! ' Then he turned the barrel so abruptly that the child was strangled and died. Carroll left the house with a command to the others that they must not touch the child until his return. Two doctors declared Carroll insane, and he was confined in a lunatic asylum. However, the fanatical spectators were certainly not insane, and provide deplorable confirmation of the sadistic basis of religious fanaticism,

[1] Archenholtz, *British Annals*, Vol. XIII, pp. 155-156.

which was similarly in evidence in the story of the cruci-
fixions at Wildisbuch[1].

Corvin[2] writes of a young girl who lived in the 'forties of
the nineteenth century in London, and who confessed that
she had no other reason for killing children and animals than
the peculiar, insane joy which she experienced when committing such acts. It gave her satisfaction to witness the
death agonies of living creatures. For years before she was
discovered she had indulged her presumably innate homi-
cidal mania, and had had many victims.

According to the usually well-informed author of *Memoirs
of a Singer*, sexual murders occurred in England comparatively frequently, and she quotes several examples[3]. The best-
known of the sexual murderers was the unknown maniac
referred to as ' Jack the Ripper ' in the 'nineties of last
century, who made the East End of London unsafe, and
who is said to have been identified as an insane student.

It is at all events a noteworthy fact that semi-erotic and
erotic literature in England during the nineteenth century
assumed a sadistic character which was, at any rate to the
same extent, alien to it up till then. Pisanus Fraxi, who was
best acquainted with this fateful metamorphosis, writes in
this connection: ' It is obvious that modern authors have
allowed themselves to be influenced by the harmful, blood-
thirsty and unnatural doctrines of the Marquis de Sade,
and have imitated the cynicism, cruelty and the unspeakable
lasciviousness which are a characteristic feature of his works,
and which, it must be admitted, he handled with masterly
skill. That is why the character of English erotic fiction
has undergone a radical change, resulting in the complete

---

[1] See *Atrocious Acts of Catholic Priests, etc.* (London, no date). Referred
to by P. Fraxi, *Index*, pp. 100-2.

[2] Corvin, *Die Geissler*, third edition (Zurich, no date), p. 341.

[3] *Memoirs of a Singer*, Vol. II (Bucarest, no date). Vol. II, p. 191.

loss of its healthy tone (if erotic literature can have a healthy tone at all)[1].'

This sadistic tendency of the later English erotic literature was considerably fostered by the thirst for sensations which is peculiar to the English, and which we encounter in every phase of life. Smollett, in *Roderick Random*, does not allow Mr. Melopoyn to succeed financially as an author before he enters this exciting field. ' I have earned many a meal with the aid of a monster; a robbery has often brought me a great deal of money; but a murder at the right time has never left me in the lurch[2].'

A few of such more recent English novels of sadistic tendency deserve to be mentioned here as being highly instructive in an investigation of the influence of the Marquis de Sade on the imaginations of their authors.

The most notorious publication of this kind bears the title *The Pleasures of Cruelty*, and is expressly described as a ' Sequel ' to the Marquis de Sade's *Justine and Juliette*. I have only seen a reprint of it[3], though it must originally have appeared before 1880, for in the third volume of the erotic periodical *The Pearl* (pp. 169-176), which was published in that year, an episode—' The Sultan's Reverie ', an extract from *The Pleasures of Cruelty*—is already quoted (Vol. II, pp. 32-52 in the reprint mentioned above). Pisanus Fraxi does not appear to have known of this work, which was written by a worthy successor of the Marquis de Sade, since it is not mentioned in his three-volume bibliography. However, *The Pleasures of Cruelty* is one of the most blatant imitations of *Justine and Juliette*, and is obviously based on a most careful reading of the latter work, scenes from

---

[1] P. Fraxi, *Catena librorum tacendorum* (London, 1885), pp. xlii-xliii.

[2] Smollett, *Adventures of Roderick Random*.

[3] *The Pleasures of Cruelty* (London and Paris, 1898). Three vols., small 8vo.

which are expressly mentioned (Vol. II, p. 8). The following analysis also confirms this view.

Sir Charles Dacre, a wealthy baronet, and one of George IV's gay companions, is already at the age of thirty-eight a completely blasé gentleman and a total physical wreck. He tries in vain to stimulate anew his jaded senses at the gaming-tables and in the brothels of Brussels, Vienna and Paris. He therefore one day requests Madame Josephine, a notorious procuress, at whose house he happens to be staying, to procure for him new sexual sensations. She offers to rejuvenate him completely on payment of a fee of £500. However, she could only accomplish this with the aid of his daughters—Sir Charles is the father of three daughters, Maud, Alice and Flora, aged eighteen, seventeen and fifteen respectively—the method being that he should rape, torture and humiliate them in every conceivable manner, which would stimulate him by the thought that he is degrading his own flesh and blood. In order to carry out this thoroughly sadistic plan without interference from the police, they go to Turkish territory, on the shores of the Bosphorus, where they rent a house. They equip in a remote part of the building a ' torture chamber ', with whips, rods, chains and other instruments of torture. In addition, Sir Charles can indulge in the sport of fishing and hunting, as the house is quite close to the sea.

' The Torture Chamber ', which constitutes the first part of *The Pleasures of Cruelty*, describes the most abominable sadistic scenes enacted by the father and Madame Josephine with the three girls, who are forced to take an active part. Interlinked with this part is a story related by Madame Josephine concerning the rape and brutal treatment of a German girl by a French libertine. In this first part flagellation and pedication are principally dealt with. In the second scene Maud is whipped to death by her own father.

[447]

Sir Charles thereupon travels to Constantinople in order to procure fresh victims on whom he can satisfy his sadistic desire. This is the theme of Part Two. Sir Charles discovers in Constantinople four orphan girls, the daughters of a Greek merchant who had shortly before lost his entire fortune and died of cholera. The girls, Haidee, Veneria, Sophia and Melissa (aged twenty-four, seventeen, thirteen and ten), are lured by the libertine to his castle, and immediately subjected to the worst sadistic practices, in which Lucidora, a former inmate of a harem, but now assistant to Madame Josephine, participates. These practices are too horrible to be mentioned here, but they are mainly imitations of descriptions to be found in *Justine and Juliette*. Here, again, various obscene episodes are intertwined, such as a story about a sadistic Sultan, about Catherine II, about an Englishwoman who makes her own daughter the subject of her sadistic pleasures, about a father who flagellates his own daughter for the same purpose.

In the third part of the book a new sadist appears on the scene, Count de Bonvit of Paris, who participates in the ' séances ' of Sir Charles, Madame Josephine and Lucidora, and carries on with the first-named obscene conversations on the *Ars amandi*, in the course of which the sexual excesses of Henry IV and the sexual adventures of a Belgian nun are related.

By the end of the third, and last, part the ' victims ' have already become enthusiastic and active sadists, and Madame Josephine is sent to Paris in order to find new active and passive female members for this sadist club.

A further sadistic publication is described as *Revelries and Devilries, or Scenes in the Life of Sir Lionel Heythorp, Bt.* (London, 1867, with seven obscene coloured etchings and a frontispiece). Four Oxford scholars and an officer, whose names are known to Pisanus Fraxi[1], though he refuses to give them, combined to write this obscene work. Each of them wrote a story, and the four stories were merged into one continuous narrative in three chapters. A great deal is said in the book about flagellation, in addition to other repulsive incidents, the most horrible of which relates to a visit to a lunatic asylum, the erotic idiosyncrasies of the inmates being described in the coarsest manner. The book concludes with a chapter entitled 'A Night in the Borough', being the description of an orgy so obscene that even the Marquis de Sade in his wildest dreams could not have thought of it.

The Inutility of Virtue (London, 1830) describes in autobiographical form the adventures of an opera singer born in Naples. On her way to Rome, where she is to marry Count Torso, she falls into the hands of a brigand, by whom she is raped. Later she marries a man whom she loves, and to whom she wishes to remain faithful. But in spite of her good intentions and her repeated assurances of fidelity, she becomes a prey to every man with whom she comes in contact. All these adventures are of the most ordinary type. The book is probably not a translation from the French, as stated on the title-page, but seems, nevertheless, to have originated from a French source.

Although cruelty and bloodthirstiness, such as the *joli Marquis* revelled in, are less pronounced in this story, the adventures related in it nevertheless remind the reader very forcibly of the idea propounded by the Marquis de Sade's *Justine* concerning the invariable misfortune that accompanies virtue. Justine, the heroine of the Marquis de Sade's story, like our singer, falls into the hands of brigands right at the beginning.

Another notorious product of sadistic imagination is the *Romance of Lust* (London, 1873). This work was also written

[1] P. Fraxi, *Catena*, p. 181.

by several authors and contains various stories, which were given continuity by a famous collector of erotic pictures and objects of art. He performed the task during a journey to Japan[1]. The book contains scenes more obscene than any in *Justine*.

Genuine sadistic ideas are also propounded in the *Experimental Lecture by Colonel Spanker* (London, 1878), a brief analysis of which is contained in the earlier part of this work. The work is a glorification of the joys to be derived from psychical and physical cruelty.

' Sensual pleasure can be excited by two things; firstly, if we believe that the object of our love approaches our ideal of beauty, and secondly, if we see the person concerned in process of experiencing the most intense sensations possible. Now, no sensation is more vivid than that of pain; the shock it produces is real and certain. It does not mislead, like the comedy of lust at which women always play but never really experience. The man who is capable of making the most powerful impression on a woman, of inducing the extreme of excitement and thrill in the feminine organism, is capable of securing the highest degree of sensual pleasure for himself.'

As a certain English bibliophile rightly observes, these sentences contain the quintessence of the entire philosophy which the Marquis de Sade has propounded in such great detail in his notorious works, in which his descriptions of sanguinary orgies, phlebotomy, vivisection and tortures of all kinds, combined with blasphemy, tend to show the importance attached to the moral humiliation of the victim. It is in this sense that in the *Experimental Lecture* a sensitive, gently nurtured young woman is subjected to the most abominable tortures. In the case of *Justine and Juliette* all thought of

[1] See P. Fraxi, *Catena*, p. 188.

reality is precluded by the large number of individuals involved in the orgies and by the murders, whereas in the *Experimental Lecture* the entire action is handled so carefully and methodically that the reader is led to believe in the reality of the proceedings described.

The endurance of pain and humiliation as a form of sexual satisfaction, known as masochism, appears in English sexual life mainly as passive submission to flagellation, but generally the English character is more inclined to sadistic acts. Nevertheless, masochistic tendencies—apart from the ' age of chivalry '—can be traced in the history of English customs. Thus there were people in the sixteenth and seventeenth centuries who swallowed sulphur and urine in order to win their adored ones, as described, for instance, in Middleton's *Dutch Courtesan.*

A well-known masochist of the eighteenth century was a ' man about town ' named Tracey who was completely dominated by his mistress, a brothel owner named Charlotte Hayes. He submitted to any indignity imposed by her, and tolerated with slavish acquiescence all her infidelities. She even entertained at his expense her various lovers at the Shakespeare or Rose Tavern, where Tracey had opened credits for her. She knew how to make herself desirable to him by wearing smart and erotically suggestive dresses, but made him pay heavily for her favours. Thus Tracey in a short time dissipated his enormous fortune and died at an early age[1].

Another masochist in the year 1791 aroused considerable attention in London by his strange end, for his death was directly due to his masochistic practices. He was a musician named Kotzwarra, and since his case is both interesting and authentic we will deal with it here in detail.

[1] See *Les Sérails de Londres,* p. 15.

J. W. Archenholtz[1] reports the affair as follows :

' A most curious incident occurred in London resulting in a criminal prosecution. There was a musician there, Kotzwarra of Prague, a man possessing extraordinary musical gifts, who played thirteen different instruments, some of them with considerable virtuosity. I knew him personally and frequently admired his talent. The famous musicians Bach and Abel, who achieved such fame in England, regarded him as unique in Europe as a performer on the contra-bass; he had also beaten all his rivals in the playing of this instrument in London, Paris and Venice. The above-mentioned musicians in the years 1769 and 1770 frequently invited him to participate in their great concerts at Hanover Square, paying him princely fees. However, Kotzwarra soon began to neglect his talents and lived a life of dissipation. He became a voluptuary of the worst kind, and thought of nothing but the artificial intensification of his sensual pleasures. He was told that a hanged person, owing to the more rapid circulation of the blood and the distension of certain vessels, enjoys a very pleasant sensation for several minutes. According to the evidence of witnesses, he had frequently tried the experiment, always in the presence of prostitutes, whom he rewarded for their assistance. In order to repeat the experiment once more he visited, one day in September, a prostitute living in the neighbourhood of Covent Garden, and requested her to hang him, but to release the rope after five minutes. The poor girl at first refused to participate in this strange performance, but Kotzwarra finally succeeded in overcoming her objections by means of persuasion and gifts of money.

' She hanged Kotzwarra, fixing the rope to the door, and releasing it at the end of five minutes. But the man gave no

[1] Archenholtz, *British Annals of the Year* 1791. Hamburg, 1793. Vol. VII, pp. 38-41.

[452]

sign of life, and although every effort was made to revive him, he remained dead. The girl, Susan Hill, was arrested for murder, and a verdict of " wilful murder " was returned against her at the preliminary proceedings by the jury, who deliberated from 5 o'clock in the afternoon till 2 a.m. the next morning. They debated the question for nine hours and finally thought that by their severe verdict they would prevent the co-operation of such girls in abnormal sexual practices. The poor girl had to stand her trial at the Old Bailey on a charge involving life or death, but the judge regarded her act not as murder but as unpremeditated man-slaughter, which was, of course, the logical view to take. She was therefore liberated immediately, with exhortations to lead a better life. The facts that came to light in the course of the trial were so subversive of modesty, and so dangerous to public morality, that the judge not only requested all the women present to leave the court, but also ordered all the documents relating to the case to be destroyed.'

Susan Hill's evidence, which is reprinted in *Modern Propensities*, etc., a pamphlet of the period, was as follows: ' That on the afternoon of the 2nd September, between the hours of one and two, a man whom she had never seen, and who was identical with the deceased, had come to the house where she was residing, the street door having been open. He asked her whether she would like to have a drink with him. She asked for port, he for brandy and water, and he gave her some money for both, also two shillings for ham and beef, which she also purchased. A little later they went to a back room, where a number of most indecent acts took place. In particular, he asked her to tear his genital organ in two, which she refused. Then he said that he would like to be hanged for five minutes and observed, while giving her the money to buy the rope, that this would increase his pleasure and produce the desired effect. She brought two thin cords

[453]

and placed them round his neck. He then drew himself up on the door of the back room, where he was hanging very low, and he drew up his legs. After five minutes she cut him down and he fell on the floor. She thought he had only fainted and called a neighbour woman living opposite to her assistance. The accused was acquitted.'

The Editor of the *Bon Ton Magazine*, in No. 31 of that periodical, dated September 1793, wrote a notice of the above-mentioned pamphlet, the frontispiece of which was reproduced, and also discussed the Kotzwarra case, adding the following dissertation on ' The Effects of Temporary Strangulation on the Human Body '.

' The strangulation of Kotzwarra, although it proved fatal, has not entirely stopped the bestial practice of suspension. The girl who assisted that eccentric lover in the operation has stated that a few seconds before his death he had shown certain signs which clearly proved the pleasant effect of this procedure.

' When this statement of the fair object of our illustration was repeated to a wealthy citizen of Bristol who, although he requires assistance in the secret affairs of Venus, is nevertheless a man of considerable public prominence, he decided to try the experiment with greater caution. Accordingly, he came to the Metropolis at the beginning of last month and immediately applied to a pretty girl in Charlotte Street, to whom he frankly revealed his impotence, informing her of the method by which this evil could be eliminated, so that he might enjoy her lovely person to the full. In order to secure her consent he brought into play the infallible argument of gold in a liberal manner, and as he had already provided himself with the stimulating rope, the process was immediately begun.'

The man stepped on a low stool, attached the sling to a ventilator, threw the other end over a cross beam, and, with the aid of his fair companion, fastened it in such a manner that the possibility of danger was eliminated. The low stool was then removed and our hero was suspended in such a manner that his feet were just touching the floor. Within thirty seconds the stimulating effect of this peculiar procedure was clearly in evidence. But suddenly he began to show alarming symptoms, so that the girl quickly released her peculiar lover. But in order to revive him completely it was necessary to invoke the assistance of the Society for Reviving Drowned Persons[1].

The Berlin masseurs also have a similar strange clientele, as many of them are equipped, in addition to their usual instruments of torture, with such ' hanging apparatus '[2].

In modern times masochism in England appears to have gained ground to a greater extent than formerly, as evidenced, in particular, by the appearance of masochist publications. As a prototype of these we may quote *Gynecocracy*, which is ' a narrative of the adventures and psychological experiences of Julian Robinson (afterwards Viscount Ladywood) under petticoat rule, written by himself' (Paris and Rotterdam, 1893). This book was translated into German and French. It deals with the systematic education of a young nobleman in masochism. The process consists in this, that a French governess, a very strict young lady, assisted by similarly energetic ladies and chambermaids, dresses him up as a woman and inculcates in him a taste for the nauseating masochistic processes which she cunningly links with sexual pleasures.

[1] The *Bon Ton Magazine*, Vol. III, p. 242.
[2] Ivan Bloch, *Beiträge zur Aetiologie der Psychopathia Sexualis*, Part II, p. 173.

CHAPTER XV

OTHER SEXUAL PERVERSITIES

ACCORDING to the author of *Memoirs of a Singer* (Vol. II, p. 188), a very widespread sexual perversity in England is exhibitionism, that is to say, the uncovering of the lower parts of the body in public for the purpose of provoking sexual excitement in the exhibitionist. This tendency was apparently responsible for the appearance of a special class of prostitutes, the so-called ' posture girls ', in eighteenth-century England. Hogarth, on the third plate of ' The Rake's Progress ', represents such a ' posture girl ', who exhibits her charms in a most remarkable manner.

According to Lichtenberg there was only one small town in England up to the beginning of the nineteenth century where a naked woman was allowed to appear in public. The name of that town was Coventry.

There was an ancient custom in Coventry, according to which, on a certain day each year, a young girl rode naked along the main street and afterwards dined—still naked—with the mayor of the town. The chronicler assures the reader that Coventry never lacked candidates in carrying out this old custom[1].

The history of English morals reveals several examples of fetishism. Archenholtz mentions a case of hair fetishism: ' I once knew an Englishman, a very nice, amiable sort of

[1] Eros, Stuttgart, 1849, Vol. II, p. 120.

man, yet, as he himself told me, he had a strange taste deeply rooted in his soul. The greatest pleasure he could conceive was to comb the hair of a pretty young woman. He had a beautiful mistress for the purpose. Love and faithfulness were of no importance to him; all he wanted from her was to be allowed to play with her hair whenever he liked. And when he wished to do this, the girl had to remove the hairpins from her hair, so that he could run his fingers through it. This gave him a voluptuous thrill all over his body[1].'

One of the queerest characters in *Venus Schoolmistress* is an old man who experiences a violent sexual agitation at the sight of a muff, and asks to be stroked with it all over his body. He also enjoys the sight of a lady with her hands in a muff.

A case of costume fetishism is described in the *Battles of Venus*, in which the author declares that he prefers to have sexual intercourse with an elegantly dressed woman than with a *femina denudata*.

Race fetishism also has numerous adherents of both sexes in England. Detailed records in *Sérails des London* (pp. 150-154) concerning the negress Harriet in London show that she always had numerous distinguished lovers.

Hogarth depicted her in his etching ' The Discovery ', in the rôle of a lover, though an involuntary one. Commenting on this etching, Lichtenberg writes: ' The extent to which black beauties are capable of fascinating white men is revealed by the genealogical trees of many mulattoes in the West Indies. And it is not only in the West Indies that distinguished men occasionally prefer negresses to white women, perhaps because brown bread is sometimes a delicacy to jaded palates.'

[1] Archenholtz, *England and Italy* (Leipzig, 1785), Vol. I, pp. 448-449.

Adrian mentions the predilection of some London ladies
for Arabs. During his sojourn in London he very frequently
saw dusky sons of the desert hanging about street corners,
and behaving exactly like female prostitutes. A man
in the know once explained to him the reason for this
phenomenon.

' Our language is not rich in decent expressions for the
indecent. London ladies sometimes have strange caprices.
By London ladies I do not mean the respectable wives of
City men or the women of the upper classes, who apparently
care little or nothing about respectability, but the women
who live in special circumstances, supported or neglected by
rich men, and naturally of easy virtue. They all appear to
be violently attracted by those supposedly strong little
bronzed men. If you have a quarter of an hour to spare,
spend it in watching one of those smartly dressed sons of the
desert. You will be sure to see either a faithful manservant
or a sly, discreet lady's maid passing him and giving him
a sign. The turbaned fellow will follow with apparent
nonchalance, take his instructions, or go straight to the
appointed place.'

Adrian further learned that these Arabs were also favoured
by London paederasts, and sometimes acted as regular male
prostitutes[1].

That tendencies to copralagnia and scatology were not
infrequent among the English will be apparent from certain
passages in Butler's *Hudibras*, a work published in the
eighteenth century, and from a book entitled *The Benefit of
Farting Explained*, and further from the fact that a rich
English bibliophile had a book written on this subject and
had it published. This book, which was printed in only
twenty copies for private circulation, bore the title, *An Essay*

[1] Adrian, *Sketches from England*. Frankfurt a.M., 1833. Vol. II,
pp. 8-10.

on Wind, with Curious Anecdotes of Eminent Peteurs, etc. Written for the edification of windbound ladies and gentlemen (Paris, Quantin, 1877)[1].

Octave Uzanne mentions scatology in England in his very clever and witty criticism of Swinburne's *A Study of Ben Jonson* (London, 1889), in which Swinburne observes in connection with Ben Jonson's scatological epigrams that it is most regrettable that such a great writer should have cultivated coprology, which is really a French speciality. To which Uzanne remarks:

' Outre que cette insistance à agiter la matière n'indigue pas une délicatesse olfactive aussi sensible que les premiers mots l'auraient pu faire supposer, M. Swinburne trouverait-il beaucoup d'écrivains anglais, du XV au XVIII siècle, qui n'aient pas fait le plongeon dont il parle, et lui serait-il bien difficile de citer même de nos jours, des écrivains anglais—oh, ceux-là de la " baser sort "—qui s'y baignent à plaisir ou s'y vautrent par métier ? ' He quotes, among others, passages from Shakespeare, Swift and Smollett, and concludes: ' Les Anglais, au surplus, le savent bien, qu'ils n'ont pas besoin de chercher en France ni ailleurs, puisqu'ils sont la " Merry England ", et que s'il faut en croire de petits papiers imprimés qui circulent parmi les couches profondes des lecteurs de la Grande-Bretagne à l'insu, sans doute du grande poète, l'homme heureux est celui qui se délecte " in the smell of his own Farts "[2] '.

In spite of this, however, Swinburne's view is well founded, since the French and Italians possess purely scatological poems, as will be seen at the merest glance at the *Bibliotheca scatologica.*

[1] Cf. J. Gay, *Bibliographie des ouvrages relatifs à l'amour, etc.* 4th edition. Lille, 1897. Vol. IV, p. 172.
[2] Cf. *Le livre moderne.* 1890. Vol. I.

Venus Cloacina, as an object of poetic glorification, is very rarely to be encountered among Germanic peoples.

Incest occurred in England with remarkable frequency. According to a number of observers, this appalling fact may be ascribed to the circumstance that the members of the family in slum districts all sleep in the same room, and often enough the same bed is used by father and daughter, mother and son, sister and brother. Countless cases of incest in England are known from reports by various authors, including Archenholtz, but we will only quote two of the most notorious instances from an early period.

The first of these relates to the trial of Thomas Weir, Mayor of Edinburgh, which took place in the year 1670. A detailed report of the trial is contained in a very rare pamphlet entitled *Ravillac Redivivus, to which is annexed an account of the Tryal of that most wicked Pharisee, Mayor Thomas Weir, who was executed for Adultery, Incest and Bestiality. In which are many Observable Passages, especially relating to the present Affairs of Church and State. In a letter from a Scottish to an English gentleman. London, printed by Henry Hills*, 1678.

Weir, who was Mayor of Edinburgh during the Rebellion, distinguished himself by his bestial cruelty to the Royalist Party, and owing to his Pharisean and hypocritical ways, he passed as a very pious man. But towards the end of his life, which was full of infamy, murder and unnatural lusts and pleasures, Thomas Weir, now a septuagenarian, was seized with a deep repentance, and made public confession to Lord Abbotshall, who was at that time Governor of Edinburgh, of all his sins.

A prosecution was instituted against Weir and his sister on the 9th April 1670, on the basis of his own evidence which, according to the physicians, Weir had given in full possession of his mental faculties. Weir's confessions were

[460]

Pl. 23]

AN EMBLEMATIC PRINT ON THE 'SOUTH SEA'

Hogarth

LOVE LAUGHS AT LOCKSMITHS.

Pl. 24]

read aloud at the trial. He had seduced his sister when she was ten years old. Subsequently he continued sexual intercourse with her at their father's house, and finally lived incestuously with her for a number of years in Edinburgh. He had likewise seduced his step-daughter Margaret Bourdon, daughter of his deceased wife, and lived with her for some time. In addition, during the lifetime of his wife, he had betrayed her with a number of married and unmarried women, especially with a certain Bessy Weems, a maidservant living in their house. In addition to adultery and incest, he had made himself guilty of the unnatural sin of Sodomism, in that he had had sexual intercourse with cows and mares, and especially with one of his mares, upon which he once rode to New Mills.

The witnesses who were examined by the court gave evidence of what they had seen with their own eyes, giving a detailed account of all they knew, and describing the situations in which they had seen the accused. In his sister's evidence the devil was mentioned a number of times.

Thomas Weir and his sister were sentenced to death. On Monday the 11th April 1670 Weir was bound to a stake and strangled, after which his body was burned. His sister, Jane Weir, was hanged the following day.

A most horrible account of incestuous acts continued for several generations is contained in the story of the Scotch robber Sawney Beane who lived in the time of James I, a story which was handed down through generations.

' Sawney Beane[1] was the son of a navvy in East Lothian, Scotland. In his early boyhood he had vicious inclinations, and as a youth he eloped with an equally vicious and depraved female. They hid themselves in a cave in the wilds of Galloway. The cave was very large and close to the sea-

---

[1] Cf. *Sawney Beane* in C. Whitehead's *Lives, Deeds and Fates of the most Notable English Robbers and Pirates.* Leipzig, 1834.

shore, so that the surrounding land was frequently flooded at high tide. There were many twists and turns in the path that led to the cave.

It was from this lair that they conducted their robberies, and in order to avoid discovery they murdered all their victims after robbing them. As the problem of provisions was causing them considerable difficulty, they decided to feed on human flesh. For this purpose they dragged the bodies of their victims into the cave, where they pickled them. They lived like this, by robbery and murder, until they had eight sons and six daughters. From the incestuous alliances of the latter sprang eighteen grandsons and fourteen granddaughters. The entire family participated in the killings and robberies, and lived by cannibalism.

In the course of the years the countryside gradually became seriously depopulated, and the disappearance of so many people finally moved the authorities to investigate. But the cannibals succeeded in evading discovery for a very long time.

When the officers of the law finally entered the cave the sight that met their eyes surpassed in horror everything that had ever been seen or heard of up till then. There were arms and legs of men, women and children dangling from the walls and roof of the cave, like so many chunks of cured animal flesh. Further quantities of human flesh were pickled in tubs. Money, gold and silver, jewellery, clothes and immense quantities of other goods lay on the floor of the cave in large piles, or hung from the walls.

The entire ghoulish family was taken into custody. The remains of the murdered people were buried on the beach, while the prisoners, together with their accumulated plunder, were taken to Edinburgh.

Crowds of people rushed to see this horrible family of incestuous ghouls, robbers and murderers, which had within twenty-five years grown in numbers to twenty-seven males and twenty-one females.

The day after their arrival in Edinburgh the entire family was executed without trial, and in the most cruel manner. The men's intestines were torn out, their hands and feet were cut off and they were then left to bleed to death. The female members of the family were burnt.

They all died without displaying the least sign of repentance, and continued to shout filthy curses to the last.

The cases of Thomas Weir and Sawney Beaue provide striking proof that the wildest imaginings of a Marquis de Sade may be equalled, and even far surpassed, by reality.

Incest is also encountered in English literature. The most famous example is John Ford's *Giovanni and Annabella*, the monstrous tragedy of sexual love between brother and sister, in which the poet does not shrink from the fact of Annabella's pregnancy through her brother Giovanni. In the last act is a dreadful, beautiful love scene between them, that ends with the brother stabbing his sister to death[1].

Quite the most horrible example of an incest novel is *Letters from a Friend in Paris* (London, 1874. Two volumes), in which one incestuous incident literally follows another. The scene of the work is in France. The author himself, the hero of the story, is a photographer who is received into a family through a mutual friend with whom he has paederistic relations. The friend is to marry a daughter of the family, after the hero himself has already enjoyed her. This family consists of father, mother, two daughters and a son, who live together incestuously and welcome the photographer as a comrade to their orgies. Next to incest,

---

[1] Cf. Prölsz, *loc. cit.*, Vol. II, pp. 15-18 (contains also a more detailed account of the incest theme in world literature). Also H. Taine, *loc. cit.*, Vol. I, pp. 397-99.

paederasty plays an important part in this product of a corrupt imagination, worthy of a Marquis de Sade.

In conclusion the ubiquitous subject of masturbation should be noticed: A very considerable literature[1] on it exists in England, as elsewhere, and, as in all other countries, the self-appointed moralists, aiming at self-advertisement and profit, are responsible for most of it. For they claim that masturbation is the cause of all possible and impossible evils and seem to prefer to make use of the subject to boost their ' wares ', partly through journals and partly by means of leaflets passed from hand to hand, the dangerously exaggerated contents of which can be seen from Ryan's quoted examples[2].

---

[1] From the eighteenth century may be mentioned: *Erononia, or the Misusing of the Marriage-bed by Er and Onan, to which is added Letters of Advice, about a Weighting of Conscience, viz., of defiling himself.* London, 1724, 8vo. *Ononia, or the heinous Sin of Self Pollution.* London, 1724, 12mo. *Ononia, or the Heinous sin of self Pollution, and all its frightful Consequence in both Sexes.* The 12th edition. London, 1727. *A supplement to the Ononia, or the Heinous sin of self Pollution. Ononia examinated and detected, by Philo Castitatis.* The second edition. 1724, 12mo. *Onanism display'd.* London, 1726, 12mo.

[2] M. Ryan, *Prostitution in London.* London, 1839. Pp. 12-13.

CHAPTER XVI

FASHION AS PROCURESS

DRESS and fashion are products of the human sexual instincts. This view, which not so long ago was opposed for example by von Schurtz in his *Philosophy of Dress*, has during the last few years been fully confirmed by scientific enquiries, which have been made by prominent anthropologists and ethnologists in particular (Steinen, Westermarck, Stratz, amongst others)[1]. As a result, dress has developed as a means of sexual attraction and, through its constant companion, fashion, is varied in every possible direction, always however falling back on the effects produced by the emphasis and exaggeration of certain features and the partial exposure of others[2]. The veiling, equally with the unveiling of certain parts, serve as sexual stimulators, according to the nature of the attractions in question, as Tasso has already recognised:

' Non copre sue bellezze, e non l'espose ' (*Do not cover her beauties nor expose them*).

In the study of the modes of different times and peoples traces are found everywhere of these two basic sexual elements, as is also the case in the study of the most important periods in the history of English fashion.

---

[1] It is interesting to learn, as regards the English mode, that as early as the previous century William Alexander, the celebrated author of the *History of Women*, affirmed the sexual origin of dress.

[2] See with regard to the main principles of fashion Iwan Bloch's *Contributions to Psycopathia sexualis*, Vol. I, pp. 139-175. Dresden, 1902. Also I. Bloch, *The Sexual Life of our Time*. London, 1909. Pp. 152-153.

One can only speak of English fashion in a limited sense, as England, to a greater extent even than other European countries, was in early days under the—in this respect—completely dominating influence of the French. Walsingham dated the introduction and spread of the French fashions in England from the siege of Calais in the year 1347[1]. Some peculiarities of English fashion have always, however remained, and especially in later times certain aspects of the mode bore the impress of the English character in many ways, as for instance the so-called Dandyism, which served to express something specifically English.

Whilst the Anglo-Saxon invaders still generally retained the primitive Germanic dress[2], the Normans had already begun to cultivate a greater refinement and more ostentation in their dress, which received a stimulus from the introduction of silk material (with the end of the thirteenth century). The wives of some nobles first appeared in silk dresses at a ball at Kenilworth Castle in Warwickshire in the year 1286[3]. At that time the over-dresses were wide and long, the under-dresses narrow and short, the former touching the ground all round. These ' trains ' were often a subject of satire. ' The ladies make their trains a thousand times as long as peacocks and magpies ', as an old English comic poem says[4]. These overlong over-dresses were slit almost half-way up the sides by the prostitutes, so that the legs clad in tight stockings might be seen.

Special pockets were made for the breasts, which were thus particularly accentuated[5].

[1] I. D'Israeli, *Curiosities of Literature*. London, 1895. P. 84.

[2] See Bruno Köhler, *Allgemeine Trachtenkunde*. Leipzig. Vol. II, pp. 188-198.

[3] Alexander, *loc. cit.* London, 1779. Vol. II, p. 133.

[4] Friedrich Hottenroth, *Implements of dress, house, field and war of the peoples of old and later times*. Second edition. Stuttgart, 1891. Vol. II, p. 133.

[5] Bruno Köhler, *loc. cit.*, Vol. II, pp. 219-220.

The true all-powerful sovereignty of the mode began in the fourteenth century, or rather in the last decades of the same. Bruno Köhler remarks: ' Ever more zealously were the fashionable frivolities of the French-Burgundians imitated in England. Formerly we had always been some decades behind the French in adopting their fashions in dress, now we kept step with them in all their modes. The tendency, which was again becoming noticeable, to invest foreign clothes with a specifically English character soon had the result that the bizarre French-Burgundian costumes became in certain ways still more atrocious in appearance and were therefore still more uncomfortable in use than in France. As the result of such a craze for luxury in dress, even the lower classes sacrificed everything in order to appear as finely clothed as possible[1].'

This luxury was particularly preposterous in the time of Richard II. Sir John Arundel possessed no fewer than fifty-two suits of gold-embroidered clothes. The prelates especially delighted in the most luxurious extravagances of the fashion. Chaucer said of them that they changed their clothes every day (had ' chaunge of clothing everie daie '). In the ' Persones Tale ' he launched his sharpest sarcasm and satire against the abominable fashions of his time, and spread himself especially over the highly serious consequences in the sexual sense of the too great " scantness " of the hose, the close fit of which emphasised in the most shameless way the buttocks and genital regions, so that with many people ' the buttockes behind ' looked ' as if they were the hinder part of a sheape in the ful of the mone '. According to Hottenroth, a fashion was set by the effeminate Richard II for the wearing of wide sleeves with tight-fitting coats, but narrow short sleeves with trailing dresses which at the same time fitted clingingly round the upper part of the

[1] Bruno Köhler, *loc. cit.*, Vol. IV, p. 26.

body, and the result was that the men, especially when seen from behind, looked exactly like the women. Over all was worn a long coat with a stand-up collar, which in front came to the chin and at the back somewhat higher, to the roots of the hair. With this attire the face was shaved to the smoothness of a woman's and no beard was worn[1]. An unusual variety of colours began to appear in the different garments, as is shown particularly in Chaucer's *Canterbury Tales*. Indeed, one and the same article of clothing would be parti-coloured—one stocking would be white above and red beneath, or white and blue, or white and black, or black and red, and so on[2]. All this was bound to lead to a softening and an effeminacy of the men and to give considerable impetus to homosexual tendencies.

Whilst under Henry VIII the smooth-shaved faces disappeared and beards took their place, a new and immoral freak of fashion appeared, the so-called ' Genital Shield ', an exaggerated padding of the hose in the vicinity of the genitals, which latter were thereby emphasised in the most indecent fashion and exposed to the lascivious gaze. Hottenroth describes the immodest hose of that period as follows: ' Hose were largely worn slit up their whole length and lined with padded under-hose of another colour. They were bound with horizontal coloured stripes of material, short distances apart, or decorated in some other way with brightly-coloured strips of material inset. Thus fashioned the hose were called " trusses ". The " genital shield," padded and slit, was put on to a three-cornered flap, and though the " trusses " were nearly covered by the coat flaps, could always be seen between the latter[3].'

---

[1] Hottenroth, *loc. cit.*, Vol. II, p. 133.
[2] D'Israeli, *loc. cit.*, p. 84.
[3] Hottenroth, *loc. cit.*, Vol. II, p. 141.

In the Elizabethan period the stiff Spanish fashion did nothing to prevent the display of glittering luxury and the adoption of various eccentricities in the world of fashion. Thus, according to I. D'Israeli, the fashion of enormous leg coverings was exaggerated to the most ludicrous extent. The dandies of that period stuffed their hose with feathers, rags and other materials till they attained an enormous width, so that they looked like great sacks, and at the public plays special seats had to be provided for these monstrous swollen extremities. On their side, the ladies in their ridiculous hooped skirts literally kept the men at their distance. In this way the dandies managed to combine the different fashions of the world in their attire[1]. Take, for example, the huge neck-ruffs of the Spanish costume, which in England were increased tenfold in size and circumference, and one can imagine how a really fashionably dressed individual burdened himself, and how glad he must have been to be rid of his clothes at least at night and to go to bed completely naked. For up to the time of James I night-shirts were very unusual. Archenholtz says: ' When this king was still a child and under the care of Lady Mar, he was taken ill in the night with colic. All the men and women servants rushed in to him stark naked, and only the Countess appeared in a half-length shirt[2].'

An example of the excess of luxury under James I was given by his favourite, the Duke of Buckingham, whose extravagance passed all bounds. Apart from the fact that he always bought the most costly materials for his clothes, such as satin, velvet, and gold and silver stuffs, he had them trimmed not only with the most expensive braiding and the richest coloured embroidery, but also with pearls, precious stones and jewelled buttons in artistic goldwork. And of

[1] I. D'Israeli, *loc. cit.*, pp. 83-84.
[2] Archenholtz, *British Annals*, Vol. I, p. 419.

these complete suits he possessed in 1625 not less than twenty-seven of which each cost about 35,000 francs, whilst for the suit he had made for the marriage of Charles I he gave 500,000 francs! [1]

This exaggerated display was followed in the frivolous and easy-going period of the Restoration under Charles II by a fashion for nakedness. The chief consideration was now not the beauty and cost of the clothes, but the service of love, and the pretty ladies of the court of Charles II vied with each other in displaying their hidden charms to the lustful gaze of their admirers. Weiss[2] characterises the fashion of this period as follows :

' Style remained generally French during the reign of Charles II, and in its details a still greater similarity developed. Encouragement was given to the prevailing fashion by the King's methods with his mistresses, introduced by himself and carried to the point of open licentiousness. The display of stuffs, in decorations and trimmings, in the use of ribbons, bows, costly braids and laces reached, as in France, the height of extravagance; but as regards outline, the more conspicuous exaggerations were at least avoided, such as the draperies of lace used for the arms and hands, the eccentric padding of the front edges of the upper-robe and so on, and this all tended to greater freedom of movement. On the other hand, none of the French methods of increasing the purely physical attractions were relinquished. As regards exposure of the neck, breast and arms, as in the use of false hair, paint and patches, not only was nothing given to the French leaders of fashion, but on the contrary, they were far outstripped.'

In fact, the shameless exposure of women's shoulders and

[1] Weiss, *Kostumkunde* (Encyclopedia of Dress). Stuttgart, 1872. P. 1028.
[2] *Ibid.*, Vol. II, pp. 1034-1035.

breasts in which, as D'Israeli tells[1], the Queen almost outdid
the other women, reached such a height that several
writers published protests against it. In 1672 a book appeared
with the title: *New Instructions to Youth as to their Behaviour,
together with a Discussion of some Novelties in the Mode;
against powdering the Hair, Naked Breasts and Patches, and
other unseemly Customs.* The author included two pictures
of women in his book, representing ' Virtue ' and ' Vice '.
The first is chastely and modestly dressed. 'Vice ' has two
great breasts sticking out from a low corset and the face
is disfigured with numerous patches of different shapes[2].
Another book denouncing nudity, which was held in some
esteem, was that published by Edward Cooke, 1678, for
which the famous theologian, Richard Baxter, wrote a
foreword. It bore the title: *A just and reasonable Reprehension of naked Breasts and Shoulders,* 1678, 8vo. Finally, in
1683 there appeared a third book entitled: *England's Vanity;
or the Voice of God against the Monstrous Sin of Pride in Dress
and Apparel,* which was called forth by the depravity of
the fashions[3].

A ridiculous custom of that time was the carrying of muffs
by the men. Samuel Pepys relates in his *Diary* that he took
an old muff of his wife's for his own use and gave her a new
one instead[4].

The sole virtue of the mode in the Restoration period was
its comparatively greater naturalness and simplicity, which,
in spite of the tendency to frivolity, had a wholesome effect.
The fashion of the eighteenth century afforded a great
contrast, with its artificiality and the rapid changes it

[1] D'Israeli, *loc. cit.,* p. 86.
[2] *Ibid.*
[3] *Ibid.* Weiss, *loc. cit.,* Vol. II, p. 1035. Gay, *Bibliographie des Ouvrages relatifs à l'amour.* Third edition. Turin, 1871. Vol. I, p. 3.
[4] Traill, *Social England,* Vol. IV, p. 485.

brought about. Georgiana Hill says: ' No century displayed so much artificiality. Clothing, customs, pleasures, talk— all showed the same rebellion against unspoilt Nature[1].' An enumeration of the eccentricities of the mode between 1700 and 1800 in the works of Malcolm should be studied, when the justice of this opinion will be recognised.

Weiss also comments upon the frequency with which the fashion changed as a typical phenomenon in England in the eighteenth century, with the early appearance of dandyism, decked in all the colours of the rainbow, the like of which was not be seen even in France[2]. W. Alexander gives a vivid insight into the fickleness of fashion as regards the dress of English women[3]. At the beginning of the eighteenth century the opinion seems to have been generally spread abroad that Nature had made the lower part of women's bodies much to big, wherefore man considered it necessary to use all the means at his disposal to restrain it and decrease its size. Towards the middle of the century the discovery was made that as regards the lower part of the female body Nature had not for some time made it as big as it ought to be. This defect was therefore remedied, and in 1759 and 1760, both old and young women looked as if they were all pregnant. Ten years later the first fashion was again the favourite. No less striking were the revolutions which the breasts and shoulders had to undergo in the different phases of the mode in the eighteenth century. At the beginning of the century it was highly indecent for the flesh to be seen two inches below the neck; in the middle of the century this part was clothed in the most elegant taste, and the greater part of the breast and shoulders exposed to view. A few years later every woman was muffled up to the

[1] G. Hill, *Women in English Life*, Vol. I, p. 307.
[2] Weiss, *loc. cit.*, Vol. II, p. 1274.
[3] W. Alexander, *loc. cit.*, Vol. II, pp. 137-138.

chin, and in the 'seventies breasts and shoulders were
again seen. A satire of the end of the century, which makes
fun most wittily of the rapid changes in the fashion, contains
the following: ' It was recently remarked with astonishment
at Drury Lane, that Lady P——'s dress was more than
a half hour out of fashion[1] '.

The principal reason for these extraordinary variations in
the fashion, which even in France were not observed to the
same extent, was the introduction of the great shops and
fashion bazaars, which as early as the eighteenth century
had developed in London to some extent, other European
towns being a long way behind in this respect. In 1792
von Schütz considers ' the smartening up of the merchants'
stores as an eccentricity of the English nation ', and ' for a
stranger it is such an unusual sight that one can spend
hours looking at it. Behind the high large-paned windows
of the lower floor, the merchant displays his wares, and many
of them are well versed in the art of arranging their shops so
attractively as to tempt many buyers[2] '.

In Cheapside and Charing Cross some of these great
bazaars and shops were in existence as early as the beginning
of the eighteenth century[3]; later, however, Old and New
Bond Street became the centre of the fashion bazaars and
were soon ' written high in the annals of luxury and the
mode ', as ' *promenoirs du caprice et du bon ton* ' and ' *colesé
de coquetterie*'[4].

The frequenting of the larger shops soon became a
necessary part of fashionable life, and as early as the middle
of the eighteenth century a new word was coined, namely
' shopping '. Alexander says: ' " Shopping ", as it is called,
is a fashionable female amusement. Two, three and some-

[1] G. Hill, *loc. cit.*, Vol. II, p. 61.
[2] Von Schütz, *Briefe über London.* Hamburg, 1792. P. 223.
[3] *The Foreigner's Guide*, p. 66.
[4] *Tableau descriptif de Londres*, p. 275.

times more ladies, accompanied by their gallants, make a round of the most celebrated shops and inspect the fashionable goods, without the intention of spending a single sixpence. Having tortured the shop people the whole morning, they return home, either without any notion of their foolishness or, what is worse, without giving a thought to the trouble and importunity they have caused in consequence of it[1].' The daily shopping was as important a fashionable occupation during the season as was in Paris the daily appearance in a box at the Opera[2]. As a rule these promenades in Bond Street began about 3 or 4 in the afternoon. Jouy divided the visitors, men and women, into three groups. The first makes genuine purchases, the second goes from curiosity and in order to be in the fashion, and the third group does it from pure boredom[3].

Highly typical was the rôle played by the men and women employees in the large fashion shops, amongst which Prichard's and Oakley's were the most celebrated, which rôle is another proof of the close connection between fashion and sex life.

As early as 1765 came the demand for strong, good-looking young men to serve in the ladies' fashion shops, who would create a market through the impression made by their personalities on the world of prominent ladies, and many scandals arose even in those days from this custom[4]. At the end of the century Boettiger says: ' As the female population of this town is not devoid of feeling for a handsome male form and fresh red cheeks, the cunning Bondstreeters look out for well-built, personable and promising shop assistants, with whom a lascivious lady might very well care to exchange a couple of dozen more words than is warranted by her

[1] Alexander, *loc. cit.*, Vol. I, pp. 98-100.
[2] *Tableau descriptif*, p. 273.
[3] Jouy, *L'Hermite de Londres*, Vol. III, p. 7.
[4] Malcolm, *loc. cit.*, Vol. I, p. 358.

business. Here lies the solution of the problem of why
fashionable women folk find it so difficult to tear themselves
away from Bond Street, and spend the whole morning
haggling and bargaining over a headdress, a couple of ells
of ribbon or a pair of shoes. It was pointed out above that
there were also many shop girls in London, of which Bond
Street had a choice supply, but it must not be forgotten
that they were greatly outnumbered by the polite good-
looking young shopmen. The more attractive the shopmen,
the more numerous and faithful the female customers[1].'

The pretty shopgirls and modistes provided a similar
attraction for the men customers. 'Toutes ces jolies mar-
chandes rivalisent entr'elles, pour fixer l'attention des
promeneurs. En achetant des bagatelles, on glisse quelque
propos d'amour; la marchande repond par un doux sourire
ou quelque furtif coup d'œil[2].'

These pretty modistes were often to be seen in the evening
at Ranelagh on the arms of their gallants, and equally often
they trod the steep path of prostitution, in which the male
dandies, who from 11 in the morning till 5 in the evening
idled their time away in the merchants' stores, the sweet
shops, fruit shops, coffee-houses, etc., ' skimming the cream
of fashion, taste and beauty[3]', were only too willing to help
them.

In the second half of the eighteenth century the luxury of
fashion developed to an astounding extent such as was seen
in no other European country. According to Archenholtz
the display in dress was so outrageous, that less thought
was given to the attire than to the pleasure of squandering
money. An everyday night-cap of the Duchess of
Devonshire cost 10 guineas, and the night-dress of the

[1] Boettiger, *London and Paris.* Weimar, 1799. Vol. IV, p. 275.
[2] *Tableau descriptif*, p. 275.
[3] *London and Paris*, Vol. IV, p. 275.

widowed Duchess of Rutland cost 100 guineas. When Colonel L. was obliged to come to an arrangement with his creditors, the account of a hat-maker, amongst others, was presented, who in the short period of seventeen months had supplied hats to the amount of £119[1]. Ladies of rank usually paid 500 guineas or more annually to their dressmakers; in addition, the fashion advisers received their honorarium. Mrs. Abington, the well-known actress, was a celebrated adviser of this sort. She drove round the town, called on certain ladies, and thereby earned £1,500 to £1,600 annually. Her ' tasteful attire on the stage was always studied by the spectators, whereby they could ensure the closest imitation of her style[2] '.

Naturally, this luxury indulged in by ladies who were unable to afford it, frequently led them into bad ways, to adultery and prostitution. They sold their attractions to the highest bidder in order to pay for their costly clothes. Hüttner says: ' For a year I have been engaged in investigating the causes leading to the many adultery trials, and have found that amongst five wives who have parted from their husbands, there are always at least three who through extravagance in dress and lack of means had been tempted, in order to pay their way, to sacrifice to the gold of the seducer that which he, through his personal attractions alone, would never have obtained of them[3].' In the middle and lower classes the same conditions prevailed. ' The wives and daughters of music masters, schoolmasters, tailors and other manual workers dress very little, if at all, differently from ladies of the front rank, and they copy not only the ostentation, but all the fashionable follies of the great[4].'

[1] Archenholtz, *Britische Annalen auf das Jahr* 1788, pp. 412-415.
[2] Archenholtz, *England und Italien*, Vol. I, pp. 165-166.
[3] Hüttner, *loc. cit.*, p. 40.
[4] *Ibid.*, p. 41.

THE GHOST OF MY DEPARTED HUSBAND.

Pl. 26]

Artist unknown

As regards the details of this fashionable luxury, the hairdressing, especially the women's, was one of the worst examples. According to Alexander this was an ancient heritage from Anglo-Saxon times, as the Anglo-Saxon women in their day regarded the coiffure as their greatest personal beauty[1]. After the middle of the eighteenth century the art of hairdressing developed enormously. Alexander declared that it was impossible to enumerate all the incredible varieties of female coiffures in use in his time. They were built up to such a size by the use of the most varied materials, such as wool, ribbons, laces, ostrich feathers, curls, combs, pins, pomades and pastes and false hair, that it was usual, when the owner stood up, for it to form a third of the total height of her body[2]! Often a complete flower or fruit garden decked the head. The actor Garrick made fun of this last fashion when he once, dressed as a woman, appeared on the stage in a coiffure built up of every sort of vegetable, in which the beetroot was particularly conspicuous[3]. Even miniature coaches, ships and animals crowned the 2-ft. high coiffure[4]. Many anecdotes were told of the consequences of this extravagant fashion. Thus it was said of a lady who complained at an evening party of a bad pain in her neck, that it came out that during the drive to the party she had been obliged to bend her head so that her chin rested on her knees, as the height of her head-dress was so much too great for the carriage. Caricatures of that time show ladies in sedan chairs with open tops from which their colossal head-dresses protruded[5].

As these artificial coiffures cost a great deal of time and

[1] Alexander, loc. cit., Vol. II, p. 114.
[2] Ibid., Vol. II, p. 139.
[3] G. Hill, loc. cit., Vol. II, p. 38.
[4] W. M. Cooper, Der Flagellantisimus und die Flagellanten. Dresden, 1899. P. 143.
[5] G. Hill, loc. cit., Vol. II, p. 37.

money, they were, when possible, dressed by the ladies themselves and naturally not taken down at night-time[1]. The result of the same coiffure remaining undisturbed for weeks at a time was that the pomades used went rancid[2], and the most insanitary condition was reached, in fact quite often vermin bred in hair which was not combed out for months on end[3].

In conjunction with the natural hair, the false, i.e., the wigs, played an important part during the whole of the eighteenth century. Georgiana Hill calls these 'the great feature of the dress of the eighteenth century[4]'. In the end they were worn, not only by men, but by women, girls and youths, and even by children of 14 years[5]. A song of the period indicates that the perruque was an indispensable adjunct of the fashionable toilette:

> And now for to dress up my beau with a grace,
> Let a well-frizzled wig be set off from his face,
> With a bag quite in taste from Paris just come,
> That was made and tyed up by Monsieur Frisson,
> With powder[6] quite grey, then his head is complete;
> If dress'd in the fashion; no matter for wit.

In May 1795 a certain Ross, who called himself ' Proprietor of the Ornamental Hair-manufactory', advertised the fact that he had received from Germany, Spain and Italy 300 lb. of glorious long hair, and that it was longer and more beautifully coloured than any that had ever been seen in

---

[1] Traill, *Social England*, Vol. V, p. 356.

[2] G. Hill, *loc. cit.*, Vol. II, p. 44.

[3] *Nocturnal Revels, or the History of the King's Place and other modern Nunneries.* London, 1779. Vol. I, p. 102.

[4] G. Hill, *loc. cit.*, Vol. II, p. 9.

[5] Hüttner, *loc. cit.*, p. 35.

[6] The powder was always perfumed, and the greatest variety of scents was sold for this purpose. G. Hill, *loc. cit.*, Vol. II, pp. 12-13.

England. He invited the ladies to come to his warehouse in Bishopsgate, where they ' would be astonished by his exceptional and tasteful assortment of hair. His chignons were of French hair, the most beautiful the imagination could picture. He had in stock about 1,000 lots, of fifty different lengths, including twenty different kinds of chestnut brown alone, and an almost endless assortment of other colours, such as black-grey, red, etc.' The prices of these chignons varied from 5 shillings to 5 guineas[1].

This mania for wigs produced a special class of thief, the wig thief, who frequented the streets of London in great numbers, and with much skill snatched their wigs from the heads of the passers-by, thereafter selling them[2].

As on their hair, great store was also set by the fair sex on their millinery. Archenholtz remarks: ' One of the chief adornments of women, however, is their hats, which are now richly trimmed with feathers and ribbons. Without these, no one, either of the upper or the lower classes, dare set her foot outside the door. No beggar woman even will be seen without a hat. They have their own way of putting them on which the ladies of other countries do not seem able to imitate successfully, and thus the effect of the hats is not so striking on them. This peculiar effect caused Linguet to say that had Homer known these attractive adornments, he would have given Venus an English hat in addition to her girdle![3] '

The most celebrated of these hats was, in conjunction with the ' mob ' and the ' Fly-cap à la Thérèse ', the ' Ranelagh-mob ', a hat which was worn by the *demi-mondaines* at Ranelagh. It consisted almost entirely of gauze which was

[1] Archenholtz, *British Annals*, Vol. XVI (1795), pp. 182-183. See also G. Hill, *loc. cit.*, Vol. II, pp. 13-14 *re* the hair merchant.

[2] Hill, *loc. cit.*, Vol. II, pp. 22-24.

[3] Archenholtz, *England und Italien*, Vol. III, p. 73.

twisted round the head, crossed under the chin, and fastened at the back of the head with the ends left hanging[1].

The fashionable extravagances of that period were also uniquely displayed in the clothing of the female bosom. On the use of the corset, George Forster remarks[2]: ' Another horror of the present-day clothing is the corset, which is worn as generally as ever, and now on account of the frightful high gauze bodices they make an excrescence of the bust, which at least does protect this delicate part from injury, but does not tend to the beautifying of the female form.' Worse than this were the artificial bosoms which were seen in London, and worn chiefly in the latter years of the eighteenth century[3]. ' It has recently been the fashion amongst women of the world to appear half naked, and to display the hidden charms of their bodies, and quite a number of these fashionable females who have no natural bosom to display, take refuge in artificial ones made of wax, so that they shall not be given away by the mode.' Madame Thiknesse relates in her newly-published morality novel *The School for Fashion*, Part II, p. 119, a true story in this connection:

' A young lady who was to be married in a few days time to a worthy man, was with her betrothed at the house of a lady of position. As the company was very numerous, the air became stiflingly hot, and caused the unfortunate girl to faint suddenly. The whole room was at once in a turmoil; they unfastened the bodice of her dress, in order to give her more air, and all at once two of the daintiest wax breasts fell to the ground from out of the gauze material of the bodice. The ladies screamed, and I do not doubt were secretly delighted at this public discovery. It can be imagined

---

[1] Traill, *Social England*, Vol. V, p. 356. Hill, *loc. cit.*, Vol. II, p. 55.
[2] *George Forster's Letters and Diaries on his Journeys on the Lower Rhine, in England and in France in the early part of* 1790. Published by Albert Leitzmann, Halle, 1893. P. 234.
[3] Weiss, *loc. cit.*, Vol. II, p. 1278.

better than described, how great was the astonishment of the
poor deceived bridegroom, who had doubtless often been
bewitched by the charms of the alabaster bosom of his
beloved. His love for the deceitful woman at once changed
to the deepest scorn; the unfortunate girl was the object of
general ridicule, and she lost at once and the same time
her lover, admiration and the esteem of her acquaintances[1].'

Further, in the course of the eighteenth century, the
peculiar fashion of false stomachs, ' pads ' or ' paddies ',
was revived. These were used for a time at the end of the
'fifties, and were seen again in the 'nineties. Archenholtz
says: ' This was the most senseless invention, against all
decency and delicacy, and disfiguring the female body;
it caused a deformity which is only seen in the female sex
during pregnancy. These decorations were called pads, and
the small ones paddies; they were usually made of tin,
and were therefore called " tin pinafores ". These artificial
stomachs were in great favour, particularly with unmarried
women, which caused the wits to say that a revolution had
taken place amongst the signs of the Zodiac, and the Twins
had come too near Virgo. But above all, these pads were the
butt of jokers, who used them unmercifully, and their use
soon had to be discontinued. Such a fashion was also in too
bad taste to last long. It was in existence in London in
February 1793, but by the end of the spring it was over in
England and went to Dublin, where it was welcomed by the
women. During the migration which took place as a result
of the French war, it was taken to Germany by refugee
English women, but was not copied there[2].'

If this artificial enlargement of the front of the lower part
of the body resembled genuine pregnancy, the enlargement

[1] Hüttner, *loc. cit.*, pp. 33-34.
[2] Archenholtz, *British Annals*, Vol. XI, pp. 240-241. On false
stomachs in France and Spain see also I. Bloch, *loc. cit.*, Part I, p. 155.

of the hips and buttocks by hooped skirts and dress-improvers certainly had as their object the arousing of some kind of perverse sexual instinct. ' How can a decent woman obtrude that vulgar part of her anatomy upon the eye? ' Wollstonecraft inquires indignantly[1], well knowing that the female posterior has a very powerful attraction for certain kinds of debauchees, and that the accentuation of this part draws the notice also of normal people to it, and must call forth perverse associations of ideas.

A monstrous enlargement of the natural outline of the pelvic region is also involved in the use of the hooped skirt. By its means the eye is drawn as it were to the hidden charms. The ' hooped petticoat ' was the subject of many satires and comic songs by the people—a song of 1721 tells with much humour of the tragi-comic fate of one such crinoline-adorned lady of fashion:

An elderly lady whose bulky squat figure
By hoop and white damask was rendered much bigger,
Without hood and bare-necked to the Park did repair,
To show her new clothes and to take the fresh air;
Her shape, her attire, raised a shout and loud laughter;
Away waddles Madam; the mob hurries after.
Quoth a wag, then observing the noisy crowd follow,
As she came with a hoop she is gone with a hollo[2].

After 1794 and before the time of the French Directorate the so-called ' fashion of nakedness ' was introduced in England, entailing the greatest possible exposure of the body[3]. Above, the bosom and neck and below, the legs were visible. Later, Lady Campbell brought in the still more

[1] Mary Wollstonecraft, *Recovery of the Rights of Women*. See also Addison's remarks on the hooped skirt in No. 80 of the *Spectator*.

[2] J. P. Malcolm, *Anecdotes of the Manners and Customs of London during the Eighteenth Century*. London, 1810. Vol. II, p. 323.

[3] Archenholtz, *Annalen*, Vol. XIII, p. 437.

revealing mode which Madame Tallien of Parisian society under the Directorate had ostracised, and which consisted of a thin transparent muslin veil as the sole clothing of the body[1]. ' You can see the outlines of her limbs quite clearly through the cloud of muslin veiling which surrounds her. Some sweet fools who have the reputation of good taste, are enchanted at the sight of the half-covered charms, and admire aloud these naked graces, lifting their round fleshy shoulders in fiery rhapsody, praising the treacherous witchery of her full dainty bust and the symmetry of her limbs; and you will see how other hateful beauties, believing that they, in order to have grace imputed to them and to attract universal admiration, have only to change their thick clothes for a muslin cloud, will in a few days fill the fashionable promenades of New Bond Street, Pall Mall, Hyde Park, Kensington Gardens, etc., with crowds of half-naked figures. When a cutting north-east wind blows, cold, illness and death are brought with the sharp air to the thinly-clothed bodies; the beauties shiver with cold, but fashion will have it not otherwise, and doctors, chemists and grave-diggers reckon on a good harvest[2].' There were numerous anecdotes and jokes on the subject of this fashion, which were chiefly put into the mouths of Quakers.

Highly remarkable and specifically English was the custom of the women to wear footgear with special devices to keep them from the dirt of the streets. Usually these were round iron contraptions, which were fastened to the shoes with straps, and taken off on entering the house[3]. This unique custom probably originated with the use of shoes made of silk and other material by the upper and middle classes, when only servants wore leather shoes[4].

[1] Archenholtz, *Annalen*, Vol. XIX, p. 292.
[2] Hüttner, *loc. cit.*, pp. 32-33.
[3] Archenholtz, *England*, Vol. III, p. 72. Schütz, *loc. cit.*, p. 222.
[4] Archenholtz, *ibid.*

Later the round contraptions were replaced by clogs with iron nails. Bornemann[1] describes very vividly the awkward, ungraceful gait of the women shod with these clogs. ' It is, as usual, a little muddy in the streets. Women and girls have therefore put on their clogs—wooden sandals secured with metal bars three inches long, fastened underneath to steel rings. On soft ground the footprint looks like that of an unknown animal with sharp uncut claws. Thus do the women go about, young and old, taking long careful steps (three feet must be the normal length) and quickly passing on their way over the mud, with a "Klipp-Klapp", which sounds like a smith shoeing a horse. The muddy places over and the ground cleaner, the wooden slippers are quickly taken off and carried daintily in the hand till it becomes necessary to put them on again. It must need a great deal of practice to walk easily in these clogs, and must have been learned in early youth, as even the youngest children wear them.'

Ladies in the highest circles in Society naturally did not make use of these very primitive means of protecting themselves from the mud, but used carrying-chairs (Sedan chairs), the number of which in 1795 was extraordinarily great, ' one more of the hundred evidences of the increasing luxury and great softness of the British '. In the fifteenth century only sick people were allowed to make use of carrying-chairs[2].

One indispensable item of the fashionable English lady's toilette in the eighteenth century was the fan.

The history of the fan in England goes back to the fourteenth century, when it first appeared under Richard II, and became very popular later in the upper classes of society, particularly under Henry VIII. Elizabeth was also very

---

[1] Bornemann, *loc. cit.*, pp. 49-50.
[2] Archenholtz, *Annalen*, Vol. XVI, pp. 176-177.

fond of the fan, and possessed one which was studded with diamonds. In the time of Shakespeare fans cost anything up to £40. In the eighteenth century the fan reached its apotheosis—every lady carried one. It became a general means of describing and depicting subjects connected with politics, the theatre, literature, art, etc.; these were all represented in the inscriptions and drawings on the fans, which were brought out according to the time of day and the occasion[1]. A young girl of the period writes in her reminiscences: ' Then I also had fans given me! One is considered enough now for a young girl, but we use fans like the Japanese, and I had one for the street, one for the morning, one for the evening and one for great occasions[2].' This extravagance in fans is referred to by a poet in the following verse:

Neat lady that is fresh and fair,
Who never knew what belonged to good housekeeping care,
But buys several fans to play with the wanton air,
And seventeen or eighteen dressings of other women's hair.

Gray wrote a celebrated poem about the fan. Many fans were inscribed or painted. When John Gay's satirical-lascivious *Beggar's Opera* appeared, prominent ladies used fans on which the airs were printed[3]. A very unusual fan had the ' history of England in a nutshell. It was divided into compartments and presented in small pictures the principal events of the last thousand years. The inventor promised that the study of history would be much facilitated

[1] G. Hill, *loc. cit.*, Vol. II, p. 52.
[2] Cooper, *loc. cit.*, p. 143.
[3] J. G. Th. Grasse, *Handbook of General History of Literature.* Leipzig, 1850. Vol. III, p. 400.

by this fan. Another fan had the likenesses of the Prince and Princess of Wales, surrounded with forty most astonishing caricatures, charades, etc[1].' Worse, however, were the obscene pictures with which the fans of many ladies were decorated, the shameless nature of which gave one lady the difficult choice—as a correspondent in a fashion journal wrote— as to whether she should blush in front of or behind her fan[2].

After the fourteenth century riding and driving became common amongst English ladies, and they have remained to this day one of the integral parts of a fashionable woman's life. Archenholtz remarks: 'Englishwomen have many peculiar customs, amongst these being their passion for riding. Thousands enjoy this pleasure daily in good weather wearing Amazon dress and sitting astride. The custom was introduced by Queen Ann, wife of Richard II, and since then it has become a custom of the country[3].' Schütz describes it as an astonishing sight at the end of the eighteenth century ' to see an English carriage containing two women, one holding the whip whilst the other manages the mettle-some steeds with grace and skill[4]'. In later times these customs provided rich material for the chroniclers of scandals, as intimate relations between the riders and their grooms often resulted from the daily ' Rotten Row ', ending frequently in an elopement. Rémo found in the newspapers one month no fewer than seventeen cases of this sort[5].

The eighteenth century and the first ten years of the nineteenth were golden days for male dandyism in England. This country is really the birthplace of true unadulterated

[1] Archenholtz, *Annalen*, Vol. XVI, p. 181.
[2] Hill, *loc. cit.*, Vol. II, p. 92. Cf. also the choice work of Lady Schreiber, *Fans and Fanleaves*, London, 1890. Addison, in the *Spectator*, No. 64, is very satirically illuminating on the rôle of the fan in love.
[3] Archenholtz, *England*, Vol. III, p. 73.
[4] Schütz, *loc. cit.*, pp. 90-91.
[5] Rémo, *loc. cit.*, p. 76.

dandyism. Here, where individual eccentricities are more
conspicuous than elsewhere, and where at the same time
boundless value is placed on external appearances, is the
best possible ground for the development of that remarkable
species of man, whose whole being was centred in his attire.
' Paraître, c'est être pour les dandys, comme pour les
femmes ', says Barbey d'Aurevilly of the English dandies[1].
But it must be borne in mind that the external appearance
referred to was not simply the ludicrous ostentation in
dress of the average fop, but that of the true English dandy
as he appeared at the beginning of the nineteenth century in
particular. His aim and object was to make his outward
appearance and his clothing as unique as possible and to set
himself in opposition as far as he could to the conventions of
fashion, thereby arousing the admiration of the crowd.

> Thus Beaux, in person and in mind,
> Excelled by those they leave behind,
> On, through the world undaunted, press,
> Backed by the Mighty Power of Dress;
> While folks less confident than they
> Stare, in much wonder—and give way[2].

In no country were so many nicknames and *termini
technici* used to designate the dandies as in England. I
know only the commonest: Beau, Buck, Maccaroni, Jessamy,
Pretty Fellow, Blood, Exquisite, Tulip, Fop, Swell, Spark,
Dandy.

The original dandies were the ' Beaux ', who celebrated
their triumph under Charles II and Queen Anne[3]. To them
belonged amongst others Sir George Hevett Wilson, the

[1] J. Barbey d'Aurevilly, *Du dandysm et de Georges Brummell*. Paris, 1862.
P. 124.

[2] Pierce Egan, *Life in London*. Edited by Camden [Hotton. New
edition. London, 1900. Pp. 176-177.

[3] Cf. the article ' Beaux ' in Misson de Valbourg's *Mémoires et
observations faites par un voyageur en Angleterre*. Haag, 1698. Pp. 28-29.

handsome Fielding (died 1712), Colonel Edgeworth, the poet Steele, and last the celebrated Nash who was called a beau by three generations, as he was born under Charles II, died under George III and now, as the poet Austey in his *New Bath Guide* says, is delighting the followers of Proserpine as a dandy in the underworld[1]. Addison left a satirical monument to this oldest generation of dandies in his well-known analysis of the brains of a dandy in the *Spectator*[2].

After the middle of the eighteenth century came the ' Maccaronis ' or ' Jessamies '[3]. The first name was given them on account of their love for the Italian dish which they enjoyed at Almack's. They founded a club which, as Horace Walpole wrote to Lord Hertford on the 6th February 1764, ' consists of much-travelled young men who wear long curls and carry lorgnettes[4] '. In 1772 they swaggered about in very tight gaily-checked jackets, waistcoats and breeches, with enormously large knots of false hair at the back of the head, ridiculously small miniature hats on top of them, red heels to their shoes, and in their hands prodigious walking sticks with long tassels hanging from them[5].

In general, men's dress in the eighteenth century underwent the same frequent changes as the women's. Every year brought a fresh mode, often radically different from that of the preceding year. The *toilettes* of the men were as much observed and criticised as those of the women.

' What! he talked to you in such an impossible coat? What a shabby oaf! ' says Evelina's dance partner in Miss Burney's *Evelina* to her on her refusing another man and sending

[1] Barbey d'Aurevilly, *loc. cit.*, pp. 45-47. Georgiana Hill, *loc. cit.*, Vol. II, p. 111.

[2] Cf. Taine, *loc. cit.*, Vol. II, p. 307.

[3] Traill, *loc. cit.*, Vol. V, p. 355.

[4] Henry B. Wheatley, *London Past and Present*. London, 1891. Vol. II, p. 453.

[5] Baker, *Streets of London*, p. 324. Leigh Hunt. *The Old Court Suburb*. Third edition. London, no date. P. 292.

him away. The author of a very rare work, *Thoughts on Gallantry, Love and Marriage*, says of the effeminate generation of men in 1750: ' There is yet another type of man who should be banned from the company of any fine-feeling woman. They are the " Fops " and " Fribbles " the " Petits Maîtres " of our time. These pretty fellows go about covered in powder, essence and perfume. What sort of a fate, I ask, could a well-bred woman reasonably expect from intimate association with a man of this contemptible breed? His own precious person is the only object of his care and anxiety; every desire of his is centred in it, and no thought of his is allowed to wander from his own ego. Here, ladies, is a subject for your wit and pleasantries; here is a target for your satire. A " Fop " is a man in a mask, and as such deserves your greatest contempt. But alas! how far from contempt is your usual treatment of these gilded playthings, these glittering nonentities? Instead of despising these " things of silk " you serve their vanity with praise and admiration[1].'

This exaggerated luxury in dress naturally led to softening and effeminacy of the men, and to the production of the ' pretty fellows ' and the ' Exquisites ' type, which in the eighteenth century were so scourged and made fun of by both English and foreign writers. Archenholtz says: ' The men resemble the women now more than in any other period. They wear their hair long and curled, sprinkled with flour and smelling of scent; they thicken and lengthen it with borrowed curls; they reject the buckles which should be worn on shoes and knee-breeches as unsuitable, and use in their place silk ribbons; the sword also is worn only where it looks most graceful, comfort is taken no account of; they cover their hands with gloves; their teeth are not only cleaned but whitened and their faces are painted. The men

---

[1] *Thoughts on Gallantry, Love and Marriage.* London, 1754. Pp. 24-25.

ride and drive whenever they can, and so their feet are unaccustomed to walking, they seek soft foods, comfortable cushions and soft beds. In order that they shall not be outdone by the women as regards dress, fine linen and laces are in daily use; they wear watches and rings and fill their pockets with trifles.' According to Hüttner, men often only differed from the women in the coverings of the legs. These dandies were anxious as a woman to set off their ' physical charms 'in every possible way, and this was done in the most repulsive manner at balls and masquerades, at the opera and concerts[1]. No wonder that these effeminate ' Exquisites ' suffered pains and sorrows which should be peculiarly feminine. Thus, one fine young man had a regular fainting fit in Bond Street on one occasion, and had to be carried into a shop. There it came out that the young man was too tightly corseted![2]

Even the flesh-coloured tights of the ballet-dancers were adopted by men. Schütz says[3]: ' Many endeavour to arouse interest by making the most ludicrous caricatures of themselves. Thus I saw some Englishmen walking up and down in St. James's Park in flesh-coloured breeches and stockings. The suits were purposely made exceptionally tight so as to give more effect to the flesh colouring. This object was attained, as from a distance I really thought some inmates of Bedlam had escaped from their keepers and had put on only shoes and coats, leaving the rest of their bodies uncovered. I should never have believed that so many dandies existed amongst the serious people of England. You can easily imagine how great was my astonishment at seeing men who, instead of sticks, carried small thick cudgels in their hands which, as they were no more than

[1] Hüttner, *loc. cit.*, pp. 78 and 82.
[2] John Bee, *Sportsman's Slang*, etc. London, 1825. P. 22.
[3] Schütz, *loc. cit.*, pp. 86-87.

half a yard long, could not be used for walking. By many, these sticks were held in the hand in the same way that women hold fans.'

Other dandies went around with coiffures in the feminine manner, wore large nosegays on their breasts, patches on their painted faces, painted their eyebrows, grinned like apes, spoke an affected French-Italian-English jargon, and in winter stuck their hands in large muffs. These last were carried by men in the middle of the eighteenth century as frequently as in the time of the Restoration. ' I am sending you a beautiful little muff which you can stick your hands into' wrote Walpole at Christmas 1764 to George Montague[1].

The curling of men's hair was a very usual custom in the eighteenth century. In the barber's shops four people were often occupied with one head of hair. ' One of them arranged the coiffure and the other three each took a part of the head, and in addition, a fifth handed the hot irons[2].' Burke called the powdered heads of the dandies by the tasteful name of ' Guinea-pigs '.

Amongst fashionable English men of the world the wearing of spectacles and eyeglasses was very popular, and was much more general than it is to-day, as it was not confined to a genuine physical need.

As to the professional classes, theology and medicine contributed a large contingent to the ranks of the dandies and gallants. ' The enormous elongated wig, the stick with its great shapeless gilt knob, the satin coat and the haughty mien of the doctor are no more to be seen, as the new disciples of Aesculapius appear in the fashionable curled coiffure, dressed in the latest mode and carrying walking sticks, and by their gallant manners they try to charm their patients. The theologians used to wear a mountain of hair on their

[1] H. B. Baker, *Stories of the Streets of London*, p. 324.
[2] Schütz, *loc. cit.*, p. 211.

heads, had black robes, serious looks and above all a worthy appearance; now they have a double row of curled locks, well covered with pomade and powder, leather breeches, boots, laces at their breast, very fine handkerchiefs and diamond rings[1].'

The artificial breasts and stomachs in the women had their counterpart in the false calves worn by the men[2]. Great care was also taken over the footwear. The calling of shoe-black enjoyed great prosperity, as many dandies had their shoes cleaned more than ten times a day[3].

The very pronounced habits of cleanliness of the English necessitated a daily change of underclothing, and only the lower classes changed these weekly[4]. But there actually existed in this country of eccentrics a ' Club of the Dirty Shirts ', the members of which opposed any necessity for cleanliness. It had underground premises in Holborn. On the invitation cards sent to the members was the postscript: ' Visiting strangers without shirts will not be admitted[5].'

Under the aegis of the Prince of Wales, later King George IV, English dandyism at the beginning of the nineteenth century reached its peak[6], at which time this prince and his friend George Brummell played the principal rôles.

The personality of the ' First Gentleman of Europe ', as George IV (1762-1830) liked to call himself, was in Thackeray's words nothing more than a coat, a wig, an affected laugh, in fact nothing but a mask. ' But this George himself, what was he? I look through his whole life and

[1] Archenholtz, *Annalen*, Vol. I, pp. 420-421.
[2] *Sérails de Londres*, p. 175.
[3] Schütz, *loc. cit.*, p. 211.
[4] Archenholtz, *England*, Vol. III, p. 141.
[5] Archenholtz, *Annalen*, Vol. I, p. 437.
[6] The word ' dandy,' according to Bee (*Sportsman's Slang* (London, 1825), p. 63), was first introduced in the year 1816, when Brummell played his rôle of the admired model for all dandies; the bodily counterpart of the word had, however, long been in existence.

recognise but a bow and a grin. I try to take him to pieces, and find silk stockings, padding, stays, a coat with frogs and a fur collar, a star and blue ribbon, a handkerchief prodigiously scented, one of Truefitt's nutty brown wigs reeking with oil, a set of teeth, a huge black stock, underwaistcoats, more underwaistcoats, and then nothing[1].' 'He celebrated his entrance into the great world by the marvellous discovery of a new shoe-buckle, an inch long and five inches wide, which covered most of the foot and reached the ground on each side. At the first Court Ball he wore a coat of shining pink silk with white ruffles, his white silk waistcoat was embroidered in various-coloured foil and adorned with a profusion of French paste: his hat was ornamented with two rows of steel beads, five thousand in number, with a button and loop of the same metal, and cocked in a new military style[2]. After 1784 the residence of this royal fop was Carlton House, the 'Focus of the Dandies' of the best society in London[3]. Amongst these, George Brummell, at the beginning of the eighteenth century, acquired a standing on an equality with the King-to-be, and played the doubtful rôle of ' dandy ' *par excellence*.

As is well known these peculiar fashions found an enthusiastic, admiring and inspired biographer in the intellectual French writer Jules Barbey d'Aurevilly, who was himself a dandy, and whose book *Du Dandysme et de Georges Brummell* (Paris, 1862) was a unique glorification of dandyism.

Brummell (born 1778) was in fact a very remarkable specimen of the genus dandy, as the following short sketch of the way and the course of his life shows.

The secret of his ' unforgettable attire ' lay, according to Georgiana Hill, in the astonishing care which he gave to the

[1] Thackeray, *The Four Georges*, pp. 113-114.
[2] *Ibid.*, p. 119.
[3] Baker, *Streets of London*, p. 325.

smallest detail. The *toilette* of a gentleman in those days was in any case a long business, but Brummell excelled everyone in this particular. Every morning he allowed at least three hours for his *toilette*. He had three hairdressers, for the front, back and sides of his head. The *clou* of his attire was his cravat, of which he had the pattern designed by a painter. If the first one was not well tied, the cravat was thrown away and another one taken. He wore three cravats daily, the last being taken off after he left the opera or the theatre, and before he had supper or played cards. In addition he changed his shirt three times a day! His washing bill was naturally colossal[1].

Brummell introduced to dandyism the principle that that which is most distinguished is at the same time the simplest. He avoided in his attire everything exaggerated or too brightly coloured, all the glaring extravagance of the fops of the eighteenth century. For this reason the use of too much perfume, pomade or oil was strongly opposed by him[2].

After the example of Brummell, the real dandy had to avoid anything ridiculous or exaggerated in his attire and in his bearing, but at the same time, by his simple exterior, to draw attention to himself. That Brummell himself succeeded in the last to such an extent was due to a unique mixture of intelligence, irony, impertinence, indolence and grace in his personality, which all the world admired[3].

From 1799 to 1814 there was no party, no gathering of society in London at which the presence of the celebrated dandy was not regarded as a triumph, his absence as a disaster. His name appeared in the papers at the head of all lists of guests. At Almack's balls, at Ascot races, he played the principal rôle. Once he himself organised in

[1] G. Hill, *loc. cit.*, Vol. II, pp. 115-117.
[2] *Ibid.*
[3] Barbey d'Aurevilly, *loc. cit.*, pp. 87, 98.

Hanover Square a party which was famous as the ' Dandies' Ball[1] '. He was Chairman of the Watier Club, of which Lord Byron was a member. He was the life and soul of the parties at Carlton House, and for a long time the bosom friend of the Prince of Wales, who recognised him alone as his equal in the domain of the *toilette*. He also knew how to captivate the great intellectuals of his time. The poet Moore sang of him, Byron often mentioned him; Barbey d'Aurevilly says that the personality of Brummell can be recognised in the latter's drawing of ' Don Juan ', as this poem had quite the ' Tone of the Dandy[2] '. The secret of Brummell's influence rested to a great extent on the circumstance that he did not make himself cheap, and in society was regarded so to speak as a passing meteor, as he never stayed anywhere long. He established as a principle of dandyism that one should only stay long enough to make an obvious impression and then leave quickly. For him, effect was only a question of time[3].

The women made a god of Brummell; the famous courtesan, Henrietta Wilson, speaks passionately of him in her memoirs[4].

The end of this celebrated dandy was sad. He had to leave England in May 1816 as he had ruined himself by gambling, and his former friend the Prince Regent (George IV) refused him all help. In Calais he was entertained for some time by friends, and his esteem as a god of fashion was undiminished. Many prominent Englishmen made pilgrimages to him to ask his advice on matters of dress, but later he was quite forgotten. King William IV appointed him Consul at Caen in 1830, of which position he was later deprived. Finally he strutted about the streets of Caen,

[1] See the *Daily Telegraph* of 19th July 1900.
[2] Barbey d'Aurevilly, *loc. cit.*, pp. 104, 107.
[3] *Ibid.*, p. 71.
[4] *Ibid.*, p. 73.

quite out of his mind, a sad ruin of his former splendour, but still trying to keep up a certain elegance; Barbey d'Aurevilly himself saw him there[1]. He died in the 'thirties[2].

It must, however, be recognised that it was this original dandyism in England which led to a general simplification of men's attire. At the beginning of the nineteenth century the English mode was almost entirely free of the all-powerful influence of the French, and had reached a much greater independence.

Thus the modern male attire of ceremony, the frock-coat[3], is essentially of English origin; at the same time European men of fashion regard London as at least as much the source of their inspiration as Paris. The former Prince of Wales, later King Edward VII, played a great part in this connection. Sombart remarked: ' The centre of fashion for men is the *entourage* of the Prince of Wales, and its authority as regards the shape of hats and the colours of ties reaches far beyond the frontiers of the two Indies[4].'

In the nineteenth century female dress still generally remained in somewhat greater dependence on the French. Bornemann mentions in 1818 the ' balloon-like dress, which in order that it should not escape notice, had a bunch of tulle planted in the middle of it[5] '. When the Empress Eugenie again brought in the crinoline, England was the first country to copy this barbaric fashion, and even when, after 1880, the ' Aesthetic ' and ' Dress reform movements ' set to work energetically to suppress the all too great tendency to copy the French extravagance, even they could not

[1] Barbey d'Aurevilly, *loc. cit.*, pp. 126, 134, 138, 154.
[2] Compare also the important description of Brummell in Calais in the Prince von Pückler-Muskau's *Letters of a Dead Man*. Munich, 1830. Vol. II, pp. 313-320.
[3] Traill, *loc. cit.*, Vol. VI, p. 95.
[4] W. Sombart, *Wirtschaft und Mode*. Wiesbaden, 1902. P. 19.
[5] Bornemann, *loc. cit.*, p. 51.

prevent the importation of the most incredible vagaries of fashion, such as, for instance, the so-called 'breast-rings'.

In the English periodical *Society* of the year 1899 there are some very remarkable details with regard to this refined fashion; these were also reported in a German book which quoted an extract from this paper[1]. They actually consisted in the piercing of the nipples and the insertion in the holes of gold rings set with brilliants. The object of this is obviously the same as the piercing of the lips and noses of savages, a purely erotic one, as by the decoration of such a significant part of the body attention is of course drawn to it when *décolletée* is worn. The breast ring competed in this connection with the corset. An Oxford Street *modiste* revealed in a letter to the publisher of *Society* some quite extraordinary details about the origin of the fashion of the breast ring. She writes: ' For a long time I could not understand why I should consent to such a painful operation without sufficient reason. I soon however came to the conclusion that many ladies are ready to bear the passing pain for the sake of love; I found that the breasts of the ladies who wore rings were incomparably rounder and fuller developed than those who did not. My doubts were now at an end. Although I am not naturally poorly-built, I had always wished for a really full voluptuous bust with a slim figure, partly because I liked it for its own sake, and also because it would be very advantageous to me in my profession. So I had my nipples pierced, and when the wounds were healed, I had rings inserted. They are naturally not especially costly or jewelled, but I am already quite satisfied with my shiny gold ones. With regard to the experience of wearing these rings, I can only say that they are not in the least uncomfortable or painful. On the contrary, the

[1] E. Neumann, *John Bull beim Erziehen.* New edition, Vol. II. Dresden, 1901. Pp. 15 *et seq.*, 24, 29 *et seq.*, 55 *et seq.*, 84 *et seq.*

slight rubbing and slipping of the rings causes in me an extremely agreeable titillating feeling, and all my colleagues to whom I have spoken on this subject have confirmed my opinion[1] '.

The custom, or rather bad custom, of the breast ring must have been in favour with the early Egyptians. Further, they are mentioned in the old Italian romances.

The breast rings are mentioned in old Spanish works as instruments of torture. The heretic girls and women had their nipples or the whole breast bored through with hot pins or nails and iron rings were inserted. The sexual element is obvious in the following sadistical description: ' The young girls, from the age of tender children to twenty years, are fastened by the rings to the whipping post naked as they were born, and whipped with rods.' The Turkish soldiers were supposed to have committed similar atrocities on the Armenian girls.

The fashion of the breast ring is common with the women of Tunis and in the Greek Archipelago. The Abyssinian women enlarge their breasts in a somewhat similar manner. They allow these to be stung by bees until they are swollen to three or four times their natural size[2].

In 1898 a Bond Street jeweller is supposed to have performed the nipple-boring operation on forty English ladies and young girls[3]; the Oxford Street *modiste* also confirmed the spread of this bad custom amongst the fashionable women of London[4].

Many ladies, instead of the rings, had small chains fastened from breast to breast. Thus a celebrated actress of the Gaiety Theatre wore a pearl chain with a bow at each end[5].

---

[1] Neumann, *loc. cit.*, Vol. II, p. 56.
[2] *Ibid.*, Vol. II, pp. 16, 30, 85-87.
[3] *Ibid.*, p. 25.   [4] *Ibid.*, p. 55.   [5] *Ibid.*, pp. 16 and 25.

CHAPTER XVII

EROTIC LITERATURE

THE conception of the erotic in literature is of the greatest importance in gauging the character of a people and in forming an opinion of a given period in its cultural development. As Georg Brandes has said: ' of all the emotions treated by literature, sexual emotion plays the most significant rôle. How it is conceived and represented is of the utmost importance for the understanding of the spirit of the age. The depth, kind and warmth of the emotional life of an entire age can be measured by the conception of the erotic, as though this were a precision instrument[1] '.

This general dictum on the importance of the erotic element in the prose and poetry of peoples may best be tested for correctness by examining its most blatant expression in erotic literature in the narrower sense. Indeed, the character of a people is very clearly reflected in its erotic literature. The extreme excrescences of the English national character, harshness, coarseness and eccentricity, obtrude even more in the erotic literature proper than in the ordinary literature of fiction and poetry, which also reveal the nature, depth, sentimentality and melancholy of the English national spirit.

Thus Boileau's statement, ' Les Anglais dans les mots bravent l'honnêteté ', only applies in the absolute sense

[1] Georg Brandes, *Die Hauptströmungen der Literatur des* 19 *Jahrhunderts* (The Main Streams of Nineteenth Century Literature). Sixth Edition. Leipzig, 1899. Vol. III, p. 230.

to obscene erotic literature, of which Pisanus Fraxi, by far the most thorough and competent observer, says: 'The English erotic stories are pitiable products from the literary point of view, which alone could excuse them in the eyes of cultured people. It seems that the English language is unsuited for the presentation of erotic themes, and that a delicate treatment is impossible in that tongue.'

He ascribes the repulsive character of English erotic literature partly to the fact that whereas in France, Italy and even in Germany, prominent thinkers and authors have not avoided the erotic field proper, in England Venus and Priapus have only been served in the literary sense by the ' veriest Grubbians ', the majority of whom were persons without any literary or artistic talent. The greatest name England can boast of is that of John Cleland, and even he is only a star of small magnitude as compared with his witty French contemporaries[1].

The position became still worse when, during the nine-teenth century, the influence of foreign, and particularly French, erotic literature had made itself felt. All the un-naturalness and subtlety of the French was taken over, but without the French delicacy of expression and form. Thus the later English erotic literature presents a repulsive mixture of degrading coarseness and crude abnormality. ' If ', says Fraxi, ' we compare stories like *Memoirs of a Woman of Pleasure* and *Memoirs of a Coxcomb* with the *Romance of Lust*, the *Experimental Lecture*, or *Lascivious Gems*, we shall find that in the first named two books the characters, scenes and incidents are natural, the style not excessively coarse, whereas in the last three works the characters and events are impossible, and the style filthy and common. Cleland's characters—Fanny Hill, the cox-

---

[1] See P. Fraxi, *Index*, p. xviii.

comb, and the procuresses and libertines with whom they meet—are described from real life, and they only do what, in the very natural circumstances into which they have been placed, they could and would have done, whereas the characters in the last named three books are the unreal products of a crazy fantasy, whose actions are either improbable or impossible[1] '.

On the whole, the erotic vocabulary of the English is rather extensive, at all events more extensive than that of the Germans, though it lacks the variety and fine shades of meaning of the obscene argot of the French. John Bee, in his *Sportsman's Slang* (London, 1825), collected numerous words of this type. The English dictionary compiled by Captain Grose is more complete. It is called *A Classical Dictionary of the Vulgar Tongue* (by Captain A. Grose, F.S.A.), London, 1785. A second edition, considerably enlarged by Pierce Egan, appeared in London in 1823.

It is undeniable that the paraphrases of sexual matters sometimes reveal a crude and original humour which, coarse and uncouth though it is, nevertheless employs the most striking similes. The numerous similes and the renaming of obscene things with other names have added a considerable fund of ambiguous expressions to the English language, which the foreigner must learn if he wishes to be sure of avoiding serious social blunders.

A further peculiarity of English erotic literature, which is not present in that of other nations, are the promising, extraordinarily long and highly spiced titles. It may safely be said that the longer the titles, the more worthless are the contents. Numerous small brochures of only a few pages, mostly in the 'fifties and 'sixties of the nineteenth century, bore on their title-pages such cunningly worded and long-winded indications of the contents, no doubt with a view to

[1] P. Fraxi, *Catena*, p. xlii.

attracting purchasers. Here is a very characteristic example of these long-winded titles:

Yokel's Preceptor: or, More Sprees in London, being a regular and Curious Show-Up of all the Rigs and Doings of the Flash Cribs in this Great Metropolis; Particularly Goodered's Saloon—Gambling Houses—Female Hells and Introducing Houses! The Most Famous Flash and Cock-and-Hen Clubs, etc. A full Description of the Most Famous Stone-Thumpers, particularly Elephant Bet, Finnikin Fan, the Yarmouth Bloater, Flabby Poll, Fair Eliza, the Black Mott, etc.: And it may be fairly styled Every Swankey's Book, or the Green-horn's Guide Thro' Little Lunnon. Intended as a Warning to the Inexperienced—Teaching them how to secure their Lives and Property during an Excursion through London, and calculated to put the Gulpin always upon his Guard.—Here will be found a Capital Show-Up of the Most Infamous Pegging Kens, Bellowsing Rooms, Dossing Hotels, Sharking Fakes, Fencing Cribs, Fleecing Holes, Gulping Holes, Molly Clubs, etc., etc., etc. To which is added A Joskin's Vocabulary of the various Slang Words now in constant use; the whole being a Moving Picture of all the New Moves and Artful Dodges practised at the present day, in all the most notorious Flymy Kens and Flash Cribs of London! By which the Flat is put Awake to all the Plans adopted to Feather a Green Bird and let him into the Most Important Secrets. With a Characteristic Engraving. Price One Shilling. London: Printed and Published by H. Smith, 37, Holywell Street, Strand. Where may be had a Catalogue of a Most Extensive Variety of every choice and Curious Facetious Work.

This very promising title is followed by a brochure of thirty-one pages of small format.

The history of English 'erotic' literature, that is to say, publications dealing with sexual matters for their own sake, begins with the Restoration period. It was only then that eroticism became a special art that was regarded as the spice, variety and intensification of ordinary love. Books were now written specially on the subject.

This deliberate, artificial stressing of sex was just as foreign to the crude naturalism of English literature that prevailed from the Middle Ages until the time of Shakespeare and his contemporaries, as the subsequent prudery, the beginnings of which may be traced to the puritanism of the Cromwellian period. From Chaucer to Marlowe and Shakespeare there was a great deal of obscenity, but it was naive obscenity. ' Prudery at that time, and for long afterwards, was unknown. It was in accordance with the spirit of the age to talk " straight from the shoulder " on all natural subjects, including sex[1].'

Wharton points out that throughout the Middle Ages not only were the worst offences against chastity allowed and taken for granted, but even the most shameful evils were regarded as harmless. It was only the conscious improvement in living that led to the discovery of new evil pleasures; but, at the same time, it also led to the prevention, in the matter of sex, of the enormities that occurred in the Middle Ages. Above all, the commission of excesses was driven from public venues into secret holes and corners[2].

Thus in the works of Geoffrey Chaucer, the first English poet, we find some obscene—very obscene—passages. Lewdness, both frank and implied, is well represented in the *Canterbury Tales*. A few passages from the ' Tale of the Wife of Bath ' will be sufficient to convey an idea of the natural coarseness of the age. For instance, the fact is enlarged upon that the genital organs are also used for passing water:

[1] Johannes Scherr, *Geschichte der englischen Literatur* (History of English Literature). Leipzig, 1874.

[2] Thomas Wharton, *History of English Poetry* (London, 1775).

Tel me also, to what conclusioun
Were membres made of generatioun,
And of so parfit wise, and why ywrought?
Trusteth right wel, they were nat made for nought.
Glose who-so wol, and say bothe up and doun,
That they were made for purgatioun,
Of urine, and oure bothe things smale,
Were eke to know a female from a male:
And for non other cause? say ye no?
The experience wot wel it is not so.
So that these clerkes be not with me wroth,
I say this, that they maked ben for both,
This is to sayn, for office and for ese
Of engendrure, ther we God not displese.
Why shuld men elles in hir bookes sette,
That man shall yelden to his wif his dette?
Now wherwith shuld he make his payment,
If he ne used his sely instrument?
Than were they made upon a creature
To purge urine and eke for engendrure.

The Wife of Bath, who has buried five husbands,
describes with extreme *naiveté* her strongly developed
appetite of the pleasures of Venus and Bacchus:

As help me God, I was a lusty one
And faire, and riche, and yonge, and wel begone:
And trewely, as min husbondes tolden me,
I had the beste queint that mighte be.
For certes I am all fulli venerian
In feling, and my herte alle marcian:
Venus me yave my lust and licorousnesse,
And Mars yave me my sturdy hardinesse.
Myn ascent was Taur, and Mars therinne;
Allas, alas, that ever love was synne!

[504]

I folwed ay min inclination:
By vertue of my constellation:
That made me that I coude nat withdraw
My chambre of Venus from a good felaw.
Yet have I a marke of Mars upon my face,
And also in another privee place.
For God so wisly be my salvation,
I loved never by no discretion,
But ever folwed min owne appetite,
All were he shorte, longe, blake or white;
I toke no kepe, so that he liked me,
How poure he was, ne eke of what degree. . . .

My fourthe housbonde was a revelour,
This is to say, he had a paramour,
And I was yonge and ful of ragerie,
Stibborne and strong, and joly as a pie.
Lord! how coude I dance to an harpe smale,
And sing ywis as any nightingale,
Whan I had dronke a draught of swete wine.
Metillius, the foule cherl, the swyn,
That with a staf by raft his wyf hir lyf
For sche drank wyn, though I hadde ben his wif,
Ne shuld he nat have daunted me fro drinke:
And after wine of Venus most I thinke.
For al so siker as cold engendreth hayl,
A likorous mouth most han a likorous tayl.
In woman vinolent is no defence,
This knowen lechours by experience.

And still more naively, without a blush, so to speak, she
relates her experiences in bed:

But in our bed he was so fresh and gay,
And so well therewithal he coude me glose,

[505]

When that he wolde han my belle chose,
That, though he had me bet on every boon,
He coude win agen my love anoon.

Unrestrained passion, the coarse and bizarre in love, the abominations of an insane lust, the most staggering aberrations of the voluptuary—all these Satanic elements of sex love are encountered in the dramas and poetical dreams of the predecessors and contemporaries of Shakespeare; in Marlowe, Greene, Ford, Webster, Massinger, etc. 'Their imaginations ran away with their intelligence.' Love becomes a delirium which, with its demented power, destroys everything around it, and finally even itself. All these poets, with whom Friedrich Bodenstedt in his valuable work *Shakespeares Zeitgenossen und ihre Werke* (Shakespeare's Contemporaries and their Works) (Berlin, 1858) deals in detail, only know the terrors and pain of love, but not its joys. Woman becomes a devil, as for instance in Webster's *Vittoria Accoramboni*, which play also bears the sub-title, *The White Devil*.

Nevertheless, these poets at times also introduce us, through individual characters, to feminine charm, to the ' true Germanic ' instinct of feminine loyalty and conjugal love. Examples of this type of woman are Beaumont and Fletcher's Bianca, Ordella, Arethusa, Juliane; Webster's Duchess of Amalfi, and also Isabella; Ford's and Green's Penthea and Dorothea[1]. The deserted Aspasia in Beaumont and Fletcher's *The Bride* is the same tender, moving figure as Shakespeare's Ophelia.

Such tender poetic characters frequently appear amidst murder, strangulation, the noise of battle and the coarsest excesses, and are therefore all the more impressive by contrast.

[1] See Taine, *loc. cit.*, Vol. I, p. 408.

The moralist of that epoch was undoubtedly Ben Jonson. While the works of the above-mentioned poets breathed a sense of living reality rooted in the coarse and abandoned nature of the times, Ben Jonson is more of a theorist. He presents vice in all its voluptuousness and lack of control, but only in order to combat it. Thus in his famous *Volpone* the ' full beauty of evil desires ' is presented to us. ' Excess, cruelty, love of gold, and brazen vice, wallow in a dazzling and uncanny poetry that is worthy of a Titianesque Bacchanalia ' (Taine). In this play a dwarf, a eunuch, and a man-woman appear as types of the city of sensual pleasure —Venice, the Queen of Vice. It is no mere coincidence that this play was illustrated by Aubrey Beardsley, an artist of the Satanistic school.

Shakespeare has represented in an inimitable and masterly manner all the phenomena and manifestations of love, its common and its ideal elements, its tragedy and its comedy, its folly and its wisdom, its excesses and its loyalties, its good and evil consequences. Finck describes Shakespeare, and rightly, as the first poet of modern love.

' It is in the works of Shakespeare that we first encounter a presentation of the various emotions, urges and moods which constitute love—sensual, aesthetic and spiritual—in their correct relationship to each other. Shakespeare's love is modern love in its full development and it is therefore understandable without the need for close analysis. It is a primeval passion, purified and ennobled by intellectual, moral and aesthetic civilisation ' (H. F. Finck, *Romantische Liebe und persönliche Schönheit* (Romantic Love and Personal Beauty), Breslau, 1894).

In Shakespeare's works love is generally a ' superhuman ' passion, something that cannot be grasped with an earthly intelligence, something that lies beyond the concept of good and evil, something that takes possession of a person against his will and drives him to commit deeds that may be noble or base. Love is an ecstasy, an exaltation, and therefore also the most powerful impulse of poetic creativeness.

Some very striking statements on the conception and significance of love in the works of Shakespeare are contained in a book by Ludwig Büchner[1].

' The greatest of all poets and men, Shakespeare, does not hesitate to describe love as divine, and to place the law of love above all human statutes and all human rules.'

No poet, not even Goethe, has created so many and such varied feminine characters as Shakespeare; their peculiar charm inspired Heine[2] and Bodenstedt[3] to write monographs on the subject. Ophelia, Miranda, Juliet[4], Desdemona, Virginia, Imogen and Cordelia are the embodiments of delicate loveliness, of true feminine tenderness and charm. They are ' charming children who feel deeply and love madly. They have fits of spontaneity, outbursts of mild temper, pretty conversation, coquettish defiances and a charming mobility, reminding us of the twittering, as well as of the beauty of birds. Whereas the heroines of the French stage are almost masculine, Shakespeare's heroines are women in the fullest sense of the word[5].'

In these women we see the expression of a romantically

[1] L. Büchner, *Liebe und Liebesleben in der Tierwelt* (Love and the Love-life in the Animal World) (Berlin, 1879).

[2] Heinrich Heine. *Shakespeares Mädchen und Frauen.* Leipzig, 1838. Vol. II, pp. 390-486.

[3] Friedrich Bodenstedt, *Shakespeares Frauencharactere*, fourth edition (Berlin, 1887).

[4] Taine, *loc. cit.*, Vol. I, p. 508.

[5] ' With whom can I compare you, Juliet and Miranda? I look again to the heavens and there seek your image. Perhaps it is to be found behind the stars, where my gaze cannot reach. Perhaps if the glowing sun were to possess the tenderness of the moon, I could compare you with it, Juliet ! Were the tender moon at the same time endowed with the sun's glow, I would then find a comparison for you, Miranda! '— Heinrich Heine, *loc. cit.*, Vol. I, p. 508.

Drawing by W. Rowlandson

A STAG AT BAY

[*Pl.* 27

ideal love in all its splendour; but Shakespeare has also
portrayed the demoniac and bacchanalian aspects of feminine
love in Cleopatra. Cleopatra ' represents the love of an
already diseased civilisation, of an age whose beauty is
already fading, whose hair, though still artificially waved and
anointed with fragrant oils, is nevertheless streaked with
grey, the love of an age which hastens to drain its rapidly
emptying cup. This love lacks faith and loyalty, but it is
none the less wild and ardent. Vexed by the knowledge that
this fire cannot be quenched, the impatient woman pours
oil upon it and throws herself with Bacchanalian abandon
into the flames[1].'

Shakespeare has not only observed the nature of human love
and its various manifestations, he was also a most realistic
observer of all the physical phenomena of love. It is true
that the famous phrase, ' the beast with two backs ', which
Shakespeare puts into Iago's mouth, is only a translation of an old French proverb, which had been used by
Rabelais, as Le Roux in his *Dictionnaire Comique* has proved[2],
but apart from that there are many other subtle observations
of physical love in Shakespeare's works.

There is, for instance, the passage in *Antony and Cleopatra*
on the sexual impulses of eunuchs:

CLEOPATRA : Thou, eunuch Mardian!
MARDIAN : What's Your Highness' pleasure?
CLEOPATRA : Not now to hear thee sing. I take no
    pleasure
    In aught a eunuch has. 'Tis well for thee,
    That, being unseminar'd, thy freer thoughts
    May not fly forth of Egypt. Hast thou
    affections?

[1] Heine, *loc. cit.*, pp. 485-486.
[2] John Davenport, *Curiositates Eroticae Physiologiae* (London, 1875),
p. 18.

MARDIAN : Yes, gracious madam.
CLEOPATRA : Indeed!
MARDIAN : Not in deed, madam; for I can do nothing
But what in deed is honest to be done;
Yet have I affections, and think
What Venus did with Mars.
(*Antony and Cleopatra*, Act I, Scene V.)

Nor has any poet emphasised as frequently as Shakespeare the evil consequences of impure love. Syphilis is referred to in many passages, and sometimes described in a very realistic and drastic manner. Thus Timon says to the courtesans Phrynia and Timandra:

. . . whore still;
Paint till a horse may mire upon your face:
A pox of wrinkles! . . .
Consumptions sow
In hollow bones of man; strike their sharp shins,
And mar men's spurring. Crack the lawyer's voice,
That he may never more false title plead,
Nor sound his quillets shrilly: hoar the flamen,
That scolds against the quality of flesh,
And not believes himself: down with the nose,
Down with it flat; take the bridge quite away
Of him that, his particular to foresee,
Smells from the general weal: make curl'd pate ruffians
bald,
And let the unscarr'd braggarts of the war
Derive some pain from you: plague all,
That your activity may defeat and quell
The source of all erection. There's more gold;
Do you damn others, and let this damn you,
And ditches grave you all!

Proksch, who has collected the passages on syphilis in Shakespeare[1], writes of this description: ' In spite of the fact that Shakespeare does not mention the name of the disease, there is not, nor will there ever be, a single trained physician who could not recognise clearly the symptoms of syphilis from the curse of Timon of Athens, written nearly three hundred years ago. . . . And only a great master could describe it as Shakespeare has done.'

Other, more humorous, references to syphilis are contained in the second part of *Henry IV* (Act I, Scene II), in *Henry V* (Act V, Scene I), in *Hamlet* (Act V, Scene I), and in *Measure for Measure* (Act I, Scene II).

The coarsely erotic and obscene literature in England began with the Restoration period, when the cult of sex for its own sake dominated the morals of the country, as well as the theatre and literature. The Titanic figures of Shakespeare and Marlowe and their contemporaries, who were also filled with the breath of genius and greatness, were followed under the reigns of Charles II and James II by a younger generation of authors, who, from Dryden to Durfey, cultivated above all the obscene and ambiguous, and exhibited a ' hard hearted, brazen and boisterous licentiousness '.

' The influence of these authors ', writes Macaulay, ' was undoubtedly harmful, but less harmful than it would have been had they been less depraved; the poison which they spread was so strong that after a short time it was eliminated by vomiting. None of them understood the dangerous art of adorning the pictures of forbidden pleasures with that which makes them attractive; none of them realised that a certain

---

[1] J. K. Proksch, *Einige Dichter der Neuzeit über Syphilis. Ein Beitrag zur Geschichte und Literatur dieser Krankheit.* (Vienna, 1881.) Pp. 4-6. Cf. the treatise by Hermann Schelenz, *Syphilis und Prostitution in Shakespeares Dramen*, in Klinische-Therapeutische Wochenschrift, 1911, No. 32.

decency is indispensable even for debauchery, that concealment attracts more than revelation, and that the imagination
is far more powerfully excited by subtle hints which challenge
it to action than by coarse exhibitions that leave it in a state
of inactivity[1].'

The most blatant representative of the eroticism of
the Restoration was undoubtedly John Wilmot, Earl of
Rochester[2], of whom the somewhat prudish Hume writes
that even his name was offensive to a sensitive ear[3]. Rochester
was, in fact, through his poems and dramas, the founder of a
new kind of erotic literature, namely, the obscene satire, in
which he probably remains unsurpassed in so far as impudent
wit, drastic outspokenness, but also elegance of metre are
concerned.

' No one has ever written ', we read in *Grammont's
Mémoires*, ' more charmingly, more subtly and more skilfully
than this lord; but in satire his pen was implacably bitter[4].'

Another contemporary, Bishop Burnet, praised Rochester's
wit, which was moulded on the pattern of Cowley and
Boileau, but which also had a peculiar malicious edge of the
author's own[5].

Even the obscene songs and plays of Rochester, according
to a contemporary biographer, have ' a peculiar beauty ', the
like of which is only to be found in Petronius and in the
' Elegantiae latini sermonis ' of Meursius[6].

The best characterisation of Rochester's work is contained in the following passage in Taine[7]:

[1] Thomas Babington Macaulay, *History of England since the Accession
of James II.*
[2] See about him earlier in this work.
[3] J. Scherr, *loc. cit.*, p. 119.
[4] *Memoirs of Count Grammont* (Leipzig, 1853), p. 187.
[5] *Works of the Earls of Rochester, Roscommon, Dorset, etc.* (London, 1714),
Vol. I, p. xxxvii.
[6] *Ibid.*, Vol. I, pp. xx-xxi.
[7] Taine, *loc. cit.*, Vol. II, p. 20.

' Rochester deprives love of all adornment, and in order to take hold of it the more securely, he converts it into a cudgel. All the noble sentiments, all the sweet dreams, all the sweet fascination, the bright, golden light that illuminates and cheers our miserable existence, the illusion that concentrates all the forces of our being and makes us see perfection in a mortal creature, and enables us to find infinite bliss in a transitory emotion—all this has vanished; all that is left is satiated lust, jaded sensuality. The worst of it is that he writes too correctly, without witty élan, without natural fire, without picturesque sensuality; his satires reveal him as the disciple of Boileau. Nothing is more repulsive than a frozen obscenity. We are able to tolerate the obscene works of a Giulio Romano and his Venetian voluptuousness, because here the sensual instinct is ennobled by genius, and the dazzling colours of his draperies turn his orgy into a work of art. We forgive Rabelais when we recognise the stream of youthful gaiety and strength that runs through his obscenities; we only need to close our nostrils, then we may follow, through mud and slime, with admiration, even with sympathy, the flow of his witty thoughts. But a man who endeavours to be elegant, and yet remains filthy and common, he who undertakes to describe the feelings of a brute in the cultured language of society, who seeks a suitable metaphor for every obscenity, who makes deliberate efforts to talk smut, who degrades his style to such purposes, without having the excuse of naturalness, élan, genius or knowledge, is like a filthy fellow who dips a precious jewel in the gutter. In the end he evokes nausea.'

But in spite of all that, Rochester as a satirist is of considerable literary importance, and we can agree without hesitation with Grässe's[1] view that had he lived longer he

---

[1] J. G. Th. Grässe, *Handbuch der Allgemeinen Literaturgeschichte* (Leipzig, 1850), Vol. III, p. 375.

would have become the greatest English satirist. Nor is he always obscene, as will be seen from the following beautiful love song:

SONG

My dear Mistress had a Heart
Soft as those kind looks she gave me,
When with Love's restless Art,
And her Eyes, she did enslave me.

But her constancy's so weak,
She's so wild and apt to wander,
That my jealous heart would break,
Should we live one day asunder.

Melting Joys about her move,
Killing Pleasures, wounding Blisses:
She can dress her Eyes in Love,
And her Lips can arm with Kisses.

Angels listen when she speaks,
She's my Delight, all Mankinds Wonder;
But my jealous Heart would break,
Should we live one day asunder.

No less tender are the following verses to his mistress:

TO HIS MISTRESS

Why dost thou shade thy lovely face? O why
Does that eclipsing Hand of thine deny
The Sun-shine of the Sun's enlivening Eye?

Without thy Light, what Light remains in me?
Thou art my Life, my Way, my Light's in thee.
I live, I move, and by thy Beams I see.

[514]

Naturally, the number of these poetic manifestations of pure love is very small as compared with that of the obscene songs which, in spite of all the ornateness and lightness of the verses, appear to have been written in a state of priapism, or in a state of physical and moral exhaustion after a night of dissipation. Now he indicates the obscene by circumlocution, now he wallows in the free use of the filthiest expressions. The first method is exemplified by the following poem :

ET CAETERA. A SONG.

In a dark, silent, shady Grove,
Fit for the Delights of Love,
As on Corinna's Breast I panting lay,
My right Hand playing with Et Caetera.

A thousand Words and am'rous Kisses
Prepar'd us both for more substantial Blisses;
And thus the hasty Moments slipt away,
Lost in the Transport of Et Caetera.

She blush'd to see her Innocence betray'd,
And the small Opposition she had made;
Yet hugg'd me close, and with a Sigh did say,
Once more, my Dear, once more, Et Caetera.

But oh! the Power to please this Nymph was past,
Too violent a Flame can never last;
So we remitted to another Day
The Prosecution of Et Caetera.

An access of 'satyriasis' appears to have inspired the following 'Wish' in the poet:

THE WISH

Oh! that I could by some new Chymick Art
Convert to Sperm my Vital and my Heart;
And, at one Thrust, my very soul translate
Into her—and be degenerate.

> There steep'd in Lust nine Months I would remain,
> Then boldly f . . . my Passage back again.

The grandiose, Satanic obscenity which appears in the latter poem has only been equalled by one more modern poet, who evidently must have read Rochester. That poet was Edmond Haraucourt, in whose *Légende des Sexes* similar crazy excesses of an unrestrained fantasy occur.

We may further mention his highly lascivious comparison of virginity with a chimney in *A Description of Maidenhead*, the drastic description of his own impotence in a love adventure in *The Disappointment*, and his account of the licentiousness of his daily life in *The Debauchee*. He thinks he is all the more entitled to employ obscene expressions in his poems because in his opinion they rather damp than intensify sensual passion.

> But obscene Words too grosse to move Desire,
> Like Heaps of Fuel do but choak the Fire.
> That Author's Name has undeserved Praise,
> Who pal'd the Appetite he meant to raise.

But better even than his lyric poetry is Rochester's satire, which was based on a highly developed caustic wit. He wrote *In Defence of Satire*, in which he expresses the following view on satire:

> And (without Doubt) though some it may offend,
> Nothing helps more than Satire to amend
> Ill Manners, or is trulier Vertue's friend.
> Princes may Laws ordain, Priests gravely preach,
> But Poets most successfully will teach.

The most famous satires of Rochester are those directed against marriage, the contents of which are clearly indicated by the closing lines of *Satire Against Marriage*:

> With Whores thou canst but venture; what thou'st
>   lost,
> May be redeem'd again with Care and Cost;
> But a damn'd Wife, by inevitable Fate,
> Destroys Soul, Body, Credit and Estate.

There is also his *Satire on the King*, in which he castigates
the King in the most impudent manner for his extraordinary
sexual exploits and his consequent impotence. He was
banished from court as a result of this satire.

But Rochester surpassed the shameless cynicism and
copious description of obscene sexual details that occur in
his lyrics and satires in his notorious drama *Sodom*, which
may be regarded as a realistic description of the paederasty
practised at the Court of Charles II. At all events, the play
is unique of its kind. I found the first reference to *Sodom*
(which seems to have escaped Pisanus Fraxi, the best
bibliographer of this play) in the travel book of Uffenbach,
which we have already mentioned. In an entry dated the
21st October 1710 he writes[1]:

'Of the Earl of Rochester we hear that his ugly satire
against King Charles II and his disgraceful comedy *Sodom*
have not been printed with his other works; in fact, the
former has not been printed at all, while the latter is very
difficult to obtain. However, it is amazing that such a godless
and shocking theme should not only have been written up by
a man, but should also have been performed in the most ugly
manner before a King in the theatre, although otherwise the
licentiousness, particularly the sexual licence, of this King,
in which the Earl of Rochester always had his share, is very
well known in England, and may be read about in the works
of the Earl of Rochester and of Burnet.'

[1] *Remarkable Journeys of Zacharias Conrad von Uffenbach, etc.* (Ulm,
1754), Vol. III, pp. 200-1.

[517]

All further records concerning *Sodom* will be found in the detailed critical investigation by Pisanus Fraxi[1], to which we will refer below.

Fraxi records the following early edition of the play:

Sodom, A Play,
By the E. of R.
Mentula cum Vulva saepissime jungitur una
Dulcius est Melle, Vulvam tractare Puellae.
Antwerp: Printed in the year 1684.

This edition was undoubtedly printed in the year stated[2]; the format was octavo, but the publication appears to have vanished in this format, as Fraxi had never seen it. He thinks that a copy of this edition had existed in the Heber collection, but had been destroyed together with other obscene books. He knows of no other printed copies of *Sodom*, but saw three manuscript copies of the play.

It has been stated that *Sodom* had been performed before King Charles II and his court, and that women were also present at the performance. This assumption is probably based on certain obscene verses in the Prologue concerning the women who ought not to be present, but were.

The true author of the play was undoubtedly the Earl of Rochester. There were some doubts about this for a time, because, like some other writers of obscene works, Rochester denied that he was the author of *Sodom*, and even wrote a scurrilous poem addressed to the alleged author, whom he gave a severe 'dressing down', apostrophising him as follows:

Tell me, abandon'd Miscreant, prithee tell,
What damn'd Power, invok'd and sent from Hell,
(If Hell were bad enough) did thee inspire?
To write what Fiends asham'd wou'd blushing hear ?

[1] Pisanus Fraxi, *Centuria librorum absconditorum*, pp. 326-45.
[2] See *Memoriae librorum rariorum*, p. 150.

And so on, continuing with foul invective and obscene abuse. He likens the tongue and mouth of the ' Moor-Fields Author ' to parts of the genital organs, then concludes with a wish as to the fate of the infamous book.

Although Rochester's denials and the above-mentioned poem led many people to attribute *Sodom* to another author, the obscure Fishbourne, even a quite superficial examination will prove Rochester's authorship. For style, wit and the words and expressions peculiar to him, and to him alone, are the same in *Sodom* as in his other works. Paederasty is mentioned with horror in the poem quoted from above, but in *Valentinian*[1], a tragedy which was produced at the Theatre Royal, Rochester glorified the practice:

'Tis a soft Rogue, this Lycias
And rightly understood,
He's worth a thousand Womens Nicenesses!
The Love of Women moves even with their Lust,
Who therefore still are fond, but seldom just;
Their Love is Usury, while they pretend,
To gain the Pleasure double which they lend.
But a dear Boy's disinterested Flame
Gives Pleasure, and for meer Love gathers Pain;
In him alone Fondness sincere does prove,
And the kind tender Naked Boy is Love.

(Act II, Scene I.)

I see further proof of Rochester's authorship of *Sodom* in the fact that his acknowledged works include a brief fragment of a similarly obscene drama to *Sodom*. The piece is entitled *Interlude*, and in Act I, Scene I, some of the characters bear similar names to those in *Sodom*.

---

[1] *Valentinian: A Tragedy. As 'tis Altered by the late Earl of Rochester, And Acted at the Theatre-Royal. Together with a Preface concerning the Author and his Writings.* By One of his Friends. Printed for Timothy Goodwin at the Maidenhead against St. Dunstan's Church in Fleet Street. 1685. The preface is by Robert Wolseley, a comrade of Rochester.

It is difficult to give even a brief outline of *Sodom* without offending the sensibilities of the least squeamish of readers. The names of the characters are, with Latin inflexions, nouns denoting the genital organs and various sexual acts, and are therefore unprintable. They are a King and his courtiers. At the rise of the curtain they appear in an ante-room whose walls are decorated with obscene pictures, and the King proclaims full sexual licence, unrestricted by any law. The courtiers receive this with clamorous gratitude, and each endeavours to say something flattering to the King. An experienced paederast gives certain advice to the King, who is eager to taste of this perverse pleasure. The King selects two of the courtiers as his lovers, and issues a pro-clamation according full licence to all paederasts and homo-sexual persons. One of the ' lovers ' reveals to the King that a certain courtier had had relations with the Queen. How-ever, the King is too kind-hearted to object and ends the scene, and the first Act, with an invitation to his ' lovers ' to come away with him.

The first and second Scenes of Act II take place in a beautiful garden decorated with statues of naked men and women in various postures. In the middle of the garden a woman standing on her head represents a fountain. The directions concerning the fountain appear to have been lifted from Rabelais. Soft music and singing is heard, then the Queen, accompanied by three ladies, enters. They complain that the King is neglecting them, but recollect that there are better men than he. The Queen declares that she is not jealous, and listens with pleasure to the praises of the masculinity of a certain courtier.

In the third Scene the ladies-in-waiting set the dildoes in motion and a discussion concerning the properties of the same develops. The Queen awaits impatiently the arrival of the courtier already referred to, and orders one of the ladies to sing an obscene song in order to help pass the time. The Act concludes with a dance by naked men and women and an orgy between them.

The third Act has little connection with the theme itself, in that it deals almost entirely with the seduction of a young prince by his sister. At the second attempt one of the ladies-in-waiting arrives in a drunken state and participates in the sexual practices of the other two, with the result that the young prince has to be taken to bed in an exhausted condition.

In the first Scene of the fourth Act we find the Queen alone with the General. She is charmed by the tests of her new lover's power, and presses for further tests, until he is incapable of acceding to her wishes, for:

> Love, like war, must have its interval;
> Nature renews that strength by kind repose,
> Which an untimely drudgery would lose.

He leaves her, and she, still unsatisfied, complains in a monologue about the scorn of this ' satiated libertine '.

The second Scene takes us back to the King and his two male ' lovers ', who are discussing the advantages of paederasty over normal sexual intercourse. Enter one of the courtiers, whom the King asks how his proclamation about sexual licence has been received. The courtier reports, among other things, that a certain woman has mated with a stallion, whereupon he, the courtier, had placed an elephant at her disposal.

One of the ' lovers ' now announces the arrival of a stranger, sent by the King of Gomorrah with forty young lads. The King is very pleased and immediately retires with one of the lads.

The first Scene of the fifth Act is the most humorous part of the whole play. The young ladies of the court complain to

Virtuoso, the supplier of dildoes, about the inferior quality of his goods, and invite him to show his own 'natural' abilities.

The last Scene, in contrast with the humour of the first, is the most tragic. The location is ' a grove of cypresses and trees in the shape of a Phallus'. After a song by a youth sitting under one of the palms, a few of the courtiers enter, followed by the King's physician, who paints in vivid colours the terrible consequences of the prevailing sexual anarchy. The Queen has already fallen a victim to her many powerful lovers. The prince is suffering from gonorrhoea, etc. The King asks the physician in alarm whether nothing can be done to stay the evil. To which the physician replies:

> To Love and Nature all their rights restore,
> —— women and let —— be no more,
> It doth the procreative end destroy,
> Which Nature gave with pleasure to enjoy,
> Please her, and she'll be kind—if you displease,
> She turns into corruption and disease.

But the King shudders at the thought of returning to a woman. He refuses to withdraw the proclamation. Thereupon the clouds burst asunder, fiery demons appear and vanish again. The ghost of one of the ladies-in-waiting reveals itself. Terrible moans and sighs rise from the earth and ghostly figures appear from the deep. The play ends with the King's declaration:

> Let heav'n descend and set the world on fire,
> We to some darker cavern will retire.

There are clouds of fire, sulphur and smoke, then the Curtain falls.

Sodom appears to have been translated into French a number of times. Soleinne had three manuscripts in his great collection of plays, two of which appear to have been translations of the English original. However, these were destroyed. Also, there are several dramas bearing the title *Sodom* which deal with sexual corruption.

An obvious imitation of Rochester's *Sodom* is the following play, written by four gentlemen in 1879:

Theatre Royal, Olimprick. New and Gorgeous Pantomime, entitled: Harlequin Prince Cherrytop and the Good Fairy F— Oxford: Printed at the University Press, 1879.

The format is octavo, thirty-one pages, with blue cover (printed in London in July 1879, in one hundred and fifty copies, price 31s. 6d.; three obscene coloured prints, which were published a little later, also belong to this volume).

The work is constructed after the pattern of *Sodom*; one character, ' a waiting maid or maid of honour ', is identical in both plays.

Harlequin Prince Cherrytop was intended as a sort of Christmas pantomime. In the first Scene we see the cave of the demon ' Masturbation ', who has subjugated Prince Cherrytop by magic, making him a martyr to masturbation. In the succeeding Scenes we witness the struggle between this abnormality and the Good Fairy, who tries to make the Prince fall in love with a Princess. An interlude presents the machinations of a King against this plan; his servants are the personifications of venereal disease in all its forms. This droll idea is very well presented, and spiced with lyrics, which are parodies of popular songs. This play, like *Sodom*, concludes with a warning that the highest bliss must be based on pure love, which is preferable to all the unnatural pleasures.

As compared with Rochester, the contemporary representatives of obscene and ' gallant ' literature, like Dorset, Roscommon, Edmund Waller, Buckingham, Otway, etc., fade into insignificance. We need only mention the characteristic fact that the women of that period also engaged in obscene authorship. There was a constellation of three feminine stars—Aphra Behn[1], Susanna Centlivre[2] and Mary Manley, whose *Atalantis*, an obscene satirical novel, may be taken as a true description of the morals of England around 1700[3]. We might also mention, in passing, the numerous cynicisms in Butler's famous *Hudibras*.

We have already discussed the absolutely erotic-frivolous nature of the dramatic literature of the Restoration period. Even a poet like Dryden was not free from it. But the peak point in this connection was reached in the plays of Wycherley, Congreve, Vanbrugh and Farquhar, the reading of which, according to Thackeray, gives the impression as though the reader were seeing the traces of an orgy at the house of Sallust in Pompeii; and according to Taine, their authors possessed all the vices they described. I refer to the brilliant analyses of these obscene comedies by Taine[4].

The first half of the eighteenth century is the period of moralising and satirical works, the age of the literature represented by the names of Defoe, Swift, Richardson, Sterne, Smollett and Fielding.

The first named deserves to be mentioned here on account of his novels of prostitutes, *Moll Flanders* and *Mother Ross*. Swift only mentions sex in order to point out its repulsive aspects. He drags love in the mud in the true sense of the term; he degrades it by an admixture of pharmaceutical and medical elements. (See 'A Love Poem from a Physician'.) Sterne, particularly in *Tristram Shandy*, which contains many objectionable passages, exhibits a similar bent. ' He loves nudity, not from an aesthetic sense like artists, nor

[1] *Poems* (London, 1684-1688, three vols.); *Plays* (London, 1702); *Histories and Novels* (London, 1696).

[2] *The Old Batchelor* (London, 1693); *The Double Dealer* (London, 1694); *Works* (London, 1752). Cf. Thornbury, *Haunted London*, p. 230.

[3] Compare O. L. B. Wolff, *Allgemeine Geschichte des Romans* (Jena, 1850), p. 227.

[4] Taine, *loc. cit.*, Vol. II, p. 86

[524]

from sensuality like Fielding, nor yet from a mania for pleasure like Dorat, Boufflers and all the other fine libertines who wrote at that period in England. When he goes to filthy places, he does so because they are forbidden and unfrequented. All he is looking for there is eccentricity and scandal. What attracts him about forbidden fruit is not the fruit but the prohibition, for those that he does dig his teeth into are quite desiccated, or at any rate wormy. That an Epicurean should take pleasure in recounting the pretty sins of a pretty woman is not to be wondered at; but that a novelist should delight in watching the bedroom of a filthy old couple, in observing the effects of a hot chestnut fallen into a man's trousers, in enlarging upon the questions of the Widow Wadman concerning the significance of wounds in the wings of the valvula—that can only be explained by an aberration of an unsound imagination, which finds pleasure in repulsive ideas[1].

Similar cynicisms and obscene innuendoes are to be found in the well-known novels of Smollett and Fielding.

Turning to the ' erotic ' literature proper of the eighteenth century, we must mention first of all the two most famous works of this type of the first half of the century, namely, Dr. William King's *The Toast* and John Cleland's *Fanny Hill, or Memoirs of a Woman of Pleasure.*

Although the distribution of *The Toast* through booksellers was not very widespread, copies of the first edition are not very rare. The British Museum possesses three copies of the quarto edition.

The author of *The Toast* was Dr. William King, son of the Rev. Peregrine King, and head of St. Mary Hall, Oxford (born in Stepney, Middlesex, in 1685, died 30th December 1763), where he was educated. In 1727 he went to Ireland,

---

[1] Taine, *loc. cit.*, Vol. II, pp. 433-4.

where he wrote the book in question. He was admired for his wit by the leading personalities of the age, and particularly by his friend Swift. He was an excellent orator, and an author of elegance, who knew Latin as well as English[1].

Dr. Johnson said: ' I clapped after Dr. King's speech so long that my hands became sore[2].' The poet Thomas Wharton describes King's brilliant talent as an orator in the following verses of his *Triumph of Isis*:

> See, on you Sage how all attentive stand,
> To catch his darting eye and waving hand,
> Hark! he begins, with all a Tully's art,
> To pour the dictates of a Cato's heart.
> Skill'd to pronounce what noblest thoughts inspire,
> He blends the speaker's with patriot's fire;
> Bold to conceive, nor timorous to conceal,
> What Britons dare to think, he dares to tell, etc.

On the other hand, there was no lack of opponents, who charged him with the spreading of revolutionary doctrines and with preaching licence, and who also cast doubts on the purity of his Latin. Churchill wrote in the *Candidate*:

> King shall arise, and, bursting from the dead,
> Shall hurl his piebald Latin at thy head.

In a poem entitled *A Satire upon Physicians or an English Paraphrase, with Notes and References, of Dr. King's Most Memorable Oration, Delivered at the Dedication of the Radclivian Library in Oxford, To which is Added, A Curious Petition to the Hon. House in Favour of Dr. King.* (*London, Printed for R. Griffiths, in Paternoster Row,* 1758), the author makes King describe himself as follows:

[1] John Nichols, *Literary Anecdotes of the Eighteenth Century* (London, 1812), Vol. II, p. 608.
[2] *Ibid.*, Vol. IX, p. 778.

In me, ah! pity to behold!
A Wretch quite wither'd, weak and old;
Who now has pass'd by heavn's decree,
The dangerous year of Sixty-three;
On asses milk and caudle fed,
I doddle on my cane to bed,
Of every step I take, afraid;
My coat unbutton'd by my maid.
My memory oft mistaking names,
For G-rge I often think of J-mes;
Am grown so feeble, frail a Thing,
I scarce remember who is King!
Th' imperial purple which does wear,
A lawful or a lawless heir!

There is a beautiful mezzotint portrait of King at the age of seventy-five, carried out by T. Hudson.

The Toast is one of the most remarkable products of English erotic-satirical literature. The fact alone is sufficiently striking that such enormous trouble and learning should have been devoted to an attack on a solitary woman who was not even prominent. Still more surprising is the further fact that such an ugly satire should have been composed by a priest. *The Toast* is the work of a genius of great learning who knew the world and its vices very thoroughly, and was a veritable master of both English and Latin. It is difficult to decide which is the more remarkable—the English verses, or the rhymed original Latin verses, or the curious prose annotations. On the whole it is an amazing piece of work, full of wit, humour, learning and satire; it is a ' poème extraordinaire ', as Sylvain van de Weyer, one of the greatest authorities on English curiosities, describes it. Octave Delepierre expresses agreement with this view in his analysis of *The Toast* in *Macaroneana*.

The motives that led to the writing of *The Toast*, as well as
the characters occurring in it, are dealt with in the article,
' By-Ways of History. History of an Unreadable Book ',
which appears in *Betley's Miscellany* (June, 1857, pp. 616-
625).

The history of the poem revolves round Lady Frances
Brudenell, the widow of the Earl of Newburgh, who in 1699
married Richard Lord Bellew, an Irish noble, to whom she
bore a son, John, who later inherited the title. Lady Frances'
second husband died in 1714, leaving the ' heavenly Myra '
of the poem in a precarious position, as the deceased was
heavily in debt. She borrowed money right and left. Her
creditors included Sir Thomas Smith, Inspector of the
Phœnix Park in Dublin and uncle of our William King, as
his half-sister had married Peregrine King.

When Sir Thomas Smith had lent Lady Bellew a substantial
amount of money, he persuaded his rich nephew, William
King, to take over his claims. King was defrauded by the
cunning Lady Bellew of many thousands of pounds, which
he was unable to recover even after protracted litigation.

The only way the learned William King could avenge
himself was by writing *The Toast*, one of the most extraordinary works of invective in existence, in which deep
learning is employed to attribute to the object of the author's
hatred the most abominable and unnatural qualities, vices
and crimes.

The characters of *The Toast*, in a peculiar mixture of
antique mythology and modern fantasy, are represented
as the dramatis personae of a poem alleged to be a translation
of Latin verses, which in turn are explained in a deeply
learned commentary. The author uses the pseudonym
Schaeffer. The male and female characters appear in mytho-
logical costume. Lady Newburgh is ' Myra ', an unnatural
and immoral old witch. Sir Thomas Smith, the author's

[528]

uncle, figures as an old, repulsive, licentious Mars, whom the author represents as the third husband of Lady Frances, by whom she has been inveigled into marriage after a long courtship, and whom she has persuaded to disinherit his nephew after defrauding him. 'Myracides' is Lord John Bellew, while Lady Allen, in the guise of 'Ali,' appears as an assistant of 'Myra'. 'Pam' is Bishop Hort, who is also referred to, in a pun on his name, as Hort-ator Scelerum. Several other contemporaries also appear under invented names. Davis and Martin wrote a special 'key' to *The Toast*, but the best key is contained in the marginal notes of a copy presented by the author to John Gascoigne in 1747. Pisanus Fraxi has dealt with the contents of this copy[1].

King evidently also intended to display his great learning in *The Toast*, in addition to writing an obscene and mordant satire against his enemies, which he later condemned himself. He began the book in anger, but, as he himself said, continued it with pleasure, and he thus created one of the most peculiar products based on classical study[2].

In order to give an idea of the nature and contents of *The Toast*, we quote the most characteristic passage, namely, the description of Myra, which was later deprecated by King himself:

> There he saw the huge Mass tumble out of her Bed;
> Like Bellona's her Stature, the Gorgon's her Head;
> Hollow Eyes with a Glare, like the Eyn of an Ox;
> And a Forehead deep furrow'd and matted grey Locks;
> With a toothless wide Mouth, and a Beard on her Chin,
> And a yellow rough Hide in the Place of a Skin;
> Brawny Shoulders up-rais'd; Cow-Udders; Imp's Teat;
> And a pair of bow'd Legs, which were set on Splay Feet.

[1] P. Fraxi, *Centuria*, pp. 320-2.

[2] He said of this last: 'I have a veneration for Virgil: I admire Horace: but I love Ovid.' Dr. William King, *Political and Literary Anecdotes of His Own Time*, second edition (London, 1819), pp. 29-30.

With the Figure the God was surprised and offended,
When he mark'd how these various defects were
    amended;
How her Back was laid flet with an Iron Machine,
And her Breasts were lac'd down, with a sweet Bag
    between;
How she shaded her Eyes, and the squalid black Beard
Was so smoothly shaved off, scarce a Bristle appear'd;
How she clear'd the old Ruins, new plaister'd her Face,
And apply'd Red or White, as it suited the Place:
With a set of Wall's Teeth, and a Cap of Deard's Hair,
Like a Virgin she bloom'd, and at sixty seem'd Fair.
Thus you see an old Hulk, many years Weather-beaten,
All the Timbers grown rotten, the Plank all Worm-eaten,
Which the Owners, who doom her to make one more
    Trip,
Scrape and calk, tar and paint, till she seems a new Ship.
But alas! for the Wretches, whose Gods have forgot 'em,
That are bound to adventure in such a foul Bottom.
Here his Godship (inclin'd to examine the whole
Which compos'd this odd Creature) look'd into her Soul.
He conceiv'd a faint Hope, that within he should find
Hidden Beauties, good Sense, and a virtuous fair Mind:
Which, he knew, for Exteriors would make full Amends,
And enrol her a Toast among Platonic Friends.
But again he was baulk'd:—For a Soul he espy'd
Ful of Envy, black Malice, base Leasing, and Pride;
Hypocritical, sordid, vainglorious, ingrate;
In her Freindships most false, and relentless in
    Hate.
He beheld, at one View, all the Acts of her Life;
How experienc'd a Miss; how abandon'd a Wife!
Then advancing Years, all her Wants she supply'd,
By an Art, which the fam'd Messalina never try'd.

Tho' her Gallants were few, or not made to her Mind;
Yet her Joyance was full, if the Jewess was kind.
While the God, that no Room might be left for Doubt,
Turn'd her upside and down, and then inside and out;
And survey'd all her Parts; many more than is fit
For the Bard to describe; but still found himself bit.

Etc.

This pleasant description of Myra continues in the same
tone. Finally, she is ready to receive her admirers, who
appear one after the other:

First approaches majestic the tall Grenadier,
All her Fury the Sight of such Manhood suppress'd;
And a train of soft Passions re-enter her Breast.
She embrac'd the great Soldier; she measur'd his
    Length;
Into Action she warm'd, and experienced his Strength:
Not so much had false Delilah's Spouse in his Locks:
Nor the Witch was more pleas'd, when she strove in the
    Box.
Introduc'd in good Order, succeed to the Fight
A Mechanic, a Courtier, a Collier and Knight:
As he finish'd to each assign'd a new Day,
And, extolling his Labours, advanc'd a Week's Pay.

But she in not satisfied with all these men; in addition,
she also pays homage to *amor lesbicus*, resorting, further,
to the rod:

O ma Vie, ma Femme! What a Shape, and a Face!
Then impatient she rush'd to a closer Embrace.
Let the rest be untold! And thus ever forbear,
Lest thy numbers, O Scheffer, offend the chaste Fair.

As a specimen of the Latin original we quote the following
verses, to which the above ' translation ' relates:

[531]

Quos puellulae calores,
Nuptae vidit quos furores!
Quae libido, cum vetu-la,
Inflat tetra et Mascu-la!
Messalina si certaret,
Messalinam superaret,
Mira, Priapeium decus,
Moechi, moechae, moecha, moechus.
Quid, quod juvenes protervi?
Quod suorum rigent nervi?
Tribadum dum Shylockissa,
Venere non intermissa,
Miram patitur, amorum
Haud indocilis novorum.

The most famous work in England's erotic literature, and one of the most excellent specimens of erotic literature in general, is John Cleland's famous novel *Fanny Hill, or Memoirs of a Woman of Pleasure*, and we must therefore give this book detailed consideration here.

Vol. 59 of the *Gentleman's Magazine* contains a long biographical note on John Cleland (1707–1789), the author of this work, which is of the greatest value from the point of view of literary history. Although a correspondent in *Notes and Queries* (Second Series, Vol. II) declares that this note is inaccurate in a number of particulars, it is nevertheless the best biographical summary we possess. We learn from it that John Cleland was the son of Colonel Cleland, the famous fictitious member of the Spectator's Club, whom Steele describes under the name of ' Will Honeycombe '.

In Swift's diary, under the date 30th March 1713, we read: ' I dined in the City at Pontac's with Lord Dupplin and a few others. Our host was a Colonel Cleland, who would like to become Governor of Barbados, and is now spreading this net for me and the others, in order to win us over in his favour. He is a real Scot.' This Colonel Cleland was one of the best known ' men-about-town ' in London at the beginning of the eighteenth century. His portrait hung in his son's library until the latter's death.

John Cleland received a good education at Westminster College, which he entered in 1722, together with Lord Mansfield. After the death of his father, whom he resembled as regards loose living, John went to Smyrna as British consul, with the remnants of the paternal fortune. It may be that it was at Smyrna that he acquired the frivolous principles which he later propounded as the author of one of the most notorious books. After his return from Smyrna he went to East India, but owing to a dispute with members of the Presidency of Bombay, he was soon obliged to come back to England almost penniless. Here he got into financial difficulties, which entailed imprisonment and other troubles.

In these circumstances he was commissioned by a publisher to write an erotic book, which commission he carried out by writing *Fanny Hill*, for which he had to appear before the Privy Council. However, the President of the Council, John, Earl of Granville, subsequently assisted him in the most generous manner by according him a yearly pension of £100, in order to render further literary activities of a similar nature unnecessary. The result was that apart from the *Memoirs of a Coxcomb*, which still belonged to the frivolous category, and the *Man of Honour*, which was a kind of literary penance for the *Memoirs of a Woman of Pleasure*, John Cleland devoted his time to political and philological publications, the latter of which mainly dealt with the Celtic languages. He lived on his pension for many years in a secluded home in Petty France, surrounded by a good library and cheered by the occasional visits of a few literary friends, who regarded him as very pleasant company. He died at the ripe old age of eighty-two years. He was a gifted conversationalist, and possessed a knowledge of many living languages, all of which he spoke fluently. As an author he displayed his talent principally as a writer of short stories, songs and essays. His political works are tedious.

Nichols observes about his works: ' In these publications Mr. Cleland has displayed a large fund of ingenuity and erudition not unworthy the education he received at Westminster[1].'

As regards the specifically literary value of his most famous book, *Fanny Hill*, we need only quote the views of two German authors, who are undoubtedly competent judges in literary matters.

J. J. Winkelmann writes that *Fanny Hill* was written ' by a master in the art, by a man of tender feelings and high ideals, and in a dignified Pindaric style[2] '. Von Murr, who quotes this passage, adds: ' And that is the truth.'

Lichtenberg, in a letter to Wolff, dated the 23rd January 1785, writes: ' I already know this swinish book (namely, *Lindamine*, Paris, 1638), only I had forgotten the title. Dieterich had brought it up one day. I am returning it immediately, within six hours of receiving it, as there is an opportunity to do so. It is very badly written. *Dom Bougre* and *The History of a Woman of Pleasure* are much better. The etchings in the latter work are really very beautiful, but the booklet is very expensive[3].'

The bibliography and bookselling history of *Memoirs of a Woman of Pleasure* are very involved and needs detailed discussion, which cannot be given within the limits of a purely bibliographical list. Ferdinand Drujon already described the bibliography of this best-known English

[1] John Nichols, *Literary Anecdotes*, Vol. II, p. 458; Vol. VIII, pp. 98, 412.
[2] Winkelmann's *Briefe au scme Freunde* (Dresden, 1777), Vol. I, p. 91.
[3] *Lichtenbergs Briefe* (Leipzig, 1902), Vol. II, p. 187.

erotic work as 'la plus obscure'. Pisanus Fraxi was unable, in spite of strenuous efforts, to find a copy of the first edition. Although he had been told that there was one at the British Museum, he was unable to trace it. James Campbell, one of the most learned authorities on erotic literature, assured him that he had never seen a copy of the first edition, which must therefore be extremely rare.

The first edition of 1749, which Pisanus Fraxi never saw, was discovered a few decades ago, and reprinted by Isidore Liseux in Paris. The original edition bears the title: *Memoirs of a Woman of Pleasure. London. Printed for G. Fenton in the Strand*, 1749. *12mo, two vols., pp.* 172 *and* 177. *With etchings.*

In the same year (1749) a second edition appeared, which was known to Pisanus Fraxi.

There is probably no erotic book which has been translated into so many European languages as Cleland's *Fanny Hill.* The novel was published in most of the principal European languages. It was only a Spanish translation that Pisanus Fraxi could not trace, but there probably was one in spite of that. Naturally, many of the foreign versions contain important modifications, abbreviations and incorrect renderings.

The Memoirs of a Woman of Pleasure, on account of which Cleland had to appear before the Privy Council, while the bookseller, Drybutter, was pilloried in the year 1757, was repeatedly banned and confiscated in England, France and Belgium. The rights were sold to the bookseller Griffiths for twenty guineas; he made £10,000 from the sale of the work.

The Memoirs of a Woman of Pleasure is the best erotic story in the English language. The construction of the story is very simple, the sequence of the scenes very natural and coherent, while the descriptive matter is vivid and impressive. The most intimate details are narrated, but always in a careful, polished style, such as we do not encounter in most of the other English erotic novels. In addition, the style is skilfully varied, so that the reader experiences neither boredom nor aversion, a difficulty which the author himself had to contend with, as he observed in the beginning of the first part[1].

The following brief analysis will give an adequate idea of the contents of the novel.

Fanny (Frances) Hill, the daughter of a poor family in a Lancashire village, comes to London by the Chester post, accompanied by a certain Esther Davis. The latter, a highly sophisticated girl, leaves Fanny in the lurch in the most shameful manner. Fanny applies to a servants' registry, where she is engaged and taken home by Mrs. Brown, an old procuress. Fanny naturally has no idea into whose hands she has fallen, and has to be enlightened by her room mate Phœbe, whom Mrs. Brown has instructed to overcome Fanny's provincial prejudices. A few days pass before Mrs. Brown finds the right lover for Fanny's virginity. He finally appears in the person of a repulsive old man, to whom the precious priority is to be sold for fifty guineas. However, in spite of Phœbe's persuasion Fanny manages to evade this attack on her chastity, preferring to entrust it to a handsome young man who is a

---

[1] ' I imagined, indeed, that you would have been cloyed and tired with uniformity of adventures and expressions, inseparable from a subject of this sort, whose bottom, or ground-work being eternally in the nature of things one and the same, whatever variety of forms and modes the situations are susceptible of, there is no escaping a repetition of near the same images, the same figures, the same expressions, with this inconvenience added to the disgust it creates, that the words " joys ", "ardours", "transports", "extasies", and the rest of those pathetic terms so congenial to, so received in the practice of pleasure, flatten and lose much of their due spirit and energy, by the frequency they indispensably recur with, in a narration of which that practice professedly composes the whole basis.' *Memoirs of a Woman of Pleasure* (Paris, 1894), pp. 187-8.

frequent visitor at Mrs. Brown's *sérail*. Charles, Fanny's hero, is both surprised and enchanted that the supposed brothel girl is in reality a *virgo intacta*. A mutual affection develops, and later the two live together in a smart flat.

However, their happiness does not last long. Charles's *affaire* is discovered and his father sends him off to one of his concerns in the South Seas. Fanny, who is pregnant, is left to her fate. Fear and worry make her ill, with consequent abortion. Hardly does she recover when her landlady, Mrs. Jones, who has carefully nursed her throughout her illness, introduces to her a certain Mr. H., whose advances Fanny in her need accepts, though with great aversion. Her new protector, though a man of noble birth, is not to Fanny's taste, and is unable to make her forget Charles. Nevertheless, she is faithful to him, until one day she discovers him in the arms of her own maid, whereupon she repays him measure for measure by seducing his servant, a young countryman. She spends a few pleasant hours in the lad's company, at the end of which she is surprised by Mr. H., who immediately discards her. The notorious Covent Garden brothel owner, Mrs. Cole, now appears on the scene.

She is ' a middle-aged, discreet sort of woman ', who has known Fanny for a long time and begs her to accept her protection. Fanny accepts and moves to a new flat near that of Mrs. Cole. Mrs. Cole's establishment constitutes a pleasant contrast to that of Mrs. Brown. There is comfort, orderliness and peace here. The brothel is screened by a smart, well-kept shop, and the girls, four in number, are well provided for and even spoilt. Under the protection of Mrs. Cole, and in the pleasant company of girls of her own age, with similar inclinations to her own, Fanny is happy for a time. Then Mrs. Cole, owing to approaching old age, gives up her establishment and retires to the country in order to spend her declining years in peace. Fanny sadly

resigns herself to the separation from her ' benefactress ',
and as she has a little money of her own, she rents a pretty
little house in Marylebone, where she represents herself as a
young wife whose husband is at sea, and calmly awaits a
fresh turn in her destinies, which proves to be a most
fortunate one.   An old gentleman whom she assists in an
accident in the field ' adopts ' her, and at his death leaves
his entire enormous fortune to her. Thus Fanny becomes
a great lady, and entirely her own mistress. Her love for
Charles has never diminished, and now it is her dearest
wish to be reunited with him. Having settled all her
affairs, she decides to visit her native village and leaves
London with that object in view. On the journey she puts
up at an inn, where two riders also take refuge from a storm.

To her infinite delight and surprise, she recognises in one
of them her lover, who has returned from his enforced
voyage. Dame fortune had not smiled upon Charles, but
Fanny has enough for two, and she places her fortune at his
disposal without reserve. She also makes a frank confession
about the life she has led during his absence. They are now
legally married, and Fanny becomes a virtuous housewife.
' The paths of vice ', the novel concludes, ' are sometimes
strewed with roses, but then they are for ever infamous for
many a thorn—for many a canker-worm: those of Virtue
are strewed with roses purely, and those eternally unfading
ones '.

Threaded into this main story there are numerous
descriptions of the life of the brothels, and also biographies
of Fanny's colleagues at Mrs. Cole's brothel. The various
sexual practices and aberrations of the male clients at the
latter brothel are also described in detail. There are many
descriptions of scenes of this kind, which include flagellation,
and contain many most obscene details.

It is said that Mrs. Cole's brothel, in particular, is very

EROTIC LITERATURE

realistically described. This procuress is supposed to be
identical with ' Mother Douglas ' of Covent Garden Market,
a notorious woman who also figures in some of Hogarth's
works. Foote brings her on the stage as Mrs. Cole in his
comedy *The Mirror*; he used to play the part himself.
Joseph Reid's Mrs. Snarewell in the farce *The Register
Office* is also said to represent this woman[1].

The reason the tendency of *Fanny Hill* is dangerous is
that the heroine ends not in hospital or in prison, as usual,
but in a happy reunion with her first love.

The name of Cleland's heroine was repeatedly used in
attempts to make otherwise worthless literary efforts more
attractive, though the contents had nothing to do with the
titles of these works. Thus already in 1773 there appeared
a novel entitled ' Memoirs of a Woman of Pleasure' in *The
Covent Garden Magazine; or Amorous Repository: Calculated
solely for the Entertainment of the Polite World*. According
to Pisanus Fraxi[2],this novel was not identical with Cleland's
story. 'Memoirs of a Maid of Honour ' also appeared in the
above-mentioned periodical.

The ' Memoirs of a Woman of Pleasure ', which appeared in
the erotic magazine *The Rambler's Magazine; or the Annals
of Gallantry, Glee, Pleasure and the Bon Ton, etc.* (London,
1783), also has nothing in common with Cleland's novel,
although the heroine's name is Fanny Hill[3].

Then there were the following worthless penny pamph-
lets: *The Pathetic Life of the Beautiful Fanny Hill, Showing
How She was Seduced, etc.* and *The Lust Legacy of Miss
Fanny Hill, a Woman of Pleasure, Containing Useful
Instructions for Young Men and Women, etc.*

[1] Fraxi, *Catena*, p. 85.
[2] *Ibid.*, p. 401.
[3] *Ibid.*, p. 332.

Finally, in the year 1880 the booksellers in Holywell Street frequently exhibited in their windows the English translation of Erneste Feydeau's *Fanny*, the word ' Hill ' being added on the cover, no doubt in order to create the impression that the book was the famous novel of John Cleland[1].

A counterpart to the *Memoirs of a Woman of Pleasure* was the *Memoirs of a Coxcomb*, published by John Cleland a few years after the former novel. (London: Printed for R. Griffiths, at the Dunciad in Paul's Churchyard. MDCCLI; 12mo, 386 pages.) Lowndes described *Memoirs of a Coxcomb* as a work of literary merit[2].

The book is written in a light, pleasant style and contains faithful descriptions of the morals of the times, but instead of the prostitute it is her male counterpart in whom the incidents centre. The coxcomb, despite his passionate hunt for sensual pleasures, develops a calm philosophy, and to a certain extent looks down on the vices in which he himself participates. The descriptions of vice and licentiousness are never obscene, so that *Memoirs of a Coxcomb* differs very considerably from the other novel.

A few other erotic writings that fall approximately within the period of Cleland's above-mentioned novels, and were to some extent influenced by them or dealt with similar vices, should be mentioned here.

A well-known work of this type is:

The Pleasures of Love—Containing a variety of entertaining Particulars and Curiosities, in the Cabinet of Venus. London: Printed in the year MDCCLV.

Small octavo, 84 pages, with 17 very beautiful etchings.

---

[1] Genuine old editions of *Memoirs of a Woman of Pleasure* rarely occur in catalogues, but a copy of the edition of 1749 appeared in the sale catalogue of the library of Count Du Bois du Bais (Paris, 1882).

[2] Lowndes, *The Bibliographer's Manual*, Vol. I, p. 477.

A VIEW ON THE BANKS OF THE THAMES.

Drawing by Rowlandson [*Pl.* 28

The frontispiece represents a stout girl drawing aside the curtain of a bed, upon which four bare legs are visible. The curtain bears the inscription: ' The Pleasures of Love, 1755.'

This extremely rare first edition was reprinted in 1872 by J. Scheible in Stuttgart (12mo, 65 pages, without illustrations, 100 copies at 1 Thaler 10 Groschen). A third edition appeared (after Scheible's reprint) in 1881 in London under the title:

The Adventures of a Rake—Containing a Variety, etc. Six Coloured Illustrations. Privately Printed. London, 1881.

Octavo, 60 pages, six very bad lithographs. 150 copies at Two Guineas. In this edition the name of the heroine was altered from Betsy to Maria.

The *Pleasures of Love* is a kind of autobiography, told by the hero, the son of a wealthy man. The value of the book is emphasised in the initial paragraph: ' There is probably no man in the world, however insignificant, whose written biography would not be entertaining', etc. Our hero is sent to the country to his uncle, and falls in love with the daughter of a farmer, whom he wishes to marry. As the union is opposed by both families, the enamoured young man elopes with his Betsy. His uncle pursues him and brings him back by force, but he has already received the greatest favour at the hands of the willing Betsy. The young man now joins a firm of solicitors in London. He detests both his chief and the law, and his restlessness, which is only intensified by his grief over his lost sweetheart, drives him into wild dissipation. He runs into his father, who forgives him, pays his debts, and apprentices him once more, but our hero soon slips back into his former ways, until, forced by necessity, he goes into service with a lady in the country. Soon after his arrival he realises that his ' services ' are to be of a very personal and intimate nature, but as the lady is young and beautiful, he is only too pleased to render those services, and he becomes her *major domo*. However, the cook and the chambermaid also enjoy his favour, so that his sexual capacity is constantly taxed. Later his mistress sends him another chambermaid from London and to his surprise and delight he finds that she is none other than his beloved Betsy, for whom he had searched in vain for a long time. At the same time he learns from a newspaper brought by Betsy that his father is dead, so that he is now master of the paternal estate. He marries Betsy and takes her back home, where they discover that Betsy is not the daughter of a mere farmer, but of a rich man, and has no less than £20,000. This concluding episode is reminiscent of the *dénouement* of Cleland's *Fanny Hill*. The *Pleasures of Love* also contains stories of the adventures of two London prostitutes with whom our hero associates, and mention is made of several well-known London brothels of the period.

A very rare and historically interesting book is the *New Attalantis,* which was published in 1762. It is a collection of five original stories, which also give a vivid presentment of the morals of the age. The full title of this work is:

New Attalantis for the Year 1762 : Being a Select Portion of Secret History ; Containing Many Facts, Strange but True!

> *The Godly dame who fleshly failings damns*
> *Scolds with her maid, or with the chaplain crams;*
> *Would you enjoy soft nights and solid dinners*
> *Faith, gallants, board with saints and bed with sinners.*
>
> *Pope.*

London, Printed for W. Morgan in Paternoster Row. MDCCLXII. Price 1s. 6d.

12mo, 100 pages. The volume concludes with 'End of the First Part', but the volume is nevertheless a complete whole.

[542]

The book contains the following stories:

1. ' The Amours of Lady Lucian.' ' This young lady ', says the text, ' was not beautiful, as she had a somewhat Dutch figure, was very stout, had ordinary features, and owed her complexion more to the chemist than to nature. . . . She lived in a state of virginity for so long that the number of her years equalled the number of her teeth. When I say that she lived in a state of virginity, I only mean that she was unmarried. For apart from actual intercourse with the male sex, it is well known that French manufacturers supply more than one instrument designed to alleviate the strict celibacy of a woman. . . . A pious and learned nobleman— Lord Lucian, bombarded her with politics, poetry and religion (in which three subjects he was equally expert) so successfully that he soon achieved the surrender of the fortress. But hardly were three minutes of the wedding night passed, than he felt himself impelled, not to fulfil the rites of Hymen, but to get up again and transcribe an epistle of Paul, which so occupied his thoughts and his time that he had no leisure that night for anything else.

' The next and the following nights passed in the same way, till the newly-married woman could no longer stand the neglect of her husband, and made a great scene in which she demanded of him something more tangible than his " sweet verses "; she did not, however, receive it from the incorrigible young poet. She now unburdened her heart to Madam Rouge, the " very incarnation of a procuress and smuggler ", who declared herself ready to help her.

' Lady Lucian was, however, afraid of the consequences of promiscuous intercourse, and the Rouge suggested to her that she should have a castrated man, as " these creatures are very easy to handle. It flatters their pride that a woman should take notice of them ", and besides their ability in external love-making is very highly developed. A rendez-

[543]

vous was therefore arranged at the house of the procuress between Lady Lucian and Signor Squalini the singer, on whom the lady had already for some time had her eye. He satisfied her in every way, and she asked him to be her music-master.　One day, however, her husband surprised them during a most tender *tête-à-tête*, with the result that the married couple parted, and Lady Lucian had " full opportunity to enjoy the society of her dear castrato without molestation ".　But Squalini soon left her and she fell into the arms of another castrated singer.　The tale ends with twenty verses, which were written by Lady Lucian " in praise of one of her maimed favourites " .'

The second tale, 'Henry and Emma', describes the love of Emma, the daughter of Albert, and Henry the husband of the beautiful Priscilla.　Emma also is not free, as she is to be married to a sailor who is not altogether antipathetic to her.　They both flee to the Continent, where their further adventures are described.　The whole is told in a dry philosophical manner, and the only interesting passage is a discourse on onanism in young girls.

In No. 3, ' The History of the Countess of B. ', is described most vividly the defloration of the young Countess of B. by her husband after he had for three weeks played the part of Knight Toggenburg, and her seven years of happy marriage, which ended all too soon with the death of the Count.　After long mourning the Countess fell violently in love with Squire Bullruddery, whom she happened to see in a very misleading situation, and who had unfortunately given her a false impression as to his virility.　The true state of affairs became evident to her soon after the wedding and gave her a very disagreeable surprise, and she refused him any further fulfilment of his marital duties.　She then compromised herself with an eighteen-year-old youth, who was, however, soon superseded by other lovers.

A similar case of a woman being thrown off her balance by the unaccustomed sight of masculine nudity forms the dramatic climax of the fourth tale of the *New Attalantis* entitled ' A Private Anecdote in the Fashionable World '. The lovely Melessa, wife of a prominent man on the Island of Angola, has for long carried on a love intrigue with the young man of pleasure, Hyppolitus. He had, however, become tired of her and involved himself with an opera dancer, and freed himself of his burdensome liaison with the help of a friend of his who was in love with Melessa, Colonel Bevil. One day, when Melessa went to visit her beloved Hyppolitus—immediately after she had dined; she scarce allowed herself time to eat, so much more valuable in her sense were the pleasures of love—on entering the room, which was darkened against the midday heat, she saw on the flower-decorated couch, in a very seductive attitude, a youth whose features she could not quite distinguish, and who appeared to be asleep. Under the kisses with which she covered her supposed Hyppolitus, he awoke, and took to himself in full measure the rights of a lover. Melessa soon discovered the deception, but was so satisfied with the Colonel that ' she bestowed upon him what she before in her own opinion, had bestowed upon Hyppolitus '. Hyppolitus then surprised the two and swore that he would never forgive the faithless lady.

The fifth tale, ' The Royal Rake; or the Adventures of Prince Yorick ', describes the extravagances of some noblemen, amongst them Prince Yorick, in the neighbourhood of Drury Lane. They get hold of a girl with the intention of seducing her, take all the prostitutes they meet in the street with them to a tavern, where they get the porter to bring in yet more harlots, till the big room is as full as the parterre of a theatre at a première. Then each one chooses a fair lady and the others are ' sent to Mother Godby to tell the tale there '. The scene then changes to a brothel where the young gentlemen are offered a rough-cheeked country girl for twenty guineas. The Prince, who drew the lucky number, paid the money and sent her back unharmed in a post-chaise to her parents.

Similar to the *Memoirs of a Woman of Pleasure* is the following new edition of an erotic book which appeared in 1769 under the title of *The History of the Human Heart or the Adventures of a Young Gentleman* (London, 1769; 12mo, 314 pages):

Memoirs of a man of pleasure; or the amours, intrigues and adventures of Sir Charles Manly. Interspersed with curious narratives and embellished with numerous elegant engravings. London: printed and published by W. Dugdale, 23 Russell Court, Drury Lane, 1827. 12mo, 306 pages, four free but not obscene copper-plates.

Another edition, issued by the same publisher with the notice ' Printed and published by J. Turner; 50 Holywell Street, Strand ' (8vo, 231 pages, six bad coloured lithographs), appeared later; also a new American edition, ' New York: Henry S. G. Smith and Co., 1855 ' (8vo, three bad woodcuts, price 50 cents).

The Memoirs of a Man of Pleasure begins with the breeding and birth of the author in the manner of Tristram Shandy, except that he also enlarges at some length on the various theories of procreation. The predilection of the hero for the fair sex, which was evident in his early youth, was explained as a sort of ' maternal impression ' given by the mother during her pregnancy. The latter had been seized by an extraordinary obscure desire for a relative who slept in the same room as herself, and this desire had been passed on to our Charles Manly, who at the early age of twelve years seduced his cousin of the same age or was seduced by her. When this was discovered he was sent for a short time to a friend of his parents, and later to travel under the care of a tutor. The latter, however, encouraged him in his excesses, and took him into bad company. Many love adventures, some of them of an incredible nature, are related, but Charles at length married a young lady, whom he had seduced and later left at The Hague, but whom he had followed to London. ' Adeline combined love and marriage with so much tender feeling that she completely took possession of the formerly wild Charles and brought him to a condition in which one hour of happiness with her was worth more to him than all the evil pleasures in the pursuit of which he had spent so much of his time, youth and money.'

In the text are to be found some interesting reports on the amusements of men of pleasure of that time, love stories of her own told by a harlot, and the like.

Two exceedingly odd examples of the satires of that time may also be mentioned here, namely the *Fruit Shop* and the still celebrated *Essay on Woman* by John Wilkes.

The title of the first, which appeared in the year 1765, is as follows:

The Fruit Shop, a tale. Vol. I.

> *Mais je l'aime et je veux que mes vers,*
> *Dans tous les coins de l'univers*
> *En fassent vivre le Mémoire;*
> *Et ne veux penser desormais*
> *Qu'à chanter dignement sa gloire.*
>
> *Volt.*

London : Printed for C. Moran in Covent Garden, 1765. Small 8vo, two vols, with irregular paging of the first volume (page xxii—Dedication, invocation, protest, caution and advice; then the text begins with pages 17 to 168). Vol. II, small 8vo, 160 pages. Vol. I contains a curious copper-plate frontispiece with the signature ' C. Trim fect.' which represents a garden scene. Before an oriental temple stands a tree in the shape of a phallus, over which two cupids hold a representation of a female genital organ. A man who is leaning against an ass points at the tree, and near him stands a boy. The man represents the ' distinguished person ' to whom the work is dedicated and against whom the author launches a violent tirade. He is the author of *Tristram Shandy*. The book takes its title from the ' Fruit Shop,' as the author calls woman, and contains a humorous-allegorical examination of every part of the female body which serves for the formation and harvesting of fruit. The author chiefly copies the art and manner of Swift and Sterne, never, however, attaining to the sarcastic wit of these authors in spite of many allusions to living persons.

Of the four parts of the book the first deals with Paradise, its true whereabouts, etc., rather wearisomely. The second tells of the events which led up to the Fall, the discovery of the fig leaf, etc., deals then with love, marriage, cuckoldry and ' unnatural beings or deserters from the fruit shop '. The third part contains a survey of the ' unwearied passion for the fruit-shop ' under the Romans, which begins with Jupiter and ends with Julius Caesar. The most remarkable of the contents are in the fourth part; for instance, the chapter on conception and celibacy, and flagellation as a ' roundabout way to heaven ', for the reason that, as a monk preaches in the latter, in flagellation the most noble part of the body becomes the lowest and the lowest the highest, in the humblest and most God-pleasing way. ' In which situation they might be sure of receiving, anon, animating impressions and missionary irradiations, if they were destined to figure among the elect.' To this the author adds further some thoroughly Jesuitical-casuistical views on the tendency to flagellation which springs from true piety, as it is expressed in the ' Nez à terre, cul en l'air '. Further, he speaks of platonic love, eunuchism and the ' Philogynists, the truly orthodox '.

The theme of the book is woman as a source of pleasure and the propagation of mankind. Those who ignore the provisions of Nature or do not make use of them, such as the celibates, onanists and paederasts, are very sharply taken to task.

In the ' Appendix ' and the ' Notes ' at the end of the second volume, amongst other things the ' fruit shop ' of St. James's Street is described, where 'matters never proceed further in this chaste domain than to a kiss or a feel, transiently and with the greatest decorum '; further, the object and title of the book are explained, and finally there are several quotations in different languages on the subject of the female breast.

Next to William King's *Toast*, the *Essay on Woman* by the celebrated politician John Wilkes, an obscene parody on Pope's *Essay on Man*, is certainly the most outstanding of the satirical erotic works of the eighteenth century.

John Wilkes was born on the 17th October 1727 in St. John's Street, Clerkenwell, London, and died on the 26th December 1797 at his house in Grosvenor Square. This is not the place to review in detail his wonderful political career, and his prosecution as publisher of the *North Briton*, chiefly on account of the notorious No. 45. With regard to his extraordinary life, the chief events of which were his expulsion from the House of Commons, his imprisonment, and promotion to be Lord Mayor of London, these can be studied in the history books, and we shall here consider in detail only the personal character of this peculiar man.

Although he himself was a man of pleasure and a debauchee, his public career was free from self-seeking and arrogance. He was a lovable father, honoured as a god by his daughter. His manners were those of a gentleman, and in spite of his ugliness[1] he was most successful with the fair sex. He was supposed to have the reputation of being able, inside of an hour, to supplant the most attractive man in a pretty woman's favour and often to have won wagers in this connection. The magnetic force of the attraction he had for women has been described, his brilliant conversation, and certain physical peculiarities belonging to the domain of so-called ' sexual osphresiology[2] '. Lord Brougham (in the *Historical Sketches of Statesmen who flourished in the time of George III*, 3rd series, *London*, 1843), Charles Johnston (in *Chrysal, or the Adventures of a Guinea: by an Adept*, London, 1821, Vol. III, Chap. 20) and Gibbon (in *Miscellaneous Works*) give some good descriptions of the personality of Wilkes, his wit, high intellectuality and unique conversational gifts. Nichols says : ' Full of wit, easy in his conversation, elegant in his manners and happy in a retentive memory, his company was a perpetual treat to his friends[3].'

A characteristic anecdote of Wilkes, which at the same time illustrates forcibly his moral unscrupulousness, is told in the *City Biography* (London, 1800, p. 110). Wilkes practised his sexual excesses also most artfully and cautiously. He once asked the legal advice of Sir Fletcher Norton as to how he could avoid an action for ' seduction ' if he took a certain girl from her father to his own house. Sir Fletcher, a very cunning lawyer, advised Wilkes, in order to get round the law, to take the girl as an upper servant, and to give her double wages; this extra pay would make it clear that something more than the ' usual

[1] Lichtenberg writes to Dieterich from London (27th October 1775): ' Wilkes has small twinkling eyes, so that you can hardly see that he squints, and about his profile there is something very distinguished and not at all disagreeable.' Lichtenberg's Letters, Vol. I, p. 231.

[2] Compare *Untrodden Fields of Anthropology*, Vol. I, p. 247

[3] Nichols, *loc. cit.*, Vol. IX, p. 477.

service' was required of her. Wilkes took the hint, and actually engaged the girl as *fille de joie* and servant for £20 a year; he then proceeded to abuse the legal profession and swore by his goddess Venus that lawyer and rogue are identical terms.

Wilkes' appearance, his tall thin form, his ugly face with the squinting eyes, made him a very good subject for caricature[1]. Hogarth's celebrated portrait only need be referred to, a gross caricature, but very like Wilkes. An epigram of the time runs:

Says John Wilkes to a lady, pray name if you can,
Of all your acquaintance the handsomest man.
The lady replied, if you'd have me speak true,
He's the handsomest man that's the most unlike you.

The most notorious of Wilkes' poems appeared in its oldest known edition (but this was not the first[2]) in the year 1763, with the title:

An Essay on Woman, by Pego Borewell Esq.; with notes by Rogerus Cunaeus, Vigerus Mutoniatus, etc., and a Commentary by the Rev. Dr. Warburton. Inscribed to Miss Fanny Murray. [Greek quotation here.] *Hom. Od. II, Vol. 6.*

Ex Archetypo saepe in Femoralibus (sic) Reverendissimi Georgii Stone, Hiberniae Primatis, Saepius in Podice Intrepidi Herois Georgii Sackville.

Small 8vo, 30 pages; the volume contains ' Advertisement by the Editor' (pp. 3-8); 'The Design' (pp. 9-12); 'An Essay on Woman' (pp. 13-22); 'The Universal Prayer' (pp. 23-26); 'The Dying Lover to His Pr . . . ' (pp. 27-28); 'Veni Creator; or the Maid's Prayer'

---

[1] *City Biography*, p. 102; *The Georgian Era* (London, 1832), Vol. I, p. 312.
[2] This consisted of twelve copies only, which Wilkes himself drew. Mr. W. F. Rae says that none of these copies is known to be in existence to-day. According to P. Fraxi, a copy of this *opus rarissimum* was known to exist in the 'fifties of the nineteenth century. P. Fraxis, *Index librorum prohibitorum*, pp. 200-201.

(pp. 29-30). In addition, many notes with the signatures 'Warburton', 'Vigerus Mutoniatus', 'Rogerus Cunaeus' and 'Burman'.

The 'Essay on Woman' contains ninety-four verses, and consists of an 'Invocation' and three parts. The 'Universal Prayer' has notes and contains thirteen stanzas each of four verses. Equally cynical is the 'Dying Lover to His Pr——" containing eighteen verses.

'Veni Creator; or the Maid's Prayer', consists of five stanzas, the first two of which contain six verses, the last three five verses. The beginning runs:

> Creator Pego, by whose aid,
> Thy humble suppliant was made, etc.

and the end:

> Immortal honour, endless fame,
> Almighty Pego! to thy name . . .

The contents of the *Essay on Woman* from the literary point of view are very poor. The notes are perhaps the best thing in it. Had Wilkes not been so disgracefully persecuted by the Government on account of this book, the wretched piece of work would never have become known nor been handed down to us. On its appearance it was most sharply condemned[1]. In the House of Lords it was described as 'a highly scandalous, obscene and godless libel, as a gross profanation of many parts of the Holy Scriptures, and a most malicious and blasphemous attempt to belittle and ridicule the person of the Redeemer'. Bishop Warburton spoke of it in the House of Lords as a book which contained the 'most hideous insults to religion, virtue and humanity and the most shocking blasphemies against the Almighty', together with

[1] On the other side, a partisan of Wilkes declared that it aroused sentiments at least comparable to those aroused by a Rochester or an Aristotle, if it did not surpass them. Compare *The Life of John Wilkes Esq. London. J. Wilkie. MCCLCXXIII (sic)*.

a ' collection of notes which for bestiality and blasphemy could not be surpassed, and would make the most hardened dweller in Hell shudder and blush with shame '. Horace Walpole calls the book ' the most shocking and blasphemous poem that was ever written ', and, further, ' a highly obscene product which represents a parody on Pope's *Essay on Man* and other poems, in which the grossest profanities are uttered '.

Kidgell wrote the most remarkable analysis on the *Essay on Woman* in his *Narrative*. This gives the best conception of the poem and, for this reason, will be quoted at length.

' This *Essay on Woman* is almost line for line a parody on Mr. Pope's *Essay on Man*.

' The title-page is followed by some pages—" Advertisement and Design "—full of the grossest indecencies as worthy preparation for the hideous language and the incredible godlessness of the text itself, for the obscene terms, the open portrayal of the most disgusting doings, with unequalled vulgarity, and the most insulting, debasing and lascivious reflections on the female sex.

' In the variations and notes to this obscene parody, the Holy Scriptures are extensively prostituted to illustrate the gross ideas of a debauched blasphemer.

' The coarseness which runs through the whole work is of an astonishing, unique and amazing originality. Many solemn passages from the Gospels are turned into obscenities by the use of double meanings. . . .

' In another of these shocking illustrations from the Scriptures the natural functions of the ass are disgustingly described. The unlearned reader is then informed that " this animal once enjoyed great regard, but has become ridiculous since it acted as the vehicle of godhead in Jerusalem ".

' The climax of obscenity and coarseness is reached in the obscene paraphrase of the " Universal Prayer " of Pope and

[553]

the memorable monologue of the Emperor Hadrian which Pope called the words of a " dying Christian to his soul " . . . '

A similar characterisation of the *Essay on Woman* appears in the 33rd volume of the *Gentleman's Magazine* (1763, p. 526).

Wilkes defended himself with great eloquence against this condemnation in a readable letter to the electors of Aylesbury[1].

That he was the sole author of the book, if he was indeed the author at all, is doubtful. The Government produced no proof, and Wilkes himself never admitted the authorship of the poem. In *Notes and Queries* (Series II, Vol. 57, pp. 1, 21, 41 and 113) there are some interesting discussions on the *Essay on Woman*, the author of which, Mr. Dilke, tries to prove that Wilkes could not have written it. This opinion was shared by Mr. W. F. Rae[2]. Horace Walpole states in the *Memoirs of King George III* that Wilkes and Potter, the son of the late Archbishop of Canterbury, together wrote this wretched work at a bacchanal, and that Wilkes afterwards had it printed himself. This Thomas Potter was the lover of the wife of Bishop Warburton, a fact which gave a unique flavour to the whole matter, and did not tend to lessen the bitterness of the Bishop.

The conduct of the Government in the prosecution of Wilkes was in any case arbitrary, illegal and partisan. On the instance of a Minister of the Crown he was brought to trial and accused of being the originator of a poem, copies of which were stolen from him by means of an illegal warrant, and the contents read by Lord Sandwich in the Upper House. No conclusive proof of his authorship could however be produced[3]. Horace Walpole contributes further

[1] *The Gentleman's Magazine*, Vol. 34, p. 580.
[2] W. F. Rae, *Wilkes, Sheridan, Fox. The Opposition under George III* (London, 1874), p. 48.
[3] Rae in *Fortnightly Review* (September, 1868).

details of the proceedings, according to which Philip Carteret Webbe first obtained possession illegally of a copy of the *Essay on Woman* from Wilkes' house. Later, the hypocritical preacher Kidgell, House-Chaplain to the infamous Duke of Queensberry (Earl of March), with the help of a traitorous printer of Wilkes, Michael Curry, got hold of some proof sheets of the poem. Later, at the instigation of the Earl of March and Lords Bute and Sandwich, Kidgell and Webbe bought the whole poem, parts of which were read by Sandwich in the House of Lords. Lords Lyttleton, Bishop Warburton and others then demanded that legal steps be taken at once against Wilkes, which demand was acceded to, but public opinion was on the side of Wilkes because of the illegal methods employed, and not less on account of the very questionable moral character of the plaintiffs. For Lord Sandwich and Lord De Spencer were two of the founders of the notorious 'Medmenham Abbey', the Duke of Queensberry was one of the most eccentric men of pleasure of his time, and William Warburton, Bishop of Gloucester, combined, according to Johnson, the strength of a giant with the morality of a debauchee; he was, however, supposed to be impotent, on which fact the poet Churchill in *The Duellist* makes play, and which also explains his wife's love affair with Potter. John Kidgell finally, the Rector of Horne and author of the wearisome novel *The Card* (London, 1755), embezzled a sum of money entrusted to him and fled to Flanders where de died, after having been admitted to the Catholic faith. Churchill wrote the following ironic lines in his poem *The Author*:

> Kidgell and I have free and modest souls:
> We scorn preferment which is gained by sin,
> And will, though poor without, have peace within.

The scandal caused by the trial of Wilkes increased the demand for the *Essay on Woman*, and several counterfeit editions were issued to meet this. Kidgell's *Narrative* also brought much correspondence[1].

One of the most interesting writers on the history of morals of the eighteenth century was George Alexander Stevens, who by his first book earned for himself a reputation as a fashionable man of pleasure. He was born in London in 1720 and died at Baldock, in Hertfordshire, on the 6th September 1784. Although a lovable personality he was a terrible good-for-nothing, a dilettante, gambler, poet, dramatic writer and actor, whom his friend Sparks regarded as the best authority on the Greeks in England. Always hard up, sometimes in prison, he experienced all extremes of good fortune and well-being as well as of poverty and want, and lived a life which in its grossness and irregularity was in no way an estimable one, though untarnished by crime. He possessed a lively wit and a very wide knowledge of mankind. Stevens was the inventor of a special type of theatrical representation, the so-called *Lectures upon Heads*, which he first gave in April 1764 in the Haymarket Theatre, and from then on earned much applause and a considerable income from it. Archenholtz relates as follows:

' An Englishman who had died the previous year, named Stevens, invented an entertainment of a peculiar kind. He called it *Lectures upon Heads*, and gave it all the winter in the Haymarket Theatre. It was a satirical-comic lecture on all ranks and classes of people of the British nation, delivered with a deep knowledge of the world and of man-

---

[1] For instance, *The Priest in Rhyme, etc.*, quarto; *An Expostulatory Letter to the Rev. Mr. Kidgell, etc. By a Layman* (London, 1763, quarto, 11 pages); *A Letter to J. Kidgell, etc.* (1763, quarto, 121 pages); *The Plain Truth, etc.* (1763, quarto), etc.

CRUELTY IN PERFECTION.

Prior. *To lawless Love when once betray'd.*
Soon Crime to Crime succeeds
At length beguil'd to Theft, the Maid
By her Beguiler bleeds.

Yet learn seducing Man! nor Night,
With all its sable Cloud,
Can screen the guilty Deed from sight,
Foul Murder! cries aloud.

Published according to Act of Parliament Feb. 1.1751.

The gaping Wounds, and blood-stain'd steel,
Now shock his trembling Soul:
But Oh! what Pangs his Breast must feel,
When Death his Knell shall toll.

Designed by W.Hogarth.

Pl. 29]

Designed by Wm. Hogarth

A Boarding-School-Miss, taking an Evening Lesson!!

Pl. 30]

Artist unknown

kind, and with wit, humour and great artistry. For his lectures he employed a number of pasteboard busts, representing the different ranks, professions and characters of mankind, which he accompanied with imitations of the speech, accent and gestures. Courtiers, doctors, lawyers, preachers, tradespeople, country people, military men, scholars, artists, court ladies and fishwives, all came into the picture. Very little that was trivial was heard, but very much that was instructive in this school of humanity which, if not for the sake of its intellectuality, which was part of the philosophy of life, then on account of the delightful mimicry, was very much sought after. He usually closed his lecture with a satire on himself, so that he might have his share of the fun he so generously distributed[1].'

These interesting lectures are collected in a little volume which is not easy to get hold of. The edition lying before me appeared in 1799, and bears the following title:

A Lecture on Heads by Geo. Alex. Stevens, with Additions by Mr. Pilon; as delivered by Mr. Charles Lee Lewes. To which is added An Essay on Satire. With twenty-four heads by Nesbit, from designs by Thurston. London; printed by T. Bensley, Bolt Court, Fleet Street, etc. 1799. 12mo, XII, 116 pages.

Amongst the descriptions of individual London types in 1770 in the *Lecture on Heads*, which were almost without exception delightful, the following deserve special mention: The effeminate or 'Master Jackey' (pp. 11-12), the Virago (pp. 12-13), the Prostitute (p. 17), the President of a Female Debating Club (pp. 33-34), the Old Youth (p. 48), the Bachelor (pp. 48-50)[2]. The description of himself, too, is delicious

---

[1] See Archenholtz, *England*, Vol. III, pp. 195-196.

[2] Of him he says: ' When they become superannuated, they set up for suitors, they ogle through spectacles, and sing love songs to ladies with catarrhs by way of symphonies, and they address a young lady with

(pp. 2-3). In two other places also he described himself very faithfully; in his poem ' Religion or the repentant Libertine ' (1751) he gives the following sketch of his own career:

> By chance condemned to wander from my birth
> An erring exile o'er the face of earth;
> Wild through the world of vice,—licentious race!
> I've started folly, and enjoyed the chace:
> Pleas'd with each passion, I pursued their aim,
> Cheer'd the gay pack, and grasp'd the guilty game;
> Revel'd regardless, leap'd reflection o'er,
> Till youth, till health, fame, fortune, are no more.
> Too late I feel the thought-corroding pain
> Of sharp remembrance and severe disdain:
> Each painted pleasure its avenger breeds,
> Sorrow's sad train to Riot's troop succeeds;
> Slow-wasting Sickness steals on swift debauch;
> Contempt on pride, pale want on waste approach.

Another autobiographical impression is given in a book which is very interesting from the point of view of the history of morals:

The Adventures of a Speculist; or a Journey through London. Compiled from Papers written by George Alexander Stevens (author of a lecture upon heads) with his Life, a Preface, Corrections and Notes by the Editor. Exhibiting a picture of the manners, fashions, amusements, etc., of the Metropolis at the middle of the eighteenth century: and including several fugitive pieces of humour, by the same author, now first collected and published. In two volumes. London. Printed for the editor, and

"Come, my dear, I'll put on my spectacles and your handkerchief for you; I'll sing you a love song:
How can you, lovely Nancy! (laughs aloud)
How droll to hear the dotards aping youth,
And tale of love's delight without a tooth! (Takes the head off.)".'

sold by S. Bladon, no. 13, Paternoster Row. MDCCLXXXVIII.
8vo. Vol. I, xxviii and 268 pages, Vol. II, 286 pages.

The *Adventures of a Speculist* is a very important and
informative composition on life and doings in London in
1760. ' A more truthful and striking picture of London life
during the middle of the 18th century it would be difficult to
find; and who knew it better than Stevens, a regular man
about town and constant frequenter of its most doubtful
haunts! ' (Pisanus Fraxi.) The ' Speculist ' begins his journey
in the City, visits Fleet prison, Exchange Alley, Jonathan's
and Bedlam Hospital, all of which he describes with lusty
humour, taking his readers into the lives of the characters
drawn. His friend Flight, who accompanied him, gave him
a manuscript, ' Authentic life of a Woman of the Town '
(Vol. I, p. 129 to the end of Vol. II), about which he remarked:
' The adventures are really lived and the observations are
correct. They furnish an excellent complement to your own
observations, so that you can form for yourself an authentic
opinion on the moral degeneration of mankind.' Then follow
humorous and interesting sketches of the taverns and night
cellars and their frequenters, some clubs like that of the
' Jolly Dog's ' the ' Damn'd High Fellows ' (Vol. II, p. 15),
the ' Momus Court ' in the White Horse, Fetter Lane (Vol. II,
p. 16). Covent Garden is described, ' as it was and as it is '
(Vol. I, p. 258), also the brothels of Jenny Douglas (Vol. I,
p. 243) and Bob Derry (Vol. II, p. 51). Further, there are
anecdotes of kept women, prostitutes, etc., and some curious
details about the ' tavern plyers ' are told. In the *Life of a
Harlot* two other tales are included, namely ' History of
a Reforming Constable ' (Vol. I, pp. 218 *et seq.*) and ' Life of
a Young Criminal ' (Vol. II, p. 196). All three are highly
entertaining, written in a lively style and impart a very
sound knowledge of contemporary corruption. In Vol. II,
p. 20, Stevens describes himself: ' That fresh-cheeked youth

who is following him is an inexplicable being. He has written some lively songs which have been fairly profitable, but spoilt them by trying to sing them himself. He has belonged to two theatrical companies, but could do nothing in either of them. He has too much intelligence for a fool and too little to be wise. He could be either better or worse than he is, if he took the trouble. George is neither incompetent nor disinclined to consider what he ought to do, but he lets things come and go, just as they happen to, too careless to regard anything as important but the present, and, like a grasshopper, enjoys half the year while the other half he is deeply unhappy.'

Stevens was also the author of five dramas, one or two poems, and of the novel *The History of Tom Fool* (1760). There are also some good examples of his muse in a small rare volume, *The Humours of London, a choice Collection of Songs*, etc., and finally, in the year 1801, appeared a collection of *Songs, comic and satirical, written by George Alexander Stevens*, etc., with many woodcuts on every page in the style of Bewick. Stevens could, as W. Davis remarked, keep an audience engrossed for four hours uninterruptedly with his lectures and recitals of his writings[1].

A similar literary personality to George A. Stevens was Samuel Johnson Pratt (born at St. Ives in Huntingdonshire on the 25th December 1749, died at Birmingham on the 4th October 1814), who wrote under the pseudonym Courtney Melmoth, which name was probably borrowed from his mistress, the actress, Mrs. Melmoth. He was an actor, poet, bookseller, reciter and author of several novels and other compositions; indeed, a ' very voluminous gentleman ', but he did not hesitate to receive financial assistance from his

[1] William Davis, *An Olio of Bibliographical and Literary Anecdotes* (London, 1817), p. 47.

above-named mistress[1]. Pratt interests us as author of the following:

The Pupil of Pleasure: or the New System Illustrated. Inscribed to Mrs. Eugenia Stanhope, editor of Lord Chesterfield's letters. By Courtney Melmoth. Versatile ingenium. Vol. I, London, printed for G. Robinson and J. Bew, in Paternoster Row. 1776.

12mo, two volumes, xv, 230 and 252 pages. New edition, 1783 (A New Edition, Corrected), with the real name of the author and a beautiful copper-plate (with signature: Dodd delin. T. Cook sculp.), two volumes, 12mo, x, 234 and 252 pages. The first edition contained 111, the second 110 letters, as letter No. 92, in which Sedley describes the seduction of a young woman in very vivid terms, was left out.

The *Pupil of Pleasure* has a moral tendency. The book refutes the maxims of Lord Chesterfield and shows by example how dangerous they may be. Sedley, a rich young man of pleasure, thoroughly saturated with Chesterfield's teaching, visits Buxton, where he succeeds in seducing two married women, Harriet Homespun and Fanny Mortimer. His roguery is at last discovered and he is killed by the furious husband, Mortimer. The story is told in 111 letters from different people, principally from Sedley and his friend Thornton. In spite of obvious originality, the *Pupil of Pleasure* is written in a style of insipid, affected sentimentality which does not suit modern taste. Although the tale is concerned solely with the seduction of women, there are no obscene descriptions or dirty words. In many ways the book reminds one of *Liaisons Dangereuses*. In the *Monthly Review* (Vol. 56, p. 232) it was described as ' unnatural and repulsive ', and impossible to read without disgust.

[1] *Notes and Queries*, Sixth Series, Vol. VII, p. 37; Vol. VI, p. 212.

Octave Mirbeau's *Journal d'une Femme de Chambre* possibly takes its theme from the French translation *Mémoires d'une Femme de Chambre* (1786) of an English original which first appeared at the end of the 'seventies or the beginning of the 'eighties, possibly under the title *The Waiting Woman or the Gallantries of the Times* (London, 1735). In any case a new edition arranged by John Duncombe in 1830 is founded on this old work, which describes the experiences of a chambermaid. For, as it says in the beginning of the book, ' the curiosity of a chambermaid has become proverbial. It was more curiosity than necessity or inclination which led me to take such a position, and so that I shall not appear to have used my talents to no purpose, I have published my "revelations" to the world for the use and the instruction of all mankind.' The chambermaid, Kitty Pry, spied out in all the houses where she was in service the secret doings of the inhabitants. Thus we get descriptions of love scenes in all classes of society, and the authoress closes with the story of two of her own adventures. The book is not badly written, and although each chapter contains an immoral episode, obscene words are avoided. Persons of position, such as the Duke of York and Cumberland, Lady Grosvenor and others, are clearly referred to, and it should not be difficult to distinguish others from the initials given.

A few other erotic works from 1780 to 1810 may be mentioned here, such as *The Woman of Pleasure's Pocket Companion*[1], the *Dialogue between a Woman and a*

---

[1] *The Woman of Pleasure's Pocket Companion. With engravings, etc. Paris (London): reprinted in the year* 1830. 12mo, 48 pages. Original edition, 1787. Contains six erotic but not indecent tales, some of them of a humorous nature. Each story has a rather bad copper-plate, some of them taken from other works, as, for instance, that belonging to the first story; ' The modern Susanna and the two Elders ' is also to be found on page 60 of *Les Bijoux du petit neveu de d'Arétin* (1791).

Virgin[1], *The Voluptarian Museum* and *The Adventures of Sir Henry Loveall*[2], *A Cabinet of Amorous Curiosities*[3] and *The Cabinet of Fancy*[4].

[1] *Dialogue between a Woman and a Virgin. Printed for R. Borewell, South Audley Street. MDCCLXXXVI. (Price two shillings).* 12mo, 35 pages. (Reprint in *Voluptarian Cabinet.*) The contents of this Dialogue, which has several different sources of origin, are as follows: Volupta, who has already ' initiated ' several girls, explains to Lydia, an immature virgin, the pleasures of sexual intercourse, and describes to her the circumstances and delights which will accompany the loss of her own virginity. Mr. Do Little, an impotent old debauchee, comes in, and for a few minutes eases his amorous state with Lydia for the sum of 100 pounds sterling. On his departure Charles, a strong young man, known to both the girls, completes the defloration of Lydia to their mutual satisfaction.

[2] *The Voluptarian Museum: or History of Sir Henry Loveall. In a tour through England, Ireland, Scotland and Wales, embellished with six highly finished prints. From beautiful paintings. Price one guinea plain, one guinea and a half in colours, etc. Paris: printed for the proprietors.* 8vo, 162 pages with good copper-plates. This is apparently the first edition of the following work, *The adventures of Sir Henry Loveall, in a tour through England, Ireland, Scotland and Wales. Embellished with ten superb coloured plates, etc. Price three guineas and a half.* 8vo, two volumes each of 68 pages, 16 coloured lithographs (8 in each volume). This is the edition published by Dugdale in 1860 of the original book, which appeared at the end of the eighteenth century, of which several good old but rare copies exist. One of the earliest contains ' 6 superb copper-plates, price 18/- '. In these pictures the women wear large round hats. Another edition is dated 1812, and is known as ' Mrs. Dawson's octavo edition '; twelve coloured copper-plates were engraved for this, one of which is very rare, as the collection seldom contains more than eleven. They are all very clever and excellently done, and signed with fictitious names such as ' Mary Wilson ', ' Sophia Cary ', ' Bolano ', etc. *Sir Henry Loveall* is written in a light conversational style, not too obscene, and contains one or two flagellation scenes and a few verses. There is nothing abnormal in it. Dugdale describes it in his catalogue as the work of ' a man of fashion, of gallantry and of adventurous daring '.

[3] *A cabinet of Amorous Curiosities. In three tales. Highly calculated to please the votaries of Venus. Tale I. The Village Bull. Tale II. Memoirs of a Feather-bed. Tale III. Adventures of a droll one; or the broke open casket. Printed for R. Borewell, South Audley Street. MDCCLXXXVI (price two shillings).* 12mo, 38 pages. There is a new edition by W. Dugdale. These three tales all deal with the same subject, the defloration of their respective heroines. In the first tale this fate overtakes two country girls who are taking a cow to the bull. In the second, Julia, the daughter of a country nobleman, is seduced by Alexander, a London fop. In the

Especially rich in erotic literature in the nineteenth century were the years between 1820 and 1840, and 1860-1880, for which, as regards the first period, publishers like Brookes, Duncombe and others were responsible, as regards the second period chiefly William Dugdale, who was indefatigable in this branch of literature. The bibliographical enumeration of the for the most part unimportant writings must here mainly suffice, with a short account of the contents. To these belong, amongst others, *The Bedfellows: or Young Misses Manual*[1], *The Modern Rake*[2], *The*

third tale, a quack doctor accomplishes the heroic act with an innocent girl under the pretext of explaining to her medically how the same events would have taken place in the case of her grandmother.

[4] *The Cabinet of Fancy or Bon Ton of the day; a whimsical, comical, friendly, agreeable composition; intended to please all and offend none; suitable to amuse morning, noon and night, writte (sic) and compiled by Timothy Tickle-Pitcher.*

> *With songs and strange extravagances*
> *He tries to tickle all your fancies.*

London: printed for J. McLaen, Ship Alley, Wellclose Square. T. Sudbury, No. 16, Tooley Street, Borough; and sold by all the booksellers in town and country. MDCCXC. 12mo, 60 pages. With a beautiful copper-plate on the title-page, ' Lady L——'s whim, or the naughty boy in dumps '. (A lady in a large hat takes a rod from a boy who wishes to punish her.) An amusing collection of pieces in prose and poetry. Tales, anecdotes, epigrams, songs, erotic but not indecent.

[1] *The Bed-fellows: or Young Misses Manuel (sic). In six confidential dialogues between two budding beauties, who have just fledged their teens. Adapted to the capacity of every loving virgin who has wit enough in her little finger to know the value of the rest, etc. Printed and published on Mons Veneris: and may be had by all who seek it there.* 12mo, 150 pages, 8 obscene, vulgar copper-plates. Four editions. The first by Dickinson in 1820, the second in 1830, the third shortly after, and the fourth in 1860 by W. Dugdale (8vo, 120 pages with 8 bad coloured lithographs). A well-written book, better than the average work of the kind. Lucy and Kate tell each other their love adventures each evening when they go to bed, describe amongst other things to the smallest details their first seduction, and intersperse these lascivious conversations with Lesbian practices.

[2] *The Modern Rake; or the life and adventures of Sir Edward Walford; containing a curious and voluptuous history of his luscious intrigues with numerous women of fashion, his laughable faux pas, feats of gallantry, debauchery, dissipation and concubinism! His numerous rapes, seductions and amatory scrapes. Memoirs of the beautiful courtesans with whom he*

Amorous Intrigues and Adventures of Don Ferdinand and Donna Marie[1], *The Seducing Cardinal*[2], *The Lustful Turk*[3] and a book which appeared later, and which was

lived; with some ticklish songs, anecdotes, poetry, etc. Enriched with many curious plates. J. Sudbury, printer, Gate Street, 1824. Large 12mo, 112 pages, 9 very obscene, clever coloured illustrations. Catalogue price three guineas. New edition a year later by J. B. Brookes. The book describes, as the title announces, the erotic adventures of a young debauchee in Paris, Spain and England till his conversion on a happy marriage. It also contains the autobiography of a French courtesan, and mention of various erotic writings such as *Fanny Hill, Letters of two cousins, Intrigues of a lady of fashion, The Ladies' Tell Tale* and *Chevalier de Faublas.*

[1] *The amorous intrigues and adventures of Don Ferdinand and Donna Marie. Ferdinand's intrigue with the innkeeper's wife. Cataline's amour with Ferdinand. Donna Marie's intrigue. Curious adventures of the Duke and Duchess of Storza, London: Printed for the booksellers.* 124 pages, about 1820 to 1830. The contents are sufficiently described in the title. The theme of ' Faublas ' is employed, a man dressed as a girl who sleeps with Donna Marie, the love of his youth.

[2] *The Seducing Cardinal or Isabella Peto. A Tale founded on Facts. London: Published as the act directs by Madame Le Duck, Mortimer Street; and to be had of all respectable booksellers.* 1830. *Price £1. 11. 6.* 12mo, 78 pages, 5 obscene coloured copper-plates. Publisher: J. B. Brookes. The ' seducing Cardinal ' is ' Johann Peter Caraffa, afterwards Pope Paul III ' (this edition is mistaken, as Pope Paul III was a Farnese and not a Caraffa, also no Giovanni Pietro C. ever existed), and Isabella Peto is an orphan of eighteen years on the point of being married to Signor Antonio Lucca. The Cardinal, who is in love with her, has her thrown into a prison of the Inquisition, so that she is obliged to sacrifice her virginity as the price of her freedom. When, a week after the marriage, Lucca is called to Candia, the Cardinal renews his intimacy with Isabella. She then travels out to join her husband, but he has been killed by the Turks in battle, and she is shut up in the harem of the Bey of Adrianopolis. She is, however, well treated there. Caraffa happens to visit Constantinople, frees Isabella and Atalide, another favourite slave of the Bey's, and takes them both to a convent. The book is very obscene.

[3] *The lustful Turk. Part the first. A History founded on Facts, containing an interesting narrative of the cruel fate of the two young English ladies, named Silvia Carey and Emily Barlow. Fully explaining how Emily Barlow and her servant Eliza Gibbs, on their passage to India, were taken prisoners by an Algerine pirate and made a present of to the Dey of Algiers; who, on the very night of their arrival, debauched Emily. Containing also, every particular of the artful plans laid by the Dey, to get possession of the person of Silvia Carey, etc. with the particulars of her becoming a victim to his libidinous desires. Which recital is also interspersed with the histories of*

similar to this, *Scenes in the Seraglio*[1], *Memoirs of Rosa Bellefille*[2], *The Favourite of Venus*[3], *How to Make*

several other ladies confined in the Dey's harem. One of which gives an account of the horrid practices then carrying in several French and Italian convents by a society of monks, established at Algiers under pretence of redeeming Christian slaves; but who, in reality, carried on an infamous traffic in young girls. Also an account of the sufferings of Eliza Gibbs from the flogging propensities of the Bey of Tunis. With many other curious circumstances, until the reduction of Algiers by Lord Exmouth; by which means these particulars became known. The whole compiled from the original letters by permission of one of the sufferers. Embellished with beautiful engravings. Published in two parts by an Arcadian, A8 (sic) the law directs; and to be had of all the principle booksellers in town and country. Price 2 guineas. 1828. Large 12mo, two parts, 99 and 94 pages, 18 coloured pictures. Publisher, J. B. Brookes. Later two new editions by Dugdale, the first 1860 or 1864. The contents of this book, with its descriptions of the worst debauchers, are enumerated in the title.

[1] *Scenes in the Seraglio. By the author of the 'Lusty (sic) Turk'. With numerous coloured plates. Price two guineas.* 8vo, 88 pages, 6 bad coloured lithographs. Appeared between 1855 and 1860. Publisher, W. Dugdale. Shortly after, a second edition appeared. Both are based on an original of 1820 or 1830 with 6 beautiful coloured lithographs. The book may very well be the work of the author of *The Lustful Turk*. Adelaide, a young Sicilian beauty, is kidnapped by the Corsair Tick, to serve as his mistress. His love for money, however, triumphs over his lust when he discovers her virginity, and he decides to sell her dearly. He therefore only forces her to put up with harmless caresses from him, and to look on at his amorous pleasures with a Countess whom he had also kidnapped. He brings his victim to Constantinople and sells her to the Sultan Achmed, who treats Adelaide with so much friendliness and delicacy that in the end she grants him his wishes of her own free will. The story of the 'Love affairs of Euphrosyne' is also included, another inmate of a harem.

[2] *Memoirs of Rosa Bellefille; or a Delicious Banquet of Amorous Delights! Dedicated to the goddess of voluptuous pleasure, and her soul-enamoured votaries, etc. Paphian Press.* 1828. 12mo, 99 pages, 6 well-executed obscene copper-plates. Published 1828 by G. Cannon in London. A new edition appeared in 1865 by W. Dugdale (M. Sullivan, printer, London. 8vo, 96 pages, 8 bad obscene lithographs, not identical with those in Cannon's edition). A rather wearisome story. Rosa, a young girl with a very highly developed erotic temperament, relates her various adventures. She runs away from school, and literally throws herself in the arms of every man she meets. She is kept by several men, but leaves them all as soon as she is tired of them or finds that her exaggerated salaciousness gives them no pleasure. Finally, she becomes a common prostitute, and takes a small lodging in the neighbourhood of Drury Lane.

Love and *How to Raise Love*[1], *The Adventures, Intrigues and Amours of a Lady's Maid* and its continuation *The Life of Miss Louisa Selby*[2], *The Ladies' Tell Tale, or*

[3] *The Favourite of Venus; or secrets of my note book: explained in the life of a votary of pleasure. By Theresa Berkley, etc. Illustrated with fine engravings. London: printed and published by J. Sudbury, 252 High Holborn.* 12mo, 78 pages. Appeared between 1820 and 1830, J. Sudbury. New edition (1870) brought out by W. Dugdale with six pictures. Descriptions of the love adventures of a shop assistant with prostitutes and kept women to whom he gives goods from his father's shop as presents.

[1] *How to Make Love, or the Art of Making Love in more ways than one, exemplified in a series of letters between two cousins. Cythera Press, 1823.* London, published by John Ascham, with 12 fine but obscene copperplates. In 1829 the same publisher issued a continuation, *How to raise love, etc.*, in two volumes. Both works together under the title *How to raise love: or mutual amatory series (sic); disclosed in a series of letters between two cousins, enriched with fine engravings. Dedicated to the voluptuous, Vol. I, London. Published for the purchasers,* 1848. Two volumes, 71 and 75 pages. (Appeared in America with lithographs.) Edition published by Dugdale between 1860 and 1865: *How to raise love; or the art of making love in more ways than one; being the voluptuous history and secret correspondence of two young ladies (cousins) handsome and accomplished, etc. With fine engravings. Part the first. Printed for the Society of Vice.* 8vo, three volumes, 104, 54 and 75 pages; 24 obscene coloured lithographs. These last editions do not correspond exactly with Ascham's; only the first twelve letters are identical, all the others being quite different. The correspondents and principal characters in *How to raise love* are two cousins, Stella and Theresa, Gabriel, a friend of Theresa, and her school-fellow, Lalotte; Charles, later the husband of Stella; Theresa's brother and a school-fellow, Frederick. It would be impossible in a short sketch to give the contents of the work. The different friends relate their adventures during their partings. Their letters deal principally with the circumstances of their first initiation into the secrets of sex. The book is not badly written, and coarse and obscene words are avoided.

[2] *The Adventures, Intrigues and Amours of a Lady's Maid! Written by herself. Never before published, etc. Embellished with engravings. London, printed by J. Ryder, Portobello Passage,* 1822. *The life of Miss Louisa Selby, being the second part of the adventures, etc. Written by herself, etc. Embellished with eight engravings. London, printed by J. Ryder, Portobello Passage.* 1822. 12mo, 132 and 169 pages. Describes the love career of Louisa Selby, the natural daughter of a country minister, by whom she was herself first seduced, in order that she should be procured by her mother. Later, she is servant maid to various mistresses, amongst them a Lesbian, is shut up in an Italian convent, has further adventures in Naples, falls into the hands of brigands and finally marries a widowed English preacher.

Decameron of Pleasure[1] and *Imitations*[2].

Amongst the large number of erotic books which appeared in England in the 'sixties to the 'eighties of the nineteenth century, those of the historian of culture and anthropologist, Edward Sellon, deserve detailed mention, as in Sellon we have perhaps the only English pornographer of the nineteenth century whose writings as regards their style and literary and historical importance may be compared with John Cleland.

[1] *The Ladies' Tell Tale; or Decameron of Pleasure. A recollection of amorous tales, as related by a party of young friends to one another. With characteristic plates. London: published by May, Wilson and Spinster, 2 Portobello Passage, Leicester Square. Price £1.11.6.* 12mo, four volumes. The first three were issued in 1830 by John Ascham, Chancery Lane, London; the fourth by W. Dugdale. Each volume has 6 bad copperplates. New edition of the first three volumes (1863), issued by W. Dugdale, the whole work (1865), in five volumes, 8vo, 109, 75, 92, 118, 55 pages and 40 bad coloured lithographs. The title here is *Love's Tell Tale*. The sub-title, *Decameron of Pleasure*, is based on the fact that the framework of the book is formed by a pornological club of ladies and gentlemen; the members of this club each relate an experience, which are collected by the president in the above-mentioned work. They are for the most part detailed accounts of the first seduction of young girls and men. The titles of the stories are: Vol. I, tale 1, 'Little Miss Curious's Tale'; tale 2, 'The Young Gentleman's Tale '; Tale 3, 'The Young Lady's Tale'. Vol. II, tale 4, 'The Traveller's Tale '; tale 5, 'The Amateur Artist's Tale '; tale 6, 'The Student in Art's Tale'. Vol. III, tale 7, 'The School Master and Mistress's Tale'; tale 8, 'The School Girl's Tale '; tale 9, 'The School Boy's Tale '. Vol. IV, tale 10, 'The Soldier's Tale '; tale 11, 'The Sailor's Tale '; tale 12, 'The Foster Brother and Sister's Tale '. Vol. V, tale 13, 'The Philosophic Sister's Tale '; tale 14, 'The Country Girl's Tale '; tale 15, 'The Country Boy's Tale '.

[2] *Bijou edition. Love's Tell Tale, The Sailor's Yarn, A delicious adventure in the Bay of Naples. Illustrated by six coloured plates. Printed for the Nihilists. Moscow (London), 1880. 8vo, 40 pages.* Issue: 150 copies. It is a new edition of tale 11 from *The Ladies' Tell Tale* (see above) with the omission of three paragraphs and changing of the names.

The Ladies' Tell Tale; or Decameron of Pleasure. A collection of amorous tales as related by a party of young friends to one another. With characteristic plates. London: H. Smith, 37, Holywell Street, Strand. Price 2/6. 12mo, 19 pages. A worthless brochure published by W. Dugdale. Contains 'Recollections of my Youth ' and four very wearisome 'facetious anecdotes '.

[568]

Edward Sellon (1818 to 1866) was one of those gifted, but at heart deeply unhappy, Epicureans who stagger from desire to gratification and from gratification to desire, not from sensuality only but for the highest of motives; in this regard his was a true Casanova nature. In him, however, was missing that optimistic comprehension of life and religious feeling, for Sellon died a convinced atheist. He himself described his life in a highly erotic book which must be placed in the forefront of his works on this subject: *The Ups and Downs of Life: A Fragment.*

> *' All the world's a stage*
> *And all the men and women merely players;*
> *They have their exits and their entrances,*
> *And one man in his time plays many parts.'*
>
> As You Like It, Act 2, Scene VII.

London, printed for the booksellers, 1867.

Sub-title: *My Life: the Beginning and the End. A Veritable History.* 8vo, 110 pages and 7 erotic coloured lithographs, an erotic picture on the title-page with the inscription: ' The Ups and Downs of Existence.' Price 2 guineas. The original signatures to the pictures still exist in one copy of the work in the possession of a London collector. There are sixteen coloured drawings, one coloured picture in the text, two etchings and one etched title drawing. As these twenty pictures could not all be included, the publisher of the book, W. Dugdale, chose eight out of them.

As stated above, this composition is the true autobiography of Captain Edward Sellon. In the original manuscript the real names of the people were given, but the editor changed them.

' As the son of a father of moderate means, whom I lost as a child, I was destined from the first for the army. I was to be taken as a cadet when I was 16, and I travelled to Portsmouth as soon as my equipment was ready, by the post on

[569]

a cold February night in the year 1834 ' (p. 3). He then went to India for ten years, and at twenty-six was given his captaincy. The greater part of this book is a description of his time in India, of a duel and various love affairs with European and native women. The Indian women attracted him far more than the English, French, German and Polish girls of all classes of society, as these could not by a long way be compared with the ' salacious, succulent houris of the far East ' (p. 42).

When he was in England on leave, Sellon found that his mother wished him to marry. Although this was not to his taste, he agreed, as the bride who had been chosen for him was a young lady of great charm, and an only daughter, heiress to a fortune of £25,000. At the wish of his parents-in-law he cancelled his return to India, and spent the winter of the year 1844 with his recently married wife in Paris. On his return to England he was unpleasantly surprised to find that she was not so well off as he had been told, and that she would only have £400 a year income. His mother-in-law also explained to him that they must economise and that she wished them to live in a pretty little cottage in Devonshire which she had taken for them. After many reproaches he left his wife and went to live with his mother in Bruton Street. During his two years' parting from his wife he consoled himself with a courtesan whom he kept in a small villa in the suburbs. Later, an understanding having been arrived at between the relatives, his wife came back to him to his mother's house.

' The first month all went well, but unfortunately I had found amongst my mother's servants a little housemaid, a sweet creature, the daughter of a merchant. She had had a pretty good education and did not resemble a servant either in manners or appearance. I had seduced this child before the return of my wife, although she was only 14 years old, and

now the difficulty arose as to how I could continue the relationship after her arrival without being discovered ' (p. 78).

Discovery soon followed. One Sunday morning, on her
return from church, his wife found Emma's hat on her bed;
her husband had complained of headache and had not got
up until after she had left the house. There was a scene at
which our hero remained unperturbed, and refused to give
any satisfactory explanation, so the furious wife lost her
temper, sprang at her husband like a panther, and gave him
a frightful box on the right ear. ' I very quietly threw the
rest of my cigar in the grate, took both her wrists in an iron
grip and put her into a chair. Now, little devil, I said, stay
there; I promise you on my honour that I shall hold you fast
like this until you humbly and sorrowfully beg forgiveness for
your insult to me.' In spite of fierce fighting and biting on the
part of the embittered wife, Sellon succeeded—but only after
several hours—in the taming of the refractory creature, and
after he himself had lost a lot of blood from the bites she had
given him; at the end of the fight he became faint and had
to be bound up that same evening by the doctor. His wife,
however, was so well cured of her jealousy that she quietly
and even smilingly let Emma, Sellon's lover, sit on his bed
with him, join them at supper and, after supper, take her own
place in the marriage bed! That did not, however, prevent
the wife, Augusta, from being also vouchsafed marital intercourse the same night. No wonder that after such an exhibition of strength Sellon fell seriously ill the next day and was
laid up for a month, during which time he was nursed by his
wife and mother. On his convalescence he went with his
wife to Hastings, Emma having previously been dismissed.

But another earlier mistress turned up again and was the
cause of a further parting from his wife. After this his
mother lost her whole fortune through fraud, and Sellon was
obliged to take up a calling in order to defray his living

expenses. Under an assumed name he drove the Cambridge post for two years, during which time he had numberless amorous adventures with his female passengers. Then he ran a school of fencing in London, where his wife sought him out, as beautiful as ever, and begged him to live with her again. 'The gods alone know how unfaithful I had been to her since we parted six years previously, but she never found out anything about it.' They took a small, pretty country house not far from Winchester in Hampshire, where they practised regular erotic orgies together, which kept Sellon faithful for three years. From this ' golden dream ' he awoke finally on account of the pregnancy of his wife, which with one blow put an end to his passion of love, especially as all his wife's tenderness was now centred in the expected child (pp. 90-91). Sellon went to London, 'indulging in every kind of debauchery', whence he returned once more to Hampshire on account of his wife, whose love for him was again aroused. This last domestic happiness, however, lasted only a short time, as Sellon was one day surprised by his wife taking the scholars from a girls' school into the wood to play ' hide and seek '. 'After this escapade I could no longer remain in Hampshire, so packed my portmanteau, and was once more a gentleman at large in London' (p. 110). The book ends here with the following note, apparently by the publisher, but in reality written by the author himself: ' The tale here breaks off suddenly and, so far as the facts are known, it appears that the author died shortly after. In any case he was not seen again by any of his many acquaintances, either living or dead.'

The sad truth was that Edward Sellon shot himself in April 1866 at Webb's Hotel, 219-220, Piccadilly (where is now the Criterion Restaurant). His friends induced the newspapers to keep silence about the unhappy end of this gifted man. Sellon had written to a friend before he com-

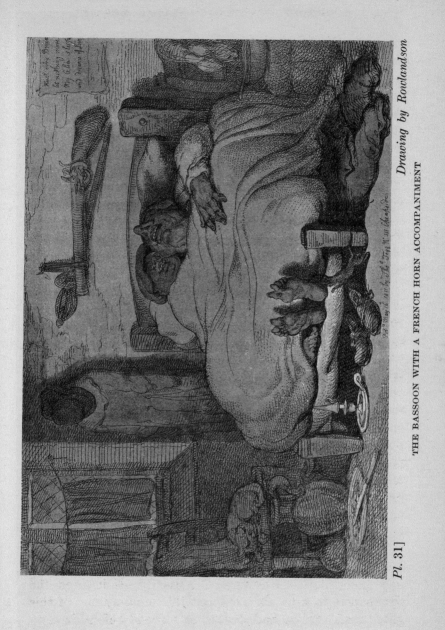

Pl. 31]

THE BASSOON WITH A FRENCH HORN ACCOMPANIMENT

Drawing by Rowlandson

WHICH WAY SHALL I TURN ME.

Pl. 32]

mitted suicide and told him of his resolution, but the letter did not arrive till the next morning, when all was over. The following verses were enclosed in it, addressed to a woman who had been very much attached to him, and who, when he was in need, had desired to help him[1].

No More!

No more shall mine arms entwine
Those beauteous charms of thine,
Or the ambrosial nectar sip
Of that delicious coral lip—
                    No more.

No more shall those heavenly charms
Fill the vacuum of these arms;
No more embraces, wanton kisses,
Nor life, nor love, Venus blisses—
                    No more.

The glance of love, the heaving breast
To my bosom so fondly prest,
The rapturous sigh, the amorous pant,
I shall look for, long for, want
                    No more.

For I am in the cold earth laid,
In the tomb of blood I've made,
Mine eyes are glassy, cold and dim,
Adieu, my love, and think of him—
                    No more.
                Vivat lingam.
                Non resurgam.

[1] This poem is also printed on p. 69 of the collection, *Cythera's Hymnal* (London, 1870).

With this melancholy swan song of an erotic, ended the career of a man who was intended for better things. Sellon died a convinced atheist and believed firmly in the truth of the words with which he closed his poem. The gap between the sudden end of the autobiography and the equally sudden end of his own life, was filled in by a letter dated the 4th March 1866, addressed to the same friend whom he warned of his suicide. In this Sellon relates very humorously how he accompanied a friend and his bride to Vienna, seduced the latter on the way, and on account of this friendly act had a terrible fight with the husband in the train shortly before reaching Vienna; how he ran through all his money in Vienna and returned to London penniless.

Before we turn to the erotic writings of Sellon, it must be mentioned that he made considerable use of his know-ledge of Indian culture which, apart from the works which are shortly to be mentioned, is evidenced by several lectures to the London Anthropological Society, printed in the reports of their proceedings. Even in his first light erotic novel, *Herbert Breakspear*[1], we are introduced very vividly to Indian life through the fortunes of two cousins, the good Herbert Breakspear and the bad Everhard, which last was betrayed by a native girl whom he had deserted, fell into the hands of the Mahratta chief and was executed as a spy, whilst Herbert, who was also imprisoned, through the magnanimity of a Mahratta whose life he had once saved, was able to return home and marry the girl he loved.

Other contributions of Sellon's to the history of Indian culture are his essays on the *Monolithic Temples of India*, his translation of the *Gita-Radhica-Krishna*, and his very

---

[1] *Herbert Breakspear, a legend of the Mahratta war. By Edward Sellon, etc. London. Whittaker and Co., Ave Maria Lane. And sold by A. Wallis and R. Folthrop, Brighton. 1848. 8vo, 143 pages.*

interesting reports on religious prostitution in India: *Annotations on the Sacred Writings of the Hindus*[1].

Sellon's transition to purely erotic writing is formed by his translation of selected passages from Boccaccio's *Decameron*, which is a very rare book to-day[2].

In the last two years of his life Sellon, apparently driven to it by necessity, wrote for the publisher, William Dugdale, several erotic books which, from the literary point of view at least, are amongst the best of their kind. The following should be given first place:

The New Epicurean; or the Delights of Sex, Facetiously and Philosophically Considered, in Graphic Letters Addressed to Young Ladies of Quality.

> ' — *domi maneas paresque nobis*
> *novem continuas fututiones*'.
>
> Catullus. *Carmen XXXII.*

A new edition. London: 1740. (Reprinted 1865.)

8vo, 92 pages. Eight coloured lithographs. This is not a ' new edition ' but the original, arranged by W. Dugdale, of which 500 copies were printed at the price of £1 11s. 6d., 1865. New edition, 1875, small 8vo, 117 pages with the same 8 lithographs. Printed in Brussels for a London bookseller. The pictures are also drawn by Sellon.

---

[1] *Annotations on the Sacred Writings of the Hindus, being an epitome of some of the most remarkable and leading tenets in the faith of that people, by Edward Sellon, author of the ' Monolithic Temples of India ', etc., etc., and editor of an English translation of the ' Gita-Radhica-Krishna ', a Sanscrit poem. London: MDCCCLXV (Printed for private circulation).* 8vo, 72 pages, printed by H. Weede, 13a High Road, Knightsbridge.

[2] *Selections from the Decameron of Giovanni Boccaccio. Including all the passages hitherto suppressed, etc. Translated from the Italian. London MDCCCLXV.* Large 8vo, viii, 78 pages. At the end of the volume is a list of ' rare editions of Boccaccio's works which exist to-day ' in seventeen numbers. The volume contains little but what is to be found in the usual translations.

In the *New Epicurean* Sellon has drawn in the person of Sir Charles a character and a way of life quite after his own heart. In the preface (pp. 3-7 in the edition of 1875) the latter, who appears in the first person, informs us: ' I am a man who, having crossed the rubicon of youth, has reached an age when his passions require a more stimulating diet than is to be found in the arms of any painted courtesan.' To this end Sir Charles rented a villa in the suburbs, the isolated idyllic position of which, behind high walls, completely protected it from the eyes of neighbours. It was surrounded by a real English park with lovely shady paths, alcoves, grottoes, fountains, beautiful lawns and flower beds, a statue of Venus in white marble in the middle of a rose bush, statues of Priapus at the ends of the shady alleys and glens, sometimes in the form of an Indian Bacchus, sometimes soft and feminine as Antinous, sometimes in the form of Hermaphrodite. In the ponds swam gold and silver fish. The interior of the villa was elegantly decorated in the style of Louis XV, hung with charming Watteaus, and provided with a choice library of erotic books, with silk-covered couches, gilt furniture, rose-coloured Venetian blinds, etc. In this Elysium Sir Charles indulged in sexual orgies of every description, principally with young girls who were brought to him by the head-mistress of a school who was a hanger-on of his. He was married, but Lady Cecilia did not disturb him at all in his love affairs and even took part in them, herself keeping a little page at her disposal. The book has, however, rather a tragic end. Cecilia had, unknown to her husband, a liaison with her cousin, Lord William. Sir Charles surprised them *in flagranti*, and a duel took place between the two men when both were slightly wounded. After this the lady entered a convent and took the veil. Sir Charles sold his villa and retired with his servants, Phœbe and Chloe,

Daphnis, Lady Cecilia's page, and the steward Jukes, to his property in Hertfordshire, where he could apply himself to the service of Venus only as a *voyeur*.

The *New Epicurean* also doubtless contains autobiographical material, and this is the case with a second erotic work of Sellon's which follows on the above, entitled:

Phœbe Kissagen; or the Remarkable Adventures, Schemes, Wiles and Devilries of Une Maquerelle, being a sequel to the 'New Epicurean, etc.' London: 1743 *(reprint)*.

8vo, 96 pages, 8 bad coloured lithographs. No new edition, but the original of 1866. Price two guineas. 500 copies printed. Sellon sent the publisher, W. Dugdale, yet a further erotic tale, as he did not consider *Phœbe Kissagen* comprehensive enough, but this was not printed with it. Its title was: *Scenes in the Life of a Young Man, a Narrative of Amorous Exploits. Phœbe Kissagen* was reprinted in January 1876 (small 8vo, 99 pages, London, 1743, reprinted 1875), without pictures[1].

Phœbe Kissagen is written in the French erotic style of the eighteenth century in the form of letters addressed to a lady of rank, Lady G . . . r. The book begins with the story of the death of Sir Charles, who had a stroke during intercourse with his favourite concubine Phœbe. The latter, and also Chloe, each received a legacy of £3,000 with which they went to London and bought a brothel in Leicester Fields. All the rooms in this brothel had peepholes through which the brothel keepers, without being seen, could themselves watch all that went on. The description of the various scenes fills the greater part of the book. The rest consists of 'Bagnio Correspondence', that is

---

[1] French translation, *Mémoires d'une procureuse anglaise. Traduits pour la première fois de l'anglais par les soins de la société des bibliophiles cosmopolites. Londres. Imprimerie de la société cosmopolite. MDCCCXCII.* Small 8vo, 136 pages.

letters which Phœbe received from her numerous men and
women clients, and in which their different passions and
perversities were revealed. Phœbe at last fell in love with a
youth called Captain Jackson, a gambler and duellist,
whom she married; he soon infected her with syphilis and
squandered her fortune, after which she left London and
retired to a quiet village[1].

St. George H. Stock, a former lieutenant in the 2nd or
Queen's Royal Regiment, specialised in works on flagella-
tion. He wrote under the pseudonyms Expert, Major
Edward Markham and Dr. Aliquis. His writings[2] enlarged

[1] Sellon wrote, in addition to the three erotic works mentioned, a story,
Adventures of a Gentleman, the manuscript of which was in the possession
of Dugdale, but was apparently destroyed later. Pisanus Fraxi possessed
four original water-colours by Sellon for this work (*Catena*, p. 427). There
are also in existence six obscene water-colours by Sellon for the *Memoirs
of Rosa Bellefille* (*ibid.*, p. 141). Finally, another erotic tale of Sellon's, in
manuscript, without illustrations, is supposed to be in existence, entitled
The Delights of Imagination. The eight obscene pictures in *The Adventures
of a School Boy* (London, 1866) are also Sellon's, and the same number of
pictures in *The New Ladies' Tickler* (London, 1866). According to Sellon's
autobiographical story, *The Ups and Downs of Life*, the title of the following erotic book also appears to have been planned: *Private recreations, or
the Ups and Downs of Life. By one who has been behind the scenes and
taken part in the performance, printed by permission, for private circulation
only*. Belfort: 1870. 8vo, 41 pages. Printed in 1879. Four chapters.
A fragment. Lord L., a debauched nobleman, has two mistresses, Lottie
and Sue, and willingly allows them to relate their love adventures and
other dirty stories, in which he encourages them by showing them obscene
pictures and photographs. These stories turn chiefly on the loss of their
virginity.

[2] *Plums without Dough; or 144 Quaint Conceits, within the bounds of be-
coming mirth. By Doctor Aliquis*, 2 Crampton Quay, Dublin, etc. 8vo,
64 pages (Dublin, 1870). *The Charm, The Night School, The Beautiful
Jewess and the Butcher's Daughter. All rights reserved*. 12mo, 30 pages
(Brussels, 1874). Four flagellantic stories. *The Sealed Letter, by Doctor
Aliquis*, 2 Crampton Quay, Dublin. *All rights reserved*. 8vo, 20 pages
(Dublin, 1870). *The Nameless Crime, a dialogue on stays, Undue Curiosity,
The Dolls' Wedding, The Way to Peel, The Jail and The Stiff Dream. All
rights reserved*. Small 8vo, 31 pages (July, 1875). Issued by Hartcupp and
Co. in Brussels. *The Romance of Chastisement; or the Revelations of Miss
Darcy, etc.* Illustrated with coloured drawings. London: printed for

monotonously always on the same theme: flagellation, of which he was a passionate devotee in his own life. He also had advertisements with double meanings inserted in the newspapers. Thus in 1871 for several weeks there appeared in the *Day's Doings* the following advertisement: ' They say that Xerxes is offering a reward to anyone who can suggest a new pleasure. Post free addresses to Aliquis, 2, Crampton Quay, Dublin. Postcards refused.'

The famous author of the *History of Civilisation in England,* Henry Thomas Buckle, has been unjustly suspected of collecting erotic, especially flagellantic books. In 1872 the publisher J. C. Hotten made a collection of seven books on flagellation which he entitled: *Library Illustrative of Social Progress. From the original editions collected by the late Henry Thomas Buckle, author of ' History of Civilisation in England '*. In a prospectus included with it, Hotten asserted that Buckle was a prominent collector of many curiosities, chiefly of flagellantic literature. From this alleged secret library of Buckle's the seven books on flagellation in the above collection were supposed to have come[1]. There was no word of truth in all this. Buckle had never collected or possessed these books. They were much more likely to have come from the library of a well-known collector, where they, in the order of their later publication

the booksellers. 8vo, 112 pages, 8 bad coloured lithographs (London, Dugdale, 1866). *The Romance of Chastisement; or revelations of school and bedroom. By an expert, etc.* (1870). Large 8vo, 128 pages and frontispiece (Dublin, 1870, printed by the author in 1,000 copies). There are also in existence many manuscripts of flagellantic stories of Stock's, mostly in the possession of London bibliophiles, such as, for example, *Harry's Holidays, A dip in the Atlantic, Castle Cara, Sam's Story, The German lessons, Did he ought to do it?, Tales out of School, The Reckoning Day, or rival recollections,* etc., etc.

[1] They were: (1) *Exhibition of Female Flagellants.* (2) *Part Second of the Exhibition of Female Flagellants.* (3) *Lady Bumtickler's Revels.* (4) *A Treatise of the Use of Flogging in Venereal Affairs* (by Meibom). (5) *Madam Birchini's dance.* (6) *Sublime of Flagellation.* (7) *Fashionable Lectures.*

by Hotten, were bound together in one volume. Hotten borrowed this volume from the bibliophile and had them reprinted without the knowledge or permission of the owner[1].

Passing over a large number of unimportant erotic books which were published in 1860 by J. and W. Dugdale, and of which only a collection of eleven highly obscene tales under the title *Lascivious Gems; set to suit every fancy, by several hands, etc. London: printed for the booksellers* (8vo, 90 pages, 8 coloured lithographs, by W. Dugdale) is worthy of mention, we must refer shortly to the most important erotic works of the last decade of the nineteenth century, written by well-known men such as James Campbell, the author of *Amatory Experiences of a Surgeon*[2] and the famous journalist George Augustus Sala, who wrote a part of the *Mysteries of Verbena House*[3].

---

[1] P. Fraxi, *Index*, p. 241.

[2] *The Amatory Experiences of a Surgeon, with eight coloured plates. Printed for the Nihilists. Moscow*, 1871. 8vo, 89 pages, 8 obscene coloured lithographs, printed in London in 150 copies. Price £3 3s. The book describes the erotic adventures of the natural son of a nobleman, who is introduced to paederasty while at school, and settles as a surgeon in a small town near where his father lived. Here his 'experiences' begin. His first liaison is with his father's mistress, but he gives her up when he surprises her in the arms of his servant. He then consoles himself with a young unmarried lady, and does away with the unwished-for result of this intercourse by a criminal abortion. All his patients were misused by him in their turn, even immature children.

[3] *The Mysteries of Verbena House; or Miss Bellasis birched for thieving. By Etonensis. Price four guineas. London, privately printed. MDCCCLXXXII.* 8vo, 143 pages, 4 obscene coloured lithographs. Pages 1-96 are from the pen of Sala, the second part was written by another London bibliophile. As Pisanus Fraxi rightly remarks, the book is the truest picture of English flagellomania we have, describing real happenings throughout, as they then existed in English girls' schools. Miss Sinclair, the principal of such an institution in Brighton, is initiated into the secrets of active flagellation by her spiritual adviser, the Reverend Arthur Calvedon, and from a chaste 'maid-matron', is in a short while turned into the 'lascivious lady of Verbena House', using the rod with true passion.

[580]

Some unique specimens of English erotic literature which we would mention briefly in closing are the erotic periodicals which are met with in no other country to such an extent as in England.

The first of these erotic periodicals appeared in 1774. It was:

1. *The Covent Garden Magazine, or Amorous Repository, calculated solely for the entertainment of the polite world*, 1774. It contained scandalous law cases, lists of prostitutes, erotic poetry.

2. *The Rambler's Magazine or the Annals of Gallantry, Glee, Pleasure and the Bon Ton; calculated for the entertainment of the polite world; and to furnish the man of pleasure with a most delicious banquet of amorous, Bacchanalian, whimsical, humorous, theatrical and polite entertainment. Vol. I for the year* 1783. *London: printed for the author and sold by G. Lister*, 46, *Old Bailey, Mr. Jackson at Oxford, etc.* 8vo, with many erotic copper-plates.

Some idea may be obtained of the multifarious contents of the periodical by the enumeration of a few of the articles. Amongst others are: 'Lecture on Propagation', an 'Essay on Woman' (in prose), an 'Essay on Manhood', an article on the 'Lovers' Doctor', notices and descriptions of wedding ceremonies in different countries, letters on flagellation, a 'Dialogue on Divorce' and 'Cytherean Discussions'. Further, memoirs of the amorous life of Cecil, Lord Burleigh, Peter Abelard, Miss Bellamy, the Duchess of Kingston, Miss Ann Catley; reports on adultery and divorce cases and finally a large number of erotic stories such as 'Adventures of a Dance Teacher', 'The Gipsy', 'Adventures of a Eunuch', 'Memoirs of an English Sérail', 'Adventures of a Man of Pleasure', 'Adventures of a Sofa', etc., etc. Dramas were also included, such as the 'Coffee-house Medley, a comedy'.

3. *The Bon Ton Magazine; or Microscope of Fashion and Folly (for the year* 1791), *Vol. I, London. Printed for the proprietors, and sold by D. Brewman,* 18, *New Street, Shoe Lane and all booksellers and news carriers in town and country.*

8vo, five volumes from March 1791 to March 1796. In every volume an index. Many beautiful copper-plates.

The *Bon Ton Magazine* is by far the most important of the gallant periodicals in England, and played the same part in the ' Scandals ' and ' High Life ' of that period, as did the *Gentleman's Magazine* in matters of greater and more general significance. Its publication was wrongly ascribed to John or Jack Mitford.

Of the contents of the *Bon Ton Magazine* may be quoted the following: Three essays, 'The Adventurer', 'The Debauchee', 'The Essayist ' ; a ' Dictionary for Good Taste ' or the ' Savoir-vivre Vocabulary '; a ' Fashionable Dictionary of Love '; ' The Love Affairs of the King of France '; ' Love Anecdotes '; biographies of actresses, thieves, 'History of the Theatre', a collection of historical essays on eunuchism, reports on scandalous trials, erotic novels such as 'Elmina or the flower that never fades', ' Life of a Modern Man of Fashion', 'Adventures and Amours of a bar-maid', 'The Black Joke', 'The Modern Lovers or the Adventures of Cupid', etc., descriptions of wedding ceremonies, flagellation scenes, peculiar clubs, descriptions of prostitution, erotic letters and poems.

4. *The Ranger's Magazine or the Man of Fashion's Companion; being the whim of the month and general assemblage of love, gallantry, wit, pleasure, harmony, mirth, glee and fancy. Containing monthly list of the Covent Garden Cyprians; or the man of pleasure's vade mecum. The annals of gallantry. Essence of trials for adultery. Crim. Con. Seduction. Doubles entendres. Choice anecdotes. Warm narratives.*

[582]

Curious fragments. Animating histories of Tête-à-têtes, and wanton frolicks. To which is added the fashionable chit-chat and scandal of the month, from the Pharaoh Table to the Fan warehouse. Vol. I, for the year 1795. London: sold by J. Sudbury, No. 16, Tooley Street, and all booksellers in Great Britain and Ireland.

4to, Volume I, from January to June 1795, 298 pages. A copper-plate in each number. The principal contents are enumerated in the title.

Twenty-seven years later a new erotic periodical appeared with the title:

5. *The Rambler's Magazine or Fashionable Emporium of Polite Literature. The fine arts, politics, theatrical excellencies, wit, humour, genius, taste, gallantry and all the gay variety of supreme Bon Ton.*

> *From grave to gay, from lively to severe,*
> *Wit, truth and humour shall by turns appear.*

Vol. I, London: Benbow, printer, Byron's Head, Castle Street, 1822. 8vo, one volume of twelve numbers from January to December 1822, viii, 570 pages, twelve copper-plates. The publisher says in the preface: ' Our principal theme is love, because as Moore says, " the whole world turns on it".' Of the very richly varied poetic and prose contents may be mentioned: ' London Hells Exposed', ' The Cuckold's Chronicle' and 'Fashionable Gallantry', extracts from the ' Golden Ass' and an incomplete erotic novel ' The Rambler; or the life, adventures, amours, intrigues and eccentricities of Gregory Griffin '.

6. *The Rambler; or Fashionable Companion for April; being a complete Register of Gallantry. Embellished with a beautiful engraved Frontispiece of the Venus de Medicis.*

> *Art, nature, wit and love display,*
> *In every page a Rambler's (sic) gay.*

[583]

London: printed and published by T. Holt, 1, Catherine Street, Strand; and to be had of all booksellers.

8vo, ten numbers from April 1824 to January 1825, when the publication of the periodical was forbidden on account of its immorality. A copper-plate in each number, including a portrait of Miss M. Tree. Many numbers have the title *The Rambler's Magazine*. Contents: Notices of theatres, scandalous stories, reports of trials, short stories, anecdotes about actresses, Canto XVII of Byron's *Don Juan* and a tale ' Maria, or the Victim of Passion '.

7. *The Original Rambler's Magazine; or Annals of Gallantry; an amusing miscellany of fun, frolic, fashion and flash. Amatory tales, adventures, memoirs of the most celebrated women of pleasure, trials for crim. con. and seduction, bon ton, facetiae, epigrams, jeu d'esprit, etc. Vol. I enriched with elegant engravings. London: printed and published by Edward Duncombe, 26 Fleet Market.*

8vo, one volume, which appeared in the year 1827, 202 pages, frontispiece and a copper-plate in each number, partly coloured and erotic. Contained chiefly biographical articles such as: ' Loves of Col. Berkeley ', ' Life, Amours, Intrigues and Professional Career of Miss Chester', 'Amours of the Duke of Wellington', 'Amours of Mrs. Thompson', ' Amour of Napoleon Buonaparte and Mrs. Billington', ' Memoirs of Miss Singleton ' (with portrait of this ' beauty of Arlington Street ' in the nude), ' Amorous Memoirs of Lady Grigsley'. In addition it contained many interesting descriptions of London brothels. Several articles bear the signature J.M. (Jack Mitford).

8. *The Rambler's Magazine; or Annals of Gallantry, Glee, Pleasure and Bon Ton: A delicious banquet of amorous, Bacchanalian, whimsical, humorous, theatrical and literary entertainment.*

Our motto is, be gay and free!
Make love and joy your choicest treasure;
Look on our book with eyes of glee,
And ramble over scenes of pleasure.

Embellished with superb engravings. Vol. I, London:
published by J. Mitford, 19, Little Queen Street, Holborn.

8vo, two volumes, 286 and 284 pages. From 1827 to
1829. Nineteen copper-plates partly coloured. The single
numbers bear the title *New London Rambler's Magazine*.
The publisher was John (Jack) Mitford, a man of good
breeding and classic appearance, who served with honour
under Hood and Nelson in the English navy, rose to be
Commander of a ship, but through his excesses was reduced
to poverty and died in 1831 in St. Giles's workhouse[1].

The chief contents of this new *Rambler's Magazine* are the
'Drawing-room Prostitutes' and the 'Bazaar Beauties',
two series of biographies of free ladies and courtesans of the
time, an essay on Madame Vestris and her portrait as she
appeared in *Midas*, the 'Love Affairs of Lord Byron', the
scandalous chronicles 'Cuckold's Chronicle' and 'Amatory
and Bon Ton Intelligence', also the erotic novel 'Helen of
Glenshiels; or the miseries of seduction' (by J. Mitford),
'Amours of London and Spirit of Bon Ton', 'The Confessions of a Methodist; or pictures of sensuality', 'The
Cambridge Larks'.

9. *The Crim. Con. Gazette; or Diurnal Register of the*
Freaks and Follies of the Present Day.

Eighteen numbers at 2d. from the 20th November 1830
to the 30th April 1831, with some woodcuts. Publisher E.
Elliott. From No. 8 on, the title was *The Bon Ton Gazette*.
The periodical contains not only reports on scandalous
cases, but also poetry, memoirs, etc. For instance, memoirs

[1] Compare W. Howitt, *Visits to Remarkable Places* (London, 1842)
Vol. II, p. 394.

of Sally Maclean, Madame Vestris, Clara Foote, Mrs. Jordan and an article on the secret love affairs of the Duke of Wellington.

10. *The Quizzical Gazette and Merry Companion.*

4to, twenty-one numbers from the 27th August 1831 to the 14th January 1832. Crude woodcuts in the text (two of them by R. Cruickshank). First published by T. Major, Bell Yard, Strand, later in Elliot's 'literary Salon', 14, Holywell Street.

A worthless collection of facetiae of the day.

11. *The Exquisite: a collection of Tales, Histories and Essays, funny, fanciful and facetious. Interspersed with anecdotes, original and select. Amorous adventures, piquant jests and spicey sayings, illustrated with numerous engravings, published weekly. Volume the first. Printed and published by H. Smith, 37, Holywell Street, Strand.*

4to, three volumes, 145 numbers at 4d., from 1842 to 1844. Numerous free and humorous illustrations, portraits of actresses, lithographs and woodcuts. Publisher, W. Dugdale. Contained chiefly novels and tales, but also a large number of erotic miscellanies of all kinds. Each number also contained poems, amongst them Wilkes' 'Essay on Woman'. Under the heading 'Stars of the Salons', 'Sketches of Courtesans' and 'Seduction Unveiled' were names, addresses and details of the appearance and careers of the favourite prostitutes, after the style of Harris's notorious list of harlots. Further, *The Exquisite* contained memoirs of Madame Vestris, Mrs. Davenport, Mlle. de Brion, Madame Gourdan, Queen Marie Antoinette, also 'Original Anecdotes and Sketches of Charles II and the Duchess of Portsmouth'.

The 'Ars amandi' was dealt with in the following essays: 'The Bride's Pocket Book', 'A Reliable Leader through the Territory of Venus', 'The Physique of Venus', 'The New Art of Loving', 'A Consideration in the Physical Sense of Man and Woman in the Marriage State', extracts from Parent du Chatelet on prostitution in Paris, a Malthusian essay, ' Seven years' experience of the practice of family limitation by the best-known methods ', letters on flagellation, articles on eunuchism and the cult of the phallus, numerous erotic tales from the French and Italian, most of them translated by James Campbell, including the three notorious romances of Andrea de Nerciat, 'The Aphrodites', 'Felicia' and 'Monrose'. Of the original English novels may be mentioned: ' Nights at Lunet; or a budget of amorous tales ', ' Where shall I go to-night? ', ' The Loves of Sappho ', ' Wife and no Wife, a tale from Stamboul ', ' The Child of Nature. Improved by Chance ', ' The History of a Young Lady's Researches into the history of the " Summum bonum " ', ' The Practical Part of Love Exemplified in the Personal History of Lucy and Helen, eminent priestesses of the Temple of Venus ', ' The Illustrious Lovers; or secret history of Malcolm and Matilda ', ' Julia, or Miss in her Teens ', ' The London Bawd '.

12. *The Pearl, a monthly journal of facetiae and voluptuous reading. Vol. I. Oxford: Printed at the University Press. MDCCCLXXIX.*

4to, eighteen parts from July 1879 to December 1882 in three volumes. Each 192 pages, title-page and index. Thirty-six obscene coloured lithographs. Printed in London. Edition, 150 copies for £25.

The Pearl is the most obscene of all English erotic periodicals; it contained chiefly poetry, facetiae and obscene stories. Of the last the most important are ' Lady Pokingham, or they all do it ', 'Miss Coote's Confession, or the voluptuous experiences of an old maid ' (a series of flagellation scenes, the ' heroine ' of which is the grand-daughter of the famous general who served in East India, Sir E—— C——), ' Sub-

umbra, or sport among the she-noodles ', also a flagellation
story, ' La rose d'amour, or the adventures of a gentleman in
search of pleasure ', ' My Grandmother's Tale, or May's
account of her introduction to the art of love ', ' Flunkeyana,
or Belgravian morals '. These erotic novels almost all contain many horrible scenes *à la* ' Justine et Juliette '. An
analysis of the first-named story, ' Lady Pokingham ', should
suffice to give an idea of what they were like. The heroine,
Beatrice, begins her tale at her school, where the usual
onanistic and tribadic malpractices were carried on. Here
the story of the seduction of her young friend, Alice March-
mont, is told. She goes with Alice to the town and lives with
a Catholic family. An episode from Lord Beaconsfield's
Lothair is then parodied, and the name of the heroine is
used. The convent flagellation scene from *Gamiani* is also
copied exactly. A pornographic assembly of the ' Paphic
Circle ' is then described, in which men and women take
part in every imaginable sort of performance. The ' Berkeley
Horse ' comes into this (cf. Chap. XII). When the distinguished gentlemen at these orgies refuse their requests, the
women fall back on the servants. Lady Beatrice Pokingham
is now introduced to the Earl of Crim-Con, an ' old man of
30 ' who ' would have been taken for at least 50 '. She
agreed to marry him, although his impotence could only be
overcome by the most unusual stimulants, and the consequences of this unnatural marriage were not long in following.
His Lordship forsook his wife for his two pages! Beatrice
surprised her husband with the two, but, however, took part
in the orgy, during which Crim-Con died. She then seduced
her brothers and heirs, and also her men servants, a housekeeper, two pages and two young maids. Her health was
undermined by these excesses, and she was sent to Madeira,
but before she went she seduced the doctor who advised her
to go. On the voyage she flagellated and seduced two naval

cadets. After a short stay in Madeira she returned to England, where she died of galloping consumption.

As supplements to the *Pearl*, without which this periodical cannot be regarded as complete, the following four publications must be mentioned:

Swivia, or the Briefless Barrister. The extra special number of the Pearl containing a variety of complete tales with five illustrations, poetry, facetiae, etc. Christmas 1879.

Sixty-four pages, four coloured pictures after French originals. Describes a wild orgy of four young men with two servants. Peculiar erotic dreams are also related and obscene songs sung.

The Haunted House, or the Revelations of Theresa Terence. 'An o'er true tale.' 'There are more things in heaven and earth than are dreamt of in our philosophy.' Being the Christmas number of the Pearl. Beautifully illustrated with six finely coloured plates, December 1880. London. Privately printed.

Sixty-two pages, six coloured lithographs. Price three guineas. The book contains a description of the sexual excesses of the old flagellant Sir Anthony Harvey; he is surprised at them by three young men, who then take part in the orgies. Defloration and flagellation are the chief themes. The ' Unveiling of Theresa Terence ', given in the title, is missing.

The Pearl Christmas Annual 1881. Containing New Year's Day, the sequel to Swivia, Vanessa and other tales, facetiae, songs, etc. Six coloured plates. London: privately printed.

Sixty-four pages, six obscene coloured lithographs. Price three guineas. Contains, with other unimportant matter, the erotic tale ' Vanessa ', the heroine of which, Phœbe, is a modern Fanny Hill, whose fortunes in the world and half-world are plausibly related.

The Erotic Casket Gift Book for 1882. *Containing various facetiae omitted in the Pearl Christmas Annual for want of space. With coloured frontispiece. London: Privately printed.*
Twenty pages (in some copies only 18 pages). Contains eight very obscene anecdotes and short stories.

After the *Pearl* two further erotic periodicals appeared:

13. No. 1. January 1851. *The Cremorne, a Magazine of Wit, etc.*

The first number of this falsely dated periodical appeared in August 1882. Each number has two obscene coloured lithographs and cost one guinea. In the table of contents are mentioned ' The Secret Life of Linda Brent ', ' A Curious History of Slave Life and Slave Wrongs ', ' Lady Hamilton, or Nelson's Inamorata. The Real Story of her Life.'

14. *The Boudoir; a magazine of Scandal, Facetiæ, etc.*

The first number appeared in June 1883, without illustrations. Price of each number 10s. 6d. Edition, 300 copies. The *Boudoir* contained numerous short anecdotes and ' eccentricities ' in prose and verse. Longer tales are: ' The Three Chums: a tale of London every-day life ', ' Adventures and Amours of a Bar-maid. A series of facts ', 'Voluptuous Confessions of a French lady of Fashion ' (after the French ' Confession galante d'une femme du monde').

CHAPTER XVIII

SEX PHENOMENA IN THE THEATRE, MUSIC, DANCING

THE task of the theatre being the portrayal of human characters and passions, it cannot help presenting the varied phenomena and the relationships of human love. Tragedy, that is to say the drama proper, has always favoured the ideal aspects of this great emotion; while comedy, and in particular farce, generally deals with the lower, sensual, purely sexual side, as witness the plays of Aristophanes, the pantomimes of ancient Rome, the profanised mystery plays of the Middle Ages, and so on, right to the present day.

That was why the Christian Church from the outset condemned the theatre as a whole, including even the most innocent pagan shows, and regarded the theatre as ' the arsenal of prostitution '.

In the same way the English Puritans of the seventeenth and eighteenth centuries condemned the comedies of the Restoration period, which were frankly based on immoral plots, as the products of an unchristian mentality. Thackeray held that ' poor Congreve's ' theatre was a temple of pagan lusts and mysteries which would only be permitted among pagans.

The appearance of women on the stage was also bound to exercise a certain influence on the nature of theatrical performances, particularly in the realm of pantomime, comedy and farce. Indeed, it was not long before the actresses entered into sexual relationships with male members of the audience. In addition, prostitutes of various degrees appear to have gravitated towards the stage from the first, in order to advertise their charms more effectively. It is a well-known fact that ' kept women ' are irresistibly drawn to the stage, partly from vanity and partly for reasons of 'business'. On the one hand, the stage gives them an opportunity to exhibit their physical charms and excite the admiration of a wide public, while on the other hand it also enables them to attract the notice of rich libertines.

In fact, the theatre was for many centuries a favourite resort of prostitutes, from the time when the surroundings of the ancient Greek and Roman theatres and circuses were infested by 'women of pleasure', down to thirty or forty years ago.

In England the early theatre had many connections with the lowest side of sex. The stage plays of ' Merry England ' were sometimes little more than sexual orgies. This was the case even with the morality plays, which were first performed in England in the twelfth century. It is a curious fact that this tendency was more apparent in England than in other Germanic countries. That was why the ' English comedians ' of the sixteenth century who came to Germany became notorious for the sexual content of their performances and the boldness of their stage dialogue. Their performances were too realistic, too true to nature. The element of sensation, or sensationalism, which was present in the English theatre up till comparatively recently, was characteristic of the plays produced by these 'English comedians'. Murder, executions, duels, battles, brilliant processions, fanfares, and the like, were all used as devices to make the plot sensational. But, above all, these actors concentrated on sex, pandering to the lowest instincts of their audiences.

The English plays of this period often contained a combination of cruelty and lust, as in *Titus Andronicus and the Haughty Empress*, in which the Empress orders her sons to rape the hated Andronica. The two young men take Andronica into a wood, and in the Fourth Act they re-appear, having carried out their mother's order and having, in addition, mutilated her.

The powerful draught that passed through the English drama of Shakespeare's period did not succeed in sweeping away entirely the smutty tone of the older comedy, yet it relegated coarseness to a secondary position as something incidental, whereas previously it had been the very essence and object of the play. The last remnants of impurity were finally eliminated under the rule of the Puritanism of the first half of the seventeenth century. The Puritans despised the drama and, like the Church in an earlier age, regarded it as the work of the Devil.

From the year 1642 until 1648 the theatre was entirely suppressed, the actors were banished or maltreated by soldiers and imprisoned[1].

All this was changed at a single stroke with the accession of Charles II. The Puritans were replaced by hedonists who expected the same pleasures from the theatre as they found in real life. The theatre, as Taine wrote, enabled them to wallow in the mire of the deepest degradation and lust. It required neither imagination nor intellect. All that was necessary was eyes to see and the capacity to remember. The filthy speeches made them laugh, while the shameless scenes tickled their fancy. The plot nearly always centred in a betrayed husband or father. The distinguished gentlemen of the audience agreed with the author in taking the

[1] D'Israeli, *Curiosities of Literature* (London, 1895), p. 281.

part of the seducer and following his actions with interest and sympathy. There were the women who were his willing victims, the almost physical demonstrations of immorality, the obscene songs, and the filthy jokes to amuse and to whet the appetites of the noble voluptuaries and libertines. The dramatists of the period represented all women as whores and all men as coarse wasters, and not only was this taken for granted, but it also became a matter of *bon ton* to indulge in all sorts of excesses. Rochester and Charles II left the theatre in an elevated state of mind, more than ever convinced that virtue was only a mask assumed by scoundrels who wanted to sell themselves dearly.

Women first appeared on the English stage in the year 1660. They soon acquired the coarse manners of their male colleagues, and behaved in the most shameless manner, publicly offering their charms for sale. It frequently happened that actresses were recruited from the brothels and returned from the stage to the brothels, or went into the King's harem, like Nell Gwynn, whom Thackeray mentions as an example of the immorality of the stage of those days.

The young—and old—gallants amused themselves with the actresses in the 'green room' in such an indecent manner that Queen Anne later found it necessary to issue a decree to the effect ' that no person of what quality soever presume to go behind the scenes or come upon the stage either before or during the acting of any play'. She also forbade the feminine portion of the audience to wear masks.

It had been the custom for women visiting the theatre to wear masks, because the action and dialogue of the plays were so obscene that no woman could hear and see them without blushing. And the ladies preferred to blush under their masks. But this peculiar device was often exploited by women of doubtful character who, protected by their masks, accosted the male members of the audience. Hence Queen Anne's decree against masks.

A strange aspect of the prostitution of the Restoration theatre was represented by the so-called 'orange girls', mostly young girls who sold oranges at the entrances of theatres. They are repeatedly mentioned in Grammont's *Mémoires*[1].

While Wycherley, Congreve, Farquhar and other dramatists put the most unrestrained sexual licence on the stage, the notorious Rochester went so far as to represent on the boards, in his play *Sodom*, the joys of unnatural love. (See Chapter XVII.)

No wonder that Jeremiah Collier[2], at the end of the century, should have subjected the immoral conditions of the theatre to merciless criticism and condemnation. First he dealt with the blasphemous habit of cursing on the stage and its frank atheism, then he flagellated the custom of playwrights to represent in every scene and in every character sexual lust. A fine gentleman, Collier wrote, was a whoring, cursing, filthy atheist. And the ladies were tarred with the same brush.

The two great theatres of the eighteenth century were Covent Garden (built in 1733) and the Drury Lane Theatre (built in 1663). The former was mainly devoted to musical performances and pantomime, while Drury Lane presented principally tragedies and comedies. In the summer season the Haymarket Theatre (built in 1720), which was mainly devoted to Italian and English Opera, played the most important part among London theatres. This was not the same as the Italian Opera House, which was also on the corner of the Haymarket.

[1] See Sanger, *History of Prostitution* (New York, 1859), p. 301.
[2] Jeremy Collier, *A Short View of the Immorality and Profaneness of the English Stage*, London, 1699 (4th edn.).

Famous actors associated with Covent Garden were Garrick (1746), Charles Kemble (1794), Mrs. Glover (1797), and later Fanny Kemble (1829), Edmund Kean, who appeared at this theatre for the last time in 1833. The 'stars' of Drury Lane were Nell Gwynn (1666), Barton Booth (1701), Mrs. Siddons (1775), John P. Kemble (1783), Harriet Mellon (1795), Edmund Kean (1814), while Henderson, Bannister, Matthews, Elliston, Liston, Young, Miss Fenton, Miss Farren, Edmund Kean, Miss Paton and Macready appeared at the Haymarket Theatre.

At the Goodman's Fields Theatre, which opened in 1729, David Garrick first appeared on the 19th October 1791 in the rôle of Richard III.

Although these representatives of the noble side of histrionic art, whose names will always live in the annals of the theatre, succeeded in raising the general level of the English theatre to a high level, they failed to banish completely the immoral tone which seems to have reached a particularly high degree of development on the English stage. The English theatre of the eighteenth century was still the customary rendezvous of the ' smart ' world, which went to the theatre for purposes other than artistic enjoyment.

Loose women still continued to appear both in the gallery and in the stalls. These creatures never missed a performance in order to entice into their net any man who appeared to be a stranger to the house. If such a man happened to be present, one or other of the prostitutes would manage to accost him, and if he responded a bargain was almost certain to be struck.

The smaller theatres, like Goodman's Fields Theatre, were cesspools of immorality which endangered the whole neighbourhood. Sir John Hawkins records that this theatre was surrounded by a whole series of brothels, a fact which is also alluded to in Foote's *Taste* (1752). Even fifty years later there were a number of brothels in the vicinity of this theatre.

Sometimes brothels were shown on the stage. Thus *The Genius* (1780) was a play about the notorious Dr. Graham and his 'Temple of Health'. Bannister portrayed Graham, and the play included his two doormen who, in gorgeous uniforms, distributed tickets at the door of the 'Temple'. The 'heavenly bed', with its glass legs, was part of the scenery. The younger Colmann and Bannister went to the 'Temple of Health' in order to study Dr. Graham and the atmosphere of the place[1].

Samuel Foote did not hesitate to complement the company of the Haymarket Theatre from the brothels. Thus, on one occasion he engaged a prostitute from the brothel of Charlotte Hayes.

It cannot be said that Shakespeare's mighty spirit dominated the stage of the nineteenth century either.

The repeated attempts to bring about a renaissance of the English drama were frustrated by the increasingly wide development of the popular predilection for sensationalism which, as we have already mentioned, was characteristic of the English taste for centuries. From the beginning of the century right to its end the English stage was dominated by the sensational play. The effect a play had on the senses of the audience was the standard of quality and lucrativeness. As early as 1815 some authors recorded the decline of the English tragedy and comedy and the prevalence of spectacular plays in the brutal sense.

This was clearly demonstrated by the theatrical posters and playbills with which the whole of London seemed to be placarded in the early part of the nineteenth century, and

[1] Thornbury, *Haunted London*, p. 103.

also, to some extent, later. These posters contained drawings of the principal scenes in the plays, which invariably dealt with murder, rape, brutal crime in general, and also, of course, with sex.

Not many decades ago plays like *A Life's Revenge* were produced at a theatre then known as the Standard Theatre in Shoreditch. In one part of the play two women fought a duel with swords, and when one of them fell wounded to the ground, her opponent fell upon her and throttled her before stabbing her to death amid the vociferous applause of the audience. The audience consisted of men, women and children—although the performances were held in the evening—and they always accompanied the proceedings on the stage with applause for the sympathetic characters and boos and hissing for the villain, as children do in the modern cinema. The love-making in *A Life's Revenge* was, to say the least, unmistakable; the kisses with which the heroine rewarded the hero sounded like revolver shots, while her caresses might better be described as ' mauling '.

But even the better-class London theatres could not entirely escape this tendency for sensationalism combined with coarseness of tone. The tone of the actresses, in particular, was most indelicate, and this fact was all the more remarkable because it contrasted so completely with the gentle, womanly character of Englishwomen in real life.

Between 1830 and 1850 the so-called ' Penny Theatres ' constituted a serious evil. Many contemporary authors complained of the ' Penny Theatres ', and Ryan described them as the ' nurseries of young thieves and prostitutes '. These cheap theatres included the Victoria Theatre in Lambeth, the Bower Saloon, Stangate, and the Rotunda in Blackfriars Road[1].

[1] H. Barton Baker, *The London Stage* (London, 1892), Vol. II, pp. 239-241.

A characteristic feature of the great London theatres, particularly in the first half of the nineteenth century, was their saloons, which served almost exclusively as the rendezvous of prostitutes.

A visitor to Covent Garden Theatre describes his impressions as follows:

' The short intervals we spent in the saloon. The saloon was full of prostitutes, whose clothes revealed more than they concealed, but whose behaviour, on the contrary, did not in any way betray their calling. A meaning look from a man is answered by the lady concerned with the handing over of a card giving her name and address and containing a tenderly worded invitation. The girls carry the cards in their bosom, and they therefore convey some of the perfume of their bodies. The offer of the cards is carried out with perfect courtesy and good taste. It is true that the saloons of the better-class theatres are only frequented by the "cream" of the prostitutes. It is a curious fact that English families, mothers and daughters as well as fathers and sons, move among these pretty ladies quite naturally, apparently unconcerned with their presence and activities. The presence of the prostitutes undoubtedly influences the sale of the half-price tickets—which they themselves must also buy—because many men only attend the theatre in order to meet them.'

But the auditorium of the theatre was also often used by prostitutes. A German writer, O. v. Rosenberg, wrote: ' Unfortunately, the audience in the entire house—I am speaking of Covent Garden and Drury Lane—is very mixed, and a duchess will often be found to be surrounded by prostitutes. The gallery is full of the latter, and they are admitted without difficulty. Indecent jokes are freely exchanged between these creatures and young men of the best families, and people do not appear to be in the least shocked even

[599]

when the men make love to the prostitutes before their eyes. During the intervals the street walkers and the young and old libertines assemble in the saloon, which is gorgeously appointed, and where refreshments are sold. The walls are lined with mirrors, and the room is furnished with ottomans and settees for the convenience of courting couples. There are hundreds of candles and candelabra to illuminate the scene.'

A bookseller named Glanville at one time published a list of the names of prostitutes who were in the habit of frequenting the saloon of the Covent Garden Theatre. The publication was called *The Fashionable Cypriad.*

Music, which a famous philosopher described as ' melody to which the world is the text ', appeals directly to the heart more than any other art. That is why music has always played such an important rôle in love. It makes the human soul receptive to erotic impulses of all kinds, whether pure or sensual. In ancient Greece and Rome they had what might be described as ' musical prostitutes '; while in modern times Italian opera-singers and musicians, some of whom were castrated, brought to the Northern countries a new kind of musical prostitution.

Nowhere was the passion for musical enjoyment of all kinds more widespread and stronger than in England: This is all the more remarkable because the English people had produced no composer of note, and hardly had a national music. The English for a long time lacked creative capacity in the field of music. But the desire for music was present to an extraordinary extent, though it was undoubtedly directed towards musical enjoyment of the wrong kind. Erasmus of Rotterdam in his *Moriae Encomium* already mentioned this peculiar musical passion of the English. All the travel authors of the eighteenth and nineteenth centuries expressed amazement at the extraordinary rôle that music played in England. Von Archenholtz's report clearly shows the connection between this passion for music and the *vita sexualis*.

' The dark, passionate emotions of the musical artist impinge on the ear in different tonal sequences, causing dark, passionate emotions to echo in our senses. That was why Plato regarded music as dangerous, banishing, in particular, soft lyric music from his Republic.

' Our time is less strict in its attitude to passion than the ancient philosopher of virtue. A voluptuous, languid crooning, performed in the silvery tones of a eunuch—that is sufficient to tickle jaded nerves to ecstasy.'

The passion of the English for song and music was not confined to the upper strata of society. Goede records the presence ' of a passionate love of music among the lower classes. The sound of any musical instrument in a London street, however inexpertly played, is sufficient to lure the people into the open from every hole and corner, and within a few minutes the street musician is surrounded by a crowd of dirty listeners, who absorb the harmonies—or disharmonies—of his music with glad ecstasy'.

As England produced no prominent composers, musicians and singers, there was an early invasion of foreign artists, who naturally found a lucrative field for their activities in this rich country.

Chief among the invaders were the two musically most gifted nations, the Italians and the Germans.

The first Italian Opera House was opened in the Haymarket on the 9th April 1705. The second, the Royal Italian Opera House, Covent Garden, was opened on the 6th April 1847, with a performance of *Semiramis*, in which the title rôle was sung by Grisi. The salaries of the artists were paid by the Government and, in addition, the opera singers were also accorded a high social status. More than one prima-donna

[601]

married into the English nobility. In the time of George II
opera singers even became political personalities of great
importance, in that the rivalries of the Whigs and Tories
were expressed in support for this or that theatrical star.

The high nobility often invited Italian singers to give
recitals at their homes. On the 17th July 1835 a concert by
Italian artists took place at Lansdowne House, the Marquess
of Lansdowne's residence. Lablache and Tamburini, the two
greatest bass singers in Europe, sang the famous duet ' Se
fiato ' from *Matrimonio secreto* by Cimarosa, and the trio
' Vadasi via di quà ' from *Cosa rara* by Martini was also
performed by Malibran, Rubini and Lablache.

The trouble was that the Italian musical eunuchs also
introduced sexual corruption into England. A contemporary
wrote about this aspect of the musical invasion as follows:

' In order to realise completely to what extent the prevailing taste has sunk, it is only necessary to visit the magnificent
theatre devoted exclusively to Italian opera—a monument
of English extravagance. Lovers of this type of public
entertainment find so much enchantment in the empty tones
that some even sacrifice their masculinity to the god of
music. The voice of nature and the expression of human
passion appears here in the form of farcical trilling and
warbling, which is called a recital, but which is neither
singing nor declamation.

' But that is not all. By supporting these emasculated
foreign singers we are promoting general moral degradation
and effeminacy, which is contagious like the pestilence and
throttles in our young noblemen all nobility of feeling.
Instead of presenting to them as examples the characters of
patriots and heroes who have performed great deeds in the
service of their country, we are shown a group of pitiable
creatures, neither men nor women, who, no matter how

[602]

highly they are praised, lack all manliness and capacity for action, which is after all the basis of dramatic expression[1].'

In addition to the Italians, German musicians and composers also played a prominent rôle in England from the end of the seventeenth century. Zacharias Conrad von Uffenbach, who saw an opera in London in the year 1710, wrote: ' The orchestra could not be better constituted. But the musicians are foreigners, mainly Germans, for the English are not much better as regards music than the Dutch, that is to say, rather bad.'

The most acclaimed German musicians in England were Handel and Weber, the former of whom lived in England for forty-nine years, from 1710 till 1759, and is buried in Westminster Abbey. Carl Maria von Weber went to London in February 1826 to attend the first performance of his *Oberon*, and died there on the 5th June of the same year. Weber was revered by the British public as a musical demigod, and his music was played and sung all over London.

In addition to the big opera-houses there were also minor temples of music in the form of music-halls of various sizes. An interesting precursor of the music-hall in the seventeenth and eighteenth centuries was the popular show-boat on the Thames.

The show-boat was a large barque, built in the form of a house, which lay in the Thames between Somerset House and the Savoy. The boat was called the 'Folly'. It contained a number of saloons, while the entire deck was used as a promenade. The four corners of the deck were decorated with turrets. This 'comic piece of architecture', as Thomas Browne described it, was constructed shortly after the Restoration. The ' Folly ' was visited by Pepys on the 13th April 1668, under which date he records in his *Diary*

[1] *A Frank Description of the Idlers and Scamps of London* (London, 1787), Part I, pp. 98-99.

that he spent a shilling on board the boat. Originally, the
' Folly ' was a musical establishment intended as a rendezvous for 'persons of quality', but very soon the ' ladies of
the town ' realised that it was an excellent place for their
purpose, and they gradually drove away the respectable
women who had used the boat as the venue of amorous
intrigues of a slightly different sort. Queen Mary, wife of
William III, paid a visit to the ' Folly ', whereupon the
owner rechristened it ' Royal Diversion ', though the
people continued to refer to the boat by its original name.
Thomas Browne describes a visit he paid to the 'Folly' in
the year 1700. As soon as he boarded the ship he found
himself surrounded by young and old women ' of all types
and sizes '. Some of these women were dancing gaily all
over the deck, while others were talking with their admirers.
However, the majority, including men armed with long
swords, who lived on the immoral earnings of the women,
crowded the saloons below deck, smoking and drinking.
Thomas Browne, who was no puritan, was so disgusted
that he immediately left the ship. In later years the
' Folly ' became the meeting place of decent artisans and
shop assistants, who went there with their sweethearts
after hours for their daily diversion.

The music-halls proper, which were characteristic of
English musical life, dated from the conclusion of the
Commonwealth period. The first music-hall in the grand
style was established by a man named Sadler in Islington.
Ned Ward, the author of *London Spy*, gave in his 'Walk to
Islington' a delightful description of the doings of a music-
hall audience in the year 1699:

We enter'd the houses, were conducted upstairs,
There lovers o'er cheesecakes were seated by pairs.
The organs and fiddles were scraping and humming,
The guests for more ale on the tables were drumming;

Whilst others, ill-bred, lolling over their mugs,
Were laughing and toying with their fans and their
    jugs,
Disdain'd to be slaves to perfections, or graces,
Sat puffing tobacco in their mistresses' faces.
Some 'prentices too, who made a bold venture
And trespassed a little beyond their indenture,
Were each of them treating his mistress' maid,
For letting him in when master's abed. . . .

The music-hall was already in the seventeenth century essentially a place for performing variety acts, so that variety, more or less as we know it to-day, first originated in England. The first programmes of the music-halls were composed of mediaeval mysteries and morality plays, so that the influence of this type of drama was perpetuated through the music-hall. The music-hall thrived to the precise extent to which the former methods of public merry-making—at annual fairs and various popular festivals—ceased to be available. The music-hall provided entertainment for the middle and lower classes, to whom it offered all the traditional elements of the old English shows—music, singing, dancing, jugglery, rope walking, etc. The author of the *Foreigner's Guide* wrote of Sadler's Wells in 1730: 'Here you are offered throughout the summer singing, music, rope walking performances, etc., and also, each evening, a farce, which anyone who pays for a bottle of wine can see.'

The famous music-halls of the eighteenth century were the 'New Pantheon', a rendezvous of prostitutes, the 'Dog and Duck' and the 'Garden of Apollo'. Prominent music-halls of the nineteenth century included Evans's Music Hall in Covent Garden, the 'Alhambra', 'Highbury Barn' in Islington, the 'Greek Music Hall' in City Road, the 'Cave of Harmony', which is mentioned by Thackeray

[605]

in *The Newcomes*, the 'Canterbury Hall' in Lambeth, and Weston's Music Hall in High Holborn.

A speciality of London music-halls until the 'seventies was the obscene burlesquing of sacred institutions. For instance, in the notorious ' Rotunda ' in Blackfriars Road, the rites of the Church were parodied in the most shameless manner, while divorce cases before the courts were also parodied, the most scandalous details being specially emphasised. One of the most notorious music-halls was the ' Coal Hole Tavern ' in the Strand where ' Baron ' Nicholson staged all the scandals of the 'fifties and 'sixties.

Another peculiar phenomenon was the appearance of negro singers.

It was in 1830 that real negroes first came to London from America in order to appear on the music-hall stage as singers. The song about ' Nelly Gray ' was brought from America by a troupe of negro singers, known as Christie's Minstrels, who first appeared at St. James's Hall and scored a great success with their negro songs. Since then a black face, a tall collar of white cardboard, blue and white striped trousers, a guitar and tambourine have become a popular ' get up ' for singers, and ' nigger minstrels ' with artificially blackened faces, which belong to genuine Londoners, and sometimes to Germans, can now be seen in the London streets singing strange songs.

In the first half of the nineteenth century it was customary among men of the 'upper classes' to visit a music-hall after an opera performance for ' supper and song '.

A music-hall of evil repute was ' Little Tom's Tavern ' in Whitechapel. But all music-halls during the first half of the nineteenth century had a bad reputation owing to the obscene songs performed in them.

Most of these songs were written by William West, a London artist and publisher, whose principal activities fall between the years 1815 and 1835. West had a shop at 13, Exeter Street, from where he later moved to 57, Wych Street, opposite the Olympic Theatre, Strand. William West's songs were performed publicly, at places to which both young and old had free access, and although they were, without exception, of an objectionable character, West was only supplying a demand.

William West's principal collection of songs appeared under the title: *The Blowen's Cabinet of Choice Songs; a beautiful, bothering, laughter-provoking collection of spiflicating, flabbergasting smutty ditties, now first printed, etc.* This collection included the following songs: ' The Magical Carrot, or the Parsley Bed ', ' Great Plenipotentiary! A most Outrageously Good Amatory Stave ', ' Katty O'Moore, or the Root ', ' The Smutty Billy Black ', ' My Woman is a Rummy Whore ', and others, even worse.

The price of these song-books was sixpence. A collection in larger format with a coloured etching as frontispiece was priced at one shilling. ' The Gentleman's Spicy Reciter ', ' The Cockatoo's Notebook ' and ' The Gentleman's Sanctum Sanctorum ' are a few of the titles appearing in this gala publication.

Another publisher of obscene songs was John Duncombe of 10, Middle Row, Holborn, who died in 1852. He published, among others, *Duncomb's Drolleries, Labern's Original Comic Song Book* and *Labern's Comic Song Book.*

A third publisher of obscene songs was William Dugdale, who published under the pseudonym H. Smith *The Coal Hole Companion, The Cider Cellar Songster,* and other similar collections.

The collection of smutty songs whose title we give below as a curiosity of cultural history is of earlier origin than the above:

The Buck's Delight, being a Collection of Humorous Songs,

Sung at Several Societies of Choice Spirits, Bucks, Free-masons, Albions and Antigallicans, with Universal Applause. Among which are a Great Variety of Choice Originals, that never Appeared in Print before. Containing also the New Songs, sung this last Season at the Publick Gardens and Theatres, and all other polite Places of Resort. To which is Added a Collection of the Most Celebrated Toasts now in Taste. The Second Edition with Great Additions. London: Printed for T. Knowles, behind the Chapter House, in St. Paul's Churchyard. (Price 1s. 6d., neatly bound in Red.)

The titles of these collections of songs, which are now extremely rare, are quoted here, because apart from their interest as songs, they also contain a great deal of the slang used between the years 1790 and 1850.

All these songs were sung at the various London music-halls in the 'forties of last century. The singing of obscene songs was only stopped when the doors of ' Canterbury Hall ' and ' Weston's Music Hall ' were opened to women. But although the musical offerings at the music-halls thereafter assumed a more respectable character, the music-halls now became convenient places of assembly for prostitutes.

The music-halls played a very important part in the musical life of the English people, yet street music was even more important, particularly in London. In no city in the world was there so much music playing and singing in the streets as in London. Players of barrel-organs and other instruments succeeded one another in the streets all day. It was amazing what atrocious performances the public not only tolerated but also enjoyed.

Street singing in London had an even longer history than street music. It dates back to the old English ballad, to the deep poesy of which Thomas Percy, Bishop of Dromore, first called attention by his famous collection.

[608]

The chief representatives of the folk-songs in Anglo-Saxon times were the bards, also called sceopas, leodhyrta or gleemen. They were poets, musicians and singers in one. But the exercise of the art was by no means confined to professionals. In Beowulf a king plays the harp, while Alfred the Great was also a bard. Later the monks showed a predilection for the profession of gleeman. When King Canute sailed past the Abbey of Ely he heard the monks singing within the Abbey.

After the Norman invasion professional singers began to be called minstrels (from the French word *menestrier*), which meant a wandering singer. The minstrels generally wrote and composed their own songs. On Sundays and holidays the men, women and children of the village assembled in a sunny clearing, or on a hill, where they were entertained by the minstrels with songs extolling the deeds of their ancestors or the romance and poetry of love.

A characteristic feature of the old English and Scottish songs and ballads was their touching simplicity and tender feeling, their understanding for love and loyalty, and a peculiar receptiveness for the beauties of nature. Naturally, rude humour and gaiety also had their rightful place in these old songs, as witness the ballads about the bold robber Robin Hood; the old historical folk-songs about Edward IV and the tanner, the King and the Miller, James I and the Tinker, are even smutty in tone.

A characteristic old English ballad is the story of the London goldsmith Shore and his unfaithful wife Jane, the mistress of Edward IV:

> To Matthew Shore I was a wife,
> Till lust brought ruine to my life;
> And then my life I lewdlye spent,
> Which makes my soul for to lament.

In Lombard Street I once did dwelle,
As London can yet witness welle;
Where many gallants did beholde
My beautye in a shop of golde.

I spread my plumes, as wantons doe,
Some sweete and secret friende to wooe;
Because chaste love I did not finde
Agreeing to my wanton minde.

At last my name in court did ringe
Into the eares of Englande's king,
Who came and liked and love requir'd,
But I made coye what he desir'd.

Yet Mistress Blague, a neighbour neare,
Whose friendship I esteemed deare,
Did saye, it was a gallant thing
To be beloved of a king.

The ballad goes on to relate how Jane Shore, driven by
her own desire and easily convinced by the arguments of
her procuress friend, became the King's mistress, whereupon her disconsolate husband left England in order not
to be a witness of her shame. Jane attained considerable
influence at Court and also practised charity with a lavish
hand, so that she was adored by the widows and orphans of
London. But with the death of her royal lover she was
overwhelmed with misfortune, as his successor on the
throne, Richard III, persecuted her by all possible means.
Her possessions were taken from her, and thereafter all her
friends turned against her. Even her old false friend, Mrs.
Blague, showed her the door. Only one man, whose life
she had once saved, stood by her, but was hanged for this

' crime '. Finally Jane Shore had to earn her living as a beggar woman in the streets of London. She died at a point in the East End of London which was thereafter known as Shore Ditch (Shoreditch). The ballad concludes with the warning:

> You wanton wives that fall to lust,
> Be you assur'd that god is just,
> Whoredom shall not escape his hand,
> Nor pride unpunished in this land.

One of the most beautiful old English ballads, in which true love is glorified in a moving manner, is ' The Bailiff's Daughter of Islington', which is included in Percy's *Reliques of English Poetry*:

> There was a youthe, and a wellbeloved youthe,
> And he was a squire's son:
> He loved the bayliff's daughter deare,
> That lived in Islington.

> Yet she was coye and would not believe
> That he did love her soe,
> Noe, nor at any time would she
> Any countenance to him showe.

The youth goes to London, where he stays for seven years without seeing his sweetheart again. All her girl friends get married, but she remains single, because she is still thinking of the young man whom she dismissed in doubt about his love. Her longing for him finally causes her to go to London. The day is swelteringly hot, and as she sits down to rest by the roadside her lover rides past:

> She started up, with a colour so redd,
> Catching hold of his bridle reine;
> One penny, one penny, kind sir, she sayd,
> Will ease me of much paine.

Before I give you one penny, sweet-heart,
Praye tell me where you were borne.
At Islington, kind sir, sayd shee,
Where I have had many a score.

I prythee, sweet-heart, then tell to mee,
O tell me whether you knowe
The bayliff's daughter of Islington,
She is dead, sir, long agoe.

If she be dead then take my horse,
My saddle and bridle also;
For I will into some far countrey,
Where noe man shall me knowe.

O staye, o staye, thou goodlye youthe,
She standeth by thy side;
She is here alive, she is not dead,
And readye to be thy bride.

O farewell griefe, and welcome joye,
Ten thousand times therefore;
For nowe I have found mine Owne true love,
Whom I thought I should never see more.

The minstrels flourished until the middle of the sixteenth century and were then superseded by inferior poets
who wrote ballads for publication. By the end of the century
the minstrels as such ceased to exist. Surviving old minstrels
were reduced to singing in the streets and outside beer-
houses. The puritanical writers of the period were constantly agitating against their ' filthy, coarse and smutty '
songs. Yet the common people still continued to listen with
pleasure to their songs.

Putenham, a courtier at the court of Queen Elizabeth,
records that these ' tavern minstrels ' mostly sang historical

songs, like the story of Sir Topas, and those of Bevis of Southampton, Warwick, Adam Bell, etc., and also other old romances. Sometimes they sang rhymes made up by themselves at weddings, taverns and beer-houses.

The ballad-singers of London in the sixteenth century had their pitch at Temple Bar, where they always had a numerous audience for their vulgar songs and ' alehouse stories '.

But the higher type ballad was not entirely lost. Thus ' Dulcina ', an erotic ballad ascribed to Sir Walter Raleigh, was very popular in the sixteenth century.

Songs of this type are also to be found in the works of Shakespeare, Ben Jonson and their contemporaries.

But folk poetry was entirely in the hands of the ballad makers, who at first printed their work on single sheets, which they sold at low prices. Later these single sheets were assembled into small volumes or ' garlands ', such as ' Garland of Joy ', ' Garland of Love ', etc.

A famous collection of songs, most of which were set to music, was written at the turn of the seventeenth century by Thomas D'Urfey. They are full of the gay, licentious, lascivious spirit of the Restoration period. A typical example of the D'Urfey songs is ' The Cumberland Lass ', the first verse of which is as follows:

> Up to my Chamber I her got,
> There I did treat her courteously.
> I told her I thought it was her Lot
> To stay all night and Lig with me.
> Oh, to Bed to me, to Bed to me,
> The Lass that comes to bed to me.
> Blith and bonny may she be,
> The Lass that comes to bed to me.

A typical London ballad of the period was the famous 'Hopeful Bargain', the full title of which was: 'The Hopeful Bargain! Or a Fare for a Hackney Coachman, giving a Comical Relation how an Ale-draper at the Sign of the Double tooth'd Rake in or near the new Palace Yard, Westminster, Sold his Wife for a Shilling, and how she was sold a second time for Five Shillings to Judge; My Lord Coachman, and how her Husband receiv'd her again after she had lain with other Folks three Days and Nights, etc. The Tune Lilly Bullero.'

The vogue of the itinerant singer reached its highest development during the second half of the eighteenth and the beginning of the nineteenth centuries. The male singers were confronted with the competition of female ballad singers, who haunted the streets of London singing obscene songs.

The sale of these street songs formed a lucrative side-line of the London book trade of the eighteenth century. Unfortunately, some of them were written, for the sake of the fee paid by the publishers, by poets of merit who lived in straitened circumstances. Oliver Goldsmith wrote ballads for street singers at a shilling each, and used to go out at night in order to hear them sung.

Collections of such obscene ballads include ' The Lovers ', at the end of *The London Bawd* (British Museum Library), and 'Love's Vocal Grove, or the Bucks in High Humour, being a Choice Collection of the Most Favourite Songs of the Town '.

However, the folk-song in the noblest sense was not entirely abandoned. Thus Bishop Percy wrote ' O Nancy ' to Anne Gutteridge in 1758. The song was set to music by Thomas Carter and was sung by Vernon at Vauxhall in 1773. It is sufficient to quote the first verse of this charming song to give an idea of its quality:

[614]

O Nancy, wilt thou go with me,
Nor sigh to leave the flaming town?
Can silent glens have charms for thee,
The lowly cot and russet gown?
No longer drest in silken sheen
No longer deck'd with jewels rare,
Say, canst thou quit each courtly scene,
Where thou wert fairest of the fair?

Other favourite and much sung English folk-songs of the
eighteenth century were ' Sweetest of Pretty Maids ',
' Sally in Our Alley ', ' Oh, the Roast Beef of Old England ',
and ' Come, Haste to the Wedding '.

Those who took pleasure in the beautiful old songs used
to congregate at the shop of the famous music-dealer
Thomson in the Strand, who knew most of the tunes, and
used to sing them to his visitors, who often included David
Garrick.

But on the whole the tendency of the eighteenth century
in the field of the folk-song was to destroy all poetic feeling
in the English people. This was the case particularly in
the cities, though an understanding of nature and a certain
poetic sense continued to maintain themselves in the country
and in the remoter industrial towns. Yorkshire and
Lancashire, in particular, had a rich fund of local legends
and songs, and many old Scottish ballads had also found
their way to these shires. In the West of England the
beautiful Christmas carols continued to survive. It was
not until the Victorian era that a new tone was re-
introduced into the English folk-song and the poetic sense
of the people was revived.

As late as the year 1860, Seven Dials, London, was the
headquarters of ballad-singers, who lived in miserable
garrets, writing ballads for the publishers, who paid them

[615]

beggarly prices calculated according to the length of the ballads. A few of these ballads became universally known and liked, and finally rose to the dignity of being sung at such places as the Argyll Rooms, and even in 'polite society'.

. A typical example of the latter kind of ballad was 'Sweet Minnie', in which the sentimental bent of the Anglo-Saxon spirit found due expression. On the other hand, there were also obscene ballads at this period, like 'The Ratcatcher's Daughter', which contained many filthy passages. This magnificent specimen of London's folk poetry had a rival in 'Polly, Won't You Try Me, Oh?' The latter song contains a characteristic feature of a certain type of English song, namely, euphonious but meaningless words and phrases.

An interesting group among London's street songs were those written in 'cant' or slang, and collected by J. S. Farmer in his *Musa Pedestris. Three Centuries of Canting Songs and Slang Rhymes* (London, 1896).

Another interesting feature of London streets, in addition to street songs, were the long-drawn and sometimes melodious street cries which were made the subject of artistic treatment and historical appreciation from earliest times.

At the end of William III's reign Peter Molyn Tempest published a number of etchings illustrating the 'Cries of London', made after the paintings of the Dutch artist, Mercellus Laroon (1653-1702).

At a later period it was the famous cartoonist Thomas Rowlandson, in particular, who paid considerable attention to the 'Cries of London'. The first of his etchings appeared in 1799 over the various cries, such as 'Buy a Trap, a Rat Trap, buy my Trap', or 'Buy my Goose, my Fat Goose', etc. Around 1810 Rowlandson published thirty more etchings on this subject, which give a very good idea of the life of London's street vendors in his time.

One of the principal pastimes of mediaeval England was dancing. Everyone, both high and low, had to be a dancer. Some kings of England wanted to be known as good dancers, and one of them, Henry VIII, was famous for his dancing. On St. Valentine's day young people in carefree gaiety danced in the streets, in the meadows and woods. Old Stow (sixteenth century) regarded the dancing of young girls out of doors, which had been customary in London in the twelfth century, and was practised until about 1530, as a preventive of ' worse things indoors '. Country girls danced all their ' rustic measures, rounds and jigs ', including the dance of the milkmaids round the Maypole, in the open.

According to Wright (*A History of English Culture*), during certain periods in the Middle Ages the passion for dancing was so widespread that it necessarily produced some serious evils and became the cause of moral corruption. Chaucer frequently mentions the ' love dances ', which were performed by two very scantily clad girls, who struck various erotic poses, exhibiting their physical charms and making certain significant movements towards each other.

There were two different types of dances in the Middle Ages, one of which may be described as ' homely ', while the other included the professional dances of the conjurers and minstrels. After the first Crusades the conjurers of Western Europe had acquired many of the tricks of their Eastern brethren and had also brought to Europe the ' Almehs ' or Eastern dancing girls. These dances formed part of the programme of the conjurers, and were nearly always coarse and indecent. The ' homely ' dances, in which men and women held hands, were comparatively harmless.

These ' folk dances ' flourished until the middle of the

sixteenth century, when they were superseded by 'social' dances, which first came into fashion at the court masquerades and balls under Elizabeth and James I. For these and also after the Restoration there was a demand for dancing instruction which was met by foreign dancing masters, mainly French.

Addison published in the *Spectator* (1711) a letter supposed to have been written by a business man concerning the dancing customs of the time. The imaginary business man takes his daughter to a ball, and while he approves of some dances as being graceful and conducive to maidenly reserve, he condemns dances like the 'Allemande', in which the dancers roll on the floor, so that the shocked business man 'could see far higher above the girl's shoes than was seemly'. Addison also mentions the 'kissing dance', in the course of which the male partner must keep his lips pressed to those of the lady for a whole minute. Addison strongly objected to the 'contre danse', which he regarded as dangerous to morals, though he was against abolishing this dance, which, if danced decently, was conducive to physical grace.

The dancing-masters of the eighteenth century had an evil reputation, for under the cloak of private dancing classes they frequently held sexual orgies of the most disgusting kind, a state of affairs to which attention was first called by Sir John Fielding.

Already in Shakespeare's time all the continental dances were known in England. One of the most popular was the so-called 'morisca', a Moorish dance imported from Spain. The dancers painted their faces black, wore Eastern costume with bells round their ankles, and hopped about so strenuously that it was seriously suggested that this dance was the cause of rheumatism and gout.

The English national dances included the 'cushion dance', which was also a game. One of the dancers placed a cushion on the floor and selected a partner by reciting a certain rhyme. The lady concerned knelt on the cushion and was kissed by her male partner. Then she repeated the process with another man, and this was continued until every young man and woman had knelt on the cushion and been kissed.

These kissing dances appear to have been popular in England for a long time before Addison. Kissing in this connection is, for instance, mentioned in *Henry VIII* (Act I, Scene 4).

Another English national dance is the hornpipe dance, in which the dancers hold the upper part of their bodies straight and stiff, and dance with a shambling movement of the legs.

The ' hunt the squirrel ' is also an English national dance, in which the partners alternately chase each other.

The dance known as the ' Anglaise ' is not an English, but a Bohemian dance. It was only in France that certain typically English steps were introduced into this dance.

On the other hand, the ' contre danse' is of purely English origin. Its French name is a corruption of country dance.

The first German valse was danced in the year 1813 at Almack's ballroom, and excited general indignation, not only among persons of the respectable middle class, but also among paragons of virtue like George Gordon Byron, who in his poem ' The Valse ' wrote:

> If such thou lovest, love her then no more,
> Or give, like her, caresses to a score,
> Her mind with these is gone, and with it go
> The little left behind it to bestow.

The dancing-masters of the nineteenth century were also in bad odour with the public. Dickens' *Dancing Academy* contains an excellent description of the true state of affairs at these dancing schools.

The ballet was first introduced in England in the eighteenth century, and was received with great enthusiasm. Noverre, one of the famous creators of the modern ballet, wrote in 1769 that dancing and ballet were ' a fashionable craze ', and that the love of ballet was so universal that not only did princes use them in their shows, but even the smallest troupes of actors and medicine vendors at fairs had ballet dancers, relying more on their performances to attract the public than on anything else they had to offer.

It was Mlle. Sallé, the famous French ballet dancer, who, in the year 1734, first brought ballet to England, scoring an outstanding success as Galathea in a Covent Garden performance of *Pygmalion and Galathea*. The enthusiasm with which the new show was received was almost pathological. The theatre was crowded to suffocation, yet prices of admission were fantastically high. At the final performance men had to fight their way to their seats. The presents showered on the dancers, including sweets which contained gold coins, amounted to a fabulous sum.

Later, Noverre came to Drury Lane and produced ballets of dazzling magnificence for those days, in which Miss Lydia Thompson collaborated, wearing Highland costume. In the second half of the century Mlle. Guimard (King's Theatre), and Parisot, Madame del Caro and Miss de Camp (Drury Lane) were the stars of ballet in England.

The English were very generous to their ballet dancers, and therefore had no difficulty in securing the services of the best exponents of the art. In 1802 the Italian Opera House counted among its members Mlle. Parisot, Mme. Laborie of the female stars, and Messrs. D'Egville, Laborie and St. Pierre of the foremost male dancers of the day. Foreign visitors to London declared that the London ballets were infinitely better than anything that could be seen in Paris.

[620]

In addition to the Italian Opera, eighteenth century London also had another theatre where ballets were performed. This was the ' Royal Circus ', near London Bridge.

Needless to say, the ' quality ' took a keen interest in ballet dancing, but not always purely from the artistic point of view. Young and old gallants used to go backstage in crowds, and sometimes filled nearly every inch of space behind the scene, in order to obtain a closer view of the artists. Naturally, this proved most inconvenient to the artists and extras. It even happened that part of the crowd was forced on to the stage itself, and at such time the gallery expressed its disapprobation in unmistakable terms.

In the 'forties and 'fifties of the nineteenth century the two most celebrated ballet dancers were Fanny Elssler and Maria Taglioni. An English critic defined the difference between the dancing of these two stars by saying that Taglioni represented ' poesy ' and Fanny Elssler ' wit '.

Fanny Elssler in 1844 performed a ballet which has since been copied many times. The story is briefly as follows: A young painter falls in love with his beautiful model, who suddenly disappears. The painter often stands gazing at the picture in deep melancholy. Finally, his mother finds the girl and brings her to the house. The girl slips into the painter's studio, takes her own portrait out of the frame and steps into its place. The painter arrives and pulls the curtain screening the picture aside, and out steps the lady of his heart.

Fanny Elssler's London appearances are also dealt with in an erotic books which describes the lady's alleged love affairs in Vienna, Paris and London. The book is entitled *Love Affairs of a Ballet Dancer. Piquantissima. Cincinatti, George Brown*, 1874.

A few decades ago London led the world in the production of magnificent ballet shows. The individual artist was denied a full opportunity to score a personal success, but the mass effects were always striking. There were lavish ballet shows, such as no other capital could provide. As early as the beginning of the 'seventies of last century a super ballet with ninety-nine performers was produced at the ' Alhambra '.

A most peculiar phenomenon in the eighteenth century and during the first thirty years of the nineteenth, were the prostitutes who danced in the streets, exhibiting their charms to passing men in this way. Adrian, in his *English Sketches*, records that one day as he was walking in Bird Cage Walk he saw a group of people forming a circle round a girl who was dancing with considerable grace and still greater abandon. When she was tired of dancing she sat down on the ground and sang obscene songs, to the great delight of the crowd. Suddenly she leapt to her feet and threw herself on the neck of a sentry at the Horse Guards Parade. With great difficulty the sentry released himself, and the girl then went dancing and singing towards the Mall. Adrian heard from someone in the crowd that the girl was a prostitute, who had started her profession as a ' high class ' courtesan, and had gradually sunk to dancing in the streets in order to find temporary lovers.

The low-class dance-halls were full of prostitutes. English and German prostitutes regularly frequented such places in the East End, singing the most abominable obscenities to the accompaniment of the dance music.

A few decades ago Maidstone, Greenwich, Gravesend, had dance-halls of doubtful reputation, where dancing was linked with prostitution, and where immoral ballets, such as the ' Drawers Ballet ', were performed.

Erotic dances were also performed at the brothels. Casanova describes a ' satyr dance ' which he witnessed at a London brothel called ' The Cannon '.

Up till a few decades ago erotic balls were held at London brothels. Nellie Cawsten, proprietress of an ' exclusive ' brothel in Brompton, gave balls which were attended by as many as 150 ' pretty ladies '. During the ball the most abominable orgies took place in the upper storeys of the house.

In addition to variety and ballet, pantomime also occupied an important place in the entertainment of Londoners in the eighteenth century. During that period pantomime was mainly performed at three of the smaller theatres: the ' Royal Circus ', ' Astley's Theatre ' and ' Sadler's Wells '. However, the big theatres, like Drury Lane and Covent Garden, were also obliged to give pantomime each evening after the ordinary programme in order to attract the poorer classes, who were admitted at half-price to this final item. With them came the girls, who during the pantomime played a similar game with the male members of the audience.

Up till about 1800 English pantomimes were on the lowest level imaginable. There was no sensible plot, and what there was was performed in a coarse or obscene manner. On the other hand, there were many changes of scenery, which appeared to satisfy the public of that day.

No less popular than pantomime were rope-walking, acrobatics and, of course, clowns. When opera was first introduced, it was found advisable to include such essentially circus ' turns '.

The English circus itself probably had its origins in ' The Three Hats ' tavern in Islington, where Tom Johnson, the ' Irish Tartar ', made his debut as an equestrian artist in the year 1758. He galloped round a circle standing first on one horse, then on two. Once he stood on his head on the back of a galloping horse. Tom Johnson's performance was once, on 17th July 1766, attended by the Duke of York and 500 other spectators.

In the summer of the same year Sampson introduced his

own wife at 'The Three Hats' as an equestrienne. He published an advertisement in the *Public Advertiser*, in which he informed the public that in addition to the usual programme he would prove to the public that the fair sex were as skilled as men when it came to horse riding. Sampson's performances continued until the year 1770.

But already in 1767 he had a serious rival in the person of a man named Price, who gave equestrian performances on 'Dobney's Bowling Green', near the present Pentonville Road, throughout the spring and summer.

Sampson and Price were followed by Coningham and Daniel Wildman, each of whom ran a separate circus.

In the nineteenth century Astley's Circus was *the* circus. The principal items on the programme were equestrian turns, but as the performances lasted from 7 till 12 p.m. each evening, it was obviously impossible to confine them to equestrianism, and time was filled in with farces, rope walking, music, competitions, etc.

Astley's Circus appears to have been a nice, homely place. Between turns the place was invaded by vendors of sausages, sweets and all sorts of other delicacies, while throughout the performance pickpockets were operating both in the auditorium and on the stage.

The first female trapeze artiste, who called herself Azella, appeared in 1869 at the Holborn Amphitheatre. She was soon followed by others, and within a short time all the London music-halls had their female trapeze artistes.

No people has such a long and eventful history of public entertainment and pastimes as the English. The golden era of public merry-making in England was the Elizabethan period, which appears to have been one long succession of festivals, processions, hunts, fairs, etc. One of the most magnificent products of English printing, which first appeared in 1788, contains a full record of the festivities organised in honour of the Queen during her many journeys through England. The book is *The Progresses and Publick Processions of Queen Elizabeth. Among which are interspersed other solemnities, publick expenditures and remarkable events during the reign of that illustrious princess. Etc. . . . Illustrated with historical notes by John Nichols.* Some of the Elizabethan public festivals were dazzlingly brilliant, others were merely grotesque.

The most characteristic English public festivals were the annual fairs. St. Edward's Fair, which was introduced by Edward III in the year 1248, continued to be held in Tothill Fields, Westminster, till 1823. Bartholomew's Fair in Smithfield was more famous. It was held several times each year, though Bartholomew's Fair proper fell in September. This Fair continued until 1855. The day after the latter Fair began Southwark Fair, which lasted fourteen days, and was mainly attended by sailors. Evelyn (in the middle of the seventeenth century) mentions among the wonders of Southwark Fair monkeys, a rope-walking ass, and the tricks of an Italian dancing girl. Pepys mentions a marionette performance and a rope-walker named Jacob Hall. The Fair ceased in 1762, but is perpetuated in the well-known etching by Hogarth.

Other London Fairs were, up till 1709, St. James's Fair and May Fair, both of which were held near Hyde Park. The latter Fair is perpetuated in the name Mayfair.

Needless to say, the shows and merry-making at the Fairs attracted, in addition to respectable citizens, the usual undesirable elements, and prostitutes were much in evidence.

Goede, a foreign visitor to London in 1800, described Bartholomew's Fair as unique in the whole of Europe. West Smithfield was packed with people and the gay tumult could be heard miles away. There were rows upon rows of stalls for the sale of cakes, rows upon rows of show booths. Each of the latter had a 'band', and the chaotic noise issuing from them was only increased by the music of all London's street musicians, who flocked to West Smithfield for the Fair. Those who had no musical instruments merely shouted at the top of their voices. All these noises merged with the gay chatter of the crowd to a steady roar that lasted for three whole days. There were also roundabouts and menageries, as well as open-air shows of all kinds and even theatres. Adjacent houses were converted into theatres for the occasion, where weird plays were performed. Naturally, each establishment had its own noise-making arrangements, whether it was a musical band or criers.

Everything was calculated to appeal to the senses of the crowd, and the crowd was only too eager to respond. Needless to say, restraint and respectability were thrown to the winds. Everything was permitted at the Fair. The Fair was invaded by crowds of prostitutes, who did a 'roaring' trade. But innocent girls also frequently fell victims to the general mood of elation, and many courtesans of that day began their careers involuntarily at Bartholomew's Fair, passing from the arms of rough sailormen into those of distinguished libertines. On the other hand, it also happened that noted courtesans visited the Fair in search of new physical sensations, such as their refined lovers could not provide. The newspapers of the time often reported such visits with great relish, though the ladies concerned took good care to disguise themselves.

Santo Domingos (Leipzig, 1826) described other London Fairs, which he compared to Sodom and Gomorrah.

Punch and Judy shows were a prominent feature of the ancient London Fairs. Punch is, of course, an abbreviation of the Italian ' Punchinello '. It was an Italian who first established a Punch and Judy show in Charing Cross. That was in the years 1666 and 1667. He paid a yearly rental to St. Martin's Church. In the year 1668 a Mr. Devon started a small theatre on the same site. An ironical song of the time concerning the delay in re-erecting the statue of Charles I, also refers to Punch:

What can the mistry be, why Charing Cross
These five months continues still blinded with board?
Dear Wheeler, inspart—we are all at a loss,
Unless Punchinello is to be restored.

Another early Punch and Judy show was at Covent Garden. It even attracted worshippers from St. Paul's Cathedral, as reported in No. 14 of the *Spectator*. In the years 1711 and 1712 attendances at the Opera were affected by the widespread popularity of the sometimes coarse, sometimes obscene Punch and Judy shows. In 1870 there were still eight big Punch and Judy ' theatres ' in open spaces in London. The best of these were in Leicester Square, Regent Street, Oxford Market and Belgrave Square. The best Punch and Judy season was the spring, but good business was also done at Christmas and midsummer.

The audiences of these shows were mostly recruited from the permanent or temporary idlers of London's streets, and pickpockets reaped a good harvest from people whose hilarious attention was riveted on Mr. Punch and the bellicose Mrs. Punch.

But the Punch and Judy shows were also watched with pleasure by distinguished Englishmen. Wyndham, the Secretary of State, never missed an opportunity to pause in front of a Punch and Judy booth on his way from Downing Street to the House of Commons.

The world of art and literature also made use of Punch as the embodiment of all the human weaknesses and follies.

In 1828 George Cruikshank drew illustrations for Payne Collier's interesting book *Punch and Judy*. Haydon painted Punch with Hogarthian wit in the year 1829, and Webster, in 1840, portrayed ' Punch in the Country '.

There was a farce entitled *Punch as Schoolmaster*. But the name of Punch has been perpetuated and given a world-wide reputation by the humorous journal of that name.

Punch, with his long nose and grotesque body—a traditional Italian figure—has become the embodiment of whatever brutality the English attribute to their national equivalent. He is a bad husband, a heartless father, a bad citizen who exercises his evil tongue freely in the field of politics, a libertine who is a bluebeard and a polygamist in one, and finally murders his wife and child and dies on the gallows. Yet the whole performance is dominated by a mood of gaiety and good humour.

Among English popular festivals the May Day and St. Valentine's Day festivals deserve to be mentioned. Stubbes, in his *Anatomy of Abuses*, relates that on the first of May men, women and children in every village go out to the woods and spend the whole night there in pleasant pastimes. In the morning they return with branches of the birch and other trees. Then they drive the Maypole into the ground, which they strew with flowers. Huts are erected near the Maypole, after which the people begin to eat, drink, dance and sing ' like heathens '. Of every hundred girls who spent the night in the wood scarce a third returned unharmed in the morning.

Towards the end of the eighteenth century London had a notorious May festival at ' The Yorkshire Stingo ' in the Marylebone Road. The festival was carried on in such an objectionable manner that it had to be banned at the beginning of the nineteenth century.

On Valentine's Day, which falls on the 14th February, all

[628]

pretty girls used to receive scores of letters which were beautifully embossed and contained declarations of love and even proposals of marriage. Unfortunately, the writers were in the habit of omitting their signatures or of altering their handwriting, so that the pretty maidens could only guess who they were. But sometimes a young man would marry the first girl he met on Valentine's Day, and according to the popular belief, such marriages were exceptionally happy.

In Wales ' trial nights ' were an accepted custom until comparatively recent times. This meant that engaged couples were allowed to sleep together for one night, and if the trial was not satisfactory they simply parted. In the contrary case the wedding followed within a few days.

In Hertfordshire there was a curious custom, which persisted until the end of the eighteenth century, and which was practised on the 10th October of every seventh year. A crowd of young men assembled in the early morning in a field and elected a leader, whom they pledged themselves to follow wherever he might lead them. Followed a cross-country tramp in the course of which the young men swung everyone they met. Respectable women kept indoors on that day, and it was loose women who allowed themselves to be swung, afterwards joining the crowd of young men and staying with them till late at night.

A custom that persisted in many parts of England till the beginning of the nineteenth century was the ducking of gossips in the river. Butler, in his *Hudibras* (seventeenth century), refers to this custom. The ducking was carried out with the aid of a ' ducking-stool ', a stool with suspension ropes. There is a document in existence from the year 1572 which contains an estimate for a ducking-stool and a charge for repairs thereon, which shows that the ducking-stool was frequently used.

In conclusion we may mention the 'shape test', a remarkable, obscene game, which was described in rhyme as follows:

The way is this, you stand erect,
Your legs together, rayther I expect;
Your shape is perfect if a sixpence lies
Between your ankles, calves, your knees and thighs.
Here are four sixpences and I'll begin,
Little Red Riding Hood shall put them in!
Not that way, stupid, stand to one side there
That everyone may see you do it fair.
Observe, I keep them firmly one and all;
I bet that you and others let them fall.

The 'Festival of Fools', with its sexual excesses, which was a custom of the Middle Ages, was in England connected with the personality of the 'Lord of Disrule', who was supposed to conduct these festivals, which took place in and around the church.

CHAPTER XIX

EROTICISM IN ART

THE principal task of Art being the representation of humanity, its activities and emotions, it has always devoted due attention to human love both in the physical and in the ideal sense.

The question whether the purely sexual aspect of love may be made the subject of artistic treatment must be answered in the affirmative, provided that the purely sexual aspect is made subservient to a higher artistic concept. Such a concept, in turn, is only possible if the object represented is considered from the general human viewpoint, the universal viewpoint, without regard to time and space, and if in the process of execution the physical side is sublimated and, to a certain extent, subjugated.

Sex is one of the most grateful subjects for humorous representation, for here the sublime indeed borders on the ridiculous, though this is due to the fact that sex is basically sublime.

The most brilliant representative of the humorous concept of sex in Art was Thomas Rowlandson. The frequent connection of lust with mysticism, which we have seen manifested in certain sexual perversions, was translated into terms of Art by Felicien Rops. And, finally, works of this type may also express the moral and moralising standpoint, which is the case with Hogarth's works.

The history of obscene and erotic works of art dates back to primitive times. The erotic sculptures of the primitive races may have originated in sexual cults, hence the sculptures of the genital organs and of the sexual act which have been found in West Africa, the Island of Bali, New Guinea, Japan, Tibet, the Philippine Islands, India, Egypt and elsewhere.

Classic antiquity produced a wealth of obscene sculptures and paintings, some of which possess considerable artistic merit. Many are now in the ' Musée secret ' in Naples.

The Renaissance period was the ' golden age ' of eroticism in Art, as witness Giulio Romano's illustrations of Pietro Aretino's *Sonetti Lussuriosi*, and Augusto and Annibale Caracci's erotic drawings representing the various ' postures ' of sexual intercourse. The castles and palaces of princes and princesses, as well as the houses of the nobility, particularly in France and Italy, were decorated with erotic frescoes and pictures. At the Palace of Fontainebleau all the rooms and galleries were covered with such obscene paintings, and Queen Anne in the year 1643 had a large number of these burned. Even in the garden and on the furniture were similar obscene representations. There was, for instance, the cup described by Brantôme. It belonged to a prince, and was embossed with obscene figures. The prince was in the habit of offering drinks to the ladies of his court from this cup.

The history of obscene art in England and France during the sixteenth, seventeenth and eighteenth centuries coincides almost entirely with the dissemination of Aretino's ' figures ', the obscene drawings of Giulio Romano and the etchings prepared from these by Marc Antonio Raimondi to illustrate the *Sonetti Lussuriosi*. There were sixteen representations of the *figurae veneris*, or the motions of sexual intercourse, illustrating the same number of sonnets by Aretino. Most of the reproductions were destroyed by Pope Clement VII, but the original copper-plates were somehow transferred to France, and during the sixteenth century a large number of copies were printed from them. Brantôme records that collections of these obscene drawings were sold freely to both men and women, married and unmarried, high and low.

Aretino had subsequently added a further four to his sixteen sonnets and the same number of new drawings were also made. Later still, a total of thirty-six ' venereal motions' were collected. In the seventeenth century all the obscene paintings and drawings were confiscated and destroyed. Nearly all Marc Antonio's etchings disappeared. The last few copies were discovered at the storming of the Bastille in the year 1789.

Aretino's drawings were probably introduced into England during the sixteenth century. At all events, it is certain that reproductions of them were made at Oxford in the year 1674. Humphrey Prideaux, in a letter to John Ellis dated 24th January 1674, wrote: ' There is often something to tell about the Press. You would hardly guess that it was used for printing Aretino's figures. I assure you we would have obtained an edition of them if the whole thing had not been destroyed last night. The gentlemen of All Souls had made copper-plates of them and used our Press to make copies. They chose for the work the hour of 4 p.m., because the Dean never came back after that hour. Yesterday, however, being very busy, he came after four, when the work had already begun. You can just imagine how he took it when he found for what purpose his Press was being used. He confiscated the copper-plates and the copies already made, and threatened to expel the owners, and I think they would deserve it if they were members of any other college than All Souls, but there, I will allow them to be virtuous that are bawdy only in pictures.'

Nevertheless, before the Dean discovered the matter sixty of the reproductions had already gone out, and were only gathered in later and destroyed by the Dean (John Fell of Christ Church).

[633]

In *Sérails de Londres* (the French translation of an English work of the eighteenth century) there is a description of the manner in which prostitutes at London brothels were practising the movements represented on Aretino's drawings of *figurae veneris*.

The first original English obscene pictures were probably those drawn by a London artist in 1755 to illustrate the erotic book *The Pleasures of Love: Containing a Variety of Entertaining Particulars and Curiosities in the Cabinet of Venus* (London, 1755, 16mo). The book, which was extraordinarily obscene, contained sixteen etchings.

John Cleland's famous obscene novel, *Memoirs of a Woman of Pleasure* (eighteenth century), was also illustrated.

The greatest English artist of the eighteenth century, who also treated erotic subjects as part of his ' moralising ' art, was William Hogarth (1697-1764). Hogarth in his erotic drawings is essentially concerned in stressing the bestial side and in pointing out the evil consequences of sensuality and licence. Hogarth was undoubtedly a moralist and did for England what Aristophanes had done for Greece in improving the morals of his age. Hogarth in his inimitable way represented the purely sexual side of love in its personal and social aspects, and in doing so he did not hesitate to be brutally frank. His pictures throw a truer light on the morals of his time than many contemporary books. Hogarth brought immorality from every hole and corner out into the revealing daylight of his art, representing not only the vice of misery but also the licence of wealth and position. Strangely enough, the greatest authority on Hogarth's works was for long the German satirist, Georg Christian Lichtenberg (1795).

' The Harlot's Progress ' series is one of the most famous of the Hogarthian etchings. They were an instantaneous

success and Hogarth sold 12,000 sets within a short time.
In addition, the 'Harlot's Progress' was copied on to coffee
cups, parasols and fans, and Theophilus Cibber even produced a pantomime on the subject. The first etching of the
series represents the heroine, Mary Hackabout, and her lay-
preacher father at the moment of their arrival in London,
where they are received by ' Colonel' Charters, one of the
most notorious procurers and brothel keepers of the eighteenth century, his assistant John Gourlay, who acts as his
tout, and an elegantly dressed procuress, in whom Hogarth
is believed to have portrayed the notorious ' Mother
Needham ', who kept a brothel in Park Place. With the
aid of this woman the girl is lured to Charters' house. In
the second etching Mary appears as the mistress of a rich
banker, in the act of helping a secret lover to escape from
her bedroom on the unexpected arrival of the banker. In
the third etching we see Mary in a miserable garret in
Drury Lane, with a representative of the law come to
arrest her for the theft of a watch. The fourth etching
shows the prostitute in her prison cell after she had been
sentenced to be ' privately whipped ' and to serve a term of
hard labour. In the fifth etching Mary is seen dead, and
we gather the cause of her death from the apparatus for a
mercury cure that is lying near her. The sixth and last
etching shows Mary in her coffin, surrounded by a group of
prostitutes and a few men of sinister aspect.

Other famous Hogarthian series are ' The Rake's Progress ' and 'Marriage à la Mode', both of which depict the
corrupt morals of the age. That Hogarth did not recoil
from a brutally plain representation of obscenity is proved
by the ninth page of ' Industry and Idleness ', where a
grenadier is seen drawing a male genital organ on the wall.

The cartoon has flourished in England since the
seventeenth century. Its popularity began at the time

of the civil uprising against Charles I, though caricatures
were then almost entirely confined to political subjects.
What led to the development of the cartoonists' art in
England was, in the first place, the abolition of absolutism.
The English citizen was able to speak his mind when the
continental nations were still, without exception, groaning
under the heel of their respective tyrants, and with freedom
of speech came the popularity of humorous expression.
But there was also another circumstance that considerably
favoured the development of caricature in England. It
was the fact that during the seventeenth and eighteenth
centuries, and also during the first half of the nineteenth
century, the cartoonist could easily find models among all
classes of society. All he had to do was to draw faithful
portraits of them, with but few modifications, for during
the periods mentioned such national characteristics as
excessive self-consciousness, a bent for eccentricity and a
strain of brutality were also reflected in the Englishman's
appearance.

Foreigners frankly admired the English caricaturists and
freely confessed that, for instance, French and German
caricaturists were tenth rate as compared with the English.

The cartoon shops of the eighteenth century and the first
thirty years of the nineteenth were regarded as public shows
and were the regular rendezvous of high and low. The greater
part of the cartoons were of a political character, but there
were also a large number of obscene cartoons. In fact, it is
recorded that apart from Mistress Humphrey's cartoon shop
in St. James's Street, the majority of such shops kept
cartoons of an immoral character.

The three greatest English cartoonists of the period in
question were James Gilray, Thomas Rowlandson and
George Cruikshank. But even they could not entirely avoid
erotic subjects. Gilray drew such cartoons as ' The Wedding

Night' and other erotic caricatures, mainly directed against the immoralities of prominent personages. Gilray also drew two flagellation scenes. One of these represents a woman flagellating a boy, with one girl holding the boy's leg and another performing a most indecent act.

By far the greatest interpreter of erotic subjects was Thomas Rowlandson. His greatness lay in the fact that he could introduce an irresistible humour even into the most obscene scenes. In portraying the sexual act he would accompany it by certain secondary circumstances that raised the whole to an artistic level. However, in spite of the fact that Rowlandson sometimes exaggerated the obscene element, he always remained natural and human, and never ventured into the realm of sexual perversion.

Of particular interest is Rowlandson's conception of the female body. At first he drew his women after the ancient Greek pattern, but later he combined bodies of Rubensian amplitude with small heads and delicate features, and small hands and feet.

The following of Rowlandson's erotic drawings were published by J. C. Hotten in 1872 in a collection entitled: *Pretty Little Games for Young Ladies and Gentlemen. With Pictures of Good Old English Sports and Pastimes. By T. Rowlandson*, 1845. *A few Copies only Printed for the Artist's Friends*.

The collection contains ten etchings:

1. 'The Willing Fair, or any Way to Please.' This is an interior with a view of a garden, in which a young man is sitting with a half-naked, buxom girl. There are a few unprintable verses beneath the picture.

2. 'The Country Squire New Mounted.' This shows an almost entirely naked woman with a plume in her hair, and a country squire dressed only in a coat. Here again there is a verse, most of which is unprintable.

3. 'The Hairy Prospect or the Devil in a Fright.' A girl raising her nightdress. The Devil is staring at her in fear and amazement. Both are standing. Underneath we read:

> Once on a time the Sire of evil
> In plainer English call'd the Devil,
> Some new experiment to toy
> At Chloe cast a roguish eye;
> But she who all his arts defied,
> Pull'd up and shew'd her sex's pride:
>
> *　　*　　*　　*　　*
>
> So much it made old Satan stare,
> Who frightened at the grim display,
> Takes to his heels and runs away.

4. 'The Larking Cull.' A bedroom, cosily furnished. A youth with *membro elephantiastico opus inter mammas peragit.*

5. 'The Toss-Off.' Represents an old Jew having sexual intercourse with a low-class girl and gazing into a looking-glass.

6. 'New Feats of Horsemanship.' Represents a man and woman having intercourse on horseback.

7. 'Rural Felicity, or Love in a Chaise.' The same, in a travelling coach.

8. 'The Sanctified Sinner.' An old man watching through a window a flagellation scene in which another old man is the passive and a young girl the active party. On the watcher's left there is an open book, *The Hypocrite Unmasked.*

9. 'The Wanton Frolic.' A beautifully furnished room. A youth is watching a girl in a very obscene manner.

10. 'The Curious Wanton.' A bedroom. A girl bending over a bed, while another is holding up a mirror to her in which she is regarding the reflection of her charms. Underneath we read:

Miss Chloe in a wanton way
Her durling (*sic*) would needs survey,
Before the glass displays her thighs,
And at the sight with wonder cries:
Is this the thing that day and night
Make (*sic*) men fall out and madly fight,
The source of sorrow and of joy
Which king and beggar both employ,
How grim it looks! Yet enter in
You'll find a fund of sweets begin.

Pisanus Fraxi collected 107 erotic etchings by Rowlandson. Many specimens of Rowlandson's obscene etchings are preserved at the British Museum.

The following etchings are not only characteristic of Rowlandson's individual humour but also interesting from the point of view of the cultural history of his age:

3. ' The Star Gazer.' A room, books and a globe on the floor. An old man in dressing-gown and slippers is watching through a telescope a man and woman disporting themselves in bed in an adjacent room, the door of which is ajar.

4. ' Carnival at Venice.' A street. A crowd of people forming a circle round a naked girl standing on all fours in a hoop. Another naked girl is passing the hat round. The onlookers are standing in obscene attitudes, while through three windows lascivious scenes are visible. At the end of the street a woman is kneeling in front of a quack, who is administering an enema.

6. ' Lady Hamilton's Postures.' This etching is described in an earlier chapter of the present work.

7. ' French Dancers at a Morning Rehearsal.' Interior of a sort of barn. There are seven persons in various obscene or erotic attitudes. One man is sitting on a chamber pot.

13. ' Inquest of Matrons, or Trial for a Rape.' An interior. This drawing is in two parts. On the right, an old woman is

examining a naked girl. On the left, the court and the defendant with his solicitor are waiting for the result of the examination, which is being observed by an incredibly ugly old man through a half-open door.

17. ' Meditation Among the Tombs.' A churchyard. A fat person is reading prayers over a grave surrounded by a number of mourners. Beneath a window of the church a peasant and a woman are disporting themselves. The inscription reads:

Life is a jest and all things show it,
I thought so once, but now I know it.

No. 18 of these etchings illustrates a fable by La Fontaine. It represents the interior of a cloister. An old nun is sitting in an armchair, surrounded by ten nuns with low-cut dresses in various attitudes. In front of them stands a young man dressed as a nun, and menacing the old nun in a peculiarly obscene manner.

19. ' Such things Are, Or a Peep into Kensington Gardens.' A most peculiar and bizarre composition. Several figures of grotesque aspect, some of them representing enormous *phalli*, are embracing in a most obscene manner. A young woman is running away, frightened. On a bench on the left, two *phalli*.

20. ' Lord Barrymore's Great Bottle Club.' An interior. Six couples sitting at a table in various attitudes. A naked girl with a punch-bowl in her hand is dancing on the table. The scene is one of drunkenness and debauchery.

23. Harlequine and Columbine, in an intimate *tête-à-tête*, are surprised by a Pierrot.

24. A strong man in the open street is balancing a vase in a most remarkable manner, while a woman is catching pennies thrown from the windows in her raised skirt. A small devil is beating a tambourine and dancing with a trumpet, which is fixed in an obscene manner.

[640]

No. 25 shows a Turk sitting on a carpet and regarding a large number of women standing in front of him in two rows.

No. 28 represents a cloister. We see a monk and two nuns, with the altar and crucifix in the background.

No. 29. 'Rural Sports, or Coney Hunting.' Three girls are admired by an old man sitting on a fence. Behind him stands a young man.

No. 30 represents a room in a castle. A young couple lying on a couch are surprised by an armed ghost.

No. 31. A young woman is being watched by an old man with a large wig through a pair of spectacles. This is an imitation of another etching entitled 'The Connoisseur'.

No. 34. A pretty girl is sitting in an armchair. In the foreground there is a person sitting on a pedestal, the bust of a woman, and a dildo.

No. 35. 'Fantocinni.' This is an interior. There is a man leaning against a barrel-organ, and in front of him a woman watching a Punch and Judy show. The man is holding a trumpet to the woman's posterior.

No. 36. A girl is being eyed by ten men in large wigs.

No. 37. A laughing girl is eyed by two men.

No. 39. An old man and a girl are swinging on two swings. The old man is very ugly and wears top boots with spurs and eyeglasses.

No. 40. Interior of a cloister. A nun with a dildo. An old man is just entering her cell.

No. 41. A young girl being eyed by six men. There is a vaseful of dildoes.

No. 43. Interior of a stable. Love scene between a hunter and a beautiful woman.

No. 44 represents an elegantly furnished room with a large antique vase. Love scene between a youth and a girl.

No. 45 is entitled: 'Empress of Russia Reviewing her Bodyguard.'

No. 46. Interior. An old man in a wig and wearing spectacles is administering an enema to a woman. On the left, three women sitting at a table. On the right, a chamber pot.

No. 47. The seashore. Two couples in a boat which is partly in the water, and partly on the beach. On the left, a stout woman shouting for help.

No. 48. A wine cellar. An old man and a girl. A ewer beneath one of the casks is overflowing.

No. 49 is entitled 'Essay on Quakerism'. A quaker and a girl who has three large plumes in her hair.

No. 50 represents a gouty old man sitting in a low arm-chair playing the violin from notes resting on the back of a girl. Two other girls are playing other instruments, and all four are singing.

No. 51. 'The Merry Traveller and the Kind Chamber-maid' represents a bedroom, in which a pretty chambermaid is placing a warming-pan into the bed in the presence of a young officer. The girl has a libidinous expression, which is rendered in a masterly manner.

No. 52. 'The Cunnyseurs' shows the interior of a cottage. A girl and three old men, with a fourth old man peeping in through the half open door.

No. 54. An interior. A youth and a girl asleep on a settee. An old man, whose face expresses uncontrollable anger, is about to stab the young man with a dagger. A woman is entering through the door which he has left ajar.

No. 55. A garden. A man on a ladder is trimming a tree shaped like a phallus. He is watched by two women. Farther away a couple on a bench. There are two tubs near them, from each of which a phallus is rising.

No. 56 represents a soldier and a peasant woman dis-porting themselves behind a hayrick. A man with a prong in his hand appears round a corner and surprises them.

No. 59 shows a man and a girl in a boat on the river. The girl is handling the oar, rowing away from an old man on the left bank who is making angry gestures. On the right bank of the river an Italian church is visible.

No. 60. A man and three girls, one of whom is swinging on a swing.

No. 61. Two girls are offering a third girl to a man. Behind the man stands a fourth woman.

No. 62. ' The Dairy Maid's Delight' represents a country girl and a negro in a dairy.

No. 64 shows a Turk sitting on a settee, and five girls.

No. 66. Four sailors and three mermaids in a cave on the seashore. A fourth sailor is busy with the boat, which is being beached, while a fifth is ready to give combat to Neptune, who is swimming towards him shaking his fist.

No. 68. A young girl is admiring herself in front of a mirror. There is an old man hiding under her dressing table.

No. 69. A youth and two girls, one of whom is holding a glass in her right hand, and a fan in her left.

No. 70. Preacher and girl under a tree, with a church in the background.

No. 72. Two amorous couples, and in front of them a vomiting woman.

No. 73. Bacchus and girl under a tree. Both are entirely nude and crowned with vine. In the background, five satyrs and nymphs dancing and playing.

No. 74. Bedroom. A very stout man and a chambermaid, who is singeing her hair with a candle. A warming-pan, the handle of which is shaped like a phallus, is on the bed.

No. 75. Two women, evidently tired with hunting, resting under a tree. They are surrounded by wild game. They are discovered by two satyrs. Behind the tree the head and shoulders of a third woman are visible.

[643]

No. 76. A pretty young woman rejecting the suit of a nude Cupid. Three obscene satyrs stand round her.

No. 77. Leda and the swan. Leda is sitting in a sort of cave and has a wreath on her head. She is embracing the swan. There are two nude children in the background.

No. 83 represents two girls. One of them is in the water up to the hips and washing the right leg of the other, who is on the point of entering the water.

No. 85. 'The Sad Discovery of the Graceless Apprentice.' A woman is begging three men and a woman to have mercy on an apprentice whom they are dragging forth from under the bed. In the confusion the chamber pot is upset.

No. 86. 'Lust and Avarice' shows a pretty girl asking a withered old man for money. The old man is putting out his tongue at her and rolling his eyes.

No. 87. 'Liberality and Desire' is a counterpart of the above. It shows a one-eyed, wooden-legged old pensioner giving his purse to a girl, pressing her breasts with one hand.

No. 91. 'New Shoes' represents a dairy, in which a milkmaid is showing her feet and ankles to a young student, who appears to be deeply absorbed in this examination.

No. 93. 'Intrusion on Study, or Painter Disturbed' shows an artist in his studio painting from a nude model. Two men burst in. The artist holds up his hand, as though asking them to be quiet, while the model bursts into tears.

No. 95. 'Symptoms of Sanctity' shows the interior of a monastery. A bald and very ugly monk is regarding with lustful eyes a beautiful young girl standing beside him with her hands folded in prayer. The holy man's right hand rests on the girl's breast, and his right on her shoulder.

No. 96. 'Touch for Touch, or a Female Physician in Full Practice', shows a pretty girl with an impudent expression receiving money from an old man, who is following her as she is about to leave. The old man's face expresses lustful desire.

No. 97. ' The Ghost of my Departed Husband, or Whither my Love, ah! Whither art Thou Gone? ' shows a churchyard. An old, extremely ugly woman has fallen on her back, evidently frightened by the watchman, who held his lantern in front of her face. Under her lies a naked, flattened ghost.

' The Discovery ' represents a pair of lovers being discovered *in flagranti delicto* by an old man with a poker. The young man is kneeling in front of him, while the girl is crying.

In ' Washing Trotters ' we see a very poorly furnished room. An ugly man and a pretty young woman are sitting facing each other, with their feet in the same tub.

' Work for Doctors' Commons.' A room. Two men, one of whom is evidently the husband, are watching from behind a wardrobe a pair of lovers who are kissing on the sofa. There is a fire burning in the room, and a guitar is lying on the floor. This etching represents General Upton and Mrs. Walsh, who were involved in a scandalous affair which caused a great stir at the time.

' Opening the Sluices, or Holland's Last Shift ' shows a few dozen stout women crouching on the beach, being offered gin by a big man. A few soldiers are standing up to the waist in the sea.

' Rural Sports, or a Pleasant Way of Making Hay ' shows two young men and three girls larking in a hayfield, while a fourth is about to throw some hay over them. In the background some men and women are loading hay.

' A View of the Banks of the Thames.' Two women, an old one and a pretty young one, are going away from the river, in which a number of naked men are bathing. But they both look back over their shoulders, the old woman remarking: ' Oh, shame on the unmannerly fellows; please tell me, Sophy, when we're far enough away? '

The above, and the following four numbers, were published by Thomas Tegg of 111, Cheapside, and sold at one
shilling for each coloured drawing.

No. 104 is ' Off She Goes '. A very stout woman, who is
about to elope with a young officer, falls to the ground from
the ladder leaned against the window. An old man wearing
a nightcap is leaning out of the window with a candle in his
hand. The driver of the stage coach is laughing.

No. 105 is entitled ' Neighbourly Refreshment '. A
young man and a young woman bend through half-open
doors, kissing. The young man is hanging up a birdcage
with his right hand, while his left is in the girl's bosom.
Behind him stands an old woman, behind the girl an old
man. A dog is attacking a cock engaged with a hen.

No. 106 is 'A Spanish Cloak'. Sentry and a young woman.
An old officer comes round the corner, surprising them.

Finally, No. 107 is ' Puss in Boots, or General Junot
Taken by Surprise'. This shows a young girl brandishing a
sword in the middle of a tent, and a man in bed apparently
calling for help.

In addition to the drawings enumerated here, all of which
appeared as etchings, Thomas Rowlandson drew countless
erotic and obscene drawings and sketches, all of which were
executed with the same graceful touch. The majority of
these works are in the possession of English collectors, in the
British Museum and in the South Kensington Museum.
The following eight Rowlandson etchings have been
described in detail by Pisanus Fraxi:

1. A naked girl lying under a tree, resting her head on
a tambourine. Two naked children, one kneeling and
playing the flute, the other, who is winged, is dancing and
also playing a flute and beating a tambourine.

2. Fourteen couples round a table. On the right the
Chairman, with a glass in his left and a bottle in his right

[646]

hand. On the left a man is vomiting. Beside him stands a drunken man. The other couples are in various attitudes.

3. ' The Road to Ruin.' A young squire is sitting at a round table with his mistress, whose breasts are bared. Both have a glass in their hands. Facing them, a captain is dealing out cards. One of the players is a sensual priest who is trying to pour the contents of two bottles into a punch bowl at the same time. This etching represents Wine, Women and Gambling.

4. An old procuress is demonstrating the charms of a young, innocent-looking girl to an old libertine, who is looking at the girl through an eyeglass.

5. Five firemen are endeavouring to extinguish a fire at a house from which a very corpulent old woman is escaping, with some domestic utensils under her skirts. The firemen watch her with lustful expressions.

6. ' Leda and the Swan.' In the background another swan is pursuing a nude woman.

7. A youth and a girl sitting on a bench. The youth has his hand on the girl's clothes.

8. ' Cricket Match at the Three Hats, Islington.' The game is played by women of all shapes and sizes, who exert their energies in a comic manner. This drawing is full of life and humour, and is characteristic of the style of this great artist.

Apart from his erotic and obscene cartoons, Rowlandson at the end of the eighteenth and the first thirty years of the nineteenth century was what Hogarth had been in the first half of the eighteenth century, namely, a great portrayer of the morals of his age. All the manifestations of the public and social life of his age are represented in his work as an artist.

The etching ' Charity Covereth a Multitude of Sins,' which shows two prostitutes leaning out of the window of a brothel just as a young officer is entering the building, reflects one side of London life. The cartoon ' The Devonshire, or Most Approved Manner of Securing Votes ' is a dig at the Duchess of Devonshire who, during the elections of 1784, literally lowered herself to the people in order to secure votes for her favourite, Charles Fox. The cartoon shows the Duchess kissing a fat butcher in the street for the sake of his vote. In ' Opera Boxes ' we get a glimpse of the doings of the ' young bloods ' at the Opera, while ' Damp Sheets ' is a protest against the filth at English inns. In ' A Little Tighter ' Rowlandson mocked at the fashion of tight lacing, while in his illustrations to Christopher Austey's ' New Bath Guide ' he poked fun at the silly fashions practised at that fashionable resort.

In a number of other remarkable drawings Rowlandson exposed the white slave traffic to India, and other evils.

Rowlandson's rivals also tried their skill in the field of the erotic and the obscene. Prominent among them were the Cruikshank family. The father, Isaac Cruikshank, drew, among others, ' The Cherub: Or Guardian of Female Innocence ', which represents a young girl standing before a soothsayer, who is pointing to a mark on her body. There is a third woman in the background, and a man is spying on them from an upper window. ' The Invitation ', also by Isaac Cruikshank, was the frontispiece of a collection of anecdotes entitled, *Useful Hints to Single Gentlemen respecting Marriage, Concubinage and Adultery, etc. By Little Isaac. London: Printed for D. Brewman, 18, Little New Street, Shoe Lane.* The drawing represents a girl sitting on a settee and talking with a man through the window. She is apparently inviting him to come in, and the man is refusing the invitation. The girl is evidently a prostitute.

Isaac's son, the great George Cruikshank (1792-1878), drew the illustrations to John Cleland's famous erotic novel

Memoirs of a Woman of Pleasure. These etchings are now very rare, and it is difficult to determine their number. It is, however, quite certain that the obscene illustrations to Cleland's obscene book were drawn by George Cruikshank.

George Cruikshank also illustrated Pierce Egan's *Life in London* (1821). It was these drawings, which were not obscene, that established Cruikshank's reputation as one of the greatest cartoonists.

George Morland (1763-1804) was another famous cartoonist. He was Rowlandson's friend, and his conception of sex was similar to that of Rowlandson. Their idea of the female body was almost identical, though Morland's style was more romantic. George Morland drew a large number of most obscene pictures, mostly in association with his brother-in-law, William Ward, and the etcher John Raphael Smith. The greater part of these artistically perfect drawings were to illustrate various famous novels of the eighteenth century.

Fielding's *Tom Jones* was illustrated by the following mezzotints, by George Morland and John Raphael Smith:

1. Tom Jones and Molly Seagrim in the Grove. Molly and Tom under a tree. Thwackum and Square regard them in amazement from the distance. Sophie Weston is climbing over a stile, assisted by the Squire.

2. Tom Jones, Molly Seagrim and Square. The young couple are surprised by Square.

3. Tom Jones and Mrs. Waters in the Inn at Upton after the Battle.

4. Lady Bellaston and Tom Jones after their return from the Masquerade.

The following obscene drawing caricatures a scene from Sterne's *Sentimental Voyage.*

5. La Fleur taking leave of his Sweethearts. This represents La Fleur with two girls. Yorick is peeping in through the window.

[649]

6. This illustrates an episode in Rousseau's *Confessions*, and represents a love scene between Rousseau and Madame de Warens. A round mirror on the back wall reflects the figure of the lady.

7. An episode from *Nouvelle Héloïse*, representing St. Preux and Héloïse, with the inscription: ' I feel you are a thousand times more dear to me than ever. O my charming Mistress! my Wife! my Sister! my Friend! By what name shall I express what I feel? '

George Morland, in association with Ward and J. R. Smith, also supplied illustrations to obscene books. The following five excellent mezzotints were for *Memoirs of a Woman of Pleasure.*

1. Fanny Hill and Phœbe. Phœbe touching Fanny in an indecent manner.

2. Mrs. Brown, the Horse Grenadier and Fanny Hill. Fanny watching through a glass door a love scene between the stout Mrs. Brown and a soldier.

3. Fanny Hill, Louisa and the Nosegay Boy. Youth and two prostitutes. Basket of flowers and rod.

4. Harriet ravish'd in the summer-house.

5. Harriet and the Barronet (*sic*). A couple on a settee, with two other couples watching them.

Another obscene mezzotint, drawn by Morland and etched by William Ward, illustrates a scene in Courtney Melmoth's *The Pupil of Pleasure.* It represents Harriet stroking Sedley's cheek with her right hand, while drawing him to herself in an indecent manner with her left. The obscene mezzotint ' Emily Palmer, afterwards Countess de Barre and Mr. de C.' was probably also Morland's work. It probably illustrates a scene from an interesting English book that appeared in London in 1771: *The Authentic Memoirs of the Countess de Barre, the French King's Mistress. Carefully collated from a Manuscript in the Possession of the Duchess of*

Villeroy, by Sir Francis N. These memoirs consist of twenty-four letters, all dated 1770, alleged to have been written by a Paris gentleman to a friend in London. They relate the love adventures of a certain Emily Palmer, who during the Regency of Richelieu was Louis XV's mistress. ' De Barre ' might have been intended to convey that the story relates to the famous Du Barry, but in reality it had no connection with her and was merely an interesting account of an ordinary love adventure. The *Monthly Review* (1771) regarded the story as ' Another heap of rubbish, swept out of Mons. Vergy's garret. This foreigner, who so impudently thrust himself into the English " Grubean " society, appears determined to fill our booksellers' shops, stalls and circulating libraries with lies and obscenity, the only studies in which he seems ambitious of excelling.'

The above-mentioned drawing illustrates a scene in which Emily is lying on a settee and trying to repel the advances of Mr. C.

According to Pisanus Fraxi, the following three obscene drawings are also the joint work of George Morland and J. R. Smith:

1. ' Mock Husband ', representing a Lesbian scene between two girls. A third girl, fully dressed, is standing behind the settee and applying the rod to the posterior of one of the others.

2. ' The Nobleman's Wife and the Taylor Crazy Tale.' A very stout man vainly trying to become the lover of a woman.

3. ' Female Contest, or, my C . . . 's larger than thine.' Five young women are being examined by a sixth.

John Raphael Smith is the sole author of the following etchings, executed as mezzotints:

1. Love scene between youth and girl on a settee.

2. Love scene between a strong youth and a coarse girl. Chamber pot in a corner.

3. Interior. *Puella cum Phallo. Cupido baculum ano inserit et muliebria titillat.*

4. Woman with long hair sitting on a bed in an attitude of grief.

5. A monk and a young girl.

6. Dutch interior. Man with tall hat and long-stemmed pipe touching a woman who is apparently asleep..

7. Interior. Woman holding her left breast with her right hand and pointing with her left to a fully dressed man.

8. Interior. A young man, bare headed but otherwise fully dressed, is touching with a bow a girl sitting on his left. There is a page of music on her right thigh.

John Grand-Carteret, in an interesting comparison between English and French erotic art at the turn of the eighteenth century, mentions, in addition to Rowlandson, Richard Newton as a master of realism in this field.

He gives reproductions of three very characteristic cartoons by Newton. The first of these is ' Which way shall I turn me? ' The drawing represents a gourmet who has the choice between the pleasures of the table and the pleasures of love, in the person of a pretty young woman lying on a settee. In 'Old Goats at the Sale of a French Kid', Cupid is auctioning a Paris beauty who is coquettishly exhibiting her charms on the auctioneer's table. A large number of men are eagerly watching her. Cupid cries: ' The last bid was fifty-two pounds a year, a carriage and pony. Come, gentlemen, make a reasonable bid for this Paris beauty. Look at her. What grace, what elegance! You're all amazed. (Admiration and amazement are portrayed by the artist in the most exquisite manner.) Five hundred a year. Thank you, sir. Five hundred it is.' The third drawing illustrates in a drastically realistic manner the physical exhaustion supervening after the sexual act. The subject is a voluptuous woman who lies exhausted in an armchair.

Perhaps Richard Newton was the originator of the eight obscene but superb mezzotints which Pisanus Fraxi places in the period of Rowlandson and Newton:

1. Interior. Love scene between a man and a woman. A kneeling boy is watching the process. He is holding his hat in one hand and making an amazed gesture with the other.

2. A young man and a girl under a tree.

3. *Coitus a posteriori*.

4. Interior. An old man sitting on a settee is caressing a girl leaning back against him. He is supporting her with his left hand, while his right is resting on her breast.

5. Interior. Man and woman in a state of sexual excitement.

6. Love scene between youth and girl in a wood.

7. Love scene between a man and a woman on a settee.

8. Interior. A man is pointing to the ample callipygean charms of a girl with his left hand, and making a gesture of admiration with his right.

9. *Coitus a posteriori*. There is a curtain falling on the back of the girl. The young man is supposed to represent George IV as Prince of Wales.

10. Bedroom. Love scene between a young man sitting on a chair and a young girl. The artist has caught their expressions of extreme ecstasy in the process of a ' seraphic kiss'. There is a bed and a door in the background.

There are also fourteen obscene mezzotints by an unknown artist illustrating Sterne's *Life and Opinions of Tristram Shandy*. The series consists of one portrait and thirteen drawings, evidently prepared for a special edition of the book, as volume and page numbers are marked on two of them. The portrait is marked ' Tristram Shandy ' and represents the head of a priest, whose nose and upper lip are shaped like a phallus. The other drawings bear various titles, such as: ' Tom's had more gristle in it ', ' Right end of a woman ', and ' A limb is soon broke in such encounters '.

The period after 1830 produced few obscene drawings of artistic merit, but countless bad coloured lithographs, some of which were published separately, but the majority of which were included in numerous erotic publications. As regards quality, an album of twelve coloured lithographs attributed to H. K. Browne, an artist of considerable merit, was an exception. The album was entitled: *The Pretty Girls of London; Their Little Love Affairs, Playful Doings, etc. By J. R. Adam, Esq., Depicted in Twelve Spirited Lithographic Drawings. By Quiz, from Designs by One of Themselves. Wm. Edwards, Importer of Parisian Novelties*, 183, *Fleet Street, London; and Paris. Price Twelve Shillings.*

These coloured lithographs are beautifully drawn and finely executed. Without being entirely obscene, they produce a highly erotic effect. The titles are as follows: (1) ' The Ballet Girl ' (On the Stage). (2) ' The Ballet Girl ' (During the Interval). (3) ' The Oyster Girl.' (4) ' Lady in a Box.' (5) ' The Waitress.' (6) ' The Fruit Seller.' (7) ' The Cigar Girl.' (8) ' The Chambermaid.' (9) ' The Servant Girl.' (10) ' The Sweetshop Girl.' (11) ' The Barmaid.' (12) ' The Children's Nurse.'

In more recent times (1877) a series of obscene illustrations to Cleland's *Memoirs of a Woman of Pleasure* was prepared by a prominent artist, whom Pisanus Fraxi ranks with Hogarth.

George Augustus Sala, the well-known author and journalist who wrote *The Mysteries of Verbena House*, a novel of flagellants, published in 1882, tried his hand at drawing scenes of flagellation. According to Pisanus Fraxi there are thirty-seven such drawings by Sala.

The renascence of puritanism during the Victorian era, which made itself felt in all fields of human activity, also produced a violent reaction against the coarse realism of English art. Nudity became taboo, and all bodily contact between the sexes was regarded as indecent. English artists were severely restricted in the representation of the nude. Hogarth dared to represent the lover in 'Marriage à la Mode' escaping half naked through the window. As late as 1860 Etty, Eastlake and Hilton were able to roam freely in the world of Titian and Rubens. But after that ' fig-leaf morals ' became the vogue, and even Watts, the great master, was obliged to explain in writing why he could not represent his Psyche and the young girl of the picture of Mammon otherwise than in the nude. The last classicists—Poynter, Tadema and Crane —continued to paint women in the nude, but their figures were completely devoid of everything even remotely carnal, and were mere marble statues. In addition, the most ' shocking ' part of their anatomy was covered over. Apart from that, the nude was only represented in pictures of babies stepping into their bath, or if the subject was a woman, her nudity had to be motivated by a religious touch. In one picture by Calderon a young nude girl is kneeling before a crucifix, swearing to renounce the vanities of the world and to follow ' naked her naked Lord '. One of the priests witnessing the scene is covering his eyes with his hand, lest he should see the graceful body of the girl!

The movement against the nude in art was far stronger in England than anywhere else. The leaders of the movement were 'Mrs. Grundy' and the old painter Horsley. In the 'eighties a violent propaganda campaign was carried on, denouncing the representation of the naked human body as indecent and immoral, thus indirectly accusing the Creator

himself of ' bad taste '. At one Royal Academy exhibition
an over-zealous anti-nudist wanted to pierce several canvases
with his umbrella because he could not bear to see the human
body in the nude.

But in spite of, or perhaps because of, the universal condemnation of the nude in art during the second half of the
nineteenth century, the artistic conception of the erotic
element received a new fillip and found expression in a new
direction. As the simple natural phenomena of love could no
longer be represented with the essentially naive naturalism
of Rowlandson, Hogarth, Morland, etc., an artificial eroticism
was evolved. It was attempted to express the erotic element
in a purely spiritual form, but this necessarily led to a subtle
kind of sensualism that was even worse than the merely
obscene yet still natural representations of the sexual act.

This movement started with the Pre-Raphaelite School,
whose most famous representatives were Holman Hunt,
Dante Gabriel Rossetti and Edward Burne-Jones. States of
mind, emotions and psychological experiences were the
principal subjects of the Pre-Raphaelites.

Dante Gabriel Rossetti (1828-1882) was the ' soul ' of the
Pre-Raphaelite School. He was also the founder of an
entirely new conception of eroticism in English art. His love
scenes of the Bible, of the *Decameron*, of the *Divine Comedy*,
and of the *Roman de la Rose* showed an entirely new kind of
' vibrant sensuality ' that had been foreign to English art
up till then.

There is no sensuality in these pictures in the antique
sense, only a voluptuous, guilty passion, of the kind that first
became known with the introduction of Christianity. The
subjects of the Pre-Raphaelite paintings were what might be
described as fatal loves. There is a great deal of kissing, but
it is kissing of a kind that desiccates the spirit. Voluptuousness is expressed by a long, slender hand, a long, slender

[656]

neck bent back by insanely passionate kisses. Rossetti's
goddess of love is always a colossal creature of cruelly disturbing beauty. Her body is vast. There is a consuming
fire in her eyes. Her full lips are always ready for demoniacal
kisses.

Rossetti rendered better than any other painter before his
time or since erotic subtleties like the fascination of a woman's
hand, cruel red lips that look like ' a poisonous flower ', or the
cruelly sensuous expression in the eyes of a lovely woman.
Rossetti was a new psychologist of love, and saw in woman
the embodiment of man's longing to escape from the drab
monotony of daily life to the fount of an eternal beauty.

The natural development of this tendency inevitably led
to mysticism and asceticism, and we find this in the pictures
of Burne-Jones. His ethereal women turn from earthly joys
to heavenly joys. The physical sensuousness which is so
powerfully expressed by Rossetti is here replaced by pure
spirituality, the voluptuous contours of the feminine form
disappear in favour of an ethereal slenderness. Thus Burne-
Jones became the idol of the aesthetes, who, having become
satiated with voluptuous curves, now began to worship
ethereal outlines. Burne-Jones's influence was so great that
it extended to real life, and the slimness of the modern
Englishwoman may be attributable to Burne-Jones's
pictures.

Aubrey Beardsley (1872-1898), who died at the early age
of twenty-six, combined in his pictures the contrasting
conceptions of the erotic represented by Rossetti and Burne-
Jones. Beardsley rendered all the subtlety of modern love,
including its Satanic element. Beardsley's first pictures were
after the style of Burne-Jones, his teacher, and his women
were angelically pure, with soft eyes, rose-bud lips and gentle
movements. Then the artist came under the influence of
Rops, who represented woman as the embodiment of lust,

the daughter of darkness, the handmaiden of the devil, and thereafter Beardsley introduced the macabre note into his work, combining heaven and hell, asceticism and lust, English prudery with modern corruption. The chaste women of Burne-Jones change into prostitutes with practised obscene lips and voluptuous outlines. It is as though an angel had suddenly begun to writhe hysterically and to use obscene language. It is this combination that lends to Beardsley's work its uncanny power. The bestial, animal side of woman was probably never expressed so strikingly as in Beardsley's ' Incipit vita nova ', ' Messalina ', and ' The Wagnerites '. In ' Incipit vita nova ' it is night, and woman has a vision of the embryo. In ' Messalina ' it is also night, and the priestess of Baal, Messalina, like an infernal fury, sets out on a tour of plunder. In ' The Wagnerites ' a horde of horrible vampire women are listening in satyriasic convulsions to the music of Tristan.

Beardsley was also a highly original cartoonist, as will be seen from his illustrations to Walter Jerrold's *Bon Mots*.

The representation of erotic subjects is only justified if it is carried out by real artists and intended for those who are capable of appreciating the artistic side. Thus as soon as erotic ' art ' is degraded to the lowest kind of pornographic representation intended for the wide masses, it ceases to be artistic, since it appeals to the very instinct which the artistic impression is supposed to overcome in the highest kind of erotic art. In England the lower type of erotic art was represented by obscene playing cards, snuff-boxes and obscene photographs. Playing cards, which were first introduced in England at the end of the fifteenth century, were after 1700 frequently painted with erotic scenes *à la* Hogarth. Thomas Heywood, of Pendleton, near Manchester, owned a set of such playing cards. One of the cards represented Cupid plucking a rose. Beneath the picture was the verse:

As when we reach to crop ye blooming rose
From off its by'r ye thorns will interpose;
So when we strive the beauteous nymph to gain,
Ye pleasures we pursue are mixed with pain.

At a later period playing cards with obscene pictures were quite common. The majority of the sets were transparent, and the obscene picture only became visible when the card was held up to the light.

Since the beginning of the nineteenth century a favourite method of spreading obscene pictures was to sell them pasted inside the lids of snuff-boxes. In the year 1816 the courts fined a merchant a large amount for selling snuff-boxes painted with obscene pictures. In September of the same year the following case occurred at Union Hall.

A certain James Price was arrested because he peddled without a licence. The inspector had seen him in Richmond going from house to house selling thread and snuff-boxes. When the snuff-boxes were examined it was found that many of them were covered with obscene drawings and etchings, some of which were of great artistic merit. Price was in the habit of offering these snuff-boxes at girls' schools, and did a roaring trade with the flappers. He was fined ten pounds with the alternative of three months in prison.

Even as late as 1830 snuff-boxes with obscene paintings on them were exhibited in London shop windows.

According to Pisanus Fraxi, no country in the world —up till a few decades ago—produced so many ' smutty photos' as England. These photographs were mostly sold in the book and paper shops in the vicinity of Leicester Square. At the beginning of the 'seventies of last century a certain Mr. Henry Hayler produced such photographs ' from life' and enjoyed a European 'reputation'. On 31st March 1874 the police suddenly stopped Mr. Hayler's doubtful trade. His studio was on that day raided by the police, who discovered no fewer than 130,248 obscene photographs and 5,000 plates, all of which were confiscated. Hayler managed to escape punishment by leaving the country in time. He reappeared in Berlin for a time, then vanished for good. The worst of the photographs confiscated by the police represented Hayler himself with his wife and two sons. The police also found a large number of letters proving that Hayler had done a world-wide trade in obscene pictures.

Remo records a most peculiar instance of the use of obscene photographs at the fashionable London brothels. The reception-room looked like the studio of a photographer, the walls being covered with photographs. Naturally, the photographs represented not old gentlemen and old maids, but pretty young ladies, including many who could sometimes be encountered in the best social circles. Each photograph was marked with a number, and the visitor could make his choice among them. At a fixed hour the procuress who owned the brothel could guarantee to bring the chosen lady to the premises. The arrangement is reminiscent of what used to be the custom at Dutch brothels.

INDEX OF BOOKS FREQUENTLY REFERRED TO IN THE PRESENT WORK

I—BIBLIOGRAPHICAL AND LITERARY WORKS

1. P. FRAXI's great bibliographies, *Index, Centuria, Catena.*
2. J. GAY—*Bibliographie des ouvrages relatifs à l'Amour, aux Femmes, au Mariage et des Livres Facétieux, Pantagruéliques, Scatologiques, Satyriques, etc. Par M. Le C. d'J* . . . *3me Edition.* Turin, J. Gay et Fils, 1871. (Better than fourth edition, from which all obscene matter is omitted.)
3. HUGO HAYN—*Bibliotheca Germanorum Erotica.* An index of the entire German erotic literature, including translations from foreign languages. Second improved and considerably enlarged edition, including Berlin and Munich erotic literature. Adapted by Hugo Hayn, Leipzig. Published by Albert Unflad, 1885. A supplement is entitled *Bibliotheca Germanorum Gynaecologica et Cosmetica.* Leipzig, Unflad, 1886.
4. EDUARD GRISEBACH—*World Literature Catalogue of a Bibliophile.* With literary and biographical notes. Berlin, Ernst Hoffmann & Co., 1898. Complementary volume, Berlin, Hoffmann & Co., 1900.
5. THOMAS BABINGTON MACAULAY—*History of England from the Accession of James II.*
6. THOMAS WRIGHT—*A History of Domestic Manners and Sentiments in England During the Middle Ages.* With illustrations from the Illuminations in Contemporary Manuscripts and other Sources, Drawn & Engraved by F. W. Fairholt, Esq. London, Chapman & Hall, 1862.
7. THOMAS WRIGHT—*A History of English Culture. From the earliest known period to modern times.* With numerous woodcut illustrations from authentic sources. London, Trübner & Co., 1874.
8. JOHANNES SCHERR—*Geschichte der englischen Literatur.* Second enlarged edition. Leipzig, Otto Wigand, 1874.
9. H. TAINE—*History of English Literature.*
10. EDWARD FORBES ROBINSON—*The Early History of Coffee Houses in England.* With some account of the first use of coffee, and a bibliography on the subject. With illustrations. London, Kegan Paul, Trench, Trübner & Co., Ltd., 1893.
11. I. D'ISRAELI—*Curiosities of Literature.* London, Routledge, 1895.
12. A FRENCH ARMY SURGEON—*Untrodden Fields of Anthropology.* Paris, 1898.

[661]

13. GEORGIANA HILL—*Women in English Life*. From mediaeval to modern times. London, Richard Bentley & Son, 1894.
14. IWAN BLOCH—*Sex Life of our Time* (' Das Sexualleben unserer Zeit in seinen Beziehungen zur modernen Kultur '). London, William Heinemann, 1908.
14a. IWAN BLOCH—*Beiträge zur Aetiologie der Psychopathia Sexualis*. Part I, Dresden, 1902. Part II, Dresden, 1903.
14b. IWAN BLOCH—*Prostitution*. Berlin, 1912.

II—LONDONIENSIA
(In Chronological Order)

15. JOHN STOW—*A Survey of London*. Written in the year 1598. A new edition, edited by William J. Thoms, F.S.A., Secretary of the Camden Society. London, Whittacker & Co., 1842.
16. (MISSION DE VALBOURG)—*Mémoires et Observations faites par une Voyageur en Angleterre, sur ce qu'il y a trouvé de plus remarquable, tant a l'égard de la religion que de la politique, des mœurs, des curiosités naturelles, et quantité de faits historiques. Avec une description particulière de ce qu'il y a de plus curieux dans Londres*. A la Haye, Chez Henri van Bulderen, 1698.
17. *The Foreigner's Guide*. Or a Necessary and Instructive Companion Both for the Foreigner and Native in their Tour through the Cities of London and Westminster, etc. London, printed for J. Pote and sold by J. Batley, at the Door in Pater Noster Row, etc., 1730.
18. *The Midnight Spy*. Or a View of the Transactions of London and Westminster, from the Hours of Ten in the Evening, till Five in the Morning. Exhibiting a Variety of Scenes in High and Low Life, with the Characters of some Well Known of both Sexes. Also the Humours of

Round Houses	Gaming Tables
Night Houses	Routes and other
Bagnios	Places of Midnight
Jelly Houses	Resort

With
General and Particular Descriptions of Women of the Town. London, Printed for J. Cooke, at the Shakespeare's Head in Pater Noster Row, 1766.

19. *L'Observateur français à Londres*. Ou lettres sur l'état présent de l'Angleterre, relativement à ses forces, à son commerce et à se mœurs. Avec des Notes et des Remarques Historiques, Critiques et Politiques de l'Editeur. Première Partie. Tome Premier. A Londres, 1769.
20. RICHARD KING—*The Frauds of London detected, or a new Warning-Piece against the iniquitous practices of that Metropolis, etc.* London, printed for Alex Hogg (1770 or 1760).
21. J. W. V. ARCHENHOLTZ—*England und Italien*. Leipzig, 1787.

A HISTORY OF ENGLISH SEXUAL MORALS

46. Max O'Rell—*Les Filles de John Bull*. Par l'Auteur de *John Bull et son Ile*. Paris, 1884.

47. Max O'Rell—*John Bull and His Island Home* (' John Bull und sein Inselheim '). Berlin, Otto Janke.

48. Hector France—*Les Va-Nu-Pieds de Londres* (Paris, 1884) and *La Pudique Albion* (Paris, 1900).

49. Hector France—*En Police Court*. Paris, 1891.

50. H. D. Traill—*Social England*. London, Cassell & Co., 1889.

51. Gustaf F. Steffen—*Aus dem modernen England*. Second edition. Stuttgart, 1896.

52. Warwick Wroth, F.S.A., of the British Museum—*The London Pleasure Gardens of the Eighteenth Century*. London, Macmillan & Co., 1896.

53. Walter Besant—*London*. A new edition. London, Chatto & Windus, 1898.

54. H. Barton Baker—*Stories of the Streets of London*. London, Chapman & Hall, 1899.

55. Pierce Egan—*Life in London, or the Day and Night Scenes*. London, Chatto & Windus, 1900.

56. Arthur H. Beavan—*Imperial London*. London, J. M. Dent & Co., 1901.

57. Walter Besant—*East London*. London, Chatto & Windus, 1901.

58. Charles Dickens—*London Sketches*.